Ivan Kapitonov
A Grammar of Kunbarlang

Mouton Grammar Library

Edited by
Georg Bossong
Bernard Comrie
Patience L. Epps
Irina Nikolaeva

Volume 89

Ivan Kapitonov

A Grammar of Kunbarlang

ISBN 978-3-11-127453-9
e-ISBN (PDF) 978-3-11-074705-8
e-ISBN (EPUB) 978-3-11-074711-9
ISSN 0933-7636

Library of Congress Control Number: 2021936236

Bibliographic information published by the Deutsche Nationalbibliothek
The Deutsche Nationalbibliothek lists this publication in the Deutsche Nationalbibliografie; detailed bibliographic data are available on the Internet at http://dnb.dnb.de.

© 2023 Walter de Gruyter GmbH, Berlin/Boston
This volume is text- and page-identical with the hardback published in 2021.
Printing and binding: CPI books GmbH, Leck

www.degruyter.com

Acknowledgements

First of all, I thank the Barlang people who kindly and patiently taught me their language. My very special thanks go to Nakangila Solomon Yalbarr and Nakangila Paul Naragoidj. I am deeply grateful to Nakangila Douglas Djalanba, Ngalngarridj Sandra Makurlngu, Ngalwamud Rita Djitmu, Ngalngarridj Millie Djamuddjana, Nakodjok Jonah Walamaka, Nakodjok Peter Gwadbu, Nakangila Jack Marilain, Alistair James, Joseph Diddo, Ngalwamud Rosemary Urbadi, Ngalkangila Nancy Namidjalmag, Nawamud Jamie Milpurr, †John James, and many others at Warruwi and Maningrida. I wish I had worked more with †George Djidurinjmak and †Frank Ambidjambidj; fascination with their language will always remain with me. It is my hope that this volume, although too brief to reflect the true richness of Kunbarlang, still offers some faithful insight into its intricate structure. May Kunbarlang language and culture remain strong for many generations to come.

This grammar is a revised version of my 2019 University of Melbourne doctoral thesis. None of this would have been possible but for my supervisors Rachel Nordlinger and Ruth Singer. Throughout my work on that project, Rachel and Ruth were incredibly generous with inspiration, encouragement, and support, and have greatly influenced my thinking about language and about how to describe it. Thank you—it is a little hard to pack my gratitude to you into words.

My thesis examiners Mary Laughren and Tony Woodbury made an important contribution to this writing, suggesting numerous improvements to the thesis. In addition to that, Mary provided an amazingly insightful and detailed feedback on all aspects of the analysis, which informed a fair share of the current revisions. Pattie Epps read the revised manuscript and made many helpful suggestions.

Isabel O'Keeffe generously shared her knowledge of Kunbarlang with me throughout my thesis years and afterwards, and would always offer to check a few important examples when she was visiting the community. Another person whose passion for Kunbarlang has influenced my work both directly and indirectly is Carolyn Coleman. She shared her work with me, which was a great head start, and the insights of her analysis had a huge effect on my thinking about many topics.

From the practical point of view, this project was made possible through the financial support of the Australian Research Council Centre of Excellence for the Dynamics of Language—ARC CoEDL (Project ID: CE140100041). This support is gratefully acknowledged. The Warruwi primary school have been very welcoming and supportive: they have provided me with accommodation and office space in the four years of visits. Many thanks to the Principals Daryll Kinnane, Keira Stewart, and Anthony Vandermolen, as well as the teachers.

I have learnt a lot about the Gunwinyguan languages, and Australian languages more generally, from discussing aspects of this work with Nick Evans, Brett Baker and Mark Harvey, whose scholarship has always been very stimulating for me.

Indeed, I have had many great discussions of various aspects of this work, and often so much more than work. For those conversations, and for the friendship, I would like to thank, in first-name alphabetical order: Alex Marley, Alice Gaby, Ana Krajinović, Aung Si, Caroline Gentens, Claire Halpert, Coppe van Urk, Cris Edmonds-Wathen (a great fieldwork buddy), Dana Louagie, Dani Diedrich, Dasha Mishchenko, David Erschler, David Pesetsky, George Moroz, Hywel Stoakes, Jake Farrell, Jean-Christophe Verstraete, Jill Vaughan (another great fieldwork buddy), John Mansfield, Jonathan Moodie, Kate Horrack (who gave me a set of toy construction blocks that became an important elicitation tool!), Katie Bicevskis, Katie Jepson, Manfred Krifka, Margaret Carew, Margit Bowler, Mary Laughren, Masha Kyuseva, Misha Knyazev, Nick Sgro-Traikovsky, Nikolaus Himmelmann, Patrick Caudal, Pavel Caha, Pavel Rudnev, Pete Nyhuis, Rebecca Defina, Sasha Wilmoth, Stefan Schnell, and Vera Hohaus. Not all of those discussions have made it to be reflected in the writing here, I'm afraid, but doubtless all of them influenced my thinking about the respective topics.

The University of Melbourne School of Languages and Linguistics has been a terrific environment to write the thesis version of the grammar, and I thank all of my colleagues there. The revised version was completed during my post-doc at the University of Cologne, and even though human interaction was severely restricted at that time, I felt the welcome and the friendly support of my colleagues there. Special thanks to Nikolaus Himmelmann for his help and encouragement.

It was a pleasure to work with Birgit Sievert, Kirstin Boergen and Charlotte Webster, who were very helpful at all stages of publication.

Last but not least, I thank my parents Sergey and Iraida, my sister Tanya, and my aunt Tatiana Sablina for their unfailing love and support and the faith they have had in me.

To Iraida and Sergey Kapitonov

Contents

Acknowledgements — V

List of Figures — XV

List of Tables — XVII

Abbreviations — XIX

Guide to recordings — XXI

1	**The language and its speakers** — 1	
1.1	The Kunbarlang people: background — 3	
1.1.1	Social organization — 4	
1.2	Kunbarlang among the Gunwinyguan languages — 7	
1.3	Fieldwork: consultants and methodology — 10	
1.4	Previous work and the contribution of this grammar — 12	
1.5	Overview of the grammar — 14	
2	**Phonetics and phonology** — 15	
2.1	Segmental units: an overview — 15	
2.2	Practical orthography — 16	
2.3	Vowels — 17	
2.4	Consonants — 18	
2.4.1	Fortis consonants — 19	
2.4.2	Phonetic description and allophonic distribution of consonants — 19	
2.4.3	Phonemic oppositions: consonants — 22	
2.5	Phonotactics — 24	
2.5.1	Syllable structure — 26	
2.5.2	Morpheme-initial position — 27	
2.5.3	Morpheme-final position — 32	
2.5.4	Whole word phonotactics — 33	
2.6	Stress — 36	
2.7	Morphophonology — 39	
2.7.1	Lenition of the initial segment of -*buk* 'person' — 40	
2.7.2	Mid vowel raising between palatal segments — 40	
2.7.3	Nasal cluster simplification — 41	
2.7.4	Manner assimilation of nasals — 44	
2.8	Reduplication — 45	
2.8.1	Non-verbal reduplication — 45

| 2.8.2 | Verbal reduplication —— 46 |

3 Grammatical overview —— 48
3.1	Typological features and grammatical functions —— 48
3.2	Parts of speech —— 50
3.2.1	Nouns —— 52
3.2.2	Adjectives —— 53
3.2.3	Adverbs —— 58
3.2.4	Verbs —— 59
3.2.5	Coverbs and preverbs —— 62
3.2.6	Noun markers —— 68
3.2.7	Pronominals —— 70
3.2.8	Numerals and other quantifiers —— 72
3.2.9	Prepositions —— 73
3.2.10	Connectives —— 74
3.2.11	Particles and interjections —— 75
3.3	Wordhood, clitics, and affixes —— 76
3.4	Argumenthood —— 77

4 Nominals —— 84
4.1	Noun class —— 84
4.1.1	Background —— 84
4.1.2	Noun class membership —— 85
4.1.3	Morphosyntax —— 87
4.2	Case —— 92
4.3	Noun markers —— 94
4.3.1	Noun markers as definite articles —— 96
4.3.2	Noun markers as linkers —— 100
4.4	Noun phrase —— 102
4.4.1	Word order —— 103
4.4.2	Analytic case marking and determining pronouns —— 106
4.4.3	The hierarchical structure of the noun phrase —— 109
4.4.4	Noun phrase discontinuity —— 113
4.5	Pronominals —— 115
4.5.1	Personal pronouns —— 115
4.5.2	Inclusory constructions —— 127
4.5.3	Demonstratives —— 128
4.5.4	Interrogatives, indefinites and ignoratives —— 134
4.6	Possession —— 141
4.6.1	Alienable possession —— 141
4.6.2	Inalienable possession —— 143
4.6.3	Typological remarks —— 147

4.7	Quantifiers —— 149	
4.7.1	Terminological and methodological preliminaries —— 150	
4.7.2	Generalized Existential (Intersective) Quantifiers —— 153	
4.7.3	Generalized Universal (Co-intersective) Quantifiers —— 157	

5 Verbs: inflectional morphology —— 162
5.1 Definitions: grammatical relations —— 165
5.1.1 Unregistered arguments —— 169
5.2 Agreement —— 173
5.2.1 The personal prefixes —— 175
5.2.2 Is third person singular subject singular? —— 188
5.2.3 Third person object prefixes —— 190
5.3 Conjugations —— 195
5.4 Tense and mood: composite morphology —— 201
5.5 Tense and mood: semantics —— 207
5.5.1 Realis forms —— 207
5.5.2 Irrealis forms —— 211

6 Verbs: derivational morphology and constructions —— 215
6.1 Argument derivation —— 215
6.1.1 Benefactive —— 216
6.1.2 Comitative —— 217
6.1.3 Reflexive/Reciprocal —— 220
6.2 Valency classes —— 234
6.2.1 Monovalent verbs —— 235
6.2.2 Divalent verbs —— 236
6.2.3 Trivalent verbs —— 237
6.2.4 Four-place verbs —— 240
6.3 Noun incorporation —— 241
6.3.1 Grammatical relations —— 242
6.3.2 External modification —— 246
6.3.3 Interaction with argument derivation —— 247
6.3.4 Productivity —— 248
6.4 Adverb incorporation —— 248
6.4.1 *baba-* 'separately, each' —— 250
6.4.2 *kaburrk-* 'COLLectively' —— 251
6.4.3 *mulmul-* 'many' —— 252
6.4.4 *nganj-* 'HITHer' —— 252
6.4.5 *mun-* 'THITHer' —— 253
6.4.6 *rnak-* 'just' —— 254
6.4.7 *warribo-* 'INADvertently' —— 255
6.4.8 *woh-* 'INComPletely' —— 256

6.5	Coverb constructions —— 257
6.5.1	Structural parallels —— 261
6.5.2	Etymology —— 264

7 Clause structure —— 269

7.1	Word order and information structure —— 269
7.1.1	Subject–Verb–Object as the default word order —— 273
7.1.2	The initial position —— 275
7.1.3	Afterthoughts —— 279
7.1.4	Word order in the noun phrase —— 281
7.2	Aspectual constructions —— 284
7.2.1	The imperfective auxiliary construction —— 284
7.2.2	Stylistic lengthening —— 288
7.3	Negation —— 290
7.4	Questions —— 293
7.4.1	Polar questions —— 293
7.4.2	Constituent questions —— 294
7.5	Imperatives —— 296
7.6	Directionals —— 297
7.7	Stative clause types —— 301
7.7.1	Ascriptive clauses —— 301
7.7.2	Possessive clauses —— 303
7.7.3	Locative and existential clauses —— 305
7.7.4	Comparative and superlative clauses —— 308
7.8	Anaphora and reference maintenance —— 312

8 Complex syntax —— 315

8.1	Clausal coordination —— 315
8.2	Subordination: preliminaries —— 317
8.3	Complement clauses —— 320
8.3.1	Causatives —— 322
8.3.2	Elements functioning as complementizers —— 325
8.3.3	Tense and mood forms in the expressions of desires —— 326
8.4	Relativisation —— 329
8.4.1	Types of Kunbarlang relative clauses —— 331
8.4.2	Arguments for relativisation in Kunbarlang —— 340
8.4.3	Accessibility hierarchy —— 342
8.5	Adverbial clauses —— 345
8.5.1	Purpose and cause clauses —— 347
8.5.2	Locative clauses —— 349
8.5.3	Time clauses —— 349
8.5.4	Conditional adverbial clauses —— 351

9	**Conclusion** —— **354**	

A	**Texts** —— **358**	
A.1	Trip to the mainland —— **358**	
A.2	Making damper —— **362**	
A.3	Spot-the-Difference game dialogue —— **365**	

Bibliography —— **371**

Index —— **383**

List of Figures

Fig. 1.1	Kunbarlang land and surrounding languages —— 3	
Fig. 1.2	"The Pama-Nyungan offshoot model", after Evans (2003b: 10) —— 7	
Fig. 1.3	The Gunwinyguan language family —— 8	
Fig. 2.1	Distribution of consonants in whole words —— 36	
Fig. 2.2	Pitch and intensity contours of *nganjrdukkume* —— 37	
Fig. 4.1	Materials: quantifier elicitation —— 152	
Fig. 4.2	Materials: quantifier elicitation —— 153	
Fig. 5.1	Verbal template in Kunbarlang —— 162	
Fig. 5.2	Verbal template in Bininj Kunwok —— 164	
Fig. 5.3	Classification of Kunbarlang objects —— 165	
Fig. 5.4	Gunwinyguan TAM categories —— 198	
Fig. 5.5	Kunbarlang TAM categories —— 198	
Fig. 6.1	Verbal template in Kunbarlang —— 249	
Fig. 7.1	Pitch contour of an afterthought —— 280	
Fig. 7.2	Pitch contour of the IAC [20060814IB03/01:00] —— 288	
Fig. 7.3	Waveform of *ka-bardi-djarrang* [20060606IB02/09:49] —— 289	
Fig. 7.4	Stylistic lengthening: *ka-bun-djarra::ng* —— 289	

List of Tables

Tab. 1	List of spontaneous discourse recordings	XXII
Tab. 2.1	Consonant phonemic inventory of Kunbarlang	15
Tab. 2.2	Vowel phonemic inventory of Kunbarlang	16
Tab. 2.3	Kunbarlang orthography	17
Tab. 2.4	Kunbarlang vocalic phoneme frequencies	17
Tab. 2.5	Kunbarlang consonantal phoneme frequencies	18
Tab. 2.6	Vowel-initial words in Kunbarlang	28
Tab. 2.7	Occurrence of consonants in morpheme-initial position	29
Tab. 2.8	Occurrence of consonants in morpheme-final position	32
Tab. 2.9	Occurrence of vowels in morpheme-final position	33
Tab. 2.10	Occurrence of consonants in word-initial position	34
Tab. 2.11	Occurrence of single consonants in word-medial intervocalic position	34
Tab. 2.12	Occurrence of consonants in word-final position	35
Tab. 3.1	Adjectival paradigm (for -*mak* 'good')	55
Tab. 3.2	A sample of Kunbarlang adverbs	59
Tab. 3.3	Kunbarlang kinship verbs	61
Tab. 4.1	Noun class paradigms	88
Tab. 4.2	Interpretive effects of various orders of NM, Adj and N	110
Tab. 4.3	Personal pronoun paradigm: Direct forms	115
Tab. 4.4	Personal pronoun paradigm: Oblique forms	118
Tab. 4.5	Coordinate and inclusory dual pronouns	126
Tab. 4.6	Kunbarlang demonstratives noun class paradigm	129
Tab. 4.7	Kunbarlang locative demonstratives paradigm	130
Tab. 5.1	Intransitive subjects: Realis Non-Future	177
Tab. 5.2	Intransitive subjects: Realis Future	177
Tab. 5.3	Intransitive subjects: Irrealis Non-Past	178
Tab. 5.4	Intransitive subjects: Irrealis Past	178
Tab. 5.5	Basic object prefixes	178
Tab. 5.6	Transitive paradigms: Realis Non-Future	181
Tab. 5.7	Transitive paradigms: Realis Future	182
Tab. 5.8	Transitive paradigms: Irrealis Non-Past	183
Tab. 5.9	Transitive paradigms: Irrealis Past	184
Tab. 5.10	Kunbarlang conjugational classes	196
Tab. 5.11	Posture verb forms in Kunbarlang	197
Tab. 5.12	Irregular conjugation verb stems in Kunbarlang,	197
Tab. 5.13	Paradigms of **pu-*	200
Tab. 5.14	Class IV IrrNonPast	201
Tab. 5.15	Tense/mood morphological combinations	202
Tab. 5.16	Example tense/mood paradigm	202
Tab. 5.17	Combinations of subject prefixes and status endings (Coleman 1982)	206

Tab. 6.1	Incorporating nominal roots —— 243	
Tab. 6.2	Kunbarlang incorporating adverbs —— 249	
Tab. 6.3	Light verbs of the coverb constructions —— 259	
Tab. 6.4	Kunbarlang coverbs with correspondence in Mawng —— 266	
Tab. 6.5	Kunbarlang coverbs with correspondence in Bininj Kunwok —— 266	
Tab. 6.6	Kunbarlang coverbs with correspondence in Dalabon —— 267	
Tab. 6.7	Kunbarlang coverbs with correspondence in Ngandi —— 267	
Tab. 6.8	Kunbarlang coverbs without established correspondence —— 268	
Tab. 8.1	Combinations of predicates with subordinate markers —— 325	

Abbreviations

1	first person	INTJ	interjection
2	second person	IRR	irrealis
3	third person	IV	class IV
A	agent	LIM	delimitative
AFOR	aforementioned	LL	land gender
ALL	allative	LNK	linker
ANIM	animate	LOC	locative
AUX	auxiliary	M	masculine
BEN	benefactive	MA	masculine gender
CAUS	causative	MED	medial
COLL	collectively	NEG	negative
COM	comitative	NEUT	neuter class
COMP	complementizer	NF	non-future
CONJ	conjunction	NM	noun marker
CONTR	contrastive	NMA	non-masculine
DAT	dative	NP	non-past
DEM	demonstrative	NSG	non-singular
DIST	distal	OBJ	object
DISTR	distributive	OBL	oblique
DU	dual	PC	past continuous
ELA	elative	PI	past imperfect
EMPH	emphatic	PL	plural
ENG	English	PLURAC	pluractionality
ERG	ergative	POSS	possessive
EXCL	exclusive	PP	past perfect
FUT	future	PRED	predicative
FV	final vowel	PROH	prohibitive
GEN	genitive	PROX	proximal
GEN	genitive	PST	past
HITH	hither	Q	question particle
I	class I	R	realis
IGNOR	ignorative	RDP	reduplication
II	class II	REFL	reflexive
III	class III	REL	relative
INADV	inadvertitive	SBJV	subjunctive
INCH	inchoative	SG	singular
INCL	inclusive	THITH	thither
INCP	incomplete	TOP	topic
INDF	indefinite	VEG	vegetable gender

Within examples:
- the parentheses around some element indicate its optionality in the given context
- the asterisk * denotes an ungrammatical form of a word or sentence (except when used in context of historical reconstruction, where it denotes the reconstructed proto-form). The combination of parenthesis and asterisk reads as follows
    - a (*x) b indicates that the form x **cannot be used** in the context of a and b (with $a\ b$ being grammatical otherwise)
    - a *(x) b indicates that the form x **cannot be omitted** in the context of a and b (that is: $a\ x\ b$ is good, but $a\ b$ is not)
- the hash-mark # denotes a form that is grammatical, but semantically anomalous in the given context (or inherently semantically inconsistent)
- the percentage sign % indicates a considerable variation in judgement among speakers
- the examples are given in the practical orthography (see §2.2) and separated into morphemes with hyphens (-); clitics are separated by the equals sign (=)
- audibly long pauses may be indicated in examples by a double pipe symbol (||)
- free translation line ends with a pointer to the source of the example, i.e. the archival collection, in the format [REC/TIME], where REC is the name of the archival item (from which fuller detail can be found out via the list of recordings), and the TIME is the location of the fragment in the recording as (HH:)MM:SS

An extra line above the example line is added in one of two cases: (i) when a phonetic transcription is in order, in which case the top line includes a transcription in the International Phonetic Alphabet (IPA); or (ii) when I wish to show the division of a longer example into clauses, in which case the practical orthography is used, but no morpheme breaks are made, and the clauses are separated by the pipeline symbol with upper indices (e.g., $|^1$).

Guide to recordings

This is the guide to recordings that have been used and referenced in this grammar.

There are two major sets of such recordings: those that I made between 2015 and 2018, and those made by Isabel O'Keeffe between 2006 and 2015. Moreover, there are several recordings made by Carolyn Coleman, three recordings made by Aung Si, and one by Ruth Singer.

The recordings that are of the format IK1-YYMMDD_XXXN are made by myself in the course of my field work (Kapitonov 2016a). They are to be found archived in PARADISEC at https://catalog.paradisec.org.au/collections/IK1. The YYMMDD field indicates the date when the recording has been made. The XXX field distinguishes different sessions within the day, typically with different speakers. Finally, the last digit ('N') distinguishes several parts within a single recording session (and if there was only one recording produced in a given session, it is trivially '1'). There are 192 recordings from my field work, made with 24 speakers of Kunbarlang. The audio files range from several lexical items to some very long (over an hour) elicitation sessions. Elicitations make up the majority of this part of my corpus; there are 13 narratives and dialogues in this collection, which are listed in Table 1 below.

The recordings that are of the format YYYYMMDD IB NN (e.g. 20060901IB03) and YYYYMMDD IOv NN (e.g. 20150413IOv01) are made by Isabel O'Keeffe. Recordings made by Aung Si are 20150212AS01, 20150212AS02, and 20150206AS03. They are archived with the Endangered Languages Archive (ELAR), see O'Keeffe et al. (2017), or see http://hdl.handle.net/2196/00-0000-0000-0002-EF13-E@view and http://hdl.handle.net/2196/00-0000-0000-000F-BF4E-0@view. There are over a hundred items in this collection, and they likewise include both grammatical elicitation and free narratives. The proportion is the opposite to my collection, i.e. narratives prevail. The recording made by Ruth Singer is RS1-140, and it is archived with ELAR at http://hdl.handle.net/2196/00-0000-0000-0013-7C8C-A@view.

Carolyn Coleman's recordings are archived with AIATSIS, see https://aiatsis.gov.au/sites/default/files/catalogue_resources/coleman_c02_finding-aid.pdf, and with ELAR, see http://hdl.handle.net/2196/00-0000-0000-000F-BF4E-0@view. When referenced here, they begin with C01 or C02. Isabel O'Keeffe's efforts in obtaining copies of these recordings are acknowledged with much gratitude.

All recordings are subject to the speakers' discretion. They may be temporarily unavailable to public access.

Tab. 1: List of spontaneous discourse recordings

Item	Topic	Speaker
IK1-150801_1PN4	Traveling along the coast	Paul Naragoidj
IK1-160510_0001	Shipwreck	†George Djidurinjmak
IK1-160513_0011	Feeding Fluffy	Sandra Makurlngu
IK1-160525_0001	Speaker's youth	Peter Waralak
IK1-160525_0011	Speaker's youth	Peter Waralak
IK1-160624_0001	Mission Centennial	Rita Djitmu and Linda Najinga
IK1-160624_0021	Outstation camping	Rita Djitmu and Linda Najinga
IK1-160719_0001	Mission Centennial	Sandra Makurlngu
IK1-160726_0011	Making damper	Sandra Makurlngu
IK1-160726_0021	Making damper	Sandra Makurlngu
IK1-170610_2SM1	Spot-the-Difference	S. Makurlngu and George Manmurulk
IK1-170615_1SY1	Feeding Fluffy	Solomon Yalbarr
IK1-170625_1PN1	Arrival of J. Watson to Mardbalk	Paul Naragoidj

1 The language and its speakers

This book is a description of Kunbarlang, an Australian Aboriginal language. The description and analysis are based on my original field work carried out in the Northern Territory, Australia, between 2015 and 2018, as well as build on the preceding body of work by other scholars. Carolyn Coleman did foundational work on Kunbarlang in central-western Arnhem Land from 1981, which resulted in the first grammar of the language (Coleman 1982). In her subsequent work in the area in the 1990s, she carried on with lexicographic research in Kunbarlang, Mawng and Maningrida languages. More recently, Dr. Aung Si (Universität zu Köln), Dr. Isabel O'Keeffe (University of Sydney), and Dr. Ruth Singer (University of Melbourne) made a number of recordings of Kunbarlang speakers at Maningrida, Warruwi, Minjilang and Darwin. These recordings provided an invaluable extension to the empirical basis of this grammar.

Kunbarlang is a nominative-accusative language with secundative indexing of objects. It belongs to the non-Pama-Nyungan Gunwinyguan language family, and like all Gunwinyguan languages is highly polysynthetic. This means that it has very rich verbal morphology: the morphosyntax of the verbal word is at the heart of the Kunbarlang structure. In fact, the verbs are so self-sufficient that any well-formed verb can be a full utterance in Kunbarlang. In the nominal domain, on the other hand, morphology is very economical—probably more so than in any other Gunwinyguan language.

However, there is much more to the Kunbarlang grammar than its polysynthetic nature and the contrasts in the morphosyntax of the verbal and the nominal domain. Kunbarlang is nowhere short of interesting properties, both from the Australianist perspective and from the broader typological point of view. In the sound system there is an unusual for an Australian language retention of retroflexion in heterorganic clusters (§2.5.2.1). Kunbarlang is agglutinating with little morphophonology, yet one finds interaction in nasal–nasal clusters that stands out against what is known as the norm of harmonic cluster resolution across Australian languages (§2.7.3).

In the area of nominal morphosyntax, Kunbarlang has a system of four noun classes (grammatical genders), which on par with Kunwinjku is the largest retained noun class system in the Gunwinyguan family (inherited from the proto-Gunwinyguan five-class system). Furthermore, Kunbarlang has two features that distinguish it within its family and indeed among most Australian languages: definite articles (§4.3.1) and a hierarchical noun phrase (§4.4.3). Kunbarlang also has a system of three cases. Although nouns do not have any case morphology of their own, there is an unusual construction with case-marked pronouns that allows nouns to be case-marked analytically (§4.2). In the course of my work I took care to investigate certain topics that do not traditionally receive close attention in grammar writing. For instance, in §4.7 I present a documentation of the wealth of quantificational devices, informed by semantic typology and theory.

The verb, and more broadly, verbal constructions in Kunbarlang offer a wealth of interesting topics both in inflection and in derivation. Polypersonal agreement morphology of the verb presents exuberant paradigmatic complexity, at the same time standing out within the Gunwinyguan family in terms of its agglutinating separability of the subject and object prefixes (§5.2.1). This inflectional system appears to be in a transitioning phase, perhaps starting to fuse certain prefix combinations into portmanteaux, but currently individual morphemes are still divisible with barely any exceptions. This complexity is further increased by the fact that subject prefixes coordinate with verbal stems in so-called composite tense and mood encoding (§5.4). Valency-changing derivations and their interaction is an area of interesting micro-variation in a single morphosyntactic domain within a genetic group of languages.

Another aspect of predicate building that makes Kunbarlang different from the other Gunwinyguan languages is the coverb construction: a particular bipartite verbal structure that is clearly related to other predicate formation options found within the family, yet is formally distinct from constructions in those other languages (§6.5.1). Interestingly, the Kunbarlang coverb construction is formally very similar to the one found in Mawng, an Iwaidjan language which has been in especially close contact with Kunbarlang for the last hundred years. One more Kunbarlang construction that has a close correspondence in Mawng is the typologically rare analytical reciprocal construction with contrastive pronouns, probably developed from a biclausal structure (§6.1.3.2).

Word order in the Kunbarlang clause is constrained by information structure, rather than grammatical function of the constituents. It shows similarity to other Australian languages where there are particular prominent positions in the clause, viz. its edges. Moreover, Kunbarlang shows a noticeable tendency for the subject–verb–object order. There are no infinitives in Kunbarlang, but it has a small array of subordinate structures of various types: complement, relative, and adverbial clauses. Since morphological (or lexical) marking of these subordinate constructions is sparce, it is interesting to investigate the formal means signalling subordination (§§8.3.2–8.3.3) and diagnostics that can be used for it (e.g. §8.4.2 on relativisation diagnostics).

The grammar concludes with an appendix that presents a selection of three texts in different genres: a narrative, a procedural text, and a fragment of a (semi-spontaneous) dialogue.

The present chapter serves as a general introduction to the Kunbarlang people and their language. In what follows, I first briefly give some ethnographic background of the Kunbarlang society (§1.1). Then in §1.2 I situate Kunbarlang within the Gunwinyguan family of languages and discuss some of its typological properties. My data collection is described in §1.3. In §1.4, I overview the previous work and motivate the extended coverage and elaboration of analysis which the present grammar offers in comparison. Finally, §1.5 concisely outlines the topics covered here.

Fig. 1.1: Kunbarlang land and surrounding languages [Map courtesy of Ruth Singer]

1.1 The Kunbarlang people: background

The traditional lands of the Kunbarlang people are in central Arnhem Land in the area stretching along the coast of the Arafura sea from the Goomadeer river in the West to the Liverpool river delta in the East. See the map in figure 1.1. On those lands, they had bordered Mawng people in the West, Ndjébbana people in the East, and Bininj Kunwok speakers (specifically, speakers of the Eastern dialects Kune and Kuninjku) in the South.

The autonym, their own name for the people and the language, is *Barlang*, in isolation pronounced more often like *Warlang* due to the initial consonant lenition. Because of the grammatical structure of the language, it must take one of a number of prefixes, forming a more specific concept that refers to a Kunbarlang person (*nabarlang* for a male, *kinbarlang* for a female), or a group of people (*kinbaddabarlang*, or reduplicated and without prefixes, *barlangbarlang*, indicating a plurality of people), or the language (*ipse*: *Kunbarlang*). In everyday English conversation people would normally refer to themselves as *Kunbarlang people*, and throughought this book I shall use the word *Kunbarlang* as both the glottonym and ethnonym, i.e. to refer to the language and the people. In other sources, slightly different spellings may be found, and even the name without the prefix: Gunbalang, Gunbarlang, Warlang. The ISO639-3 code for Kunbarlang is WLG.

In the course of the 20th century, the Kunbarlang people have moved off their traditional lands and spread in two primary directions: West and East. The movement westwards began with the establishment of a Methodist mission on traditional Mawng lands in South Goulburn island (Warruwi) in 1916, which attracted a large number of Kunbarlang people. The eastwards trajectory formed with the establishment, across the Liverpool river, of the trade post of Maningrida (Manayangkarirra) after World War II, which in 1957 became a government-run settlement. This settlement grew rapidly and also attracted a number of Kunbarlang people. Moving off of their traditional lands has probably been a factor accelerating linguistic assimilation, foremost by Ndjébbana speakers.

The exact number of speakers is not possible to establish,[1] but my best estimate is that today there are close to 30 Kunbarlang speakers living in Warruwi and around a dozen speakers in Maningrida. There is a fair amount of migration and marriage between people in Warruwi and Minjilang (Crocker island, located West of South Goulburn, near the Cobourg peninsula), and I know of at least two speakers who live in Minjilang. The city of Darwin is the major attracting hub in the area, providing access to healthcare, shops, nursing homes etc., and at the moment of writing I know of three people who permanently live in Darwin. The 2011 census reports 20 speakers of Kunbarlang in Australia, 19 of them in Warruwi.[2] In 1969, Kinslow Harris (1969b: 1) reported approximately 125 speakers of Kunbarlang.[3] In 1982, Coleman (1982: ii) reported an estimate of "probably fewer than one hundred first-language speakers" living primarily in Warruwi, Gunbalanya (Oenpelli) and Maningrida.

The ages of speakers range between late 20s and early 70s. As far as I can tell, no children are acquiring Kunbarlang at the moment. Likewise, not all Kunbarlang people speak the language. All speakers of Kunbarlang are fluent in Mawng: even the Kunbarlang people of Maningrida have childhood or other family connections to Warruwi. The Kunbarlang who live in Maningrida also speak Ndjébbana. Most adults are also fluent in Bininj Kunwok, and individual repertoires may include other Australian Aboriginal languages as well. All the speakers that I know of speak Aboriginal English, with somewhat varying degree of fluency. In the course of my work with Kunbarlang speakers I heavily relied on their competence in English, which I discuss in more detail in the methodology section (§1.3).

1.1.1 Social organization

1.1.1.1 Kinship

As in all Australian Aboriginal societies, kinship is the central organisational principle of social relations among the Kunbarlang people. Kin relations determine interpersonal behaviour models, and these kinship relations are extended beyond one's biological

---

[1] Evans (2001) discusses the difficulties in determining the exact extent of speakers in a language with small numbers, from the point of view of how a given social system determines one's rights to count as a speaker.
[2] Australian Bureau of Statistics website (http://quickstats.censusdata.abs.gov.au/census_services/getproduct/census/2011/quickstat/SSC70198?opendocument&navpos=220), retrieved on 2018/10/02.
[3] Cf. her slightly smaller figure of "about 100 [Kunbarlang] speakers residing mostly at Goulburn Island and Maningrida, with smaller groups in Oenpelli, Mudginberry and around Goomadeer Creek" (Kinslow Harris 1969a: 4).

family to their entire social universe, with the potential to include strangers. This is known as 'classificatory kinship' or 'universal kinship', i.e. a system of relations where everyone in the social universe is classified as kin (see McConvell 2018 and references therein, as well as other papers in that volume). For instance, one's biological mother's sisters are classified as one's mothers—and further, by extension, their children (i.e., *cousins*, from the English-language point of view) are classified as one's siblings.

1.1.1.2 Language and land

The basic unit of social grouping and organisation is a patrilineal clan, or PATRICLAN, like elsewhere in western Arnhem Land (cf. Evans 2003a: 40 ff).[4] In Kunbarlang they are called *nguya* (cf. Kune *kun-nguya*). These patriclans have names and their own territories within the broader Kunbarlang country. One's ownership of a language is effectively mediated by their *nguya* in the following way: the language is directly associated with the land, and thus an individual inherits the rights to their father's language *through* their affiliation with the patrilineal clan's territory. When speaking English, my consultants would refer to the *nguya* as "mobs" or "tribes".

These are the patriclans that I have heard of (with the name of their land when it is known): Djindibi (Mawuludja), Djumbilirri, Kamulkbarn (Nakalarramba),[5] Kumungkurdu (Mayirri and Bat island), Kurduwala (Kubarnbangku), Kurikuri, Mandjulngunj (Mirrangkangku / King River),[6] Mardbarrdjiyi (Mayirri), Marrabandja (Karrabbu), Marrabangku, Mayirrkulij. Additionally, the dictionary mentions Marranumbu and Murruwarn patriclans (Coleman 2010: 66,78).

Although I have little to say about dialectal variation in Kunbarlang, it does appear that these patriclans are associated with some characteristic linguistic differences, i.e. *patrilects*. The only known differences are lexical. Thus, for instance, the word for 'dog' is *durduk* ([duɖuk]) in Kunkurduwala, but *nakarrken* ([naharken]) in Kunkamulkbarn; the Kunkamulkbarn word for 'rain' is *marnki* ([maŋgi]), while in other dialects it is *balmad* ([balmat]). While referring to members of a patriclan or to their patrilects, some of the clan names may take on class prefixes, according to the standard rules of noun class assignment: classes I/II for men and women, respectively, and class IV for the language (as in *Kunkurduwala* earlier in this paragraph). Interestingly, it seems that not all clan names allow this. I do not have the exhaustive picture, but to the best of my knowledge, prefixes can be attached to *Kamulkbarn, Kurduwala, Mardbarrdjiyi, Marrabandja* and *Marrabangku*, and may not be attached to *Mandjulngunj*.

---

[4] A recent description of these topics with reference to western Arnhem Land can also be found in O'Keeffe 2016: §3.1

[5] Also spelt *Nagalarramba*, this is the land where the photographer Axel Poignant took the celebrated series of shots in 1952 (Poignant 1996).

[6] My understanding is that this clan connects Kunbarlang and Mawng people, since King River is west of the Kunbarlang traditional lands, in Mawng territory.

It is hard to tell if there are any differences in the sociolinguistic status of these different patrilects, and more generally what the speakers' perception of the lects is. My impression is that *Kunkurduwala* is often singled out for some reason. People will refer to it as the 'hard' (*kunrayek*) or 'real' (*djininj*) Kunbarlang, and often furnish it along the lines of "there are two tongues: Kurduwala and the other/plain one", also pointing out they are "different, but still the same"—which I interpret as acknowledging dialectal difference within one language, intelligible for everybody regardless of their *nguya*. The metaphor typically offered for the division between Kunkurduwala and other varieties of Kunbarlang is the goanna's (*nadjanarr*) split tongue. Besides the Kunkurduwala, in one of Isabel O'Keeffe's recordings (ID: 20060831IB03), a speaker also refers to Mandjulngunj as *kunrayek* 'hard'.

Besides the dialects and patrilects, there are also dedicated registers for special circumstances: the respectful trirelational kin term system of *kun-derbi*, the avoidance, or 'Mother-in-law', register *kun-kurrng*, and the bereavement register *marrdjukkun lerrk*, used by widows during the mourning period (O'Keeffe et al. 2017). Some kun-derbi and kun-kurrng terms are documented in Coleman (2010), but the sociolinguistic particulars of these special registers have not been described, and it is likely that their use is dramatically declining. Evans (2003a: 59–67) details the structure and use of the Bininj Kunwok registers *kun-debi* and *kun-kurrng*, and Garde (2013: ch.4) provides an in-depth ethnographic account of *kun-debi* in Bininj Kunwok; both give further references for the broader Australian context.

1.1.1.3 Subsections and moieties

The extension of kinship to the individuals outside of one's immediate family, and further still, outside of one's usual social network, is enabled by a more abstract overarching system of SUBSECTIONS, commonly known in Australia as 'skins'. In this part of Australia there are eight subsections, which determine marriageability, avoidance, terms of address and other aspects of social behaviour. One's subsection is determined based on that of one's mother, and in this way they form two disjoint matrilineal succession cycles (*Mardku* and *Ngarradjku*). These succession cycles form the binary system of *matrimoieties*. There is also a patrilineal counterpart to it, the *patrimoieties Duwa* and *Yirriddja*. While the matrimoiety system is ancient in western Arnhem Land, the patrimoiety system has been spreading as a borrowing from the Yolŋu in eastern Arnhem Land (Evans 2003a: 47–8).

The subsection system spread across northern Australia—the system which Kunbarlang also is a part of—includes eight named units ('skins') of people. This system is a product of amalgamation of two independent *section* systems (i.e. ones that have four named units) that came into contact, and in this combined state spread into Arnhem Land (McConvell 1985).

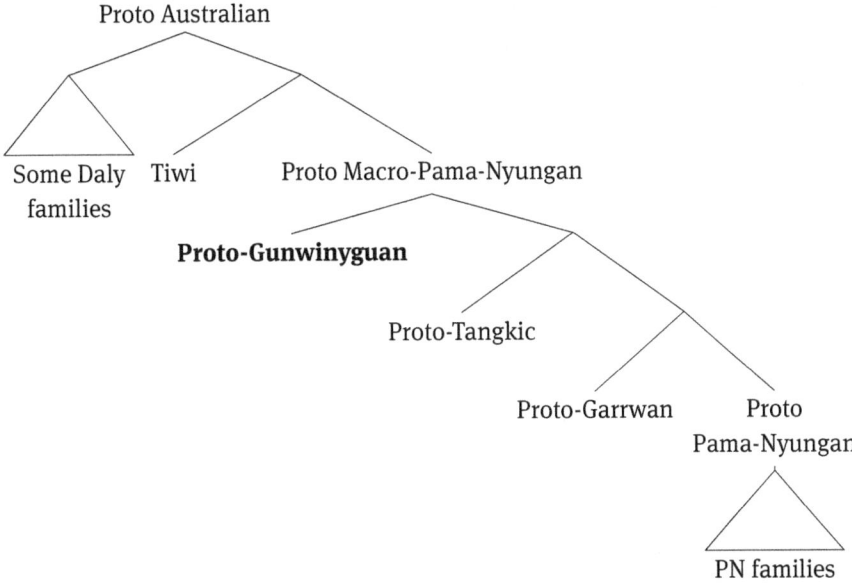

Fig. 1.2: "The Pama-Nyungan offshoot model", after Evans (2003b: 10)

1.2 Kunbarlang among the Gunwinyguan languages

Kunbarlang genetically belongs to the Gunwinyguan family, which is a non-Pama-Nyungan family of Australian languages spoken across Arnhem Land. Its similarity to "Gunwinggu" was already recognized by Capell (1940). The placement of the Gunwinyguan languages within the higher-level Australian family, according to the so-called "Pama-Nyungan offshoot model", is shown in figure 1.2.

I adapt a number of sources to illustrate the further subdivision of the Gunwinyguan family. This is primarily based on Alpher, Evans & Harvey (2003: 309), but also includes elaborations in B. Baker 2004 and van Egmond (2012: ch.9) concerning the Eastern/*bak* group. B. Baker (2004) also argues against the unity of the "*bak*"-group and against inclusion of Dalabon in the Central group; figure 1.3 presents Alpher, Evans & Harvey's (2003) analysis in these respects. The dashed lines reflect the tentative inclusion of Kungarakany and Mangarayi in the Gunwinyguan family. See Merlan 2003 for an argument that Mangarayi belongs to the Marra-Alawic family.

Kunbarlang is a fairly representative member of the family, sharing a number of characteristic typological traits with the other Gunwinyguan languages. They include:
- prevalence of head marking
- high degree of polysynthesis, in particular
  - noun and adverb incorporation
  - polypersonal agreement

- valency-changing derivations
- templatic organisation of the verbal word
- noun class system
- discourse-configurationality

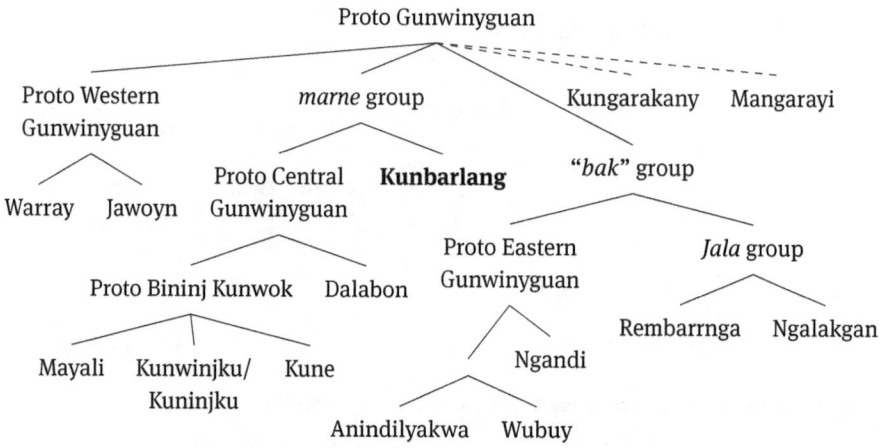

Fig. 1.3: The Gunwinyguan language family

Polysynthesis is one of the striking features of many non-Pama-Nyungan language families, the Gunwinyguan languages among them (Evans 2017). The elaboration of the verbal word is such that it allows one to express a full proposition with a fair amount of modifying details in a single phonological word. This is possible mainly due to the polypersonal agreement and incorporation. The former means that the person and number features of subject and (in case of the polyvalent verbs) an object are indexed in the verb (1.1a). The latter refers to the option of incorporation into the verb of a number of other lexical roots, both of nominal and of adverbial nature (1.1b).

(1.1) a. Ngunda **ngay-buddu**-wuni.
 not 1SG.IRR.PST-3PL.OBJ-give.IRR.PST
 'I didn't give it to them.' [IK1-160729_0001/03:20]

 b. Ka-**nganj-kanak**-bingki.
 3SG.NF-HITH-sun-exit.NP
 'The sun is rising.' [IK1-160612_0011/10:34]

In (1.1a) the agent and the recipient of the giving event are encoded by prefixes on the verb. In (1.1b) there is a directional adverbial and the subject of the verb, both contained within the verbal word. Moreover, some further argument relations can be encoded via verbal morphology, in particular the benefactive/implied (1.2) and the comitative participants.

(1.2) Nga-**ngun**-**marnanj**-kinjang neyang.
1SG.NF-2SG.OBJ-BEN-cook.PST food
'I cooked food for you.' [IK1-180522_2SM1/18:37]

On the other hand, there also are some important differences between Kunbarlang and the other Gunwinyguan languages. These include:
- different organisation of the TAM system
- coverb constructions
- minimal nominal morphology
- hierarchical noun phrase

Gunwinyguan languages feature rather complex TAM systems. They differ in whether there are any mood/modality distinctions in the agreement prefixes: Anindilyakwa, Kunbarlang, Mangarayi, Warray, Wubuy do have at least a realis/irrealis distinction, while Bininj Kunwok, Ngalakgan and Ngandi use suffixes instead (Verstraete 2005 via van Egmond (2012: 134)). Dalabon marks realis with a dedicated morpheme -*h*- that immediately follows the subject prefix (Evans 2006: 37). The specific inventory of TAM categories varies between languages, Kunbarlang's being one of the smallest and organised in a way different from others (§5.3 and also §5.4).

Kunbarlang has a type of complex predicate called coverb construction, which is a bipartite verbal construction. In (1.3), for example, there is a complex predicate that means 'to acquire', which is built from an inflecting verb -*rna* 'to sit', which inflects for tense, and an uninflecting element *bard*. Although it is related to the ways of forming complex predicates in the other Gunwinyguan languages, it is formally quite distinct and has a closer resemblance to the Iwaidjan language Mawng than any of the Gunwinyguan (§6.5).

(1.3) Neyang **ka-rninganj**=**bard** kandidjawa.
food 3SG.NF-sit.PST=acquire bread
'He bought food, flour.' [20060620IB04/11:59–12:03]

Although a number of inflectional categories are relevant for the Kunbarlang noun phrase, the nouns have scarcely any morphology, in stark contrast to the rich Kunbarlang verbs. At the same, the systematicity of word order patterns and interpretive effects associated with them betrays the very principled noun phrase structure. This is remarkable in comparison with other Gunwinyguan languages, where absense of noun phrase construal has been reported (see Evans (2003a: 229–31) for Bininj Kunwok and Heath (1986) for Wubuy). Chapter 4 covers a variety of topics in the noun phrase, showing how much information can be expressed via syntactic means.

1.3 Fieldwork: consultants and methodology

Most of the present descripton is based on orginal field work carried out by the author in Darwin, Maningrida and Warruwi in 2015–2018. This work was done in four trips:
- July–August 2015 (two weeks, Warruwi and Darwin)
- April–August 2016 (four months, Warruwi, Maningrida and Darwin)
- May–June 2017 (six weeks, Warruwi and Darwin)
- May–June 2018 (six weeks, Warruwi and Darwin)

Additional invaluable data come from the recordings made by Dr. Isabel O'Keeffe, Dr. Aung Si and Dr. Ruth Singer in the period from 2006 to 2015 in Warruwi, Darwin, Maningrida and Minjilang. They generously made these recordings and the existing transcriptions available to me, which expanded considerably the amount of data, especially from the spontaneous production. These sources are outlined in the list of recordings below.

I have had a chance to work, at least briefly, with the majority of the present-day Kunbarlang speakers. At the same time, there was a small group of people who I worked with particularly intensively. Nakangila Solomon Yalbarr and Nakangila Paul Naragoidj have been tireless and patient teachers for me, and Kunbarlang data as they speak it constitute a considerable part of the empirical basis of this grammar. The wealth of linguistic repertoire of Ngalwamud Rita Djitmu is another major constituent in the recordings both of my own and by others. Ngalngarridj Sandra Makurlngu and Nakangila Douglas Djalanba have been sharing invaluable insights into the intricacies of meaning and use of Kunbarlang expressions. I cannot name every speaker individually here, but refer the reader to the acknowledgements.

My recordings have taken place in diverse settings, depending on the circumstances. Although I have always aimed to record indoors (e.g. at the Warruwi Language centre) for the best possible quality, some recordings have been made in people's front yards, or other outdoor settings. Thus, the text about making damper (bush bread) in appendix A.2 was recorded during a short bush trip.

My main method was elicitation, which was extensively complemented by the analysis of recordings of different genres (primarily narrative). The elicitation involved direct translation of English prompts into Kunbarlang and elicitation from non-verbal prompts (pictures, videos, construction blocks set-ups), as well as grammaticality judgements of word forms and sentences constructed by myself in order to test specific hypotheses in the process of work. Thus, the forms that were judged ungrammatical in the language constitute an important part of the analytical material in this work, and are used throughout the book to illustrate specific grammatical restrictions. The notation used is customary in the field (see the list of abbreviations and conventions on page XX ff.). Another note is in order about glossing of examples. I choose to use consistent glosses for polysemous morphemes, rather than contextually appropriate ones. For instance, the verbal root *-djin* 'to consume' can be used to mean 'to eat', 'to burn' or 'to bake' on different occasions. Instead of using different glosses, I consistently gloss it with the concise 'eat'. Another verb where the gloss may not always be entirely transparent is *-ngundje* 'to say/do'. It is highly polyfunctional, with such meanings as 'to do', 'to be', 'to say', or 'to think', depending on the context, collocation, or its own morphological make-up. However, it is consistently glossed as 'do'.

When working on the matters crucially involving fine semantic judgements, I often employed the truth value judgement task (TVJT; Crain & Thornton 1998). This method involves constructing a model of a particular state of affairs in the real world, against which the target sentence is evaluated for acceptability. The model can be constructed via presenting a speaker with a verbal context, or a picture/video representation of the target situation. Then the speaker can be asked to describe the stimulus, but also, crucially, a particular form can be offered for the speaker to judge its appropriateness in that context. Thus aspects of semantics can be studied in a controlled fashion and without reliance on the analytical intuitions of the speaker or their competence in the intermediary language. A more detailed discussion of the TVJT with specific illustrations can be found in the section on quantifiers (§4.7).

The elicitation and the analysis of spontaneous speech recordings (narratives, dialogues, and storyboards) were employed in a complementary fashion. Direct elicitation was used to probe specific aspects of the Kunbarlang grammar in the minute detail, while text analysis helped broaden the scope of language constructions that may have been overlooked in elicitation for various reasons. Moreover, text analysis made it possible to estimate the actual rate of use of particular constructions, as well as the relative frequency in cases when competing forms of expression were available.

All samples of spontaneous production and all elicitation sessions were recorded in .wav format with the minimum sample rate of 44100Hz and the minimum bitrate of 16 bit.[7] The texts were also filmed with a digital camera (raw format .MTS, subsequently converted to MP4 v2). All of the recordings are archived with PARADISEC (see *Guide to recordings* above for details).

The time-aligned transcriptions of the recordings (full in case of texts, partial in case of elicitations) were created with the help of ELAN (ELAN 2020; ver. 4.8–6.0), and archived together with the audio files. Plain text files typed in the course of elicitation (or created later based on the notebook notes) also accompany the recordings in the archive. Acoustic analyses, i.e. the spectrograms and waveforms presented here, were done in Praat (Boersma & Weenink 2016).

---

[7] Sometimes the speakers would hesitate to be recorded at the outset of a session, and in those cases I had to work only with text files or pen and paper until they were comfortable with the recorder on.

I have used a range of materials to aid both text collection and elicitation of particular grammatical topics. These were:
- MPI videos on reciprocal situations (Evans et al. 2004)
    - see http://fieldmanuals.mpi.nl/volumes/2004/reciprocals/
- storyboards from the Totem Storyboards Project
    - http://totemfieldstoryboards.org/; esp. TFS Working Group (2012)
- Nordlinger & Kidd's (2018) materials for word order production in picture description
- Kyuseva's (2020) Spot-the-Difference materials, which I used as a task to record dialogue
- Bruening's (2008) quantifier scope stimuli

These materials are mentioned in those sections where relevant for the data presented.

1.4 Previous work and the contribution of this grammar

As mentioned above, Arthur Capell (1940: 271–2) gave the earliest characterisation of Kunbarlang. He noted that the "general structure of the Gunba:lang language is similar to that of Gunwinggu", provided about 25 lexical items, and mentioned that there is incorporation and "a system of tenses and a negative indicated by variable suffixes, while the prefixes remain the same".

Joy Kinslow Harris carried out the first large-scope analysis of Kunbarlang: based on her field work at Maningrida, Oenpelli Mission (Gunbalanya) and Warruwi in 1965–66, she published a tagmemic grammar (Kinslow Harris 1969b), which is the only dedicated publication on Kunbarlang in the XX century. Combining data from narratives and elicitation, this grammar covers the basics of the verbal and nominal morphosyntax, as well as a range of phrasal and clausal level constructions, such as imperatives, interrogatives, adjectival predicates, and some clause combining strategies. Most of the generalisations are presented as formal statement of TAGMEMES, i.e. rewrite rules, which are supposed to comprise a generative grammar of the language: supplied by a dictionary of roots and affixes, such grammar would produce all well-formed sentence of the language. This description also comprises a chapter in her dissertation (Kinslow Harris 1969a), in which she uses Kunbarlang as the baseline for a comparative analysis of morphosyntactic constructions in a range of Arnhem Land languages: Bininj Kunwok (Kunwinjku, Kundjeyhmi, and Kundedjnjenghmi varieties), Dalabon, Jawoyn, Ndjébbana, Mengerrdji, and Mawng.

Kinslow Harris's preliminary grammar is rather brief and includes only a small data set, yet it is of considerable interest: her and my data collection occurred 50 years apart, and her data are the earliest available records. Thus, the constructions that Kinslow Harris cites provide a valuable diachronic point of reference. The fact that her generalisations are largely valid for the language in its present state suggests that—in the areas of grammar she describes—Kunbarlang has been reasonably stable in these 50 years.

A specific aspect of that general interest concerns the possible influence of English on the grammatical structures of Kunbarlang. In the introduction to her dissertation, Kinslow Harris (1969a: 9) explains that in her data collection "Gunwinggu was used as the contact language and 'situation elicitation' was used instead of 'translation elicitation' in order to obviate English-conditioned responses". Additionally, she notes that the texts and the items of her questionnaire were recorded from non-English speakers, with only the (verbal) paradigms elicited from a speaker with some English competence (Kinslow Harris 1969b: §0.1). This, therefore, precludes not only the immediate 'translation bias', but also any direct contact influence of English on Kunbarlang. One of the relevant findings emerging from this is that the word order of subject–verb–object has been the neutral one (in the face of word order freedom) even prior to expansion of contact with English (see §7.1).

The fullest description, going into the detail of many core grammatical topics, is Carolyn Coleman's unpublished Honours thesis (1982), based her field work in Maningrida in 1981–82. It has a broad scope, including phonology, morphology and syntax. Its main focus, however, is grammatical relations as manifest both in the verb and in the phrasal level constructions, and the insightful treatment that many of them are given has influenced numerous aspects of my analyses in this book. Coleman's analysis is largely informed by Foley and Van Valin's Role and Reference Grammar, and the presentation frequently follows the logic of that framework, either unifying phenomena that belong to the same *layer* (nuclear, core, or peripheral), or to the same type of relation. Thus, cosubordinate nexus (Coleman's §2.3.4), which cross-cuts all layers, includes purposive constructions (at the peripheral layer; see §8.5.1 of the present grammar), viewpoint aspect constructions with an auxiliary posture verb (at the core layer; §7.2.1 here) and verbal reduplication (at the nucleus layer; §2.8.2 here).

Some of the aspects of Coleman's (1982) description have been summarised briefly in a manuscript (Coleman n.d.), which also includes more comprehensive paradigm tables and a discussion of various pronominals. Coleman has been compiling a comprehensive dictionary over the course of her work. It has not been published at the moment of writing this, but she generously made the manuscript available to me, and it will be drawn upon and referred to throughout this grammar as Coleman 2010.

I do not aim to give a summary, let alone a review, of the preceding work here in the introduction. Suffice it to say that despite that very important groundwork, a range of topics remained that were not covered in sufficient detail, or which were not covered at all, and the goal of this current grammatical description is to both broaden and deepen those previous ones, as well as verify the existant analyses. In a number of cases my work led me to revise previous analyses significantly. For instance, the area of pronominal prefixes and tense/mood suffixes of the verb has been completely reanalysed. Related to that, I describe pronominal prefix paradigms in transitive verbs that have never been described before (§5.2). I indicate throughout the text where I am building on that preceding work, and where my data or interpretation differ from it. In citing data from those previous works, I retain the authors' transcription of Kunbarlang, but represent it in the orthography adopted in this book, and provide my own glossing for the cited examples.

Looking beyond the grammatical structures, Isabel O'Keeffe (2016) in a recent thesis in musicology investigates ceremony and musical practices in western Arnhem Land, in particular the Kunbarlang song tradition (*manyardi*). Further documentation work of the language is currently being carried out within an ELDP-funded project (O'Keeffe et al. 2017).

1.5 Overview of the grammar

This grammar consists of eight chapters and an appendix. Chapter 1 is the general introduction to the Kunbarlang people and their language, the data and methodological aspects of the present work. Chapter 2 is devoted to the sound inventory of Kunbarlang and its phonological and morphophonological processes. Chapter 3 gives an introductory grammatical overview and describes the Kunbarlang parts of speech. Chapter 4 focuses on the constituents of the noun phrase. That chapter also provides a discussion of the noun phrase constituency and the categories of noun class (grammatical gender) and case in Kunbarlang. Discussion of the verbal morphosyntax is divided between the two following chapters. Agreement and tense and mood, i.e. the inflectional categories, are described in Chapter 5, while Chapter 6 treats derivational morphology and constructions. Chapter 7 discusses the structure of a simple clause and the phenomena relevant at the clause level, such as negation and question formation. Finally, multiclausal constructions made either by coordinating or by subordinating clauses are presented in Chapter 8. Chapter 9 provides a summary and indicates directions for further research. The Appendix gives a selection of glossed Kunbarlang texts in different genres.

2 Phonetics and phonology

2.1 Segmental units: an overview

This section identifies the sets of consonantal and vocalic phonemes in Kunbarlang. Their phonetic characteristics and distribution, as well as phonotactics more generally, will be the subject of the following sections.

The 'long and thin' consonant inventory of Kunbarlang, with its many places of articulation but neither fricatives nor voice contrast in obstruents, is quite typical for an Australian language. The Kunbarlang vowel inventory is somewhat larger than the more standard three-vowel set, but is typical for the languages of the north. The distribution of vowels conforms to the standard vowel triangle. The consonant phonemic inventory of Kunbarlang is in table 2.1. Table 2.2 below gives the vowel inventory.

The consonantal inventory of Kunbarlang is similar to those of other Gunwinyguan languages. Kunbarlang lacks dental consonants (t̪, n̪, l̪) found in Ngandi and Wubuy, otherwise having all the consonants present in the maximal inventory of the family Harvey (2003: 206). The fortis/lenis contrast is found in Kunbarlang and in Bininj Kunwok (Evans 2003a, Stoakes 2013); see 2.4.1 for more on fortis. As is common in Australian languages (e.g. Fletcher & Butcher 2014: 101), there are no contrastive fricatives ([-son,+cont] in Chomsky & Halle 1968 style phonological features) and no phonemic voicing contrast in the stop series, but instead there are multiple place of articulation contrasts. Besides that, there is a corresponding nasal for every place of articulation. Thus, each of the five places of articulation (excluding glottal) shows the three-way stop contrast: lenis–fortis–nasal. There are also two glides (the labio-velar /w/ and the palatal /j/) and four liquids, comprising two laterals (the alveolar /l/ and the retroflex /ɭ/) and two rhotics (the alveolar tap/trill /r/ and the retroflex /ɻ/). The labio-velar glide is placed in the labials (rather than velars) column throughout this chapter, and when quantitative measures are given, is counted together with labials. Given that labials and dorso-velar consonants are grouped together as 'peripherals' for most phonotactic purposes, there are no significant consequences of such treatment of /w/, as opposed to, say, counting it together with velars.

Tab. 2.1: Consonant phonemic inventory of Kunbarlang

	Labial	Alveolar	Retroflex	Palatal	Velar	Glottal
Lenis	p	t	ʈ	c	k	ʔ
Fortis	p:	t:	ʈ:	c:	k:	
Nasal	m	n	ɳ	ɲ	ŋ	
Lateral		l	ɭ			
Rhotic		r	ɻ			
Glide	w			j		

Tab. 2.2: Vowel phonemic inventory of Kunbarlang

	Front	Central	Back
High	i		u
Mid	e		o
Low		a	

Kunbarlang has five out of six vowels attested in the Gunwinyguan family (table 2.2), i.e. all except the mid-high central vowel found in Dalabon and Rembarrnga. To sum up, there are 22 consonant and five vowel phonemes in Kunbarlang. Consonants demonstrate an apical contrast (between alveolar and retroflex coronals) without a laminal one (the so-called 'double-apical' pattern). In terms of manner, there is a phonemic distinction between lenis and fortis oral stops. Its peripherals include both labial and dorsal consonants. Peripherals (as opposed to coronals) form a recurring natural class in Australian phonologies (Dixon 2002: 63); in Kunbarlang, peripherals behave as a natural class in consonant clusters (see §2.5.1).

2.2 Practical orthography

The practical orthography adopted in this grammar is based on the conventions in the previous work by Coleman (1982, 2010) and is fairly standard for Australian linguistics. The orthography for vowels is straightforward and is the same as reflected in table 2.2. As for the consonants, velar fortis and lenis stops are written with the unvoiced series symbols, while stops in all other places of articulation employ voiced series symbols. This achieves a certain phonetic accuracy, as the velar stop's realisations are phonetically more often voiceless than those of other stops (which are typically closer to the voiced end of continuum). Further practical motivation comes from the need to disambiguate the velar nasal, spelled *ng*, from the nasal–stop cluster, spelled *nk*. The spelling of consonants is provided in table 2.3, with the IPA symbols in forward slashes (i.e. "/p/ b" means that the phoneme /p/ is spelled in the orthography as *b*). Note that the fortis consonants are spelled as the corresponding lenis doubled up, except retroflexion and palatalisation are only marked once, i.e. /ʈː/ is spelled *rdd*, not *rdrd*.

Stress is not systematically marked in the orthography, but where needed, primary stress will be indicated by an acute accent and secondary by a grave accent, on the relevant vowels. In what follows, this practical orthography will be used for rendering Kunbarlang, except for discussions of phonological rules and phonetic matters, where IPA symbols are used. These are enclosed in forward slashes (/a/) for phonemic and square brackets ([a]) for phonetic representations, as is customary. The practical orthography in the examples is used phonemically, not reflecting the variable phonetic

Tab. 2.3: Kunbarlang orthography

	Labial	Alveolar	Retroflex	Palatal	Velar	Glottal
Lenis	/p/ b	/t/ d	/ʈ/ rd	/c/ dj	/k/ k	/ʔ/ h
Fortis	/pː/ bb	/tː/ dd	/ʈː/ rdd	/cː/ ddj	/kː/ kk	
Nasal	/m/ m	/n/ n	/ɳ/ rn	/ɲ/ nj	/ŋ/ ng	
Lateral		/l/ l	/ɭ/ rl			
Rhotic		/r/ rr	/ɻ/ r			
Glide	/w/ w			/j/ y		

realisation of the phonemes (see the following two sections), nor the morphophonological processes (see §2.7).

2.3 Vowels

Table 2.4 provides counts of Kunbarlang vowel frequencies based on 1900 entries in the dictionary (Coleman 2010).

Tab. 2.4: Kunbarlang vocalic phoneme frequencies

	Front	Central	Back	Total	% of total
High	i, 1160		u, 1326	2486	43
Mid	e, 689		o, 428	1117	19
Low		a, 2226		2226	38
Total	1849	2226	1754	5829	
% of total	32	38	30		

The mean vowel frequency is 1165.8, with the high front /i/ being closest to that figure. The vowel with most occurences in the dictionary is the low central /a/. It can be seen from the table that the vowels are not uniformly distributed, with the mid vowels /e/ and /o/ being noticeably less frequent. While there do not seem to be any categorical restrictions in occurrence of the mid vowels in any position in stems, there is a dispreference against them appearing in stems with the vowels of another height, particularly high ones.

Phonetic realisations of vowels are overall rather straightforward. There is little or no variation in vowel quality depending on metrical strength (such as reduction or centralisation in unstressed syllables), which is similar to the findings in other Australian languages, in particular other Gunwinyguan languages (Kuninjku: Bishop 2002: 233; Dalabon: Fletcher & Evans 2002). All vowels appear nasalised after nasal consonants, especially after the velar nasal /ŋ/. There is, however, some variation in the low vowel /a/. While most of the time it is pronounced as a low central [a], there are cases where it is realised as a higher and more front variant, closer to [æ] or [ɛ]. These, however, appear to be variable, rather than well-defined by the context (2.1): it does not occur systematically, but in random tokens.

(2.1) a. [kaˈkiɲʸaŋ] / [kaˈkiɲʸæŋ] 's/he cooked it'
b. [ˈmaɾɛk] / [ˈmɛɾɛk] 'not'
c. [-d͡ʒalaɻk-] / [-d͡ʒalɛɻk-] 'alive' (bound morpheme)

An experimental phonetic study could reveal more about the vowel space and vowel acoustics in Kunbarlang, but this is outside the scope of the present grammar.

2.4 Consonants

Table 2.5 gives counts of consonantal phonemes frequency based on 1900 entries in the dictionary (Coleman 2010).

Tab. 2.5: Kunbarlang consonantal phoneme frequencies

	Labial	Alveolar	Retroflex	Palatal	Velar	Glottal	Total	% of total
Lenis	p, 894	t, 262	ʈ, 250	c, 598	k, 1183	ʔ, 74	3261	39
Fortis	pː, 104	tː, 32	ʈː, 28	cː, 43	kː, 186		393	5
Nasal	m, 820	n, 396	ɳ, 227	ɲ, 336	ŋ, 465		2244	26
Lateral		l, 557	ɭ, 280				837	10
Rhotic		ɾ, 733	ɻ, 82				815	10
Glide	w, 472			j, 363			835	10
Total	2290	1980	867	1340	1834	74	8385	
% of total	27	24	10	16	22	1		

With a grand total of 8385 phoneme tokens and 22 types, this gives a mean of 381 token per phoneme. The phonemes /n/ and /j/ are closest to the mean, on the upper and the lower sides, respectively. The most frequent consonant is /k/ (1183 tokens), and the least frequent one is /ʈː/ (28) tokens. It can be noticed that the fortis stops are all roughly by an order of magnitude less frequent than the corresponding lenis stops. Another remarkable contrast is between the two rhotics: the tap /ɾ/ is much more heavily used in the lexicon than the retroflex rhotic (733 vs. 82 tokens). The glottal stop /ʔ/ in Kunbarlang has a low count and does not form minimal pairs. Overall, in terms of the manner of articulation, lenis stops are the most frequent and fortis stops are the least frequent consonants. In terms of the place of articulation, labials are the most frequent and retroflex consonants are the least frequent ones.

2.4.1 Fortis consonants

Kunbarlang displays a contrast between audibly short and long oral stops at all places of articulation except glottal. The phonemic contrastive status emerges on the basis of minimal and near-minimal pairs in tautomorphemic contexts (§2.4.3.2). The phonotactic distribution of fortis consonants, however, is captured most economically if heterosyllabic attachment is assumed. This is the analysis I follow in the discussion of Kunbarlang syllable structure (§2.5). This analysis extends naturally to the distribution pattern of the fortis, which are found in morpheme-initial and morpheme-medial positions, but not morpheme-finally. The heterosyllabic attachment thus systematically creates complex codas with morpheme-initial fortis when the preceding syllable is closed. These resulting clusters generally follow the restrictions on admissible complex codas that are independently motivated in the analysis of Kunbarlang phonotactics. It should be borne in mind, however, that the precise phonetic nature of the long stops is open to further acoustic study, possibly one along the lines of Stoakes's (2013) acoustic and aerodynamic analysis of the corresponding consonants in Bininj Kunwok. One of the questions for such a study would be about the acoustic difference between phonemic fortis consonants (*nukka* 'he') and the heteromorphemic homorganic stop clusters (*-kuk-karlyung* 'long'), which are also realised as audibly long stops.

2.4.2 Phonetic description and allophonic distribution of consonants

Since voicing is not a contrastive feature for obstruents, there is noticeable freedom of allophonic variation along that dimension. Just as in Bininj Kunwok (Evans 2003a: 79), oral lenis stops have a tendency to be realised as voiced syllable-initially and as voiceless syllable-finally. However, there is further variation by place of articulation: for instance, the velar /k/ seems more often voiceless, but the labial /p/ through to the palatal /c/ are more often realised as voiced. For instance, see (2.2a) for the voiced allophones of /k/ and /p/ in the syllable-initial position, and (2.2b) for the voiced allophone of /t/ and the voiceless allophone of /k/, again syllable-initially. A voiceless allophone of /t/ in the syllable-final position is shown in (2.2c).

(2.2) a. /ŋunci-ɲaɲ-kapurk-ka/ → [ˌŋuɲd͡ʒiɲaŋgaˈburkːa] 'you two will come here' [IK1-160505_0011/28:41]

b. /ka-kitaɲ/ → [ˈkakidaɲ] 's/he/it went' [IK1-150724_1SY1/16:22]

c. /na-wamut/ → [naˈwamut] 'Nawamud [skin name]' [IK1-160829_0001/53:08]

Fortis stops are audibly longer than the lenis ones. They tend to be realised as voiceless, even though they only appear prevocalically (see §2.5 for more on syllable structure). Stops are usually unreleased word finally, especially the oral ones. Velar lenis and nasal stops often undergo lenition. The context for lenition of /k/ is intervocalic, in which environment it is realised as [ɣ]/[x] or as [w] (preceding the high back vowel /u/). An example of each realisation, including an unlenited realisation [k] preceding a high front vowel, is given in (2.3):

(2.3) a. /ka-kitaɲ/ → [ˈkakidaɲ] 'he/she/it went'
 b. /jika/ → [ˈjiɣa] 'some'
 c. /na-kuci/ → [ˈnawud͡ʒi] 'one'

The velar nasal /ŋ/, on the other hand, lenites primarily in word-initial position, e.g. in personal pronouns and in personal prefixes on verbs, but also intervocalically. It may lenite to [ɣ̃] or to [w̃] or even stronger, with only some creaky voice or nasalisation of the following vowel betraying its presence in the phonemic representation (2.4a), or all the way through to complete phonetic erosion (2.4b). For comparison, Bininj Kunwok shows massive rates of complete deletion of the initial /ŋ/ in closed-class morphemes (noun and verb prefixes and free pronouns), reaching 49% of the time in noun class/gender prefixes (Marley 2020: 102ff.).

(2.4) a. /ka-ŋan-ʈukbaɲci-ŋ/ → [ka a̰ɳʈukˈbaɲd͡ʒiŋ] 's/he showed it to me'
       [IK1-170620_1SY2/00:36]
 b. /ŋaɲ-puʈːu-wu-ɲ/ → [aɲbuʈːuˈwuɲ] 'I'll give it to them'
       [IK1-160505_0011/33:50]

The labio-velar glide /w/ lenites strongly in the environment between a nasal stop and the high back vowel /u/. This particular constellation of /Nwu/ has a low type-count, but a reasonably high token-count due to the frequency of the verbal root/thematic /wu/ 'to give'. When it is preceded by nasal-final personal prefixes or prepounds, the glide disappears (2.5). This happens very clearly and systematically; in all examples cited in orthography I give the phonemic form -wu-.

(2.5) a. /ka-pun-wu-j/ → [ˈkabunuj] 's/he gave it to him/her/it'
       [IK1-150724_1SY1/46:00]
 b. /-woɭŋ.wu-ɲ/ → [-woɭŋuɲ] 'to heat'   [IK1-170615_1SY2/51:13]

In the nominal lexicon, there is the word *manwurrk* 'bushfire', which is most often pronounced [ˈmanuɻk], but occasionally the form [ˈmanwuɻk] can be heard (both variants, uttered by two speakers, can be heard in [20140703IOv03/00:28–30]).

Moving on to apicals, word- or utterance-initial position is not contrastive for them in Kunbarlang, and their occurrence word-initially is noticeably low (see §2.5.4). There are no optional prefixes that can be added to the few apical-initial words that there are, in order to create a contrastive environment. The fact that current existing transcriptions make a distinction between alveolar vs. postalveolar apicals probably is a historical analytical accident (for instance, *durduk* 'dog' vs. *rdubburdubbe* 'many'). The least controversial option available at present is to conceive of the initial apicals as representing an archiphoneme with allophonic variants as to how advanced or retracted their articulation is (cf. Butcher 1995). Typically for an Australian language (B. Baker 2014b: 142), utterance-initially apicals' realisation in Kunbarlang appears alveolar and phrase-medially, especially after vowels, postalveolar/retroflexed (2.6a–b, the 'archiphoneme' represented as a capital letter).[1] Very untypically for an Australian language, however, (i) Kunbarlang apicals often receive a retroflex realisation in word-initial, phrase-medial positions even after heterorganic consonants (2.6c), and (ii) Kunbarlang phonemic retroflexes that follow heterorganic consonants word-medially across a morpheme boundary retain their retroflexion. I further address this issue of robust retroflexion in §2.5.2.1, and take up the question about neutralisation in §2.5.2.2.

(2.6) a. /Lama ɳaʈːa-cu-ŋ/ → [ˈlama aˈdːa-d͡ʒuŋ] 'we speared it with a shovel spear'
 [20140703IOv02-FA/09:06]

 b. /ka-ca Nawalak/ → [ˈkad͡ʒa ˈɳawalak] 'she's pregnant'
 [IK1-150801_004/01:54]

 c. /ɳaʈːa-cu-ŋ Lama/ → [aˈdːa-d͡ʒuŋ ˈɭama] 'we speared it with a shovel spear'
 [20140703IOv02-FA/09:04]

The laminopalatal nasal /ɲ/ tends to have a phonetic off-glide when preceding a [-high,-back] vowel (/a/ or /e/), e.g. /ka-kiɲaŋ/ 'he/she/it cooks it' [kaˈkiɲʸaŋ]. Nasal place of articulation behaviour in heterorganic clusters is slightly variable but with the overall tendency to resist anticipatory assimilation. Thus, an alveolar nasal /n/ when preceding a palatal stop may retain its place (2.7a–2.7b) or sometimes take on palatalisation (2.7c). Notice that (2.7b) and (2.7c) exemplify different realisations of the same subject prefix *ngundji-* '2DU.IRR'.

(2.7) a. /ka-pun-caraŋ/ → [ˌkabunˈd͡ʒaraŋ] 'he/she/it ate him/her'
 [20140703IOv01-ShM/01:06–09]

 b. /ŋunci-na-ɲ/ → [ˈŋund͡ʒiɲaɲ] 'you two look [at me]!'
 [IK1-160613_0001/16:08–11]

 c. /ŋunci-ɲaɲ-kapurk-ka/ → [ˌŋuɲd͡ʒiɲaɲgaˈburkːa] 'you two will come here'
 [IK1-160505_0011/28:40–42]

---

1 It would be superfluous to posit yet another phoneme, however (e.g. a place-underspecified apical consonant at least for each of lenis, nasal, and lateral manners). Thus, the majority of apical-initial words are transcribed with an alveolar phoneme, as the citation forms suggests.

Another characteristic feature of consonant phonetic realisation that is evident in (2.7) is the spirantisation of the laminal alveopalatal stop /c/, resulting in the affricate [d͡ʒ] and even, rarely, [d͡z] (2.8). This is also a recurring phonetic feature in Australian languages (Fletcher & Butcher 2014: 103).

(2.8)   /ŋanci-cin/ → [anˈd͡zid͡zinʲ] 'we two will eat it'   [C02-026608/24:40]

Intramorphemically, there is a phonetic on-glide when the alveopalatal stop follows [a]. Some of the frequent morphemes that show this effect are the interjection *adju* 'I don't know' (2.9a), the pronoun *-ngadju* 'she.GEN' (2.9b) and the noun *wadjbud* 'sand' (the on-glide is absent in careful pronounciation), but this on-glide never appears in this phonetic environment when there is a morphological boundary between [a] and [d͡ʒ], e.g. (2.9c).

(2.9)   a.   /acu/ → [ˈaʸd͡ʒu] 'dunno'

     b.   /ŋacu/ → [ˈŋaʸd͡ʒu] 'she.GEN'

     c.   /ka-cu-ŋ/ → [ˈkad͡ʒuŋ] 's/he chopped it'

2.4.3 Phonemic oppositions: consonants

Phonemic oppositions for consonants are illustrated with minimal pairs. However, a strict minimal pair can not be found for all of the phonemic contrasts in Kunbarlang, and a retreat to near-minimal pairs is sometimes necessary. The oppositions are given with regards to the place of articulation (§2.4.3.1) and the manner of articulation (§2.4.3.2).

The glottal stop (*h* in the orthography, see table 2.3 in §2.2 for orthographic conventions) has low frequency in Kunbarlang and I am not aware of any minimal pairs where it would contrast with other consonants. It is restricted to the syllable-final position. Its distribution, however, is lexically conditioned and cannot be reduced to a phonological environment; thus, it may be present or absent in a morphophonologically similar context, being specified for a given lexeme (2.10):

(2.10)   a.   ka-wo**rrh**me 's/he is kindling something'

      b.   ka-ka**rr**me 's/he / it is holding something'

2.4.3.1 Place of articulation contrasts

Kunbarlang distinguishes five places of articulation for non-continuants (obstruents and nasals) and three for approximants. The following sections illustrate the contrasts.

2.4.3.1.1 Lenis stops: b, d, rd, dj, k
1. b ~ rd ~ dj ~ k: *kabeye* 'he/she/it bites it' vs. *kardam* 's/he puts something down' vs. *kadja* 'he/she/it is standing' vs. *kaka* 'he/she/it goes'
2. b ~ rd: *babi* 'after' vs. *bardi-* 'liquid' (incorporated nominal)
3. b ~ d ~ dj: *barbung* 'fish' vs. *darrbuk* 'possum sp.' vs. *djanarr* 'goanna sp.'
4. d ~ rd: *nganjrduka* 'I'll look' vs. *kanganjdukulungale* 'wind is coming'
5. d ~ k: *durduk* 'dog' vs. *kurrula* 'sea' and *wadjbud* 'sand'

2.4.3.1.2 Nasals: m, n, rn, nj, ng
1. m ~ n ~ ng: *mayi* vs. *nayi* vs. *ngayi* 'noun marker of class III / I / II'
2. n ~ rn: *kabunbum* 's/he hit him/her/it' vs. *kaburnbum* 's/he finished'
3. n ~ ng: *ninda* 'I class proximate demonstrative' vs. *nginda* 'II class proximate demonstrative'
4. nj ~ m: *kanganjwonj* 's/he is returning' vs. *kanganjwom* 's/he returned'
5. nj ~ ng: *kanjnganjwonj* [kaɲaɲwoɲ] 's/he will return' vs. *kanganjwonj* [kaŋaɲwoɲ] 's/he is returning' (see §2.7.3 for the interaction of adjacent nasals)
6. rn ~ nj: *-barndje* 'to seal, stick' vs. *-rdukbanjdje* 'to show, teach'
7. rn ~ ng: *karnadjinj* 's/he saw her-/himself' vs. *kangandjin* 's/he's eating me'

2.4.3.1.3 Laterals: l, rl
Both laterals are found intervocalically, for instance inside of these verbal stems: *kamabulunj* 'he/she/it likes it' vs. *kardenburlume* 'he/she/it is breaking it'.

2.4.3.1.4 Glides: w, y
The glides, or semivowels, contrast in various environments, including word-initially: *walaya* 'cliff' vs. *yalbi* 'country'.

2.4.3.2 Manner of articulation contrasts
Kunbarlang distinguishes six manners of articulation, with maximal subsets of five in alveolar and retroflex consonants. The contrasts are illustrated in the following sections.

2.4.3.2.1 Labials: p, bb, m, w
1. b ~ bb: *ngarrabu* 'I might hit it' vs. *Karrabbu* (toponym)
2. b ~ m ~ w: *barramimbanj* 'woman' vs. *marrakkak* 'seagull' vs. *warri* 'because'
3. b ~ w: *ngawunj* 'I'm giving it to him/her/it' vs. *ngabunj* 'I'm hitting him/her/it'
4. bb ~ m: *dolobbo* 'stringybark' vs. *komorlo* 'white egret'
5. bb ~ w: *nabborrongkorlk* 'rock wallaby' vs. *kawokdja* 's/he / it is talking'

2.4.3.2.2 Alveolars: d, dd, n, l, rr
1. d ~ dd ~ n ~ l ~ rr: *didirna* 'cicada' 'vs. *kaddikkaddik* 'oyster-catcher' vs. *djininj* 'properly' vs. *marnilikarrng* 'star' vs. *ka-birrinja* 'it's the same'
2. dd ~ l ~ rr: *djaddi* 'come here!' vs. *mayali* 'knowledge' vs. *warri* 'because'
3. dd ~ n: *djiddawurr* 'crow' vs. *djawina* 'friend'

2.4.3.2.3 Retroflexes: rd, rdd, rn, rl, r
1. rd ~ rn ~ rl: *kardam* 's/he puts it down' vs. *karna* 's/he / it is sitting' vs. *karlakka* 's/he throws it'
2. rd ~ rdd ~ rn ~ r: *djarderre* 'mouth' vs. *kardderre* 'honey in trees' vs. *yimarne* 'like' vs. *narrambareng* 'honey in the ground'
3. rdd ~ rl: *kurdduk* 'faeces' vs. *kaburlume* 's/he is smashing it'
4. rl ~ r: *djubirlk* 'whelk' vs. *berk* 'legless lizard'

2.4.3.2.4 Palatals: dj, ddj, nj, y
1. dj ~ ddj ~ nj ~ y: *mabidja* 'fireweed' vs. *middjaba* 'knee' vs. *ka-birrinja* 'it's the same' vs. *miyarrul* 'fighting stick'
2. dj ~ y: *kadjawunj* 's/he is feeding him/her' vs. *kayawanj* 's/he searching for something'
3. nj ~ y: *njunjuk* 'water' vs. *yuk* 'northern brown bandicoot'

2.4.3.2.5 Velars: k, kk, ng
1. k ~ ng: *korro* 'locative medial demonstrative' vs. *ngorro* 'class IV medial demonstrative' and many others (e.g., third vs. first person personal prefixes)
2. k ~ kk: *beka* 'tree goanna' vs. *bekka* 'arafura file snake'

2.5 Phonotactics

This section deals with Kunbarlang syllable structure and phonotactics more broadly. I begin with a brief review of the word templates, which are the common practice in Australian phonotactics descriptions, but then argue for a simpler syllabic analysis of Kunbarlang, i.e. one via monosyllabic templates (§2.5.1).

It is customary in the Australianist literature to analyse phonotactics in terms of word templates with five distinct consonant positions, rather than in terms of prosodic licensing, i.e. syllable onsets and codas (see Hamilton (1996: ch. 3), Dixon (2002: §12.1.3), B. Baker (2014b: 143ff)). The standard presentation of the template, as given by Hamilton (1996: 75) (after Dixon 1980: 159ff.), is in (2.11):

(2.11) $C_{init} V C_{inter} V (C_{fin})$
$C_{init} V C_1 . C_2 V (C_{fin})$

The motivation for this approach comes from three main factors. One is that monosyllabic words are notoriously infrequent in Australian languages. Another is that consonant clusters are often confined to word-medial, intervocalic environments, but not found word-initially or word-finally. Most importantly, however, in the majority of languages it is the intervocalic position (the C_{inter}) where the consonants show the most place of articulation contrasts. Thus, for instance, the apicals—that is, alveo-apical and apico-retroflex consonants in those languages where the distinction is phonemic—typically only contrast in C_{inter}, with neutralisation in other positions (cf. B. Baker 2014b: 142). The argument, then, is that a mere reference to a syllable onset would not be enough to state this aspect of phonotactics, since C_{init}, C_2 and C_{inter} are all onsets, but the latter has a special status in comparison to the other two.

While Kunbarlang phonotactics can be described with word templates, it can be equally well described in prosodic terms with only minimal qualifications, and therefore I will adhere to that as a simpler option. With respect to the pro-template arguments listed above, Kunbarlang has a fair number of monosyllabic words; there is a range of legal syllable-final clusters, which are essentially insensitive to word-medial vs. word-final positioning; and the place of articulation contrasts do not seem limited to the intervocalic environments (see especially §2.5.2.1 on lack of apical neutralisation in clusters).

The general description of syllable structure will be followed by more specific discussion of onsets (§2.5.2) and codas (§2.5.3) in morphemes, and then the full range of prosodic positions in whole words in §2.5.4. Let us, however, first briefly review the question of the minimal word.

Words in Kunbarlang can be as short as an open monosyllable (CV), although these are very few and clearly are not a preferred word structure. The attested ones are the conjunctions *ba* 'so' and *la* 'and' and the interjection *ke* 'oh really?' No phonetic lengthening of the vowel appears to be necessary for these words. The number of monosyllabic words of the shape CVC, a closed syllable, is however considerable. They occur in various categories, such as nouns (*muk* 'fly; bee', *wam* 'honey'), interjections (*bonj* 'alright'), and quantifiers (*djal* 'only', *ngob* 'all'). There are also predicative lexical clitics (coverbs), many of which are monosyllabic (e.g. *ngurr* 'wash', *kerd* 'carry'); it is not their weight that determines their clitic status, as there are polysyllabic coverbs that observe similar positional restrictions (e.g. *kubirribirrkuk* 'steal').

From the point of view of syllable structure, Kunbarlang phonotactics can be captured with a monosyllabic template. The analysis offered here is much in the spirit of Evans's (2003a: 89ff.) analysis of Bininj Kunwok syllable structure (although the particular structures are, obviously, different). Kunbarlang has a set of admissible complex codas, in the order of 20, and the majority of syllables are CV(C)(C), the particular details to follow presently. Only minor qualifications are required, viz. regarding the omissibility of onsets word-initially and the assumed syllabification of fortis consonants.

For the reader interested in the quantitative distribution of the various segments and their classes, three kinds of counts are provided in this chapter. The counts for the overall relative functional load of the segments in the lexicon were given in §§2.3–2.4 (for vowels and consonants, respectively). For the different classes of consonants with respect to their occurrence in the composition of morphemes, there are counts of the MORPHEME-initial and MORPHEME-final positions in sections 2.5.2 and 2.5.3, respectively. A general result is that the distribution of consonant classes in the different prosodic positions largely follows the harmonic scale preferences described by Hamilton (1996). These counts are carried out on the dictionary, as the most complete and representative collection of Kunbarlang morphemes. Thus, a note on the structure of the dictionary currently used (Coleman 2010) is in order. Kunbarlang is a polysynthetic language abundant with bound morphology. In the headwords, those nominal roots that are bound are given without the relevant class prefixes and all verbal roots are given without the inflectional prefixes, albeit often with several derivational morphemes attached. One consequence is for the word edges: verb-initial segments as they appear in speech are limited to the onsets of bound subject prefixes (see section 5.2.1) and thus are only a subset of what is allowed morpheme-initially. Likewise, verb-final segments are confined to what the tense and mood suffixes end in (that is, open syllables and a small subset of consonants; see section 5.3). Another consequence is that a number of morphemes will appear in the data repeatedly. Because of that, the counts in §§2.5.2–2.5.3 should be taken to indicate, not the text frequencies of the segments or frequencies in a complete and non-redundant set of morphemes, but the frequencies of segment occurrences in stems, i.e., nominal roots, uninflected verbs and functional categories.

These figures, however, are only of interest specifically from the morphophonological point of view, and they are crucially dependent on the present morphological analysis. With this in mind, I provide a third quantitative analysis in §2.5.4, namely that of the full-formed, well-formed lexemes from my recordings. Accordingly, there are three types of positions represented by this third count: WORD-initial, WORD-final and intervocalic. This discussion of whole word phonotactics completes the picture of the phonological shapes of Kunbarlang.

2.5.1 Syllable structure

Kunbarlang syllables typically are CV(C)(C). With only a few exceptions (see table 2.6 below), syllables begin in a consonant. All classes of consonants are allowed in the onset except for the glottal stop. However, only some of the fortis are attested in onsets in the data. The asymmetries between different consonant classes in the onset position are further taken up in §2.5.2 and §2.5.4. Turning to codas, we find that they may consist of zero, one, or two consonants. Open syllables are quite frequent in Kunbarlang. This can be seen especially vividly in §2.5.4, where empty codas are shown to make up nearly half of the word-final codas, and in the intervocalic positions single consonants (syllabified as onsets) also prevail considerably. Simple codas may consist of any consonant but fortis; the relative frequencies of the different classes will be discussed in §2.5.3 and §2.5.4. Finally, about 20 biconsonantal combinations comprise complex codas, which may either be tautosyllabic or arise through resyllabification of a fortis onset across the syllable boundary. There are no triconsonantal codas in Kunbarlang.

(2.12) a. $C_i V \left\{ \frac{C_f}{C_1 C_2} \right\}$, where

b. C_i is any consonant but the glottal stop /ʔ/
C_f is any consonant but fortis
C_1 is any approximant
C_2 is any peripheral oral stop, or the alveolar stop /t/, in which case C_1 is alveolar (homorganic)

For completeness, in (2.13) I provide the list of the coda clusters that have been encountered in the data at least once (in orthography).

(2.13) wk, ld, lk, lng, lh, rrd, rrk, rrng, rrh, rlk, rlng, rlh, rk, rng, rh, yk, lb, yb, rlb, rrb

The first consonant in a cluster, C_1, is most typically a liquid. The glide /w/ has so far been found in one word only (*marawk* 'friarbird'); the glide /j/ occurs rarely and only in codas created by resyllabification of the following fortis (2.14a). The latter is also true of all clusters with /p/ as the C_2 (2.14b).

(2.14) a. nawa**yk**kan → na.wa**yk**.kan 'agile wallaby' [Coleman 2010: 90]
b. ka**rrb**bere → ka**rrb**.be.re 'mangrove worm' [20060620IB03/00:50]

2.5.2 Morpheme-initial position

Although there are vowel-initial morphemes in Kunbarlang, these are very few and their striking majority begin with /a/.[2] The words containing vowel-initial morphemes are

---

[2] Textual numbers of vowel-initial tokens are predicted to be relatively high due to pervasive lenition of the velar nasal in the word-initial position—a frequent configuration due to many verbs beginning with that nasal. However, this phonetic detail is not reflected in the transcriptions used for the counts here, and thus is not reflected in the frequency counts given for initials in §2.5.4.

Tab. 2.6: Vowel-initial words in Kunbarlang

a	adjak	'sickness'
	adju	'dunno'
	alabbikka[4]	'flatback turtle'
	alidjalidj	'harpoon'
	Alkbarn Ka-yuwa	place name
	andawulmurra	'little hawksbill turtle'
	angbardi	'expert hunter'
	arladjirr	'ark shell'
	arriwawanj	'waterspout'
	Ayinkudji	place name
e	eh[5]	'huh?'
i	ilurrk	'cuttlefish'
	Indjalkkudji	place name
o	obobo	'sugar gall'

listed in table 2.6. These words are primarily monomorphemic, only *alidjalidj* 'harpoon' being a clear reduplication. Vowel hiatus is prohibited, and the only vowel-initial syllables are also the word-initial ones.[3]

Turning to consonants, the frequency distribution of the place of articulation classes in Kunbarlang word onsets conforms fully with Hamilton's (1996: 213ff.) generalisation that the preference for a given consonant in the onset decreases along the continual harmonic ordering of places in C_{init} (2.15). The scale is expressed in terms of the active articulator, thus lumping together alveolar and retroflex consonants under the label *apical*.

(2.15) LABIAL, DORSAL > LAMINAL > APICAL

That is, labials are the best possible onsets, and they are the most frequent class in Kunbarlang onsets (counting 779 out of 1858, or 42%). Apicals are the least optimal onsets, and indeed, they are the least frequent class in Kunbarlang, alveolar and retroflex apicals together making up for 273 (or 15%) onsets in the used dataset.

Table 2.7 presents counts of occurrence of consonants in the morpheme-initial position in Kunbarlang in a dataset of 1858 entries.

It can be seen from table 2.7 that all classes of consonants (but the glottal stop) are permitted morpheme-initially, but the fortis series is extremely restricted: only a few labial and retroflex fortis are found morpheme-initially. Some other consonants

---

[3] Apparently, this is a phonological restriction, rather than phonetic one. Occasionally, hiatus sequences may be created as a result of intervocalic lenition of /ŋ/, see e.g. (2.4a).
[4] With the variant *kalabbikka*.
[5] Typically realised with an initial glottal stop.

Tab. 2.7: Occurrence of consonants in morpheme-initial position

	Labial	Alveolar	Retroflex	Palatal	Velar	Average
Lenis	p, 303	t, 38	ʈ, 42	c, 194	k, 364	188
Fortis	p:, 5	∅	ʈː, 4	∅	∅	5
Nasal	m, 315	n, 69	ɳ, 49	ɲ, 10	ŋ, 147	118
Lateral		l, 42	ɭ, 21			32
Rhotic		r, 7	ɻ, 5			6
Glide	w, 161			j, 82		122
Average	196	31	24	72	170	88

are highly restricted in this position, too, most notably the two rhotics and the palatal nasal. These are especially scarce word-initially. B. Baker (2014b: 143) points out that in Australia "there are clear asymmetries in the manner of articulation of consonants permitted in initial position... [l]iquids are very commonly highly restricted in this position" and "[o]nly a small number of Australian languages allow the tap/trill /r/ in word-initial position." Indeed, in Kunbarlang not only the rhotics but also the lateral liquids show very low counts compared to stops, nasals and the glides /w/ and /j/, both *morpheme*-initially, as shown here, and word-initially, as will be demonstrated in section 2.5.4.

2.5.2.1 Retroflexion retention following heterorganic consonants

Australian languages that show the apical contrast, i.e. the phonemic contrast between alveolar and postalveolar/retroflex stops, are reported to show it intervocalically, with neutralisation patterns elsewhere (B. Baker 2014b: 142). This can be tied, at least in part, to the main perceptual cue of the retroflexion, namely the sharp decline in the F3 of the preceding vowel (Ladefoged 2003: 159–68). Against this backdrop, Kunbarlang seems unique among Australian languages in that the apical contrast is retained following heterorganic consonants. That is, retroflex apicals are phonologically realised as retroflex in word-medial, morpheme-initial position, even when preceded by a non-retroflex consonant. Examples of that are in (2.16): in (2.16a) audible retroflexion is retained after an apical nasal and in (2.16b), after a palatal nasal. Note that in general Kunbarlang nasals do not show anticipatory assimilation of their place of articulation either (see also §2.7.3 for more on nasal interactions).

(2.16) a. /ka-ŋan-ʈukbaɲciŋ/ → [kaˈɳanʈukˌbaɲɟiŋ]
          3SG.NF-1SG.OBJ-show.PST

          '[He] taught me.' [lit. 'He showed it to me.']   [20150413IOv01/07:10–11]

      b. /ŋa-manaɲ-ɭakwaŋ/ → [ˌɳamanaɲˈɭakwaŋ]
            1SG.NF-BEN-throw.PST

          'I shaved him.' [lit. 'I threw [it] off him.']   [IK1-160818_0021/40:46–48]

I have recorded a variety of word-medial clusters where a retroflex consonant follows one with another place of articulation in the best acoustic conditions I could create in the field. To the best of my hearing, retroflexion on the C_2 is retained in the majority of cases, with only a few exceptions. The first exception is that nasal–nasal clusters are simplified to a single nasal, chosen in accordance with the nasal hierarchy (n > ɳ > ɲ > ŋ), which is discussed in detail in §2.7.3. Second, variation is more pronounced if C_1 is /n/ or /l/, suggesting that alveo-apicals have a stronger effect on realisation of the following retroflex. This might have to do with the transition being too small to be discerned. Specifically, /nɖ/ comes out varying between [nɖ] and [nd] (IK1-170620_1SY2: 00:31–37 and 03:28–33, resp.; cf. (2.16a)); and /lɖ/ → [ld] (ibid./05:42–47), /lɭ/ → [ll] (ibid./05:24–30). Finally, while the velar nasal does not affect the following retroflex, in most cases the velar oral stop does. However, this is not uniform either, and appears contingent on the broader context: the retroflex is neutralised to the alveolar realisation when it follows /rk/; but in an example where /k/ itself follows a vowel — /...pakɖu.../ — retroflexion is not lost and the velar stop is significantly lenited. This further suggests a particular effect of a preceding alveo-apical on the retroflex neutralisation. In the remaining pairs the retroflexion on the second consonant is rather distinct; these are [mɭ ɳɖ ɲɭ ɳɖ ɳɭ].

This data set under discussion is not large enough for any quantitative measurements, as the controlled low-noise environment recordings come from a single speaker. Most of the clusters in the same word forms were recorded from another speaker as well, but in a noisier setting. Moreover, it must be noted that I am relying on my own perception of the acoustic qualities of the consonants under discussion.[6] Visual inspection of spectrograms does not reveal any clear patterns in F3 of the neighbouring vowels for Kunbarlang retroflexes,[7] whether as C_2 or elsewhere, even when they are heard distinctively. An experimental study of acoustic and articulatory properties of Kunbarlang consonant clusters would be instrumental for better understanding of phonotactics in this language.

This retention of retroflexion appears extremely unusual in Australia, where "[m]ost languages are reported to have apico-retroflex realisations of [the] neutralised segments in phrase-medial context, following a vowel, but apico-alveolar realisations otherwise (i.e., utterance-initially, and following consonants other than retroflex)" (B. Baker 2014b: 142). On the other hand, the behaviour of the nasals, which do not assimilate, is quite typical among the Australian languages (see, e.g., Fletcher & Butcher (2014: 107–8) on resistance to anticipatory place of articulation assimilation in Australian languages), although apicals appear more prone to coarticulation ef-

---

[6] This perception has been confirmed by two colleagues of mine, too.
[7] Sharp decline of F3 of the preceding vowel is the most distinctive feature of retroflexes in spectrography (Ladefoged 2003: 159–168).

fects, which is also consistent with the behaviour of alveolar+retroflex clusters in Kunbarlang.

2.5.2.2 Apical initials and the question of neutralisation

The preceding section shows that retroflexion is unusually robust in Kunbarlang and does not neutralise word-medially following heterorganic consonants. At the same time, the utterance-initial position is not contrastive for the apicals in Kunbarlang. In line with the major pattern, as cited above, the only apicals found utterance-initially have alveolar realisations. To wit, retroflex-initial free morphemes, which would not be 'covered' by a prefix or would not encliticise to a host, are virtually non-existent. An example of such a noun is *rlama* 'shovel spear'. There are several tokens in the recordings, and to my best judgement the retroflexion can be heard when preceded by another word (even consonant-final), but not when utterance-initial (see (2.6) for a nice example of two contrasting tokens produced side by side by one speaker). The picture for the utterance-initial position in Kunbarlang is very much in line with findings of Butcher's (1995) palatographic study of several Australian languages. He concludes that "it is in any case highly probable that both the APICAL and the LAMINAL archiphonemes represent an original single phoneme that has failed to 'split', rather than... a merging of two originally contrasting sounds" (p. 34). He also points out, from a practical point of view, that since "Australian writing systems have all been developed pretty recently... [they] represent the current state of the spoken language and offer no clues as to candidate pairs of words which might be investigated for partial neutralisations" (ibid.)—of course, unless clever manipulation of context gives away an active neutralisation pattern, but there is no such opportunity for this in Kunbarlang, as we have seen.

Butcher's (1995) general findings with regards to the articulatory realisations of coronals in his sample also provide a meaningful context for such variation as described above for the word-/utterance-initial position in Kunbarlang. He found that word-initially in double-apical languages (i.e. in a non-contrastive position) articulatory realisations of the allegedly neutralised segments are intermediate between the two distinct articulations of the "un-neutralised" targets—*ein Mittelding*, as he calls this following Trubetzkoy. Namely, these segments share the postalveolar place with the retroflexes of the respective languages, but the gesture of the active articulator is apical, rather than subliminal—unlike in retroflexes. Butcher (1995: 34) suggests that the allophonic variation is likely 'the perceptual consequence of co-production of the consonant' with the surrounding sounds. This appears a likely scenario for Kunbarlang as well, where apical protophonemes probably did not clearly differentiate into either of the phonemicaly contrastive descendants.

Tab. 2.8: Occurrence of consonants in morpheme-final position

	Labial	Alveolar	Retroflex	Palatal	Velar	Glottal	Average
Lenis	p, 26	t, 41	ṯ, 23	c, 57	k, 233	ʔ, 26	68
Nasal	m, 64	n, 75	ṉ, 20	ɲ, 198	ŋ, 102		92
Lateral		l, 35	ḻ, 24				30
Rhotic		r, 87	ɻ, 4				46
Glide	w, 6			j, 20			13
Average	32	60	18	92	168	26	61

2.5.3 Morpheme-final position

Fortis consonants are the only consonants prohibited in the morpheme-final position (more generally, they do not occur syllable-finally in Kunbarlang). With the exception of the alveolar /r/, approximants show very low frequency, especially so /ɻ/, which ends four morphemes (one of them a monosyllabic coverb), and /w/, which ends six. The velar stop /k/ is the most frequent consonant in the morpheme-final position in Kunbarlang. The second most frequent consonant in that position is the palatal nasal /ɲ/; this contrasts markedly with its very low frequency in morpheme-initial position. Table 2.8 provides counts for the morpheme-final occurrences of Kunbarlang consonants (including the C_2 of consonant clusters) on the basis of 1893 entries from the dictionary (Coleman 2010). The row for fortis stops, unattested in syllable-final position, is omitted.

In terms of the frequency in the lexicon, morpheme-final position in Kunbarlang does not as neatly correspond to Hamilton's (1996) generalisation as the morpheme-initial position. The harmonic scale for C_{fin} (2.17; Hamilton 1996: 228) is a near-reverse of that for C_{init} (2.15).[8] Again, the preference for a consonant in the morpheme-final position decreases rightwards along the scale:

(2.17)   APICAL > LAMINAL > DORSAL > LABIAL

In Kunbarlang, however, we find that the two dorsal consonants—the velar lenis stop /k/ and the velar nasal /ŋ/—are more frequent than the two classes of apicals taken together (335 vs. 302, or 32% and 29%, respectively). The remaining three place of articulation classes in their respective ranking conform to the scale (2.17), labials being the least frequent ones, making up 9% of the morpheme-final consonants. Besides, 852, or 45% of the items, end in an open syllable.

Finally, I give some counts for vowels; however, I only provide them for the morpheme-final position, i.e. not including the word-medial syllable-final occurrences.

---

[8] Hamilton's (1996) scale for C_{fin} is totally ordered, while the one for C_{init} is only partially ordered, as the dorsals and labials are not ordered with respect to each other.

Tab. 2.9: Occurrence of vowels in morpheme-final position

	Front	Central	Back	Average
High	i, 267		u, 111	189
Mid	e, 159		o, 37	98
Low		a, 285		285
Average	213	285	74	172

The low central vowel /a/ is the most frequent Kunbarlang phoneme to end a morpheme (285 morphemes out of 1893, or 15%). Other morpheme-final vowels are rather evenly distributed, as is shown in table 2.9, with the exception of the mid back /o/, which only counts 37 instances. This is not surprising, given the relatively low functional load of /o/ in Kunbarlang (see table 2.4).

A comparison of tables 2.8 and 2.9 gives a rough idea of the relative proportion of closed and open syllables in Kunbarlang. One finds that they are almost equally frequent, with open ones constituting 45.4% of the total.

2.5.4 Whole word phonotactics

As suggested above, the quantitative descriptions of the morpheme-edge positions are artificial to the degree that they rely on a specific morphological analysis, and—more importantly—reflect on the properties of an analytic construct, rather than full-blown Kunbarlang words. To this end, I conclude the quantitative description of phonotactics with counts of word-edge and word-medial positions of full-formed words as used in speech. The dataset comprises the current ELAN transcriptions of my elicitation and spontaneous production recordings (at the moment of writing), and as such reflects a more actively used part of the lexicon as compared to the full dictionary. On the other hand, due to a relatively high proportion of elicitations in these data, it cannot be taken to reflect a fully 'natural' pattern of frequencies. For that reason the lexemes are collapsed by type, to compensate for repeated occurrences of certain tokens in elicitation transcriptions and other possible side-effects. There are thus 1079 lexeme types, for which I report counts of consonantal segments in word-initial, word-final, and intervocalic contexts. Let us begin the survey with the consonants in the word-initial position, summarised in table 2.10. In these data, there are 1065 (types of) words beginning with consonants, the remaining 14 beginning with vowels.

Looking at the word-initial position, one immediately notices the effect of the morphological make-up of Kunbarlang that was mentioned above: the initials attested in spontaneous and semi-spontaneous production are overwhelmingly dominated by the velars /k/ and /ŋ/. This is not the least bit surprising given the prevalence of verbs in the polysynthetic clause of Kunbarlang and the fact that verbs begin just with these two phonemes (with a handful of exceptions in case the subject is of the second person;

Tab. 2.10: Occurrence of consonants in word-initial position

	Labial	Alveolar	Retroflex	Palatal	Velar	Average
Lenis	p, 45	t, 3	∅	c, 23	k, 531	120
Nasal	m, 59	n, 50	ɳ, 2	ɲ, 9	ŋ, 307	85
Lateral		l, 4	ɭ, 1			3
Rhotic		∅	ɻ, 1			1
Glide	w, 17			j, 13		15
Average	40	15	1	15	419	67

Tab. 2.11: Occurrence of single consonants in word-medial intervocalic position

	Labial	Alveolar	Retroflex	Palatal	Velar	Average
Lenis	p, 194	t, 26	ʈ, 52	c, 51	k, 83	81
Fortis	pː, 8	tː, 126	∅	cː, 9	kː, 31	35
Nasal	m, 78	n, 33	ɳ, 70	ɲ, 24	ŋ, 134	68
Lateral		l, 48	ɭ, 33			41
Rhotic		r, 83	ɻ, 7			45
Glide	w, 91			j, 78		85
Average	93	63	32	41	83	60

see the detailed paradigms in §5.2.1). The average total for these two velars outranks that for any other place of articulation at least by an order of magnitude.⁹ On the other hand, the retroflex apicals are virtually absent from this position. The overall picture for word-initial consonantal onsets thus conforms to Hamilton's (1996) harmonic scale for onsets (2.15): labial, dorsal > laminal > apical.

I analyse single intervocalic consonants as syllable onsets; the individual figures for such consonants, as well as averages for place and manner of articulation classes are provided in table 2.11. Given that words are polysyllabic, there are more intervocalic datapoints than there are words; the total for the single consonants is 1259.

Since the consonants in table 2.11 are onsets, the same harmonic scale (2.15) of peripherals over laminals over apicals is relevant for them as well. The pattern is almost upheld, with the main divergence being the relatively high incidence of the alveolar apicals, especially when compared to rather fewer lamino-palatals. However, if the two subclasses of onsets (i.e. tables 2.10 and 2.11) are combined, it is easy to see that

---

9 In fact, the picture is further complicated by the fact that the initial velars of the personal prefixes often lenite, sometimes leaving what is perceived as an 'uncovered' vowel word-initially. However, the data used for these statistics do not reflect that detail, so an idealised picture of slightly higher incidence of velars is reported.

Tab. 2.12: Occurrence of consonants in word-final position

	Labial	Alveolar	Retroflex	Palatal	Velar	Glottal	Average
Lenis	p, 6	t, 8	ʈ, 4	c, 5	k, 42	ʔ, 6	12
Nasal	m, 59	n, 22	ɳ, 1	ɲ, 217	ŋ, 114		83
Lateral		l, 5	ɭ, 4				5
Rhotic		r, 7	ɽ, 1				4
Glide	w, 1			j, 57			29
Average	22	11	3	93	78	6	33

apicals do not outrank the laminals, but they form roughly equivalent classes; I do not provide calculations, which the interested reader can carry out easily.[10]

Finally, let us turn to the word-final position (table 2.12), i.e. codas, for which the harmonic scale (2.17) is virtually a mirror image of the onsets one; thus: apical > laminal > dorsal > labial.

Word-finally, there were 488 open syllables (45%, exactly matching the figure for morpheme-final codas) and 559 simple codas (52%), the remaining 3% provided by a few complex codas. Among the simple codas, the figures for which are reported in table 2.12, there are four ones that stand out: /ɲ/, /ŋ/, /m/, /j/. These four happen to be just those consonants that all verbs end in (unless they end in an open syllable), which can be seen in the conjugation tables 5.10 and 5.12 in Chapter 5 (for regular and irregular verbs, respectively). In part due to that, nasals as a group are noticeably ahead of other manner of articulation classes.

In terms of the harmonic scale, its predictions are borne out with the exception of the apicals. Instead of being the most frequent kind of word-final syllable coda, they are the rarest kind (with the average of 7 for alveolars and retroflexes taken together). However, similarly to the above discussion in regards the onsets, here too a consideration of the word-medial syllable codas from the intervocalic clusters and the ambisyllabic attachment of the fortis puts the proportions in accord with the harmonic scale preference (see figure 2.1). Thus, the apparent "disharmonic" phonotactic effects of the word edges can be seen to stem primarily from morphological factors. This is an interesting observation, and it can be investigated further whether it is accidental that it is specifically apicals that seem to be at heart of the divergence for both the onset and the coda patterns.

Figure 2.1 summarises the descriptive statistics for this dataset of whole words.[11]

---

10 In fact, once the C_2 of the intervocalic clusters are taken into account as well, the results fit the harmonic scales generalisation about onsets even better. This is evident from the examination of figure 2.1.

11 I am very grateful to George Moroz for his generous assistance with the production of this chart, as well as for helpful discussion of syllable structure in general. The chart visualisation was done using the R package ggplot2 (Wickham 2016).

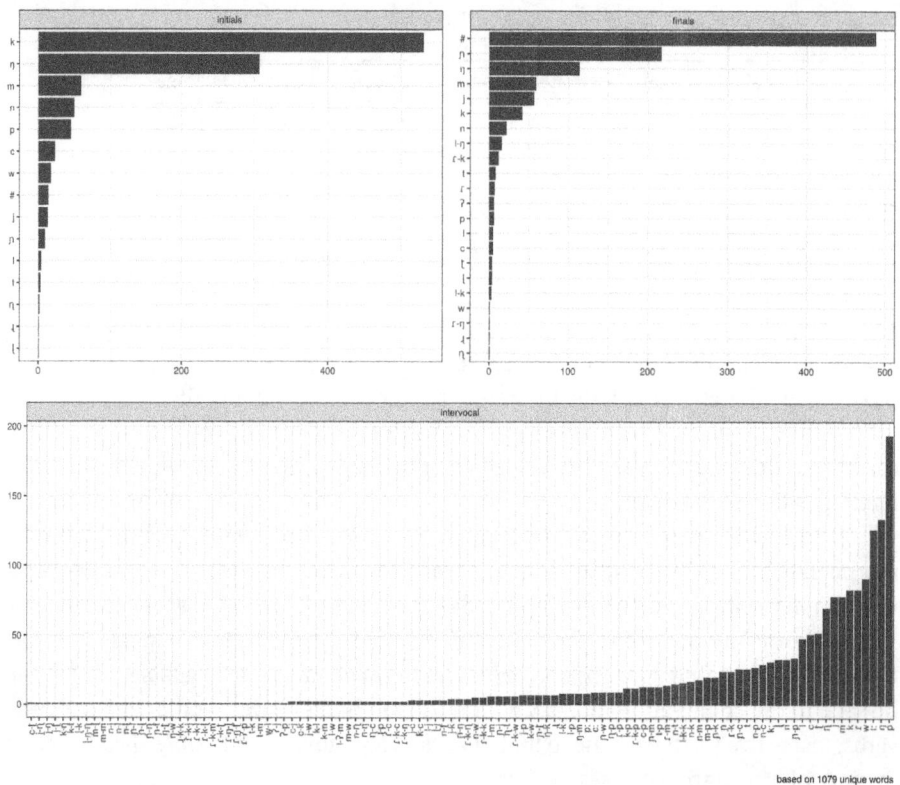

Fig. 2.1: Distribution of consonants in word-initial, word-final, and word-medial intervocalic positions

2.6 Stress

Within the Gunwinyguan family, the two languages with the most thoroughly studied metrical structure are Bininj Kunwok and Ngalakgan. Both languages show metrical systems that are intricately connected to the morphological make-up of words. Interestingly, according to the analyses, footing operates differently in these two languages. In Bininj Kunwok feet are unbounded and (usually) aligned with morphemes (Evans 2003a: 99; Bishop 2002: 120). This means that there is no secondary stress in morphemes that are longer than two syllables. In contrast to that, in Ngalakgan feet are binary (specifically, bimoraic trochees; B. Baker 2008b: 71ff.). Therefore, a morpheme consisting of four open syllables (for instance) receives a primary and a secondary stress on its first and third syllables (with some variation as to which is which).[12]

---

[12] Considering other languages of the area, Nakkara has a rather intricate system of stress placement rules (Eather 2011: 35–42).

2.6 Stress

This section presents some preliminary observations on stress in Kunbarlang; a quantitative, instrumental study needs to be carried out in order to verify the claims made here and for a fuller undestanding of the metrical structure of Kunbarlang. The examples discussed here are from a range of contexts, some recorded in isolation and some taken from connected speech. To the best of my knowledge, there is very little variation in stress placement across variable contexts, and thus there should not be any confounds when word tokens are taken from narratives.

Acoustic correlates of metrical strength are not straightforward in Gunwinyguan languages, cf. the following quote from Bishop (2002: 240): "it needs to be emphasised that the relative magnitudes of duration, intensity and F0 in accented/stressed vs unaccented/unstressed syllables do not always (or unambiguously) indicate the metrically strong syllable in a foot in BGW. For example, the accent-related F0 peak occurs on the unaccented, post-stress syllable in delayed or late peak accents." The general picture, however, seems to be that intensity (in Dalabon (Fletcher & Evans 2002) and, with caveats, in Kuninjku) and pitch accent (in Kuninjku and probably Ngalakgan) are the most reliable exponents of lexical stress in these languages, while vowel length varies independently of stress and there are no systematic changes in vowel quality (although see B. Baker 1999 for Ngalakgan).

Stress in Kunbarlang is not contrastive, i.e. it does not serve a differentiating function. It is signalled primarily by higher pitch of the stressed syllable vowel and also by greater intensity (in dB). Vowel length does not seem to pattern together with these metrics, and where there is a mismatch, I find identification of primary stress placement rather challenging. Figure 2.2 below shows the spikes of both pitch (specks) and intensity (contour line) on the stressed antepenultimate syllable in the verbal word *nganjrdukkume* 'I'll cut it', realised as [ãɲˈɖukːume].

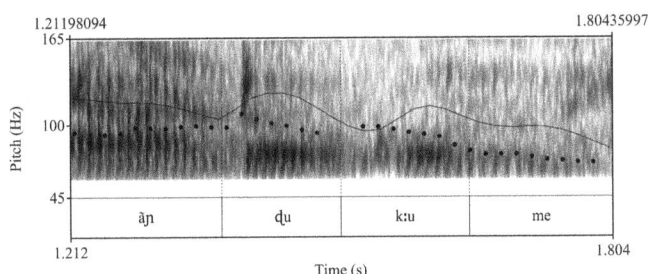

Fig. 2.2: Pitch and intensity contours of *nganjrdukkume* [IK1-170620_1SY2/09:08]

The stressed antepenult in figure 2.2 notwithstanding, the most robust pattern is for the primary stress to fall on the penultimate syllable, if the word is longer than one syllable. In monosyllables the stress will fall on the only syllable. Examples of words of different length and varied morphological structure are given in (2.18): two syllables

(2.18a–c), three syllables (2.18d–f), four syllables (2.18g–j), five syllables (2.18k–m), six syllables (2.18n).

(2.18)   a.   ká-ka 's/he goes'

   b.   ná-wuk 'male person'

   c.   kédjurr 'mud'

   d.   yiwárrudj 'church'

   e.   ka-ngúnda 's/he says/does'

   f.   na-wúk=bonj '(that) male person'

   g.   bàrramímbanj ~ bárramìmbanj 'woman'

   h.   ngàdda-rdáyinj 'we entered'

   i.   kà-bukáyinj 's/he got out [e.g. of the boat]'

   j.   man-kuk-kárlyung 'long [class IV]'

   k.   ka-bìrr~birrínja '[it's] the same'

   l.   kàdda-nganj-kánginj 'they brought [him] over here'

   m.   ngàrrk-buddu-yákbum 'our kids' [lit. 'we dropped them / gave birth to them']

   n.   kàdda-bàba-rnékbe 'they're dancing separately'

However, frequently there are exceptions. Let us focus on verbs, which can get very long and also offer complex morphological structures. As stated above, probably the most frequent pattern is for the primary stress to be penultimate (2.19).

(2.19)   ngaddá-rdam 'we are putting it down'

Notice that in (2.19) stress is on the personal prefix, not the (monosyllabic) stem (likewise in (2.18a)). Example (2.20) shows that the prefix may be stressed even if the stem is disyllabic.

(2.20)   ká-kidanj 's/he / it went'

Other examples of the primary stress falling on non-penultimate syllables are the antepenultimate on the stem (2.21a), final (also on the stem; 2.21b), or both (primary on the final and secondary on the antepenultimate syllable; 2.21c):

(2.21)   a.   ngà-bak-rdúkkume 'I'm cutting it lengthwise'

   b.   ngàdda-djarráng 'we ate'

   c.   kìdda-nganj-rlàkwaní 'they would throw it down'

Sometimes it appears to me that the prefix has the primary stress and the stem—the secondary (2.22):

(2.22) ngadda-ngánj-mayìnj 'we came across'

The antepenultimate stress, as in (2.21a), does not systematically originate in stress shifting off from a light syllable.[13] Example (2.23) shows that it does not have to even when the next one left is potentially heavier (CVC vs. CV):

(2.23) kaddà-karrmíli 'they would get them'

Clash of the primary and the secondary stress appears possible sometimes, albeit not at all often; (2.24) is one example. Notice that this one is an adjective (-*burrinj* 'pleasant') with a noun incorporate (*wurrng*- 'blade').

(2.24) man-rdawùrrng-búrrinj 'the one with a sharp blade'

In what concerns the secondary stress placement, it tends to go leftwards on alternating syllables from wherever the primary stress is placed, as in (2.21a) or (2.23), but in longer words gaps get larger, as in (2.25). I am not aware of any words with more than three audibly stressed syllables.

(2.25) ngàdda-makàrninjdjánganj 'we sang'

This variation does not seem to betray any systematically organised metrical structure. At the present stage of research, I find that Kunbarlang primary stress is fixed lexical, with a tendency towards penultimate. This means that all morphemes are inherently specified for stress location (no-stress specification being one possibility), with some limited variation possible in discourse (the limits of which variation would be a matter for future prosodic work). Furthermore, from the current data it appears plausible that stems take precedence over affixes, so that the primary stress falls on the stem, and affixes receive secondary stress. Stems must be allowed the no-stress specification, in which case an affix receives the primary stress, as in (2.20). In §2.7.1 below I discuss a special case of systematic stress variation along with changes in the morphological structure in the pronominal -*buk* 'person'.

2.7 Morphophonology

The surface realisation of phonemes and morphemes in Kunbarlang is relatively straightforward and does not involve many complex rules. This degree of agglutination

---

[13] Evans (2003a: 103–4) describes occasional retraction of stress leftwards from light syllables in Bininj Kunwok.

is similar to Bininj Kunwok, cf. Evans's remark that Bininj Kunwok "morphology is almost lego-like" (2003a: 106). Some of the alternations described in this section are exceptional and morpheme-specific (the lenition in -*buk* 'person', §2.7.1, and nasal hardening, §2.7.4), while others appear to be manifestations of the general phonological preferences in Kunbarlang that however only become obvious on morpheme boundaries (mid vowel raising, §2.7.2, and nasal cluster simplification, §2.7.3).

2.7.1 Lenition of the initial segment of -*buk* 'person'

There is a pronominal root -*buk* in Kunbarlang that is used for human referents only (§4.5.1.1). It carries an obligatory gender prefix, viz. *na*- for masculine and *ngal*- for feminine referents. The stress in the standalone (citation) form is on the prefix (2.26a–2.26b). However, this pronoun can also receive information-structural morphemes, namely the enclitic *bonj* 'exactly' or the contrastive suffix -*ma* (§4.5.1.2). Both of these morphemes shift stress from the gender prefix onto the root -*buk*. That leads to morphophonemic lenition of the stem-initial /p/ from the clear stop realisation [b] to [w], which in the feminine form is further eroded after /l/ up to inaudibility (2.26a–b vs. 2.26c–d). Such a stark contrast between post-tonic and pre-tonic realisation of consonants—/p/ in particular—is not attested elsewhere.

(2.26) a. /na-puk/ → [ˈnabuk]
       b. /ŋal-puk/ → [ˈŋalbuk]
       c. /na-puk=poɲ/ → [naˈwukboɲ]
       d. /ŋal-puk-ma/ → [ŋalˈukma]

In the feminine form this is lenition (just like in the masculine), rather than categorical deletion: there are instances where the labiovelar glide realisation of the /p/ is clearly audible, such as (2.27):

(2.27) [ŋalˈwukma] [IK1-160809_0001/09:03–05]

The same speaker in the same recording session has produced multiple tokens of [ŋalˈukma] and [ŋalˈukboɲ] with complete erosion of the /p/.

2.7.2 Mid vowel raising between palatal segments

The unrounded mid vowel /e/ in Kunbarlang has a wide distribution, occurring before and after consonants of all classes. In particular, it is found following palatals (2.28a) and preceding them (2.28b). As a reminder, the palatal consonants in Kunbarlang include /c/, /cː/, /ɲ/ and /j/.

(2.28) a. /kapurunmac:e/   → [kaburunmaɟ:e]
            3PL.NF+3DU.OBJ+pierce.NP
            'It's attacking them two.'   [IK1-170530_1SY1/12:24]

        b. /kat:aɲemejiɲ/   → [kad:aɲem**e**jiɲ]
            3PL.NF+smear+REFL.PST
            'They painted themselves [with clay].' [IK1-160624_0001/03:38]

However if /e/ has a palatal immediately on each side, it is realised as the high front allophone [i]. The typical context for this is in the reflexive/reciprocal forms, where the palatal-initial suffix -*yi* attaches after the verbal root (2.29):

(2.29) /ŋark-ɲil-mac:e-ji/   → [arkɲilmaɟ:**i**ji]
        1.INCL.NF-eye-pierce-REFL.NP
        'glasses [lit. what we put around the eyes]'   [IK1-160816_0001/29:32]

Notice that although it may appear as regressive assimilation of the vowel height before the high vowel in the suffix, this is unlikely so, as no assimilation is found in (2.28b) in a similar context. A context with a different following vowel is difficult to construct given the morphological inventory of Kunbarlang. A lexicon search reveals that there are no tokens of [e] between two palatals elsewhere in the words, which suggests that this raising alternation reflects a general dispreference in Kunbarlang against the [e] between two palatal consonants.

2.7.3 Nasal cluster simplification

Kunbarlang shows an interesting pattern in simplifying heterorganic nasal clusters. While there is a scale similar to the harmonic scale of Hamilton 1996, the Kunbarlang one operates on a different principle, being position-independent. In terms of description, I report a more complex simplification pattern than in the previous work by Coleman.

Coleman (1982: 15–16) makes two observations regarding the nasals:
1. nasals do not assimilate in the place of articulation to the adjacent consonants
2. normally, two adjacent heterorganic nasals are retained, but in personal prefix combinations, the second of two juxtaposed nasals is deleted

My findings are similar regarding the place of articulation retention in nasals, see remarks on that in §2.5.2 and see Fletcher & Butcher (2014: 107–8) on resistance to anticipatory place of articulation assimilation in Australian languages more generally.[14] Example (2.30) shows retroflex and alveolar nasals not assimilating to the following labial stop, either intramorphemically (2.30a) or intermorphemically (2.30b).

(2.30) a. [gaˈbuɳbum]
Ka-burnbum.
3SG.NF-stop.PST
'S/he stopped.' [IK1-160712_0001/01:30:48]

b. [gaˈbunbum]
Ka-bun-bum.
3SG.NF-3SG.OBJ-hit.PST
'S/he hit someone.' [ibid./01:31:11]

Concerning the simplification of heterorganic nasal clusters, here I describe a slightly more complicated pattern than Coleman (1982) does. The main domain of this process is indeed the personal prefixes (i.e. the inflectional morphology), partly because they offer most of the opportunities to create such clusters. However, there are a few other combinations involving incorporated nominals, and this process is strikingly evident in possessive pronouns with the prefix *kin-* 'I/II'. The interactions seem to be restricted to the [-labial] nasals, as the [m] is found in a variety of contexts (at least, following [n], [ɲ], [ŋ] and preceding [ŋ]). The remaining four nasals, however, seem to form a hierarchy as in (2.31):

(2.31) n > ɳ > ɲ > ŋ   where > means 'wins over'

The hierarchy in (2.31), rather than recourse to the linear order of the segments, is motivated by the cases where the first nasal is deleted and the second, kept (2.32).

(2.32) [ɲaɳaɳaɳaɲ]
Nganj-rna~rna~rnanj   bi-rnungu.
1SG.FUT-RDP~RDP~see.NP DAT-he.GEN
'I'll look after him/her/it.' [IK1-170615_1SY1/02:10]

Thus, in (2.32) the stem-initial retroflex nasal overrides the preceding palatal nasal, which is the coda of the monosyllabic personal prefix. The root/affix relation does not play a role here: if the personal prefix ends in a "stronger" consonant than the initial of the stem (i.e. the root and, optionally, derivational affixes), then the cluster is simplified to the detriment of the stem-initial consonant (2.33).

---

14 There are, however, *manner* of articulation sandhi in Kunbarlang coverb constructions, namely hardening (§2.7.4).

(2.33) a. [kabunaɻ]
Ka-bun-**rn**ay.
3SG.NF-3SG.OBJ-see.PST
'He saw her.' [IK1-160518_0011]

b. [kiɲibuɲ]
Ki**nj**-**ng**ibunj.
2SG.FUT-name.NP
'Say his name!' [20060620IB03/27:38]

The hierarchy (2.31) is reminiscent of Hamilton's (1989) place markedness scale for Australian languages (2.34):

(2.34) The place scale (Hamilton 1989, cited in Hamilton 1996: 110):
Labial > Dorsal > Laminal > Apical

The work on the scale (2.34), such as Hamilton (1993, 1996), regards this scale as crucially *position-dependent*. Features to the right on the scale are less marked than features to the left if the segment occurs as the first consonant in the cluster (C_1) or in word-final position (C_{fin}). Markedness relation is reversed for the second consonant in the cluster (C_2) and the syllable-initial position (C_{init} and C_{inter}): features to the right in (2.34) are *more* marked in these positions. Importantly, in Kunbarlang the hierarchy (2.31) is *position-independent*. This means that the relation (2.31) between the nasals holds regardless of the order they come in, and the resolution of the cluster is **not** done according to the markedness as in (2.34). Consider example (2.32), where the nasal cluster contains a lamino-palatal /ɲ/ as the C_1 and an apico-retroflex /ɳ/ as the C_2. According to (2.34), the C_1 in this cluster is relatively unmarked, but the C_2 is, on the contrary, marked. However, the cluster is resolved in favour of the more marked apico-retroflex C_2. The pattern cannot be explained by saying that the more marked segment is selected, because (2.33a) shows the opposite pattern, with the less marked segment selected.

The nasal clusters between derivational morphemes, however, are not simplified, even though the resulting clusters sometimes violate the Australian-wide harmonic generalisations (Hamilton 1996: 109ff.). This is the case with nasal clusters occurring both between two derivational prefixes (2.35a) and between a derivational prefix and the root (2.35b).

(2.35) a. [kad:aɲaɲŋoʅŋkidaɲ]
Kadda-nga**nj**-**ng**orlng-kidanj.
3PL.NF-HITH-group-go.PST
'They were coming in a bunch.' [IK1-160719_0001/15:12]

b. [kad:aɲolŋŋa]
Kadda-ngorl**ng**-**rn**a.
3PL.NF-group-sit.NP
'They are sitting in a group.' [IK1-170608_1SY1/08:38]

The cluster in example (2.35b) is very marked according to Hamilton's (1996) generalisations, discussed above and reflected in the scale (2.34). That is, both a dorsal in the C_1 and an apical in the C_2 are highly marked. The cluster, however, is not simplified.[15] This might be connected to the exceptional abundance of dorsals on the C_{fin} in Kunbarlang, cf. §2.5.3.

2.7.4 Manner of articulation assimilation in the coverb constructions

There is sandhi in Kunbarlang that appears specific to the coverb constructions (i.e. complex predicate constructions where a coverb is encliticised to an inflected verb; see §6.5). In this sandhi, the final nasal of the verb hardens preceding a stop (2.36):

(2.36) [kabu**bd**ol]
Ka-bu**m**=**d**ol.
3SG.NF-hit.PST=obstruct
'It was closed.' [IK1-170615_1SY1/31:03]

Only a subset of nasals are affected, and only a subset of stops trigger the hardening. The nasals are the palatal /ɲ/ and the labial /m/ (hardening to [ɟ] and [b], respectively).[16] The stops are the alveolar /t/ and the velar /k/ (2.37).

(2.37) [kaˈɟaŋaɟkolk]
Ka-djanga**nj**=**k**olk.
3SG.NF-stand.PST=cut
'S/he was chopping [them].' [IK1-160504_0001/01:03:05]

It is interesting to note that with the exception of the combination [ɲd], all three other combinations are found elsewhere in the language, and thus the hardening does not seem to reflect a phonotactic restriction:

---

15 The quality of the recording is borderline: both the dorsal and some apical articulation immediately following it are audible, but having more examples with better sound quality would be beneficial for further analysis.
16 The dictionary (Coleman 2010) cites forms like -*buddob* (< /puɲ=top/) 'burst smth.', where the palatal nasal appears to harden to an alveolar, rather than palatal, stop. I have not heard such forms as of yet, but it is quite possible that there is variation.

md *mimdom* 'old person'
mk *kunmimke* 'night time'
ŋk *nga-nganj-kidanj* 'I came'

B. Baker (2014b: 147–8) points out that in coverb constructions "there can be special phonological rules applicable to the boundary between… the coverb, and… the inflected finite verb". He cites Marra, where there is manner dissimilation between two nasals on the coverb/verb boundary.

Furthermore, in Kunbarlang the hardening seems to be the typical realisation, but not an obligatory one, because there are occasional exceptions, such as (2.38):

(2.38) -[ɲaleɲked]
Ka-nganj-ngale**nj**=**k**erd~kerd.
3SG.NF-HITH-spread.PST=RDP~carry
'She carried [something].' [20060814IB01/01:42]

The fact that the hardening is the normal realisation of the relevant nasals in the coverb constructions, testifies to the tightness of their nexus. One may hypothesise that this sandhi has developed as a morphophonemic by-product of this special morphosyntactic construction. Another possibility is that this is a case of a morpho-phonological pattern borrowing, which could come from Mawng, which also has both coverb constructions and a hardening pattern (see Capell & Hinch 1970: 41–42).

2.8 Reduplication

This section outlines reduplication patterns found in Kunbarlang, their form and meaning. In Kunbarlang there is a divide with respect to reduplication between coverbs and verbal morphemes, on the one hand (i.e. morphemes related to verbal predication), and all other morphemes, on the other hand. Firstly, only for verbs and coverbs is reduplication somewhat productive. Second, the patterns differ slightly, with only the non-verbal morphemes showing full reduplication. I therefore discuss them separately.

2.8.1 Non-verbal reduplication

There is a considerable number of non-verbal morphemes in Kunbarlang that have reduplicated form. They can be nouns (*kodjkodj* 'head'), adverbs (*bonj~bonj* 'still; too'), or numerals (*kudji~kudji* 'one each'). For the absolute majority of these, only the reduplicated form exists, so the process is not productive. There are five exceptions that I am aware of:
1. the particle *bonj* 'right; exactly; enough' is reduplicated to *bonj~bonj* 'still; too'

2. the numeral *-kudji* 'one' is reduplicated for a distributive reading
3. the noun *mimdom* 'elder' is reduplicated to yield a plural term (the only noun to do so)
4. the adverb *munguy* 'a_lot' is reduplicated for emphasis
5. the adverb *rlobberl* 'outside' can be reduplicated without any discernible difference in meaning; some speakers say that "you don't need to say it twice"

In terms of the form, the reduplicant is copied to the left of the base. With all of these elements reduplication is always full (i.e. the reduplicant is a full copy of the base) up to the final vowel (see below). All bases are either monosyllabic (*kekkek* 'bone') or disyllabic (*karlurrkkarlurrk* 'kookaburra').

When a disyllabic base ends in an open syllable and the two vowels differ, the final vowel of the reduplicant undergoes assimilation to the initial vowel of the base, e.g. *welewelu* 'mosquito' (cf. *rlobberlrlobberl*, where the base ends in a consonant and hence the second vowel of the reduplicant does not change).

2.8.2 Verbal reduplication

Verbs and coverbs are similar to the rest of the reduplicating morphemes with respect to the directionality—the reduplicant is copied to the left of the base. However, only coverbs show full reduplication (*kerdkerd* 'carry'; *munumunu* 'squash'). The only monosyllabic verb that I know to undergo copying always retriplicates: *-rnanj* 'to see' → *-rna~rna~rnanj* 'to look after'. All the other verbs are di- and trisyllabic.

The major pattern with the polysyllabic verbs is that the reduplicant consists of a copy of the first syllable and the initial CV of the second syllable.[17] Similarly to what has been said above about the non-verbal reduplication, the final vowel of the reduplicant usually assimilates to the first vowel of the base, althought exceptions will be pointed out. Consider examples in (2.39) and (2.40):

(2.39)   a.   -kinje~kinje 'to cook habitually, always' (< -kinje 'to cook')

         b.   -ngibi~ngibunj 'to call names of places, one after the other' (< -ngibunj 'to call a name')

         c.   -rleme~rlemang 'knocked on something a lot' (< -rlemang 'knocked')

---

17 The same pattern is reported in Diyari, Ngiyambaa, and Yugambeh-Bandjalang by Parncutt (2015). In fact, there may be a further similarity between Kunbarlang and Ngiyambaa: as I have noticed above, there is only one monosyllabic verb in Kunbarlang known to retriplicate; in Ngiyambaa, monosyllabic roots are prohibited from copying, because verbal reduplicants must be disyllabic (Donaldson 1980: 198–9).

(2.40) a. -bili~bilayi 'to sway a lot' (< -bilayi 'to sway')
   b. -rdukku~rdukkume 'to cut a lot of something' (< -rdukkume 'to cut')
   c. -yakbi~yakbiyinj '[many teeth] fell out' (< -yakbiyinj 'fell out')
   d. -barra~barrkenrdam 'to load a lot of something somewhere'
      (< -barrkenrdam 'to load something somewhere')

Examples in (2.39) show reduplication of disyllabic bases and examples in (2.40)—of trisyllabic bases. I have included some forms with exceptions. In (2.39a) the mid vowel /e/ does not assimilate to the following high /i/. I do not have a different verb with a similar phonemic composition to cross-check. In (2.40c) the high front vowel /i/ does not assimilate to /a/, perhaps because of the intervening glide /y/, which is articulatorily close to /i/. Finally, in example (2.40d) we see lenition of /rk/ to /r/. This lenition seems to be regular: -barra~barrkidbe 'all the different ones' is a repeatedly attested form, whereas the base-faithful form *kun-barrki~barrkidbe* has been attested only once [C01-015539/18:31].

It will be apparent from the above examples that reduplication of verbal stems has a distinct function of encoding pluractionality, i.e. event plurality. It can be due to multiple participants (2.40c), repetitive/iterative action (2.39c) or habitual action (2.39a).

3 Grammatical overview

In this chapter I discuss several fundamental topics of Kunbarlang grammar, which also facilitate reading of individual chapters. The first of these is a short introduction to the grammatical functions and the general grammatical features of Kunbarlang. The grammatical functions receive a fuller treatment in §5.1, but a brief overview here will give the reader the necessary definitions of terms used throughout the grammar. That is followed by a classification of the Kunbarlang lexicon into parts of speech, with a general overview of their properties and classification criteria. In the next short section 3.3 I build on the presentation of the parts of speech to make explicit the criteria I used for wordhood and to distinguish clitics from words, on the one hand, and from affixes, on the other hand. I conclude with a discussion of argumenthood in section §3.4, where I argue that Kunbarlang is a pronominal argument language. This discussion relies crucially on the presentation of grammatical functions and main characteristics of the parts of speech, but also heavily references a wide range of topics throughout the grammar; thus, depending on the reader's personal style, it can be read either as a preview of themes to come, or be later returned to as a summary of some core aspects of Kunbarlang general architecture.

3.1 Typological features and grammatical functions

The clause in Kunbarlang is heavily polysynthetic (for general background on polysynthesis see Murasugi 2014, Fortescue, Mithun & Evans 2017; for specific reference to northern Australia, see Evans 2017). The verb (§3.2.4, Chapters 5 and 6) carries enough information about the event and argument structure to express a full proposition even when it is the only element in the clause (see Chapter 7 on the basic clause structure). Indeed, Kinslow Harris (1969b: 4) calls it "a minimal clause". Other words, such as nominals and adverbials, may add extra specification to the event decriptions, but they are never obligatory. When they are present, they are ordered with respect to each other and the predicate with a significant degree of freedom (although the preference for SVO is evident). That is to say, word order does not encode grammatical relations. Nor are grammatical relations systematically indicated by cases: the case system of Kunbarlang is reduced to the nominative/genitive/dative distinction in the personal pronouns (§4.5.1), but full NP core arguments are not marked for case. The pair of examples in (3.1) shows that the word *kirdimarr* 'man' is the same whether it is agent or patient (and the demonstrative *ninda* that modifies it does not vary either).

(3.1) a. **Ninda** kirdimarrk ka-karlangwanj pikipiki.
DEM.PROX.I man 3SG.NF-chase.NP pig
'This man is chasing a pig.' [IK1-170609_2SM1/01:00:18–24]

b. **Nginda**   barramimbanj ka-**bun**-rnay   **ninda**
   DEM.PROX.II   woman   3SG.NF-3SG.OBJ-see.PST DEM.PROX.I
   kirdimarrk.
   man
   'This woman saw this man.'   [IK1-150724_1SY1]

The rich verbal morphology partially contributes to argument structure representation. Certain referential characteristics of up to two core arguments are encoded by the personal prefixes on the verb (namely, person and number); see, however, §5.1.1 on the class of unregistered arguments, which cannot be cross-referenced in the verb. Unlike the majority of Gunwinyguan languages, Kunbarlang does not extensively use subject-object portmanteaux in the personal prefixes, instead combining subjects and objects in an agglutinating way (§5.2). Syntactic alignment is nominative-accusative, and with respect to objects it is secundative (§5.1). *Nominative-accusative* means that the single argument of an intransitive predicate is indexed in the verb similarly to the agent (and differently from the patient) of a transitive predicate. *Secundative* means that the patient of a transitive predicate is indexed in the same way as the recipient (rather than the patient) of a ditransitive predicate (Haspelmath 2005). This is illustrated in (3.2), where the third person plural object is indexed by the prefix *buddu-* whether it is the theme (3.2a) or the recipient (3.2b).

(3.2) a. Nga-**buddu**-rnay.
         1SG.NF-3PL.OBJ-see.PST
         'I saw them.'   [IK1-160828_0001/07:01]

      b. Ngayi nga-**buddu**-wuy   neyang.
         I   1SG.NF-3PL.OBJ-give.PST food
         'I gave them food.'   [IK1-160503_0001/57:54–57]

In what follows I call patients of transitives and recipients of ditransitives (i.e. the objects indexed in the object slot) PRIMARY objects, and the patients of ditransitives, SECONDARY objects. Some of the argument derivation morphology (§6.1) creates new predicates of increased valency by adding a participant to the underlying verb (the benefactive §6.1.1 and the comitative §6.1.2). The verbal reflexives and reciprocals in Kunbarlang are of valency-conserving type, and they only target the primary object (3.3). These patterns are discussed in detail in §6.1.3.

(3.3) Ngarrki-**wu-dji**   ngob.
      1.INCL.FUT-give-REFL.NP   all
      'We'll share it, all of us.' [lit. 'we shall give it to ourselves']
                                                         [IK1-170610_1SY2/11:38]

A wide array of grammatical roles can be relativised in Kunbarlang, even up to the possessor (§8.4).

The following section elaborates the brief grammatical sketch through discussing form and function of the various word classes I distinguish in Kunbarlang. After presenting these word classes, I briefly touch upon wordhood criteria and the question of clitics in §3.3. Finally, at the end of the chapter, I return to the issue of general grammatical architecture and discuss the problem of argumenthood in Kunbarlang (§3.4).

3.2 Parts of speech

There are a number of categories (parts of speech) that can be distinguished in Kunbarlang, among them ADJECTIVES, ADVERBS, CONNECTIVES, COVERBS (LEXICAL CLITICS), DEMONSTRATIVES, INTERROGATIVES, NOUN MARKERS (DETERMINERS), NOUNS, NUMERALS, PARTICLES, PREPOSITIONS, PREVERBS, PRONOUNS, QUANTIFIERS and VERBS. They are exclusive, in the sense that each word normally only belongs to one category. There is only one derivational morpheme that changes part of speech of the base, the inchoative *-mi*, which turns adjectives into verbs (see more on this in §3.2.2). No other means of conversion between categories have been found.

The parts of speech can be classified into open and closed class ones:
open adjectives, adverbs, connectives, nouns, numerals, and preverbs
closed coverbs, demonstratives, interrogatives, noun markers, prepositions, pronouns, quantifiers, and verbs

This distinction refers to the ability of a given category to acquire new members, either via productive rules or via lexical borrowing (as is nearly always the case in Kunbarlang). It does not, however, refer to the absolute size of the category, nor is it intended to coincide with that between content and function words. Indeed, both classes include content as well as function words—in other words, some functional categories are open class and can be borrowed. I find the open~closed class distinction to be more useful of the two and adhere to it in this description.

Open class parts of speech can acquire new members, e.g. through borrowing. Closed class ones are so called because their list is not expandable. Among the closed class categories, coverbs (§6.5) are exceptional in that they are best analysed as lexical clitics and not free words. This accounts for their strict placement and the sandhi unique to the coverb construction (§2.7.4), and is in accord with their being a closed class. There are a few probable loans from e.g. Iwaidjan languages, but it is not possible to establish the timeline of the borrowing—it could have happened just as the construction arose in Kunbarlang. Even though they are not a word class in the proper sense, they are still included in this section because of their lexical semantics, their contribution to complex predicate formation, and certain formal similarities to adverbs and preverbs (from which they must thus be delineated).

The verbs are also a closed class (albeit a large one, in the order of 450 members), which is a common feature of the Gunwinyguan languages (cf. Harvey 2003: 206–7). New verbal words are not borrowed into Kunbarlang with the same status as the native roots, but rather with the aid of a construction with preverbs (somewhat similar to the coverb construction): usually the root form of the loaned English verb is placed left-adjacent to the inflected Kunbarlang verb *-ngundje* 'to do' (3.4).[1] There are, however, some variations, discussed in §3.2.5.2.

(3.4) Ngorro   ngadda-djin,   **share ngadda-ngundje.**
       DEM.MED.IV   1PL.EXCL.NF-eat.NP   share 1PL.EXCL.NF-do.NP
       'Then we eat it, we share it.'   [IK1-160726_0021/01:15–19]

Adjectives (3.5a) and nouns (3.5b) are loaned readily.

(3.5) a. Badjubadju nayi **yellow, blue** and **white.**
           shirt   NM.I ENG   ENG   ENG
           'A shirt that is yellow, blue and white.'   [IK1-160624_0001/06:47–51]

       b. **Picture** ninda   ngorro   ka-dja.
           ENG   DEM.PROX.I   DEM.MED.IV   3SG.NF-stand.NP
           'He is on the [t-shirt] print [lit. 'stands in the picture'].'
                                                          [ibid./06:59–07:02]

Connectives and numerals are quite often borrowed from English, especially in those cases when English makes finer lexical distinctions than Kunbarlang. For instance, where English speakers use *and* and *but*,[2] Kunbarlang speakers have only one lexeme *la* 'CONJ'. Thus, the loan *but* (3.6a) is quite frequent in Kunbarlang speech (perhaps because *but* is more specific than *and*, and Kunbarlang *la* is more strongly associated with the latter). Another connective, *or*, and the particle *only* are seen in (3.6b). Similarly, since the numeral system of Kunbarlang is small, English numerals are readily borrowed when large precise numbers need to be expressed (3.6b).

---

1 An interesting question concerns the possible sources of such preverb borrowing. I am not aware of any instances of preverb constructions where the preverb is from another indigenous language.
2 Abstracting somewhat, the same logical connector with different pragmatic shades.

(3.6) a. Yimarne   kadda-ngunda=barr   na-bareng,   **but**   nukka   ngorro
    like   3PL.NF-do.PST=open   I-dangerous   ENG   he   DEM.MED.IV
    karlu,   nukka ngorro   na-mak,   Christian man.
    NEG.PRED   he   DEM.MED.IV   I-good   ENG   ENG
    'They thought he was dangerous, but he wasn't, he was good, a Christian man.' [IK1-160624_0001/03:05–12]

b. Ngana-kalng   **only   three hundred   or   two hundred**.
    1DU.EXCL.NF-get.PST   ENG   ENG   ENG ENG
    'We bought it for only $300 or $200.'   [20060901IB03/02:30–33]

In the following sections I discuss the diagnostics for the different parts of speech in Kunbarlang.

3.2.1 Nouns

The main distinguishing property of nouns in Kunbarlang is their inherent specification for NOUN CLASS (or GRAMMATICAL GENDER; see §4.1). This is an easily applicable heuristic because nouns head noun phrases, triggering noun class agreement on all modifiers (see examples (3.11) and (3.12) in §3.2.2), as well as on the adjectival predicates (3.7). The class I and IV nouns (*kirdimarrk* 'man' and *lakamurrng* 'night', respectively) govern the appropriate class agreement on the adjective *-kukkarlyung* 'long' in the predicative function in (3.7).

(3.7) a. Ninda   **kirdimarrk** **na**-kukkarlyung.
    DEM.PROX.I   man[I]   I-long
    'This man is tall.'   [IK1-160818_0001/02:53–55]

b. Ngondo   kilabenbe   kun-djuhmi   la   **lakamurrng**
    DEM.PROX.IV   daylight   IV-short   CONJ   night[IV]
    kun-kukkarlyung.
    IV-long
    '[In the dry season] the day is short and the night is long.'
                                         [IK1-170606_1SY2/14:02–07]

Nouns are the main part of speech modified by adjectives (§3.2.2) and possessor phrases (§4.6), and this is a useful practical diagnostic, but it is not absolutely reliable as the only test, since (i) it is possible that not all nouns can be easily construed as possessed, and (ii) in the absence of an overt noun a possessive phrase could appear to modify another modifier, such as an adjective. Thus, even though in (3.8) it may seem as though *bingaybu* 'mine' is modifying the word *mayi*, that is in fact a noun marker and not a noun.

(3.8) Kundulk bi-nungku   man-djuhmi, la   **mayi**   **bi-ngaybu**
      tree   DAT-you.SG.GEN   III-short   CONJ NM.III   DAT-I.GEN
      man-kukkarlyung.
      III-long
      'Your stick is short and mine is long.'   [IK1-160818_0001/19:54–20:02]

Kunbarlang nouns do not have any productive morphology, except the limitative suffix -*wu* (3.9). Apart from nouns, it has been attested with adverbs, so this is not a good test for nounhood.

(3.9) Lorrkon kirdimarrk-**wu** kanjbadda-rnanj.
      L   man-LIM   3PL.FUT-see.NP
      'Lorrkon ceremony is only for men to see.'   [IK1-170525_2SY1/25:26–27:18]

In terms of their usage and semantics, nouns are prototypical arguments and denote individuals (3.7a) and entities (3.8), as well as more abstract notions (3.7b, 3.10).

(3.10) Kanjyuwa ki-ngundje   kuyi   kukka, ngayi ka-ngan-karrme
       PROH   2SG.NF-do.NP   NM.IV   it.IV   I   3SG.NF-1SG.OBJ-hold.NP
       kundji.
       shame
       'Stop fooling around, I'm ashamed of you.' [lit. 'Stop doing that, shame holds me.']   [IK1-160513_0001/44:18–50]

In the next section I turn to the Kunbarlang adjectives.

3.2.2 Adjectives

Adjectives constitute a distinct part of speech in Kunbarlang (cf. Dixon (1980: 271–5) on the weak noun/adjective distinction in many Australian languages). The criteria that can be used to distinguish Kunbarlang adjectives from nouns include the following:
(i) nouns function in an NP as referential heads, while adjectives function as attributive modifiers (cf. Louagie 2020: 68)
(ii) nouns belong to a particular noun class (or, rarely, two classes), and do not appear as the target of agreement (but instead control agreement on the modifiers), while adjectives obligatorily agree (as targets) in noun class with a head noun (3.11–3.12)
(iii) inchoative -*mi* combines with adjectives but not nouns (3.14) vs. (3.15)
(iv) nouns may be incorporated into adjectives, but not into nouns, and not vice versa (3.16)

The category of noun class (§4.1) permeates the whole of the noun phase, being an agreement category defined on all nominals (i.e. constituents of the noun phrase; see Chapter 4). There is a clear asymmetry, however, in that only nouns are inherently specified for the noun class, and all[3] of the modifiers of the head noun agree with it. As a special case, the head noun can be elided. Adjectives do not have an inherent noun class and can inflect for all classes of the head noun (3.11–3.12).

(3.11) Third person singular forms of -*mak* 'good'
    a. na-mak 'good (e.g. man)'
    b. kin-mak 'good (e.g. woman)'
    c. man-mak 'good (e.g. food)'
    d. kun-mak 'good (e.g. liquid)'

Most adjectives have a paradigm like -*mak* 'good' in (3.11), i.e. classes II–IV prefixes end in the alveolar nasal. However, a few adjectives that do not seem to form any natural class have a paradigm where those prefixes end in a vowel, without the nasal (3.12). See §4.1.3 for some more detail.

(3.12) Third person singular forms of *buke* 'old' (Coleman 2010: 20)
    a. banikkin   ki-buke
       dish/vessel[II] II-old
       'an old billy-can'

    b. mandjawak ma-buke
       knife[III] III-old
       'an old knife'

    c. kuyi ku-buke
       NM.IV IV-old
       'in olden times; long ago'

Noun class is a feature of the third person. Adjectives, however, are not limited to description of third person referents. In predicative function, for instance, they can have any person/number combination. Interestingly, the first and second person forms take prefixes from the irrealis non-past verbal subparadigm (table 5.3 in §5.2.1). Third dual and plural have prefixes similar to the irrealis ones, but slightly distinct. No other verbal prefixes are possible on adjectives (or any other nominals). Table 3.1 gives the

---

3 Some quantifiers, such as the numeral 'two' (*kaburrk*), the universal quantifier *ngob*, and occasional instances of *yika* 'some', make an exception in that they do not decline (§4.7).

Tab. 3.1: Adjectival paradigm (for -*mak* 'good')

		Singular	Dual	Plural
First	Exclusive	ngarra-mak	ngana-mak	ngadda-mak
	Inclusive		ngarrak-mak	
Second		kirri-mak	ngunu-mak	nguddu-mak
Third		see (3.11)	**kinbarra**-mak	**kinbadda**-mak

full set of forms for the adjective -*mak* 'good'. Third person non-singular forms, distinct from the verbal paradigm, are in boldface. Examples of the first person 'inclusive' and the second person singular forms are given in (3.13).

(3.13) a. Ngudda ngayi **ngarrak-mak**.
     you.SG   I   1.INCL-good
     'You and I are good, kind.'   [IK1-160704_0001/04:18]

   b. Ngudda **kirri-ngongokwarri** la   kinj-rna-dji   karra
     you.SG 2SG-dirty   CONJ 2SG.FUT-see-REFL.NP DEM.MED.LOC
     badumang!
     glass
     'You are soiled, look at yourself in the mirror!' [IK1-180521_1SY1/26:30]

While derivation in the Kunbarlang nominal domain is extremely limited, many adjectives can combine with the inchoative morpheme -*mi* to form inchoative verbs (3.14).

(3.14) a. Kun-mak ngob ka-**mak-minj**.
     IV-good   all   3SG.NF-good-INCH.PST
     'S/he's **got well** (again).'   [IK1-160704_0001/09:14]

   b. Manda   kandiddjawa ka-**rayek-minj**.
     DEM.PROX.III bread   3SG.NF-hard-INCH.PST
     'This bread has **dried**.' [speaker's comment: "It's like frozen"]
                                                       [IK1-160704_0001]

   c. Lakamurrng ka-**kuk-karlyung-minj**   kuyi kunmimke.
     night   3SG.NF-length-big-INCH.PST NM.I overnight
     '[In the dry season] the night was getting longer day by day.'
                                                   [IK1-170606_1SY2/18:55–58]

Nouns cannot combine with this morpheme (3.15a). Instead, the inchoative meaning has to be expressed periphrastically; one possibility is (3.15b).

(3.15) a. *Djarrangalanj kadda-**kirdimarrk-minj** / kinbadda-**kirdimarrk-minj**.
boy　　　　　3PL.NF-man-INCH.PST　　3PL-man-INCH.PST
intended: 'Boys became men.' [in the context of initiation]
[IK1-170525_1JW1/54:58–55:18]

b. Djarrangalanj kadda-warre　　kadda-kalbi-yi　　kirdimarrk.
boy　　　　　　3PL.NF-occur.NP 3PL.NF-get-REFL.NP man
'Boys become men.'　　　　　　　　[IK1-170525_1JW1/57:44–58:03]

In Kunbarlang nouns can incorporate into predicative categories, viz. adjectives and verbs (3.16; see further in §6.3). Adjectives, however, do not incorporate into nouns.[4]

(3.16) a. Na-**rnil-mak**.
I-eye-good
'[He has got] good eyes.'　　　　　　[IK1-160715_0001/28:21–23]

b. Na-buk　na-**karlmu-warri**.
I-person I-ear-bad
'He is bad in the ears, hard of hearing.'
[Coleman 2010: 51; glosses mine—IK]

c. Kenda　　　　kun-**ngundek-burrinj**.
DEM.PROX.LOC IV-country-pleasant
'This is beautiful country.'　　　　　　[IK1-170606_1SY1]

This set of morphosyntactic properties clearly delineates adjectives as a category distinct from nouns. Kunbarlang adjectives are also consistent with traditional understanding of adjectival semantics, as they denote qualities, such as these:
- size, e.g. *-ngana* 'large', *-djuhmi* 'short'
- age, e.g. *-kerrkung* 'young; new', *-buke* 'old'
- perceptual characteristics, e.g. *-djelmi* 'warm', *-rdulmuk* 'heavy'
- evaluative characteristics, e.g. *-burrinj* 'pleasant', *-mak* 'good'

Some interesting outliers are quantificational adjectives (e.g. *-kudji* 'one', *-rleng* 'much', *-worrbam* 'few'; §4.7, esp. §4.7.2), the interrogative adjective *-kaybi* 'which [person]' (discussed together with true interrogatives in §4.5.4) and the adjective *-kang* 'from' (3.17), which is used to talk about provenance of objects or people.

---

[4] Body part and generic nominals can be incorporated into adjectives in other Gunwinyguan languages, too; see, for instance, Baker & Nordlinger 2008 on Ngalakgan, Wubuy and Bininj Kunwok.

(3.17) a. Nganj-ka nganj-kali lorre **kun-kang** Bottle Rock.
　　　　1SG.FUT-go.NP 1SG.FUT-get.NP ground[IV] IV-from [toponym]
　　　　'I'll go get sand/soil from Bottle Rock.' [IK1-170525_2SY1/41:20–28]

　　b. Ngayi **ngarra-kang** Karrabbu.
　　　　I 1SG-from [toponym]
　　　　'I'm from Karrabbu.' [20150212AS01/00:48–55]

Accordingly, typical adjectival meanings are usually expressed in Kunbarlang by lexemes in the category of adjectives. A prominent exception is colour: there are no dedicated adjectival expressions for concepts in this domain. The closest ones are -*karrkeyang* 'clean; white' and -*ngongokwarri* meaning 'dirty; dark; blackened' (3.18), which are not dedicated colour adjectives.

(3.18) Mulurrmulurr ngayi kin-**karrkeyang** la mulurrmulurr ngayi
　　　 ibis　　　　 NM.II　 II-clean　　　 CONJ ibis　　　　　 NM.II
　　　 kin-**ngongokwarri**.
　　　 II-dirty
　　　 'The white ibis and the black ibis.' [20060620IB04/06:46–50]

The concept 'white' is lexicalised as the verb -*walarrbunj* 'to be white' (3.19).

(3.19) a. Kurrana ka-ngan-marnbunj **nga-walarrbunj**.
　　　　 moon 3SG.NF-1SG.OBJ-make.NP 1SG.NF-white.NP
　　　　 'The moon makes me shine and appear white.' [IK1-160523_0011/42:56]

　　b. Picture **ka-walarrbum** ngob.
　　　　 ENG 3SG.NF-white.PST all
　　　　 'The picture is bleached ("whitened").' [ibid./35:47–8]

All other colours are expressed in a phrasal construction with the similative *yimarne(k)* 'like' and a reference object: e.g. *yimarnek mulubin* 'red' (lit. 'like blood'), *yimarnek maworord* (or *mirlak*) 'green' (lit. 'like leaf/grass'), *yimarnek kuyunu* 'blue' (lit. 'like cloud'), and used in the quality-forming construction with the verb -*ngundje* (3.20):

(3.20) Ngayi kodbarre korro kaddum, barninda, ka-**ngundje** **yimarne**
　　　 I　　 house　 DEM.MED.LOC top　　 IGNOR 3SG.NF-do.NP like
　　　 mulubin.
　　　 blood
　　　 'In my picture, the roof of the house is red [lit. 'it does like blood'].'
　　　　　　　　　　　　　　　　　　　　　　　　 [IK1-170610_2SM1/01:44–02:00]

3.2.3 Adverbs

Adverbs, like nouns, are morphologically inert (except for the derivational limitative suffix *-wu* that can mark both nouns and adverbs; see example 3.21a). However, unlike nouns, adverbs don't have an inherent noun class (to be precise, noun class as a grammatical category is not defined on adverbs at all). They fulfil functions typically associated with the category of adverbials, i.e. adjuncts that modify the verb or verbal phrase. Semantically, there are primarily adverbs of manner (*morrehmorre* in 3.21a) and adverbs of time, i.e. temporal location (*balkkime* in 3.21a), as well as frequency and duration (3.21b).

(3.21) a. Ka-yambi-burrdje **balkkime**-wu **morrehmorre**.
3SG.NF-swag-wrap.NP today-LIM slowly
'S/he's packing slowly just today.' [IK1-180522_3SY1/15:33–36]

b. Nga-kidanj **waken** la ngunda ngayi-yu
1SG.NF-go.PST while CONJ not 1SG.IRR.PST-lie.IRR.PST
kenda.
DEM.PROX.LOC
'I went there for a while, I didn't sleep there.' [IK1-160802_0011/10:27–38]

There are also adverbs that speakers can use to encode their estimation of probability of some event, i.e. an epistemic meaning (3.22).

(3.22) Nguddu-yung **mandjang** ki-nguddu-bu.
2PL.IRR.NP-lie.IRR.NP perhaps 3SG.IRR.NP-2PL.OBJ-hit.IRR.NP
'If you sleep [in the house] you might get hurt.'
[20060614IB/00:30–33; translation mine—IK]

Adverbs enjoy considerable freedom of placement. When modifying a verb, they can be linearly separated from it and can appear on either side of it; cf. the temporal adverb *balkkime* in (3.23) and further examples in section 3.2.5.1 below, e.g. (3.37).

(3.23) a. And ngarrk-warre ngorro **balkkime** kenda.
ENG 1.INCL.NF-move.NP DEM.MED.IV now DEM.PROX.LOC
'And we who are here now.' [IK1-160424_0001/01:27–29]

b. And **balkkime** kenda ngarrk-dja.
ENG now DEM.PROX.LOC 1.INCL.NF-stand.NP
'And today we are here.' [ibid./01:58–02:00]

Adverbs most typically modify verbs, as in (3.21), but can also associate with nominals (3.24)—but even in that case they do not take noun class morphology.

Tab. 3.2: A sample of Kunbarlang adverbs

Class	Adverb	Meaning
Temporal	babi	later
	benbe	yesterday
	malayi	tomorrow
	ngulamngulam	morning
	wularrud	already
Manner	bidkumbel	by hand
	burudjang	pointlessly
	morrehmorre	slowly
	mungu	accidentally
	rnimirnimi	backwards
	werrk	immediately
Locative	djingakab	far away
	kaddum	above
	rlobberl	outside
Probability	badjuk	suppose
	kukkangundje	perhaps

(3.24) Kinj-ka   kinj-kali   [mayi kundulk **djininj**].
       2SG.FUT-go.NP 2SG.FUT-get.NP NM.III tree   properly
       'Go get **the proper tree** [e.g. for making fire]!'   [IK1-170531_1YF1]

A sample of Kunbarlang adverbs of different semantic classes is given in table 3.2.

There is another class of uninflecting items in Kunbarlang which combine with verbs, viz. coverbs (see §3.2.5.1). However, coverbs are lexical clitics with a fixed position, and this restriction provides an operational test for distinguishing between adverbs and coverbs.

3.2.4 Verbs

The verbs in Kunbarlang are the part of speech that is easiest to recognize. They carry obligatory personal prefixes which are very distinctive and which no other part of speech carries.[5] The full paradigms can be found in §5.2.1, and the rich template for the verbal word in the beginning of chapter 5. The personal prefixes can have a complex polysyllabic structure as in (3.25a) or be as short as a CV syllable (3.25b).

---

[5] Adjectives agreeing with first and second person pronouns have the agreement prefixes that are formally identical to one of the verbal subject paradigms, the one I call irrealis non-past (see table 5.3 in §5.2.1). However, the remaining three subject prefix paradigms are not available for adjectives.

(3.25) a. Ngandjidda-ka.
1PL.EXCL.FUT-go.NP
'We [without you] shall go.' [20060620IB04/13:55–56]

b. Ka-ka.
3SG.NF-go.NP
'S/he / it is going.' [IK1-170610_2SM1/10:25–26]

The verbs are prototypical predicates, they have full propositional force and often are the only element in the clause (as for instance in (3.25) above). Verbs denote states and activities. They provide tense and mood information for the clause (§5.5). They can be semantically rather specific, such as -*burrdjuwa* 'to tell; divulge' (3.26), or, on the contrary, very general, like -*ngundje*, which by and large means 'to perform' (3.27).

(3.26) Ngondo nganj-**burrdjuwa**...
DEM.PROX.IV 1SG.FUT-divulge.NP
'Now I'm going to tell [a story]...' [20150413IOv01/00:11–13]

(3.27) a. Yimarnek ngayi-kangkayini kabbala la nga-**ngunda** eh-eh.
like 1SG.IRR.PST-go.IRR.PST boat CONJ 1SG.NF-do.PST INTJ
'I was like, *maybe I'll go on the boat*, but then I was like, *nope*.'
[20060620IB05/02:26–30; translation mine—IK]

b. Birlinj ka-**ngundje** ki-karrme nakarrken?
how 3SG.NF-perform.NP 2SG.NF-hold.NP dog
'How many dogs do you have?' [IK1-170525_2SY2/27:08]

Kunbarlang verbs can have between one and four argument positions. The different valency classes (both underived and derived) are extensively exemplified in §6.2. Another internal subdivision of verbs is in terms of the multiple conjugational classes, discussed in §5.3. In the following section (§3.2.4.1) I present a particular subset of Kunbarlang verbs, used to express kinship relations.

3.2.4.1 Kinship verbs

Kunbarlang, similarly to Bininj Kunwok, Dalabon, and some Iwaidjan languages, has a set of KINSHIP VERBS, i.e. lexical items that are morphologically verbs but have the meaning of 'be K to', where K stands for a variety of kinship relations (e.g. -*kalng* 'be a mother to'; 3.28). See Evans 2000 (esp. §3.5) for a typology and a comparison of the Iwaidjan and Gunwinyguan languages to the Amerindian ones, where kinship verbs are also widespread.

Tab. 3.3: Kunbarlang kinship verbs

Kinship verb	Meaning	Corresponding nominal term
-djanganj 'stood'	siblings	*yabok* 'EZ', *kokok* 'EB', *mabidj* 'YB' etc.
-kalng 'got'	mother	*karrard* or *ngayingana* 'M'
-karrmeng 'held'	father	*ngabbard* 'F'
-rna 'sit'	spouse	*ngalbininjkobeng* 'wife' etc.
-yakbum 'dropped'	parent	*karrard* 'M', *ngabbard* 'F'

(3.28) ngayi ka-ngan-kalng
       I   3SG.NF-1SG.OBJ-get.PST

       'my mother' [Field notes, SY 2016-04-27]

Similar to what one finds in Bininj Kunwok (e.g. 3.29), all Kunbarlang kinship verbs are metaphorical extensions of verbs with other, more basic meanings. In Evans's (2000) terms, these verbs have etymologies relating to "kinship defining events" (e.g. p. 140).

(3.29) Bininj Kunwok (Evans 2000: 140, ex. (62a))

       ngan-yawme-y
       3/First-conceive-PP

       1. '(the one that) she conceived me.'
       2. 'my mother'

One sign of high specialisation of these Kunbarlang forms in the kinship function is that they all are fixed to a particular tense. Most of them are realis past form, except for *-rna* 'spouse' is realis present.[6] The correct tense forms is how I cite them in table 3.3.

Examples in (3.30) show that prefixes can have any person/number combination.[7]

(3.30) a. ki-ngan-karrmeng
           2SG.NF-1SG.OBJ-hold.PST

          'you are my father' [Field notes, PN 2016-04-24]

     b. ki-(*bun)-karrmeng
           2SG.NF-(3SG.OBJ)-hold.PST

          'you are his father' [Field notes, PN 2016-04-24]

---

[6] This probably relates to their etymology stemming from the "kinship defining events", where parental relations are defined by the event of birth, which for a living person lies in the past, but spousal relations are defined as ongoing. However, on such an interpretation the relations of siblings (also encoded by the past tense verb) would need extra explanation. Perhaps further etymological study could shed light on this.

[7] The verb *kakarlmukarrmeng* in (3.30d) is a neologism for 'drove a car'; literally 'he held [its] ears', where "ears" is a metaphor for the steering wheel.

c. ngadda-karrmeng
    1PL.EXCL.NF-hold.PST
    'we are his fathers'   [Field notes, PN 2016-04-24]

d. **Ka-ngan-karrmeng**   ka-karlmu-karrmeng (ka-kidanj).
    3SG.NF-1SG.OBJ-hold.PST 3SG.NF-ear-hold.PST 3SG.NF-go.PST
    '**My father** [lit. 'the one who held me'] drove (away).'
                                                     [Field notes, SY 2016-04-27]

Examples (3.30d) and (3.31) show the kinship verbs used in context, in argumental positions, available to them because they are free relative clauses (see §8.4.1.2).

(3.31) Nginda   **ngayi ngana-rna**   kikka Mirrangkangu.
        DEM.PROX.II I   1DU.EXCL.NF-sit.NP   she   M
        '**My wife**, she is of the Mirrangkangu patriclan.' [20150413IOv01/02:26–29]

In (3.31), for instance, the free relative means roughly 'who I sit with', and is the subject of the sentence. This is an inclusory construction (§4.5.2) and it is not immediately clear what grammatical role is relativised: I classify this as subject relativisation, but note that the free relative refers only to one of the pair of referents. Example (3.32) shows the kinship verb for 'be siblings'.

(3.32) Kabarra-djanganj Naragoidj.
        3DU.NF-stand.PST N
        '(She is) sister of Naragoidj.'   [IK1-170610_2SM1/19:51]

3.2.5 Coverbs and preverbs

Both coverbs and preverbs are uninflecting elements that only occur in construction with the verb. In such a construction they form a kind of a complex predicate, i.e. a predicate whose semantics and argument structure are built jointly from multiple lexical morphemes, or, in other words, "the information normally associated with the [lexical—IK] head of a verbal predicate is spread over several parts of the predicate" (Bowern 2014: 264); see also Baker & Harvey (2010). Consider an example of a preverb (3.33a) and a coverb (3.33b) construction in Kunbarlang:

(3.33) a. Ngal-buk=bonj   ka-kidanj   ngorro   **married ka-ngunda**
           II-person=exactly 3SG.NF-go.PST DEM.MED.IV married 3SG.NF-do.PST

   Nganeyokkarrama.
   N

   'She went and **got married** to a man called Nganeyokkarrama.'
   [20150206AS03/06:37–40]

   b. **Ka-bun-rlakka=dilirr**   ninkareyak ka-bun-walkki-bukayi
      3SG.NF-3SG.OBJ-throw.NP=drift current   3SG.NF-3SG.OBJ-COM-rise.NP

   karra   wadjbud.
   DEM.MED.LOC sand

   'The current carries him/her taking him/her to the shore.'
   [IK1-180605_1SY1/01:04:34–40]

Despite the functional and formal similarity between the two classes, there are also a number of important formal differences that motivate keeping them separate.
- coverbs only occur in the postverbal position, while preverbs occur on either side with a preference for preverbal position
- preverbs are, effectively, an open class category for borrowing English verbs, while the coverbs are a closed class of morphemes that either are retained from the proto-Gunwinyguan stage or were borrowed from other indigenous languages during some previous contact (the judgment about this is usually made based on occurrence of similar forms in other languages from the Gunwinyguan family or elsewhere; §6.5)
- coverbs are best analyzed as lexical clitics, while preverbs can be considered a word class

3.2.5.1 Coverbs

Coverbs are a closed class in the order of a hundred members. They are morphologically inert and only appear in a particular construction (i.e. the coverb construction, §6.5), where they encliticise to an inflected verb. As mentioned in section §3.2.3, coverbs are prone to confusion with adverbs.[8] This is because they combine with verbs (all of which are also attested independently) and the apparent semantics often resembles that of adverbials. Consider example (3.34):

(3.34) a. Merlbedj ka-**dja**=**bokob.**
           seaweed 3SG.NF-stand.NP=float

   'Seaweed is ['stands'] underwater.'   [IK1-160615_0011]

---

8 In fact, this is how they are classified in Coleman's (2010) dictionary: "adverb:bound".

b. Nayi ka-**rna**=**bokob**   ninda   bidju Karrabbu.
    NM.I 3SG.NF-sit.NP=float DEM.PROX.I EMPH K
    'That very one that is sitting in the water, at Karrabbu.'
                                               [IK1-160510_0001/02:36–39]

The word *bokob* seems to have an adverbial-like semantics 'in the water', combining freely with predicates and contributing to their meaning compositionally. However, unlike adverbs, the coverbs are not free words but rather enclitics, and as such are not freely placed. They must always follow the verb immediately, and thus cannot be separated by an adverb, for instance.[9] This test is shown for *bokob* in (3.35) and for another coverb, *kulkkulk* 'run', in (3.36).[10]

(3.35) a. Nga-rna=**bokob**   bonj~bonj.
           1SG.NF-sit.NP=float   RDP~exactly
           'I'm still sitting in the water.'   [IK1-180522_1PG1/12:22–25]

       b. *Nga-rna   bonj~bonj   **bokob**.
           1SG.NF-sit.NP RDP~exactly float
           intended 'I'm still sitting in the water.'   [ibid./12:15–20]

(3.36) a. Ka-ka=**kulkkulk**   karra   wadjbud.
           3SG.NF-go.NP=run   DEM.MED.LOC sand
           'He/she/it is running to the beach.'   [IK1-180522_3SY1/01:45–48]

       b. *Ka-ka   karra   wadjbud **kulkkulk**.
           3SG.NF-go.NP DEM.MED.LOC sand   run
           intended: 'He/she/it is running to the beach.'   [ibid./01:49–54]

       c. *Nganj-ka   balkkime **kulkkulk**.
           1SG.FUT-go.NP now   run
           intended: 'I'm going for a run now.'   [IK1-150803_1PN1/14:29–38]

---

9 There are occasional instances of coverbs placed in the preverbal position. It appears that the coverbs that allow this are the monosyllabic, probably ideophonic ones: *dob* 'smash', *budj* 'thud', *bard* 'grab'. This is probably related to the Gunwinyguan excorporation (see §6.5.1), but more work is required on this both in Kunbarlang and in the other languages which manifest the phenomenon. Note, however, that in both Bininj Kunwok and Dalabon it is precisely the ideophonic elements that can alternate between the prepound (within-stem) position and the preverbal occurrence.

10 Data appear variable on some lexical items: O'Keeffe, Coleman & Singer (toappear) report that certain items classified as coverbs by Kapitonov (2019a) (and Coleman 2010—although she does not make the strong claim about inseparability) are allowed by some speakers to be separated from the verb. For instance, *marrmarr* 'happy' could be separated by *ngob* 'all' and *djininj* 'properly'.

This contrasts with the greater placement freedom of adverbs, illustrated in section §3.2.3 above and in (3.37) with *morrehmorre* 'slowly'. This adverb is shown to be separated from the verb by another adverb (3.37b) or by a coverb (3.37c).

(3.37) a. Nukka ka-ka **morrehmorre**.
 he 3SG.NF-go.NP slowly
 'He's walking slowly.' [IK1-180522_3SY1/11:36–39]

 b. Ka-yambi-burrdje balkkime-wu **morrehmorre**.
 3SG.NF-swag-wrap.NP now-LIM slowly
 'S/he's packing slowly just today.' [ibid./15:33–36]

 c. Ka-ka=kulkkulk **morrehmorre**.
 3SG.NF-go.NP=run slowly
 'He/she/it is running slowly.' [ibid./16:20–22]

Notice also that coverb constructions, such as *-ka=kulkkulk* 'to run' in (3.36a), are distinct from verb-noun idioms, such as *-ka barbung/mamukunbid* 'to go fishing' (lit. 'to go fish' or 'to go fishing line'), as shown by the same position test in (3.38): the adverb *balkkime* can be placed between the verb and the noun in an idiom.

(3.38) Nga-**ka** balkkime **barbung/mamukunbid**.
 1SG.NF-go.NP now fish/fishing_line
 'I'm going fishing now.' [IK1-150803_1PN1/12:42, 15:53]

The semantics of the coverb can be relatively transparent, as in the case of *bokob* 'float', or very little so. The situation is exacerbated in cases when there is only one inflected verb available for a given coverb and there are no cross-combinations; for instance, the coverb *kolk* 'cut' can only be analysed given one construction, that is with the verb *-dja* 'to stand' (3.39). In the constructions above the semantics of the whole is a narrowing of the semantics of the inflecting verb: *-dja=bokob* ['stand' + *bokob*] 'to stand floating' is a type of standing, and *-ka=kulkkulk* ['go' + *kulkkulk*] 'to run' is a kind of directed motion. On the other hand, *-dja=kolk* ['stand' + *kolk*] 'to cut' is not a type of standing.

(3.39) [kaˈɟaŋaɟkolk]
 Ka-djanganj=**kolk**.
 3SG.NF-stand.PST=cut
 'S/he chopped it [e.g. a tree down].' [IK1-170623_1PN1]

Given that the base inflecting verb in (3.39) simply means 'stood', the semantics of *kolk*—or indeed the whole construction—is non-compositional. This example also demonstrates the high degree of nexus between the verb and the coverb, showing in the sandhi between them (the final palatal nasal of the verb hardens before the initial stop of the coverb); this is not a frequent morphophonemic alternation in Kunbarlang (see §2.7.4).

Finally, we notice here the formal diversity within the coverbs: they range from monosyllabic, such as *kolk* (3.39), to rather large polysyllabic ones, such as *kubirribirrkuk* 'steal' (3.40):

(3.40) Ka-ngan-marnanj-yambi-kalng=**kubirribirrkuk**.
3SG.NF-1SG.OBJ-BEN-swag-get.PST=steal
'S/he / it stole a swag from me.' [IK1-160715_0001/10:44]

To summarise, coverbs are lexical enclitics, and their fixed position offers a reliable metric to distinguish them both from adverbs and from preverbs, to which I turn now.

3.2.5.2 Preverbs

PREVERB here is a descriptive term for how English verbal lexemes are borrowed into Kunbarlang; all Kunbarlang preverbs are English loans. Since the class of the verb roots in Kunbarlang is small and closed, i.e. does not admit new members, the borrowing proceeds via a phrasal PREVERB CONSTRUCTION. In this construction, which is a type of complex predicate,[11] the verb *-ngundje* 'do' provides the verbal predicate scaffolding and the loan, placed adjacent to it, provides the semantics. Unlike the coverbs, the preverbs can appear on either side of the verb (3.41), but have a preference for preverbal position—unlike the coverbs, which are restricted to the postverbal position. Notice also that the verb *-ngundje* 'do' is used in *coverb* constructions as well, such as for instance *-ngundje=marrmarr* 'be happy', illustrated in (3.42) below.

---

11 There is ample literature on the light verb / complex predicate construction as a means to loan verbs in typologically diverse languages. In the Australian context, it is often the coverb constructions, and it has been observed that coverbs are freely borrowed (Bowern 2014: 288). McConvell (2010) discusses the scenario where coverb constructions are developed to accommodate the loans, specifically in some Pama-Nyungan languages (e.g., Gurindji) for borrowings from non-Pama-Nyungan ones. See Mansfield (2016: §2) for an overview of the idea that some light verb constructions arise to provide syntactic structure for loans. More historical work is required to determine how Kunbarlang coverb and preverb constructions may have arisen, but see some more discussion in §6.5. One of the notable parallels taken up in that section is that Bininj Kunwok uses the same type of 'satellite' construction for English borrowings (Evans 2003a: 587).

(3.41) a. Some   dry   ngadda-djarrang,   sometime
            ENG   ENG   1PL.EXCL.NF-eat.PST   ENG

   njunjuk **mix** ngadda-**ngundje**.
   water   ENG   1PL.EXCL.NF-do.NP
   'Some (times?) we consumed it straight, sometimes we mix it with water.'
                           [20060830IB08/01:15–19; translation mine—IK]

b. Nga-**ngundje mix** with coffee, sometime coffee nga-bardi-djin
   1SG.NF-do.NP ENG   ENG   ENG   ENG   ENG   1SG.NF-liquid-eat.NP

   nga-mabulunj   milk.
   1SG.NF-like.NP ENG
   'I mix [milk] with coffee, sometimes I drink coffee and I want milk.'
                                                [20070108IB01/26:13–18]

Out of 59 instances observed in naturalistic speech, 34 (which is roughly 58%) occur in preverbal position. Interestingly, 18 out of the 25 postverbal occurrences were contributed by a single speaker with a strong preference for such placement (only one preposed preverb is found in his speech).[12]

The freedom of placement that distinguishes Kunbarlang preverbs from coverbs is also manifest in their separability. As demonstrated in (3.35) and (3.36) above, coverbs cannot be separated from the verb. Preverbs, on the other hand, allow interruption by other material. The contrast is illustrated in (3.42), where the universal quantifier *ngob* can intervene between a verb and a preverb, but not between a verb and a coverb:

(3.42) Ngadda-ngunda   ngob **celebrate**, la   ngadda-ngunda   (*ngob)
       1PL.EXCL.NF-do.PST all   ENG   CONJ   1PL.EXCL.NF-do.PST   all

   marrmarr (ngob).
   happy   all
   'We all were celebrating, we (all) were happy.'   [IK1-180604_1SM1/10:02–22]

Kunbarlang adverbs, discussed in §3.2.3 above, are also uninflecting and can be arranged freely in the clause. However, preverbs differ from adverbs in three important ways. First and foremost, adverbs are modifiers that do not affect argument structure of the verb. By contrast, in preverb constructions the argument structure is that of the English loan, not of *-ngundje*, which by itself is used as a speech verb. Consider example (3.43), where the preverb *heading* licences a goal location.

---

[12] If this speaker is excluded from the counts, the proportion of preverbal position rises to 33/40 (82.5%).

(3.43)   **Heading** ngarrk-ngunda   Kurridja.
         ENG   1.INCL.NF-do.PST   K
         'We were heading to Kurridja.'   [IK1-160624_0001/01:13–16]

Second, preverbs only combine with the verb *-ngundje*, while adverbs do not have restrictions apart from semantic combinability. Thus, in (3.43) above the event is not classified as a type of 'going' by using the verb *-ka* 'to go'; compare this to the coverb *kulkkulk* in (3.36a) above.[13] Third, there can be multiple adverbs (3.44), but only one preverb in a clause.

(3.44)   **Kukkangundje** nganj-kali   **malayi**.
         maybe   1SG.FUT-get.NP tomorrow
         'Maybe I'll get it tomorrow.'   [IK1-170609_1SY1/36:50–54]

The verb *-ngundje* can be both in present and past tense. Most of the time the borrowed verb is in its root form (as in the examples above). However, one speaker used a past tense form *married* twice, and the gerund is frequently used by a few speakers. The gerund forms encountered are *camping, cheating, handling, heading, playing around, repairing, roasting, shopping, waiting* and *writing*. Sometimes particle verbs are borrowed, the other ones being *look after, pack up, pass away* and *rush in*. Other instances of multi-part loans are *get wild* and *kick him out*, although it becomes difficult to decide whether such fragments are loans or instances of code-switching into English.

A good number of various preverbs used in spontaneous narrative can be found in the text sample in appendix A.1.

3.2.6 Noun markers

There is a class of adnominal elements in Kunbarlang that have two main functions: the definite article and the linker. Following Coleman (n.d.), I call this part of speech NOUN MARKERS (NM). They agree with the head noun in number (semantically) and, in the singular, in noun class (3.45). An example of a plural noun marker is in (3.46):[14]

(3.45)   Nga-djarrang   man-rnungu   **mayi**   kandiddjawa.
         1SG.NF-eat.PST III-he.GEN   NM.III   bread[III]
         'I ate his damper.'   [IK1-180601_1SY1/45:00]

---

[13] I do not have ungrammatical examples with other verbs, but I have not seen a similar combination of an English verb with any other Kunbarlang verb.
[14] The plural NM is homophonous with the class II 'feminine' one, which is probably a non-accidental homophony, cf. the similar pattern for demonstratives in Table 4.6. They are also homophonous with the first person free pronoun 'I'.

(3.46) Ngunda kidda-kalbing djininj mayali, **ngayi** barrayidjidj.
not 3PL.IRR.NP-get.IRR.NP properly sense NM.PL kids[PL]
'They don't hold the knowledge tight, the kids.' [IK1-160424_0001/03:27–30]

The noun markers do not have a deictic component: unlike demonstratives or personal pronouns, they cannot be uttered accompanied only by a pointing gesture. Semantically, they mark nominal phrases that are definite or attributive modifers that are restrictive (§4.3). In both of these uses they play an important role in the syntax of the noun phrase, as is detailed in §4.4.3. The noun markers appear freely placed within the noun phrase, except being prohibited from the NP-final position. In §4.3 I show that the position of the NM has distinct interpretive effect; thus, the apparent freedom of placement may be regarded as a side effect of the existence of different constructions.

(3.47) a. Belebbele **nayi** nadjorleng   NOUN-NM-ADJ
crab_apple NM.I I-ripe

ka-mankang korro lorre.
3SG.NF-fall.PST DEM.MED.LOC ground
'A ripe crab apple fell to the ground.'   [IK1-150728_001/06:00–02]

b. na-djorleng **nayi** belebbele   ADJ-NM-NOUN
I-ripe NM.I crab_apple
'the ripe crab apple'   [IK1-150728_001]

c. **kuyi** hospital ku-buke   NM-NOUN-ADJ
NM.IV hospital IV-old
'the old hospital'   [20060620IB03/25:02–04]

d. **nayi** na-rlengbinbin nguya bi-ngadju   NM-ADJ-NOUN
NM.I I-big patriclan DAT-she.GEN
'her big patriclan'   [20150413IOv01/07:50]

e. *na-djorleng belebbele **nayi**   ADJ-NOUN-NM
I-ripe crab_apple NM.I
intended: 'a ripe crab apple'   [IK1-150728_001]

f. *belebbele na-djorleng **nayi**   NOUN-ADJ-NM
crab_apple I-ripe NM.I
intended: 'a ripe crab apple'   [IK1-150728_001]

A frequent use of a noun marker is as a relativiser, turning a clausal phrase into a nominal one (3.48):

(3.48) Ngayi ngunda ngarra-mabulu [_RC**mayi** ngal-buk=bonj
 I not 1SG.IRR.NP-like.NP NM.III II-person=exactly
 ka-kinje].
 3SG.NF-cook.NP
 'I don't like what she cooks.' [IK1-160628_1RD1]

By itself, the string *ngalukbonj kakinje* is a clause that means 'she cooks [something]' or 'she is cooking [something]'. The function of the noun marker in (3.48) is to relativise over the object of the verb 'to cook', turning that string into an object relative clause (which then occupies the object position of the matrix verb *-mabulunj* 'to like'). The syntax and semantics of noun markers are further discussed in §4.3 and their utility in constructing relative clauses—in §8.4.

3.2.7 Pronominals

I use 'pronominals' as a term for the group of noun phrase constituent elements that primarily have to do with referential functions and do not have the rich lexical semantics of nouns and adjectives: personal pronouns, demonstratives, and interrogatives (which also serve as the basis for indefinites). A feature common to all Kunbarlang pronominals is that they can function as determiners within a noun phrase (§4.5).[15] The pronominals are organised into paradigms, and each class has a slightly different set of categories relevant for it.

3.2.7.1 Personal pronouns

The personal pronouns refer to individuals and objects, like 'we', 'she' or 'it' in English (§4.5.1). The categories of the personal pronouns are: person, number, case, and noun class (only in the third person). The paradigms are given in tables 4.3 and 4.4 in §4.5.1.

(3.49) a. **Ngayi** Nawodjok, Pastor.
 I N pastor
 'I am Nawodjok, Pastor.' [IK1-160430_0001/00:20–24]

---

15 This does not uniquely identify them, as noun markers also do that. Also, the 'human pronoun' *-buk* is exceptional in that it cannot function as a determiner (§4.5.1.1).

b. Balkkime **bedbe** balanda la **ngarrka** kirdimarrk
    now   they   whitefella CONJ we.INCL man

   ngarrk-ngunda join.
   1.INCL.NF-do.PST ENG

   'Now they white people and us Aboriginal people, we've joined.'
   [20070108IB01/18:29–34]

Personal pronouns are the only part of speech in Kunbarlang for which case is a morphological category (§4.2) and which can host the dative prefix *bi-* (3.50).

(3.50) A: **Bi-nganungka** kabbala.
         DAT-we.DU.EXCL.GEN boat

         'That's our (two's) boat.'   [IK1-170516_2DDj1]

      B: Oh, **bi-nungunungka** kabbala!
         INTJ DAT-you.DU.GEN boat

         'Oh, it's your two's boat!'   [ibid.]

As will be explained in §4.5.1, the dative form (used in (3.50) in the possessor function) is formed by adding the dative prefix *bi-* to the genitive stem.

3.2.7.2 Demonstratives

The demonstratives are deictic, i.e. they used for 'pointing' to real world objects or entities in discourse, like 'this' or 'those' (§4.5.3). The relevant categories in the paradigm of demonstratives (see table 4.6) are: distance, number and noun class (only in the singular number).

(3.51) a. Na-buk=bonj **narnda** bonj balanda.
         I-person=exactly DEM.DIST.I exactly whitefella[I]

         'That whitefella.'   [IK1-160624_0001/04:37–39]

      b. **Manda** mayi welenj ka-ka=kulkkulk.
         DEM.PROX.III NM.III road[III] 3SG.NF-go.NP=run

         'This road is running along.'   [IK1-170610_2SM1/14:34–36]

Like with all noun modifiers, noun class is not inherent for demonstratives, but is an agreement category, as seen in (3.51).

3.2.7.3 Interrogatives

The interrogatives are a set of forms that have several functions depending on the operator that takes scope over them. By default they are used in constituent questions, where they encode the ontological category of the referent that the question is about, e.g. THING, MANNER etc. (§4.5.4). They are non-inflecting (3.52).

(3.52) **Barda** ninda   ki-karrme?
what   DEM.PROX.I 2SG.NF-hold.NP
'What have you got there?'   [IK1-160613_0001/01:20]

The question word for 'who', -*kaybi*, is an adjective, and as all adjectives agrees with its restrictor in number and noun class (with the default being masculine singular). This means that the person asking about an identity can specify that s/he means a woman or a plurality (3.53).

(3.53) Kinbadda-**kaybi** kadda-bing?
3PL-who   3PL.NF-exit.PST
'Who [plural] have arrived?'   [IK1-160610_0011/32:10]

They can also be used, either in the bare form or with the suffix -*nuk*, as indefinites, see §4.5.4.

3.2.8 Numerals and other quantifiers

As in other languages, expressions of quantification (i.e. expressions dealing with numbers and quantities) in Kunbarlang are very diverse morphosyntactically. Formally they are a somewhat heterogeneous class that consists of adjective-like agreeing words (e.g. -*yika* 'some'), uninflecting adverbs (e.g. *kirdirrkkirdirrk* 'always'), and even affixes (e.g. the prefix *mulmul-* 'many'). The semantic and formal diversity of Kunbarlang quantifiers is the subject of §4.7.

However, numerals and quantifiers proper can be individuated as categories in their own right. The class of numerals is open: the inherited numerals system is small, but they are readily loaned from English. The numeral -*kudji* 'one' agrees with the noun head in noun class like an adjective, but unlike adjectives can coordinate with the uninflecting numeral *kaburrk* 'two' (3.54). See §4.7.2.1.1 for more details.

(3.54) Kadda-rna   **kaburrk la**   **kin-kudji**.
3PL.NF-sit.NP two   CONJ II-one
'There are three females.'   [IK1-160809_0001/45:37–41]

Quantifiers proper are a small and closed class of uninflecting words that can combine with nouns. They are *ngob* 'all' (3.55), *ngobbu* 'both', *nunu* 'all', and *yika* 'some' (the latter can optionally agree with the noun, see §4.7.2.1).

(3.55) Kadda-mulmul-kalng **ngob** kikakkin.
 3PL.NF-many-get.PST all meat
 'They got all the meat.' [IK1-160429_0001/1:22:24–26]

Like other nominal modifiers, quantifiers are often found self-standing, i.e. without an overt noun head. See §4.7.

3.2.9 Prepositions

There is only one dedicated preposition in Kunbarlang, *walkki* 'with' (3.56).

(3.56) Kirdimarrk **walkki** waliman ka-rdulkarrawarribinj.
 man with axe 3SG.NF-tire.PST
 'The man with the axe is tired.' [IK1-170526_1SY1/41:48–55]

The comitative prefix in Kunbarlang has the same form and function (§6.1.2), and thus I analyse *walkki* as a preposition that can be incorporated.

(3.57) Ngayi ngabbard ka-ngan-**walkki**-rnirdam.
 I father 3SG.NF-1SG.OBJ-COM-place.PST
 'My father gave me [the language].' [lit. 'placed it with me']
 [20070108IB01/02:36–38]

Prepositional phrases headed by *walkki* can modify both nouns (3.56) and verbs (3.58).

(3.58) Na-kudji monkey ka-djarrkrdam norno **walkki** kundulk.
 I-one ENG 3SG.NF-lift.NP snake with tree
 'A monkey is lifting a snake with (i.e. using) a stick.'
 [IK1-170530_1SY1/03:21–34]

It is rather conspicuous that Kunbarlang does not have locative adpositions, especially given that there are no locative cases, either. The locative demonstrative *korro/karra* 'DEM.MED.LOC' (§4.5.3) is frequently used as a generic locative preposition (3.59), but this use does not warrant analysing it as belonging to two different parts of speech, so I treat it consistently as a demonstrative.

(3.59) Ngadda-rdam **korro** nguluk.
 1PL.EXCL.NF-put.NP DEM.MED.LOC ash
 'We put it into the ashes.' [IK1-160726_0021/00:47–49]

Whichever analysis of *korro* is best, it is a single word that does not differentiate any locational nuances. From this point of view, the absence of an inventory of functional locative markers (i.e. adpositions or cases, in contrast to periphrastic ways of expression) is remarkable.

3.2.10 Connectives

The connectives in Kunbarlang are *la* 'and; but', *bala* 'and', *warri* 'because', and *anu* 'so that'. They are used to conjoin constituents of various types. The connective *bala* is only used in the composite numerals involving *-kudji* 'one', e.g. *kaburrk bala na-kudji* 'three [lit. two and one]'. The connective *warri* is used to combine clauses where the second one describes the reason and the first one—the consequence (3.60). The most versatile connective is *la*, which can conjoin constituents of diverse types (see (3.61) below).

(3.60) |¹ Nga-rnay |² kunwaral ka-djanganj |³ nga-nganjwom |⁴ warri munun.

Nga-rnay   kunwaral ka-djanganj   nga-nganj-wom
1SG.NF-see.PST spirit   3SG.NF-stand.PST 1SG.NF-HITH-return.PST

warri   munun.
because   darkness

'I saw a spirit standing and returned because it was dark.'
[IK1-160610_0001/45:38–46:03]

From the point of view of combining clauses in discourse, (3.60) shows a number of other characteristic properties. Most strikingly evident is the default strategy to juxtapose clauses without any morphosyntactic marking: there is only one connective between the four clauses. The difficulty in deciding whether there is any syntactic subordination shows in the absence of any formal marking between clauses 1 and 2. Finally, clauses in discourse tend to be very short, often consisting of a single predicate (which is all clauses in (3.60) but clause 2). These topics are taken up in greater detail in chapters 7 and 8.

The connective *la* 'CONJ' can coordinate various types of phrases, including nominals (3.61a), verbs (3.61b),[16] and clauses (3.61c).[17]

---

[16] Since every well-formed verb in Kunbarlang can function as a standalone clause, in cases of same-subject verbs it is a complex decision whether one deals with verb or clause coordination.

[17] The verb *kabundjin* in (3.61c) is translated 'it bakes', although it literally means 'it [the heat] consumes it [the damper]'. I made the decision to use a uniform gloss in those cases when the polysemy is reasonably transparent. Here, for instance, I stick with the concise gloss 'eat' for the root *-djin*, which can mean 'eat; consume', 'burn' (as an extension of the idea of consumption), or 'bake' (as an extension of the idea of burning).

(3.61) a. **Nadjanal** la **kudjarra** ngadda-kalng.
goanna_sp. CONJ long-neck_turtle 1PL.EXCL.NF-get.PST
'We caught goanna and long-neck turtle.' [IK1-160624_0021/08:11–13]

b. **Ngandjidda-kinje** neyang la **ngandjidda-djin** babi.
1PL.EXCL.FUT-cook.NP food CONJ 1PL.EXCL.FUT-eat.NP later
'We [without you] are going to cook food and eat it afterwards.'
[IK1-150728_001]

c. Bonj ngorro ka-bun-djin, **man-djorleng**, la
exactly DEM.MED.IV 3SG.NF-3SG.OBJ-eat.NP III-ripe CONJ
ngadda-nguluk-kali.
1PL.EXCL.NF-ash-get.NP
'Then it bakes, and when it's ready, we take it out from the ashes [lit. 'it is ready and we take it out'].' [IK1-160726_0021/01:03–11]

When *la* connects clauses, it can also have a more specialised interpretation than coordination. A frequent use is to connect the reason and the consequence, as in (3.62) (the consequence clause comes first; see more in §8.5.1):

(3.62) Kinj-worrhme wirdidj **la** kun-bondjek nga-warr-mi.
2SG.FUT-kindle.NP fire CONJ IV-cold 1SG.NF-bad-INCH.NP
'Light a fire, because I'm cold!' [IK1-170615_1SY2/50:06–09]

3.2.11 Particles and interjections

Besides the word classes listed above, there is also an array of interjections and particles in Kunbarlang. The interjections serve a range of communicative functions, such as indicating ignorance (*adju* 'dunno'), agreement (*ma/yoh* 'yes'), surprise (*ardu* 'oh!'), or request the utterance to be repeated (*eh?* 'huh?'). All of these interjections are independent utterances and they are not syntactically integrated with other clausal material.

Unlike interjections, particles are those uninflecting words that are integrated into the clause and cannot form independent utterances (except for *bonj* in the sense 'enough'). This latter property also sets them apart from adverbs (§3.2.3). Another point of difference is the fact that adverbs are modifiers describing events and probability estimation, whereas particles fulfil grammatical/structure functions (such as negation or question formation, or marking similarity constructions).

There is a range of particles, most of which are discussed in other chapters, based on their function. These include the intensifier *bidju*, used in emphatic reflexives (§6.1.3.1);

the prohibitive particle *kanjyuwa*, used in negative imperatives (§7.5); the negators *ngunda* and *marrek* (§7.3); the interrogative particle *yidok*, used in polar questions (§7.4.1); the similative *yimarne(k)* (§8.3); and the particle *wali*, which combines with an array of nominals to form the 'turn'-construction (§4.5.1.3). There is also the particle *bonj* 'exactly; right; enough', which has a wide array of functions and can be both uttered independently meaning 'enough' or 'Thanks, I'm good', as well as cliticised to pronouns and demonstratives to encode emphasis (3.63).

(3.63) Q: Kenda?
           where
           'Where?'   [IK1-160510_0001/02:12]

        A: Korro,   **korro=bonj**.
           DEM.MED.LOC DEM.MED.LOC=exactly
           'There, right there.'   [ibid./02:14]

In addition to that, it can be reduplicated, and then it is used as 'too' or 'again' (3.64).

(3.64) Kun-barrkidbe   kunmimke   kadda-djarrang   **bonj~bonj**   nayi   wam.
        IV-other   overnight 3SG.NF-eat.PST   RDP~exactly   NM.I   honey
        'They ate the sugar bag the next day too.'   [20060830IB02/01:37–40]

On the use of *bonj* in analytic reflexive formation, see §6.1.3.1.

3.3 Wordhood, clitics, and affixes

In Kunbarlang, there are no strong phonological criteria for delimiting a word: stress is not understood well enough at the present stage of research, and (morpho-)phonological processes are too few to serve as a diagnostic distinguishing words from affixes. However, two morpho-syntactic criteria appear sufficient to define wordhood for all parts of speech: the 'stand-alone' criterion and the free ordering criterion. The former refers to the ability of items in some categories to stand alone as full utterances. These categories are: adjectives, adverbs, nouns, numerals, pronominals, quantifiers, verbs, and interjections. Words in some other categories cannot form full utterances on their own, primarily due to semantic reasons, but they have a certain degree of freedom of placement. Such categories are: connectives, preverbs, and noun markers. Affixes pass neither of these two diagnostics.

In this grammar, I analyse several (classes of) morphemes as clitics. They are defined as such on a variety of grounds, rather than a single uniform criterion. There are the following five types of enclitics in Kunbarlang (vaguely following the order of their appearance in examples in the grammar), with explanations of their clitic status:

1. coverbs, which rigidly follow verbs (§3.2.5.1): they have rich lexical semantics and induce consonantal manner assimilation which is not found with any bound morphemes (§2.7.4)
2. the particle *bonj* 'exactly' (§3.2.11): it can stand alone (unlike any affix), but when encliticised to the pronominal *-buk*, it triggers a stress shift (§2.7.1; unlike in phrasal constructions)
3. oblique personal pronouns (§4.5.1), which have pronominal semantics and are bound roots: they must either encliticise to an inalienable possessum (§4.6.2) or carry a prefix
4. the clitic =*wali* 'turn' (§4.5.1.3): it adjoins to a whole range of nominals and thus can be considered cross-categorial, in contrast to affixes
5. the directional clitics =*bi* and =*way* (§7.6): similarly to =*wali* (and unlike typical affixes), they are cross-categorial, attaching to both demonstratives and verbs

The only Kunbarlang preposition *walkki* (§3.2.9), according to the outlined criteria, may be classified as a phrasal proclitic, because it immediately precedes the noun phrase. That is, if there is a modifier before the noun, such as a noun marker, the preposition precedes that modifier (3.65). However, for ease of presentation throughout this thesis, I will represent *walkki* as an independent word rather than a clitic.

(3.65) **walkki** mayi   nguk=rnungu
        with   NM.III intestine=he.GEN
        'with the guts'   [20140703IOv01-ShM/03:14]

3.4 Argumenthood

As has been alluded to above, and as will become more evident in later chapters (especially Chapters 6 and 7), the verb with its rich morphology is the central constituent part of the Kunbarlang clause—in a sense, a self-sufficient one. Kunbarlang is among the languages that are interesting and challenging for an analysis of how the participants in the verb's argument structure are licensed as constituents in the actual clause. My goal in this section is to give an account of argumenthood that is fully explicit, internally coherent and consistent with the available data, and at the same time relies on theoretical constructs as little as possible.

Kunbarlang is interesting in that it uses a very compact case system even in comparison to most head-marking non-Pama-Nyungan languages (§4.2). In particular, (a) case is morphologically marked only on free personal pronouns and on verbal personal prefixes, and (b) case marking on nominals is not used to distinguish among the arguments of a polyvalent verb. Even though both show a two-way distinction, the morphological case on free pronouns is not isomorphic to that on bound pronouns (personal prefixes). Free pronouns distinguish verbal arguments (direct form) from non-argument NPs (oblique form, a.k.a. genitive; an additional prefix derives dative on the basis of that). Bound pronouns only index verbal arguments, whereby they distinguish subjects from a variety of objects. The bound pronouns themselves do not differentiate between the types of objects, but these distinctions are, arguably, preserved once applicative morphology is included in the picture. Thus, for instance, the benefactive applicative *marnanj-* can be viewed as the "verbal dative".

Essentially, I argue that it is hard to maintain that the free occurring nominals are the true arguments of the verb in Kunbarlang (what I shall call *the NP-argument view* for convenience). Instead, I advocate the view that Kunbarlang is a *pronominal argument* language, following the spirit, if not the letter, of Jelinek (1984). First, here are some reasons behind the claim about nominals just made:

(i) the noun phrases show characteristic nonconfigurational behaviour: are freely omitted, rather freely ordered, and sometimes split (see §4.4.4 and §7.1 for details; see Hale (1983) for foundational work on nonconfigurationality in Warlpiri and Nordlinger (2014: §6) for a recent overview in Australian-wide context)
(ii) when they are omitted, it makes little sense to talk about 'agreement' on the verb, on the NP-argument view, since there isn't anything to agree with
(iii) likewise, in inclusory constructions (§4.5.2) there is necessarily an agreement mismatch on the NP-argument view
(iv) full nouns do not show number distinctions (§3.2.1), yet the verb shows full 'agreement' for number in both the subject and the object slots (§5.2)

The pronominal argument view put forth here holds, crucially, that in Kunbarlang only the bound pronouns are true arguments of the verb. Free NPs are licensed in clauses through association with those bound pronouns on the verb. I shall first explain the mechanics of this view and how it stands up to the issues in (i–iv), and also discuss some apparent counter-arguments. Then, at the end of the section, I give an interpretation as to why a language might work this way.

Let us appreciate that the problems listed in (i–iv) do not arise on this pronominal argument view. With regards to nonconfigurationality issues, as stated in (i), the solution afforded by the pronominal argument hypothesis is to consider all free nominals syntactically adjoined. This move provides for all three aspects of nonconfigurationality: NPs can be freely omitted, because adjuncts are optional, and they can be freely ordered because their structural position does not bear on their grammatical function. Splitting of noun phrases is rather restrained in Kunbarlang, essentially confined to an afterthought configuration, so it's not a major challenge for either analysis in any event. In section §7.1 I discuss word order in relation to its communicative function, and address the question about the significance of the word order of free NPs on the view that they are all adjuncts.

This is how the (lexical or derived) argument structure of a given predicate is realised in the clause. Argument NPs bear the direct (unmarked) case and are construed with verbal prefixes via an agreement-like relation (see more on that below), being licensed by this construal. Non-argument NPs are licensed in the clause by an appropriate case, which is always marked by a free pronoun in that case form. All in all, the case form of an NP is always structurally predictable, i.e. there are no lexical case assigners.[18]

By way of an example, consider (3.66). It shows a first person subject that is only instantiated by the bound subject pronoun *nga-*, and an object which is indexed in the verb and is also elaborated by an NP with some complex internal structure. The object is a benefactive (oblique) object. It is headed by the noun *durduk*, which on the present analysis is licensed by the benefactive applicative *marnanj-* on the verb, and thus it is an argument nominal in the direct case. In contrast to it is its possessor *Kamarrang*: as a non-argument nominal, it is obligatorily marked by the dative pronoun *birnungu*. See section 4.6 on possessives and sections 6.1.1 and 6.1.2 on applicatives.

(3.66) Nga-marnanj-bareng-mi [ninda durduk [nayi Kamarrang
 1SG.NF-BEN-dangerous-INCH.NP DEM.PROX.I dog NM.I K
 *(bi-rnungu)]].
 DAT-he.GEN
 'I'm angry with Kamarrang's dog.' [IK1-180605_1SY1/09:28–35]

An immediate problem for this view of licensing of NPs is presented by the existence in Kunbarlang of *unregistered* arguments (§5.1.1). These are 'additional' arguments of some predicates, which are not, and cannot, be cross-referenced in the verb. The problem, therefore, has to do with constraining their occurrence: under what conditions are they allowed and what keeps their number to only one such extra argument per predicate. Similar *quasi* or unregistered objects were brought up as a serious problem for pronominal argument analyses of other languages (e.g. Austin & Bresnan 1996 for Warlpiri and Davis & Matthewson 2003, 2009 for St'át'imcets). However, this phenomenon seems equally problematic for any model of Kunbarlang clause structure, and presents a genuine descriptive quirk that cannot be used to adjudicate between different models at the moment. Further work will, hopefully, shed more light on the nature of Kunbarlang unregistered arguments. Perhaps they could be explained in terms of a regular verbal lability-like diathesis change, and the class of verbs undergoing it could be constrained on principled grounds. But for now I tentatively conclude that it is not prohibitive of the pronominal argument analysis offered here, and leave it at that.

The issues in (ii–iv) above all pertain to the analysis of the verb's *agreement*, or feature sharing between the verb and the argumental NPs. In traditional grammatical

---

[18] Possessive constructions can use either of the oblique case forms, i.e. either genitive or dative (§4.6). This is not a lexically conditioned variation, however; the reasons behind the variation are yet to be discovered.

analysis, personal prefixes are exponents of that feature sharing. In a language where nominal arguments are exempt from overt presence in the clause, adjustments to the analysis have to be made. On the pronominal argument view advocated here, the personal prefixes on the verb are bound pronouns that *instantiate* the arguments (in other words, *saturate* the predicate's argumental valencies). Thus, on the NP-argument view a range of agreement puzzles arise that do not plague the pronominal argument analysis. Obviously, when overt nominals are absent (ii), an explanation is required as to what the verb agrees with: phonologically null *pro*'s? full NPs that are deleted afterwards? While such options are conceivable, they hardly seem preferable on any grounds. Next, there are inclusory constructions in Kunbarlang, where the bound pronoun on the verb has a 'larger' number than is warranted by the overt nominal, and—somewhat worse—can have a different person. This is shown in (3.67), where the third person singular (as seen from the pronoun) NP is semantically part of the subject, and it is the only overt nominal material related to the subject, and yet the subject is of the first person plural.

(3.67) **Ngadda**-kidanj   [ngal-buk ngayi Georgina].
1PL.EXCL.NF-go.PST   II-person NM.II G
'We went, including Georgina.' [lit. 'We-went that Georgina.']
[20060814IB03/00:09–13]

Worse still is the very general fact about the distribution of the number feature across categories: of all nominals, only free personal pronouns have full number paradigms; nouns do not have number. To be sure, they admit of non-singular construal, and there is even one lexically plural noun *barrayidjidj* 'kids',[19] but (a) nouns do not change form depending on construal, and (b) even though agreeing modifiers have a non-singular form, they never distinguish the dual. The only other category of morphemes besides the free pronoun roots that show the full disctinction of singular–dual–plural are the bound pronouns on the verb. It would be obvious by now that on the view that the bound pronouns are true arguments, no 'agreement' paradoxes arise: they express the maximal specification of the arguments' person and number, and free NPs, when present, are specified in their construal through the association with / licensing by the verbal morphology.

Let us turn now to another issue that has been brought up in reference to other languages as problematic for the pronominal argument analysis. It has to do with referential characteristics of bound pronouns, where we find a mirror-image situation

---

[19] There is a possibility that the string *barra* in *barrayidjidj*, and possibly also in *barramimbanj* 'woman', is related to Ndjébbana number prefix *barra-* 'third person augmented', which only marks number on three noun roots, viz. 'children', 'women' and *muya* 'dead person, spirit' (but it is also a productive agreement prefix, e.g., on 'nominals' like *-karrowa* 'many'). See McKay (2000: 193) for Ndjébbana. Kunbarlang *barramimbanj* does not have the same inherent plurality as *barrayidjidj*.

compared to the category of number in Kunbarlang. In Warlpiri (Austin & Bresnan 1996: §4.1), as well as in Northern Straits Salish (Davis & Matthewson 2009: 1110–1), bound pronouns are always definite when by themselves, while NPs 'coindexed' with them can be definite or indefinite. This situation is not captured by the pronominal argument view, on which the 'argumental' bound pronouns should encode at least as much (grammatical) information as 'adjunct' free overt NPs.[20] Kunbarlang is similar in this respect: in the absence of an overt NP, bound pronouns are interpreted as definite,[21] while NPs normally have either construal. The contrast is illustrated in (3.68), where in the absence of a free NP the object is interpreted as definite.

(3.68) a. **Kadda-Ø-kalng** ngorro kadda-worrhmeng bi-rnungu.
3PL.NF-get.PST DEM.MED.IV 3PL.NF-kindle.PST DAT-he.GEN
'They got him/*someone and made a fire for him.'
[IK1-16010_0001/04:44–49]

b. Ka-kidanj wadjbud **ka-Ø-kalng** **barda-nuk**.
3SG.NF-go.PST sand 3SG.NF-3SG.OBJ-get.PST what-INDF
'He went to the beach and got something.' [IK1-150724_1SY1/12:17–23]

c. **Ka-bun-rnay** ka-nganj-ka.
3SG.NF-3SG.OBJ-see.PST 3SG.NF-HITH-go.PST
'S/he / it saw him/her/it (BUT NOT: someone/something) coming.'
[20060606IB02/04:23]

d. Ngayi **nga-Ø-rnay** **na-kaybi-nuk**.
I 1SG.NF-3SG.OBJ-see.PST I-who-INDF
'I saw someone.' [IK1-150724_1SY1/07:15]

On the one hand, Austin & Bresnan (1996) rightfully argue that the verbal-morphology-as-agreement view offers the most straightforward treatment of such definiteness mismatch. On the other hand, they also point out the possibility that pronominal arguments behave as *e-type* pronouns in these cases. This is a general descriptive term for (a type of use of) pronouns that are neither (co-)referential nor bound by an operator[22] (see Nouwen 2020 for a contemporary discussion of Gareth Evans's original work), but which are paraphrasable with definite descriptions. For instance, on the

---

20 Evans (2002) constructs the opposite line of attack. He shows that in Bininj Kunwok object personal prefixes have a *wider* array of interpretations than free personal pronouns do in English or indeed in Bininj Kunwok itself, concluding that the bound pronouns cannot be equated with free pronouns in the way suggested by (some versions of) the pronominal argument hypothesis.
21 There is one notable exception of the third person plural prefixes, which have a non-specific indefinite reading (similar to the English impersonal *they* in *As they say...*).
22 Note the two entirely different uses of "*bound*": a variable *semantically* bound by an operator in this instance, and a *morphologically* bound form elsewhere in the ongoing discussion.

e-type interpretation of the object bound pronoun in (3.68d) it would amount to (*there is*) *someone; I saw them*. In other words, the Kunbarlang bound pronouns may refer to a dislocated quantificational phrase if that has "sufficient descriptive content"; I assume here that what counts as sufficient may vary between languages. Austin & Bresnan also highlight the following contrast between an empty set-denoting NP (3.69b) and one which denotes a possibly non-empty set (3.69a):

(3.69) Austin & Bresnan (1996: 238)

    a.   Every man she meets, she tells him her life story.

    b.   *No man she meets, she tells him her life story.

In Kunbarlang, there is no comparable effect of 'negative quantified' NPs (3.70a). Notice that without an overt NP the object takes wide scope with respect to negation (3.70b).

(3.70)   a.   Ngunda [na-kaybi [ki-buddu-rnani /
                not   I-who   3SG.IRR.PST-3PL.OBJ-see.IRR.PST

               ki-bun-rnani]].
               3SG.IRR.PST-3SG.OBJ-see.IRR.PST

               'He didn't see anyone.'   [IK1-160628_0001/09:28–10:08]

    b.   ...la   ngunda ngay-∅-rnani.
                CONJ   not   1SG.IRR.PST-3SG.OBJ-see.IRR.PST

               '...so I didn't see him/her/it (BUT NOT: someone/something).'
                                                                 [IK1-180521_2SY1/32:08]

However, this does not compromise the e-type solution for the definiteness mismatch, because such negative NPs in Kunbarlang are existentials in the scope of higher negation, as indicated by brackets in (3.70a). This means that an example like (3.70a) literally is composed along the following lines: 'it's not the case that [for some person, [I saw them]]'. Calling upon the e-type reading of the bound pronouns may be somewhat more complex than invoking a simpler agreement analysis, but I maintain that considering the benefits offered by the pronominal argument analysis for the system overall, this added bit of complexity is worth it.

The views presented here are not at all novel. My analysis of argumenthood in Kunbarlang owes to the vast scholarship on the topic, and specifically to the *Pronominal Argument Hypothesis* (Jelinek 1984), as already mentioned, and its subsequent interpretations such as those by M. C. Baker (1996) and, especially, Pensalfini (2004). This latter paper offers a theory of why certain languages show such nonconfigurational effects; I briefly summarise it here, referring the reader to the source for all details and a deeper theoretical background. In Pensalfini's (2004) theory, nonconfigurational languages are those which at the core clause level separate *formal information* required for (narrowly construed) grammatical operations from *encyclopedic information*, which has to do with the referential function of language. The former type of information is used for the computational function of language, that which gives language its generative capacity and infinite nature. It comprises, roughly, the grammatical categories found across languages: person, number, tense, aspect, etc. The latter type of information is what usually is conceived of as the realm of lexical semantics: such distinctions as there are between rowing and paddling, or between a crow and an osprey, which are crucially important in communication, but normally do not play any role in the grammar. Now this separation may take place in the nominal as well as in the verbal domain. Kunbarlang is a language that separates them in the nominal domain. Thus, in core syntax only 'grammatically relevant' information is admitted, i.e. such information about participants as is encoded by the pronominal elements within the Kunbarlang paradigm. Other—encyclopedic—information is banned from argument positions and may only enter clauses in the right of syntactic adjuncts.

4 Nominals

Many Australian languages do not have a clear division between nouns and adjectives as distinct word classes, as they show identical morphological possibilities (Dixon 1980: 272). When they form a single word class, they are usually referred to as "nominals"; Nordlinger (2014: 237–8) further points out that this nominal word class may include pronouns, demonstratives and locational terms. This is not the use of the term that I intend here: as is shown in §3.2, all of these are distinct classes in Kunbarlang. Instead, I use "nominals" as the general term for the syntactic class that includes the constituents of the noun phrase in Kunbarlang, i.e.: nouns, adjectives, noun markers, personal pronouns, demonstratives and interrogatives/indefinites.

The grammatical categories relevant for the nominals in Kunbarlang are case, noun class, number and person. Both noun class and number manifest themselves in agreement of the modifiers with the head noun. Their nature, however, is different: while noun class is an inherent grammatical category of the noun, number is a feature of semantic construal of the noun phrase. Noun class may or may not be marked on the noun with a prefix; there is no productive morphological marking of number on the nouns.[1] Person and grammatical case are only defined on personal pronouns. Person and number, but not noun class, are categories which participate in feature sharing between the bound pronouns on the verb and the corresponding free noun phrases. There is a system of possessive classification, which partitions nominal lexemes into two classes according to their alienability.

4.1 Noun class

4.1.1 Background

Systems of overtly distinguishing subclasses of nouns, collectively referred to as *nominal classification*, are widespread in Aboriginal languages of northern Australia (Harvey & Reid 1997a). The particular types, or systems, of classification are often thought to form a scale, with *classifier* systems being on its "lexical" end and *noun classes* (also known as *grammatical gender*)—on its "grammatical" end.[2] The latter kind of systems, noun classes, is a category frequently attested in non-Pama-Nyungan languages (see Louagie 2020: 48–49). Such systems are found in the majority of Gunwinyguan languages, except Dalabon and Rembarrnga (Evans & Merlan 2003: 270). I shall briefly exemplify from Kunbarlang (4.1) before discussing the system in full below.

---

1 Reduplication can sometimes mark plurality, but its scope is restricted.
2 See, e.g., McGregor (2002: 4–10); he prefers to call classifier systems *category* systems.

(4.1) a. Ka-karrme **nayi na-rleng durduk**.
 3SG.NF-hold.NP NM.I I-much dog[I]
 '[she] has many dogs.' [IK1-160818_0001]

 b. Ka-karrme **ma-rleng mayi burru**.
 3SG.NF-hold.NP III-much NM.III arm[III]
 '[the tree] has many branches.' [IK1-170522_1SM1/44:50–53]

The two examples in (4.1) show how the modifiers in the noun phrase—the detemiser and an adjective—change form based on the noun class of the head noun (class I in (4.1a) and class III in (4.1b)).

There are four noun classes that Kunbarlang nouns can have. These are inherent to the noun and the nouns are distributed on a semantic basis, detailed in §4.1.2 below. The majority of the nouns belong to one class only; roots that allow for cross-classification are rare (see §4.1.2). Morphologically, the noun class is only marked on the modifiers within the noun phrase, but not on the noun (4.1). In the glosses in the rest of this section, I indicate the class of the nouns in a square bracket near the root.

4.1.2 Noun class membership

The distribution of nouns across the four noun classes in Kunbarlang is semantically based, as is typical for Australian noun class systems (Harvey & Reid 1997a, Gaby & Singer 2014).

I 'MASCULINE': male humans, most animals, fish and shellfish, some birds, some introduced objects (*badju-badju* 'shirt' or *djurra* 'paper', both loans from Austronesian languages in the course of contact with Macassans (see Evans 1992 and references therein)), all honey, meat; also the default class assigned to novelty items
II 'FEMININE': female humans, many birds, some shellfish, insects, crabs, snakes, rats, jellyfish, sun and heat
III 'VEGETABLE': plants, plant food and derivatives, blood, woven clothes, tools, weapons and household items, song, custom
IV 'NEUTER': land and places, all liquids, body parts, weather, abstract notions (e.g., *burrudjang* 'sorcery type'), language, rocks/stones

Although many birds belong to class II, there is an argument from the grammar that they are prototypically classified as class I, as most animals. The word that means 'wing' in Kunbarlang is *burru=rnungu*, literally 'his arm' (see §4.6.2 on the inalienable possession construction). The pronoun *rnungu* that cliticizes onto the noun *burru* 'arm' has to agree in class with possessor, and in this case we find class I agreement.[3] Many languages of northern Australia show a similar pattern, where animals normally belong to the 'masculine' class, but a high proportion of birds (and fish, unlike in Kunbarlang) belond to the 'feminine' class; see Harvey (1997) on the 'domain of experience' principle applied to such 'anomalous' patterns of classification (following such classic work on the Dyirbal nominal classification as Dixon 1972 and Lakoff 1986, and extending and generalising it). The general idea behind this principle is that the gender opposition may be used to mark culturally significant domains through assigning them to the opposite, anomalous class. For instance, exceptional classification of birds (and fish) may reflect the opposition of the prototypical ground-dwelling fauna and creatures that inhabit the air or water. Another way in which this opposition may be used is to single out a member of a set that has a salient property compared to other members, e.g. salient 'harmfulness'.

There are occasional exceptions to the generalisations in the above list. For instance, some artefacts that one might expect to belong to class III are found in other classes: *borndok* 'woomera', class I (through association with men); *djerr* 'women's pubic apron', class II (perhaps as a women's attribute). Fauna can sometimes belong to classes other than I/II, cf. *mayama* 'itchy caterpillar', class III (perhaps through association with trees, or to highlight its harmfulness). Novel fruit are class I, rather than III, e.g. *nayi lemen na-mak* [NM.I lemon I-good] 'tasty lemon'/'the lemon is tasty'.

Like in other Gunwinyguan languages, there are several lexicalised terms for wallaroos of specific sex, e.g. *djukerri* 'female black wallaroo' (generic for black wallaroo is *nadjinem*), *karrurrken* 'adult female antilopine wallaroo' (generic for antilopine wallaroo is *karndakidj*), which are class II. These specific female wallaroo names are fixed to class II and do not partake in cross-classification. Overall, roots that allow cross-classification by different prefixes are extremely scarce. Some nouns appear to carry a class prefix, e.g. **nadjanarr** 'floodplain goanna' or **kundjorlok** 'creek' (see the adjectival prefixes in table 4.1). These quasi-prefixes usually match the class of the noun, although there are some rare exceptions, such as *kundulk* 'tree', which is class III, but looks like carrying class IV prefix *kun-*. However, these sequences are at best frozen to the stems, and in other cases are probably coincidental. Cross-classification by prefixes on nouns is virtually non-existent. There are two terms for kinship relations and their participants that show noun class inflection (without class III):

(4.2) a. *na-kobeng* [I] 'husband', *ngal-kobeng* [II] 'wife', *kun-kobeng* [IV] 'marriage'

b. *na-kurrng* [I] 'father- or son-in-law', *ngal-kurrng* [II] 'mother- or daughter-in-law', *kun-kurrng* [IV] 'the "Mother-in-law" language register'

---

3 Incidentally, *burru=ngadju* [lit. 'her arm'] means 'branch', where we observe superclassing of classes II and III in the oblique pronoun stem. Superclassing is explained in §4.1.3 below.

The few examples apart from that are better analysed as conventionalised or lexicalised uses of certain adjectives as head nouns, cf. (4.3):

(4.3) a. *na.bareng* [I] 'policeman; soldier', *kun.bareng* [IV] 'alcohol' — from *-bareng* 'dangerous'

   b. *na.walak* [I] 'child', *ku.walak* [IV] 'rock' — from *-walak* 'small'

The only systematic noun class alternation that I am aware of is found with body part terms. While originally, i.e. as body parts, they are class IV (4.4a), they also admit of the construal as a part of an animal intended for food, in which case they govern class I agreement (4.4b). Additionally, those body parts that undergo metaphorical extension receive an appropriate construal in that case as well, e.g. class III when the extension is into the plant domain (4.4c).

(4.4) a. **kun-ngaybu djanga**
      IV-I.GEN   foot[IV]
      'my foot' [IK1-170525_2SY1/06:39]

   b. kalakalak **kin-ngaybu** nayi **djanga**
      chicken   I/II-I.GEN   NM.I foot[I]
      'my chicken leg(s)' [ibid./07:57]

   c. Ka-karrme   **ma-rleng** mayi **burru**.
      3SG.NF-hold.NP III-much   NM.III arm[III]
      '[the tree] has many branches.' [IK1-170522_1SM1/44:50–53]

4.1.3 Morphosyntax

The category of noun class permeates the Kunbarlang noun phrase, being an obligatory agreement feature, i.e. all modifiers must agree with the head noun. Formally, there are a number of sub-paradigms of class prefixes and the choice of the form depends on the given modifier. I analyse this as a single system with some allomorphy, conditioned by the category of the stem. There are also curious cases of syncretism or superclassing. I summarise the prefix system in table 4.1, with examples following it. The semantics of the classes is discussed in §4.1.2.

There are four main categories of stems that select noun class prefixes, called 'agreement probes' in table 4.1. They are: adjectives (§3.2.2), possessor genitive pronouns (where the prefix tracks the noun class of the possessum; §4.6), noun markers (§4.3) and terms for people, such as skin names and the human pronoun *-buk* (§4.5.1.1). Adjectives are further divided into two groups with respect to presence/absence of an

Tab. 4.1: Noun class paradigms

Agreement probe	I	II	III	IV	Example
Adjective	na-	ki(n)-	ma(n)-	ku(n)-	(4.5), (4.6)
Possessor		kin-	man-	kun-	(4.9)
Noun marker (SG)	na-	nga-	ma-	ku-	(4.11)
People's gender	na-	ngal-	—	—	(4.12)

-*n* at the end of the noun class prefix (see below). Although demonstratives also decline for noun class, their morphology is less regular (in part due to the somewhat idiosyncratic vocalism). I therefore describe their declension as synchronic stem suppletion. However, for the classes I–III the initial formatives are immediately recognizable: *n-*, *ng-*, *ma-*, compare the noun marker row in table 4.1. The paradigm for demonstratives can be found in table 4.6 in §4.5.3.

Evans (2003a: 34–5) proposes that a proto-Gunwinyguan gender prefixation system can be reconstructed with five classes and case-conditioned suppletion. The system includes masculine *na-* with a genitive suppletive form *ki-*, feminine *ngal-* (genitive *(k)iny-*), vegetable *ma-* (genitive *nga-*), and two "neuters", *ku-* and *ra(k)-*. These distinctions have been neutralised to a variable extent in all descendant languages. One may hypothesise that in Kunbarlang the *ra(k)-* neuter was merged with the *ku-* neuter. The form *ngal-* is only preserved in the pair terms like *na-buk* 'man' ~ *ngal-buk* 'woman' and in subsection (skin) names, e.g., *Ngal-ngarridj* 'female of the Ngarridj skin'. A recent reconstruction of the class morphology at the proto-Australian level suggests that the Kunbarlang class III and IV prefixes are reflexes of the proto-Australian forms **ma-* and **ku-*, respectively (Harvey & Mailhammer 2017).

Here is what noun class morphology looks like on different agreement probes. There are two sets of adjectives that differ in the shape of the prefix they take. Coleman (n.d.) calls them 'old' and 'new' adjectival paradigms. The prefixes that the 'old' ones take are all of the shape CV, i.e. end in a vowel (4.5). The 'new' ones have an [n] at the end of the class prefix (and thus a CVC shape) in classes II, III and IV (4.6).

(4.5)   a.   **na**-rleng dolobbo
                 I-much   stringybark[I]
                 'a lot of stringybark trees.'   [IK1-180601_1SY1/01:39:20]

         b.   **ki**-rleng [kindjalarrk]
                 II-much   cockles[II]
                 'a lot of cockles'   [20060814IB05/00:41]

c. **ma**-rleng kunem
　　III-much paperbark[III]
　　'a lot of paperbark trees'　　　　　　　　　　[IK1-180601_1SY1/01:39:24]

d. **ku**-rleng lerrk.
　　IV-much word[IV]
　　'a lot of words'　　　　　　　　　　　　　　[20150413IOv01/11:54]

(4.6) a. **na**-kudji kirdimarrk 'one man[I]'

b. **kin**-kudji marnilikarrng 'one star[II]'

c. **man**-kudji kubbunj 'one canoe[III]'

d. **kun**-kudji kunmimke 'one night[IV]'

The choice between the allomorphs is not phonologically conditioned (4.7) and appears to be a matter of lexical conditioning.

(4.7) "Old" vs. "new" adjectives (in Coleman's (n.d.) terms): Not phonologically conditioned allomorphy

a. ku-buke 'old' vs. kun-burleng 'dry'

b. ku-wanjak 'little' vs. kun-warri 'bad'

The adjectives that select for the CV-allomorphs (as in (4.5)) are a very small class: *-buke* 'old', *-rleng* 'much' and its derivatives (such as *-rlengbinbin* 'big, grown up'), *-ngana* 'big', and *-wanjak* 'little'. Coleman (2010) lists also *-lerreburrinj* 'even [of surface]', *-lerrewarri* 'uneven [of surface]', and *-murrbenben* 'fat' this type, but I do not have examples of the former two, and have encountered forms like *kin-murrbenben* 'fat [female]', which is the 'new' type.

Possessive constructions in Kunbarlang (§4.6) include an oblique pronoun (§4.5.1) encoding the possessor. This pronoun reflects the noun class of the possessor in the following way: class I *-rnungu* 'he.GEN', classes II and III *-ngadju* 'she.GEN'. Class IV remains a missing form, as I was not able to find a suitable class IV possessor. Class I–III possessors are exemplified in (4.8).

(4.8) a. Nga-nguddu-wuy　　　　lerrk bi-**rnungu Ngabbard** ngundji-kanj.
　　　　1SG.NF-2PL.OBJ-give.PST word DAT-he.GEN father[I]　　2DU.FUT-take.NP
　　　　'I gave you the Father's words, now take them.'
　　　　　　　　　　　　　　　　　　　　　　　　[IK1-160430_0001/04:13–17]

b. Mary   ka-rnay   nayi   djurra   korro   kun-bodme
    M[II]   3SG.NF-see.PST NM.I   paper   DEM.MED.LOC   IV-back
    bi-**ngadju**.
    DAT-she.GEN
    'Mary found the book behind her.'   [IK1-160513_0001]

c. **kundulk**   la   merre=**ngadju**
    tree[III]   CONJ   hair=she.GEN
    'the tree and its leaves'   [IK1-160819_0001/13:30–34]

Examples (4.8a) and (4.8b) show the dative possessive construction, in which the prefix on the possessor pronoun is invariable. However, there is another, genitive possessive construction, in which the noun class of the *possessum* is shown on the pronoun with a noun class prefix. Consider examples in (4.9).

(4.9) a. Ninda   nayi   **djurra**   **kin**-ngaybu / *__na__-ngaybu.
         DEM.PROX.I   NM.I   paper[I]   I/II-I.GEN   I-I.GEN
         'This is my book.'   [IK1-170522_1SM1/26:06–15]

    b. **kin**-ngarrku   **madj**
        I/II-we.INCL.GEN   octopus[II]
        'our octopus'   [IK1-170525_1JW1]

    c. Manda   mayi   **neyang**   **man**-ngaybu.
        DEM.PROX.III NM.III food[III]   III-I.GEN
        'This food is mine.'   [IK1-170522_1SM1/24:52–54]

    d. Djindibi   **kun**-budbe   **yalbi**.
        Dj   IV-they.GEN   country[IV]
        'It's Djindibi country.'   [20060620IB04/12:20]

Notice that class I and II possessums (as well as plural ones) trigger agreement prefix *kin*-, as SUPERCLASSING into class II. The prefix *na*- used for class I on adjectives is disallowed from these. Superclassing is the phenomenon of systematic 'disagreement' between a nominal head and its modifiers, reported in a number of Australian languages with grammatical gender systems (see a recent overview in Meakins & Pensalfini 2016, and an extensive analysis of superclassing in Bininj Kunwok, where it has a broader scope than in Kunbarlang, in Evans, Brown & Corbett 2002). Interestingly, it seems to be a common pattern across these languages for the masculine class to be the default for animates (i.e. feminine class nouns can have a masculine class-marked modifiers, but not the other way round), while in Kunbarlang it is the opposite.[4]

Consider the noun phrase *ngayi kin-ngadju nawalak* in (4.10). It is semantically plural, as is evident from the verbal agreement, i.e. the plural prefix *kadda-*. However, this is not marked in the form of the noun, as there is no number morphology on Kunbarlang nouns.

(4.10) Nginda ngayingana ngayi **kin**-ngadju nawalak **kadda**-baba-yuwa.
DEM.PROX.II mother NM.PL I/II-she.GEN child[I] 3PL.NF-DISTR-lie.NP
'Her [lit. 'this mother's'] kids live separately.' [IK1-160819_0001]

The modifiers track semantic plurality for human referents, and the plural form is systematically identical to the class II form (see §4.5.3 for demonstratives and §4.3 for noun markers; personal pronouns also show this pattern, cf. §4.5.1). In demonstratives and noun markers this syncretism is easy to detect, because the masculine class noun is modified by a feminine-like class form (cf. *ngayi* instead of *nayi* in (4.10)). In the possessive agreement, with its superclassing of class I and II possessums into the form *kin-*, I am making an analytic extrapolation. Morphosyntax of possessive constructions is discussed in detail in §4.6.

The form of the noun markers suggests that they are also built with the class prefixes attached to the stem *-yi* (4.11). Notice that class II in this case is not *ki(n)-* but rather *nga-*, probably related to the form *ngal-* in people's gender pairs (4.12), with [l] lost due to the following glide.

(4.11) Noun marker class agreement
   a. nayi kirdimarrk 'the man[I]'
   b. ngayi barramimbanj 'the woman[II]'
   c. mayi mankarre 'the law[III]'
   d. kuyi njunjuk 'the water[IV]'

---

[4] There is, possibly, a historic explanation for the unusual Kunbarlang pattern. This prefix *kin-* could be a reflex of the proto-Gunwinyguan genitive masculine form *ki-*, postulated by Evans (2003a: 34–35), or a merger of that and the proto-Gunwinyguan genitive feminine form *(k)iny-* (ibid.). Bininj Kunwok does not have a similar form; however, Kunbarlang seems to have a more conservative system of noun class, which speaks in favour of this historical hypothesis. On the other hand, the systematic syncretism of the feminine and the plural forms in Kunbarlang (see page 91) might call for a unified synchronic explanation that would favour the unusual feminine-oriented superclassing. I leave it at this speculative point to a further historical investigation.

(4.12) People's gender
>   a. na-bininjkobeng 'husband'
>   b. na-wamud 'male of Wamud skin'
>   c. ngal-bininjkobeng 'wife'
>   d. ngal-wamud 'female of Wamud skin'

Demonstratives in Kunbarlang have, in addition to the four noun class series that participate in the regular head–modifier agreement, one more series, the locative. This series bears certain resemblance to the noun class paradigm of the demonstratives, and probably relates to the noun class system historically. However, synchronically the locative demonstratives, unlike the agreeing adnominal ones, do not interact with the noun class of the nouns, and thus I analyse them as a separate locative series, unrelated to the category of noun class. They always have locative semantics, albeit quite broad. The precise choice of meaning between essive, lative or elative depends on context. See §4.5.3 for details and for the full paradigms of the Kunbarlang demonstratives.

4.2 Case

Although Gunwinyguan languages are highly polysynthetic and primarily head-marking, they nevertheless have rather rich CASE (or case-like) systems. Bininj Kunwok is representative of the family in this respect. In Bininj Kunwok, these cases do not mark grammatical function of the core constituents and are often not obligatory, their foremost use being to mark adjunct roles. Evans calls them in the Bininj Kunwok grammar 'role affixes' for that reason (2003a: 136ff.). However, the array of these role affixes is considerable, including over a dozen affixes.

The category of case plays a relatively minor role in the grammar of Kunbarlang. The case system of Kunbarlang is reduced compared to other Gunwinyguan languages. Case is a morphological category only for personal pronouns. There are three grammatical cases in Kunbarlang, which I label DIRECT,[5] GENITIVE and DATIVE. The direct case is the morphologically unmarked form and in syntax it marks core arguments of predicates (4.13); the dative marks benefactive objects (§5.1) and alienable possession (§4.6.1); and genitive is only used in the adnominal function in possessive constructions (§4.6). Nouns can only be case-marked in construction with pronouns, discussed in §4.4.2. I will sometimes refer to the genitive and dative together as OBLIQUE cases; this grouping is made on the morphological grounds, since the two share the oblique pronominal stem (table 4.4 in §4.5.1), as opposed to the direct case, which uses the direct forms

---

5 This is the term traditionally used in Indo-Aryan linguistics for the case that marks both subjects and objects—as opposed to the peripheral, or oblique, grammatical cases. Cf. Blake (1994: 34–35).

(table 4.3 *ibidem*). There are also two directional clitics in Kunbarlang that attach to verbs and demonstratives (§7.6); due to their idiosyncratic combinatorics I do not analyse them as (locative) cases.

(4.13) a. **Ngudda ki**-nganun-wuy.
you   2SG.NF-1DU.OBJ-give.PST
'**You** gave [something to] us two.'   [IK1-160505_0011/00:57–01:01]

b. Nga-∅-rnay   **kikka**/*bi-ngadju.
1SG.NF-3SG.OBJ-see.PST she/DAT-she.GEN
'I saw **her**.'   [IK1-160622_0001/21:46–22:03]

c. Na-wuk=bonj   ka-**ngan**-wuy   (*bi-ngaybu).
I-person=exactly 3SG.NF-1SG.OBJ-give.PST DAT-I.GEN
'He gave it **to me**.'   [IK1-160616_0001]

d. Ka-ngun-wuy   **ngayi** ngudda=bonj
3SG.NF-2SG.OBJ-give.PST I   you=exactly
'She gave **me** to you.'   [IK1-160618_0001/45:38–40]

Subject (4.13a), primary object (4.13b–c) and secondary object (4.13d) are all core grammatical functions in Kunbarlang (see §5.1 for definitions and discussion), and such arguments must be in the direct case. As (4.13b) shows, only the direct form *kikka* 'she' is allowed as a free-standing pronominal Theme argument, and not the dative form *bi-ngadju* 'DAT-she.GEN'. The contrast between (4.13c) and (4.13d) shows the same effect for the Goal primary objects.

A dative pronoun can occur with an underlying ditransitive verb only if its reference is disjoint from the verb's core objects (4.14).

(4.14) Ninda   Bill ka-**bun**$_i$-wuy   **bi-ngadju**$_j$.
DEM.PROX.I Bill 3SG.NF-3SG.OBJ-give.PST DAT-she.GEN
'Bill gave it to him/her$_i$ for her$_j$.'   [IK1-160616_0001]

The interpretation of (4.14) is that the dative personal pronoun *bi-ngadju* 'DAT-she.GEN' is necessarily disjoint in its reference from the personal prefix *bun-*: *ka$_i$-bun$_j$-wuy bi-ngadju$_{k/*j}$*. Notice that the same does not hold of the direct free pronouns, as the examples in (4.13) show. In these examples the person and number information about one participant occurs twice, encoded both within the free pronoun and within the corresponding personal prefix.

From the point of view of the form, oblique pronominal stems are suppletive, e.g. *ngudda* 'you' ~ *-nungku* 'you.GEN'. Full paradigms are given in tables 4.3 (p. 115) for direct and 4.4 (p. 118) for genitive pronouns. The oblique stems are bound roots: they must have a prefix or themselves cliticise onto a possessum noun. The dative case is built on the basis of the genitive by adding the prefix *bi-* 'DAT'.[6] This is similar to the case containment structures, frequently found in Australian languages (Schweiger 1995). For example, Austin (1995) describes the 'derivational double case' in some Western Australian languages (Kanyara and Mantharta groups), whereby some of the local cases (e.g., ablative) are built on the basis of the locative (Jiwarli) or the dative (the Kanyara languages).

There is no case morphology for other nominals (nouns, adjectives and other types of pronouns). A noun phrase in a case position, such as the possessor (4.15a) or the oblique object (4.15b), is case marked through inclusion of a free pronoun (see §4.4.2 for a detailed description).

(4.15) a. Mary ka-rnay nayi djurra korro kunbodme=**rnungu**
 M 3SG.NF-see.PST NM.I paper DEM.MED.LOC back=he.GEN
 nawalak.
 kid
 'Mary found the book behind the child's back.' [IK1-170606_1SY1]

b. Ngayi nga-bareng-minj **bi-rnungu** nukka kirdimarrk.
 I 1SG.NF-dangerous-INCH.PST DAT-he.GEN he man
 'I got angry with him.' [IK1-160615_0011/46:48–51]

Example (4.16) combines both the dative and the genitive in one nominal phrase.

(4.16) Nga-bareng-mi **bi-rnungu** durduk nayi Kamarrang
 1SG.NF-dangerous-INCH.NP DAT-he.GEN dog NM.I K
 kin-rnungu.
 I/II-he.GEN
 'I'm angry with Kamarrang's dog.' [IK1-180605_1SY1/13:15–21]

See §5.1 for a discussion of grammatical functions in Kunbarlang, as well as for further examples of case marking.

4.3 Noun markers

Kunbarlang has in its noun phrase a functional category that appears innocuous, and yet—in the face of virtual absence of morphology in the nominal domain—is burdened

---

[6] This seems to be a part of a broader tendency: "in Australian languages syncretism of genitive and dative is common" (Schweiger 1995: 339). Furthermore, the pattern where dative derives from genitive is also typologically common (Caha 2009: 10).

with a good deal of syntactic and semantic work. These determiners are involved in matters of reference, information structure, relative clause formation and, more generally, phrase structure of the NP. This section focuses on the semantics of noun markers, while their syntax will be taken up in section 4.4 (especially the hierarchical analysis of the noun phrase). What is important here in terms of syntax is that they have two main functions. On the one hand, these elements are articles in the sense of Himmelmann (2001), more precisely definite articles, as I show below. On the other hand, they have the linker function (*Gelenkartikel* of Himmelmann (1997: §5.1)), often occurring between a noun and its modifier. Due to this duality, I stand by Coleman's (n.d.) convention of calling them noun markers (rather than, say, articles). After a brief illustration of their basic morphosyntactic properties, the two functions are discussed in §§4.3.1–4.3.2.

The noun markers (NMs) agree with the head noun in noun class (§4.1; example (4.11), repeated here).

(4.11) Noun marker class agreement
    a. nayi kirdimarrk 'the man'
    b. ngayi barramimbanj 'the woman'
    c. mayi mankarre 'the law'
    d. kuyi njunjuk 'the water'

In elicitation, they can occupy any position within a nominal phrase, except the final/rightmost ((4.17); see other examples and discussion in §3.2.6 and §7.1.4), and can occur more than once in one nominal phrase ((4.17e) and (4.18)).

(4.17) IK1-180601_1SY1/38:21–43:22
    a. Nga-djarrang [**mayi** man-rnungu kandiddjawa].
       1SG.NF-eat.PST NM.III III-he.GEN bread[III]
       'I ate his biscuit.'
    b. Nga-djarrang [**mayi** kandiddjawa man-rnungu].
    c. Nga-djarrang [kandiddjawa **mayi** man-rnungu].
    d. Nga-djarrang [man-rnungu **mayi** kandiddjawa].
    e. Nga-djarrang [**mayi** man-rnungu **mayi** kandiddjawa].
    f. *Nga-djarrang [kandiddjawa man-rnungu **mayi**].
    g. *Nga-djarrang [man-rnungu kandiddjawa **mayi**].

(4.18) Mandjulngunj but Mirrangkangu [**nayi nguya   nayi na-rlengbinbin**].
M   ENG M   NM.I patriclan NM.I I-big

'[She is] Mandjulngunj, but Mirrangkangu is the big *nguya* (patriclan).' [or perhaps more literally, '[She is] Mandjulngunj, but [at the same time] of the big patriclan Mirrangkangu.'—IK]   [20150413IOv01/02:30–33]

The noun markers cannot be the single constituent of the noun phrase (4.19) and thus are not used as independent anaphoric pronouns.

(4.19) Q: Sandra ka-kinje   neyang?
           S   3SG.NF-cook.NP food

'Is Sandra cooking food?'   [IK1-170613_1SM1/29:49–53]

A: Yoh, ngal-buk=bonj   ka-kinje   mayi   *(neyang).
   yes II-person=exactly 3SG.NF-cook.NP NM.III food

'Yes, it is she [who is cooking food].'   [ibid./31:40–32:04]

The requirement that there be other nominal material following a noun marker is a useful test for presence of noun phrase structure; for instance, it is applied in relative clause identification (§8.4.2).[7]

4.3.1 Noun markers as definite articles

In their first function noun markers immediately precede the noun. They pass Himmelmann's (2001: 832) definition of ARTICLES, which includes these three criteria:
1. this grammatical element occurs only in nominal expressions
2. its position within such expressions is fixed relative to the head
3. this element cannot be used independently of some nominal head

As I have shown, the first and the third criteria are essential for the noun markers in Kunbarlang. The second criterion is trickier, as they can go on either side of the noun. However, in section §4.4.3 I advance an analysis according to which noun markers always precede their immediate scope, and in that sence can be said to precede the head. They are interesting from this point of view, since articles as a functional category are extremely rare in Australian languages (cf. Louagie 2020: 184–5).[8] Thus Kunbarlang contributes data to the emerging typology of article-like elements in Australia, indeed, in the languages of Arnhem Land. B. Baker (2008a) argues that noun class prefixes in the

---

[7] The articles, or noun markers, in Mawng also have the relative clause-marking function (Forrester 2015: 80).
[8] Cf. also Dixon (2002: 66), who stated it more categorically as a complete absence of articles.

Gunwinyguan languages Ngalakgan and Wubuy, as well as article+prefix combinations in Marra, another non-Pama-Nyungan language from southeast Arnhem Land, function similar to the articles of European languages. However, they indicate topicality of the referent and the scope of clausal operators, rather than categories like definiteness or specificity. In Mawng the article prevails in the post-verbal NPs, but not in the ones in the pre-verbal position (Forrester 2015: ch. 5). Forrester suggests that it may be related to information structure sensitivity, potentially an avoidance of non-discourse neutral positions in front of the verb (e.g. p. 12). At present I have seen no indication of a similar clause-level information structure sensitivity in the Kunbarlang noun markers.

When the NMs immediately precede the noun, their semantic-pragmatic contribution has to do with matters of reference and, typically of this domain, is quite elusive. For want of a better characterisation, I analyse them as marking DEFINITENESS. This, of course, needs further clarification, as there are quite different views on the content of that label, see Lyons (1999: 1–12) for an introduction. The Kunbarlang NMs do not fall neatly into just one of the familiar categories: uniqueness, identifiability, or familiarity (or its subtypes, such as bridging, anaphoric, or situational familiarity). At the same time, they without doubt are connected to those categories. Let me introduce some relevant data, after which more discussion of their nature will follow.

Importantly, the discussion of subtle semantic matters in this and the following section (definiteness, novelty/familiarity, intersective readings, contrastive focus, etc.) crucially relies on interpreting nominal expressions in context. For that reason, all conclusions presented here are based on CONTEXTUALISED examples, primarily spontaneous narratives, or carefully constructed examples (such as (4.20a)). Many examples elsewhere in the grammar come from elicitation focused on other grammatical features and due to that are oblivious to, e.g., the familiarity effect—and thus the free translations of such elicited examples may occasionally diverge from the generalisations stated here, which should not be taken as counterexamples.

First, we observe that in contexts where the intended referent is NOVEL/non-familiar, such as the *de dicto* object in (4.20a) or the phrase denoting the price (rather than any specific money) in (4.20b), NMs do not naturally occur.

(4.20) a. Ngayi **nga-yawanj** doctor la nga-rdukkumi-yinj.
I 1SG.NF-seek.NP ENG CONJ 1SG.NF-cut-REFL.PST
'I am looking for a doctor because I cut myself.'
[IK1-170620_1SY1/13:41–45]

b. **Na-wanjak rrubbiya** ngana-kalng mayi man-kang Adelaide,
I-little money 1DU.EXCL.NF-get.PST NM.III III-from A
cheap one.
ENG ENG
'We got it for little money, the one from Adelaide, a cheap one.'
[20060901IB03/02:24–30]

As soon as the same nouns are in a context where they have a familiar (definite) referent, they appear with noun markers (4.21, 4.22b).

(4.21) The speaker recounts her visit to a hospital and conversation with the doctor— the doctor is thus preestablished in the context:

Karlu ngayi nga-ngun-wakwanj nga-ngunda.
NEG.PRED I 1SG.NF-2SG.OBJ-ignorant.NP 1SG.NF-do.PST

Nga-marnanj-ngunda **nayi doctor.**
1SG.NF-BEN-do.PST NM.I ENG

'No I don't know you, I said. I told the doctor.' [20060901IB02/07:10–14]

The pair in (4.22) is particularly telling: the first instance of the noun *rrubbiya* is novel, and is a bare noun, but it creates a *discourse referent*, and so the second instance is familiar, and thus marked with a NM.

(4.22) a. **Rrubbiya** ka-nganj-kanginj, ka-nganj-kidanj
money 3SG.NF-HITH-take.PST 3SG.NF-HITH-go.PST

ka-ngan-wuy.
3SG.NF-1SG.OBJ-give.PST

'He brought some money for me, he came and gave it to me.'
[20060620IB03/25:36–40]

b. Ka-ngan-marnanj-ngunda **nayi kin-nungku rrubbiya** nayi Japani
3SG.NF-1SG.OBJ-BEN-do.PST NM.I I/II-you.GEN money NM.I Japanese

ki-kelkkuyinj.
2SG.NF-work.PST

'He told me, *Your money, which you [earned when you] worked for the Japanese.*' [ibid./25:40–46]

The next example (4.23) further confirms that the relevant semantic feature is definiteness (and not, for instance, specificity). This is the beginning of a short narrative about the tradition of collecting *mabudj* 'cheeky yam'. The first mention of *mabudj* is with a bare noun, as it is novel. The yams themselves remain non-specific throughout the story, i.e. there are no specific yam bulbs that are being referred to. But the first mention of *mabudj* 'yam' in (4.23a) creates a discourse referent, a discourse entity independent of the real-world referent. It is by virtue of that discourse referent that the topic of the story, the yam, is treated as familiar and from then on is tracked by NMs. Notice that in this I follow the view, originating with Ihsane & Puskás (2001), that definiteness and specificity are independent of each other.[9]

---

9 One class of examples that motivate the dissociation includes NPs whose referent is hypotetical or potential, such as that in (i) from Lyons (1999: 9):

(4.23) 20060830IB01/00:09–18 (translation mine—IK)

    a. Kadda-kidanj ngayi mimdom~mimdom kadda-kidanj kadda-bum
       3PL.NF-go.PST NM.PL RDP~old.person 3PL.NF-go.PST 3PL.NF-hit.PST

       mabudj kadda-rda-yinj korro djunguyu.
       cheeky_yam 3PL.NF-put-REFL/PST DEM.MED.LOC bush

       'People of old used to go gather yams, they entered the bush.'

    b. Kadda-warrenj kadda-yawang **mayi mabudj**.
       3PL.NF-move.PST 3PL.NF-seek.PST NM.III cheeky_yam

       'They browsed around looking for the yam.'

Noun markers can combine with proper names, which is compatible with their suggested semantic import.

(4.24) Nga-ngunda bi-ngadju **ngayi Sylvia**.
       1SG.NF-say.PST DAT-she.GEN NM.II S

       'I said to Sylvia.'   [20060901IB02/01:38–41]

Now let us once again consider the characterisation of the noun markers as definite. There are two issues with it that should be kept in mind. The first is that there is certain optionality to the occurrence of the NMs, which makes them appear rather unlike the definite articles in the Germanic languages, for instance. Optionality is very typical of determiner elements across Australia (Louagie 2020: 182–3), and in fact it is not all too uncommon for definite articles in other languages (cf. discussion of Hausa in Lyons 1999: 52–3). The second issue is that it is not yet clear which exactly definiteness-related semantic category the noun markers encode. Sometimes a noun phrase with a noun marker does not have a unique or an identifiable referent, but it is familiar (such as the anaphorically familiar *mayi mabudj* in (4.23b) above). Sometimes it can be the other way around, i.e. the referent is not familiar, but is identifiable, for instance due to its restrictive modifier, as is the case in (4.25). Here, the noun *nuna* is modified by the restrictive clause, which renders it identifiable.

(4.25) Kadda-ngan-marnanj-ngunda ngayi kadda-ngan-rnay X-ray **ngayi**
       3PL.NF-1SG.OBJ-BEN-do.PST NM.PL 3PL.NF-1SG.OBJ-see.PST X-ray NM.PL

       nuna.
       white_woman

       'The white women who saw me for the X-ray told me.'
                                                [20060901IB02/04:11–15]

(i) **The man who comes with me** will not regret it.

This second issue is familiar from the analyses of English, where a single-feature account of definiteness is yet to reach. It should not be taken as problematic for analysing the noun markers as definite articles, but rather as indicative that further work on the Kunbarlang noun phrase is required to establish the semantic joints along which these NMs carve. Crucially, the presence of a noun marker normally signals some definiteness-related category, and the reverse holds: when a noun in spontaneous discourse is not marked by a NM, its referent is neither familiar, nor identifiable, nor unique. An important caveat is that NMs are not the only markers of definiteness, which in their absence can also be signalled e.g. by possessives or demonstratives.

There is no dedicated indefinite article that would be in a paradigmatic opposition to this function of NMs, but the numeral *-kudji* 'one' (§4.7.2.1.1) is sometimes used as an indefinite article (4.26).

(4.26) **Kun-kudji kurrambalk** ka-bun-djin   wirdidj korro
        IV-one   house   3SG.NF-3SG.OBJ-eat.NP fire   DEM.MED.LOC
        yirrk.
        inside
       'A house is burning from the inside.'   [IK1-170530_1SY1/10:44–48]

The cognate numeral 'one' in Bininj Kunwok has a similar use (Evans 2003a: 244).

4.3.2 Noun markers as linkers

In their second function noun markers appear immediately preceding modifiers, most importantly adjectives and relative clauses. The modifier phrases formed with them are obligatorily INTERSECTIVE and in fact RESTRICTIVE.[10] I offer a more detailed discussion of the theoretical content of these notions in Kapitonov submitted and here I primarily concentrate on the relevant data patterns. The most important observation connected to the duality of NMs (as definite articles or linkers) is that the position of the NM within the nominal phrase has an effect on the interpretation; this is why both in this and in the preceding section I describe the position of the NM in terms of immediate precedence. I argued above that when immediately preceding nouns, NMs signal definiteness. The next important observation is that when the NM does not immediately precede the noun, it does not signal definiteness of the NP; consider example (4.27):

---

[10] There are one or two apparent counterexamples to the restrictive interpretation, but these are not uncontroversial, i.e. might not be true counterexamples. Spontaneous discourse is not rich in nominal phrases that have both a noun and an adjective, and ultimately careful elicitation will be needed to clarify the issue.

(4.27) [Mulurrmulurr **ngayi** kin-karrkeyang] la [mulurrmulurr **ngayi**
wading.bird NM.II II-clean CONJ wading.bird NM.II
kin-ngongokwarri].
II-dirty
'The white ibis [or spoonbill; Threskiornitidae] and the black ibis.'
[20060620IB04/06:46–50]

As part of the recall of various birds that used to be the typical game, the two conjoined nominal phrases in (4.27) refer to novel/indefinite kinds (not individuals, nor pluralities of individuals). Unlike in English, in Kunbarlang reference to kinds does not invoke definite marking.

The point becomes even clearer with prenominal adjectives, such as in example (4.28). The order here is *noun marker – adjective phrase – noun*, and even though the noun marker precedes the noun, it does not *immediately* precede it. The situation described in (4.28) is hypothetical, and even though horses are an ongoing topic at that moment, this hypothetical horse is a novel discourse referent (thus, indefinite).

(4.28) Yoh if ki-karrme **nayi** [$_{AP}$**real quiet**] **djarrang**, kun-mak.
yes ENG 2SG.NF-handle.NP NM.I ENG ENG horse IV-good
'Yeah if you get a REALLY quiet horse, that's good.' [20070108IB01/21:42–46]

What is common to examples like (4.27) and (4.28), where the NM immediately precedes the attributive modifier, is the restrictive reading of that modifier. This means that the adjectives in the above examples do not merely describe their respective nouns, but also presuppose a contrast with some other, excluded referents; for instance, 'real quite' horses are contrasted with the 'wild' ones. In fact, this effect of reference restriction is found when the modifier is another noun (4.29b), although such examples are quite rare.

(4.29) a. Ka-rninganj ka-burrun-ngunga::ng man-barrkidbe ka-kalng.
3SG.NF-sit.PST 3SG.NF-3DU.OBJ-growl.PST III-other 3SG.NF-get.PST
'He sat there growling at them, then he got another one.'
[20150212AS01/05:12–15]

b. **Kundulk mayi mulurr** mukka ngorro.
tree NM.III driftwood it.III DEM.MED.IV
'A log that was a driftwood, that is.' [ibid./05:17–19]

Thus, the second function of the noun markers in Kunbarlang is to signal the intersective, restrictive reading of an attributive modifier. Since such NMs often occur between the noun and the following modifier, I refer to this function as the linker (see Himmelmann (1997: §5) for a typological view). Notice, however, that this is not a one-to-one correspondence: NM+modifier combination is always intersective (and a non-intersective modifier may not occur with a NM), but it is *not* the case that the absence of a NM *entails* a non-intersective reading. Cf. the discussion of optionality of NMs in their definite article function in §4.3.1 above.

As one might expect, the two functions can be combined within a single nominal phrase: in this case there are multiple noun markers. Examples of this are (4.18) above and (4.30). The nominal phrases in these examples are definite, and the modifier with the NM is construed as restrictive. In the case of (4.30) it is an ad hoc borrowing of an English prepositional phrase.

(4.30) Like ku-rleng **kuyi** shop **kuyi** in Adelaide.
        ENG   IV-much   NM.IV   ENG   NM.IV   ENG ENG
        'Like, boy, many are the shops [that are] in Adelaide!'
        [20060901IB02/08:31–35]

It is possible that a unified analysis can be given to the two functions of the Kunbarlang noun markers described here. I anticipate that in pursuing such an approach, insights about one function can inform a better understanding of the other. That task, however, is beyond the scope of this grammar; see Kapitonov (submitted) for additional discussion. In section 4.4.3 I return to the noun marker patterns presented here and argue that these data provide strong support for a hierarchical analysis of the Kunbarlang noun phrase.

4.4 Noun phrase

Phrase structure constituency and even the very existence of the noun phrase as a syntactic unit in Australian languages has been under debate since the seminal work on configurationality and constituency in some of these languages (such as Hale 1983, Blake 1983, Heath 1986; see Nordlinger 2014 for an overview of the issues and a comprehensive bibliography). The reasons for this include the freedom of word order often found among the potential constituents of the noun phrase (i.e. the head noun and the modifiers that semantically relate to it), as well as the existence of discontinuous noun phrases, which featured prominently in the nonconfigurationality debate since Hale (1983). Discontinuity is the configuration in which the nominals that semantically belong together are interrupted by other material (such as the verb, for instance).

Recent typological study of these and other aspects of the noun phrase structures by Louagie (2020) suggests that these structures are in fact more constrained. Louagie surveyed a 100-language sample for criteria dealing with NP constituency from the point of view of its external morphosyntax (i.e. how it functions in larger structures; for instance, the locus of case marking, clausal word order, prosody), as well as its own integrity (foremost, word order *within* the NP, and discontinuity). Her findings indicate that the majority of languages at least admit of NP construal, and often strongly support it.

The existence of the noun phrase in Kunbarlang is strongly supported by the following considerations:
- word order within the noun phrase is relatively fixed, with some categorical restrictions (§4.4.1)
- case marking in the oblique case positions suggests a phrasal construal (§4.4.2)
- reordering of attributive modifiers and noun markers with respect to the noun and to each other yields systematic interpretive effects that reveal hierarchical organisation (§4.4.3)

4.4.1 Word order

Kunbarlang is a nonconfigurational language (see references above) in which word order is not constrained by the grammatical function of syntactic constituents, but rather is connected to discourse-pragmatic functions (information structure; this is elaborated in §7.1). Within the Kunbarlang noun phrase, word order is not completely rigid, but there are some clear regularities. First, the noun markers are prohibited at the absolute end of the NP, as was shown in (4.17) (repeated here).[11]

(4.17) IK1-180601_1SY1/38:21–43:22

    a. Nga-djarrang [**mayi** man-rnungu kandiddjawa].
        1SG.NF-eat.PST NM.III III-he.GEN bread[III]
        'I ate his biscuit.'

    b. Nga-djarrang [**mayi** kandiddjawa man-rnungu].

    c. Nga-djarrang [kandiddjawa **mayi** man-rnungu].

    d. Nga-djarrang [man-rnungu **mayi** kandiddjawa].

    e. Nga-djarrang [**mayi** man-rnungu **mayi** kandiddjawa].

    f. *Nga-djarrang [kandiddjawa man-rnungu **mayi**].

    g. *Nga-djarrang [man-rnungu kandiddjawa **mayi**].

---

11 The grammatical examples in (4.17) differ in their prosodic properties. While the one with the order det–GEN-possessor–noun (4.17a) is clearly within the same prosodic contour, examples (4.17b–d) seem to have a slight pause within the alleged NP, in each case after the first nominal. It raises the possibility that those involve marked information structure, or, alternatively, are combinations of a NP with a following afterthought. Importantly, if this were the case, it would indicate an even more rigid word order within the NP then my analysis here suggests. This issue is hard to resolve without studying Kunbarlang syntax-prosody interface at a level beyond the limits of this grammar.

Second, the permutations like those in (4.17) primarily come from elicitations. Noun phrases that occur in their "natural habitat" in spontaneous production (especially in longer texts with clear context) show rather principled organisation. In §4.4.3 I argue that it reflects the hierarchical structure underlying the noun phrase in Kunbarlang.

Also, in spontaneous discourse noun phrases are always very short, i.e. do not have more than one or two modifiers. In fact, adnominal attributive adjectives are outright rare. The presentation of the noun phrase structure proceeds as follows. First I give a flat template that captures the ordering of NP constituents in the first descriptive approximation. Then I illustrate the position of modifiers with a few examples and point out some apparent exceptions. After that I leave the questions of ordering for a moment in order to present another topic, namely the use of personal pronouns as determiners and case-markers within the Kunbarlang noun phrase (§4.4.2). Then I return to the question of NP structure and offer some suggestions about how the ordering facts, the determining pronouns, and the noun markers can be brought together (§4.4.3). Finally, this section concludes with a consideration of *NP discontinuity* (§4.4.4).

The template that emerges from observing various nominal phrases is in (4.31). NM stands for 'noun marker' (§3.2.6) and RC, for 'relative clause' (§8.4).

(4.31) pronoun — demonstrative — quantifier — NM — GEN-possessor — HEAD NOUN — adjective — DAT-possessor — RC

It has a certain degree of abstraction to it, and in the face of the syntactic complexity of the Kunbarlang noun phrase will not meet the surface facts of every example. Most importantly, however, as we will see soon, Kunbarlang likes its NPs cut into very small servings. This is one reason behind the fact that examples (4.32) illustrate one type of modifier each, and thus mainly show the ordering of those relative to the head noun, rather than relative to each other. An example of a dative possessor is in (4.36a) and of a genitive one in (4.40) in the next subsection.

(4.32) a. **Nukka nayi kirdimarrk** kanj-bun-beye nayi nakarlyung.
he NM.I man[I] 3SG.FUT-3SG.OBJ-bite.NP NM.I crocodile
'The crocodile is going to bite the man.' [IK1-170609_2SM1/52:46–53]

b. Nganj-ngun-walkki-karrme **ninda djalakkiradj**.
1SG.FUT-2SG.OBJ-COM-hold.NP DEM.PROX.I fishing_spear
'I'll borrow that spear from you.' [IK1-180518_1SY2/23:44]

c. Or **kun-kudji kunbid la kaburrk nayi djurra** ay birlinj?
ENG IV-one hand CONJ two NM.I book ah how
'Or seven books, or what?' [IK1-170610_2SM1/26:27–31]

d. **Bilem   ma-rlengbinbin** ngadda-kanginj.
   bark_canoe III-big   1PL.EXCL.NF-bring.PST
   'We brought a big canoe.'   [20140709IOv05/03:56]

Next, consider an example that looks rather different (4.33). The noun phrase is in the square brackets.[12]

(4.33) And ngana-rnay   [nayi kirdimarrk nayi ka-warrminj   nayi
        ENG 1DU.EXCL.NF-see.PST NM.I man   NM.I 3SG.NF-sick.PST NM.I
        na-kang Kunbarlanja].
        I-from   Gunbalanya
        'And we saw a man from Gunbalanya who was sick [or 'who has passed away'—it is not clear which point in time the relative clause refers to].'
                                    [20060901IB03/00:10–15; translation mine—IK]

The most striking feature of (4.33), viz. the noun markers that precede every modifier, will be elaborated on in §4.4.3. For now, notice that when both the adjective and the relative clause have a linker noun marker, their mutual order does not have to conform to that stipulated in the template (4.31) (here the adjective phrase *nakang Kunbarlanja* 'from Gunbalanya' follows the RC).

Another type of noun phrase with adjectival (and sometimes other) modifiers that is recurrent in the data and will inform the analysis is in (4.34):

(4.34) La   ma-wanjak mayi   welenj?
        CONJ III-little NM.III road
        'The SMALL road?'   [IK1-170610_2SM1/54:04]

The important features of (4.34) are its word order "Adj–NM–Noun" and the focus on the adjective (indicated by small capitals in translation). I hear a pitch accent on the adjective in such examples, but have not made any instrumental measures. I shall return to the orders as in (4.33) and (4.34), as well as the connection with focus, in §4.4.3.

Also, although up until this point I have been choosing examples that demonstrate an overt head noun, it is important to keep in mind that very often it is absent in Kunbarlang (cf. 4.35). That is, any modifiers, alone or in a group, can constitute a noun phrase. Whether in such cases there is a phonologically null nominal head or it is genuinely absent is a matter of theoretical considerations, and I do not wish to make a strong claim here. However, there are several conceptual advantages to postulating

---

[12] Despite its ablative preposition-like appearance in the translation, *-kang* 'from' is an adjective in Kunbarlang. See also §3.2.2.

null nominals. One is, they preclude the question of what exactly heads the phrase and what category the projections are in the absence of an overt noun. The other is, they allow for a principled and transparent approach to referential interpretation of the nominal phrases, whereby such null nominals are the referential loci of their elliptical NPs (for instance, discourse-anaphorically). A related benefit is the convenience they afford in the analysis of discontinuous NPs (see §4.4.4 below). Alternative solutions for either of the issues are conceivable, but they pertain to the theoretical exercise alluded to above, which I shall not engage in here. I shall thus assume null nominals here, and use them sparingly.

(4.35) La [ninda nabarrkidbe nayi korro kunkun], ngondo
CONJ DEM.PROX.I I-other NM.I DEM.MED.LOC IV-right DEM.PROX.IV
kenda=way mayi kurrambalk ka-dja.
DEM.PROX.LOC=HITH NM.III house 3SG.NF-stand.NP
'And **this other one** [picture] **on the right**, there is a house in it.'
[IK1-170610_2SM1/49:32–39]

The preliminary ordering data pointed out above speak in favour of the NP construal, rather than a flat, appositional analysis (cf. Blake 1983, Heath 1986). In the remainder of this section I strengthen the case for a well-organised noun phrase in Kunbarlang, and provide some suggestions about its hierarchical organisation.

4.4.2 Analytic case marking and determining pronouns

The other argument for the noun phrase construal comes from the case marking of a nominal group in oblique case positions. There are two kinds of such positions, viz. the possessor (§4.6) and adjuncts NPs (adjunct to a verb (4.37a–b) or to a noun (4.37c)). Noun phrases in those positions have to be case-marked, but case is only morphologically present on personal pronouns (§4.5.1). In such cases Kunbarlang employs an analytic construction, whereby a genitive or dative case-marked pronoun is combined with the morphologically inert noun. Examples in (4.36) illustrate this for possessives and those in (4.37), for dative adjuncts.

(4.36) a. Nga-nguddu-wuy lerrk **bi-rnungu Ngabbard**.
1SG.NF-2SG.OBJ-give.PST word DAT-he.GEN F
'I gave you the Father's word.' [IK1-160430_0001/04:13–16]

b. more language, **kun-ngarrku ngarrka Kun-barlang**
ENG ENG IV-we.INCL.GEN we.INCL IV-Warlang
'and more language, that of us Kunbarlang people'
[IK1-160424_0001/06:00–05]

(4.37) a. Ngadda-dja   Kunngoninj   **bi-rnungu nukka ngorro**
       1PL.EXCL.NF-stand.NP ceremony_name DAT-he.GEN he   DEM.MED.IV
       kirdimarrk ngadda-yurrkbungu njunjuk la   kadda-yurrkbungu.
       man   1PL.EXCL.NF-bathe.NP water CONJ 3PL.NF-bathe.NP
       'We have the cleansing ceremony for that [deceased] man, we have a shower with water and they have a shower.'
       [20060901IB08/01:55–02:02]

   b. Ngayi balkkime nga-nganj-kidanj   nganj-yolyolhme **bi-ngadju**
      I   today   1SG.NF-HITH-go.PST 1SG.FUT-tell.NP DAT-she.GEN
      Ngalbangardi.
      N
      'Today I came to speak to Ngalbangardi.'   [20070108IB01/00:11–17]

   c. our memories **barrayidjyidj bi-budbe**
      ENG ENG   children   DAT-they.GEN
      'our memories for children'   [IK1-160424_0001/06:28]

Such analytically oblique case-marked NPs are always contiguous, and provide support for the NP construal in Kunbarlang: the head noun being able to be case-marked by virtue of associating with the pronoun, forming a constituent with it.[13]

It is likely that this analytic case construction is formally related to the 'determining' use of the personal pronouns within NPs. This is a typologically prominent feature in Australian languages, where personal pronouns may co-occur or compete with other determiner-like elements in the noun phrase (see Hale 1973, Blake 2001 and Louagie (2020: ch. 5) for typology and analysis). Across those Australian languages that have them, the adnominal pronouns "are markers of definiteness and/or specificity, or they have a function relating to discourse management" (Louagie 2020: 188). In Kunbarlang they seem to occur in definite noun phrases. However, referential semantics is a very fine matter, and this claim about their referential/discourse contribution should be taken as tentative until a further, focused semantic study. These adnominal pronouns are exemplified with *kikka* 'she' and *mukka* 'it' in (4.38) below; further examples can be found in §4.5.1, §4.5.3, and elsewhere throughout the grammar.

---

13 This is almost the opposite of what one finds in the languages that have morphological case on each nominal word and few constraints on the order and contiguity of those nominals (like Kalkatungu; see Louagie (2020: ch. 6) for a typology), where the case-marking perhaps facilitates interpretation of the dispersed constituents of the nominal group, and constructing the functional representation of the clause in general, through *unification* (Nordlinger 1998).

(4.38) a. **Kikka** Ngalbangardi ka-wokdja Kunbarlang kun-mak
she.II N 3SG.NF-speak.NP K IV-good
ngadda-ngayinj.
1PL.EXCL.NF-hear.PST
'As we heard, that Ngalbangardi speaks Kunbarlang well.'
[20070108IB01/25:22–26; translation mine—IK]

b. **mukka** bonj kurrambalk
it.III exactly house
'that house [the church]' [IK1-160719_0001/00:19]

Notice that they can be used with personal names (4.38a). Skin names, although commonly used functionally as proper names, are quite ambiguous in virtue of being a small set, and thus being frequently repeated within a community. The addition of a determining personal pronoun as in (4.38a) signals or emphasises definiteness (more specifically, identifiability).

In this 'determining' use pronouns compete with other elements in the syntactic category of determiners in Kunbarlang: noun markers and demonstratives. The following generalisations (somewhat tentative, given the notoriously delicate semantic matter) can be made based on the occurrence of noun phrases in context:

1. different determiner classes can co-occur within one noun phrase, but normally do not
2. noun phrases with noun markers are *definite* (this, however, depends on the position of the NM; see 4.3)
3. noun phrases with determining pronouns or demonstratives are *definite* (by virtue of the definite deictic reference of personal pronouns and demonstratives)
4. *non-specific* noun phrases usually do not have determiners

None of these generalisations is a categorical rule, probably. Although usually a noun phrase that has a determiner will only have one of the personal pronoun, demonstrative or noun marker, occasionally speakers do combine them. All pairwise combinations are attested: pronoun and noun marker (4.39a), demonstrative and noun marker (4.39b), pronoun and demonstrative (4.39c). The noun phrases in all three examples in (4.39) contain either a determining pronoun or a demonstrative and are all definite.

(4.39) a. **Nukka nayi kirdimarrk** kanj-bun-beye nayi nakarlyung.
he NM.I man[I] 3SG.FUT-3SG.OBJ-bite.NP NM.I crocodile
'The crocodile is going to bite the man.' [IK1-170609_2SM1/52:46–53]

b. **Manda mayi welenj** ka-ka=kulkkulk.
DEM.PROX.III NM.III road[III] 3SG.NF-go.NP=run
'This road is running along.' [IK1-170610_2SM1/14:34–36]

c. **Na-buk=bonj   narnda=bonj   balanda.**
   I-person=exactly DEM.DIST.I=exactly whitefella[I]
   'That very whitefella.'   [IK1-160624_0001/04:38]

In fact, the direct form pronouns do not only co-occur with full nouns in the determining function. They even co-occur with the case-marking oblique pronouns, as the pronominal possessor (4.40). This extensive use of personal pronouns within larger noun phrases may be indicative of their incipient grammaticalisation.

(4.40) Korro   **ngudda kun-nungku** yalbi   kadda-bum   ninda.
        DEM.MED.LOC you   IV-you.GEN   country 3PL.NF-hit.PST DEM.PROX.I
        'This is your country where they killed this [crocodile].'
                                                      [20060620IB04/11:36–45]

It is important to notice that the direct case pronouns, such as the ones in (4.38), contrast with the oblique case marking ones discussed above: the direct case ones are optional and used for semantic/pragmatic purpose, while the oblique ones have the grammatical function of marking a noun phrase for case, and as such are obligatory. One consequence for the semantic composition is that the oblique ones are not as immediately associated with definiteness as direct ones are; example (4.104) in §4.5.4.1, for instance, features an oblique (i.e. grammatically obligatory) pronoun as part of a patently non-specific, non-referential interrogative NP.

4.4.3 The hierarchical structure of the noun phrase

In this section I bring together noun marker placement data from §4.3 and the ordering of adjectives with respect to the noun to argue for hierarchical phrasal structure in the Kunbarlang nominal phrases.

Recall that the noun markers in Kunbarlang have two distinct functions, depending on what the NM immediately precedes. When directly followed by the noun, the NM functions as the definite article, and when directly followed by an attributive modifier, as the linker forming restrictive modifiers. This in itself strongly suggests a hierarchical structure: if the noun phrase had been flat, one would rather expect the same semantic effect regardless of the position of the NM. Before I elaborate on this, let us also consider the position of the adjective in the NP.

The descriptive nominal phrase template in §4.4.1 places adjectives as the first constituent following the noun. However, as I indicated in that section, the picture is somewhat more complex, and adjectives can in fact occur both before and after nouns. The judgements are rather delicate, but as I summarise it in Kapitonov (submitted), the postnominal position corresponds to an information-structurally neutral reading

Tab. 4.2: Interpretive effects of varying the word order of noun marker (D), adjective, and noun

order	definite	restrictive	emphatic
N A			
A N			✓
D N A	✓		
A D N	✓		✓
D A N		✓	✓
N D A		✓	

(4.41), while the prenominal position (4.42) conveys a sense of emphasis on the adjective (which I tentatively associate with focus).

(4.41) **Bilem** **ma-rlengbinbin** ngadda-kanginj.
bark_canoe III-big 1PL.EXCL.NF-bring.PST
'We brought a big canoe.' [20140709IOv05/03:56]

(4.42) a. Ngalngarridj ninda Mandjulngunj but Mirrangkangu [nayi
N DEM.PROX.II M ENG M NM.I
na-rlengbinbin nguya bi-ngadju].
I-big patriclan DAT-she.GEN
'Ngalngarridj is Mandjulngunj but Mirrangkangu is her BIG *nguya* (patriclan).' [20150413IOv01/07:47–51]

b. **Na-warri nginjeng**, nga-rlakwang, nga-woh-karrmeng...
I-bad thing 1SG.NF-throw.PST 1SG.NF-INCP-handle.PST
'BAD thing, I chucked it, I got it by mistake...' [RS1-140/24:02–05]

One exception concerns the existential quantifiers, many of which morphologically are adjectives 4.7.2.1. Unlike attributive adjectives, they precede the noun by default. For instance, out of the 37 examples of adnominal numerals 'one' and 'three', both of which include the agreeing form *-kudji* 'one', they occur to the left of the noun in 33 cases (or 89% of the time). Based on this, it seems most plausible that existential quantifiers occupy a different base position than attributive adjectives. I identify it here as NUMP (NUMBER PHRASE), in line with the established practice in the typological generative literature (see Cinque 2005 among many others). This projection is above the NP, which I here assume to include attributive adjectives.

Combining the interpretive effects of noun markers with the positional effects of attributive adjectives, we obtain the pattern in table 4.2, with noun markers indicated as D (from *determiner*) for readability. Based on these generalisations, I treat N–Adj as the basic order, and the opposite, i.e. Adj–N, as derived from that. Thus, I analyse the basic structure of NP with simple modification as in (4.43).

(4.43) a. [$_{NP}$ bilem$_N$ [$_{AP}$ marlengbinbin]]

b.
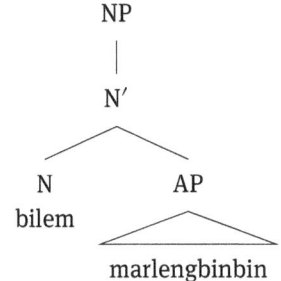

Given the apparent systematic interpretive effects, namely focusing of the adjective in the prenominal position, I analyse that position as derived from the basic by displacement of the adjective. Displacement is a well-known and widespread correlate of information-structural markedness (Mallinson & Blake 1981: 152, Erteschik-Shir 2007), and Kunbarlang seems no exception to that generalisation. Particulars of the formal execution thereof are not pertinent here, see Kapitonov (submitted) for a proposal.

Interestingly, the clause-initial position in Kunbarlang is also associated with pragmatic markedness (see §7.1.2), which suggests a parallel displacement effect at the clausal level. However, unlike the NP, the Kunbarlang clause does not seem to have such a strict word order, so it is somewhat trickier to make the argument; see §7.1 for discussion of the clausal word order and §3.4 for the pronominal argument hypothesis in relation to Kunbarlang. What is more important here is that the focused adjectives do not have to occur at the left edge of the clause (4.42a), which I take to mean that there is some information-structural activity not only at the clausal level, but also at the level of the NP.

The patterns in table 4.2 strongly suggest the presence of a hierarchical structure, which gives rise to the systematic interpretive effects. Had that not been the case, the observed sensitivity to the order of composition of the noun markers would be hard to explain. Assuming the movement analysis of the adjective–noun order, as I did above (albeit without full formalisation), the following structures (4.44) emerge as the most economical way to capture the semantic effects of the different word orders:

(4.44) a. [N [NM A]]
b. [NM [N A]]
c. [[NM A]$_i$ N t_i]
d. [A$_i$ [NM [N t_i]]]

It was shown in §4.3 and §4.4.1 that there can be more than one noun marker in a noun phrase. Indeed, linker noun markers become obligatory once there is more than one modifier. Kapitonov (submitted) offers the following generalisation:

(4.45) In Kunbarlang, a modifier can combine with the noun directly (i.e. without a linker noun marker), but such composition renders the resulting noun phrase inaccessible to further *direct* modification. Modification using linkers remains available.

Attempts to use two modifiers that both do not have a linker NM result in grammaticality (4.46):

(4.46) *manda **man-warri man-rnungu** mayi mabudj
DEM.PROX.III III-bad NM.III III-he.GEN NM.III
intended: 'this bad yam that belongs to him' [IK1-180606_2SY1/01:07:50–57]

The noun marker in the definite article function is regulated by the definiteness considerations independently of the generalisation in (4.45). Some examples of this *determiner spreading* (i.e. the recurrence of NMs on modifiers) are (4.33) above and (4.47):

(4.47) a. [**Mulurrmulurr** [ngayi kin-karrkeyang] [$_{RC}$ngayi ka-karrmi
wading.bird NM.II II-clean NM.II 3SG.NF-get.NP

spoon]] kikka ngorro ngadda-buni.
spoon she DEM.MED.IV 1PL.EXCL.IRR.PST-hit.IRR.PST

'The white *mulurrmulurr*, the one with the spoon [i.e. royal spoonbill, *Platalea regia*], that one we hunted.' [20060620IB04/07:05]

b. [**Manda mabudj** [mayi man-warri] [mayi nabuk
DEM.PROX.III cheeky_yam NM.III III-bad NM.III he

man-rnungu]] ka-rna ka-ngarrkun-wunj.
III-he.GEN 3SG.NF-sit.NP 3SG.NF-1.INCL.OBJ-give.NP

'He keeps giving us these yams of his that are rubbish.' [the speaker's comment: 'These yams, it's belong to him, it's no good, he's always giving us.'] [IK1-180606_2SY1/01:09:50–55]

To generalise somewhat, it appears that Kunbarlang avoids large noun phrases altogether, and in the conspicuously rare cases when these are produced, their constituents have to be syntactically 'parcelled' with the help of linkers. This phenomenon requires considerable further in-depth work, including testing the analyses offered here and gathering more data on the possible combinations of various modifiers—a clear lacuna in the current corpus.

Considering the other elements listed in the noun phrase template (4.31), we find that pronouns and demonstratives do not show similar variation, but occupy the leftmost position in the noun phrase. The tree in (4.48) provides the first approximation to a wholistic NP structure for Kunbarlang.

(4.48)

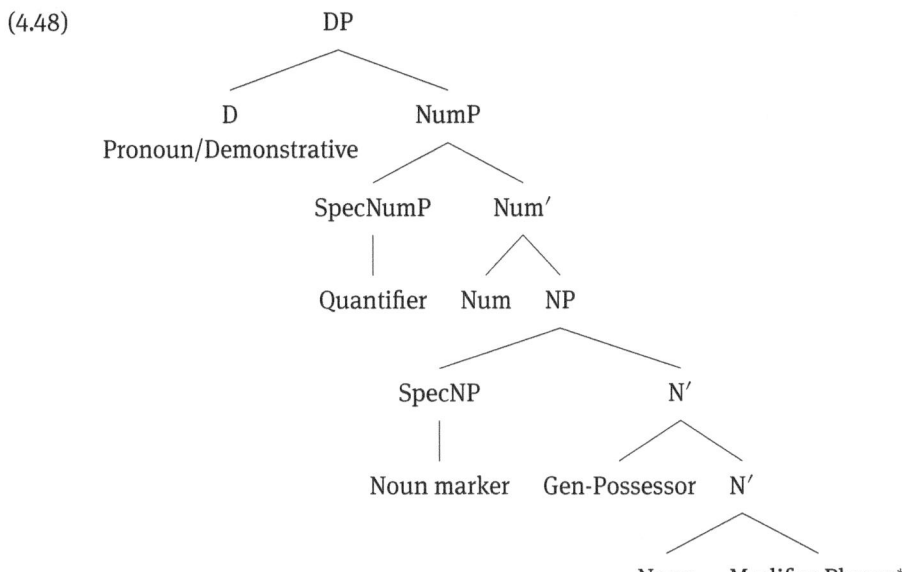

The "Modifier Phrase*" stands for one or more of (i) adjective phrases, (ii) dative possessors, and (iii) relative clauses. The general architecture here is more important than the specific labels. It remains to be seen if the DP hypothesis (as suggested by the top layer of the tree) provides the best account for the Kunbarlang data, especially in light of the broader conceptual difficulties it faces (Bruening 2009). Likewise, there is more work to be done on the syntax of possessors, especially given that (i) the GEN-possessor may occur to the left of the NM, and (ii) the functional distinction between the genitive (agreeing) and the dative construction is still ill-understood (§4.6). Finally, for the details of implementing the focus displacement of the adjective into the prenominal position, I direct the reader to Kapitonov (submitted).

4.4.4 Noun phrase discontinuity

Evidence has been mounting both from language-specific (e.g. Schultze-Berndt & Simard 2012 on Jaminjung) and typological work (Louagie & Verstraete 2016) that coreferential discontinuous nominals do not necessarily indicate nonconfigurationality and/or absence of NP constituency in a language. Schultze-Berndt & Simard 2012, for instance, argue that (i) 'true' discontinuity should be distinguished from other constructions that may be similar in appearance (e.g., two separate coreferential NPs), and (ii) this true discontinuity is not random but highly constrained, e.g. by information-structural factors.

Kunbarlang data are in line with this argument. Firstly, nominals that are coreferential but interrupted by other material are infrequent, appearing in the data very occasionally. Second, they all seem to be of one kind, viz. a modifier in right-peripheral apposition, typically an adjective. In this construction (4.49), the right-dislocated modifier is offset by a short pause or pitch reset. I analyse this as two separate coreferential NPs. However, here I remain agnostic with respect to the exact syntactic mechanism responsible for separation and for coreference of the two parts, as nothing seems to hinge on it.

(4.49) a. Bedbe-rrema **wirdidj** kadda-worrhmeng **ma-ngana**.
they-CONTR fire[III] 3SG.NF-kindle.PST III-big
'The others made a fire, a big one.' [20060606IB02/11:30]

b. June 19th kenda ngorro **murlil** ngarrki-karrme
ENG ENG DEM.PROX.LOC DEM.MED.IV ceremony 1.INCL.FUT-hold.NP
ku-rlengbinbin.
IV-big
'On June 19th we'll have here a celebration, a big one.'
[IK1-160430_0001/01:28–38]

The adjective *ma-ngana* 'big' in (4.49a) describes the referent encoded by the noun *wirdidj* 'fire', but they are not adjacent. I analyse this adjective as a separate noun phrase headed by a zero anaphor noun and located in the right-peripheral 'afterthought' position; see §7.1.3. Example (4.49b) is exactly parallel. Thus, under this treatment, the Kunbarlang NPs in (4.49) are no more discontinuous than the ones in the English translations given. The only difference is that Kunbarlang allows any nominal to constitute a noun phrase without the need for a(n overt) head noun.

Notice that the second noun phrase, consisting of the adjective, adds specification to the description of the referent. In the broader picture, it seems that those Australian languages that freely allow for discontinuous coreferential nominals show a preference for the more general elements (e.g. a determining pronoun or a generic noun) to appear earlier in the clause, and the more specific ones (e.g. an adjective or a specific noun) to occur later, narrowing the description and making it more precise. Blake (2001: 419–20) illustrates this for Kalkatungu and lists references to other languages that exhibit a similar pattern. Kunbarlang appears in agreement with this tendency.

Under the afterthought analysis, there are no discontinuity data in Kunbarlang that compromise postulating the noun phrase. Taking this together with the discussion of word order in §4.4.1 and case marking in §4.4.2 above, I conclude that Kunbarlang does have the noun phrase as a syntactic unit.

4.5 Pronominals

4.5.1 Personal pronouns

Kunbarlang personal pronouns encode person, number and case. Besides that, in first person non-singular a distinction is made with respect to whether the referent includes the second person (i.e. the addressee) or not. This distinction is often labelled as 'clusivity' in grammatical descriptions. The labels 'inclusive' and 'exclusive' are more convenient than person combination descriptions like '1+2' and '1+3', and thus are used throughout the grammar. Third person singular pronouns distinguish noun class. There are two case forms of the pronoun stems: direct and oblique. The direct ones are used for all core arguments, i.e. subjects and primary and secondary objects, while the oblique ones are used for oblique case functions, i.e. benefactive objects and possessors; see §4.2 for more on Kunbarlang case and §5.1 for a discussion of grammatical roles. The paradigm for the direct forms is given in table 4.3 (after Coleman (n.d.: 1, 10)).[14] There are three persons (first, second and third) and three numbers (singular, dual and plural).[15] The forms in parentheses are the allomorphs used with the contrastive suffix -*ma* (§4.5.1.2). The paradigm for the oblique forms can be found below in table 4.4.

Notice that there is no number distinction for inanimates, as reflected in class III and IV rows. Example (4.50) shows that with a plural 'vegetable' referent (ensured by a plural quantifier) the form *mukka* is used, and the form *kikka* cannot be. Likewise, the verbal agreement is singular. These facts indicate that inanimates are inherently morphosyntactically singular.[16]

Tab. 4.3: Personal pronoun paradigm: Direct forms

		Singular	Dual	Plural
First	Exclusive	ngayi (nganj-)	nganangka	ngadbe
	Inclusive		ngarrka	
Second		ngudda (nji-)	nungunungka	nukudbe (ngudbe-)
Third	Class I	nukka	benengka / kikka	bedbe / kikka
	Class II	kikka		
	Class III	mukka	—	—
	Class IV	kukka	—	—

---

14 These forms differ slightly from those given by Coleman (n.d.). I hear the first person inclusive as *ngarrka* (instead of *ngarrkka*), without the fortis consonant, and also I have added the form *kikka* for the third person dual and plural, which she did not include.
15 Coleman includes the coordinate dual forms into the same paradigm. I discuss them separately in §4.5.1.4 below.
16 An alternative analysis could be that singular, dual and plural forms are merely homophonous in classes III and IV.

(4.50) Dolobbo, {mukka / *kikka} ma-rleng ka-warre ka-dja.
stringybark it.III they III-much 3SG.NF-occur.NP 3SG.NF-stand.NP
'There are many stringybarks.' [IK1-170602_1SY1]

There is significant formal similarity between some of the free pronouns in table 4.3 and the realis subject personal prefixes in the verb (table 5.1 in §5.2), cf., for instance, the first person exclusive dual in (4.51). This is not true across the board, however—compare the third person plural in (4.52).

(4.51) **Nganangka ngana**-rninganj bonj~bonj Adelaide ngayi la ||
we.EXCL.DU 1DU.EXCL.NF-sit.PST RDP~exactly A I CONJ
Ngalkodjok.
N
'We were still there at Adelaide, myself and Ngalkodjok.'
[20060901IB03/01:11–15]

(4.52) **Bedbe kadda**-nganj-wom **kadda**-nganj-kidanj kenda=bonj.
they 3PL.NF-HITH-return.PST 3PL.NF-HITH-go.PST DEM.PROX.LOC=exactly
'They returned, came back here.' [20060620IB03/07:32–35]

In third person, the distinction between the use of *kikka* as opposed to *benengka* or *bedbe* (in dual or plural, respectively) is not a sharp one. It seems that there is no categorical difference between these forms, in fact. My impression is that *benengka/bedbe* (4.52, 4.53) are the preferred forms for humans, and *kikka* for non-humans (provided they admit of plural number expression), as in example (4.54), where the protagonists are a Brahminy Kite and an Osprey. Syncretism of *kikka* between class II singular, on the one hand, and all plurals, on the other, reflects a systematic syncretism pattern, found also in the demonstratives (§4.5.3) and noun markers (§4.3).[17]

(4.53) a. **Benengka** bi-burnungka.
they.DU DAT-they.DU.GEN
'It belongs to them two.' [IK1-170516_2DDj1/23:24–26]

b. **Bedbe** kirnda=bonj kadda-rninganj.
they.PL DEM.AFOR.LOC=exactly 3PL.NF-sit.PST
'They stayed over there.' [20060620IB03/20:33–35]

---

17 And arguably in possessum agreement, see discussion in §4.1.3.

(4.54) La **kikka** ngorro kabarra-wandarrkbum.
CONJ they DEM.MED.IV 3DU.NF-err.PST
'And **those two** made a mistake.' [20150212AS01/07:24–26]

The personal pronouns in argument positions are usually redundant because of the pronominal prefixes on the verb, and therefore full pronouns can be dropped. Nevertheless, they may also appear overtly: cf. the pair in (4.55), where in the two contiguous fragments of the narrative the first person pronoun is first absent and then overtly present. There does not seem to be any clear motivation for its absence in one case and presence in another. In some pro-drop languages, such as Hungarian, Latin or Polish, the use of full pronouns is a marked option, typically only used under certain conditions, e.g. contrastive focus. Mushin & Simpson (2008) show that it is also the case in a number of Australian languages where there are obligatory bound pronouns which make features of the referent clear. This does not seem to be the case in Kunbarlang, where using free pronouns is not marked.

(4.55) a. Ngadda-rda-yinj, ngadda-djarrang,
1PL.EXCL.NF-put-REFL.PST 1PL.EXCL.NF-eat.PST

ngadda-makarninjdjanganj.
1PL.EXCL.NF-sing.PST

'We went in, we ate and we sang.' [IK1-160624_0001/01:18–22]

b. Ngemek **ngadbe** ngadda-makarninjdjanganj.
yet we.EXCL.PL 1PL.EXCL.NF-sing.PST

'We sang more.' [ibid./01:23–25]

The third person singular forms of the direct pronouns can be used for the whole range of referents from human to inanimate ones, as long as the noun class is appropriate. Examples of inanimate or non-human animate reference for class I (*nukka*) and class II (*kikka*) are in (4.56). Note that personal pronouns can be in a group with nouns, as in (4.56a). This is the 'determining' use of pronouns, discussed in §4.4.2.

(4.56) a. **Nukka** ngorro **cyclone** ngorro ka-nganj-kidanj ready.
he.I DEM.MED.IV cyclone DEM.MED.IV 3SG.NF-HITH-go.PST ready
'That cyclone was ready and approaching.'
[IK1-160624_0021/02:06–09]

b. **Na-rrambareng nukka** Duwa.
I-ground.honey he.I Duwa
'Honey in the ground is Duwa (moiety).' [20060620IB03/03:01–05]

c. Barninda **kikka**, **bingkibingki**.
   IGNOR she.II baler.shell
   'What's her name, baler shell.'
   [20060620IB04/03:20–22; translation mine—IK]

The direct personal pronouns serve as the base for emphatic pronoun formation, achieved by adding the particles *bonj* 'exactly', *bidju* 'EMPH', or their combination to the pronoun (4.57). Such emphatic pronouns are used in (emphatic) reflexives (§6.1.3.1).

(4.57) **Bedbe=bonj** **bidju** kadda-nganj-kidanj.
   they.PL=exactly EMPH 3PL.NF-HITH-go.PST
   'They came by themselves.' [IK1-160513_0001/53:50]

The paradigm for the oblique personal pronoun stems is given in table 4.4 (based on Coleman n.d.: 12).[18] The oblique stems are bound. To be realised they may be prefixed by either *bi-* 'DAT' or one of the noun class prefixes *kin-* 'I/II' / *man-* 'III' / *kun-* 'IV' (in the situation of alienable possession), which agrees with the possessum head noun (4.58),[19] or else they are right-attached to the inalienable possessum head noun (see §4.1 on the noun classes and §4.6 on possession).

Tab. 4.4: Personal pronoun paradigm: Oblique forms

		Singular	Dual	Plural
First	Exclusive	-ngaybu	-nganungka	-ngadbe
	Inclusive		-ngarrku	
Second		-nungku	-nungunungka	-nungudbe
Third	Class I	-rnungu	-burnungka	-budbe
	Class II	-ngadju		
	Class III	-ngadju	—	—
	Class IV	?	—	—

(4.58) a. Manda mayi neyang **man-ngaybu**.
   DEM.PROX.III NM.III food[III] III-I.GEN
   'This food is mine.' [IK1-170522_1SM1/24:52–54]

---

18 Coleman gives the form *-benengka* as the third person dual, however I hear *-burnungka* in all recordings; the form is exemplified in (4.60). Similarly, for the second plural I consistently hear *-nungudbe* instead of Coleman's variant *-nukudbe*, see (4.61).
19 See §2.7.3 on the simplification of the nasal clusters that affects many of such pronouns.

b. Korro   **kun-nungku** yalbi   kadda-maddjing.
   DEM.MED.LOC IV-you.GEN   country[IV] 3PL.NF-pierce.PST
   'That's your country where they speared it.'   [20060620IB04/11:52–55]

Notice again that there is no number distinction for inanimates, as the rows for class III and IV show. Example (4.59) shows that when the inanimate referent is non-singular, the singular form of the pronoun is used nevertheless. This is consistent with the verbal patterns of noun marking, where inanimates normally do not trigger non-singular agreement either (see §5.2).

(4.59) a. Merre=**ngadju** ka-bun-djarrang   kaburrk mayi   kundulk.
          hair=she.GEN   3SG.NF-3SG.OBJ-eat.PST two   NM.III tree
          'Foliage of two trees burned down.'   [IK1-170531_1YF1]

      b.?/* Merre=**burnungka** ka-bun-djarrang   kaburrk mayi   kundulk.
          hair=they.DU.GEN   3SG.NF-3SG.OBJ-eat.PST two   NM.III tree
          intended: 'Foliage of two trees burned down.'   [IK1-170531_1YF1]

(4.60) Kun-kudji ngayingana bi-**burnungka**.
       IV-one   mother   DAT-they.DU.GEN
       'One mother for both of them.'   [IK1-160424_0001/07:56–58]

(4.61) Kukka ngorro   nga-ngunda   bi-**nungudbe** la   bonj.
       it.IV DEM.MED.IV 1SG.NF-say.PST DAT-you.PL.GEN   CONJ exactly
       'That's what I've told you and that's it.'   [20150413IOv01/12:34–37]

Originally Coleman proposed that there is a distinction between the dual *-ngarrku* and the plural *-ngarrkunungu* in the first person inclusive forms. It appears, however, that the latter is not a form in its own right, but rather *-ngarrku nunu*, i.e. a combination of the only inclusive form with the quantifier *nunu* 'all' (§4.7.3), added to emphasise plurality. This is in agreement with the observation that there is no dual/plural distinction in the first inclusive throughout the paradigms of personal prefixes in the verb (§5.2.1). As example (4.62) shows, the form *-ngarrku* may be used with clearly plural (rather than dual) reading:

(4.62) Ngarrka bi-**ngarrku**   history ngorro   kanj-yuwa   karra
       we.INCL DAT-we.INCL.GEN   history DEM.MED.IV 3SG.FUT-lie.NP DEM.MED.LOC
         djurra.
         paper
       'Our history will be in the book.'   [20150413IOv01/09:17–21]

As can be seen from table 4.4, there are only two known oblique forms for the third person singular, *-rnungu* and *-ngadju*. The former is only for class I (4.58b), whereas the latter is a syncretic form for classes II (4.63) and III (4.59a). I could not find a context to elicit a class IV oblique form, which thus remains a gap in the table.

(4.63) Ninda bi-**ngadju** nayi banikkin.
DEM.PROX.I DAT-she.GEN NM.I cup
'This is her cup.' [IK1-170522_1SM1/22:12–14]

It has been discussed above that direct free pronouns do not contribute emphasis just by virtue of being used as opposed to pro-dropped (see example (4.55)). The same is true for argumental oblique pronouns.[20] Example (4.64) shows the two options used in turn one after the other by the same speaker with the same verb *-ngundje* 'say/do': first, he uses an oblique free pronoun *bi-ngaybu*, and after that, a personal prefix introduced by the benefactive derivation (*ngan-marnanj-*):

(4.64) a. Kadda-ngundje **bi-ngaybu** "kikka Ngalbangardi ka-wokdja
3PL.NF-do.NP DAT-I.GEN she.II N 3SG.NF-speak.NP
Kunbarlang kun-mak ngadda-ngayinj".
Kunbarlang IV-good 1PL.EXCL.NF-hear.PST
'They tell me: "We heard that Ngalbangardi speaks Kunbarlang well."'
[20070108IB01/25:21–26; translation mine—IK]

b. Yoh, nga-ngunda, ngayi ngorro teach im.
yes 1SG.NF-say.PST I DEM.MED.IV [Kriol]
Ka-**ngan-marnanj**-ngunda "Ah aku!"
3SG.NF-1SG.OBJ-BEN-say.PST ah ok
' "Yes", I told them, "I teach her." They said to me "Ah okay!"'
[ibid./25:26–29; translation mine—IK]

The oblique pronouns are used to mark possessors and oblique arguments, the latter including beneficiaries and maleficiaries, addressees (4.64a), stimuli (4.65) etc. The oblique arguments are overviewed in section 5.1; the possessives are discussed in section 4.6.

(4.65) Kadda-rninganj korro rlobbel~rlobbel kadda-rdukidanj **bi-rnungu**.
3PL.NF-sit.PST DEM.MED.LOC RDP~outside 3PL.NF-look.PST DAT-he.GEN
'They were sitting outside looking/waiting **for him**.'
[20060620IB06/2:14–2:19]

---

20 However, recall from §4.4.2 that the oblique pronouns marking a larger noun phrase for case *are* obligatory. See also examples later in the present section.

Since Kunbarlang nouns do not have any case marking whatsoever, the oblique pronominal forms (genitive and dative) can also be used to mark the whole noun phrase as an oblique argument or possessor (4.66). Such a pronoun is obligatory (4.66b; see §4.6 on possessives and §4.4.2 for a discussion of this marking as an argument for NP constituency in Kunbarlang).

(4.66) a. Mary ka-rnay   nayi djurra korro   kun-bodme=**rnungu**
         M   3SG.NF-see.PST NM.I paper DEM.MED.LOC IV-back=he.GEN
         nawalak.
         kid
         'Mary found the book behind the child's back.'
                                                   [IK1-170606_1SY1/30:53–31:28]

   b. *Mary ka-rnay   nayi djurra korro   kun-bodme **nawalak**.
        M   3SG.NF-see.PST NM.I paper DEM.MED.LOC IV-back   kid
        intended: 'Mary found the book behind the child's back.'
                                                   [ibid./31:19–28]

In the following subsections I discuss the human-only pronominal *-buk* 'person' (§4.5.1.1), the contrastive suffix *-ma* (§4.5.1.2) and a coordinate pronominal construction encoding dual referents (§4.5.1.4).

4.5.1.1 The human pronoun *-buk*

There is another pronominal stem which is dedicated to third person human referents (and Dreamtime story characters) only: *-buk* 'person'. This word carries the masculine prefix *na-* or the feminine prefix *ngal-*.

(4.67) a. **Na-buk** kordokmeng ka-kidanj.
         I-person first   3SG.NF-go.PST
         'He went first.'   [IK1-160811_0001/18:33–36]

   b. **Ngal-buk** ki-rnak-kudji.
      II-person   II-LIM-one
      'Just she alone.'   [20060621IB01/01:23–25]

It appears somewhat intermediate between nouns and pronouns (see §3.2.1 and §3.2.7, respectively), and the lexical gloss chosen for it is meant to reflect that status. Among its "noun-y" properties are the prefixes that it takes and the somewhat richer semantics. The prototypical pronouns, such as *nukka* 'he.I' and *kikka* 'she.II' only encode the number and class features of the referent, but *-buk* also specifies that the referent is human, i.e. it has an extra semantic feature compared to those other ones. However, it is analysed here as a pronoun, too, because it does not combine with modifiers typical of nouns (4.68), it is used in the asyndetic pronominal construction (see §4.5.1.4 below) and it takes the pronominal contrastive suffix -*ma* that nouns do not take (example (4.69) and §4.5.1.2).

(4.68)   a.   *kaburrk na-buk 'two men'   [IK1-160523_0011/09:00–03]

        b.   *na-buk ngob 'all men'

        c.   *nukka ngob 'all men'

Example (4.68) shows that -*buk*, just like other singular pronouns (4.68c), cannot combine with quantifiers denoting pluralities. Nouns do not have such restrictions because they are not marked for number and normally allow for both singular and non-singular construal. The following example shows that nouns do not take the contrastive suffix -*ma* often found on the -*buk* pronouns:

(4.69)   a.   **Na-buk-ma**   ka-makarninjdja,   **ngal-buk-ma**   ka-rnekbe.
             I-person-CONTR   3SG.NF-sing.NP   II-person-CONTR   3SG.NF-step.NP
             'He is singing, she is dancing.'   [IK1-170530_1SY2/38:52–56]

        b.   **Djarrang**(*-**ma**) ka-ka=kulkkulk,   **nakarrken**(*-**ma**) ka-ngokmirdam.
             horse-CONTR   3SG.NF-go.NP=run   dog-CONTR   3SG.NF-bark.NP
             'The horse is running, the dog is barking.'   [ibid./48:13–32]

Moreover, there are signs that the forms *nabuk* 'male person' and *ngalbuk* 'female person', on the one hand, and *nukka* 'he' and *kikka* 'she', on the other hand, are in competition in a certain sense. Namely, the -*buk* pronouns are used with the clitic *bonj* 'exactly' about twice as often as the -*kka* pronouns (4.71), and only the former but not the latter are used with the contrastive suffix -*ma* (§4.5.1.2). At the same time, only the -*kka* forms, but not the -*buk* ones, are used in a determiner-like function in multiword noun phrases (as in 4.71b; see further §4.4.2). Interestingly, both *bonj* and -*ma* shift stress from the class prefix *na-/ngal-* onto the stem -*buk*. That in turn leads to lenition of the stem-initial /p/ from the clear stop realisation [b] to [w], which is further eroded after /l/ up to inaudibility (2.26a–b vs. 2.26c–d). Such a stark contrast between post-tonic and pre-tonic realisation of consonants, or /p/ in particular, is not attested anywhere else (see §2.7).

(4.70)   a.   /na-puk/ → [ˈnabuk]

        b.   /ŋal-puk/ → [ˈŋalbuk]

        c.   /na-puk=poɲ/ → [naˈwukboɲ]

        d.   /ŋal-puk-ma/ → [ŋalˈukma]

(4.71) a. **Ngal-buk=bonj** ka-bun-merre-rnanj
 II-person=exactly 3SG.NF-3SG.OBJ-hair-see.NP

   la ngal-buk-ma=wali.
   CONJ II-person-CONTR=turn

   'They (two girls) are delousing each other in turn.' [lit. 'She$_j$ is looking at her$_k$ hair and it's her$_k$ turn.'] [IK1-160809_0001/09:32–36]

 b. **Mukka=bonj** kurrambalk, ka-ngunda turn hundred years old.
   it.III=exactly house 3SG.NF-do.PST turn hundred years old

   'That house [church], it turned one hundred years old.'
   [IK1-160719_0001/00:19–25]

Two following subsections discuss constructions characteristic of the *-buk* pronouns, viz. the contrastive use with the suffix *-ma* and the asyndetic dual coordination.

4.5.1.2 Contrastive *-ma*

Kunbarlang personal pronouns can take a contrastive/emphatic suffix *-ma*; consider (4.72), where the first person protagonist in the second part (b) contrasts with the third person agent set up in the context (4.72a). This suffix probably is cognate with the Bininj Kunwok formative *-man*, which occurs in the emphatic pronominal series (Evans 2003a: 263).

(4.72) a. Kun-kudji ngarrki-rnilakka kanj-ka ka-rna
   IV-one 1.INCL.FUT-send.NP 3SG.FUT-go.NP 3SG.NF-sit.NP

   kanj-bunj.
   3SG.FUT-hit.NP

   'We'll send him back to get more.' [20150212AS01/03:59–04:02]

 b. La **ngarrka-ma** ngarrki-kali mulurr ngarrki-ka.
   CONJ we.INCL-CONTR 1.INCL.FUT-get.NP driftwood 1.INCL.FUT-go.NP

   'And us mob, we'll get driftwood and we'll go.' [ibid./04:02–06]

This suffix attaches only to direct forms and never to oblique ones. The suffix has a plural allomorph *-rrema* (4.73).[21]

---

[21] There is one attested form *ngadma* 'we (exclusive, contrastive)' [C02-026607/01:42–44]. This suggests historical separability of the formative *-be* common to the plural forms of all persons except the first person inclusive (cf. table 4.3; the inclusive free and bound forms are in fact numberless, see §5.2.1 on the latter). In this light it is quite probable that *-be* is historically a plural marker, and that the original allomorphy is *be~berre*, rather than *ma~rrema*. See also footnote 19 on page 80. Despite the plausibility of this historical analysis, the synchronic picture is more economically captured by the analysis offered in the body text.

(4.73) **Ngudbe-rrema** la   **ngadbe-rrema**.
        you.PL-CONTR   CONJ   we.EXCL.PL-CONTR
        'You guys and we.'   [20150413IOv01/08:18–21]

It also selects for idiosyncratic stem allomorphs of the first and second person singular pronouns and the second person plural one, not found on any other contexts. The pronoun *ngayi* 'I' has the contrastive allomorph *nganj-* (4.74), the pronoun *ngudda* 'you (SG)' has the allomorph *nji-* (4.74b), and *nukudbe* 'you (PL)'—*ngudbe-* (4.73). The clitic =*wali* 'turn' is discussed in §4.5.1.3.

(4.74) a. Na-buk   werrk   ka-rdokme   babi   la   **nganj-ma**=wali
           I-person   immediately   3SG.NF-leave.NP   later CONJ I-CONTR=turn
           nganj-rdokme.
           1SG.FUT-leave.NP
           'He goes first and then it's my turn to go.'   [IK1-170525_1SY1]

        b. Ka-birrinja   kuyi   ngarrk-burrun-karrme,   **nji-ma**   la
           3SG.NF-same.NP   NM.IV   1.INCL.NF-3DU.OBJ-get.NP   you.SG-CONTR   CONJ
           nganj-ma.
           I-CONTR
           'It is similar what we've got [dog-wise], you and I.'
                                                           [IK1-180606_1SM1/08:14–20]

4.5.1.3 The 'turn' construction

Kunbarlang has a clitic that yields the meaning 'X's turn'. It is most often found with contrastive personal pronouns (4.75a; see §4.5.1.2), but has also been recorded with nouns (4.75b), demonstratives (4.75c; §4.5.3), and ignoratives (4.75d; §4.5.4).

(4.75) a. Kun-kudji   kinj-ka   kinj-kali   **nji-ma=wali**.
           IV-one   2SG.FUT-go.NP   2SG.FUT-get.NP   you.SG-CONTR=turn
           'Go once again and get [some more fish], it is your turn.'
                                                           [20150212AS01/05:59–06:01]

        b. Nakangila   ka-mangarninjdjanganj   ka-burnbum,   yirrkbonj
           N   3SG.NF-sing.PST   3SG.NF-finish.PST   then
           Nawamud=wali   ka-mangarninjdja.
           N=turn   3SG.NF-sing.NP
           'Nakangila sang, he stopped, now Nawamut is singing in his turn.'
                                                           [IK1-170601_1SY1/04:27–37]

c. Ka-bun-djinj werrk kaddum babi la kuyi
   3SG.NF-3SG.OBJ-eat.NP immediately above later CONJ NM.IV
   karnda=way=wali ngadda-ngorrordam ka-bun-djinj
   DEM.DIST.LOC=HITH=turn 1PL.EXCL.NF-turn.NP 3SG.NF-3SG.OBJ-eat.NP
   ngob.
   all
   'It [the damper] bakes first on the top and then on the other side in turn, we turn it around and it bakes completely.' [IK1-160726_0021/00:50–01:01]

d. Ngadda-bakdjungi **barninda=wali** karrbbere.
   1PL.EXCL.IRR.PST-descend.IRR.PST IGNOR=turn mangrove_worm
   'We would go down [to the beach to get] whatsit now, mangrove worms.'
   [20060620IB03/00:51–55; translation mine—IK]

The use with the ignorative in example (4.75d) does not seem to literally relate to the position of the referent in an ordered sequence, but rather appears to be employed to structure the narration. That is, it is used to say something along the lines of "what is the next topic in turn?", rather than "after doing this and that we'd go down for the mangrove worms".

This 'turn' construction is structurally identical to the Bininj Kunwok 'turn'-construction, which uses a cognate clitic =*wali* (Evans 2003a: 258). Mawng also has a similar construction, and the particle *ali* clearly appears related (Singer 2006: 39).

4.5.1.4 Dual pronouns: asyndetic coordinate construction

In addition to the dual forms in table 4.3 there is an asyndetic coordinate construction for pronominal expression of the dual referents, listed in table 4.5. When the two referents are of different person, it is in essence juxtaposition of two personal pronominals in the order SECOND–FIRST–THIRD PERSON (4.76).

(4.76) a. **Ngayi na-buk** ngana-yunganj hospital.
        I I-person 1DU.EXCL.NF-lie.PST hospital
        'He and I slept in hospital.' [20060620IB03/25:10–12]

     b. Babi la ngarrki-rna ngarrki-wokdja lerrk Kunbarlang
        later CONJ 1.INCL.FUT-sit.NP 1.INCL.FUT-speak.NP word K
        ngudda ngayi.
        you.SG I
        'And then we'll sit and speak Kunbarlang language, you and I.'
        [IK1-160828_0011]

c. **Ngudda ngal-buk** ngundji-nganj-ka.
you   II-person   2DU.FUT-HITH-go.NP
'You and she, you two will come.'   [IK1-170601_1SY1/53:25–30]

For the case when both referents are of the third person, however, two singular pronouns cannot be juxtaposed. Instead, a dual third person pronoun must be used, either alone (4.77a) or in the inclusory construction (4.77b and §4.5.2; see also Singer 2001). The difference between the asyndetic construction (as in (4.76)) and the inclusory construction (IC; 4.77b) is that the former expresses semantic coordination, whereas the latter combines expressions for a set and its subset. Thus, in (4.77b) the referent of *ngalbuk* 'she' is a (singleton) subset of the dual referent of *benengka* 'they two'.

(4.77) a. **Benengka-ma** wularrud ngorro   kabarra-djirrkkanginj.
         they.DU-CONTR already   DEM.MED.IV   3DU.NF-push.PST
         'They two have already pushed off [the driftwood].'
                                                           [20150212AS01/04:31–34]

b. Kabarra-rna=lorr   **benengka ngal-buk**.
    3DU.NF-sit.NP=lean   they.DU   II-person
    'They two (one of them a woman) are sitting leaning against each other.'
                                                       [IK1-160812_0001/37:17–20]

Although I analyse these third person dual forms as an inclusory construction, I include them in table 4.5 for reference.

Tab. 4.5: Coordinate and inclusory dual pronouns

First & Second	ngudda ngayi	'you I'
First & Third	ngayi nabuk	'I he'
	ngayi ngalbuk	'I she'
Second & Third	ngudda nabuk	'you he'
	ngudda ngalbuk	'you she'
Third & Third	benengka nabuk	'they (two) he'
	benengka ngalbuk	'they (two) she'

Coleman (n.d.: 10) lists the form *beneka* for the third & third combination, but I have encountered only one instance of that variant (see example 4.78 below). When asked about the correct form, my speakers give *benengka*. It's not likely to be a dialect difference, as other speakers of the same clan (Kunkamulkbarn) as the speaker of (4.78) confirm the variant *benengka* (4.77). Perhaps *beneka* is an older variant, or one dialectal variant taking over, or even an occasional feature of faster speech.

(4.78) **beneka** la   Ngal-bulanj
        they.DU CONJ N
        'those two [Matt and Ngal-bulanj]'   [20060814IB01/02:26–29]

Notice also that in example (4.78)—unlike the forms cited in table 4.5—there is a free conjunction *la*. This seems to be unusual in the context of Australian inclusory constructions, as Singer (2001: 48) notes: "The use of free conjunctions in Australian ICs seems to be rare. For example, although these participate in nominal coordination in [Wubuy], Dyirbal, Arrente, Lardil and Warlpiri they do not normally participate in ICs." The ICs in Kunbarlang are taken up more generally in §4.5.2. Given that this is a one-off example, however, it is more likely to be a 'sloppy' occasional use of the conjunction in comitative, rather than additive, sense.

My speakers inform me that when one member of the pair is female and the other male, either of *nabuk/ngalbuk* is appropriate. Thus, *benengka ngal-buk* really means something along the lines of 'these two, including a woman', and *benengka na-buk*, conversely, 'these two, including a man' (see example (4.81) in section §4.5.2).

4.5.2 Inclusory constructions

Similarly to many Australian languages (Singer 2001), Kunbarlang has INCLUSORY CONSTRUCTIONS. Consider examples in (4.79):

(4.79) a. Mabidj **ngandji**-burrk-ka.
            yB   1DU.EXCL.FUT-COLL-go.NP
            'Younger brother and I shall go (together).'   [IK1-160427_1SY1]

        b. Kirnda   **ngana**-kalbi-yinj   Ngalngarridj.
            DEM.AFOR.LOC   1DU.EXCL.NF-get-REFL.PST   N
            'There Ngalngarridj and I married.' [lit. 'got each other']
                                                          [20150413IOv01/07:39–41]

In (4.79a) there is only one singular noun phrase *mabidj* 'younger brother', but the verb shows dual number first person agreement. The use of the inclusory construction allows the speaker to construe the set of two referents (the speaker and his *mabidj*, reflected in the subject prefix), while only using a nominal to refer to a *subset* of that set. Likewise, in (4.79b) the name *Ngalngarridj* refers to a subset of the two-member set denoted by the subject prefix *ngana-*. As (4.79) shows, the *superset* (expression denoting the maximal set) in Kunbarlang can be expressed by the bound pronominal only, without a free pronominal (Singer's (2001) *Type 2*). I have encountered one example where the inclusory construction expresses a possessor within a noun phrase (4.80).

(4.80) Nayi nawalak ka-kanginj djabirrk **bi-burnungka** **nayi**
NM.I child 3SG.NF-take.PST swag DAT-they.DU.GEN NM.I
kabarradjanganj korro manberrk.
sibling DEM.MED.LOC bush

'The boy took his and his brother's swags and went to the bush.' [lit. 'the swag(s) of theirs (dual) his sibling'] [IK1-160513_0021/14:37–44]

The oblique pronoun *burnungka* 'they.DU', which marks the noun phrase as possessive, is showing the actual number of referents as two, although *kabarradjanganj* 'sibling' is construed as singular, as is evident from the form of the noun marker (since on the non-singular construal it would have been *ngayi* 'NM.PL'). This example is interesting because on the first impression it may be classified as Singer's (2001) *Type 1*, but in fact the free pronoun may be analysed as a dative case marker (see §4.4.2), rather than a proper constituent of an inclusory noun phrase. Since this is the only available example of such a structure, it is not clear at present whether it can be subsumed under one of Singer's (2001) types (her database does not contain adnominal uses of the IC).

Finally, we find cases where both a free pronoun and a bound pronoun encode the superset, as in (4.81):[22]

(4.81) Ngayi nga-kalng na-worrkbam barbung, la **benengka na-buk**
I 1SG.NF-get.PST I-few fish CONJ they.DU I-person
kabarra-kalng na-rleng.
3DU.NF-get.PST I-much

'I caught little fish, and those two guys caught plenty.' [IK1-160819_0001]

The superset is expressed by the dual pronoun *benengka* and the dual subject prefix *kabarra-*, and the human pronoun *na-buk* is encoding that one of the referents is male ('they two, including a man').

4.5.3 Demonstratives

According to Coleman (n.d.: 8–9) Kunbarlang demonstratives encode four degrees of referential distance: proximal, medial, distal and aforementioned. The first three have to do with physical proximity, and the last one with referential proximity. Besides that, the demonstratives in adnominal function agree with the head noun in the noun class (see 4.1). Some examples are given in (4.82) below, illustrating the four referential distance series:

---

22 This is the rare *Type 3* of Singer 2001.

Tab. 4.6: Kunbarlang demonstratives noun class paradigm

Class	Proximal	Medial	Distal	Aforementioned
I	ninda	nirra	narnda	nirnda
II	nginda	ngirra	ngarnda	ngirnda
III	manda	marra	marnda	marnda
IV	ngondo	ngorro	ngarnda	ngornda
Plural	nginda	?	?	ngirnda

(4.82) a. **Manda**   mankarre ngadbe   kirdimarrk.
   DEM.PROX.III law   we.EXCL.PL man
   '**This** is the law for us aboriginal people.'
   [RS1-140/05:03–06; translation mine—IK]

b. **Nirra**   nayi binana ka-dja   korro   clinic.
   DEM.MED.I NM.I banana 3SG.NF-stand.NP DEM.MED.LOC clinic
   'There are banana trees near the clinic.'   [IK1-170516_1SY1]

c. Ka-kidanj   korro   **narnda**   Jimmy ka-yuwa.
   3SG.NF-go.PST DEM.MED.LOC DEM.DIST.I J   3SG.NF-lie.NP
   'S/he went to where **that** Jimmy is camping.'
   [IK1-160811_0001/25:48–52]

d. Madjarkadj ngulamngulam ngadda-rlakwang
   [toponym]   morning   1PL.EXCL.NF-throw.PST

   ngirnda=bonj.
   DEM.AFOR.PL=exactly

   'In the morning we left Madjarkadj and those [people that I have just mentioned].'   [20140709IOv05/03:46–50]

e. **Nginda**   karrakenda kabarra-kidanj?
   DEM.PROX.PL where   3DU.NF-go.PST
   'Where have **those two** gone?'   [20150212AS01/05:04–06]

The paradigm of all the noun class forms is in table 4.6. The plural forms are my addition to Coleman's (n.d.) paradigm (4.82e). The proximal series is the default one.

Plural reference of a demonstrative can also be constructed by adding the suffix -*dju* 'COLL' on the singular form of a demonstrative (4.83).

(4.83) **Ninda-dju**   ngob kadda-rnekbe   (barramimbanj kirdimarrk).
   DEM.PROX.I-COLL all   3PL.NF-step.NP   woman   man
   'They're all dancing (women and men).'   [IK1-170530_1SY2/38:00–04]

In addition to the four series that agree with the head noun in adnominal function, there is another series of demonstratives in Kunbarlang, viz. the *locative* demonstratives. In their pronominal/standalone use they mean 'here', 'there', etc.; the medial *korro/karra* also has an adnominal use, for which see below. This series shows the same four distance gradations as the other demonstratives, and has formal similarities to the noun class series (see table 4.7).

Tab. 4.7: Kunbarlang locative demonstratives paradigm

Series	Proximal	Medial	Distal	Aforementioned
LOC	kenda	korro/karra	karnda	kirnda

However, the locative demonstratives do not interact with the noun class system: they retain the same form regardless of the class of the noun they occur with (4.84). Thus, the medial locative demonstrative *korro* is used with a class I noun in (4.84a) and a class IV noun in (4.84b). For this reason, I describe the locative series as synchronically separate from the noun class system.

(4.84) a. Ngarrk-ngundje mawamawa, and **korro** **mawa**, ngabbard.
1.INCL.NF-do.NP FFF ENG DEM.MED.LOC FF[I] F
'[From the one that] we call great-grandfather, and to the grandfather and father.' [IK1-160424_0001/01:02–08]

b. Nga-ka **korro** **kodbarre**.
1SG.NF-go.NP DEM.MED.LOC house[IV]
'I'm going towards the house.' [IK1-180518_1SY1/12:28–30]

Furhermore, it is only the medial locative demonstrative *korro/karra* which productively combines with a wide range of nouns, as in (4.84). Such constructions look and function like prepositional phrases with a generic locative preposition,[23] but an analysis of it as ambiguous between a demonstrative and a preposition is not warranted (cf. §3.2.9). The syntax of these combinations is of yet ill-understood; but this use of the medial demonstrative together with a nominal constituent figures prominently in locative relative clause formation (§8.4.1). The other demonstratives only combine with place names and inherently locational expressions (4.85).

(4.85) **Kenda** Warruwi.
DEM.PROX.LOC W
'Here in Warruwi.' [IK1-160525_0001/00:31]

---

[23] Interestingly, the neighbouring Mawng has the locative/allative preposition *tuka*, formally identical to the Land gender proximal demonstrative (Singer 2016: 34).

The locative demonstratives, like the other ones, can combine with the collective suffix *-dju* (4.86):

(4.86) Yimarne **korro-dju** kun-barndanganj.
 like DEM.MED.LOC-COLL IV-wide
 'Like everywhere in a big area.' [C02-026607/02:32–35]

It is plausible that this series of demonstratives is historically related to the noun class system. Evans (2003a: 34–5) mentions an ancient (at least at the level of proto-Gunwinyguan) gender prefixation system of five classes, which included masculine, feminine, vegetable, and two "neuter" classes, with prefixes *ku-* and *ra(k)-*. This system collapsed in several descendant languages, including Kunbarlang, which now only distinguishes four classes of nouns. Perhaps the fifth class, the archaic *ra(k)-*, collapsed with class four (*ku(n)-*) for all Kunbarlang nominals but the demonstratives. Indeed, Coleman (n.d.: 2) analyses the locative series as noun class V. Additional corroboration for the view that all demonstratives are things of a same kind may come from the fact that combinations of a locative demonstrative with an agreeing adnominal one do not occur in spontaneous discourse and are dispreferred in elicitation. However, the idiosyncratic non-agreeing behaviour of the purported 'class LOC' demonstratives, taken together with the absence of any correspondence to that class in Kunbarlang nouns, leads me to treat these demonstratives as a separate, locative series.

Notice that there are two forms for the medial locative demonstrative in table 4.7: *korro* and *karra*. This is not regular allophony of /o/ or /a/ (§2.3), and there does not seem to be any semantic difference between the variants; currently the reason why there are these two variants is unclear.

There are certain collocations where demonstratives co-occur with each other or with other pronominals. This occurrence of the medial class IV demonstrative *ngorro* as the second word in a group of pronominals is a major pattern (4.87). In such combinations, *ngorro* remains invariant; it does not function as a demonstrative, but rather modifies the other pronominal (see also §4.5.3.1 below on its discourse functions). The first word, which agrees with the head noun, can be either a third person pronoun (one of *nukka/kikka/mukka/kukka*) (4.87a), or another demonstrative (4.87b).

(4.87) a. Kunkarrnim, yoh, kabarra-walkki-bukayinj **mukka ngorro**
 K yes 3DU.NF-COM-rise.PST it.III DEM.MED.IV
 kubbunj.
 canoe[III]
 'They landed with that canoe at Kunkarrnim.'
 [IK1-160624_0021/03:22–26]

b. **Ninda ngorro** badjubadju ngadda-rda-yinj.
    DEM.PROX.I DEM.MED.IV shirt[I]   1PL.EXCL.NF-enter-REFL.PST
    'This is the shirt we were wearing.' [IK1-160624_0001/06:29–32]

In both examples in (4.87), the first element in the construction agrees with the head noun in the noun class: *mukka kubbunj* "it.III canoe[III]", *ninda badjubadju* "this.I shirt[I]". On the other hand, *ngorro* does not change.

This use of *ngorro* appears to indicate GIVENNESS of the referent (Chafe 1976, Krifka 2008), and may be related to its discourse functions discussed in §4.5.3.1 below. This is not, however, the recognitional use of the demonstrative, since that by definition is *hearer old*, but *discourse new* (Himmelmann 1996, Diessel 1999: 106). Recognitional use is not a prominent use of demonstratives in Kunbarlang at all, as far as I can tell; this is perhaps somewhat surprising given that Himmelmann (1996) finds it as an important function across the languages in his sample. Moreover, he points out that a number of Australian languages have special series of recognitional demonstratives (1996: 231–3). Probably the closest to a recognitional use in Kunbarlang would be the distal *narnda* in (4.82c); this agrees with Himmelmann's finding that it is usually the distal series that has this function.

An interesting property of Kunbarlang demonstratives is that when they are used to talk about the location of a referent (e.g., in a response to the question, *Where is X?*), they still have to agree with the referent's noun class, rather than have the locative form. To make a crude parallel, this would be as if in response to *Where is the pen?* one said *This (one)*. The following set of examples (4.89) illustrates the actual pattern of (some) conceivable answers to the question (4.88).

(4.88) Karrakenda nayi pencil?
       where   NM.I pencil
       'Where is the pencil[I]?' [IK1-170516_1SY1/45:29–31]

(4.89) Answers to (4.88): [IK1-170516_1SY1/45:33–51:09]

    a. **Ninda** ka-yuwa.
       DEM.PROX.I 3SG.NF-lie.NP
       'Here it is.' [lit. 'This (class I) is lying.']

    b. ***Kenda /** ***Ngondo** (ka-yuwa).
       DEM.PROX.LOC DEM.PROX.IV 3SG.NF-lie.NP
       with pointing, intended: 'Here it is.' [cf. e]

    c. **Ninda** ka-yunganj kenda.
       DEM.PROX.I 3SG.NF-lie.PST DEM.PROX.LOC
       'It was here.'

d. **Kenda** ka-yunganj.
   DEM.PROX.LOC 3SG.NF-lie.PST
   'It was here.' [can be said if one infers the pencil's former location from e.g. seeing a stain it left]

e. **Kenda** ka-yuwa.
   DEM.PROX.LOC 3SG.NF-lie.NP
   'That's where I keep it.' [cf. b]

The key contrast is between (4.89a) and (4.89b): in the former the demonstrative agrees in the noun class with *pencil* (class I), while in the latter it is from the locative series or shows 'country/places'-class (IV) agreement, both of which are out if the speaker is pointing at the sought pencil.[24] The options (4.89d) and (4.89e) show additionally that the locative demonstrative *kenda* can be used only when it refers to the *place* itself, i.e. the former or the habitual location of the referent in question. This suggests that Kunbarlang demonstratives have a strong locative component to their semantics, such that even in the situation where identification not of the *referent*, but of *its location* is at stake, the demonstrative nevertheless agrees in noun class with that referent.[25]

4.5.3.1 Discourse functions of the demonstrative *ngorro*

The class IV medial demonstrative *ngorro* is used for discourse coherence functions. One of these functions is marking the logical connection between propositions, typically the consequential connection (4.90), or indication of inference (4.91). Notice the position of *ngorro* in the apodosis clause of (4.90): it occupies the second position, as linkers often do in Kunbarlang (see §8).

---

[24] Given that *pencil* belongs to noun class I, the 'country' class IV is inappropriate here anyway, and in other examples only the locative *kenda* is shown.

[25] Two interesting points of comparison are to be made. In Mawng, the proximate demonstrative sometimes appears to mean 'here' rather than 'this' (Ruth Singer, p.c.), quite similar to Kunbarlang. On the other hand, in Bantu an adnominal determiner will show locative agreement (class 17) when its head noun is contained within a prepositional phrase (i), being the inverse of Kunbarlang:

(i) Kom (Grassfields Bantu; Chia 1983:83 via Watters 2003: 244)

a. ndō   *yèā/**zia**   mà tí   yūin.
   CL.9.house *CL.17.that/CL.9.that   I   PAST:3 buy
   'the house that I bought'

b. ndō   **yèā**/*zia   mà tí   yūin.
   CL.9.house CL.17.that/*CL.9.that   I   PAST:3 buy
   'in the house that I bought'

(4.90) Kuyi ngudda kinj-rnekbe nayi djang, ngarrki-warr-mi
NM.IV you.SG 2SG.FUT-step.NP NM.I dreaming.site 1.INCL.FUT-bad-INCH.NP
ngob, ngarrka **ngorro** ngarrki-warr-mi.
all we.INCL DEM.MED.IV 1.INCL.FUT-bad-INCH.NP
'If you step on that dreaming site, we all will die.'
[IK1-160802_0001/40:58–41:12]

(4.91) Ngunda ngarra-rna ngalkordo, **ngorro** karlu njunjuk.
not 1SG.IRR.NP-see.IRR.NP brolga DEM.MED.IV NEG.PRED water
'I don't see brolgas, therefore no water.' [IK1-160726_0001/14:31–37]

In this use *ngorro* is optionally accompanied by the class IV free pronoun *kukka*, whereby the two form a complex expression similar to 'that's it':[26]

(4.92) Ngunda ngarra-rna ngalkordo, **kukka ngorro** njunjuk
not 1SG.IRR.NP-see.IRR.NP brolga it.IV DEM.MED.IV water
karlu.
NEG.PRED
'I don't see brolgas, therefore no water.' [IK1-160726_0001/13:59–14:16]

Diessel (1999: 125) observes that demonstratives to sentence connectives is a well-attested grammaticalisation scenario. Within Australia, for instance, McConvell (2006) describes a variety of such complementizers in the Ngumpin-Yapa languages.

4.5.4 Interrogatives, indefinites and ignoratives

There is a set of four forms whose primary occurrences are either as question words or as indefinites. I call these forms INTERROGATIVES, for the least marked form arguably is the one with the constituent question word function (in accordance with strong typological finding that indefinites may derive from interrogatives, but not the other way around; see Haspelmath 1997). Essentially they are narrow scope existential pronouns, whose reading depends on the operator that takes immediate scope over them.[27]

Example (4.93) shows their three main uses: interrogative (4.93a), existential indefinite (4.93b), and 'negative indefinite' (4.93c), illustrated by the root *birlinj*, whose core

---

[26] This composite expression, *kukka ngorro* 'that's it', is also used as an exhaustive narrative marker, e.g. at the end of the story.
[27] Mushin (1995) coins the term *epistememe* for the forms that serve as ontological categorisation of discourse referents and that may take on interrogative, indefinite, hesitation and complementising functions. She suggests that their epistemological contribution is the basis for such functional development.

category is *manner* 'how', but its felicitous free translations include also 'when' and 'what'. A further interesting (and fairly coincidental) feature of the collection in (4.93) is that it illustrates the polyfunctionality of the verb *-ngundje* 'do'.

(4.93) a. La   na-barrkidbe **birlinj** ka-ngundje? Na-wanjak?
CONJ I-other   how   3SG.NF-do.NP I-little
'And what is the other like? Little?'   [IK1-170610_2SM1/01:02–08]

b. Ninda   **birlinj-nuk** ka-bun-marnanj-ngunda.
DEM.PROX.I how-INDF   3SG.NF-3SG.OBJ-BEN-do.PST
'This one said something to him.'   [IK1-170624_1PN1/30:37–42]

c. Nga-mikwang.   **Ngunda birlinj ki-ngundje**   la
1SG.NF-stuck.PST   not   how   3SG.IRR.NP-do.IRR.NP CONJ
ngarra-bing.
1SG.IRR.NP-exit.IRR.NP
'I'm stuck. Can't do anything to get out.' [lit. 'It **wouldn't do anyhow** so that I would get out.']   [IK1-180521_2SY1/08:52–58]

In (4.93a) *birlinj* is in a question, and thus functions as a question word that marks the focus of the question (constituent question formation is further discussed in 7.4.2). The interrogative in (4.93b) is in the scope of the existential operator marked by the suffix *-nuk*, and thus it has an existential indefinite reading 'somehow'/'something'. Finally, in (4.93c) *birlinj* is in the scope of negation, and since the interrogative always takes narrow scope, the reading is that of a negated existential.[28]

4.5.4.1 Interrogatives proper
The INTERROGATIVES in Kunbarlang include five major ontological categories, lexicalised as four main interrogative expressions:
- *-kaybi* 'which [person]', 'who' (an adjective)
- *barda* 'what'
- *birlinj* 'how; when'
- *karrakenda* 'where'

The person interrogative, *-kaybi* is an adjective and agrees in person and number with the understood referent. I discuss it here due its similarity in function, including the ability to take the indefinite suffix *-nuk* (see below). Its meaning is best captured as 'which [person]', but since it occurs without an overt noun most of the time, I chose to

---

[28] While negation always is overt, the question operator is covert and the existential operator may be covert, too (4.106).

gloss it consistently as 'who' throughout the grammar. The default agreement is the singular masculine prefix *na-* (4.94a), but the question word can also be construed as asking about a female (4.94b) or a plural individual (4.94c).

(4.94) a. **Na-kaybi** ninda?
    I-who   DEM.PROX.I
    'Who's that?'   [IK1-160624_0001/01:45–47]

  b. **Kin-kaybi** ki-marnanj-ngunda?
    II-who   2SG.NF-BEN-do.PST
    'Who was that woman you spoke with?'   [IK1-170606_1SY1/44:33–34]

  c. **Kinbadda-kaybi** kadda-nganj-kidanj?
    PL-who   3PL.NF-HITH-go.PST
    'Who all came?'   [IK1-160610_0011/25:35–37]

Being an adjective, it can modify overt noun heads (4.95):

(4.95) **Kin-kaybi barramimbanj** ka-nganj-kidanj?
    II-who   woman   3SG.NF-HITH-go.PST
    'Which woman came?'   [IK1-160610_0011/23:53–56]

If the referent is not third person, as in the question *Who are you?* (4.96), the prefix is selected accordingly:

(4.96) Adju, ngudda **kirri-kaybi**?
    dunno you   2SG-who
    'Hey, who are you?'   [IK1-180520_1DDj1/01:11:28–29]

The interrogative *barda* 'what' is used to ask about inanimate objects (4.97). It is also used to inquire about reason, meaning 'what for' or 'why'. In that case it takes on the genitive case by attaching the genitive masculine pronoun *-rnungu* as an enclitic (4.98).

(4.97) La   **barda** ngemek kirnda   ki-karrme?
    CONJ what   yet   DEM.AFOR.LOC 2SG.NF-hold.NP
    'And what else have you got there?'   [IK1-170610_2SM1/27:25–28]

(4.98) **Barda=rnungu** ki-kalng   kekkek?
    what=he.GEN   2SG.NF-get.PST bone
    'Why did you buy a bone?'   [IK1-170615_1SY1/04:39–41]

The interrogative *birlinj* is rather multifunctional. Its core meaning is probably 'how', as in *Birlinj ki-ngundje?* 'How are you doing?', perhaps a calque from the English greeting. Besides, it is extensively used in combination with the verb *-ngundje* 'say/do' to inquire about qualities, functioning as 'which; what kind'. Example (4.99) is a fragment from a recording of a spot-the-difference game, where the participants employed this construction frequently:

(4.99) IK1-170610_2SM1/07:17–27

    A: Ngudda mandjad?
         you   straight
         'Is your [road] straight?'

    B: Yoh.
         yes
         'Yes.'

    A: Ngayi karlu.
         I   NEG.PRED
         'Mine isn't.'

    B: **Birlinj ka-ngundje?**
         how   3SG.NF-do.NP
         'What is it like?' [lit. 'How does it do?']

It can be used to inquire about the reason (4.100):

(4.100) **Birlinj** kabarra-karlung?
        how   3DU.NF-dig.PST
        'Why have they two dug [the pit]?'   [IK1-170625_1PN1]

It is also used to talk about time (4.101). This example also shows that interrogatives can combine with nouns in a determiner-like fashion: the structure here is [[[birlinj kanak] kangundje] kinjka].

(4.101) **Birlinj kanak** ka-ngundje   kinj-ka?
        how   sun   3SG.NF-do.NP   2SG.FUT-go.NP
        'What time are you going?'   [IK1-170626_1PN1/49:10–13]

It is even found in the spatial interrogative use, i.e. in asking 'where'. However, this is only used to request details (e.g., the name) of an aforementioned location (4.102), and not to ask about location of sought objects.

(4.102) A: Korro kun-rnungu yalbi.
DEM.MED.LOC IV-he.GEN country
'In his country.' [20060831IB03/05:20–22]

B: **Birlinj** kenda?
how DEM.PROX.LOC
'Where is that?' [20060831IB03/05:28–29]

A: Mayirri.
M
'Mayirri.' [20060831IB03/05:30]

The conventional way to ask about location of objects and events is using *karrakenda* (4.103), which seems to be a lexicalised combination of a medial and a proximal locative demonstratives.

(4.103) A: **Karrakenda** mukka kabarra-bum marderr?
where it.III 3DU.NF-hit.PST creek
'Where did those two make that creek?' [20150212AS01/02:06–07]

B: Manda.
DEM.PROX.III
'There.' [ibid./02:08]

There are no possessive interrogatives. Instead, the person interrogative *-kaybi* is marked for genitive (4.104) or dative, as in a regular possessive construction; see §4.2 above for case marking and §4.6 below on possession.

(4.104) **Na-kaybi kin-rnungu** ninda djurra?
I-who I/II-he.GEN DEM.PROX.I paper
'Whose book is this?' [IK1-160427_1SY1]

The following subsection discusses the use of interrogatives in the indefinite reading in declaratives.

4.5.4.2 Indefinites
As stated above, Kunbarlang indefinites are formed from base form interrogatives. There are two main indefinite readings: existential and negative. The existential indefinites are used to refer to individuals and objects that the speaker cannot identify, or can, but decides not to. Normally they are formed with the suffix *-nuk* 'INDF' (4.105), although see below for bare forms.

(4.105) a. La nga-mabulunj **na-kaybi-nuk** kanj-bun-wunj neyang
CONJ 1SG.NF-like.NP I-who-INDF 3SG.FUT-3SG.OBJ-give.NP food
Fluffy kuyi nganj-ka.
F NM.IV 1SG.FUT-go.NP
'And I want someone to feed Fluffy when I go.'
[IK1-160513_0011/01:58–02:21]

b. Kinj-wunj mayi neyang kanj-djinj or barbung or
2SG.FUT-give.NP NM.III food 3SG.FUT-eat.NP or fish or
barda-nuk kinj-wunj.
what-INDF 2SG.FUT-give.NP
'Give him food to eat or fish or something [i.e., share it with him].'
[RS1-140/04:31–36]

c. Adju ngawakwanj, **birlinj-nuk**.
dunno 1SG.NF-ignorant.NP how-INDF
'I don't know when, some time.'
[IK1-170614_1PG1/35:29–31]

d. Wigu **karrakenda-nuk** kukka-dju: Anjaminali, Andiwarnmalk,
W where-INDF it.IV-COLL A A
Wiala welenj ngadda-bum.
W road 1PL.EXCL.NF-hit.PST
'We made roads at Wigu and elsewhere: Anjaminali, Andiwarnmalk, Wiala.'
[20060620IB03/14:46–15:00]

In example (4.105d) the indefinite *karrakendanuk* 'somewhere' combines with *kukka-dju*, class IV personal pronoun with collective suffix, which means roughly 'all [the locations]'. The resulting meaning is 'somewhere [else] in all those places', or just 'elsewhere'.

Very occasionally bare interrogatives can receive the existential indefinite reading.

(4.106) **Birlinj** ka-bun-marnanj-ngunda.
how 3SG.NF-3SG.OBJ-BEN-do.PST
'He said something to him.'
[IK1-170624_1PN1/30:48]

The negative reading of indefinites is used to negate existence of individuals or objects (4.107). The form is the bare interrogative form preceded by a negative particle (*ngunda* or *marrek/merrek*).

(4.107) a. **Ngunda na-kaybi** ki-rlakwani.
not I-who 3SG.IRR.PST-throw.IRR.PST
'No one would just throw it [rubbish on the ground].'
[20070108IB01/13:07–08]

b. **Ngunda barda** ngemek.
   not what yet
   'There's nothing else.' [20060901IB02/04:36–37]

c. **Ngunda birlinj** kidda-ngundje
   not how 3PL.IRR.PST-do.IRR.NP

   la kidda-woh-kidang.
   CONJ 3PL.IRR.PST-INCP-go.IRR.NP

   'They can neither do anything nor walk properly.'
   [20060614IB/01:21–24]

d. **Merrek karrakenda** ngarra-kidang.
   not where 1SG.IRR.NP-go.IRR.NP
   'I can't go anywhere.' [IK1-180525_1DDj1/29:20]

Such a construction must precede the verb (4.108), presumably due to the the fact that (i) negation marker has to precede the predicate, and (ii) the indefinite itself has to be in the scope of that negation.

(4.108) IK1-180525_1DDj1/32:35–33:10

a. **Merrek na-kaybi** ngay-rnani.
   not I-who 1SG.IRR.PST-see.IRR.PST
   'I didn't see anyone.'

b. *Ngay-rnani merrek na-kaybi.
   1SG.IRR.PST-see.IRR.PST not I-who

4.5.4.3 Ignorative

The IGNORATIVE is *barninda* 'whatsit' (4.109), which perhaps historically is a contraction of *barda* 'what' and *ninda* 'DEM.PROX.I'. It is used to substitute for words that the speaker cannot remember (effectively, a hesitation marker). It may also be used together with a personal pronoun of appropriate noun class, as in (4.109c).

(4.109) a. Na-kudji kirdimarrk ka-bunj donkey walkki **barninda** ||
          I-one man 3SG.NF-hit.NP ENG with IGNOR
          stockwhip.
          ENG
          'A man beats a donkey with whatsit, a stockwhip.'
          [IK1-170530_1SY1/03:59–04:11]

b. Kadda-marnbum ‖ **barninda** ‖ karra   kadda-rdukidanj.
   3PL.NF-make.PST   IGNOR   DEM.MED.LOC   3PL.NF-look.PST

   'They made this, what's it called, where they were looking from.'
   [20060620IB03/08:23–30]

c. Kidda-maddjingi   la   **barninda** ‖ **barninda** kikka,
   3PL.IRR.PST-pierce.IRR.PST   CONJ   IGNOR   IGNOR   she.II

   bingkibingki.
   baler.shell

   'They used to spear it and what else... what's her name, baler shell.'
   [20060620IB04/03:16–22; translation mine—IK]

As is evident in (4.109), *barninda* is often followed by a pause, during which the speaker is presumably searching for an appropriate expression.

4.6 Possession

In Kunbarlang noun phrase possession is expressed by the genitive and dative pronouns.[29] They encode the possessor and either carry a prefix or are themselves encliticised to the possessum. Kunbarlang has a system of POSSESSIVE CLASSIFICATION, whereby the choice of a possessive construction partitions the nominal lexicon into two classes. These two classes in Kunbarlang are customarily called ALIENABLE and INALIENABLE (Nichols & Bickel 2013c).[30] Altogether there are three possessive sub-constructions with the personal pronoun
- genitive pronoun encliticised to the possessum noun (inalienable possession)
- genitive pronoun prefixed with a class marker agreeing with the possessum, where classes I and II are super-classed with prefix *kin-* and classes III and IV take the usual prefixes *man-* and *kun-*, respectively (alienable possession)
- dative pronoun with the prefix *bi-* 'DAT' (alienable possession)

I discuss these constructions below grouped by alienability of the possessum.

4.6.1 Alienable possession

Alienable possessive constructions in Kunbarlang involve prefixed oblique forms of personal pronouns, which encode the possessor features. The prefix is either the invari-

---
[29] On the verbal ways of expressing possession see 7.7.2.
[30] This is somewhat idealised. In fact, certain nouns, in particular body parts, are inalienable by default, but can be coerced into the alienable interpretation by the context.

ant dative *bi-* (4.110) or a noun class agreement (*kin-* for classes I and II, *man-* for class III, and *kun-* for class IV; see §4.1 for more), agreeing with the possessum (4.111). I have not found any difference between the dative and the genitive possessive constructions other than the word order preference: the dative possessor tends to follow the head noun, while the genitive possessor tends to precede the head (§4.4.1).

(4.110) korlonj *(**bi**)-rnungu
       patriline.child DAT-he.GEN
       'his child' [IK1-160822_0001/21:31]

Example (4.110) shows that the prefix cannot be omitted when the possessum is alienable (which kinship terms are, as is often the case in Australian languages (Dixon 1980: 293)).

(4.111) a. Kanjyuwa ki-karrme, **kin-ngaybu durduk**, merrek ngudda
           PROH   2SG.NF-hold.NP I/II-I.GEN dog, not you.SG
           kin-nungku.
           I/II-you.SG.GEN
           'Don't touch it, it's my dog, not yours!' [IK1-160829_0001/08:40–57]

       b. Mawuludja, <...> **kun-budbe yalbi** Djindibi mob. Djindibi,
          M   IV-they.GEN country Dj   mob Dj
          kun-budbe yalbi.
          IV-they.GEN country
          'Mawuludja, [unclear] it's Djindibi country. Djindibi, it's their country.'
          [20060620IB04/12:11–20]

Example (4.111b) shows a possessor expressed by a full noun, the clan name *Djindibi*. As shown, it can appear on either side of the head noun and genitive pronoun complex.

Coleman (1982: 78, n.d.) recognized that the form *ki-* was used indistinguishably for possessums of classes I and II, and postulated a possessive prefix *ki-* (the nasal segmented with the base). This was probably due to lack of class III and IV possessums in her data. I reanalyse this as agreement, which both accounts for the prefixes *man-* and *kun-* (e.g. (4.111b)) on those possessums, and treats possessive morphology as uniform noun class agreement within the noun phrase.

Unlike with the body parts (see example 4.118), possessor raising is unavailable in the alienable constructions (4.112), whether with *bi-* or noun class prefix:

(4.112) a. *Nayi durduk {bi/kin}-ngaybu ngayi **kadda-ngan-bum**.
           NM.I dog   DAT/I/II-I.GEN   I   3PL.NF-1SG.OBJ-hit.PST
           intended: 'They hit my dog.' [IK1-170525_2SY1/12:45–13:30]

b. Nayi durduk {bi/kin}-ngaybu ngayi **kadda-bum.**
    NM.I dog   DAT/I/II-I.GEN   I   3PL.NF-hit.PST
    'They hit my dog.'   [ibidem]

Also notice that the possessor pronoun cannot agree with the subject when it is functioning as a predicate. It strictly has to agree with the possessed nominal, or else be in the dative (4.113):

(4.113) a. *Ngayi **ngarra**-nungku djadja.
            I   1SG-you.GEN   MB
            intended: 'I'm your uncle.'   [IK1-180520_1DDj1/01:11:40]

         b. Ngayi bi-nungku   djadja.
            I   DAT-you.GEN MB
            'I'm your uncle.'   [ibid./01:12:09–13]

4.6.2 Inalienable possession

The main inalienable possessums in Kunbarlang are body parts.[31] Oblique pronouns just encliticise to these to mark the possessor (4.114). There are only two forms for the third person singular oblique pronouns, viz. -*rnungu* 'he.GEN' and -*ngadju* 'she.GEN', and the inanimates use the latter (as in (4.114d); see §§4.1.3 and 4.5.1).

(4.114) a. Nayi ring ka-mankang   korro   **kunbid=ngadju.**
             NM.I ring 3SG.NF-fall.PST DEM.MED.LOC hand=she.GEN
             'The ring fell off her finger.'   [IK1-160728_0001/48:23–27]

         b. Kenda   kun-bondjek la   **kunbid=ngadbe** kun-bondjek.
             DEM.PROX.LOC IV-cold   CONJ hand=we.EXCL.PL   IV-cold
             'It's cold here and our hands are cold.'   [IK1-170606_1SY1]

         c. **Barramimbanj** nga-rnay   **djanga=ngadju.**
             woman   1SG.NF-see.PST   foot=she.GEN
             'I saw a woman's footprint.'   [IK1-160827_0001/29:51–55]

         d. kundulk la   **merre=ngadju**
             tree[III] CONJ hair=she.GEN
             'the tree and its leaves'   [IK1-160819_0001/13:30–34]

---

[31] Kin terms, which typologically often are another group of inalienable lexemes, are alienable in Kunbarlang.

Example (4.114c) shows that the possessive construction may be linearly disrupted by the predicate. Metaphorical extensions of the body parts to the domain of inanimate referents are also treated with the same inalienable construction (4.114d). Notice that class II pronoun *-ngadju* 'she.GEN' is used for the inanimate class III possessor *kundulk* 'tree'.

The possessors expressed by a full noun are placed adjacent to the possessed (i.e. the head noun). The oblique pronoun of the same noun class as the possessor encliticises to the possessum, just like in the case of a pronominal possessor (4.114a).

(4.115) Nga-rdam   **kalakalak kodjkodj=rnungu** korro   kun-bondjek.
         1SG.NF-put.NP   chicken[I]   head=he.GEN   DEM.MED.LOC   IV-cold
         'I'm putting the chicken's head into the refrigerator.'
                                                              [IK1-170621_1SY1/07:00–05]

The dative-marked possessor is not normal for the inalienable nouns, and does seem to suggest alienation (see discussion of (4.121) below). I have not seen it used in narratives. However, it may occasionally occur in production during elicitation, such as in example (4.116) and in (4.120) below.

(4.116) Ngayi nganj-bunj=ngurr   **kodjkodj bi-ngaybu**.
         I   1SG.FUT-hit.NP=rippled   head   DAT-I.GEN
         'I will wash my head.'   [IK1-160518_0011/14:54]

The possessor pronoun must attach to the possessum head noun on the right (4.117a–b).

(4.117) a. **Djanga=ngaybu** wularrud nga-rdulkkarrawarribin.
             foot=I.GEN   already 1SG-tired
             'My feet are tired.'   [IK1-170525_2SY1/03:47–51]

         b. *ngaybu djanga
             I.GEN   foot
             intended: 'my foot/feet'   [IK1-170525_2SY1/06:24–26]

One of the interesting aspects of example (4.117a) is POSSESSOR RAISING (e.g. Payne & Barshi (1999), who use the term EXTERNAL POSSESSION). This is a morphosyntactic phenomenon when the possessor of a semantic argument of the predicate functions as the morphosyntactic argument. In Kunbarlang this is most evident in the agreement patterns, because overt nominal arguments of a given predicate can be missing. In (4.117a) we see that the adjectival predicate *-rdulwarribin* 'tired' agrees with the first person possessor (object pronominal prefix *ngan-*), rather than with the 'feet' (in which case the object prefix would have been ∅-). Another example of that is (4.118), where the object agreement with the possessor is obligatory (4.118a vs. b).

(4.118) a. Ka-**ngan**-rlemang   kunbodme=ngaybu.
        3SG.NF-1SG.OBJ-punch.PST back=I.GEN
        'S/he punched me in the back.'   [IK1-170525_2SY1/15:05–08]

   b. *Ka-rlemang   kunbodme=ngaybu.
        3SG.NF-punch.PST back=I.GEN
        intended: 'S/he punched my back / me in the back.'
                                                  [IK1-170525_2SY1/15:33–39]

Still another example shows that one's shadow is also inalienable in Kunbarlang grammar, and likewise gives rise to possessor raising (4.119):[32]

(4.119) Nga-wundji-yinj   la   ka-**ngan**-rnay   **kiwayuk=ngaybu**.
        1SG.NF-hide-REFL.PST CONJ   3SG.NF-1SG.OBJ-see.PST shadow=I.GEN
        'I was hiding but s/he saw my shadow.'   [IK1-170606_1SY1/40:51–41:12]

The dative construction does not support possessor raising.

(4.120) a. Nga-wundji-yinj.   Ka-nganj-kidanj   ka-ngan-bawuy
        1SG.NF-hide-REFL.PST   3SG.NF-HITH-go.PST   3SG.NF-1SG.OBJ-pass.PST

        ngunda **ki-rnani**   **bi-ngaybu kiwayuk**.
        not   3SG.IRR.PST-see.IRR.PST   DAT-I.GEN   shadow
        'I was hiding. S/he walked past me and didn't notice my shadow.'
                                                  [IK1-170606_1SY1/48:15–25]

   b. *Ka-nganj-kidanj   ka-ngan-bawuy
        3SG.NF-HITH-go.PST   3SG.NF-1SG.OBJ-pass.PST

        ngunda ki-rnani   **kiwayuk=ngaybu**.
        not   3SG.IRR.PST-see.IRR.PST shadow=I.GEN
        intended: '[I was hiding.] S/he walked past me and didn't notice my shadow.'   [IK1-170606_1SY1/48:56–59]

As the grammatical variant (4.120a) shows, the pronoun is marked by the dative prefix *bi-* and the verb lacks an object pronominal prefix for the possessor. The inalienable construction with the genitive pronoun cliticising onto the possessum noun is ungrammatical here (4.120b).

The inalienability of body parts is not exactly a hard-wired property of all lexemes, but rather for some nouns it can interact with semantics of the whole event description.

---

[32] While not necessarily being body part nouns, certain person's representations are frequently treated as inalienable in Australian languages. These include nouns meaning 'shadow', 'reflection', 'name', 'footprint'. See, for example, McGregor (1996: 257–8) on Nyulnyul.

Thus, body parts can be coerced into alienable interpretation, with an appropriate change of the possessive construction. The case in point is the difference in the treatment of *one's own* body parts and *someone else's* body parts that one owns. Example (4.121) provides a contrast to (4.117a) in this respect:

(4.121) a. **Djanga {bi-ngaybu / kin-ngaybu}** yiwanj nganj-kinje.
foot DAT-I.GEN I/II-I.GEN DISC.PTCL 1SG.FUT-cook.NP
'Maybe I'll cook the [e.g. chicken] leg(s) that I have.'
[IK1-170525_2SY1/05:00–06:00]

b. **kalakalak kin-ngaybu** nayi **djanga**
chicken I/II-I.GEN NM.I foot
'my chicken leg(s)' [IK1-170525_2SY1/07:52–58]

When a body part is not the possessor's own inalienable body part, as in (4.121), it can be described by an alienable possessive construction. Note that the word *djanga* 'foot' is class I in this case, as evident in the choice of class I noun marker *nayi* in (4.121b). This suggests that it is not construed as much a body part as simply meat, class I being appropriate for animal food.

4.6.2.1 Proprietive and other extended usage

Interestingly, some of these body-part-plus-possessor combinations develop idiomatic meanings. These may be more or less compositional. On the one end of the scale there are the idioms denoting classes of objects based on their salient "possessive" characteristic (4.122a-b).[33] A clear case of a less compositional idiom is shown in (4.122c), where there is no obvious semantic component of possession (see also example (7.70a) in §4.6).

(4.122) a. djanga=rnungu
foot=he.GEN
'car' [lit. 'his foot']

b. kumu=ngadju
eye=she.GEN
'Cycas calcicola' (cycad sp.) [lit. 'her eye(s)']

c. merre=rnungu
hair=he.GEN
'comb, hairbrush'

---

[33] This resembles the functioning of the PROPRIETIVE ('having'), which is a grammeme often found in case inventories of Australian languages (Nordlinger 2014: 242).

Notice that in (4.122c) there is no possessor semantically; rather, the idiom is a metonymic one, acknowledging a connection between the tool and its object of application. This is unlike (4.122a), where the car is described as something that has "feet", or (4.122b), where a cycad is referred to as 'her eye(s)', probably because of its ovoid seeds being a traditional food.[34] Both idioms are semantically exocentric, however, as they denote something different than a subtype of the head noun denotation. Other languages of the region have similar PROPRIETIVE-like use of the possessive construction: for instance, Mawng (Singer 2006: 40), Nakkara (Eather 1990: 375ff.) and Ndjébbana (McKay 2000: 196–7).

This pattern appears to be productive to a certain extent (rather than being a frozen list of lexicalised combinations). While translating a storyboard that included a reference to a rabbit, one speaker made the following suggestion (4.123):

(4.123)   *Rabbit* I don't know... **karlmu=rnungu**?
                                        ear=he.GEN
'[Kunbarlang word for] 'rabbit' I don't know... "the one with the ears"?' [lit. 'his ear']   [IK1-160513_0011/07:01–07]

Thus, she used the inalienable possessive construction to innovate a Kunbarlang term for 'rabbit' based on its salient characteristic.

Possessive classification (i.e. the alienability distinction) is one of the important parameters of cross-linguistic variation in possessive constructions. Kunbarlang exhibits a clear picture here, with two well-defined classes (proviso the coercion possibilities illustrated in (4.121)). The following section discusses another parameter whose value is not as easy to determine in Kunbarlang: the locus of marking.

4.6.3 Typological remarks

One of the main parameters of the typological description of possessive constructions (alongside the possessive classes, such as alienability classes discussed above) is the locus of morphosyntactic marking in possessive noun phrases (Nichols & Bickel 2013a).[35] Kunbarlang possessive constructions are interesting in that they combine traits of both head marking and dependent marking types.

---

34 Masha Kyuseva (p.c.) notes that *djanga=rnungu* 'car' and *kumu=ngadju* 'cycad sp.' can be metonymic—or even meronymic—as well. On this scenario, first the car's wheels (or cycad's seeds) are conceptualised as feet/legs (resp., eyes), and then the expression is extended from a part to the whole object.
35 And conversely, Nichols & Bickel (2013b: §3) list locus of marking in possessive phrase with noun possessor as one of two most informative phrase types in defining the whole-language locus type.

On the one hand, typologists tend to classify possessive constructions with a free pronominal word marking the possessor features as a head marking type. Thus, Dryer writes:

> There are still other languages in which a word intervenes [between] the possessor and possessed noun, which is not an adposition but a pronominal word varying for features of the possessor, as in [(4.124)] from Loniu (Hamel (1994)), an Austronesian language of Papua New Guinea. (Dryer 2007: 180)

(4.124) Loniu (Hamel 1994 via Dryer 2007: 180)
  ɲatama iy   pihin
  father   3SG.POSS woman
  'the woman's father'

"This type of construction is probably best viewed as a variant of the head-marking construction... except that the pronominal morpheme is a separate word in Loniu rather than an affix." (Dryer 2007: 180)

Likewise, Nichols & Bickel suggest that

> [head] marking using a separate word is illustrated by [(4.125)] from Tiwi, where the marker of possession is the uninflected pronoun *ŋara* 'he'. That it is syntactically attached to the head noun 'tail' and not the possessor noun 'crocodile' is shown when the order of possessor and possessed nouns is inverted: in ([4.125]a-b) 'he' immediately precedes 'tail' regardless of the latter's position relative to 'crocodile'. (Nichols & Bickel 2013a: §1.4)

(4.125) Tiwi (Osborne 1974: 74–75)

    a. jərəkəpai ŋara tuwaɹa
         crocodile   he   tail
         'the crocodile's tail'

    b. ŋara tuwaɹa jərəkəpai
         he   tail   crocodile
         'the crocodile's tail'

Indeed, the pronominal word in Kunbarlang is normally found next to the possessum noun. In fact, in the inalienable constructions it cliticises onto the head noun, and in (4.114c) one even finds the possessor (i.e. the dependent) noun discontinuous from the possessum-*cum*-pronoun complex. These facts are consistent with classifying Kunbarlang possessive NPs as head marking.

On the other hand, there are at least two arguments against such a decision. One is related to linear (dis-)continuity. Firstly, the fact that the pronoun encliticises to the head noun can be reduced to the requirement that there is a morpheme to the left of the oblique pronoun stem, which appears to be a correct generalisation. Discontinuity as in (4.114c) is not critical, as it is a regular property of Kunbarlang NPs. Moreover, examples can be adduced where the pronoun is separated from the possessum head by other material, such as the noun marker in (4.126):

(4.126) Mary burdubburdub ka-bunj=ngurr **John bi-rnungu** nayi
M often 3SG.NF-hit.NP=rippled J DAT-he.GEN NM.I
badjubadju...
shirt
'Mary usually washes John's shirt...' [IK1-160513_0021/06:36–41]

The second argument comes from considering the function of the genitive pronouns to mark the whole NP as genitive, as discussed above in §4.4.2. Nouns in Kunbarlang do not have case morphology and the case-marked pronouns are used in construction with nouns to build analytically case-marked NPs. If that is indeed the function of the genitive pronoun in larger noun phrases, then arguably it is a dependent marking trait of the possessive construction as well.

Perhaps the most appropriate typological classification of Kunbarlang possessive NPs in terms of the locus of marking is one of Nichols & Bickel's (2013a) minor types, namely HEADWARD-MIGRATED DEPENDENT MARKING. They describe this intermediate type as follows, contrasting it to the above example from Tiwi: "a fully inflected dependent (typically a pronominal argument) cliticises to the head, as in Bororo (Macro-Gê; Mato Grosso, Brazil)".

(4.127) Bororo (Crowell 1979: 197 via Nichols & Bickel 2013a)
barae eno moto
Brazilians 3PL.GEN land
'Brazil' (lit. 'Brazilians' land')

"This is different from [(4.125)] in that the pronominal piece in [(4.127)] is case-inflected and is therefore a syntactic word, while that in [(4.125)] has no case and can therefore be regarded as a phonologically word-like grammatical formative." (Nichols & Bickel 2013a: §1.5)

Indeed, the pattern is similar to the pattern in Kunbarlang. The oblique pronominal forms in the Kunbarlang alienable construction carry the dative prefix or agree with the possessum in noun class. This shows their status as syntactic words rather than mere morphological markers indexing the possessor's features.

4.7 Quantifiers

Quantifiers in Kunbarlang stand out among other constituents of the noun phrase in terms of freedom of their placement (this is in line with the general picture of noun phrases in Australian languages (Louagie & Verstraete 2016: 51–52; Louagie 2020: 158; see also §4.4.4 of the present grammar). Like most other constituents of the noun phrase, (D-)quantifiers can be selfstanding in Kunbarlang, meaning that there may be no overt nominal head.

4.7.1 Terminological and methodological preliminaries

This section is mainly structured around a recent comprehensive semantic questionnaire on quantification designed for cross-linguistic comparison by Keenan & Paperno (2012) and Keenan (2012). *Semantic* means here that the basis for selecting the expressions as quantificational is the meanings that they express, rather than a particular form, part of speech or otherwise. Following Keenan & Paperno (2012), I utilize their adaptation of Partee's (1995) distinction between A-quantifiers and D-quantifiers, which is a morphosyntactic distinction. Thus, the A-type includes those quantifiers which typically combine with predicates, such as adverbials or verbal affixes. On the other hand, those quantifiers that combine primarily with nominals or form nominal expressions are classified as belonging to the D-type.

Since this choice to use Keenan's (2012) questionnaire involves some technical terminology and notions from the field of formal semantics, I feel that it needs to be explicitly motivated. The primary motivation for this choice is the precision that if offers. The field of quantification is essentially semantic, and as such, relies most crucially on interpretation, which may often be very subtle. Thus a precise notional system in tandem with controlled methodology is instrumental for establishing the exact semantics of quantity.[36] In sum, the quasi-formal apparatus is employed here not to impose a specialised theory on the language and the reader, but to supplement the usual explanations with mathematically precise characterisation. I discuss methodology right after I explicate the notion of quantifier assumed here.

4.7.1.1 Quantifiers: a definition

Intuitively, quantifiers are expressions related to counting and measuring quantities. For our purposes here it is sufficient to think of quantifiers more formally as follows: a quantifier is an expression whose meaning is a particular relation between two (or sometimes more) sets (along the lines of the GENERALIZED QUANTIFIER THEORY; see Barwise & Cooper 1981). This assumes that most other natural language expressions, such as noun and verb phrases, denote sets of things. Consider, by way of example,

---

[36] I underscore that we are primarily targeting the semantics of *quantity* here. There may be further overtones to the meanings of these expressions that the questionnaire is not designed to capture, such as the spatial connotations of Bininj Kunwok A-quantifiers (Evans 1995a). It must be pointed out, however, that understanding the semantics of quantification proper of these items is prerequisite for any further inquiry into their meaning.

the English sentence *Several cats are sleeping*. The quantifier *several*, according to our theory, relates two sets here, viz. the set of cats and the set of sleeping things, as relevant in the context of the utterance. More specifically, it requires the intersection of these two sets to include more than one element—then the resulting sentence truthfully describes the state of affairs. We may write the following to express that condition in the language of set theory:

SEVERAL(C)(S) is TRUE iff $|C \cap S| > 1$, where C is the set of cats and S the set of sleeping things

In the ensuing discussion, however, nothing relies on the reader's understanding of set theory, its notation, or the generalized quantifier theory. Rather, this is included here for the reader eager to get as precise an understanding of the Kunbarlang quantifying expressions as possible.

4.7.1.2 Quantifiers: a methodology

As was suggested above, fine semantic judgements require a particularly rigorous and reliable methodology. The main methods that I used to study the interpretation of quantifiers were direct elicitation and the truth value judgement task (TVJT; Crain & Thornton 1998, Matthewson 2004). In this task the speaker is asked to judge whether a given sentence is truthful and appropriate given a particular state of affairs. I used pictures and a toy construction set to represent the states of the world, and either asked what the best way was to describe that in Kunbarlang, or asked whether a particular Kunbarlang expression (which was either previously elicited, or modified from that, or just constructed by myself) was felicitous in that circumstance.

An example of using this technique is as follows, cf. figure 4.1. The picture in figure 4.1 represents a man fishing by a lake. The construction blocks represent fish. By manipulating the amounts of fish in the man's bucket and in the lake various configurations of interest are produced. Thus, figure 4.1 can be described by (4.128a), but neither by (4.128b) nor by (4.128c):

(4.128) a. **Kaburrk** ka-kalng.
two 3SG.NF-get.PST
'He caught **two** [fish].' [IK1-170606_1SY2/54:53–55]

b. Ka-kalng na-**worrbam**, la na-**barrkidbe** nayi **nguyuyi**
3SG.NF-get.PST I-few CONJ I-other NM.I many
ngunda ki-kala.
not 3SG.IRR.PST-get.IRR.PST
'He caught a **few**, but **many others** he didn't catch.'
[IK1-160701_0001/56:21–28]

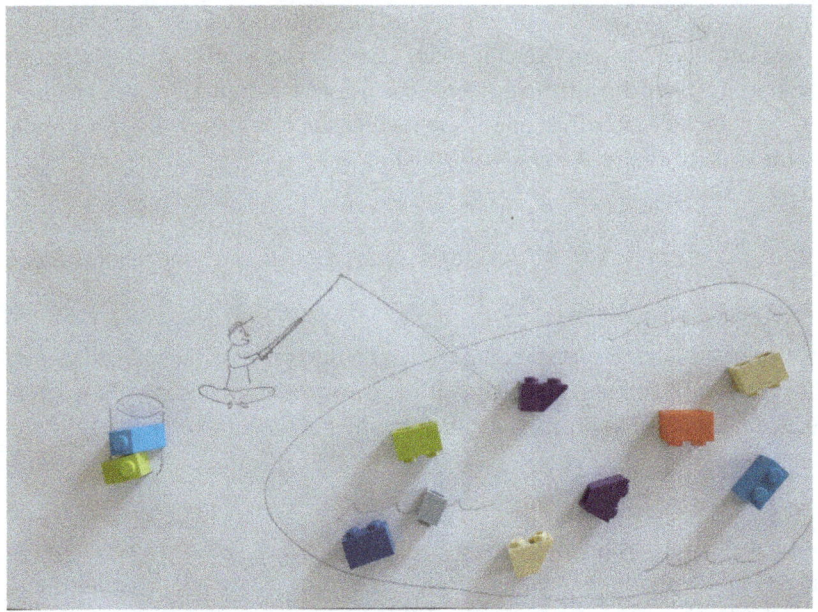

Fig. 4.1: Materials: quantifier elicitation

    c. Ka-**mulmul**-kalng.
        3SG.NF-many-get.PST
        'He caught **many**.'   [IK1-170606_1SY2/55:39–40]

One of the conclusions we may draw from (4.128b) is that while -*worrbam* translates as 'few', it does denote a cardinality larger than two. Next, given the prompt (4.128c), the speaker rearranges most of the fish from the lake into the bucket as in figure 4.2 and utters (4.129).

(4.129) Ka-**mulmul**-kalng   ninda   la   ka-baybum   **kaburrk bala**
           3SG.NF-many-get.PST DEM.PROX.I CONJ 3SG.NF-leave.PST two   LNK
           na-kudji.
           I-one
           'He caught **a whole lot** and left **three**.'   [IK1-170606_1SY2/56:07–12]

Proceeding in such a fashion, researchers can use their judgement of the relevant meanings and semantic subtleties, such as scopal possibilities of the quantifiers and other operators etc. An obvious improvement in using the technique would be to videotape the manipulations with the elicitation materials to facilitate future (re-)analysis.

Fig. 4.2: Materials: quantifier elicitation

4.7.2 Generalized Existential (Intersective) Quantifiers

These quantifiers are characterised by the common property that to evaluate a sentence formed with such quantifier relating sets A and B, one should consider the intersection of A and B: A ∩ B. In other words, these quantifiers deal with (non-)existence of entities and their cardinality.

4.7.2.1 D-Quantifiers

The existential D-quantifiers in Kunbarlang are the bound roots *-rleng* 'much; many' (4.130),[37] and *-worrbam* '(a) few' (4.130b), the free root *yika* 'some; few' (4.130a), and the cardinal numerals (see §4.7.2.1.1 below). See also example (4.140) for a D-quantifier usage of *mulmul* 'many', which seems to be an A-quantifier primarily.

---

[37] It seems a recurring pattern in Australian languages that some adjectives, in particular 'big', can also function as quantifiers. Similarly, in Kunbarlang *-rleng* is polyfunctional between the quantifier meaning 'much; many', but the inchoative and resultative forms derived from it build upon the other meaning, viz. 'big'. Thus, *-rlengmi* means not 'multiply' but 'grow', and *-rlengbinbin* means not 'multiplied' but 'grown up'. Also, *-wanjak* 'small, little' can quantify mass nouns meaning 'little' (similar to English). Cf. Anindilyakwa adjectives *arvma* 'big' and *adhvrrungwarrna* 'huge' "to express plurality... for non-count nouns" (Stokes 1982: 45 via van Egmond 2012: 126); Gooniyandi (McGregor 1990: 260) *nyamani gamba* 'a lot of water' [lit. "big water"]; cf. also Louagie (2020: 106).

(4.130) a. **Kinbadda-rleng kirdimarrk** kadda-nganj-kidanj korro
3PL-much man 3PL.NF-HITH-go.PST DEM.MED.LOC

yiwarrudj, la **na-yika kirdimarrk** kadda-makarninjdjanganj.
church CONJ I-some man 3PL.NF-sing.PST

'Many people came to the church, but few [of them] sang.'
[IK1-160802_0001/01:47–55, 02:34–40]

b. **Kinbadda-rleng** kadda-nganj-kidanj **barramimbanj la**
3PL-much 3PL.NF-HITH-go.PST woman CONJ

kirdimarrk yiwarrudj, kadda-makarninjdjanganj
man church 3PL.NF-sing.PST

kinbadda-worrbam la **kinbadda-yika** karlu.
3PL-few CONJ 3PL-some NEG.PRED

'Many women and men came to the church, a few sang and some didn't.'
[IK1-160802_0011/01:31–02:31]

Like most D-quantifiers in Kunbarlang, the ones in (4.130) have adjectival morphology, in that they agree with the head noun in person, number and noun class (in singular). Notice, however, that plural number agreement is optional, in the sense that some speakers do not use it, hence the form *na-yika* with a singular class I prefix but plural reference in (4.130a).

The quantifier *yika* may or may not be prefixed with a class marker. The former option is found in examples like (4.130). The non-prefixed form is examplified in (4.131) below:

(4.131) **Yika** ngay-ngayini.
some 1SG.IRR.PST-hear.IRR.PST

'Only **a little bit** [Ndjébbana] I can understand.' [RS1-140/20:40–43]

In fact, the non-prefixed form is the more frequent option, with only 4 out of 25 forms (=16%) found in the corpus having a class prefix. For some of these non-prefixed uses it is not entirely clear whether it is D- or A-quantification, see for instance (4.132):

(4.132) Ngemek **yika** karlu njunjuk ki-yawani...
yet some NEG.PRED water 3SG.IRR.PST-search.IRR.PST

'Yet **sometimes** there is no water so they would look for it.'
[20150212AS02/01:52–54]

In (4.132), *yika* could be used in an adverbial function, i.e. as an A-quantifier, or alternatively could be modifying a null/elliptical nominal head meaning something like 'times', thus still being a D-quantifier. This interesting polysemy of an existential quantifier between A- and D-quantifier use is found in at least three other languages (Djinang, Mawng and Yir Yoront) in Bowler & Kapitonov's (forthcoming) 125-language sample.

4.7.2.1.1 Cardinal numerals

Cardinal numerals are a special case of existential quantifiers. The cardinal numerals in Kunbarlang include the simple ones *-kudji* 'one', *kaburrk* 'two' (4.128a), (*kun-kudji*) *kun-bid* 'five' (<*kun-bid 'hand') and the complex ones derived from them, e.g. *kaburrk bala nakudji* 'three' (lit. 'two and one'; example 4.129), *kaburrk la kaburrk* 'four' (lit. 'two and two'), *kaburrk kun-bid* 'ten' (lit. 'two five'), etc. The only numeral that agrees with the head noun in noun class is *-kudji* 'one' (including in composite forms), the rest are invariant.

The numeral *-kudji* 'one' is a frequently used, polyfunctional word. Besides the core use as a numeral, it is sometimes employed to express the meaning 'another / one more', as in an important fieldwork phrase *Ki-mabulunj kun-kudji (tea)?* [2SG.NF-like.NP IV-one (tea)] 'Would you like another cup of tea?' Sometimes it is used as an indefinite article (this is never obligatory; compare *barramimbanj* and *kirdimarrk* in (4.133), both of which are indefinite):

(4.133) **Kin-kudji barramimbanj** ka-bun-rlakwang kirdimarrk
II-one woman 3SG.NF-3SG.OBJ-throw.PST man
ka-mankang korro lorre.
3SG.NF-fall.PST DEM.MED.LOC ground
'**A woman** pushed a man and he fell to the ground.'
[IK1-170530_2SY1/07:23–31]

It can also be used as restrictive focus marking. Thus, the form *ngana-kudji* [1DU.EXCL-one] in (4.134) means 'only we two':

(4.134) Yimarnek **ngana-kudji** ngana-djarri but balanda
like 1DU.EXCL-one 1DU.EXCL.IRR.PST-eat.IRR.PST but whitefella
ngemek kabarra-djarrang bonj~bonj.
yet 3DU.NF-eat.PST RDP~exactly
'[We thought] like only we would eat that, but the whitefellas ate it too!'
[20150413IOv01/03:49–53]

The numeral *-kudji* can also be reduplicated to mark distributivity. In such use, it does not necessarily have scope over an argument of the predicate, but can scope over events, effectively behaving as an adverbial (4.135). When quantifying over repeated events, the agreement is with "times", i.e. class IV.

(4.135) Nga-mabulunj nganj-ka=kulkkulk **kun-kudji~kudji**.
1SG.NF-like.NP 1SG.FUT-go.NP=run IV-DISTR~one
'I like to go for a run **from time to time**.' [IK1-170606_1SY2/26:59–27:04]

4.7.2.2 A-Quantifiers

The existential A-quantifiers in Kunbarlang quantify both time intervals and individuals. The temporal ones are the free forms (*burdub~*)*burdub* 'often, a lot' (4.136) and *waken* 'for a while' (4.137), and the 'times'-construction with *burru* 'arm'. The individual are the verb prefixes *kaburrk-* 'two / COLL' (see section §6.4.2 for examples) and *mulmul-* 'many' (see §6.4 on incorporated adverbials in general).

(4.136) a. **Burdub~burdub** ngay-kangkayini barbung...
RDP~a_lot 1SG.IRR.PST-go.IRR.PST fish
'I used to go fishing often/a lot...' [IK1-160819_0001/38:14–16]

b. Ngadda-warrenj **burdub** ngondo ngorro.
1PL.EXCL.NF-move.PST a_lot DEM.PROX.IV DEM.MED.IV
'We stayed there [out in the bush] a lot.' [20060620IB03/16:15–19]

(4.137) Nga-kidanj **waken** la ngunda ngay-yu kenda.
1SG.NF-go.PST while CONJ not 1SG.IRR.PST-lie.IRR.PST DEM.PROX.LOC
'I went there for a while, I didn't sleep there.' [IK1-160802_0011/10:27–38]

To express that some event took place *x* many times, Kunbarlang metaphorically extends the word *burru* 'arm' in two slightly different constructions: *x burru=rnungu* (4.138a) and *x kuyi burru* (4.138b).

(4.138) a. Ka-kidanj **ku-rleng burru=rnungu**.
3SG.NF-go.PST IV-much arm=he.GEN
'S/he / it went there many times.' [IK1-170525_2SY2/18:00–04]

b. **Kaburrk bala kun-kudji kuyi burru** ngana-wom
two LNK IV-one NM.IV arm 1DU.EXCL.NF-return.PST
kuyi Adelaide.
NM.IV A
'We went back to Adelaide three times.' [20060901IB02/04:41–46]

The quantifier *mulmul-* 'many' can be incorporated into the verb (4.139) or be freestanding (4.140). Its combinations are highly lexically restricted: only two verbs have been found to combine with this quantifier. They are -*ka* 'to go' (the subject-oriented use) and -*kali* 'to get' (the object-oriented use). The subject-oriented use is exemplified in (4.139a), object-oriented in (4.139b), and (4.139c) displays it quantifying over the object in combination with the universal D-quantifier *ngob* 'all', which is always freestanding.

(4.139) a. Kadda-nganj-**mulmul**-kidanj.
3PL.NF-HITH-many-go.PST
'A lot of people came.' [IK1-160802_0001/14:20–22]

b. Kadda-**mulmul**-kalng apple kadda-wu-djinj.
3PL.NF-many-get.PST apple 3PL.NF-give-REFL.PST
'They got a bunch of apples and shared them.'
[IK1-160429_0001/1:28:33–36]

c. Kadda-**mulmul**-kalng **ngob** kikakkin.
3PL.NF-many-get.PST all meat
'They got all the meat.' [IK1-160429_0001/1:22:24–26]

In the following example (4.140) the quantifier *mulmul* is freestanding, used in combination with *ngob* 'all' again. In this case it is not immediately clear whether it is still an A-quantifier or is used as a D-quantifier.

(4.140) Kadda-nganj-kidanj **mulmul ngob**.
3PL.NF-HITH-go.PST many all
'Everyone came.' [IK1-160802_0001/14:40–43]

4.7.3 Generalized Universal (Co-intersective) Quantifiers

Generalized universal quantifiers have in common that to evaluate a sentence formed with such quantifier relating sets A and B, one should consider the complement of A to B, i.e. the result of subtracting all Bs from As: A−B (in other words, As that are not Bs). Typically, a universal quantifier would require this complement to be an empty set. For instance, *All cats are sleeping* is true iff in the relevant context one cannot find a cat that is not sleeping. Thus, these quantifiers deal with inclusion.

4.7.3.1 D-Quantifiers
The universal D-quantifiers in Kunbarlang are the very frequent *ngob* 'all' (4.141), and the very rare *ngobbu* 'both' (4.142) and *nunu* 'all' (4.143). There are many examples of *ngob*:

(4.141) a. Ngadda-wom **ngob** Kurridja korro.
1PL.EXCL.NF-return.PST all K DEM.MED.LOC
'We all returned to Kurridja.' [IK1-160624_0021/08:15–18]

b. Ngarrki-rlakka **ngob** lerrk there ‖ ngarrki-marnbunj djurra.
1.INCL.FUT-throw.NP all word ENG 1.INCL.FUT-make.NP paper
'We'll all throw in words in there, we'll make a book.'
[IK1-160424_0001/09:44–48]

c. Kadda-djarrang na-wanjak nayi kikakkin, la marrek
3PL.NF-eat.PST I-small NM.I meat CONJ not
kidda-bularrbuni **ngob nayi kikakkin**.
3PL.IRR.PST-finish.IRR.PST all NM.I meat
'They ate a little bit of the meat, but didn't finish it all.'
[IK1-160802_0001/52:15–26]

d. Kadda-kalng kuyi njunjuk **bi-ngarrku ngob**.
3PL.NF-get.PST NM.IV water DAT-we.INCL.GEN all
'They brought water for us all.' [IK1-160802_0001/08:49–56]

The quantifier *ngobbu* 'both' appears to be related to *ngob*, given the similarity of its form and function. The formative *-wu* is attested as a restrictive focus suffix 'only' (see §3.2.1). It can only tentatively be identified as a constituent of *ngobbu* since is hard to see a plausible semantic development for the combination, nor am I certain whether its initial labio-velar glide hardens after /p/ (it does not after /k/, for instance).[38]

(4.142) Ngayi nga-ngundje mawa **ngobbu** Kurlinjmarr Ledjeledjel
I 1SG.NF-say.NP FF both K L
kabarra-wundji-yinj.
3DU.NF-hide-REFL.PST
'My grandmother and grandfather Kurlinjmarr and Ledjeledjel both hid themselves.' [20150206AS03/06:12–17]

There are only two instances of *nunu* found in texts (4.143), but its semantics is confirmed in elicitation. This morpheme is also mentioned as a component of the plural form of the oblique first person inclusive pronoun *-ngarrkku-nunu* by Coleman (n.d.: 12); see §4.5.1 for an argument against such an analysis.[39]

---

[38] At the same time, the Mawng quantifier *yirrkju* 'both' has the same structure, i.e. a universal quantifier with a suffix 'only' (Singer et al. 2015).
[39] The function of *korro* in (4.143b) is not clear at present.

(4.143) a. Kenda   ngorro   ngarrki-rna   **nunu**.
          DEM.PROX.LOC DEM.MED.IV 1.INCL.FUT-sit.NP all
          'We're all going to stay here.'   [IK1-160624_0021/01:48–51]

   b. Korro   **kunbuy nunu** kadda-djarrang.
      DEM.MED.LOC ant.nest all   3PL.NF-eat.PST
      'They ate all those ant nests.'
                           [20060814IB05/01:25–29; translation mine—IK]

The universal D-quantifiers are not specified for distributivity. Thus, we find collective uses of *ngob* 'all' (e.g. (4.141c)), but it is compatible with distributive use as well, cf. (4.144):

(4.144) Barrayidjyidj kadda-kali   kaburrk sandwich **ngob**.
        children   3PL.NF-get.NP two   sandwich all
        '[at school for lunch] Children get two sandwiches **each**.'
                                                    [IK1-170601_1SY1/43:26–32]

It does not, however, enforce a distributive interpretation. This can be achieved through the use of the A-quantifier *baba-* 'DISTR' (see §§ 4.7.3.2 and 6.4.1) or the reduplicated numeral *kudji* 'one' (see subsection 4.7.2.1.1).

4.7.3.2 A-Quantifiers

The universal A-quantifiers in Kunbarlang are the prefix *baba-* 'DISTR' (4.145) and the free word *kirdirrkkirdirrk* 'always' (4.147). The verbal prefix *baba-*, like the rest of the verbal quantificational prefixes, has scope over arguments, rather than events. It provides a distributive reading of some plural participant of the verb (agent in (4.145a) and theme in (4.145b)); see also §6.4.1.

(4.145) a. Kadda-**baba**-kali   kaburrk mayi   sandwich.
          3PL.NF-DISTR-get.NP two   NM.III sandwich
          'They get two sandwiches each.'   [IK1-170607_1SM1/01:07:48–59]

   b. Nga-**baba**-kalng.
      3SG.NF-DISTR-get.PST
      'I have got some of each.' [Speaker demonstrates by pulling one block from each of three piles of construction blocks]   [IK1-160429_0001/05:06–12]

This prefix requires some plural participant, i.e. it does not just mean 'separately': compare the ungrammatical (4.146a), where the only participant is singular, and (4.146b). Other devices are available to express meanings like 'alone', e.g. the numeral 'one' (4.146c).

(4.146) a. *Nga-nganj-baba-kidanj.
1SG.NF-HITH-DISTR-go.PST
Intended: 'I came alone.' [IK1-160429_0001/16:14–16]

b. Ngana-nganj-baba-kidanj.
1DU.EXCL.NF-HITH-DISTR-go.PST
'We two came here separately.' [IK1-160429_0001/17:20–22]

c. Ngarra-kudji nga-nganj-kidanj.
1SG-one 1SG.NF-HITH-go.PST
'I came alone.' [IK1-160429_0001/18:55–57]

The adverbial *kirdirrkkirdirrk*, on the other hand, quantifies over events:

(4.147) a. Ka-ka=kulkkulk **kirdirrkkirdirrk**.
3SG.Real-go.NP=run always
'S/he goes running always/every day.' [IK1-160719_0011/06:28–29]

b. Nga-ngundje exercise **kirdirrkkirdirrk**.
1SG.NF-say.NP exercise always
'I do exercise every day.' [IK1-170606_1SY2/24:34–44]

It is notably more difficult to verify the quantificational force of the quantifiers over events, as the precise scenarios are not as easily constructed with visual stimuli. Thus, the division between meanings like 'often' and 'always' is always more tentative in the present discussion than, for instance, the division between 'many' and 'all'.

4.7.3.2.1 Quantifier *munguy* 'a long time'

At the moment I refrain from a determinate classification of the quantifier *munguy* (and its reduplicated form *munguymunguy*) according to its force. It is most often found as an adverbial (thus, an A-quantifier), the core meaning of which appears to be 'a long time' (4.148).

(4.148) a. Ngayi nga-wom Marnawukan **munguy**.
I 1SG.NF-return.PST Maningrida a_lot
'I went back to Maningrida [and stayed there] **for a long time**.'
[20060620IB03/20:47–50]

b. Ngadda-kidanj **munguy~munguy** ngadda-bing.
1PL.EXCL.NF-go.PST RDP~a_lot 1PL.EXCL.NF-exit.PST
'We went on **for ever** and then we arrived.' [20140704IOv02/00:18–20]

This idea of a prolonged time period gives rise to several developments, such as 'still' (4.149a) or the universal reading 'always'/'every day' (4.149b).

(4.149) a. Doctor ka-ngan-marnanj-ngunda na-wanjak wam kinj-rdam
doctor 3SG.NF-1SG.OBJ-BEN-say.PST I-small honey 2SG.FUT-put.NP

karra tea, la karlu, **munguy** nga-rdam
DEM.MED.LOC tea CONJ NEG.PRED a_lot 1SG.NF-put.NP

ki-ngana.
II-big

'Doctor told me to put less sugar in my tea, but in vain, I still put a lot.' [speaker's rendering: "I'm still putting big mob"]

[IK1-160802_0021/16:50–18:01]

b. Ka-ka=kulkkulk **munguy**.
3SG.Real-go.NP=run a_lot

'S/he goes running always/every day.' [IK1-160719_0011/06:08–10]

The D-quantifiers described in §§4.7.2.1 and 4.7.2.1 above are constituent parts of noun phrases. Within noun phrases, they are often found co-occurring with noun markers (e.g. *kaburrk mayi sandwich* 'two sandwiches' in (4.145a)). Noun markers are discussed in section 4.3.

5 Verbs: inflectional morphology

The verb is arguably the most complex and morphosyntactically elaborate part of the Kunbarlang grammar. The verb features templatic organisation with a prevalence of prefixes, but also a few suffixal slots; these affixes represent inflectional categories and derivational possibilities. There is little in the way of morphophonology in Kunbarlang (§2.7), with affixes combining in an agglutinating fashion. This simplicity, however, is generously compensated by the large number of conjugational classes and formidable agreement paradigms.

I divide the presentation of the Kunbarlang verb and certain associated constructions into two chapters: the present chapter covers the phenomena in the domain of inflection, while Chapter 6 deals with the morphosyntax of derivation within the verbal domain. The areas relevant for inflection of the Kunbarlang verb are, essentially, agreement and expression of tense/mood values, and these two main areas are interconnected to the extent that the obligatory subject prefixes encode part of the tense/mood information within a system of so-called *composite TAM marking*. The personal prefixes, which appear at the verb's left edge, are the subject of §5.2. The tense and mood system of the verbal stem, which gives rise to a sizeable set of conjugational classes, is described in §5.3. Section 5.4 discusses the combinatorial nature of the tense and mood expression in Kunbarlang, and section 5.5 goes into the detail of what temporal and modal meanings this system encodes. Chapter 6 on derivational morphosyntax continues the discussion of the verb from the point of view of argument structure alternations and other ways of modifying event descriptions in Kunbarlang.

The verbal template is shown in figure 5.1. Its general structure is fairly typical of the languages in the Gunwinyguan family: the leftmost prefixes are the agreement with the verb's arguments, between them and the stem there is an array of incorporation and argument derivation slots, and after the stem there are suffixes for the reflexive/reciprocal derivation and TAM categories. Compare the (somewhat more elaborate) verbal template of Bininj Kunwok in figure 5.2 below, which shows that in Bininj Kunwok the general structure of the verbal word is very similar to that in Kunbarlang.

The leftmost two slots of the Kunbarlang verb are the personal prefixes, which are obligatory (see below for more on the portmanteau nature of the subject slot).

-10	-9	-8	-7	-6	-5	-4	-3	-2	-1	0	+1	+2
Subject	Object	Benefactive	Delimitative	Directionals	Incorp. Qfr.	Inadvertitive	Incorp. noun	Incompletive	Comitative	Stem	RR	TAM

Fig. 5.1: Verbal template in Kunbarlang

Valency-increasing derivations of the benefactive and the comitative are marked in slots -8 and -1, respectively. Slots -7, -6, -5, -4, and -2 host incorporated adverbials, and slot -3 hosts incorporated nominals. The RR (slot +1) stands for the reflexive/reciprocal suffix. The TAM morphology in Kunbarlang is an area where division into morphemes is complicated due to the great number of conjugational classes and the remainder of the irregular verbs; see §5.3 for details. In examples below, which illustrate some combinations of verbal affixes, I separate the TAM suffix of the regular verbs, and show TAM values of the irregular stems as cumulative. The convention throughout this grammar, however, is to show all TAM values of the stem as cumulative, e.g. *-bingki* "-exit.NP".

Some of the ordering options are exemplified in the following examples. The subject slot is present in every verb, being the leftmost prefix. Example (5.2) shows slots -7 and -3: Example (5.1) also shows the object prefix in slot -8, the incompletive prefix in slot -2, and a TAM suffix in slot +2.

(5.1) Nga-buddu-woh-wu-y.
       1SG.NF-3PL.OBJ-INCP-give-PST
       'I gave them a part [of something].'   [IK1-160503_0001/01:13:52]

(5.2) Ngayi   nganj-rnak-kodjkodj-bingki.
       I   1SG.FUT-LIM-head-exit.NP
       'I'll only stick out my head.'   [IK1-180601_1SY1/23:16–19]

Example (5.3) shows slots -8 and -3:

(5.3) Nganj-ka   nganj-marnanj-bardi-kali   njunjuk.
       1SG.FUT-go.NP   1SG.FUT-BEN-liquid-get.NP   water
       'I'll go get water for him/her/it.'   [IK1-180605_1SY1/30:02–05]

Example (5.4) shows prefixal slots -6 and -1, and suffixal slots +1 and +2.

(5.4) Kinj-nganj-walkki-rda-yi-∅   korro   yirrk!
       2SG.FUT-HITH-COM-put-REFL-NP   DEM.MED.LOC   inside
       'Bring it inside!'   [IK1-180518_1SY1/37:14–16]

The arrangement of incorporated adverbials amongst themselves and with respect to the other prefixes is further illustrated in §6.4.

As in other Gunwinyguan languages (Evans 2003a: 336), Kunbarlang verbal stems can be simple or complex.[1] The simple ones are monomorphemic. The complex ones

---

[1] Kinslow Harris (1969b: 6) calls them 'simple roots' and 'compound stems', respectively, but her compound stems also include productive combinations with incorporated adverbials.

-12	-11	-10	(-9)	(-8)	(-7)*	(-6)	(-5)*	(-4)	(-3)	(-2)	(-1)	(E-4)	(E-1)	(E-0)	(E+3)	0	(+1)	+2	+3
Tense	Subject	Object	Directional	Aspect	Miscellaneous 1	Benefactive	Miscellaneous 2	Gener.inc.nom.	Body part inc.nom.	Numerospatial	Comitative	Gener.inc.nom.	Comitative	Stem [open]	Incorp. verb form	Stem [open]	RR	TAM	Case

Fig. 5.2: Verbal template in Bininj Kunwok

appear monomorphemic synchronically, but historically have been bimorphemic. They consist of a so-called PREPOUND and THEMATIC (the terms are Evans's (ibid.)). Thematics are essentially the same elements as the simple stems, and they determine the conjugation class.[2] For instance, there is the verb -*bunj* 'to hit' (5.5a).[3] Besides being a simple stem on its own (5.5a), it serves as the thematic in a multitude of complex stems (5.5b–c).

(5.5)   a.   Ki-buddu-**bu**-∅.
               3SG.IRR.NP-3PL.OBJ-hit-IRR.NP
               'It would kill them.'   [20150206AS03/07:16]

       b.   Mabidj kinj-**ngi.bu**-nj   na-kaybi nukka.
              YB   2SG.FUT-call-NP   I-who   he.I
              'Call your little brother's name.'   [20060620IB03/27:37–41]

       c.   Kadda-rnak-**marn.bu**-m but merrek kidda-**bularr.bu**-ni.
              3PL.NF-LIM-make-PST   ENG not   3PL.IRR.PST-finish-IRR.PST
              'They only partially built that house, but didn't finish it.'
                                                          [IK1-150725_0011/09:29–33]

All tense/mood suffixes in (5.5) are determined by the thematic -*bunj*, i.e. they are the same that the simple verb 'to hit' would have in the respective tenses. Kunbarlang prepounds derive from a variety of historical sources: incorporated nouns that froze together with the thematic (such as *ngi* in (5.5b) from *kingi* 'name', which has a historical class II prefix *ki*; see §6.3 on noun incorporation and its productivity criteria), secondary predicate incorporation (e.g. -*djarrak.rna* 'to be alive' from *djarrak* 'healthy'; this is not a productive process in Kunbarlang, but is in Bininj Kunwok (Evans 2003a: 481)), or unidentifiable, perhaps, cranberry morphs (such as *marn* and *bularr* in (5.5c)).

Verbs (i.e. verbal stems) are a closed class category in Kunbarlang. As discussed in §3.2, this refers to the fact that new words cannot be added to this class: new predicates

---

[2] There is one thematic that does not occur as a simple stem, but only in complex stems, *dje*; see §5.3.
[3] The citation form for verbs is the stem with the realis non-past suffix.

are loaned from English as uninflecting preverbs to be used in the preverb construction (§3.2.5.2). Thus, the class of verbs is finite, but it is not small: currently about 450 verbs have been recorded, including 50 simple stems, on the basis of which the rest are built. The simple stems are diverse both formally and semantically (the majority among them are the verbs of motion, perception, transfer, consumption, and destruction). This diversity can be appreciated in §5.3 (tables 5.10 and 5.12), along with complexity of the conjugational classes that these verbs are divided into.

Before exploring the verbal form in greater detail, I discuss grammatical relations in Kunbarlang (§5.1), understanding of which is instrumental for most of the other topics.

5.1 Definitions: grammatical relations

Following Bickel (2010), who emphasises the construction-specific nature of grammatical relations, I understand them here as classes of arguments treated the same way by some construction in the given language. Based on three diagnostic properties in Kunbarlang—verbal agreement, selection, and noun incorporation—I distinguish the following five grammatical roles in Kunbarlang: SUBJECT, PRIMARY OBJECT, SECONDARY OBJECT, BENEFACTIVE OBJECT, and COMITATIVE OBJECT. The subject is set apart from the four objects because of its distinct behaviour regarding agreement: it is cross-referenced in the dedicated subject slot (see figure 5.1 for the verb's morphological template). The four objects compete for being indexed in the verb's only object slot, but are classified by their relation to verbal selection, agreement, and noun incorporation, as is detailed in the rest of this section. Figure 5.3 offers an economical way to present these four classes of objects. This is not an exhaustive list of the objects' properties, but should be taken as a heuristic for classifying a given argument, like a decision tree read from left to right.

Within the argument structure of a given predicate as used in speech, it is useful to draw a distinction between the core arguments and the oblique arguments. The former ones include all arguments that can be subcategorised for by the verbal stem: the subject and the primary and secondary objects. The latter ones include the remaining two objects, which are not subcategorised for but are promoted to the argument status from

Selected				
	yes	Index in Obj.slot	yes	primary
			no	secondary
	no	Incorporation	yes	comitative
			no	benefactive

Fig. 5.3: Classification of Kunbarlang objects

the benefactive and the comitative adjuncts, respectively. The applicatives involved in this promotion are discussed in §§6.1.1 and 6.1.2.

Stepping back and looking at the family level, one finds that the notion of grammatical relations appears somewhat elusive in the Gunwinyguan languages, at least with respect to the distinction between direct and indirect objects. For instance, Evans defines the 'true objects' (i.e., direct ones) in Bininj Kunwok as those that are neither subjects nor indirect objects. The latter ones are in turn defined in terms of agreement: an IO is "that argument of a ditransitive verb which is represented in the second pronominal prefix slot" (Evans 2003a: 391).[4] To avoid problems with thematic role to grammatical function matching, I adopt a different approach and instead of direct and indirect objects use the terms PRIMARY and SECONDARY OBJECT (in Dryer's (1986) terminology; they are also sometimes called *first* and *second* objects). But first I shall define the subjects, which seems the easiest and therefore a good place to start (5.6).

(5.6) SUBJECTS are the arguments cross-referenced in the subject slot.

Every verb has a subject in the sense of (5.6) (that is, it is not necessarily expressed by an overt nominal). In Kunbarlang, there are no subject-demoting transformations, such as the passive voice. Having confined the subject arguments to those indexed in the subject slot (the leftmost prefix slot of the verb), we turn to the object slot, which follows immediately.

(5.7) a. PRIMARY OBJECTS are the underlying objects cross-referenced in the object slot. These are, basically, the Goal/Source arguments of the ditransitives and Themes of monotransitives;

b. SECONDARY OBJECTS are the (overt or understood) underlying arguments of ditransitives which are not cross-referenced in the object slot.

It is important in the definition (5.7) that these two objects are *underlying*, i.e. part of the verbal stem's argument structure unmodified by any argument derivations. In terms of the place of Kunbarlang in the object alignment typology, (5.7) amounts to the generalisation that Kunbarlang shows SECUNDATIVE ALIGNMENT (or, more specifically, SECUNDATIVE INDEXING) of objects, i.e. the Patient-like arguments of monotransitives are treated in the same way as the Recipient/Goal/Source-like arguments of ditransitives with respect to **agreement** (Haspelmath 2005). The following pair of examples shows that the second person Theme of the transitive verb *-burrbunj* 'know' (5.8a) receives the same object agreement as the Goal of the ditransitive verb *-wunj* 'give' (5.8b):

---

4 It is worth noting that the Gunwinyguan languages are not unique in this respect, and difficulties arise in some other Australian languages, esp. with regards to the definition of the indirect objects (e.g., Evans (1995b: 97–99) on grammatical relations in Kayardild) and sometimes objects more broadly (e.g., Nordlinger (2011) on the bivalent constructions in Murrinhpatha).

(5.8) a. Ngayi **nga-ngun-burrbunj** Mary.
I 1SG.NF-2SG.OBJ-know.NP M
'I know you, Mary.' [20060901IB02/07:07–09]

b. Korro ngudda kun-nungku yalbi kadda-bum ninda
DEM.MED.LOC you IV-you.GEN country 3PL.NF-hit.PST DEM.PROX.I
la **rrubbiya** balkkime **kanjbadda-ngun-wunj.**
CONJ money today 3PL.FUT-2SG.OBJ-give.NP
'This is your country where they killed this [crocodile] and they will give you money today/now.' [20060620IB04/11:36–45]

We see in (5.8b) that the Goal-like argument of -*wunj* 'give' is indexed in the object slot of the verb, but the Patient-like argument, i.e. the object of the transfer, is only expressed by a free NP, and is not indexed in the verb. The same pattern is found with other (underived) ditransitive verbs, which are listed in §6.2.3.1.

Only the primary (5.9a) object can be bound by the reflexive/reciprocal (RR) suffix (§6.1.3).

(5.9) a. Lerrk kabarra-wu-dji.
word 3DU.NF-give-REFL.NP
'They are talking [lit. 'giving each other words'].' [IK1-160809_0001/29:50]

b. Kudjurn kadda-ngeme-yinj kenda.
white_clay 3PL.NF-paint-REFL.PST DEM.PROX.LOC
'They painted themselves with clay here.' [IK1-160624_0001/03:39–41]

The ability to interact with the reflexive/reciprocal derivation is the other major difference between the primary and the secondary object, in addition to indexing in the agreement slot. It also sets the primary object apart from the oblique objects, i.e. the benefactive and the comitative ones, which cannot be bound by the RR regardless of their indexing; see §6.1.3 for details. I introduce these two grammatical functions in turn.

I chose BENEFACTIVE (§6.1.1) as the representative of a considerable range of thematic roles, which can be realised via one of two alternative constructions.[5] One construction involves a dative-marked free NP adjunct to the verb (5.10a). The other is with the benefactive applicative (5.10b), whereby the verb has the prefix *marnanj-* 'BEN' and the free NP is promoted to an object and is in the direct case (see §4.2 on case and §6.1.1 for more on the benefactive applicative).

---

[5] This family of thematic roles may be termed AFFECTED participant; cf. Horrack (2018: 6–9), who uses the term AFFECTEE in her discussion of Wubuy.

(5.10) a. Ngayi nga-bareng-minj **bi-rnungu nukka kirdimarrk.**
I 1SG.NF-dangerous-INCH.PST DAT-he.GEN he man
'I got angry with him.' [IK1-160615_0011/46:48–51]

b. Ka-**bun-marnanj**-bareng-minj, kukkangundje
3SG.NF-3SG.OBJ-BEN-dangerous-INCH.PST maybe

ki-bun-rnak-bu.
3SG.IRR.NP-3SG.OBJ-LIM-hit.IRR.NP
'He's so angry with her, he might just hit her.'
[IK1-160728_0001/09:28–39]

For completeness, compare (5.10a) with (5.11). In the former, there is no benefactive prefix on the verb, and the noun phrase has to be case-marked with the help of the dative pronoun in order to be licensed and construed as a type of benefactive role. In (5.11), however, the noun phrase appears in the direct case, due to the presence of *marnanj-* in the verb.

(5.11) Ngana-**marnanj**-kelkkuyinj **na-wuk**=bonj **Paspaley.**
1DU.EXCL.NF-BEN-work.PST I-person=exactly P
'We two worked for Paspaley [in the pearling industry].'
[20060620IB03/09:43–47; translation mine—IK]

Benefactive arguments do not incorporate into verbs; see §6.3.3.

Finally, there is another thematic role relevant for the grammatical function inventory of Kunbarlang, the COMITATIVE (5.12).

(5.12) a. Kadda-bu-djinj **walkki rlama.**
3PL.NF-hit-REFL.PST with shovel_spear
'They were fighting with shovel spears.' [IK1-180605_1SY1/25:45–47]

b. Ka-kalng nayi djurra la **ka-walkki-bing**.
3SG.NF-get.PST NM.I paper CONJ 3SG.NF-COM-exit.PST
'He bought a book and walked away with it.'
[IK1-160505_0011/15:46–49]

The comitative both bears similarity to and shows difference from the benefactive (affectee) role(s). Similarly to the benefactive adjuncts/objects, *semantically* it is not subcategorised for, and is almost always interpreted compositionally, bearing a fixed thematic role regardless of the particular predicate it is added to (for details, see §6.1.2). Its usual meaning is the comitative, whence the name.

Another similarity to the benefactive is that there are two alternative constructions for the comitatives. One is the comitative adjunct with *walkki* 'with' functioning as a preposition (5.12a). The other is the promotion of that participant to the comitative object, whereby *walkki-* occurs in the comitative slot of the verb, as an applicative (5.12b). In the latter case the comitative NP appears as an argument marked for the direct case (5.13).

(5.13) Ka-ngan-**walkki**-rnay **kun-bareng** nayi   djamun   la
        3SG.NF-1SG.OBJ-COM-see.PST IV-dangerous NM.I policeman CONJ
        nga-wundjinj.
        1SG.NF-hide.PST
        'The policeman saw me with grog and I hid it.'   [IK1-160816_0001/33:09–15]

Similarly to the benefactive, comitative objects cannot feed reflexive/reciprocal derivation (see §6.1.2). What distinguishes them from the benefactives, though, is that comitative objects can incorporate into verbs (5.14):

(5.14) Nganj-**lerrk**-**walkki**-**wonj**   bi-rnungu   balanda.
        1SG.FUT-word-COM-return.NP   DAT-he.GEN   whitefella
        'I will translate [lit. '**return with words**'] for the whitefella.'
                                                 [IK1-180601_1SY1/01:16:32–37]

The five grammatical functions defined here for Kunbarlang were discussed with the syntax–semantics mapping in mind, even though formally I held on to the purely distributional idea about "arguments treated the same way by some construction" (following Bickel's (2010) lead, as pointed out at the beginning of the section). In particular, secondary objects are systematically associated with the Theme role of three-place predicates. In the next section (§5.1.1) I discuss a class of *quasi* objects in Kunbarlang, which neither are captured neatly by "some construction", nor show a clear-cut thematic role association, and yet can be said to constitute a distinct class of arguments. Afterwards, in §5.2, I move on to discuss the morphosyntax of the verbal personal prefixes system, armed with the definitions and taxonomy established here.

5.1.1 Unregistered arguments

Secondary objects are postulated based on the small class of ditransitive verbs, necessitated by their lexical argument structure with three participants (e.g. WHO gives WHAT TO WHOM). However, they can be viewed as a subtype of UNREGISTERED ARGUMENT (Coleman's (1982: 65–9) EXTRA OBJECTS) found in Kunbarlang with a broader variety of verbs of various underlying transitivity.[6] Unregistered arguments are those noun phrases that (i) **are arguments,** in the sense that they appear semantically selected by the predicate and bear the direct case, but (ii) **are not** (and **cannot**) be indexed in the verb by the pronominal cross-referencing morphology. It is worth pointing out that in all of these respects Kunbarlang unregistered objects closely resemble unregistered arguments in Warlpiri (Austin & Bresnan 1996: 242–3) and the Salish language St'át'imcets (called also *quasi objects* and analysed in detail by Davis & Matthewson 2003). On the other hand, these Kunbarlang objects parallel very closely the *unaffixed nominal adjuncts* of Bininj Kunwok (Evans 2003a: 588–90), including in particular the adjunct roles that are thus expressed (see below).[7] The important difference, however, lies in the fact that in Bininj Kunwok, these adjuncts can receive optional role marking, e.g. with the instrumental, ablative, or locative affixes. As discussed in §3.4, in Kunbarlang these objects present a problem for the analysis of clause structure advanced here—or for most analyses of clause structure, for that matter.

Instruments and locatives seem to be two primary types of the unregistered argument in Kunbarlang (Themes of ditransitives aside); they are illustrated in (5.15) and (5.16), respectively.

(5.15) a. Kinj-rnanj kanj-ngun-**dja**=**kolk** waliman.
2SG.FUT-see.NP 3SG.FUT-do.NP=cut axe
'You watch him, he's gonna chop you up with an axe!'
[IK1-160504_0001/57:20–22]

b. Nukka ngorro **dardken** ngadda-**rdukkumili,** wirdidj,
he DEM.MED.IV stone_axe 1PL.EXCL.IRR.PST-cut.IRR.PST fire
barda-nuk.
what-INDF
'We used to cut [stuff] with a stone axe—firewood, anything.'
[20060620IB03/31:00–31:05]

c. Kanjyuwa ngunu-**maddje** **mandabul** nga-burrun-marnanj-ngunda
PROH 2DU.NF-pierce.NP barrel 1SG.NF-3DU.OBJ-BEN-do.PST
la ngundji-baybunj ngarrki-**maddje** **bakkay.**
CONJ 2DU.FUT-leave.NP 1PL.FUT-pierce.NP spear_type
'*Don't shoot it with a gun,* I told them, *leave it, we'll spear it with a bakkay spear.*'
[20060620IB04/08:50–55]

---

6 Indeed, it is Coleman's (1982: 67) analytical preference to treat ditransitive Themes as 'extra objects' of divalent verbs. Even though they are not cross-referenced by personal prefixes, Coleman considers them arguments because of their ability to incorporate (op. cit.:41–2, 170).
7 As Evans & Marley (forthcoming) note, "the prevalence of such role-unmarked NPs is greatest among the two languages ([Bininj Kunwok] and Kunbarlang) most closely in contact with the Iwaidjan family, where this is normal".

(5.16) a. **Kuberrk** ka-**yunganj**.
            dry_land 3SG.NF-lie.PST
            'It was lying on dry land.' [20060620IB04/09:05]

   b. **Iliwan** ngadda-**rninganj**.
       I   1PL.EXCL.NF-sit.PST
       'We were staying at Iliwan.' [20060620IB03/19:26]

There is no definitive list of verbs that allow such objects, but it seems safe to say that not just every verb does. It is my impression that most verbs related to exertion of force that affects their Theme admit of an unregistered Instrument. Here are some with which such objects have been attested: *-bunj* 'to hit', *-rlemang* 'to punch' [both IK1-160829_0001/51:44–48], *-rdukkume* 'to cut' (5.15b), *-djuwa* 'to stab, pierce' [20060831IB10/01:05], *-maddje* 'to pierce' (5.15c). The Instruments show clear signs of lexical selection by the verb; thus, there is a correspondence between the type of traditional tool or weapon and the appropriate destruction verb: *rlama* 'shovel spear' (for hunting land animals and fighting) is used with *-djuwa* 'to stab, pierce' [IK1-180605_1SY1/49:21], thinner spears like *djalakkiradj* 'three-pronged fishing spear' and bullets (5.15c) with *-maddje* 'to pierce', and *dardken* 'stone axe' with *-rdukkume* 'to cut' (5.15b). The unregistered locative arguments, in turn, occur foremostly with posture verbs (5.16).

However it is not only Instruments of destruction verbs and Locations that may be expressed by unregistered arguments in Kunbarlang. There are other cases when such an object can occur and receive a plausible construal. Consider two examples of the (normally, intransitive) verb *-kelkkuyi* 'to work' in (5.17), which show that it can take unregistered arguments with different thematic roles, viz. an incremental theme and then two types of occupation, one via the describing the workplace, the other via direct naming of the job.

(5.17) a. Kirnda   ngorro   kanjbadda-**kelkkuyi djurra** and **lerrk**.
            DEM.AFOR.LOC DEM.MED.IV   3PL.FUT-work.NP   paper and word
            'Over there, they'll be working on the book and the language.'
            [IK1-160424_0001/09:27–30]

   b. Yoh nga-**kelkkuyinj kabbala**, diving boat.
       yes 1SG.NF-work.PST boat   ENG   ENG
       'Yes, I worked on a boat, a diving boat.' [20070108IB01/21:12–15]

c. Nga-nganj-warrenj   after nga-ngunda   finish nga-**kelkkuyinj**
    1SG.NF-HITH-move.PST ENG   1SG.NF-do.PST ENG   1SG.NF-work.PST
    stockman job.
    ENG   ENG

'I was doing that and after I finished that, I worked as a stockman.'

[ibid./21:15–20]

Judging from translations and based primarily on positive data, one can make the following observation regarding these objects. It is common to the Kunbarlang unregistered arguments—other than secondary objects—that they up the list of participants in a given clause by one. That is, while the secondary objects are semantically selected and obligatory, the rest of the unregistered arguments are semantically selected, but not at all obligatory.

Unregistered objects are not the only way Instruments are expressed in Kunbarlang. The comitative (§3.2.9) has this as one of its functions; example (5.18) shows that some verbs that are used with unmarked Instruments can also take an Instrument with a preposition (compare this to (5.15b) above). See also (3.58) for another example of this function of the comitative, with a different verb. It is hard to tell if this is the original Kunbarlang point of variation, of the use of the comitative preposition is calqued from English.

(5.18) Nganj-**rdukkume** kikakkin **walkki mandjawak**.
        1SG.FUT-cut.NP   meat   with   knife

'I'll cut the meat with a knife.'   [IK1-170620_1SY1/42:58–43:01]

In terms of word order, unregistered arguments resemble object noun phrases, in that very often they are found in the immediate postverbal position, without being confined to it (cf. (5.15b)). In fact, the available data are consistent with the hypothesis that there can be *at most one overt non-dislocated* unregistered argument per clause, including secondary objects. This would be a more principled explanation of occurrence of *walkki* with Instruments than blaming the contact with English. However, the data are not sufficient to confirm this with certainty at present, and more testing of (im)possible configurations has to be carried out to prove this hypothesis. Word order in Kunbarlang is further discussed in §7.1.

The rest of this chapter is structured as follows. The morphology of verbal agreement is described in section 5.2. Conjugational classes and the construction of composite TAM marking are the subject of sections 5.3 and 5.4. The range of modal and temporal meanings that these composite forms express is discussed in §5.5.

5.2 Agreement

The verb in Kunbarlang exhibits polypersonal agreement with the ability to index (up to) two of its arguments with personal prefixes, just as in other Gunwinyguan languages. At the same time, one argument is marked obligatorily in every verb, i.e. there are no verbs without any participant cross-reference. This means that every verbal word has one or two personal prefixes in it—the subject and an object, if the verb has one. See section 5.1 for an exposition of the grammatical functions relevant for Kunbarlang. The personal prefixes paradigm has separate morphemes for subject and object arguments throughout (5.19), which appears almost unique among the Gunwinyguan languages. Warray also has largely separable subject and object morphemes, where the subject ones also encode TAM distinctions, but the ordering of S and O differs from that in Kunbarlang (Harvey n.d.). The other languages in the family have extensive fusion of subject and object into portmanteaux (along with certain combinations of separate morphemes), as in the Dalabon example (5.20).[8]

(5.19) a. Nawalak **ka**-malakkidjanganj.
child   3SG.NF-laugh.PST
'The child laughed.'   [IK1-160505_0011/1:19:26–1:19:31]

b. **Ka-ngun**-rnirlakwang.
3SG.NF-2SG.OBJ-send.PST
'S/he sent you something.'   [IK1-160504_0001/28:11–28:13]

(5.20) Dalabon (Evans, Brown & Corbett 2001: 206)
dja-h-ngabbong
3/2-R-givePP
'she bin give you' [i.e. 'She gave it to you'—IK]

As can be seen from the contrast of (5.19b) and (5.20), in Kunbarlang, but not in Dalabon there are separate morphemes for the subject and object arguments. The pair (5.19) also shows that Kunbarlang follows the nominative-accusative alignment in the personal prefixes. In other words, the subject personal prefix of a given person and number is formally expressed by the same element (with a caveat discussed presently), whether it is the subject of an intransitive or a transitive verb (and that is different from the form used for the object).

However, Kunbarlang has its own form of complexity in the organisation of the pronominal prefix paradigms, namely an exuberant multitude of forms. One facet of this complexity has to do with the mood expression in the subject (see §5.2.1 below).

---

8 In the original source, *h*- is misglossed as IRR in (5.20).

This is a part of the grammatical content of the subject prefix, and thus is always readily visible. The other facet only shows in those transitive verbs whose subject and primary object are both non-singular. Consider (5.19b) again, which has two singular number arguments cross-referenced in the verb, and then compare it with the examples in (5.21), which all have the same person arrangement of the subject and object as (5.19b), but vary in their number values. In (5.21a) the object is plural, but the singular subject is *ka-*, the same form as that in (5.19b). In (5.21b), the subject is plural, but the singular object is *ngun-*, the same form as in (5.19b). In (5.21c), both the subject and the object are plural; however, neither of them has the same form as the (same-person) plural prefixes in the other examples in (5.21). This variation of the prefix form, which depends on the number features of *both* the subject and the object simultaneously, permeates the entire transitive paradigm in Kunbarlang.

(5.21) a. **Ka-nguddu**-baba-wuy.
3SG.NF-2PL.OBJ-DISTR-give.PST
'S/he gave you all something, one each.' [IK1-160513_0001/01:53]

b. **Kadda-ngun**-rnanj kekkek=nungku.
3PL.NF-2SG.OBJ-see.NP bone=you.GEN
'They are looking at your bones [i.e. the X-ray].'
[IK1-170608_1SY1/44:29–33]

c. **Kabarr-ngun**-midjbunj.
3NSG.NF-2NSG.OBJ-wait.NP
'They are waiting for you mob.' [IK1-180529_1SY1/2:00:23]

In the situation as in (5.21c) the dual/plural distinction of both the subject and the object is neutralised. Despite the degree of regularity that arises this way, the extent of allomorphy is remarkable. Taking into account the four mood series of the subject, the number of exponents for a particular person/number value can reach 13 (e.g. for the third person plural; out of the logical maximum of 28). This dimension of allomorphy in the transitive paradigms has been heretofore undescribed for Kunbarlang.

In the next section I present the morphology of these personal prefixes in two steps: first, the forms that are used in intransitive verbs and the transitive verbs with a singular agreeing argument; then the non-singular transitive verbs. I argue, based on the regularities both in the specific forms and in the overarching pattern, that these forms are better analysed as allomorphy than as subject-object portmanteaux, although the system appears to be in a transitionary state. Then I show that the third person singular subject is *numberless* (§5.2.2) and review the conditions on the expression of the third person singular object (§5.2.3). Taken together, these facts about the agreement paradigms reflect the recurrent number neutralisation in Kunbarlang.

5.2.1 The personal prefixes

Despite the systematic parsability of subjects and objects, discussed above, Kunbarlang prefixes are not purely agglutinating. They pack together information about the argument PERSON and NUMBER, and the subject series also encodes one of the four TENSE/MOOD values. There are some subregularities in these subject-TAM portmanteaux which suggest that the tense/mood formatives had been placed between the subject and the object before they fused with the subject forms. In fact, this deconstruction would probably necessitate person and number separation as well. Thus, a form like *ngandjidda-* '1PL.EXCL.FUT' may be hypothesised to derive historically from **nga-* '1', **nj(dji)-* 'FUT', and **dda-* 'PL', which then could be followed by an object prefix.[9] Currently, however, the degree of fusion is remarkably high, which led me to pack the subject+tense/mood forms into a single slot without pursuing a decomposition. While prefixal TAM morphology is found in many neighbouring languages, the order of tense/mood intervening between the subject and the object is rather unusual. At a broader typological scale, however, such order is not at all uncommon. For instance, it is found in Bantu languages (see Riedel 2009: 28–31 for Sambaa examples) and in Athabaskan (albeit in the mirror order; see Hale 2003: 14–16). It should be pointed out that such subject-TAM portmanteaux are also not typical of northern Australia (although subject-object fusion is common in Gunwinyguan languages, as noted above).

The mood and the tense of the subject interact with those of the stem in a combinatorial fashion to yield the full tense/mood specification of the verb; see §5.4 and §5.5). There are three persons: first, second and third. The number system encodes three numbers: singular, dual and plural. There is also the CLUSIVITY distinction in Kunbarlang, which is a further elaboration of the first person non-singular forms with regards to whether the referent *includes* the addressee (i.e. the second person) or *excludes* them. This is illustrated below with a paradigmatic opposition (5.22): the availability of the overt personal pronouns highlights the difference in readings.

(5.22) a. Ninda (la) ngayi ngana-ka korro wadjbud.
DEM.PROX.I CONJ I 1DU.EXCL.NF-go.NP DEM.MED.LOC beach
'He and I, we [exclusive] are going to the beach.'
[IK1-160518_0011/22:49–23:11]

b. *Ngudda ngayi ngana-ka korro wadjbud.
you I 1DU.EXCL.NF-go.NP DEM.MED.LOC beach
'You and I, we [exclusive] are going to the beach.' [ibid./22:16–33]

---

9 Indeed, this is the way Kinslow Harris (1969b: 8–9) analyses forms like *kanjbadda-* '3PL.FUT': *ka-nj-badda* (person+tense+number). While attractive for certain forms, this leaves a number of other forms, such as *djidda-* '2PL.FUT', in a need of additional explanation.

c. Ngudda (la)   ngayi ngarrki-ka   korro   wadjbud.
   you   CONJ I   1.INCL.FUT-go.NP DEM.MED.LOC   beach
   'You and I, we [inclusive] are going to go to the beach.'
   [ibid./21:56–22:06, also 24:04–08]

d. *Ninda   ngayi ngarrki-ka   korro   wadjbud.
   DEM.PROX.I   I   1.INCL.FUT-go.NP   DEM.MED.LOC   beach
   'He and I, we [inclusive] are going to go to the beach.'   [ibid./23:54–24:08]

Manipulating the conjoined subject between 'you and I' and 'he and I' in (5.22) allows to unveil the clusivity distinction in the prefixes *ngana-* (dual exclusive) and *ngarrki-* (non-singular inclusive). The exclusive prefix "blocks" the addressee (i.e. the second person pronoun *ngudda*) from forming a set with the speaker (*ngayi*)—hence the ungrammaticality of (5.22b). Conversely, the inclusive prefix requires the addressee to be included. Noteworthy is that even the non-singular is interpreted as dual in the presence of an overt subject that mentions two people. This is evident in (5.22d), where the exclusion of the addressee from the list together with an inclusive prefix produces the infelicity effect. If that was not the case—and given that Kunbarlang has the inclusory construction, see§4.5.2—the addressee should have been able to be construed as implicitly included, and the number as plural: "he and I, and, implicitly, you".

To summarise, the categories expressed in the personal prefixes are:
- grammatical function (subject or object)
- person (three persons and the additional clusivity distinction in first person non-singular)
- number
- tense/mood (in subject prefixes)

I have mentioned above that there is considerable allomorphy of the prefixes in the transitive paradigm. This allomorphy is mostly related to the configurations where both arguments of a transitive verb are non-singular,[10] although there are some first and second person combinations that have allomorphs even when both prefixes are singular (discussed and exemplified below). I introduce the paradigms in two steps. First, in tables 5.1–5.4, I give the forms of the subject that are used with intransitive verbs (and with most transitive verbs that have at least one singular agreeing argument); each table shows a different tense/mood subparadigm. Object prefixes for the transitive verbs with a singular subject or object are listed in table 5.5. The tables are based on Coleman (n.d.: 13–15), although I have changed a few forms that differed in my fieldwork. The forms that differ are listed in the paragraphs below. One general distinction, which I shall not repeat for each table, is that I hear and transcribe a lenis, rather than fortis,

---

[10] That is, dual or plural, but not the first person inclusive. This falls out naturally from the analysis of the inclusive forms as *numberless*; see the discussion below.

velar stop in all of the first person inclusive forms, i.e. *ngarrk-* [ŋaɾk] instead of *ngarrkk-* [ŋaɾk:] in realis non-future etc.

Tab. 5.1: Intransitive subject pronominal prefixes—Realis Non-Future

		Singular	Dual	Plural
First	Exclusive	nga-	ngana-	ngadda-
	Inclusive		ngarrk-	
Second		ki-	ngunu-	ngudda-
Third		ka-	kabarra-	kadda-

Tab. 5.2: Intransitive subject pronominal prefixes—Realis Future

		Singular	Dual	Plural
First	Exclusive	nganj-	ngandji-	ngandjidda-
	Inclusive		ngarrki-	
Second		kinj-	ngundji-	djidda-
Third		kanj-	kanjbarra-	kanjbadda-

Realis Future: Coleman (n.d.: 13) cites the form *ngundjidda-* for the '2PL.FUT'. I have only encountered that form once in my work (see example (5.76)), hearing *djidda-* otherwise, and even have been explicitly corrected to this shorter variant from the longer one (5.23). Perhaps the longer form results from some speakers' regularisation of the paradigm given the first person dual and plural forms and the second person dual form.

(5.23)   IK1-180529_1SY1/01:32:10–23

   a.   *Ngundjidda-yambi-burrdje.
        2PL.FUT-swag-wrap.NP
        intended: 'Pack up you mob!'

   b.   Djidda-yambi-burrdje.
        2PL.FUT-swag-wrap.NP
        'Pack up you mob!'

Irrealis Non-Past: Coleman (n.d.: 15) lists first person exclusive dual and plural with a final *u* (i.e. *nganu-* and *ngaddu-*), but I hear and transcribe them with a final *a*. Also, for third person dual and plural she gives the forms *kinbarra-* and *kinbadda-*, respectively. Those are the adjectival forms (see §3.2.2), and the verbal ones are *kibarra-* and *kidda-*, e.g. (5.24):

Tab. 5.3: Intransitive subject pronominal prefixes—Irrealis Non-Past

		Singular	Dual	Plural
First	Exclusive	ngarra-	ngana-	ngadda-
	Inclusive		ngarrak-	
Second		kirri-	ngunu-	nguddu-
Third		ki-	kibarra-	kidda-

(5.24) Ngunda **kidda**-kalbing djininj mayali, ngayi barrayidjidj.
not 3PL.IRR.NP-get.IRR.NP properly sense NM.PL children
'They don't hold the knowledge tight, the kids.' [IK1-160424_0001/03:27–30]

Irrealis Past: Coleman (n.d.: 15) gives *ki(yi)-* for the second person singular and *kayi-*

Tab. 5.4: Intransitive subject pronominal prefixes—Irrealis Past

		Singular	Dual	Plural
First	Exclusive	ngay-	ngana-	ngadda-
	Inclusive		ngarrki-	
Second		ki-	ngunu-	nguddu-
Third		ki-	kibarra-	kidda-

for the third person singular. I have only ever encountered the form *ki-* for both of these. Also, I transcribe the first person singular prefix as *ngay-*, rather than *ngayi-*.

Tab. 5.5: Object pronominal prefixes for singular subjects

		Singular	Dual	Plural
First	Exclusive	ngan-	nganun-	ngaddu-
	Inclusive		ngarrkun-	
Second		ngun-	ngunun-	nguddu-
Third		bun-/Ø-	burrun-/Ø-	buddu-/Ø-

Object prefixes: Coleman (n.d.: 15) lists the plural forms of objects with a final alveolar nasal *-n*, similar to the dual forms (i.e. *ngaddun-*, *nguddun-*, and *buddun-*). I find that the plural objects do not have that nasal and end in a vowel instead (like the form *buddu-* in (5.25); but not the numberless inclusive *ngarrkun-*, to be discussed presently).

Along with the few instances of syncretism that are probably accidental, there is one clear systematic pattern: first person inclusive forms are always identical in dual and plural. That is, number distinctions are collapsed in all contexts when an argument's referent includes the speaker and the hearer (5.25).

(5.25) Adjak   ka-karrme   ki-buddu-bu
sickness   3SG.NF-hold.NP   3SG.IRR.NP-3PL.OBJ-hit.IRR.NP

    ki-**ngarrkun**-bu.
    3SG.IRR.NP-1.INCL.OBJ-hit.IRR.NP

'It has a sickness, it would kill them, it would kill us (all).'
                                            [20150206AS03/07:14–17; translation mine—IK]

The object form *ngarrkun-* in (5.25) is underspecified for the number of referent—it could potentially be dual or plural. Since this number semantics—cardinality greater than one—already follows from the meaning of the inclusive form (which by definition involves at least the speaker and the hearer), I regard the inclusive forms as *numberless*. That is, number as a category is undefined on first person inclusive forms. This patterns well with the fact that inclusive forms are exempt from the number-triggered allomorphy patterns, as discussed below. See §5.2.2 for arguments in favour of numberless analysis of third person 'singular' subject prefix.

In this section I am not attempting to exemplify every possible combination of subject and object prefixes, suffice it to give a few more diverse examples (5.26–5.30). Many other combinations can be found elsewhere in the present grammar.

(5.26) Kun-mak kuyi **ngundji**-nganj-kaburrk-ka.
IV-good   NM.IV 2DU.FUT-HITH-two-go.NP
'Good that you two will come together.'   [IK1-160505_0011/28:39–41]

(5.27) Mayi man-kuk-karlyung **nganj-ngun**-wunj   mayi kundulk.
NM.III III-length-big   1SG.FUT-2SG.OBJ-give.NP NM.III tree
'I'll give you a long stick.'   [IK1-160824_0001/01:00:48–59]

(5.28) Ngunda **kirri**-kelbung;
not   2SG.IRR.NP-afraid.IRR.NP

    karlu,   ngunda **ngarra**-kelbung   **nga**-ngunda.
    NEG.PRED not   1SG.IRR.NP-afraid.IRR.NP 1SG.NF-do.PST

'[They said] Don't be frightened; No, I'm not frightened, I said.'
                                                    [20060901IB02/04:15–18]

(5.29) **Kidda**-kangkayini   **kidda**-ngayini   djarrebe
3PL.IRR.NP-go.IRR.PST   3PL.IRR.NP-hear.IRR.PST   far

ki-wardidji,   **ki**-dji   kordorrkordorrk.
3SG.IRR.NP-shout.IRR.PST   3SG.IRR.NP-stand.IRR.PST   ONOMATOPOETIC

'They used to go along hearing them [brolgas] from far away calling out, calling "kordorrkordorrk".'   [20150212AS02/1:33–38]

(5.30) a. Ngunda **ngay-buddu**-wuni.
not   1SG.IRR.PST-3PL.OBJ-give.IRR.PST
'I didn't give it to them.'   [IK1-160729_0001/03:20]

b. Ngunda **ki-ngan**-wuni.
not   3SG.IRR.PST-1SG.OBJ-give.IRR.PST
'He didn't give it to me.'   [IK1-160729_0001/03:32]

As I have mentioned above, Kunbarlang personal prefixes exhibit prolific allomorphy in the transitive forms where neither of the prefixes is singular. The full transitive paradigms are presented in tables 5.6–5.9. The tables are followed by a general discussion of the major patterns found in these paradigms.

Tab. 5.6: Transitive paradigms: Realis Non-Future

O	S	First SG	First DU	First PL	First INCL	Second SG	Second DU	Second PL	Third SG	Third DU	Third PL
1	SG					ki-ngan	ngunu-n	nguddu-n	ka-ngan	kabarra-ngan	kadda-(nga)n
1	DU					ki-nganun	Ø-ngarrun	Ø-ngarrun	ka-nganun	kabarr-ngan	
1	PL					ki-ngaddu			ka-ngaddu		
1	IN								ka-ngarrkun	kabarra-kun	kadda-kun
2	SG	nga-ngun	ngana-ngun	ngadda-ngun					ka-ngun	kabarra-ngun	kadda-ngun
2	DU	nga-ngunu		ngarr-ngun					ka-nukun	kabarr-ngun	
2	PL	nga-nguddu							ka-nguddu		
3	SG	nga-Ø	ngana-Ø	ngadda-Ø	ngarrk-Ø	ki-Ø	ngunu-Ø	nguddu-Ø	ka-bun	kabarra-Ø	kadda-Ø
3	DU	nga-burrun		ngarr-bun	ngarrk-burrun	ki-burrun	ngurr-bun	ngurr-bun	ka-burrun	ka-burrun	ka-burrun
3	PL	nga-buddu			ngarrk-buddu	ki-buddu			ka-buddu		

Tab. 5.7: Transitive paradigms: Realis Future

S	O	First				Second			Third		
		SG	DU	PL	INCL	SG	DU	PL	SG	DU	PL
1	SG					nj-ngan			kanj-ngan	kanjbarra-ngan	kanjbadda-ngan
1	DU					nj-ngarrun	ngundji-n	djidda-n	kanj-nganun	kanjba-ngarrun	kanjba-ngarrun
1	PL					nj-ngaddu	djidda-ngan	djidda-ngan	kanj-ngaddu	kanjibarra-kun	kanjbadda-kun
1	IN								kanj-ngarrkun		
2	SG	nganji-ngun	ngandji-ngun	ngandjidda-ngun					kanj-ngun	kanjbarra-ngun	kanjbadda-ngun
2	DU	nganji-ngunu	nganjidjirr-ngun	nganjidjirr-ngun					kanj-ngungun	kanjbarra-ngun	kanjbarra-ngun
2	PL	nganji-nguddu							kanj-nguddu		
3	SG	nganji-∅	ngandjidda-∅	ngandjidda-∅	ngarrki-∅	kinj-∅	ngundji-∅	djidda-∅	kanj-bun	kanjbarra-∅	kanjbadda-∅
3	DU	nganj-burrun	ngandjirr-bun	ngandjirr-bun	ngarrki-burrun	kinj-burrun	djirr-bun	djirr-bun	kanj-burrun	kanj-burrun	kanj-burrun
3	PL	nganj-buddu			ngarrki-buddu	kinj-buddu			kanj-buddu		

Tab. 5.8: Transitive paradigms: Irrealis Non-Past

O	S	First SG	First DU	First PL	First INCL	Second SG	Second DU	Second PL	Third SG	Third DU	Third PL
1	SG					kirri-ngan	ngunu-n	nguddu-n	ki-ngan	kibarra-ngan	kidda-(nga)n
	DU					kirri-nganun	Ø-ngarrun	Ø-ngarrun	ki-nganun	kiba-ngarrun	kidda-ngarrun
	PL					kirri-ngaddu			ki-ngaddu		
	IN								ki-ngarrkun	kibarra-kun	kidda-kun
2	SG	ngarra-ngun	ngana-ngun	ngadda-ngun					ki-ngun	kibarra-ngun	kidda-ngun
	DU	ngarra-nungun	ngarr-ngun	ngarr-ngun					ki-nungun	kibarr-ngun	
	PL	ngarra-nguddu							ki-nguddu		
3	SG	ngarra-Ø	ngana-Ø	ngadda-Ø	ngarrak-Ø	kirri-Ø	ngunu-Ø	nguddu-Ø	ki-bun	kibarra-Ø	kidda-Ø
	DU	ngarra-burrun	ngarr-bun	ngarr-bun	ngarrak-burrun	kirri-burrun	ngurr-bun	ngurr-bun	ki-burrun	ki-burrun	
	PL	ngarra-buddu			ngarrak-buddu	kirri-buddu			ki-buddu		

Tab. 5.9: Transitive paradigms: Irrealis Past

O	S	First SG	First DU	First PL	INCL	Second SG	Second DU	Second PL	Third SG	Third DU	Third PL
1	SG					ki-ngan	ngunu-n	nguddu-n	ki-ngan	kibarra-ngan	kidda-(nga)n
	DU					ki-nganun	∅-ngarrun		ki-nganun	kiba-ngarrun	
	PL					ki-ngaddu			ki-ngaddu		
	IN								ki-ngarrkun	kibarra-kun	kidda-kun
2	SG	ngay-ngun	ngana-ngun	ngadda-ngun					ki-ngun	kibarra-ngun	kidda-ngun
	DU	ngay-nungun	ngarr-ngun						ki-nungun	kibarr-ngun	
	PL	ngay-nguddu							ki-nguddu		
3	SG	ngay-∅	ngana-∅	ngadda-∅	ngarrki-∅	ki-∅	ngunu-∅	nguddu-∅	ki-bun	kibarra-∅	kidda-∅
	DU	ngay-burrun	ngarr-bun		ngarrki-burrun	ki-burrun	ngurr-bun		ki-burrun	ki-burrun	
	PL	ngay-buddu			ngarrki-buddu	ki-buddu			ki-buddu		

As can be seen from the tables, in each tense/mood subparadigm the singular forms of the subject are systematic within each respective person column, and so are the singular forms of the object, within each respective person row. Essentially, they are the forms from the 'intransitive subject' tables 5.1–5.4 and the object table 5.5 above. The notable exclusions are found when a second person subject acts on a first person object:

1. throughout the subparadigms, 1SG.OBJ prefix *ngan-* is reduced to *n-* when the subject is second person dual or plural
2. the 1SG.OBJ prefix *ngan-* is also reduced when the subject is third person plural, especially so in realis non-future
3. in realis non-future and irrealis past, the second person non-singular subject is null
4. in realis future, the 2SG subject monosyllabic prefix *kinj-* is reduced to its coda *-nj-*. By the law of nasal cluster resolution (§2.7.3), this palatal nasal overrides the velar initial of the object prefix: /ɲ-ŋan/ → [ɲʸan] etc.

However, when both the subject and the object carry a number feature of either dual or plural, their shapes rarely match the dual or plural forms of that person/number combination. Irregular, phonologically fused and hard to separate forms for subject/object combinations are widespread in other Gunwinyguan languages, and are customarily analysed as portmanteaux. That potentially could be a simple synchronic analysis for Kunbarlang, due to the irregularities and the disparity of the intransitive and the transitive paradigms. I prefer to discuss these paradigms here in terms of allomorphy. The choice of this label over calling them portmanteaux is not particularly important, but I wish to highlight the regularities found in these formidable transitive paradigms.

Indeed, this allomorphy is not completely random. First of all, there is regularity in the shape of the four paradigmatic tables: there is a very systematic neutralisation of the dual/plural distinction in both subjects and objects, such that regardless of the tense/mood and person, there is always one form for a dual or plural subject acting on a dual or plural object. I gloss these forms as "NSG" to reflect this fact (5.31).[11]

(5.31) a. **Kanjbarra-ngun**-midjbunj.
3NSG.FUT-2NSG.OBJ-wait.NP
'They (dual or plural) will be waiting for you (dual or plural).'
[IK1-180608_1PN1/42:27]

---

[11] A similar—although less pervasive—phenomenon is found in Bininj Kunwok, where just those cases when the object is the first or second person, "the distinction between augmented and unit augmented subjects is neutralised everywhere" (Evans 2003a: 409).

b. Ngunda **ngarr-ngun**-midjbu.
    not   1NSG.EXCL.IRR.NP-2NSG.OBJ-wait.IRR.NP
    'We (dual or plural) can't wait for you (dual or plural).'
    [IK1-180531_1SY1/39:04]

Second, although the variation in form is considerable, there is enough recurrence of form to regard these forms as agglutination of subject and object, so that portmanteaux analysis is not necessary from the point of view of divisibility. For instance, the form *ngarrun-* (see realis non-future and irrealis past; second person acting on first) appears highly irregular and it may be tempting to analyse it as a portmanteau—but one finds that it is also the 1NSG object form with the 3NSG.IRR.NP subject. Taking into account other facts of the second person subject prefix erosion with the first person object (e.g. in the future subparadigm), it seems most natural to analyse *ngarrun-* as the first person object with a null second person subject. Looking further at the paradigm tables, one finds that the form *ngarrun-* as the first person non-singular object is found with the third person non-singular subject in the future and in the irrealis non-past. Thus, there are enough cross-combinations of subjects and objects to guarantee their divisibility, i.e. agglutination. There is one form that in some speaker's production fuses beyond separation: the regular combination *ngarra-nungun-* (1SG.IRR.NP subject and 2SG object) may be contracted to *ngarnakun-*.

Third, there are a couple of other syncretism regularities. One is that the 3NSG subject plus 3NSG object form is always the same as 3SG subject with a 3DU object of the respective tense/mood subparadigm. The non-singular object always has the same form as the singular object (of the same person) in the following combinations (writing $n > m$ for n^{th} person subject and m^{th} person object) : 1>2, 1>3, 2>3, 3>2.

Finally, a consideration of the first person inclusive forms supports the view that these allomorphy patterns are specifically triggered by the morphosyntactic feature of NUMBER. Semantically they are all non-singular, by virtue of the inclusive semantics, necessarily adding at least the hearer to the speaker. But whereas all other non-singular forms give rise to the allomorphy patterns discussed above, the inclusive ones do not:[12] when it is the subject, it is fully regular, and as the object it (i) combines with the regular SG–DU–PL subject forms, and (ii) has two allomorphs whose distribution is morphophonologically conditioned, the longer one appearing with monosyllabic subjects, and the short one—with polysyllabic subjects, arguably being a truncated variant of the longer one. This is explained naturally under the analysis of Kunbarlang inclusive forms as morphosyntactically numberless, which was motivated above by their underspecification patterns.

I have suggested above that this complex system of personal prefixes is in a transitionary state. This view is motivated primarily by the impression of the less-than-perfect

---

12 Realis future forms are somewhat aberrant, but the data on these forms are rather scarce, and I have decided to leave these forms aside until further opportunity for checking.

regularity of forms (i.e. the allomorphy just discussed), as well as the stark contrast between Kunbarlang and the other Gunwinyguan languages, which feature numerous portmanteaux, as well as different linear ordering principles for the segmentable combinations (object before subject in Dalabon or person-based order in Bininj Kunwok). We do not have a historical record of Kunbarlang sufficient to make demonstrable claims about its verb's evolution. Yet it is interesting to compare the current system to the description by Kinslow Harris (1969b: 8–13). Her full transitive paradigms only include the realis system (i.e. the irrealis subject forms are given as a list of the intransitive forms, without enumerating all of the context-dependent allomorphs) and within those make only a limited distinction between exclusive and inclusive forms. However, the forms reported by her are nearly completely identical in their segmental composition to the ones given here, and the subject and object markers are also treated as separable (although her segmentation occasionally differs from mine—but this is of purely analytical interest). The second important finding is that Kinslow Harris's data reflect similar patterns of syncretism, albeit with caveats. The main similarity that is evident is the fact that the subject DU and PL distinctions neutralise in NSG>NSG combinations. For example, the distinct forms *ngunjdji-* '2DU.FUT' and *djida-* '2PL.FUT',[13] used with singular objects, are replaced by the neutralised form *djirra-* '2NSG.FUT' with 3NSG objects. Thus the resulting combination, presumably,[14] is *djirrabun-*, corresponding to my *djirrbun-* '2NSG>3NSG:FUT' (see table 5.7 above).

The main difference that I find in Kinslow Harris's (1969b) paradigms compared to mine, concerns the (non-singular) objects. Whereas in my field work I found thoroughgoing syncretism in all NSG>NSG cells, this appears more variable in her data. Thus, in the future tense non-singular third person objects show the DU/PL distinction with 2SG subject (*kinjburru-* and *kinjbudu-*, respectively), but neutralise it with the non-singular second person subject (the form *djirrabun-* presented above). However, in some other tense/person/number combinations, it appears as if the number distinction of the object may be retained. One such example involves the non-future 2>3 combinations. In Kinslow Harris 1969b: 10–11, these are *ngurrubun-* '2NSG>3DU' and *ngurrukun-* '2NSG>3PL', which correspond to my uniform *ngurrbun-* '2NSG>3NSG' (see table 5.6 above). Taken at face value, this may be interpreted as a sign of a currently ongoing regularisation of the personal prefixes system.

The next two sections deal with the question of number in third person subject morphemes (§5.2.2) and the patterns of third person object agreement (§5.2.3), which deserve a special mention.

---

[13] I change Kinslow Harris's orthography to the one used in this book, preserving her segmental analysis. Also, I use my labels for categories: my 'future' and 'non-future' in the subject prefixes correspond to her 'present' and 'past'.

[14] "Presumably" because I have composed the form from two paradigm cells—the combination as a whole is not listed. Importantly, all of these forms are given as distinct subject and object prefixes in separate tables, with only several (rather trivial) forms shown in actual combination.

5.2.2 Is third person singular subject singular?

In the presentation of the personal prefixes above they were offered as a set of tables, each combining person and number values. The values of the category PERSON in Kunbarlang are: first, second and third. Those of NUMBER are: singular, dual and plural. However, it seems that not all prefixes are specified for both of these categories. In §5.2.1 it was suggested that first person inclusive forms are in fact unspecified for number. The present section aims to adduce evidence for a similar conclusion about the third person 'singular' subject prefixes, namely: realis non-future *ka-*, realis future *kanj-*, and irrealis (past/non-past) *ki-*.

The main evidence to be discussed here comes from the quite widespread use of these 'singular' prefixes for non-singular referents, both non-human and human.[15] Consider example (5.32), where the first three instances of the subject prefix cross-referencing a plural referent (one and the same, as it appears) are 'singular' and the fourth one appears to be elaboration that provides more exact detail:[16]

(5.32) Kenda=bonj **ka**-nganun-yakbum nayi Japani
DEM.PROX.LOC=exactly 3SG.NF-1DU.EXCL.OBJ-drop_off.PST NM.I Japanese

ka-ngaddu-yakbum la **ka**-wom,
3SG.NF-1PL.EXCL.OBJ-drop_off.PST CONJ 3SG.NF-return.PST

kadda-wom.
3PL.NF-return.PST

'The Japanese brought us and dropped us here [at Goulburn Island] and they went back.' [20060620IB03/09:52–10:01]

This number neutralisation, shown in the narrative fragment (5.32), is a recurring pattern, even if not an overwhelmingly frequent one. It is also typical that the underspecified forms occur next to ones with a proper number specification. Both the plural (5.32) and the dual (5.33) can be reduced to the *ka-* form.

---

[15] Making this assumption also allows for a neat analysis of the third person singular object morpheme distribution (subject of the next section).
[16] The attentive reader will notice that the two object prefixes also encode different number values, first dual and then plural. It is less clear from the narrative what its actual cardinality should be. One possibility is that the speaker first focusses on just two persons, himself and another Warlang man, and then clarifies that there were others.

(5.33) Mayirri,   then start **ka**-ngunda   kubbunj **kabarra**-bum   old man,
       place.name ENG   ENG   3SG.NF-do.PST   canoe   3DU.NF-hit.PST ENG ENG
       mammam,   two, two   mammam, Kodjok and   Kunarr mammam.
       MF   ENG   ENG   MF   K.   ENG   K.   MF

'[We were/arrived at] Mayirri, then they two started to make a canoe, the two old men, two grandpa's, Kodjok and Kunarr.'   [IK1-160624_0021/00:45]

The underspecification is found with non-human referents as well, e.g. brolgas in example (5.29) above, or buffaloes in (5.34) below. Often the referent indexed by such underspecified prefixes may have a generic construal or flavour, or some sort of reduced individuation of the members of the plural referent. Notice, however, that this is not a requirement (cf. example 5.33), nor are these referents to be interpreted as kinds (i.e. as *the Leadbeater's possum* in *The Leadbeater's possum is endangered*).

(5.34) Na-rleng nganabbarru **ka**-dja   korro   man-berrk.
       I-many   buffalo   3SG.NF-stand.NP DEM.MED.LOC III-dry.land
       'There are many buffaloes on the mainland.'   [IK1-160715_0001/01:37:22–40]

In (5.34) the quantifier *na-rleng* 'many' is used, which ensures that the subject is not misconstrued as denoting a singular referent. Most of the examples in this section are in realis mood, but the phenomenon is not confined to it (5.29). Interestingly, these examples always come from spontaneous discourse. As soon as a speaker's attention is drawn towards this issue during elicitation, they would prohibit the 'singular' prefix form and demand the appropriate one—dual or plural. This is probably a pragmatic effect, some kind of preference for the most specified form when the speaker is making a conscious effort to speak 'correctly', i.e. normatively. Various patterns of number neutralisation are found in many languages of the area. For instance, in Ndjébbana, "for nominals with multiple non-human referents number may be neutralised and the gender contrast retained if the number of referents is non-specific. If, however, the plural non-human referents are individuated or enumerated... the appropriate augmented or unit augmented pronominal affixes are used. Finally number may be neutralised for human referents when sort of general/habitual statement is made without specific referents in mind" (McKay 2000: 192). In the next section I also review some relevant data from Bininj Kunwok.

In the light of the data presented in this section, I suggest that it is best to analyse the third singular subject prefixes as actually unmarked, or unspecified, for number. The following subsection (§5.2.3) is concerned with a similar issue in the third person object prefixes, where the morphological (non-)realisation of the prefix is dependent on its number value.

5.2.3 Third person object prefixes

The paradigm of object prefixes is given in table 5.5. From the table it is immediately obvious that the third person objects differ from first and second person ones: their cells contain zeroes (∅).[17] Let us first discuss dual and plural third person objects, and then we'll turn to the singular ones, whose pattern is somewhat more complicated.

The relevant notion for the dual and plural objects is ANIMACY. Thus, with an inanimate object in (5.35a) there is no object prefix on the verb, while it is obligatory with an animate object in (5.35b).

(5.35) a. Nga-rnay. (CONTEXT: There are many cars in Darwin.)
        1SG.NF-see.PST
        'I saw them.'   [IK1-150805_0002/15:19]

    b. Nga-**buddu**-rnay. (CONTEXT: A big mob is coming to fight us.)
        1SG.NF-3PL.OBJ-see.PST
        'I saw them.'   [ibid./13:26]

It is not straightforward whether animacy needs to, or even can, be considered a grammatical category in Kunbarlang. No other manifestations of it have been detected so far. Even in the domain of agreement, there is no clear division of the nominal lexicon into the animate and inanimate classes: rather, there are *bona fide* animates (live humans) and *bona fide* inanimates (properly inanimate objects), and there is some vagueness in between, in the domain of animals, forming a scale from 'animate' dogs to 'inanimate' fish and bugs.

The same property is relevant for the singular objects as well. Inanimate objects are never cross-referenced with the object morpheme -*bun*- (5.36a), and animates are (5.36b):

(5.36) a. Mary **ka-rnay**   nayi djurra korro   kun-bodme
         Mary 3SG.NF-see.PST   NM.I paper   DEM.MED.LOC   IV-back
         bi-ngaydju.
         DAT-she.GEN
         'Mary saw the book behind her.'   [IK1-160513_0021/29:12–40]

    b. Fred **ka-*(bun)-rnay**   Mary.
       Fred 3SG.NF-3SG.OBJ-see.PST Mary
       'Fred saw Mary.'   [IK1-160518_0011/19:29–20:07]

---

[17] The ∅'s in table 5.5 are used for a practical purpose rather than an ontological commitment to zero-allomorphs. Should the reader want to construct a verb using the paradigm tables, the ∅'s may serve as a reminder of the variation described here.

The object marker is obligatory for the singular animate referent in (5.36b). However, the pattern underlying the distribution of the singular object marking is more complex. Its overt (non-)appearance is dependent not only on the properties of the object, but also on those of the subject. Consider the following pair of examples in (5.37):

(5.37) a. Korlonj   **ki-rnanj**   kirdimarrk ka-rna…
         patriline.child 2SG.NF-see.NP man   3SG.NF-sit.NP
         'Son, [when] you see a man sitting…'   [RS1-140/04:25–27]

   b. Ka-rnay   **ka-bun-rnay**   ka-nganj-ka.
      3SG.NF-see.PST 3SG.NF-3SG.OBJ-see.PST 3SG.NF-HITH-go.NP
      'S/he looked and saw him/her coming.'   [20060606IB02/04:22–24]

The difference between (5.37a) and (5.37b) is in the features of the subject: in the former the subject is second person, while in the latter it is third person. Accordingly, the object marker for the third person singular object is only present in the latter case. The generalisation about *bun-* can be stated as follows:[18]

(5.38) BUN- GENERALISATION: Kunbarlang third person singular object marker *bun-* (i) only cross-references animate referents, and (ii) appears on the verb iff the subject is third person singular (*ka-*).

Indeed, if the subject is other than third person singular, *bun-* may not appear in the object slot. (5.37a) above provides an example of a second person subject, and (5.39a) below illustrates the point for a first person subject. Note that there is no such effect between, e.g., first person subject and second person object (5.39b).

(5.39) a. Ngunda **ngay-(*bun)-rnani**   na-buk.
         not   1SG.IRR.PST-see.IRR.PST I-person
         'I didn't see him.'   [IK1-160704_0001/51:21–33]

   b. Aku ngayi **nga-ngun-burrbunj**,   ka-ngan-marnanj-ngunda.
      ok I   1SG.NF-2SG.OBJ-know.NP 3SG.NF-1SG.OBJ-BEN-do.PST
      'OK, I know you, he told me.'   [20060901IB02/07:21–24]

Non-singular (i.e., dual or plural) subjects preclude the appearance of *bun-* regardless of their person. This effect of third person dual and plural subjects is exemplified in (5.40a) and (5.40b), respectively:

---

18 This generalisation, referring to properties of both the subject and the object, may appear at first as a case of subject/object portmanteau '3SG.SBJV:3SG.ANIM.OBJ'. However, this does not seem to be the correct analysis, both on theoretical grounds (which I do not pursue here, but see Kapitonov 2016b) and on language-internal considerations, for which see below.

(5.40) a. Benengka yiwanj **kanjbadda-rnanj** ngal-buk malayi...
they.DU DISC.PTCL 3DU.FUT-see.NP II-person tomorrow
'They two will see her tomorrow...' [IK1-160712_0001/04:48–05:14]

b. Na-buk yimarnek ki-buddu-karlkkandji la **kadda-rnay**
I-person like 3SG.NEG-3PL.OBJ-stalk.IRR.PST CONJ 3PL.NF-see.PST
la **kadda-bum**.
CONJ 3PL.NF-hit.PST
'He was going to sneak up on them, but they saw him and beat him.'
[ibid./00:42–01:40]

At the same time, the non-singular object markers always cross-reference animate objects, regardless of the subject's featural content; see example (5.35b) above. The following example offers a near-minimal pair of a verb with first person singular subject and third person singular (5.41a; no marker) or plural object (5.41b; marker present).

(5.41) a. **Nga-mu-rnilakwang** korro nukudbe.
1SG.NF-THITH-send.PST DEM.MED.LOC you.PL
'I sent someone to you.' [IK1-160503_0001/33:42–46]

b. **Nga-buddu-rnilakwang** korro nukudbe.
1SG.NF-3PL.OBJ-send.PST DEM.MED.LOC you.PL
'I sent them to you.' [ibid./35:14–19]

The generalisation (5.38) is relevant for all arguments that are cross-referenced in the object slot. Thus, it does not matter what the object's θ-role is, so the patterns described above hold of Recipient object just as well (5.42):

(5.42) a. Ngayi **nga-wuy** ngal-buk=bonj.
I 1SG.NF-give.PST II-person=exactly
'I gave it to her.' [IK1-160610_0001/11:25–27]

b. Ngal-buk=bonj **ka-bun-wuy** djurra John.
II-person=exactly 3SG.NF-3SG.OBJ-give.PST book John
'She gave a book to John.' [ibid.]

Likewise, the objects that are introduced by valency-changing derivations exhibit the same behaviour. In (5.43) realisation of the benefactive argument is contrasted with a first person and a third person subject.

(5.43) a. Ki-rnay   nayi kirdimarrk nayi **nga-marnanj-rlakwang** djirrka?
       2SG.NF-see.PST NM.I man   NM.I 1SG.NF-BEN-throw.PST   beard
       'Have you seen the man who I shaved?'   [IK1-160818_0021/40:44–48]

   b. Ngal-buk **ka-bun-marnanj-ngunda** John kuyi na-buk=bonj
      II-person 3SG.NF-3SG.OBJ-BEN-say.PST J   NM.IV I-person=exactly
      bidju.
      EMPH
      'She told John about himself.'   [IK1-160513_0021/26:02–24]

Recall that there are other items in the Kunbarlang agreement inventory that invite a numberless analysis:
- Kunbarlang third person singular subject prefix *ka-* is best analysed as numberless (§5.2.2)
- all first person inclusive forms in Kunbarlang are numberless as well (§5.2.1)

In sum, we have seen that there is no particular reason to adopt the portmanteau semantics for the personal prefix *bun-* over the simpler analysis as an object marker. In fact, the simpler analysis pontentially has a desirable conceptual advantage on a syntactic view of agreement. Namely, object agreement does not need to look ahead: only the object's features matter, not the subject's features (Kapitonov 2016b). Next, I review a relevant fragment of Bininj Kunwok agreement system.

Interestingly, in Bininj Kunwok there is a similar in spirit, but less grammaticalised inverse-like system (Evans 2003a: 417–25). The personal prefix *bi-*, which marks the combination of third minimal subject and third minimal object (we can call this object agreement for convenience), is only used when the object is of a comparable or higher animacy than the subject on the scale (5.44). Otherwise the intransitive prefix is used (roughly speaking, *ba-* or Ø-, depending on the dialect and on the verbal tense). These are the inverse and the direct forms, respectively.

(5.44) Malevolent spirits > humans > other animates > inanimates
                                          [Evans 2003a: 422, ex.10.96]

Thus, animals, which **do not** trigger the *bi-* form with human subjects (5.45a), do so with inanimate subjects (5.45b).[19]

---

[19] The notation '3/3' denotes the third minimal subject acting on third minimal object in portmanteau prefixes. The glosses H and L stand for 'higher' and 'lower', respectively, referring to the position of the object on the scale (5.44) w.r.t. the subject. Boldface mine—IK.

(5.45) Bininj Kunwok (Evans 2003a: 421)

a. Bininj Ø-ngune-ng duruk.
man 3/3L.PST-eat-PP dog
'The man ate the dog.' [ex.10.85b]

b. Gunj / Duruk gun-dulk **bi**-bom.
roo dog IV-stick 3/3H.PST-hit.PP
'The stick hit the kangaroo/dog.' [ex.10.91]

Conversely, humans, which **do** trigger the *bi-* form (5.46a) with human subjects, in combinations with spirit subjects fail to support object agreement (5.46b).

(5.46) Bininj Kunwok (Evans 2003a: 421)

a. Daluk **bi**-bom.
woman 3/3H.PST-hit.PP
'S/he hit the woman.'
OR 'The woman hit him/her.' [ex.10.82]

b. Daluk **ba**-bu-ni na-bulwinjbulwinj.
woman 3/3L.PST-hit-PI MA-spirit
'The spirit killed the woman.'
NOT: 'The woman killed the spirit.' [ex.10.89]

However, the system seems not fully grammaticalised, as there are occasional examples where the described principles are not operating, and, more generally, "there are border-line cases, such as babies or higher [animates—IK], where the speaker enjoys considerable latitude to manipulate the Ø vs *bi-* choice to communicative ends" (Evans 2003a: 425).

Crucially, Kunbarlang lacks the inverse effects. Thus, the object agreement does not appear in the combinations of an inanimate subject with an animate (i.e., higher) object, if that object NP does not normally support object agreement (5.47).

(5.47) Ninda na-warri mandjang **ki-bu** barbung.
DEM.PROX.I I-bad perhaps 3SG.NEG-hit.IRR.NP fish
'This poison would kill fish.' [IK1-160715_0001/01:05:38–43]

Fish, as a low animacy referent, never triggers object agreement, and so it does not in an inverse context in the presence of a 'lower' subject. In contrast to Kunbarlang data in (5.47), such combinations give rise to object marking in Bininj Kunwok (5.48):

(5.48) Bininj Kunwok (Evans 2003a: 422 ex.10.99)
Mawurrumbulk **kabi**-bu-n   ka-dowe-n.
fish.poison   3/3H-kill-NP 3-die-NP
'The fish poison kills the fish.'

I conclude that while there are very good reasons to conceive of the Bininj Kunwok object agreement pattern as a kind of an inverse system, the same analysis would be unjustified for the superficially similar Kunbarlang facts. Given the formal similarity of the markers involved—*bi-* in Bininj Kunwok and *bun-* in Kunbarlang—it is plausible that the two systems are slightly different developments of a common inheritance. It is possible to speculate further that Kunbarlang, with its complex but thoroughly agglutinating paradigms (§5.2.1), represents an innovation against the background of other Gunwinyguan languages whose paradigms are full of portmanteaux.[20]

In the broader picture, it is apparent that in the organisation of the Kunbarlang agreement paradigm the feature of number has a profound effect due to its tendency for neutralisation. At the descriptive level, it has been involved in the discussion of the third person 'singular' subject and object prefixes, the first person inclusive prefixes, and the allomorphy patterns in the transitive paradigms. I leave the exploration of its theoretical significance, as well as a formal analysis, for a separate occasion.

5.3 Conjugations

Common irregularities of the verbal conjugations are one of the major arguments in favour of the Gunwinyguan family (Alpher, Evans & Harvey 2003). The Gunwinyguan languages all have elaborate systems of verbal conjugation, with many subclasses organized around the subregularities. Wubuy provides one of the most spectacular examples with approximately 27 different subclasses of the eight more general patterns (Heath 1984: 408–411). Kunbarlang follows this common structure with its multiple conjugational classes of small size. On the present analysis, seven different classes (with a total of 12 subclasses) are recognised.[21] The classes are summarised in table 5.10, which shows the sets of suffixes characteristic of each conjugational class and lists the class members. The members shown are all bound morphemes—thematics (see the beginning of this chapter on the structure of the verbal word). The form of the verb root is obtained by combining the thematic from the 'Members' column with the desired suffix. Thus, for example, the four forms of the root -*beye* 'to bite' (class I.B) are:

---

[20] I'm grateful to Nick Evans for bringing up that point.
[21] Coleman (1982: 45,102) mentions a figure between 10 and 12 conjugations, but does not give a full list of those, nor of the verbs that group together.

-beye, -beyang, -beye and -beyerli. The semantics of the tense/mood forms is discussed in §5.5.

Tab. 5.10: Kunbarlang conjugational classes

Class		Realis Non-past	Realis Past	Irrealis Non-past	Irrealis Past	Members
I	A	∅	nj	∅	li	INCH -mi
	B	e	ang	e	erli	bey 'bite', kinj 'cook', ngem 'smear', rlem 'knock', rlum 'break'[a]
	C	e	eng	e	ili	karrm 'hold', larlm 'separate',[b] rdukkum 'cut'[c]
II		∅	ing	∅	ingi	all verbs ending in -dje,[d] birrayi 'reach'
III		∅	nj	∅	ni	bukayi 'climb, rise up', kelkkuyi 'work', mayi 'go across', ngayi 'hear', warre 'move', warribi 'deteriorate',[e] REFL -dji/-yi
IV	A	nj	ng	∅	ni	mikwa 'be stuck', wa 'wander'
	B	nj	m	∅	ni	bu 'hit', wo 'return'
	C	nj	y	∅	ni	djarrakbu 'save', mabulu 'want', rdawu 'cut', rna 'see', wu 'give'
	D	nj	y	ng	ni	rlu 'cry'
V		wa	ng	ng	ngi	dju 'stab', karlu 'dig', rluklu 'wake'
VI		a	nganj	ng	i	dj 'stand', rni 'sit', yu 'lie'
VII		be	dang	be	dana	rnek 'step', yi 'empty'

[a] The RP is rlumung, with -u, presumably from assimilation.
[b] The RNP is larlma, with -a.
[c] The RP is rdukkumung, with -u, presumably from assimilation.
[d] Except for ngundje 'say; do', which is irregular, and burrdje 'wrap', which shows variation in the irrealis forms: NP burrdjing, PST burrdjingi~burrdjerli.
[e] The RP varies between -nj and -n.

The distribution of thematics into classes is not strictly determined by any factors, whether phonological, semantic, or the thematic's transitivity. However, there are some regularities in certain classes:

class I the majority of thematics end in -m; it could be the case that all of these contain a proto-Gunwinyguan thematic (e.g. *ma; Alpher, Evans & Harvey 2003: 329–33), but it is not obvious

class III all thematics end in a front non-low vowel (e/i)

class IV all thematics end in a vowel other than front non-low (a/o/u)

class v all thematics end in *-u*

class vi contains the three posture verbs; this grouping is common among Gunwinyguan languages

This last class vi needs some further clarification in regard of the vocalism of the stems. Although it is clear that these three verbs share a common conjugation pattern, the choice of the vowel between the root and the suffix is hardly predictable. The full forms of these three stems are listed in table 5.11.

Tab. 5.11: Posture verb forms in Kunbarlang

Realis		Irrealis		
Non-past	Past	Non-past	Past	Gloss
dja	djanganj	djang	dji	'stand'
rna	rninganj	rning	rni	'sit'
yuwa	yunganj	yung	yu	'lie'

The analysis in table 5.10 leaves a set of 15 irregular verb thematics that do not belong to any of the above verb classes: *bingki* 'exit', *birrinja* 'be same', *djin* 'eat', *ka* 'go', *kali* 'get', *kanj* 'take', *kelbungu* 'be afraid', *ngadjbe* 'grind', *ngale* 'spread', *ngunga* 'threaten', *ngundje* 'say/do', *rdam* 'put', *rduka* 'look', *rlakka* 'throw', *yurrbungu* 'wet'. Almost all of these are very frequent verbs. The full list of forms is in table 5.12.

Tab. 5.12: Irregular conjugation verb stems in Kunbarlang,

Realis		Irrealis		
Non-past	Past	Non-past	Past	Gloss
bingki	bing	bing	bingkini	'exit'
birrinja	birrinjanganj	birrinjinj	birrinjinj	'be same'
djin	djarrang	djang	djarri	'eat'
ka	kidanj	kidang	kangkayini	'go'
kali	kalng	kalbing	kala	'get'
kanj	kanginj	ka	kandji	'take'
kelbungu	kelbunganj	kelbung	kelbunguni	'be(come) afraid'
ngadjbe	ngadjbum	ngadjbe	ngadjbuni	'grind'
ngale	ngalenj	ngaleng	ngaleni	'spread'
ngunga	ngunga	ngunga	ngungarli	'threaten'
ngundje	ngunda	ngundje	ngunda	'say/do'
rdam	rdam	rdam	rdana	'put'
rduka	rdukidanj	rdukidang	rdukarli	'look'
rlakka	rlakwang	rlakwa	rlakwani	'throw'
yurrbungu	yurrbunganj	yurrbu	yurrbunguni	'get wet'

Kunbarlang differs from other Gunwinyguan languages in terms of the inflectional categories that characterise the tense and mood of the stem. In particular, it differs from Dalabon (Evans & Merlan 2003) and Bininj Kunwok (Evans 2003a: ch. 9), the two languages it groups together with (see also Alpher, Evans & Harvey 2003: 310–313). In other Gunwinyguan languages, typically, irrealis is one form counterposed to a system of realis, which includes non-past and past, the latter also showing aspectual contrast between perfective and imperfective. This may be schematically represented as in figure 5.4 (cf. Alpher, Evans & Harvey 2003: 311; *imperative* is in parentheses since a distinct form is not found in many languages).

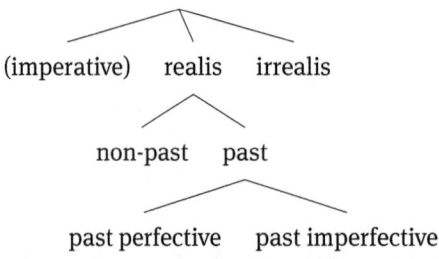

Fig. 5.4: Structure of Gunwinyguan TAM inflectional categories

The TAM categories of Kunbarlang are organised in a different fashion, showing a main opposition of realis and irrealis systems, each with non-past and past forms; cf. figure 5.5 and §5.4. Notice that the aspectual distinction (perfective vs. imperfective) is not grammaticalised in Kunbarlang. The mood, rather than the tense, is analysed here as a higher-level division, because of the restrictions on the combination of subject prefixes with TAM suffixes: they may have different tense specification, but must have the same mood specification (see §5.4 on the composite TAM forms in Kunbarlang).

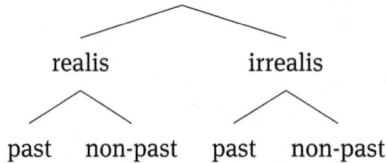

Fig. 5.5: Structure of Kunbarlang TAM inflectional categories

Out of these four Kunbarlang TAM forms shown in figure 5.5, three clearly continue the proto-Gunwinyguan (pGN) forms as reconstructed by Alpher, Evans & Harvey (2003, henceforth AEH), and suggestions are made below regarding the historical origins of the fourth form, the irrealis non-past. Kunbarlang data were not used in AEH's reconstruction: "The verbal suffix system of Kunbarlang is so aberrant that we decided not to integrate it into our reconstruction at this stage" (op. cit.: 308). From the formal and functional similarity it is clear that the Kunbarlang realis non-past and past, as categories, have developed out of the non-past and past perfective, respectively. Kunbarlang irrealis past developed out of the pGN past imperfective. It has retained some of the original semantics, still being used in past habituals (see §5.5.2.1), but also extended to such irrealis meanings as negation and counterfactuals. It seems to be a relatively common development; as the authors of the reconstruction notice, "many languages have lost the distinction, or blurred or exchanged forms between the irrealis and the past imperfective" (p. 312). The past imperfective suffix in the majority of pGN conjugations is /niɲ/, and the corresponding Kunbarlang form is /ni/, i.e. Kunbarlang has systematically dropped the final palatal nasal (similar to Bininj Kunwok, Ngandi, Wubuy and Mangarayi).[22]

An illustrative example of a Kunbarlang stem paradigm against the background of other Gunwinyguan languages is the verb 'hit', given in table 5.13 (forms from languages other than Kunbarlang are (a subset of) those in Alpher, Evans & Harvey (2003: §2), except for Anindilyakwa from van Egmond (2012: 353); orthography unified, with the initial labial stop systematically represented by *p*, palatal nasal by *ny* and the glottal stop by *q*).

The origin of the fourth Kunbarlang stem form—irrealis non-past—is far from obvious and would require separate research, but a hypothesis can be made here. Alpher, Evans & Harvey (2003: 312) observe that the Bininj Kunwok irrealis form has cognates in Dalabon, Ngandi (the evitative) and Wubuy (the non-past 2). They remark that the irrealis series is probably reconstructable for pGN, but "so many languages have lost the distinction, or blurred or exchanged forms between the irrealis and the past imperfective, that the reconstruction is complex" and is not attempted in that paper. Kunbarlang does not have any morphology immediately resembling the elaborate BGW irrealis forms, but connection seems easier to establish to the Dalabon irrealis (Evans & Merlan 2003) and the Ngandi evitative (Heath 1978: ch. 9).

Kunbarlang IrrNP is identical to the realis non-past for classes I, II and III (table 5.10). In the remaining classes the IrrNP formative is either -∅ or -*ng*.[23] Among the

---

22 On the other hand, Kunbarlang irrealis past bears formal similarity to the irrealis forms of Ngalakgan and Rembarrnga, cf. WLG *rna-ni* "see-IRR.PST"~ NIG *nani* "see-IRR" (B. Baker 2004: 321). This appears to be coincidential, for two reasons: (i) B. Baker (op. cit.: 323) argues that the irrealis form is a recent innovation in Ngalakgan and Rembarrnga, and there is no reason to subgroup Kunbarlang with them, and (ii) the unusual irrealis past forms of Kunbarlang conjugation I, which have a lateral in them, are easier to explain on the hypothesis that these forms indeed continue the pGN past imperfective of *-*ma*- 'do; say'/thematic.
23 There are some other forms occasionally, which I disregard for the moment.

Tab. 5.13: Paradigms of *pu-

Language	Non-past	Past (perf.)	Past Ipf.
Kunbarlang	pu-ny	pu-m	IrrPst: **pu-ni**
Jawoyn	pu-n	pu-m	pu-nay
Warray	pu-n	pu-m	pu-n-iny
Bininj Kunwok	pu-n	po-m	pu-ni
Dalabon	pu-n	po-ng	pu-niny
Ngalakgan	pu-n	poq-po-∅	pu-n-iny
Rembarrnga	pu-n	puwa	pu-n-iny
Ngandi	pu-nung	poo-m	pu-ni
Wubuy		pa-ng	pi-ni
Mangarayi	pu-n	pu-p	pu-ni
Anindilyakwa		pa-ma	
pGN	*pu-n	*po-m~*po-ng	*pu-n-iny

verbs in the table, the -*ng* form characterises the posture verbs (class VI.A), *rlunj* 'to cry' (class IV.E), and class V verbs, such as *djuwa* 'to stab'.

Dalabon irrealis is "mostly based on the present stem" (Evans & Merlan 2003: 277). The main pattern is that either -*i* is added after the present tense suffix, or the glide -*y* substitutes for that suffix. Additionally, in several verbs the irrealis is -*ngi*; these are the three posture verbs, *dong* 'chop' (cognate to WLG *djuwa* 'stab'), and three more which do not seem to have cognates in Kunbarlang.

The pGN non-past continues in Ngandi as future. It typically carries a suffix that contains a nasal. The evitative formatives in Ngandi are -∅, -*yi* and -*ngi*; they are never added on top of the future, but are in complementary distribution with the future ones.

The correspondences across the three languages are these:
1. in the three posture verbs the reflex of the pGN irrealis suffix is /-ŋi/; Kunbarlang and Dalabon, but not Ngandi also have that reflex in their respective forms of pGN *do-; few other modern verbs show that velar nasal
2. in Kunbarlang and Ngandi the reflexive/reciprocal forms take zero suffix in IrrNP (resp., evitative); if Ngandi thematics -*ḍu* and/or -*ḍa* are cognate to Kunbarlang thematic -*dje*, then there is further similarity here
3. there is a pattern where the Dalabon/Ngandi verbs that have present (resp., future) suffix with the apical -*n*, have the irrealis reflex with a glide (-*y*/-*yi*); this corresponds to Kunbarlang verbs with present suffix -*nj* and IrrNP -∅ (see table 5.14; clear examples of such verbs are *bunj* <*bu-* 'hit', *rnanj* <*na-* 'see', and *wunj* <*wo-* 'give')

While this would need to be confirmed by a thorough reconstruction, I conclude here that Kunbarlang irrealis non-past, as well as Dalabon irrealis and Ngandi evitative, instantiate modern reflexes of the proto-Gunwinyguan morphological category of irrealis. Given that all three languages are non-contiguous, this further confirms the sugges-

Tab. 5.14: Kunbarlang class IV correspondences with Dalabon and Ngandi

	Reflex of the pGN	
	non-past	irrealis
Dalabon	-n	-y
Ngandi	-n(uŋ)	-yi
Kunbarlang	-nj	-∅

tion made by B. Baker (2004: 674–5) that "Dalabon and Ngandi [and Kunbarlang—IK] preserve the essential details of the Irrealis category from pGN, which has become reshaped in various daughter languages such as Bininj Gun-wok and the Jala group".

5.4 Tense and mood: composite morphology

The tense and mood values in Kunbarlang are marked morphologically in a composite way, by the combination of the values of the subject prefix and the verb stem form (Australian composite TAM marking, in particular, counterfactual forms, are investigated in Verstraete 2005).[24] There are four series of subject prefixes (§5.2.1), and four forms of the verb stems (§5.3). These are cross-combined in a restricted way, yielding five morphological combinations (six for some younger speakers). Viewpoint aspect can only be marked analytically (§7.2). This section outlines the inflectional morphology on the verb that serves for the expression of tense and mood meanings. The semantics of these forms is discussed in detail in §5.5, along with other, analytical, ways of encoding tense and mood. My analysis of the Kunbarlang tense/mood forms differs significantly from Coleman's (1982); in what follows I first present the system as I found it in my fieldwork, and afterwards compare this description with Coleman's.

Table 5.15 below gives the combinations that proved well-formed in my fieldwork. On the present analysis, the verb forms are divided into two major groups, viz. REALIS and IRREALIS forms. Both prefixes and stems have that division, and must agree in mood with each other.

By way of illustration, table 5.16 shows the forms for the verb *-djin* with the first person singular subject, arranged in the same way as the table 5.15.

Two of the subject prefix series and two of the verb stem types are realis. The realis categories are the past (5.49a), the present (5.49b), and the future (5.49c). The irrealis

---

[24] Terminological notes: I use the term *mood* here for the binary opposition between realis and irrealis (also called "reality status" sometimes), rather than for the sentence moods, which have to do with illocutionary force. For a recent overview of the competing terminology, as well as for references, see Nikolaeva (2016).

Tab. 5.15: Permitted tense/mood combinations of subject prefixes and verb stems

	Subj. prefix	Verb stem Realis Past	Realis Non-past	Irrealis Past	Irrealis Non-past
Realis	Future		✓		
Realis	Non-future	✓	✓		
Irrealis	Past			✓	
Irrealis	Non-past			(✓)	✓

Tab. 5.16: A tense/mood paradigm of -*djin* 'to eat'

	Subj. prefix	Realis Past	Realis Non-past	Irrealis Past	Irrealis Non-past
Realis	Future		nganj-djin		
Realis	Non-future	nga-djarrang	nga-djin		
Irrealis	Past			ngay-djarri	
Irrealis	Non-past			(ngarra-djarri)	ngarra-djang

forms occur in modal contexts, including under negation (see below). The prefix and stem must agree in whether they are realis.

(5.49) a. ngana-rninganj
       1DU.EXCL.NF-sit.PST
       'we two (exclusive) were sitting'   [20060901IB02/04:52–53]

   b. ngana-rna
       1DU.EXCL.NF-sit.NP
       'we two (exclusive) are sitting'   [20150413IOv01/02:27–28]

   c. ngandji-rna
       1DU.EXCL.FUT-sit.NP
       'we two (exclusive) will sit'   [IK1-160811_0001/19:55–56]

The two realis subject prefix series are FUTURE (table 5.1) and NON-FUTURE (table 5.2). The realis stems are PAST and NON-PAST. The combination of the future prefix and past stem is prohibited, presumably on semantic grounds. The remaining three combinations yield future, present and past temporal reference (5.49). At least for the future, the temporal reference may be relative (5.50).

(5.50) a. La   babi **ka-kidanj**   kun-barrkidbe yalbi **kanj-marnbunj**
            CONJ later 3SG.NF-go.PST IV-other   country 3SG.FUT-make.NP
            yiwarrudj. La   ngunda ki-marnbuni,   babi la
            church   CONJ not   3SG.IRR.PST-make.IRR.PST later CONJ
            ka-warr-**minj**.
            3SG.NF-bad-INCH.PST

   'Later he **went** to another country **to build** a church. But never built it, as he **died**.' [copybook notes]

   b. Nga-mabulunj **nganj-ka**=kulkkulk kun-kudji~kudji.
      1SG.NF-like.NP 1SG.FUT-go.NP=run IV-DISTR~one
      'I like to go for a run from time to time.' [IK1-170606_1SY2/26:59–27:04]

In (5.50a), the reference of the future form *kanj-marnbunj* is not to the future of the speech time (i.e. absolute), but to the future relative to the past tense reference of the verb *ka-kidanj*. That is confirmed by the following sentence, which states the death of the protagonist in the past (of the speech time). Similarly, the running event in (5.50b) is not at a future point relative to the speech time (as would be with absolute future), but a habitual event that has instances both prior and posterior to the speech time.

The division in the irrealis forms is between PAST (5.51a) and NON-PAST (5.51b). For some speakers, the subject and verb stem are in a one-to-one correspondence, i.e. for them only two combinations are possible, where the subject prefix and the stem bear the same value. These are irrealis past and irrealis non-past. The respective subject prefix paradigms can be found in tables 5.3 and 5.4.

(5.51) a. Ngunda **ngay-rnani**.
            not   1SG.IRR.PST-see.IRR.PST
            'I didn't see him/her/it.' [IK1-180531_1SY1/02:10:18]

   b. Karlu,   ngunda **ngarra-rna**.
      NEG.PRED not   1SG.IRR.NP-see.IRR.NP
      (i) 'No, I don't see him/her/it.'
      (ii) 'No, I shan't see him/her/it.' [IK1-160704_0001/49:39]

   c. *Ngunda ngay-rna.
      not   1SG.IRR.PST-see.IRR.NP
      intended: 'I don't/didn't see him/her/it.' [IK1-180531_1SY1/02:10:25–29]

   d. *ngarra-rnani
      1SG.IRR.NP-see.IRR.PST
      Speaker's judgement is that this is not a word.
      [IK1-160704_0001/52:34–41]

Other—younger—speakers allow combining the non-past prefix with the past stem (5.52b).[25] The resulting meaning is the same as for the combination of the past prefix with the past stem, i.e. past tense reference. The fact that these two are two equal options to express the irrealis past leads me to conclude that for them this prefix is only specified as irrealis, but (for these speakers) may not be specified for tense. The three irrealis forms that are grammatical for these younger speakers are not isomorphic to the three realis forms, i.e. they are not negative polarity conditioned allomorphs of the realis forms. See table 5.15: crucially, the two realis combinations are with the non-past forms of the verb stem, and the two irrealis ones are with the past forms of the stem. Example (5.52c) shows the more standard form, in which the prefix and the stem match in both mood and tense.

(5.52) a. Ki-mabulunj bilmu?
2SG.NF-like.NP barramundi
'Do you like barramundi?' [IK1-160722_0011/06:50]

b. Nga-wakwanj, ngayi marrek **ngarra djarri** bilmu
1SG.NF-ignorant.NP I not 1SG.IRR.NP-eat.IRR.PST barramundi
wularrud.
already
'I don't know, I've never tried it.' [ibid./06:53-58]

c. Nga-wakwanj, ngunda wularrud **ngay-djarri**.
1SG.NF-ignorant.NP not already 1SG.IRR.PST-eat.IRR.PST
'I don't know, I have never tried it.' [IK1-160704_0001/01:20:22-38]

The irrealis forms are obligatory under negation, that is with the negative particles *ngunda* 'not' and *marrek* 'not' (5.52b). In the absence of the negative particles they convey modal meanings. The non-past forms have an epistemic possibility meaning (5.53a) and can occur in the protasis of a real conditional (5.54). When used to indicate epistemic possibility, the non-past verb forms are often accompanied by the word *mandjang* 'perhaps', which immediately precedes the verb (5.53a). Notice also in (5.53a) that the future form is used in imperatives. Negative imperatives use the present form with a prohibitive marker (§7.5); there's no dedicated imperative mood marking.

---

25 The speaker of this example is in her early 40s. The negated experiential perfect reading arises in the presence of the adverb *wularrud* 'already'. Without that adverb the verb (with the negative particle) is ambiguous between that reading and negating a particular event ('I didn't eat it').

(5.53) a. Kinj-rnanj   nukka nakarrken mandjang
       2SG.FUT-see.NP he   dog   perhaps
       ki-ngarrkun-beye.
       3SG.IRR.NP-1PL.OBJ-bite.IRR.NP
       'Watch out, that dog might bite us.'   [IK1-170609_1SY1/24:37–41]

   b. Karlu   **ngunda ki-ngarrkun-beye.**
      NEG.PRED not   3SG.IRR.NP-1PL.OBJ-bite.IRR.NP
      'No, it won't bite us.'   [ibid./26:40–43]

(5.54) Kuyi   **ki-ngan-beye**   nganj-bunj.
       NM.IV 3SG.IRR.NP-1SG.OBJ-bite.IRR.NP 1SG.FUT-hit.NP
       'If it bites me, I will kill it.'   [IK1-160828_0001/03:37–41]

The past irrealis forms have an even more diverse array of functions. On the one hand, those forms can have counterfactual meaning (5.55). On the other hand, they can refer to remote past habitual situations (5.56, repeated from 5.29 above).[26]

(5.55) Ngudda benbe   yimarne **ki-nganj-kangkayini**   ngayi
       you.SG yesterday   like   2SG.IRR.PST-HITH-go.IRR.PST   I
       ngay-ngun-wuni   bilmu   ki-djarri.
       1SG.IRR.PST-2SG.OBJ-give.IRR.PST barramundi 2SG.IRR.PST-eat.IRR.PST
       'Had you come yesterday, I would've given you barramundi to eat.'
                                                  [IK1-170609_1SY2/10:43–54]

(5.56) **Kidda-kangkayini**   **kidda-ngayini**   djarrebe
       3PL.IRR.PST-go.IRR.PST 3PL.IRR.PST-hear.IRR.PST far
       ki-wardidji,   **ki-dji**   kordorrkordorrk.
       3SG.IRR.PST-shout.IRR.PST 3SG.IRR.PST-stand.IRR.PST ONOMATOPOETIC
       'They used to go along hearing them [brolgas] from far away calling out, calling "kordorrkordorrk".'   [20150212AS02/01:33–38]

The meanings and functions of the permitted combinations are discussed at length in §5.5.

The previous analysis by Coleman (1982) rests on a somewhat different pattern in the data. Her table of permitted combinations includes six to seven forms (Coleman

---

[26] Although not the most frequent combination of functions, counterfactuals and past habituals may in fact be closely enough related. Classical New Persian had the suffix -*i* used exactly and only for past habituals and counterfactuals (Lazard 2006: 65). Also, counterfactuals are very often built on the basis of past tense (Iatridou 2000, Verstraete 2005).

1982: 104; see table 5.17 here, with the original order of columns and rows adjusted for the ease of comparison with table 5.15).[27] For Coleman, the prefixes are MODAL and are grouped into two classes: the ones concerned with 'performance' proper (*performative* and *non-performative* ones) vs. the ones concerned with the 'intent towards performance' (*intentional* and *non-intentional*) (p. 99). The verb stems are divided first by STATUS (realis vs. irrealis; correspond to my use of *mood*), and then (i) realis has a TENSE distinction (past and non-past), but (ii) irrealis has a 'PROBABILITY' distinction (possible vs. impossible).

Tab. 5.17: Permitted combinations of subject prefixes and status endings (Coleman 1982)

Subject prefix	Stem status			
	Realis		Irrealis	
	Past	Non-past	Improbable	Impossible
Intentional		✓		
Performative	✓	✓		
Non-intentional		✓	✓	
Non-performative	(✓)			✓

My analysis is informed by somewhat different data. Most importantly, there are two combinations reported by Coleman, but not confirmed in my fieldwork. One is of a non-intentional prefix with a non-past suffix, which in my terms is irrealis past and realis non-past (5.57):

(5.57) Malayi   ngayi **ngayi-kali**.
tomorrow I   1SG.IRR.PST-get.NP
'I might get it tomorrow.'   [Coleman 1982: 97; gloss mine—IK]

The other form is a combination of a non-performative prefix with a past suffix, which in my terms is irrealis non-past and realis past (5.58):

(5.58) Ngayi ngunda **ngarra-djarrang**   kandiddjawa.
I   not   1SG.IRR.NP-eat.PST   damper
'It wasn't me who ate the damper.'   [Coleman 1982: 93; gloss mine—IK]

---

[27] The two tables have the same order and position of forms, even though they are differently named. This allows one to 'overlay' one table on top of the other. Visual inspection reveals immediately three points of discrepancy in the data: Coleman's table has two combinations in the lower left block that mine does not; these two combine what I call irrealis prefixes with the realis stems. My data, on the other hand, have one combination in the lower right block that is missing from her data. This is the alternative past form that I found only some younger speakers to accept.

Both examples were rejected by several of my informants. It is very hard to tell if a change has occurred since, or whether it is just a transcription error in the first place. Neither of these two combinations appear frequently in Coleman's (1982) thesis.

5.5 Tense and mood: semantics

The morphological resources of the verbal paradigm that make up the various tense and mood forms are described in §5.4. As mentioned in that section, by *mood* I refer here to the opposition between realis and irrealis (sometimes termed *reality status*). The choice of term is partially driven by the wish to de-emphasize the semantic component of *actualization* of some state of affairs, often implied in the "reality status" (Nikolaeva 2016: 80). In Kunbarlang, realis and irrealis are, first of all, two morphological subsystems in the system of expressing temporal and modal meanings. While the two subsystems largely coincide with the actualized/non-actualized distinction, the inclusion of future tense within the realis system may be viewed as a wrinkle on the actualization divide. I refer the reader to the section on the future forms (§5.5.1.3) for further discussion.

In this section I deal in greater detail with the meaning and functions of the synthetic forms described in §5.4 and discuss analytical constructions that further convey TAM semantics. Under the analysis outlined, the major division is between two moods, realis and irrealis. Within those, there are further tense distinctions, such that, broadly speaking, there are past, present and future forms within the realis system, and past and non-past forms in the system of irrealis. Viewpoint aspect is not systematically encoded by the verbal morphology, but it can be expressed via stylistic lengthening or serial verb constructions (§7.2). Kunbarlang Aktionsart has not been studied extensively, this would be a topic for future in-depth lexicographic work on the aspectual semantics.

5.5.1 Realis forms

Realis mood forms are built with realis subject prefixes and realis verb stems, and include three combinations: past, present and future.

5.5.1.1 Realis past
The main function of past tense realis forms is to convey past tense reference, i.e. talk about events that took place in the past; consider (5.59), a fragment of the narrative about the speaker's camping trip in Arnhem Land during the 1974 cyclone Tracy.

(5.59) a. Ngorro balanda **ka**-nganj-**kidanj**, **ka-wokdjanganj**,
DEM.MED.IV whitefella 3SG.NF-HITH-go.PST 3SG.NF-speak.PST
ka-burrdjung dukulu, cyclone.
3SG.NF-divulge.PST wind ENG
'That whitefella came, and talked, and told about the wind, the cyclone.'
[IK1-160624_0021/06:15–20]

b. But **kabarra-ngunda** "*karlu*" ngayi two old people, "*oy kun-mak*
ENG 3DU.NF-do.PST no NM.PL ENG ENG ENG INTJ IV-good
ngadda-rna".
1PL.EXCL.NF-sit.NP
'But the two old men said "No, we're fine here."' [ibid./06:22–28]

c. Ngorro bonj **ka-wom**.
DEM.MED.IV exactly 3SG.NF-return.PST
'So he went back.' [ibid./06:30–32]

The past is unspecified for perfective/imperfective interpretation. The event normally is understood as being complete or finished, but this can be cancelled (5.60).

(5.60) **Ka-borrkkidanj** la ngunda ki-burnbuni la munguy
3SG.NF-dance.PST CONJ not 3SG.IRR.PST-finish.PST CONJ a_lot
ka-borrkka.
3SG.NF-dance.NP
'He was dancing and didn't finish, and is still dancing.'
[IK1-170616_1SY1/07:04–20]

5.5.1.2 Realis present

Present tense realis forms are built with realis non-future prefixes and realis non-past suffixes. The present tense is used to refer to events whose time overlaps with the moment of speech: both specific events which are simultaneous with the moment of speech, translated with the English Present Continuous (5.61), and generic events (5.62), including present tense habituals (5.62b–c).

(5.61) Manda man-djelmi la **ka-worrhngunj**.
DEM.PROX.III III-lukewarm CONJ 3SG.NF-heat.NP
'That [food] is lukewarm and s/he's reheating it.' [IK1-170615_1SY2/51:09–14]

(5.62) a. Namaddba, nayi nukka ngorro mukka mangrove
        oyster   NM.I he.I DEM.MED.IV NM.III mangrove
        ka-dja.
        3SG.NF-stand.NP
        'Oysters, they live in the mangroves.'   [20060814IB02/00:27–32]

   b. **Ka-kelkkuyi** korro   office, **ka-bihbunj** djurra.
      3SG.NF-work.NP DEM.MED.LOC office 3SG.NF-write.NP paper
      'S/he works at an office. S/he writes letters.'
        [IK1-160428_0001/07:42–48; after Dahl's (1985) Questionnaire item (25)]

   c. **Ka-ka**   **kulkkulk** munguy.
      3SG.NF-go.NP run   a_lot
      'S/he goes running always/every day.'   [IK1-160719_0011/06:08–10]

The present is also used in talking about events that do not have a specific temporal value, such as in example (5.63), taken from a procedural text on making damper.

(5.63) a. Bonj   ngorro   **ka-bun-djinj,**   man-djorleng, la
      exactly DEM.MED.IV 3SG.NF-3SG.OBJ-eat.NP III-ripe   CONJ
      ngadda-nguluk-kali.
      1PL.EXCL.NF-ash-get.NP
      'Then it bakes, and when it's ready, we take it out from the ashes.'
                                                         [IK1-160726_0021/01:03–11]

   b. **Ka-yuwa,**   **ngadda-rdukku~rdukkume,** ngorro
      3SG.NF-lie.NP 1PL.EXCL.NF-PLURAC~cut.NP DEM.MED.IV
      ngadda-djinj,   share **ngadda-ngundje.**
      1PL.EXCL.NF-eat.NP share 1PL.EXCL.NF-do.NP
      'It sits [cooling down], we cut it in pieces, then we eat it, we share it.'
                                                               [ibid./01:12–20]

Realis present is the verbal form that is used in negative imperatives (§7.5), together with the obligatory prohibitive marker *kanjyuwa* (5.64):

(5.64) Kanjyuwa **ki-rnanj!**
      PROH   2SG.NF-see.NP
      'Don't stare at him/her/it!'   [IK1-180521_1SY1/25:03]

5.5.1.3 Realis future

The future tense form of the verb is morphologically related to the present tense form, because both are built from the realis non-past stem; the future, however, uses the future subject prefix series. These forms are used when the event time follows the utterance time (5.65).

(5.65) a. Kadda-burrdjung kuyi **kanj-mankanj** nayi balmad malayi.
3PL.NF-divulge.PST NM.IV 3SG.FUT-fall.NP NM.I rain tomorrow
'They said [on the radio], it will rain tomorrow.'
[IK1-160516_0001/04:00–04]

b. Kukkangundje **kanjbadda-rna kanjbadda-wonj** malayi, la
maybe 3PL.FUT-sit.NP 3PL.FUT-return.NP tomorrow CONJ
ngarrk-wakwanj.
1.INCL.NF-ignorant.NP
'Maybe they'll be going back home tomorrow, but we don't know.'
[IK1-170615_1SY2/09:59–10:09]

c. **Nganj-ka** korro kaddum korro Ngabbard
1SG.FUT-go.NP DEM.MED.LOC above DEM.MED.LOC F
ka-rna. Yiwanj **nganj-nganj-wonj**.
3SG.NF-sit.NP DISC.PTCL 1SG.FUT-HITH-return.NP
'I will go to Heaven where Father sits. Later I will return.'
[IK1-160430_0001/03:57–04:09]

Examples above show absolute time reference (although (5.65a) may be relativised to the speech verb in that sentence, if the future form is understood as direct speech), but the future forms can also have relative reference (5.66):

(5.66) La babi ka-kidanj kun-barrkidbe yalbi **kanj-marnbunj**
CONJ later 3SG.NF-go.PST IV-other country 3SG.FUT-make.NP
yiwarrudj. La ngunda ki-marnbuni, babi la
church CONJ not 3SG.IRR.PST-make.IRR.PST later CONJ
ka-warr-minj.
3SG.NF-bad-INCH.PST
'Later he went to another country **to build** a church. But never built it, as he died.' [copybook notes]

Kunbarlang future tense form is also the only form used in positive imperatives (5.67, 5.74b; see §7.5 on imperatives) and in the hortative function (5.68).

(5.67) **Kinj-wunj** na-buk!
2SG.FUT-give.NP I-person
'Give it to him!' [IK1-180521_1SY1/21:36]

(5.68) **Ngarrki-ka**   ngorro   barbung!
        1.INCL.FUT-go.NP DEM.MED.IV   fish
        'Let's go fishing!'   [20070108IB01/16:22]

The proper analysis of the Kunbarlang future is unclear at the moment, and needs further work on its temporal and modal semantics. On the one hand, future tense is morphologically related to the proper realis categories of the present and the past, through sharing the realis non-past stem with the present form of the verb. On the other hand, as mentioned in the introduction to this section, realis is often thought of as having to do with actualized events; future tense reference, however, is non-actualized. Before further work can be done, I offer the following analysis.

The Kunbarlang future is a tense category, not a modal category (as Comrie (1985: 44) points out, "[it] is... possible to have future time reference which is not necessarily modal"). The realis/irrealis divide in Kunbarlang has to do with the possible worlds semantics (Lewis 1986). All forms of the realis subsystem make reference to the actual world. The irrealis forms (see the sections below) all involve quantification over possible worlds. As a tense that belongs to the realis system, future has to do with statements about a future reference point (i.e. speaker's predictions).

Some potential complication comes from the fact that the Kunbarlang future is occasionally found in what functionally are conditionals (5.69):

(5.69) a. Ngayi **nganj-djinj**   kun-mak mayi   kumungadju?
            I   1SG.FUT-eat.NP IV-good NM.III   berry
            'I'll be OK if I eat this berry?' [lit. 'I shall eat this berry fine?']
                 [IK1-160618_0001/34:18–21; after Dahl's (1985) Questionnaire item (81)]
        b. Ngudda **kinj-djinj**   **kinj-weddjuwa**.
            you.SG   2SG.FUT-eat.NP 2SG.FUT-vomit.NP
            'If you eat it you'll vomit.'   [ibid./33:50–54, also 34:22–25]

Although the future can be found in conditionals, it appears less common in this function than the non-past irrealis form (§5.5.2.2; the usual form used in conditionals). Moreover, there is a possibility that the modal flavour of the conditional is not inherent to the semantics of the Kunbarlang future. Perhaps the literal meaning of (5.69b) is akin to the English *You eat this and you'll vomit*—where the conditional reading arises contextually, since there is no formal conditional marking.

5.5.2 Irrealis forms

Irrealis mood forms are built with irrealis subject prefixes and irrealis verb stems. For some speakers, the tense specification of the prefix and the stem must match, for other speakers, the non-past prefixes may combine with the past stems. In either case, the composite verb forms have only a two-way distinction, viz. between past and non-past. The contrast between present and future, observed in the system of realis, is neutralised in irrealis.

5.5.2.1 Irrealis past

The irrealis past in Kunbarlang is used in a variety of irrealis contexts, specifying past tense reference. This form is obligatory (for the events preceding the speech time) in the scope of negative particles (*ngunda* 'not' and *marrek* 'not', the latter having similar forms in Bininj Kunwok and Mawng).

(5.70) Yoh la **ngunda ngarrki-kangkayini**, karlu.
yes CONJ not 1.INCL.IRR.PST-go.IRR.PST NEG.PRED
'Yes, but we didn't go, nothing. [Because there was no car.]'
[20060830IB02/02:09–11]

This form is also used in counterfactual conditionals (5.55, 5.71).

(5.71) Kuyi **ngarrki-kangkayini** hammer **ngay-karrmili** or
NM.IV 1.INCL.IRR.PST-go.IRR.PST hammer 1SG.IRR.PST-hold.IRR.PST or
rrabbi... la karlu.
file CONJ NEG.PRED
'If we had have been going to go, I would've taken a hammer or a file... but nothing.' [20060814IB02/01:12–18]

Still another function of the irrealis past form is the past habituals. This occurs particularly frequently in older people's stories about the olden times and traditional activities, such as the fragments in (5.72) and (5.73).

(5.72) a. Kingarduld **ngadda-karlungi**.
venus.clam 1PL.EXCL.IRR.PST-dig.IRR.PST
'We used to dig [scratch the surface of the sand/mud] for venus/tapestry clams.' [20060620IB03/01:19–24]

b. **Ngadda-worrmili** wirdidj,
1PL.EXCL.IRR.PST-kindle.IRR.PST fire

kunkeba **ngadda**-wirdidj-**djungi**.
fire.drill 1PL.EXCL.IRR.PST-fire-stab.IRR.PST
'We used to make fire, we twirled the fire drill.' [ibid./01:30–35]

c. **Ngadda-kinjerli** barbung.
1PL.EXCL.IRR.PST-cook.IRR.PST fish
'We would cook fish.' [ibid./01:36–38]

(5.73) **Ki-warreni**   **ki-wokdji**
        3SG.IRR.PST-move.IRR.PST 3SG.IRR.PST-speak.IRR.PST

   ki-yawani   njunjuk bonj~bonj.
   3SG.IRR.PST-seek.IRR.PST   water   RDP~exactly

   'They [brolgas] would go along crying out, looking for water again.'
   [20150212AS02/01:59–02:03]

Some scholars point out that habituals have a modal component to them (Boneh & Doron 2010), which explains the use of irrealis in Kunbarlang on the proposal made above that Kunbarlang irrealis is inherently modal, i.e. has to do with possible worlds.

5.5.2.2 Irrealis non-past

Kunbarlang irrealis non-past is used in irrealis contexts, specifying present or future tense reference. Similarly to its past tense counterpart (see above), it is obligatory in the scope of negation.

(5.74) a. **Ngunda kidda-kalbing**   djininj mayali, ngayi barrayidjidj.
          not   3PL.IRR.NP-get.IRR.NP   properly sense   NM.PL children

   'They don't hold the knowledge tight, the kids.'
   [IK1-160424_0001/03:27–30]

   b. Na-mak kinj-karrme   la   **ngunda ki-ngun-beye.**
      I-good 2SG.FUT-hold.NP   CONJ not   3SG.IRR.NP-2SG.OBJ-bite.IRR.NP

   'It's good, hold it and it won't bite you.'   [IK1-170615_1SY2/18:08–12]

Other uses of this form include the protasis of a conditional (5.75a) and other modal contexts, in particular, expressing epistemic possibility (5.75b).

(5.75) a. The police warns the local population about the coming cyclone. They say, among other things:

   Nguddu-yung   mandjang **ki-nguddu-bu.**
   2PL.IRR.NP-lie.IRR.NP   perhaps   3SG.IRR.NP-2PL.OBJ-hit.IRR.NP

   'If you sleep [in the house] you might get hurt.'
   [20060614IB/00:30–33; translation mine—IK]

   b. Kukkangundje **ki-bun-rnak-bu.**
      maybe   3SG.IRR.NP-3SG.OBJ-LIM-hit.IRR.NP

   'S/he might just hit him/her/it.'   [IK1-160728_0001/15:32–34]

Deontic modality does not have any specific form of expression in Kunbarlang. It may be expressed with future/imperative (5.76), or with the irrealis non-past if modalised through the use in a conditional (5.77b).

(5.76) **Ngundjidda-ka** ngorro.
2PL.FUT-go.NP DEM.MED.IV
'You can go now.' [E.g., said by a teacher after the class is over.]
[IK1-170522_1SM1/02:51]

(5.77) a. Ngudda ngunda **kirri-rna**.
you.SG not 2SG.IRR.NP-see.IRR.NP
'You won't find it.' [IK1-170609_1SY1/22:47–49]

b. Ngarra-mabulu **ngarra-rna**.
1SG.IRR.NP-want.IRR.NP 1SG.IRR.NP-see.IRR.NP
'If I want to, I can find it.' [ibid./21:40, 22:54]

Perhaps a type of epistemic modal meaning of the irrealis non-past is the adversative use as in (5.78):

(5.78) Kanjyuwa ki-kali la **ki**-ngun-**djang**!
PROH 2SG.NF-get.NP CONJ 3SG.IRR.NP-2SG.OBJ-eat.IRR.NP
'Don't get it, it'll burn you!' [IK1-170530_1SY2/21:26–30]

This review of the functions that the various Kunbarlang tense/mood forms have concludes the discussion of the verbal inflectional morphology. In the next chapter I turn to the ways of extending the Kunbarlang verb by means of derivational morphology and special verbal constructions.

6 Verbs: derivational morphology and constructions

This chapter presents a variety of morphological devices that can alter the verb's argument structure and modify the event description. These include valency increasing prefixes (§6.1), noun incorporation (§6.3) and a variety of incorporated adverbials (§6.4), and valency-conserving reflexive/reciprocal suffix (§6.1.3). Section 6.2 reviews the valency classes found in Kunbarlang, taking into account both underived predicates and predicates formed through the application of argument structure derivations. The last section (§6.5) discusses a particular type of complex predicate construction found in Kunbarlang, viz. the coverb construction. This construction is unusual in the Gunwinyguan family but is structurally very similar to the Mawng coverb construction. However, there is interesting correspondence between the Kunbarlang coverb construction and certain features of predicate building in the Gunwinyguan languages, in particular, the complex stems and the phenomenon of excorporation.

6.1 Argument derivation

Thanks to its rich polysynthetic morphology, Kunbarlang has an array of morphological means to change the predicate's valency and argument structure. It has both valency increasing and conserving derivations. The former include the benefactive (§6.1.1) and the comitative (§6.1.2), expressed by prefixes. The reflexive/reciprocal suffix represents a valency-conserving derivation—I argue in (§6.1.3) that it does not lower valency of the predicate in the general case. However, due to a restriction on anaphoric binding of secondary objects there is a valency reduction-like side-effect of reflexivisation of ditransitive Themes. Even though the reflexive/reciprocal does not alter the valency of the predicate, it is still discussed here among argument derivations, because it (i) derives a new predicate from the base verb by (ii) acting on its argument structure.

A predicate can be formed via successive application of derivations, and interpretation of the resulting predicates suggests that the reflexive/reciprocal always applies before the benefactive or the comitative. This is the opposite of the restriction found in Anindilyakwa, Bininj Kunwok, Ngandi, and Wubuy, whereby the reciprocal cannot precede other argument derivations (Horrack 2018: 266–8). The two Kunbarlang valency-increasing derivations do not interact with each other, and in that sense are unordered.[1]

---

[1] Derivation of predicates and interaction of applicatives in a such morphosyntactically rich language as Kunbarlang is a complex topic, and within the scope of this grammar I cannot do full justice to its exploration. Recent work on another Gunwinyguan language Wubuy by Horrack (2018; see esp. ch. 7) reveals an intricate system of interaction of valency-changing processes and their effects

6.1.1 Benefactive

The benefactive is introduced by the prefix *marnanj-* (6.1a) in the slot -8 (see table 5.1 at the beginning of chapter 5). It is cognate with the benefactive prefixes in Bininj Kunwok and Dalabon (the "*marne* group" of Alpher, Evans & Harvey 2003).

(6.1) a. Ka-**ngan-marnanj**-yawanj djurra, nayi kin-ngaybu.
3SG.NF-1SG.OBJ-BEN-seek.NP paper NM.I I/II-I.GEN
'S/he's looking for my book for me.' [IK1-170602_1SY2/01:18–25]

b. Yoh ngal-buk=bonj njunjuk **ka-yawanj**.
yes II-person=exactly water 3SG.NF-seek.NP
'Yes, she looks around for water.' [20150212AS02/01:41–44]

Its main function is to add an extra argument to the verb's frame (compare the benefactive-marked derived ditransitive predicate in (6.1a) with its monotransitive base verb in (6.1b)). The thematic role of the new argument can be the beneficiary (6.1a), the addressee (6.2a), the goal (6.2b), the stimulus (6.2c), or the maleficiary (6.2d). I decided to use the traditional label 'benefactive' here, but it may be more transparently called AFFECTEE to reflect the range of thematic roles it introduces (that is the terminological choice made for the similar derivation in Wubuy by Horrack (2018: 6–9)). Coleman (1982: 37) calls this derivation IMPLICATED ARGUMENT.

(6.2) a. Kabarra-**marnanj**-ngunda that two mammam: *Bonj*
3DU.NF-BEN-do.PST ENG ENG MF exactly
ngandjidda-rna kun-mak.
1PL.EXCL.FUT-sit.NP IV-good
'The two mammam told him [John Hunter]: *Ok, we'll be fine.*'
[IK1-160624_0021/02:15–20]

b. Kabarra-**marnanj**-bing old man kakkak Bungorro.
3DU.NF-BEN-exit.PST ENG ENG MMB B
'They two came to the old man Bungorro.' [ibid./03:35–38]

c. Kadda-**marnanj**-borrkkidanj njunjuk.
3PL.NF-BEN-dance.PST water
'They went dancing for that water.' [IK1-160726_0001/10:28–32]

d. Ka-**ngan-marnanj**-yambi-kalng=kubirribirrkuk.
3SG.NF-1SG.OBJ-BEN-swag-get.PST=steal
'S/he / it stole a swag from me.' [IK1-160715_0001/10:44]

---

on the realisation of verbal arguments. Further work on Kunbarlang would be beneficial for a deeper understanding of how argument structure is built and modified.

The benefactive derivation effectively promotes dative adjuncts into argument status (in particular, enabling their cross-referencing in the object slot). Consider two consecutive clauses from a narrative, where both devices are used in turn to express a beneficiary (6.3):

(6.3) a. Kadda-kalng ngorro kadda-worrhmeng **bi-rnungu**.
3PL.NF-get.PST DEM.MED.IV 3PL.NF-kindle.PST DAT-he.GEN
'They got him and made a fire for him.' [IK1-16010_0001/04:44–49]

b. Ka-**buddu-marnanj**-worrhmeng ngob.
3SG.NF-3PL.OBJ-BEN-kindle.PST all
'They made fire for them all.' [ibid./04:49–51]

This additional non-subcategorised benefactive/affectee role must be expressed either as a dative adjunct (6.4a) or a benefactive object (6.4b), but the two constructions cannot be mixed, as shown by the ungrammaticality of (6.4c), where there is both a prefix in the verb and a free dative pronoun instead of the object prefix.

(6.4) IK1-160618_0001/46' ff.

a. Kunj ka-bum **bi-ngaybu ngayi**.
kangaroo 3SG.NF-hit.PST DAT-I.GEN I
'S/he killed a kangaroo for me.'

b. Kunj ka-**ngan-marnanj**-bum ngayi.
kangaroo 3SG.NF-1SG.OBJ-BEN-hit.PST I

c. *Kunj ka-**marnanj**-bum bi-ngaybu ngayi.
kangaroo 3SG.NF-BEN-hit.PST DAT-I.GEN I

The benefactive appears fully productive, i.e. it combines with a large number of diverse verbs. The interpretation of the thematic role of the introduced argument arises based on the base verb semantics.

6.1.2 Comitative

The comitative, like the benefactive, increases the valency of the verb, but it bears a number of important differences to it, which I explain below. It occupies slot -1 in the verbal template and is expressed by the prefix *walkki-* (6.5).[2]

---

[2] For some speakers, the initial glide of the comitative prefix hardens to [b] after stops; I do not reflect that in the transcriptions given here.

(6.5) **Ka-ngan-walkki-rnay** **kunbareng** nayi djamun la
3SG.NF-1SG.OBJ-COM-see.PST alcohol NM.I policeman CONJ
nga-wundjinj.
1SG.NF-hide.PST
'The policeman saw me with grog and I hid it.' [IK1-160816_0001/33:09–15]

In (6.5), the comitative licenses the unmarked noun *kunbareng* as the comitative argument. By contrast, without the comitative applicative, the noun has to be an adjunct in a prepositional phrase with *walkki* (6.6).

(6.6) Kadda-bu-djinj **walkki rlama**.
3PL.NF-hit-REFL.PST with shovel_spear
'They were fighting with shovel spears.' [IK1-180605_1SY1/25:45–47]

The absolute majority of examples with the comitative derivation include an animate Theme and an inanimate comitative (as in (6.5)), so the latter is not indexed in the object agreement slot. Examples in (6.7) show that the comitative argument is indexed by a personal prefix in the object slot, when not overridden by other objects.

(6.7) a. Nga-wom nga-buddu-rnay djarrangalanj ngudda
1SG.NF-return.PST 1SG.NF-3PL.OBJ-see.PST boy you.SG
ki-buddu-walkki-rleng-minj.
1SG.NF-3PL.OBJ-COM-much-INCH.PST
'I went back and saw the boys that you were growing up with.'
[IK1-170621_1SY1/28:05–12]

b. Ngayi ngabbard **ka-ngan-walkki-rnirdam**.
I father 3SG.NF-1SG.OBJ-COM-place.PST
'My father gave me [the language].' [lit. 'placed it with me']
[20070108IB01/02:36–38]

Furthermore, with verbs whose comitative argument is the Recipient, it gets indexed in the object slot over the Theme (6.8):

(6.8) **Ka-buddu-walkki-baybum** nayi nawalak.
3SG.NF-3PL.OBJ-COM-leave.PST NM.I child
'She left the child with them.' [IK1-180529_1SY1/01:22:14–20]

The comitative argument can also be incorporated, like the generic incorporated nominal *bardi-* 'liquid' in (6.9):

(6.9) Ka-bun-**bardi-walkki-rnay**   kunbareng.
       3SG.NF-3SG.OBJ-liquid-COM-see.PST   alcohol
       '[The policeman] saw him/her with grog.'   [IK1-180601_1SY1/01:22:08–11]

The comitative seems to be less frequent than the benefactive and combines with fewer verbs. Although the present data do not suggest any particular semantic restriction on the type of the base verb, my impression is that the majority of uses include a motion verb, e.g. *-bingki* 'to exit', *-bukayi* 'to rise', *-wonj* 'to return' etc.

(6.10) Ngadda-bum=munumunu   ngob, bonj   la
       1PL.EXCL.NF-hit.PST=squash all   exactly CONJ
       ngadda-walkki-bakdjung.
       1PL.EXCL.NF-COM-descend.PST
       'We made it all squashed in together, then we went down to the sea with it.'
                                           [20060620IB04/02:04–08]

Another important difference is that the comitative has a free-standing counterpart of the same phonological form, which serves as a preposition (6.6, 6.11; see also §3.2.9).

(6.11) Makubarrkidj   ka-bun-djarrang   nayi   drum [_PP_**walkki** mayi
       separately(?) 3SG.NF-3SG.OBJ-eat.PST NM.I   drum   with   NM.III
       nguk=rnungu].
       intestine=he.GEN
       'We put a separate drum on fire with the guts.'
                          [20140703IOv01-ShM/03:09–14; translation mine—IK]

Semantically, the comitative typically encodes a possessive, 'having', meaning. The possessor can be the subject (6.7a, 6.10) or the object of the base verb (6.5). There are, however, occasional examples that do not clearly fall into the comitative interpretation (6.12),[3] which may be idiomatic.

(6.12) Mamu   ka-ngaddu-karlangwang   yakarni   kikka ngorro
       devil 3SG.NF-3PL.EXCL.OBJ-chase.PST magpie_goose   she.III DEM.MED.IV
       ngadda-walkki-bu-djinj.
       3PL.EXCL.NF-COM-hit-REFL.PST
       'Devil was chasing us, we were fighting over those magpie geese.' [lit., perhaps: 'hit each other, having the geese']   [20060620IB04/05:01–06]

---

[3] Evans (2003a: 397) calls the isomorphic Bininj Kunwok verb *-yi-bun* 'to hit o over/for the possession of COM' (where the root *-bun* is cognate with the Kunbarlang *-bunj* 'to hit', but the comitative prefix *yi-* is not cognate with any Kunbarlang morphemes, to my knowledge) a 'potential comitative', commenting that the object is construed as possessing the COM at the outset of the event.

Additional evidence for the idiomatisation of the comitative in (6.12) comes from the fact that an adjunct comitative phrase does not have the same meaning (6.13):

(6.13) Kadda-bu-djinj **walkki** yakarni.
3PL.NF-hit-REFL.PST with magpie_goose
'They were fighting, and each mob had magpie geese.'
NOT: 'They were fighting over the magpie geese.'
[IK1-180605_1SY1/25:40–43]

There is also one known idiom with it, -*walkki-karrme* 'to help' ((6.14); lit. 'to hold it with X').

(6.14) Ngunda ngarra-mabulu **ngarra-ngun-walkki-karrme**.
not 1SG.IRR.NP-like.IRR.NP 1SG.IRR.NP-2SG.OBJ-COM-hold.IRR.NP
'I don't want to help you.' [IK1-170602_1SY2/05:29–39]

As discussed in more detail in §6.1.3, the comitative cannot be input to the reflexive or reciprocal derivation in Kunbarlang. The only examples where the comitative prefix and the reflexive/reciprocal suffix -*dji~-yi* co-occur are the non-transparent ones, like (6.12) above (where the RR has to apply first, to the extent that a compositional interpretation may be suggested) or (6.15) below, where the verb means 'to work together' or 'to help each other', but hardly literally 'to hold something with each other':

(6.15) **Ngarrki-walkki-kadbi-yi** so ngarrki-bularrbunj quick.
1.INCL.FUT-COM-hold-REFL.NP ENG 1.INCL.FUT-finish.NP ENG
'We'll work together so that we finish quick.' [IK1-180518_1SY2/26:56–27:00]

This fact about the interaction of the two derivations can be accounted for by a fixed ordering of the derivations: the RR always applies before the comitative does. With this in mind, let us turn to the reflexive/reciprocal derivation.

6.1.3 Reflexive/Reciprocal

Similarly to the majority of Gunwinyguan languages, Kunbarlang has a suffix that is used to form reflexives and (with non-singular subjects) reciprocals.[4] Along with the morphological strategy that is ambiguous between the reflexive and the reciprocal readings, Kunbarlang has unambiguous analytic constructions for both readings. Even though these do not pertain to the domain of verbal morphology, I review them here as

---

4 Anindilyakwa, Warray and Wubuy have separate markers for reflexive and reciprocal derivations.

the alternative means of expression of similar semantics. I begin with general information on the reflexive/reciprocal (RR) suffix that is common to both readings and then discuss each of them in more detail in §6.1.3.1 (reflexives) and §6.1.3.2 (reciprocals).

As is frequently the case in Australian languages (Evans, Gaby & Nordlinger 2007: §2), the same exponent serves both the reflexive and the reciprocal derivation in Kunbarlang. That is the suffix in slot +1 with two allomorphs *-yi* and *-dji*.[5] The distribution of the allomorphs is phonologically conditioned as follows:

1. after the high back vowel /u/ they are found to be in free variation, with some of the tokens being intermediate between the glide and the stop realisations
2. *-yi* is used after the high front vowel /i/ (6.16b)[6]
3. *-dji* is used elsewhere (6.16a)[7]

(6.16)   a.   Nga-djirrka-rlakwa-**djinj**.
                1SG.NF-beard-throw-REFL.PST
                'I shaved [myself].'   [IK1-160818_0021/20:37–39]

        b.   Kabarra-djalerrkkalbi-**yinj**.
                3DU.NF-embrace-REFL.PST
                'They two hugged each other.'   [IK1-160809_0001/06:03–05; MPIR:07]

Example (6.17), with a plural subject, illustrates the aforementioned reflexive/reciprocal ambiguity: it is ambiguous between the reading where everyone is working on their own hair and the other where everyone is helping each other.

(6.17)   **Kadda**-merre-marnbu-**dji**.
         3PL.NF-hair-make-REFL.NP
         'They$_i$ are doing up their$_i$ hair.'   [IK1-160819_0001/30:08]

There is a parameter of typological variation in anaphoric binding constructions which has to do with the transitivity of the clause resulting after the binding takes place. Thus, there is a distinction between valency-conserving and valency-reducing strategies, and the majority of Australian languages are reported to follow the latter (Dixon 2002: 320;

---

[5] Dixon (2002: 206–7) reconstructs a hypothetical suffix *-*dharri*, which, he suggests, has a very long history, in contrast to the more recently developed causative and applicative morphology.

[6] Some of the reciprocal examples in this section were elicited using the video stimuli from Evans et al. (2004). In those cases I cite the number of the video in the set as follows: *MPIR:nn*, where *nn* is the number.

[7] There is further detail regarding the RR realisation with /e/-final stems. If that front mid vowel is preceded by a palatal consonant, it raises to [i] between the two palatals, feeding the choice of the *-yi* allomorph (see discussion in §2.7.2). Otherwise the vowel does not change and the stop-initial allomorph *-dji* is selected.

see also Evans, Gaby & Nordlinger 2007 specifically on reciprocals). In Kunbarlang, the object prefix of the base verb (6.18a) goes away when the RR suffix is applied (6.18b).

(6.18) a. **Ngarr-bun**-wuy.　　　　　　　　　Kirnda　　　　ngorro　　　money
　　　　1NSG.EXCL.NF-3NSG.OBJ-give.PST DEM.AFOR.LOC DEM.MED.IV ENG
　　　　ngadda-kalng.
　　　　1PL.EXCL.NF-get.PST
　　　　'We gave [the crocodile] to them, we got some money there.'
　　　　　　　　　　　　　　　　　　　　　　　　　　　　　[20060620IB04/10:28–33]

　　　b. Ngarrki-kinje　　　　neyang ngorro　　　**ngarrki**-wu-**dji**
　　　　1.INCL.FUT-cook.PST food　　DEM.MED.IV 1.INCL.FUT-give-REFL.NP
　　　　korro=way　　　　　kenda=way.
　　　　DEM.MED.LOC=HITH DEM.PROX.LOC=HITH
　　　　'We'll make food and then share it/exchange it with each other [lit. 'give it to ourselves'].'　　　　　　　　　　　　　　　　　[IK1-180522_2SM1/16:52–17:02]

Although at the first glance this may seem as transitivity reduction, I argue that it should not be analysed as such. Rather, in descriptive terms, the object prefix is (functionally) substituted by the RR suffix: since the object is anaphorically bound by the subject, their person and number feature values are equated, and no separate object agreement arises. There is an empirical argument for classifying Kunbarlang RR construction as a valency-conserving one, coming from body part noun incorporation.[8]

As will be discussed in section 6.3, body part (BP) noun incorporation in Kunbarlang follows the absolutive pattern. This means that a BP can incorporate if it is possessed by (or itself is) an intransitive subject or an object, but never an Agent. The cases of BP noun incorporation into RR-derived predicates show a similar pattern. Example (6.19a) provides a baseline with an incorporated BP noun, which is necessarily interpreted as object-oriented; (6.19b) and (6.19c) show such incorporated BP nouns in RR-derived verbs with the reflexive and the reciprocal interpretations, respectively (although the latter admits of the reflexive reading, too).

(6.19) a. Ka-ngan-**bid**-karrmeng.
　　　　3SG.NF-1SG.OBJ-hand-hold.PST
　　　　'S/he shook my hand.' (NOT: 'She shook me with her hand.')
　　　　　　　　　　　　　　　　　　　　　　　　　　　　　[IK1-160809_0001/18:40]

---

8 This is similar to Dalabon, with the difference that in Dalabon the portmanteaux personal prefixes behave as if the clause was in fact intransitivised, and so it is classed as a *mixed* system (Evans, Gaby & Nordlinger 2007).

b. Nga-mabulunj nganj-**merre**-ngeme-yi   ngarra-merre-ngongokwarri.
   1SG.NF-like.NP 1SG.FUT-hair-paint-REFL.NP 1SG-hair-black
   'I want to dye my hair [so that] I have black hair.'
   [IK1-170610_1SY1/17:36–41]

c. Kabarra-**merre**-rna-dji.
   3DU.NF-hair-see-REFL.NP
   'They two are delousing each other (simultaneously).'
   [IK1-160809_0001/48:29; MPIR:45]

Presumably, for the object-oriented construal of the incorporated body part, the object itself should remain available at some level of syntactic representation after the reflexive/reciprocal derivation has applied.[9]

Further—albeit somewhat less direct—evidence comes from incorpororation of generic noun Themes. This kind of incorporation is possible with RR-derived predicates (with a bound Recipient), suggesting that it is not the case that all objects must be removed for RR to apply. Consider (6.20):

(6.20) Ka-**bardi**-kaybu-yinj.
       3SG.NF-liquid-deprive-REFL.PST
       'S/he deprived him-/herself of grog.'   [IK1-160518_0011/01:18:39]

Incorporation of *bardi-* in (6.20) suggests that the secondary object remains in the (underlying) argument structure of the RR-derived predicate.

The RR suffix identifies (binds) the primary object with the subject, requiring them to be coreferential. The primary object is the only grammatical function that can be reflexivised or reciprocalised (6.21). This is evident in the behaviour of ditransitives. The recipient/goal participant of a ditransitive is normally expressed as its primary object, and as such it is readily bound by the RR suffix (6.21a). However, if the theme participant has to be bound, the recipient must be expressed either as a dative-marked external nominal (6.21b) or as a benefactive object, reintroduced by the applicative (6.21c). Notice also that the only possible binder is the subject.

(6.21) a. Kadda-wu-**yinj**.
          3PL.NF-give-REFL.PST
          'They gave each other something.'   [IK1-160512_0001/17:52]

---

[9] There are certain RR-derived predicates that have lexicalised to an extent, while retaining transparency of the derivation, e.g. *-rdayi* 'to enter' [lit. 'to put oneself (inside)'. These resemble antipassive uses of the reflexive, and semantically may be the furthest away from a prototypical transitive situation. Yet even these retain the BP incorporation capacity, e.g. *-djanga-rdayi* 'to insert one's feet'. See also §6.2.3.2.

b. Nga-rdukbanjdji-**yinj** **bi-rnungu**.
   1SG.NF-show-REFL.PST DAT-he.GEN
   'I showed myself to him.' [IK1-160715_0001/30:51–54]

c. Nga-**marnanj**-rdukbanjdji-**yinj**.
   1SG.NF-BEN-show-REFL.PST
   'I showed myself to him/her/it.' (NOT: 'I showed her to herself.')
   [ibid./32:41]

Examples in (6.22) show that (6.21b) is not just an effect of morphology whereby the external dative pronoun is required to mitigate the ambiguity that may arise because the third person singular object prefix is incompatible with the first person subject one (see §5.2.3). The problem with (6.22a) is not a morphological, but a syntactic one, and has to be resolved by the retreat to an external dative pronominal again (6.22b).

(6.22) a. *Ka-**ngan**-rdukbanjdji-yinj.
       3SG.NF-1SG.OBJ-show-REFL.PST
       Intended: 'S/he showed her-/himself to me.' [IK1-160818_0011/31:15]

b. Ka-rdukbanjdji-yinj **bi-ngaybu**.
   3SG.NF-show-REFL.PST DAT-I.GEN
   'S/he showed her-/himself to me.' [ibid./32:02]

Interestingly, RR-derivation can bind both underlying objects of *-rdukbanjdje* at once (6.23): both the Theme *and* the Goal are bound by the subject. (This suggests that there is possibly nothing wrong with binding of the ditransitive Theme per se.)

(6.23) Kabarra-rdukbanjdji-yinj.
       3DU.NF-show-REFL.PST
       'They two showed themselves to each other.' [IK1-160715_0001/34:09]

This verb is probably the only one that shows the effect—it also is the only one ditransitive for which this would yield a sensible interpretation. The exact mechanism and significance of this effect have to be explored further. One possibility, not explored yet, is that the RR suffix is an unselective binder: applied early to the lexical verb, it binds all available objects to the subject, producing the 'double-binding' effect in (6.23). This hypothesis would also explain the facts about binding of the ditransitive Themes illustrated in (6.21b) and (6.22) above: the Recipient is 'evacuated' in those cases in order to avoid being bound. On such a view, however, the timing of noun incorporation in examples like (6.20) needs to be taken into consideration. Clearly, intricacies of Kunbarlang argument structure warrant further investigation.

As was pointed out above, the only possible binder (antecedent) is the subject. Example (6.21c) above shows that the benefactive object cannot bind the secondary object. Examples in (6.24) show that the primary object cannot either: for instance, to express 'to show X$_i$ to each other$_i$', a periphrastic construction with a causative has to be used (see §8.3.1 on causatives).

(6.24)   a.   *Nga-burrun$_k$-rdukbanjdji-yinj$_k$.
               1SG.NF-3DU.OBJ-show-REFL.PST
               intended: 'I showed them two$_k$ to each other$_k$.'   [IK1-160715_0001/36:33]

          b.   Nga-burrun$_k$-marnbum   kabarra$_k$-kuk-rna-djinj$_k$.
               1SG.NF-3DU.OBJ-make.PST   3DU.NF-body-see-REFL.PST
               'I made them two$_k$ see each other$_k$.'   [ibid./38:26–30]

Derived objects (i.e. the benefactive and comitative ones) cannot bind the reflexive, nor can they themselves be reflexivised or reciprocalised. Instead, one must use circumlocutions. Example (6.25) illustrates this for the comitative and example (6.26) for the benefactive.

(6.25)   a.   *Ngarrk-walkki-baybu-yinj.
               1.INCL.NF-COM-leave-REFL.PST
               intended: 'We've exchanged something [lit. 'left something with each other'].'   [IK1-180518_1SY2/16:12]

          b.   Ngayi   nganj-ngun-walkki-baybunj   ninda,   la   ngudda
               I   1SG.FUT-2SG.OBJ-COM-leave.NP   DEM.PROX.I   CONJ   you.SG
               nj-ngan-walkki-baybunj   ninda.
               2SG.FUT-1SG.OBJ-COM-leave.NP   DEM.PROX.I
               'I'll give this to you, and you give this to me.'   [ibid./15:20–30]

(6.26)   Kadda-marnanj-kinje-dji.
         3PL.NF-BEN-cook-REFL.NP
         'They are cooking each other (for somebody).'
         NOT: 'They are cooking for each other.'   [IK1-180522_3SY1/38:46–49]

The fact that the underlying themes and goals, licensed by the verb's predicate-argument structure, can be reflexivised/reciprocalised, but the derived objects cannot, highlights their different status. Despite being indexed by a bound pronoun in the object slot, derived objects differ syntactically from underlying (primary or secondary) objects.[10]

---

[10] This parallels the pattern in Warlpiri, where EXTERNAL OBJECTS show syntactic behaviour distinct from that of the verb's underlying objects, although both kinds are registered by clitics in the auxiliary complex (Simpson 1991: 381–95). I am grateful to Mary Laughren for stressing that observation.

Placing the verb under contrastive focus in coordination does not facilitate a form like *ka-marnanj-kalbi-yinj* [3SG.NF-BEN-get-REFL.PST], and free pronouns are used for the reflexive Goal instead (6.27):

(6.27) Ka-ngan-marnanj-kalng kikakkin la ngal-buk=ma ka-kalng
3SG.NF-1SG.OBJ-BEN-get.PST meat CONJ II-person=CONTR 3SG.NF-get.PST
bi-ngadju.
DAT-she.GEN
'She bought meat for me and for herself.' [IK1-180522_2SM1/23:26–36]

This is in contrast with other Gunwinyguan languages. In Bininj Kunwok, there is a difference between the reflexive and the reciprocal, such that only the latter, but not the former can bind derived objects (Evans 2003a: 439–40). We see that in Kunbarlang the reciprocal is not able to bind a derived object (6.25). In Wubuy, Anindilyakwa, and Ngandi, similarly to BKW, the reciprocal can apply after the valency-increasing derivations, but not before them (Horrack 2018: 266–8).

Another, perhaps a little more trivial, consequence of the restriction of the RR-derivation to primary objects is that monovalent predicates are incompatible with it, even when denoting a semantically reciprocal situation (6.28). Example (6.28a) illustrates the coverb construction meaning '(to be placed) leaning against something', and is ambiguous between a reciprocal reading ('leaning against each other') and a non-reciprocal one ('leaning against something separately'). Example (6.28b) shows that it is impossible to add the RR suffix to such a construction to disambiguate it in favour of the reciprocal reading. The resulting verb form (without the coverb) can only be interpreted as containing a different root (6.28c).

(6.28) a. Kabarra-rna=lorr benengka ngal-buk.
3DU.NF-sit.NP=lean they.DU II-person
'They two (one of them a woman) are sitting leaning [against each other *or* against something else].' [IK1-160812_0001/37:17–20]

b. *Kabarra-rna-dji=lorr.
3DU.NF-sit-REFL.NP=lean
Intended: 'They two are sitting leaning against each other.'
[ibid./45:00–02]

c. Kabarra-rna-dji.
3DU.NF-**see**-REFL.NP
Only: 'They are looking at each other.'
NOT: 'They are sitting (leaning) against each other.' [ibid./43:55–57]

It is possible to disambiguate (6.28a), but only in favour of the non-reciprocal reading, using the distributive prefix *baba-* (6.29):

(6.29) Kabarra-baba-rna=lorr.
3DU.NF-DISTR-sit.NP=lean
'They are sitting separately, leaning against something.'
[IK1-160812_0001/45:58–46:00]

In the next two subsections I discuss separately the properties of reflexives and recirocals that are peculiar to them, including the ways to express either reading unambiguously.

6.1.3.1 Reflexives and the intensifier *bidju*

The forms derived with the RR suffix are ambiguous between the reflexive and the reciprocal readings when the subject is non-singular, as was noted above (6.17). The reflexive reading, however, can be enforced by using the emphatic construction "pronoun=*bonj bidju*" (6.30).

(6.30) Kadda-widrna-dji **bedbe=bonj bidju.**
3PL.NF-hate-REFL.NP they=exactly EMPH
'They hate themselves.' [IK1-160513_0001/52:53–58]

Such use of a free personal pronoun with a focus clitic *bonj* 'exactly' and the emphatic particle *bidju* 'EMPH' forces the reflexive reading and thus disambiguates the predicate. I analyse the combination (*bonj*) *bidju* as an adjunct intensifier (König, Siemund & Töpper 2013), more specifically composed of the focus clitic *bonj* and the anaphoric intensifier *bidju*. To wit, *bonj* is optional in this construction, i.e. *bidju* can combine with a pronoun by itself (6.31).[11]

(6.31) Balkkime **ngudda bidju** kinj-bu-yi=ngurr.
today you EMPH 2SG.FUT-hit-REFL.NP=rippled
'Today you are washing (yourself) yourself! (i.e., I am not helping you).'
[IK1-160513_0001/35:45–50]

Furthermore, the clitic *bonj* alone does not convey the same emphasis. Compare the intensified reading of (6.34a) below to example (6.32), where the pronoun without *bidju* merely spells out the subject.[12]

---

[11] According to König, Siemund & Töpper (2013), many languages use an identical form for reflexives and intensifiers (differing only in their distribution; for instance, the English *x-self*), while in others these are formally differentiated (for instance, the German *selbst* or the Russian *sam*); Kunbarlang clearly falls into the latter group. The worldwide distribution of these two possibilities is 94/74 (identical/differentiated), with Australian languages in their sample closely reflecting that ratio (5/4, not counting Kunbarlang).

[12] It could potentially convey identificational focus, for instance, in an answer to the question *Who saw it?* (but this particular example was elicited without larger discourse context).

(6.32) Ka-rnay **na-wuk=bonj**.
3SG.NF-see.PST I-person=exactly
'He saw it.' [IK1-160513_0021/01:23]

Finally, the particle *bidju* must adjoin to a pronoun and cannot modify the verb on its own (6.33):

(6.33) *Fred ka-rnay bidju.
F 3SG.NF-see.PST EMPH
'Fred saw himself / saw it himself.' [IK1-160518_0011/01:53–02:04]

There are two interesting and important properties to notice:
(i) the pronominal intensifier construction itself cannot substitute for the reflexive/reciprocal suffix, where the structural conditions of the suffix are met
(ii) the particle *bidju*, however, imposes a coreference requirement (the NP containing it must be coindexed with the local subject; see below), which in certain configurations yields the reflexive interpretation in the absence of the RR suffix

To appreciate these two points let us first confine our attention to the verb's objects. In the absence of the RR suffix the construction serves for intensification without contributing the reflexive semantics (6.34). Example (6.34a) has only the emphatic, but not the reflexive, reading, and example (6.34b) demonstrates an overt object present, which would be eliminated in a reflexive clause.

(6.34) a. Ka-rnay **na-wuk=bonj bidju**.
3SG.NF-see.PST I-person=exactly EMPH
'He saw it himself, with his own eyes.'
NOT: 'He saw himself.' [IK1-160513_0021/01:53–58]
b. I feed my dogs, but...
Ngayi kinbadda-bareng yiwanj **kanjbadda-yawanj neyang**
NM.PL 3PL-dangerous DISC.PTCL 3PL.FUT-seek.NP food
bedbe=bonj bidju.
they=exactly EMPH
'The wild [dogs] will search for food themselves.'
[IK1-160513_0001/57:35–58:07]

Recall that *bidju* always appears as a constituent of a NP (6.33). As I noted above, the particle *bidju* ensures that the NP that contains it is coindexed with the local subject. The following data demonstrate that this is the correct analysis. First, observe the impossibility of *bidju* in (6.35), confirming that it must be coindexed with the local subject:

(6.35) a. Mary ka-rnay   nayi djurra korro   kun-bodme
        M   3SG.NF-see.PST NM.I paper DEM.MED.LOC IV-back
        bi-rnungu (***bidju**).
        DAT-he.GEN   EMPH
        'Mary saw the book behind him/*himself.'   [IK1-160513_0021/33:36–48]

   b. *[Na-wuk=bonj   ka-ngan-wardam]   [la   nganj-walkki-karrme
       I-person=exactly   3SG.NF-1SG.OBJ-ask.PST CONJ 1SG.FUT-COM-hold.NP
       bidju].
       EMPH
       '*He asked me to help himself.'   [IK1-180522_3SY1/55:11–20]

Adding *bidju* to (6.35a) is impossible, because it establishes obligatory coreference of the NP containing it with the subject, and they clash in gender features in this case. In (6.35b) the potential antecedent of *bidju* is in a different, conjoined clause, which renders it inaccessible.[13] Thus, we see that this intensifier is not merely a type of focus, neither is it a logophor. Rather, it is a local anaphor. When there is no gender clash, the presence of *bidju* enforces (through coindexation with the subject) a reflexive reading of a structure that is otherwise ambiguous due to the referential ambiguity of the pronoun (6.36).

(6.36) a. Mary ka-rnay   nayi djurra korro   kun-bodme
        M   3SG.NF-see.PST NM.I paper DEM.MED.LOC IV-back
        bi-ngadju.
        DAT-she.GEN
        'Mary$_m$ found the book behind her$_{m/j}$.'   [IK1-160513_0021/32:00–17]

   b. Mary ka-rnay   nayi djurra korro   kun-bodme
      M   3SG.NF-see.PST NM.I paper DEM.MED.LOC IV-back
      bi-ngadju   **bidju**.
      DAT-she.GEN   EMPH
      'Mary$_m$ found the book behind herself$_{m/*j}$.'   [ibid./32:18–38]

Normally *bidju* is subject-oriented, as in the examples above; however, in elicitation a benefactive is allowed as its antecedent (6.37).

---

[13] There is another problem with (6.35b), that is, the absence of a pronoun (see discussion of example (6.33) above). My informants usually pick up such mistakes easily, so I venture that this is not the main problem here. To be sure, no examples are known where *bidju* is in a different clause from its antecedent.

(6.37) Nga-buk   ka-kidanj   ka-bun-rnay   John, la   nukka John
        II-person   3SG.NF-go.PST   3SG.NF-3SG.OBJ-see.PST   J   CONJ   he.I   J

   ka-**bun-marnanj**-ngunda   kuyi   **ngal-buk=bonj**   **bidju**.
   3SG.NF-3SG.OBJ-BEN-do.PST   NM.IV   II-person=exactly   EMPH

   'She went to see John, and he told her about herself.'

   [IK1-180531_1SY1/02:34:30–42]

Within the clause, *bidju* does not have to be a co-argument of its antecedent. For instance, it can be the possessor within an adjunct locative phrase (6.38):

(6.38) Ki-djung   mayi   kundulk [**korro**   **ngudda bidju kin-nungku**
        2SG.NF-stab.PST   NM.III tree   DEM.MED.LOC   you   EMPH   I/II-you.GEN

   karra   kodbarre].
   DEM.MED.LOC   house

   'You felled a tree near your own house.'   [IK1-180531_1SY1/23:16–27]

To sum up the above discussion, Kunbarlang has an intensifier construction with (*bonj*) *bidju*, which serves to emphasise reflexive readings in cases of ambiguity and has the general intensifying function otherwise. What is particularly interesting about this construction is that it has some properties of an anaphoric pronoun without being one. Thus, it is involved in establishing referential coindexing between two NPs, but it does not affect the argument structure of the predicate, behaving consistently as an adjunct even when modifying arguments (e.g. 6.34a).

6.1.3.2 Reciprocals

The morphological reciprocal (just like the reflexive) is valency-reducing in terms of Evans, Gaby & Nordlinger (2007), which means that the verbal construction resulting from the application of the RR suffix to a base verb is one valency lower. More specifically, an object that is bound by the reciprocal cannot be instantiated. Typically (i.e. in the case of a transitive verb), this is manifest in the absence of object agreement. Consider the pair of examples in (6.39), which show the object agreement in the verb *-ngeme* 'to paint' and that it disappears in a reciprocal situation.

(6.39) a. Kinj-**ngan**-ngeme   balkkime, la   ngayi
            2SG.FUT-1SG.OBJ-paint.NP   today   CONJ   I

            nganj-**ngun**-ngeme   malayi.
            1SG.FUT-2SG.OBJ-paint.NP   tomorrow

       'You paint me now, and I'll paint you tomorrow.'

       [IK1-160712_0001/10:32–37]

b. Ngarrki-ngeme-yi.
   1.INCL.FUT-paint-REFL.NP
   'Let's/we'll paint each other.' [ibid./09:32]

In addition to the morphological construction with the reflexive/reciprocal suffix -*yi*/-*dji*, described above, there is an analytic construction. Formally it looks like an elliptical clause, one from which everything is elided but for the subject, expressed by a contrastive pronoun (6.40).

(6.40) Ka-bun-rnay **la** na-wuk-ma.
       3SG.NF-3SG.OBJ-see.PST CONJ I-person-CONTR
       'They looked at each other.' [IK1-160809_0001/29:07–09; MPIR:33]

As can be seen, in terms of morphosyntax this construction is valency-conserving (Evans, Gaby & Nordlinger 2007), as the verb retains the agreement in the object slot.

The morphological reciprocal is preferrably used for simultaneous situations (6.41a), although its use in sequential ones is also often admitted. There is, however, a preference to give longer explicit descriptions (e.g. via the analytic construction) for the sequential situations (6.41b). A simultaneous situation is one where the participants perform as agents of the relevant action at the same time. A prototypical simultaneous situation is when two people embrace. A sequential situation, by contrast, is one where a similar event iterates over time with the participants alternating in the agent role. A prototypical sequential situation is when two people chase each other in turn (or in fact anything that is done *in turn*). Note that events of most kinds can be manipulated to skew them towards one or the other kind of situation, and this is one of the reasons why video stimuli are immensely useful for elicitation and checking of reciprocal constructions: they are maximally unambiguous with respect to the number of participants, their agentivity and the temporal course of events.

For instance, there are several videos that present events of delousing. In one of them, there are two participants, who are browsing each other's hair simultaneously, and that is best described by the morphological reciprocal (6.41a). In another video, however, the two participants are taking turns in looking at each other's hair, and the preferred description for that is with the analytic construction (6.41b).

(6.41) a. Kabarra-merre-rna-dji.
          3DU.NF-hair-see-REFL.NP
          'They are looking at each other's hair / delousing each other [simultaneously].' [IK1-160809_0001/48:29; MPIR:45]
       b. Ka-bun-merre-rnanj la ngal-buk-ma.
          3SG.NF-3SG.OBJ-hair-see.NP CONJ II-person-CONTR
          'They are looking at each other's hair / delousing each other [taking turns].' [IK1-160809_0001/09:04; MPIR:10]

The analytic reciprocal strategy (as in (6.40) and (6.41b)) seems fully constructionalised, with its three constituents—the verb, the conjunction *la* and the emphatic pronoun—occurring in this order under a single intonational contour. It is interesting to note that unlike the morphological strategy, which requires the base verb to be transitive (see example (6.28) and related discussion), this construction admits intransitive verbs as well, cf. (6.42):[14]

(6.42) Pat la   Stacey **ka-nganj-yuwa**   la   **na-wuk-ma**.
        P   CONJ S   3SG.NF-HITH-lie.NP   CONJ   I-person-CONTR
        'Pat and Stacey are neighbours (i.e., live near each other).'
        [IK1-160513_0011/00:44–50]

The construction is sensitive to the number of participants in the reciprocal event and to its internal composition (simultaneous or sequential subevents; Evans et al. 2004). The number of participants is tracked by the grammatical number of the verb's personal prefixes and of the contrastive personal pronoun. Thus, examples (6.40) and (6.42) unambiguously describe situations with two participants (and thanks to the gender specification of the singular pronoun *nawukma* 'he.CONTR', also indicate that at least one of the participants is male). If the event involves more participants, both the verb and the pronoun reflect that (6.43).

(6.43) Ka-**buddun**-karlangwanj la   **bedbe**-rrema.
        3SG.NF-3PL.OBJ-chase.NP   CONJ   they-CONTR
        'They are chasing each other.'   [IK1-160809_0001/35:38–40; MPIR:43]

The analytic reciprocal only suits descriptions of simultaneous reciprocal events, but not sequential ones. This is illustrated by the unacceptability of this construction in (6.44a), when the prompt video shows two men hugging one another in turn. This prompt, like all other markedly sequential events, invites an explicit description instead (6.44b).

(6.44) a. *Ka-bun-djalarrkkarrmeng   la   na-wuk-ma.
            3SG.NF-3SG.OBJ-embrace.PST   CONJ   I-person-CONTR
            Intended: 'They hugged each other in turn.'   [IK1-160812_0001/33:12–25]

---

14 It is not clear at present why the posture verb *-yuwa* 'to lie' (meaning 'to live' here) has the directional prefix *nganj-* 'HITH'. It may serve as locative (rather than directional) with stative verbs; there are also examples of this prefix used with the other posture verbs in my recordings, albeit few.

  b. Na-buk werrk   ka-bun-djalarrkkarrmeng yirrkbonj
    I-person immediately 3SG.NF-3SG.OBJ-embrace.PST then

    ka-ngorrodjanganj   na-wuk-ma=wali
    3SG.NF-turn_around.PST I-person-CONTR=turn

    ka-bun-djalarrkkarrmeng.
    3SG.NF-3SG.OBJ-embrace.PST

    literally: 'He hugged him first, then he turned around and hugged him in his turn.' [ibid./32:38–54; MPIR:58]

Interestingly, the neighbouring Iwaidjan language Mawng (as well as Iwaidja, spoken on Croker Island) uses a structurally similar construction as its main reciprocal strategy (Singer 2011). It also includes a conjunction and a contrastive pronoun (6.45) and appears to have developed from a biclausal construction; Singer notes that this structural type is cross-linguistically rare (2011: 234, citing Evans 2008).

(6.45) Mawng (Singer 2011: 238)

   Ngi-wu-ng   la ngapimung.
   1SG>3M-hit-PP CONJ 1SG.CONTR

   'We (two) hit each other.'

In Mawng, there is a hierarchy (6.46) that determines the person of the contrastive pronoun (Singer 2011: 238).

(6.46) $1 > 2 > \frac{3M > 3F}{3PL}$

Consider (6.45): the subject of the verb is of the first person, and the contrastive pronoun is also of the first person. The literal rendition of that would not amount to *I hit him, and then he [hit me]*; the choice of the pronoun does not intuitively reflect the reciprocal, turn-taking nature of the event. However, the contrastive pronoun must be of the first person, which overrides the third person on the hierarchy (6.46).

  Similarly to Mawng, Kunbarlang has a hierarchy, but unlike Mawng, the third person outranks the second in Kunbarlang (6.47):

(6.47) $1 > 3 > 2$

The datapoint that illustrates this is in (6.48a), where the pronoun is third person, like the subject of the verb. Example (6.48b) confirms that the person of the pronoun is not just tied to that of the subject.

(6.48) a. Ngudda na-buk kanj-ngun-rnanj la
you I-person 3SG.FUT-2SG.OBJ-see.NP CONJ

na-wuk=ma/*nji=ma.
I-person=CONTR/you=CONTR

'You and he, you'll see each other.' [IK1-180530_JW1/01:24:05–07]

b. Ka-ngan-bum la nganj=ma.
3SG.NF-1SG.OBJ-hit.PST CONJ I=CONTR

'We fought / hit each other.' [IK1-180522_3SY1/44:42–45]

Given the typological rarity of such a reciprocal construction and the close connections between Kunbarlang and Mawng speakers (including the fact that all Kunbarlang speakers are proficient in Mawng), it is highly plausible that the homology of this reciprocal strategy in the two languages is not accidental, but has been the result of language contact. Taking into account the presence of a similar construction in Iwaidja and in no other Gunwinyguan languages, one may conjecture that it has been borrowed from Mawng into Kunbarlang.

6.2 Valency classes

Australian languages are well-known typologically for their lack of lability (Dixon 1980: 278; with the notable exception of Mawng (Singer 2006: 63–5)). In Kunbarlang, as well, the stems have fixed transitivity and thematic role grids, and the argument frame of a verb can only be altered via valency-changing derivations (§6.1). There are a few prepounds which show a causative-inchoative alternation depending on the choice of the thematic (-*wunj* 'to give' or -*mi* 'INCH'; see §8.3.1), but they are a small and closed class. The following pattern with the intransitive (6.49) and the transitive (6.50) verbs meaning 'to break' is typical and illustrative: one of them is strictly transitive, the other is strictly intransitive, and their argument frames cannot be mixed and matched.

(6.49) a. Ninda banikkin ka-mankang, **ka-rdakdjung**.
DEM.PROX.I cup 3SG.NF-fall.PST 3SG.NF-break.PST

'The cup fell down and **smashed**.' [IK1-160505_0011/01:10:40–44]

b. *Mary ka-rdakdjung nayi banikkin.
M 3SG.NF-break.PST NM.I cup

intended: 'Mary smashed the cup.' [ibid./01:11:27–35]

(6.50) a. Mary **ka-rdenburlumung** / **ka-rlumung**   nayi banikkin.
       M   3SG.NF-smash.PST / 3SG.NF-break.PST NM.I cup
       'Mary **smashed** the cup.'   [IK1-160505_0011/01:11:34–01:12:39]

   b. *Ninda   banikkin ka-mankang,   ka-rlumung.
      DEM.PROX.I cup   3SG.NF-fall.PST 3SG.NF-break.PST
      intended: 'The cup fell down and smashed.'   [ibid./01:13:00–05]

The predicates in Kunbarlang can have between one and four argument positions. No Kunbarlang verbs are known to be avalent, i.e. to have zero argument positions. In particular, there are no specialised weather verbs found, such as exist, for instance, in Germanic languages (e.g., English *to rain*) or in Bininj Kunwok (e.g., *mayhke* 'to lightning'; Evans 2003a: 393). Rather the nouns that denote atmospheric conditions combine with intransitive posture (6.51b) and motion verbs (6.51c), (6.52). As is discussed in §3.2 on parts of speech, nouns characteristically cannot have personal prefixes (6.51a).

(6.51) IK1-160513_0001/16:26–18:52

   a. *Ka-balmad.
      3SG.NF-rain
      intended: 'It's raining.'

   b. Balmad ka-dja /   *ka-rna /   *ka-yuwa.
      rain   3SG.NF-stand.NP 3SG.NF-sit.NP 3SG.NF-lie.NP
      'It's raining.'

   c. Balmad ka-bakdjuwa.
      rain   3SG.NF-descend.NP
      'It's raining.'

(6.52) Dukulu ka-ka=kulkkulk.
       wind   3SG.NF-go.NP=run
       'The wind is blowing.'   [IK1-160512_0011/53:28–30]

6.2.1 Monovalent verbs

Monovalent verbs have just one argument. Regardless of its thematic role it is obligatorily cross-referenced by the appropriate personal prefix out of the "subject set" and I call this only argument the subject. Monovalent verbs can be formed from intransitive stems only, as there are no decreasing derivations.

(6.53) a. **Ka-malakkidjanganj**.
3SG.NF-laugh.PST
'S/he laughed.' [IK1-160505_0011/01:19:30]

b. Ka-ngan-ngungang la ngunda **ngay-kelbunguni**.
3SG.NF-1SG.OBJ-threaten.PST CONJ not 1SG.IRR.PST-afraid.IRR.PST
'S/he threatened me but I didn't get scared.' [IK1-180521_2SY1/54:19–23]

c. **Kinj-wonj** kinj-yawanj.
2SG.FUT-return.NP 2SG.FUT-seek.NP
'Go back and look for it!' [IK1-170516_2DDj1/59:13–16]

6.2.2 Divalent verbs

Divalent verbs are those that have two arguments, viz. the subject and an object. Divalent predicates show the most diversity in the ways they can be formed, which can be one of the following:
– having a monotransitive verbal stem unmodified by any argument derivation
– derived from a monovalent predicate via application of the benefactive or the comitative prefix (where the monovalent predicate can be an intransitive verbal stem or itself derived)
– derived from a ditransitive verbal stem via application of the reflexive/reciprocal suffix

6.2.2.1 Underived divalent verbs

There are very many transitive stems in Kunbarlang. They form divalent verbs if not modified by any of the argument derivations.

(6.54) a. Malayi ngunda **ki-ngan-rluklung**.
tomorrow not 3SG.IRR.NP-1SG.OBJ-wake_up.IRR.NP
'S/he won't wake me up tomorrow.' [IK1-180521_2SY1/29:19–22]

b. **Nga-yawang, nga-kalng**.
1SG.NF-seek.PST 1SG.NF-get.PST
'I looked for it [the lost dog], I found it.' [IK1-160829_0001/06:47–52]

The primary (and only) object of an underived monotransitive verb is cross-referenced in the object slot in the verb (as in (6.54a)), unless that is a third person singular object acted upon by a subject other that third person singular (6.54b).[15] See §5.2 for a full explanation of the verbal agreement system.

6.2.2.2 Increasing valency to two

The intransitive stems may serve as the basis for valency-increasing derivations and thus form divalent verbal forms. There are two valency-increasing derivations in Kunbarlang, viz. the benefactive and the comitative (§6.1). They can combine with a wide variety of verbal stems, the main restriction generally being the viability of the semantic interpretation.

One of the relatively frequent verbs that is formed in this way is *-marnanj-bingki* 'to arrive to (meet) someone', derived by applying the benefactive to the intransitive stem *-bingki* 'to arrive; to exit'.

(6.55) a. **Ka-burrun-marnanj-bing** ka-burrun-rnay ninda
3SG.NF-3DU.OBJ-BEN-exit.PST 3SG.NF-3DU.NF-see.PST DEM.PROX.I

kabarra-rna.
3DU.NF-sit.NP

'He found those two and he saw them sitting down.'
[20150212AS01/05:27–31]

b. **Nganj-walkki-wonj**.
1SG.FUT-COM-return.NP

'I'll bring it back.' [IK1-160829_0001/06:58–07:00]

The comitative derivation in (6.55b) is the idiomatic way of expressing the meaning 'to bring something back'.

6.2.3 Trivalent verbs

Trivalent verbs have three arguments, viz. the subject, a primary object and a secondary object. Trivalent predicates in Kunbarlang can be formed from underlyingly ditransitive stems, be derived from a monotransitive stem via a valency-increasing argument derivation (i.e. the benefactive or the comitative), or sometimes be derived from an intransitive stem via applying both valency-increasing derivations.

---

[15] Inanimate objects do not get a cross-referencing personal prefix either, regardless of the nature of the subject.

6.2.3.1 Underived trivalent verbs

At present six underived trivalent verbs (i.e., ditransitive stems) are known. The most frequently used one is *-wunj* 'give' (6.56a). The other five are these (6.56): *-barndje* 'stick' (6.56b), *-berrekbunj* 'promise in marriage' (6.56c), *-kaybunj* 'withhold' (the primary object's role here is closer to Source; 6.56d), *-rdukbanjdje* 'show' (6.56e), and *-yikali* 'take away' (the primary object's role here is closer to Source; 6.56f).

(6.56) a. **Nga-buddu-wuy** kekkek nakarrken la na-kudji ngunda
1SG.NF-3PL.OBJ-give.PST bone dog CONJ I-one not
ngarra-wu nayi nakarrken.
1SG.IRR.NP-give.IRR.NP NM.I dog
'I gave bones to [all] the dogs but I won't give a bone to this one.'
[IK1-170610_1SY2/19:23–30]

b. Nayi barrawidjwidj **ka-ngan-barndje** keddjurr.
NM.I kid 3SG.NF-1SG.OBJ-stick.NP mud
'The kid is sticking mud on me.' [IK1-160518_0011/39:25]

c. Ngayi **nga-ngun-berrekbunj** kenda[?].
I 1SG.NF-2SG.OBJ-promise.NP DEM.PROX.LOC
'I promise you so and so.' [ibid./01:01:41]

d. Nga-wardam la na-buk **ka-ngan-kaybum**.
1SG.NF-ask.PST CONJ I-person 3SG.NF-1SG.OBJ-withhold.PST
'I asked him/her [for something], but s/he didn't give [it to] me.'
[ibid./01:15:56]

e. And **ka-ngan-rdukbanjdjing** yalbi.
ENG 3SG.NF-1SG.OBJ-show.PST country
'[My father] taught me the country.' [lit. 'He showed the country to me.']
[20150413IOv01/07:10–11]

f. **Ka-bun-yikalng** karlurru barda-rnuk.
3SG.NF-3SG.OBJ-take.away.PST cigarette what-INDF
'He took from him smokes or something.' [IK1-160510_0001/03:25–29]

In all examples in (6.56), except for (6.56d), there is a Theme/Patient object present in the form of a free standing NP (the *secondary* object), but without any cross-reference in the verb. This is because a Goal or a Source is the *primary* object, i.e. the preferred argument for indexing in the object slot. However, there is another possibility for indexing the secondary object on the verb, namely, noun incorporation (more on noun incorporation in §6.3).

6.2.3.2 Increasing valency to three

Underlying transitive stems can take on the benefactive or the comitative and thus yield trivalent predicates.

(6.57) a. **Ka-ngun-marnanj-djarrang**.
3SG.NF-2SG.OBJ-BEN-eat.PST
'S/he ate it on you (to your detriment).' [IK1-180601_1SY1/35:50]

b. **Ka-buddu-walkki-baybum** nayi nawalak.
3SG.NF-3PL.OBJ-COM-leave.PST NM.I child
'She left the child with them.' [IK1-180529_1SY1/01:22:14–20]

A felicitous combination of the benefactive with the comitative is extremely rare, but a good example is the verb -*marnanjwalkkiwonj* 'to return something to someone', derived from the intransitive stem -*wonj* 'to return (intr.)', illustrated in (6.58). The felicity of this combination is partially due to a subpart of it, -*walkkiwonj*, seemingly developing the idiomatic meaning 'to bring back'.

(6.58) Ninda nganj-ngun-wunj djurra, yiwanj babi la
DEM.PROX.I 1SG.FUT-2SG.OBJ-give.NP paper DISC.PTCL later CONJ
nj-ngan-marnanj-walkki-wonj.
2SG.FUT-1SG.OBJ-BEN-COM-return.NP
'I'll give you this book, then afterwards return it to me.'
[IK-180531_1SY-01/02:12:23–33]

It is also possible to apply a valency-increasing derivation and the valency-conserving RR-derivation to a transitive stem and thus get a trivalent derived predicate as the result. I cannot assess the extent of productivity of such a derivation: the known examples are the cases where a particular derived form of a verb seems to undergo lexicalisation, but is still transparent enough. The order of derivations is such that the reflexive/reciprocal always precedes the valency-increasing derivations (§6.1.3). Thus, in (6.59a) and (6.59b) the original stem -*rdam* 'to put' is turned by the reflexive into 'to enter' (-*rdayi*), and afterwards its valency is increased to a three-place predicate by the benefactive or the comitative prefix, respectively. In (6.59c), on the other hand, the original stem is -*bunj* 'to hit', first reciprocalised to mean 'to fight each other', and then made three-place by a somewhat idiosyncratic use of the comitative (see also §6.1.2).

(6.59) a. Ngayi Ngalngarridj **nga-marnanj-lerrk-rda-yinj**.
NM.II N 1SG.NF-BEN-word-put-REFL.PST
'I called Ngalngarridj.' [IK1-160628_0001/04:01–04]

b. Ninda   mutikang nayi kin-ngaybu ngunda
   DEM.PROX.I car   NM.I I/II-I.GEN not

   ngarra-walkki-rda-yi.
   1SG.IRR.NP-COM-put-REFL.IRR.NP

   'I cannot drive my car inside [of this shed].' [lit. 'I cannot get myself inside with the car.']   [IK1-170616_1SY1/01:05:08–17]

c. Mamu   ka-ngaddu-karlangwang   yakarni   kikka
   devil 3SG.NF-3PL.EXCL.OBJ-chase.PST magpie_goose she.II

   ngorro   **ngadda-walkki-bu-djinj.**
   DEM.MED.IV   3PL.EXCL.NF-COM-hit-REFL.PST

   'Devil was chasing us, we were fighting over those magpie geese.'
   [20060620IB04/05:01–06]

6.2.4 Four-place verbs

There are no underived four-place verbs in Kunbarlang. Ditransitive stems, in principle, can increase their valency by one when the benefactive or the comitative is attached. However, such forms have not been registered in spontaneous discourse and the judgements of these forms are mixed, with some speakers accepting, for instance, the benefactive derivation of -*wunj* 'to give', while others reject it (6.60).

(6.60) a. **Nganj-ngun-marnanj-wunj** ninda   djurra kinj-marnanj-kanj
          1SG.FUT-2SG.OBJ-BEN-give.NP DEM.PROX.I paper 2SG.FUT-BEN-take.NP

          Jackie.
          J

          'I'll give you this book to take to Jackie.' [lit. 'I'll give you this book for him, you'll take it to Jackie.']   [IK1-180522_3SY1/23:55–24:02]

       b. *Nga-ngun-marnanj-wuy.
          1SG.NF-2SG.OBJ-BEN-give.PST

          intended: 'I'll give it to you for him/her.'   [IK1-180522_2SM1/03:42–45]

I am led to conclude at this point that four-place predicates are a marginal phenomenon that belongs to the Kunbarlang grammar, but is not really a part of people's language use. No transitive stems increased by both the benefactive and the comitative (parallel to (6.58)) are known.

6.3 Noun incorporation

Kunbarlang has a rich system of noun incorporation, whereby nominal roots can under certain circumstances appear linearly within the verbal word (6.61). Noun incorporation is one of the hallmarks of polysynthesis (M. C. Baker 1988, 1996, Evans 2017, Mithun 1984b) and within the Gunwinyguan family is found in all languages (except Kungarakany and Mangarayi (Evans 2003a: 33), if these are to be included in the family).

(6.61) a. Korro   Gove kikka benbe   kadda-**kodbarre**-bum.
           DEM.MED.LOC G   they yesterday 3PL.NF-shelter-hit.PST
       'At Gove they later made houses.'   [20060620IB03/32:44–50]

       b. Kunbid=rnungu ka-**birri**-rdami-yinj.
          hand=he.GEN   3SG.NF-hand-put-REFL.PST
       'He left a handprint.'   [IK1-170606_1SY1/38:24–26]

Bininj Kunwok is well-known for its elaborate productive system of noun incorporation (Evans 2003a: §10.4). It has a very wide variety of incorporated nominals, and allows a vast array of external modification of those. In comparison with Bininj Kunwok, the Kunbarlang system is more modest; in particular, external modification is very restricted. Another difference is that whereas Bininj Kunwok has two clearly distinct subtypes of incorporated nominals, viz. body parts and generic nouns,[16] which can co-occur and occupy distinct slots in the verb, Kunbarlang does not seem to have grounds to make this distinction. Specifically, the two seem unable to co-occur.

Some of the important parameters of variation in the domain of noun incorporation are the grammatical relations that can be incorporated and the set of the forms that incorporate. I discuss the grammatical relations after listing the forms. The forms of the nouns are usually identical to the freestanding forms of those nouns, with a few exceptions, such as for instance the word *djabirrk* 'swag', whose incorporated form is *yambi-*, or the word *njunjuk* 'water', whose incorporated form is *bardi-* 'liquid' (or *ngambi-* 'water' in the Kumungkurdu dialect (Coleman 2010: 92)).[17] An important caveat is that the nouns that historically bear noun class prefixes (§4.1.3) drop them so that only the root is incorporated (6.62).

---

16 And possibly also a separate category of incorporated nouns serving as secondary predicates, see Evans (2003a: 458ff.) for details.
17 The 'water'-suppletion seems to be a familial trait of the Gunwinyguan: the same is the case in Kundjeyhmi and Kunwinjku (*gukku ~ bo-*), Kune and Kuninjku (*kunronj ~ kolk-*), Ngandi (*ku-djark ~ bun-*), and in Ngalakgan (*we? ~ binyi-*), according to Evans (2003a: 332). Evans further notices that in Ngalakgan, as in Mayali, this is the only suppletive incorporated nominal in the language (ibid.: fn. 5).

(6.62) a. La   mayi   **kundulk** ka-dja   mayi   kaburrk.
         CONJ NM.III tree   3SG.NF-stand.NP NM.III two
         'As for trees, there are two.'   [IK1-170610_2SM1/03:04–12]

   b. Ka-**dulk**-dja.
      3SG.NF-tree-stand.NP
      'A tree is standing.'   [IK1-160505_0011/01:22:46]

Table 6.1 lists a large selection of incorporated roots with their meaning and the full free form, when one is attested. The free forms are in boldface in case there is suppletion. The list is to be read as non-exhaustive, since body parts incorporate productively (as in Bininj Kunwok), and it is likely that other incorporating noun roots may be found.

Some individual combinations have lexicalised, so that the predicate as a whole does not compositionally relate to the verb-plus-noun, nor can the incorporate be taken out of such a combination; e.g. -*yalbi.rdakdjuwa* 'to sprint', whose meaning is not a function of *yalbi-* 'country' and *-rdakdjuwa* 'to break'. The only metaphorical extension I am aware of is *djarda-* 'mouth' extending to mean topological entrances, such as the door or the brim of a jug. In all other cases the incorporate retains its meaning.

6.3.1 Grammatical relations

Kunbarlang allows for a wide variety of grammatical relations to incorporate into the verb. That includes
- the core set of arguments
    - intransitive subject (6.62b), (6.63)
    - primary object (6.65)
    - secondary object (6.66)
- locative adjuncts, in particular
    - essive locatives (6.68)
    - ablative (source) locatives (6.69)

The incorporation of arguments follows the absolutive pattern, i.e. objects and intransitive subjects (6.63) can incorporate, but not agents/transitive subjects (e.g. 6.64; see M. C. Baker 1996: 291–2). In fact, among the incorporating nominal roots few have semantics that goes well with agentivity.[18] The predicates in (6.63a)–(6.63c) may look agentive, but it is also possible that their only arguments are construed as non-volitional figures moving on a trajectory. In the absence of tests, at present, this has to be left open.

---

18 Compare: "the overwhelming majority of incorporable nouns are inanimate in Gunwinyguan languages" (B. Baker 2014a: 248).

Tab. 6.1: Incorporating nominal roots

Root	Meaning	Free form
bak	long and rigid	
bardi	liquid	**njunjuk**
bim	white clay	**kudjurn**
bid/birr(i)	hand	**bid**
bodme	behind	kunbodme
burru	arm	burru
dukulu	wind	dukulu
dulk	tree	kundulk
djakbu	trace	
djarda	mouth	**djarderre**
djanga	foot	djanga
djorlk	waterway	kundjorlk
rdawurrng	blade	
kakkin	flesh	kikakkin
kanak	sun	kanak
karlmu	ear	karlmu
kodbarre	shelter	kodbarre
kodj	head	kodjkodj
kuk	body	**kiburrk**
lerrk	word	lerrk
lorre	ground	lorre
merre	hair	merre
mirl	nose/face	**kumerle**
njil	spirit	
ngambi	water	**njunjuk**
ngorlng	group	kingorlng
nguluk	ash	nguluk
nguk	internal organs	nguk
ngundek	country	**yalbi**
ngundu	arm	**burru**
rnil	eye	**kumu**
yalbi	country	yalbi
yambi	swag	**djabirrk**

(6.63) a. Njunjuk ka-**bardi**-ka=kulkkulk.
water 3SG.NF-liquid-go.NP=run
'Water is running down.' [IK1-160808_0001/07:41–43]

b. Ngorro kadda-**bardi**-bing njunjuk.
DEM.MED.IV 3PL.NF-liquid-exit.PST water
'Water was coming up.' [20060606IB02/13:04–06]

c. Ka-nganj-**kanak**-bingki.
3SG.NF-HITH-sun-exit.NP
'The sun is rising.' [IK1-160612_0011/10:34]

d. Ka-**dulk**-rdakdjung.
3SG.NF-tree-break.PST
'A tree broke.' [IK1-180601_1SY1/01:41:15]

(6.64) a. Dukulu ka-rlakwang.
wind 3SG.NF-throw.PST
'Wind broke it [the tree].' [IK1-180529_1SY1/11:59]

b. *Ka-**dukulu**-rlakwang.
3SG.NF-wind-throw.PST

Concerning objects, it is the Themes that incorporate, that is, the primary objects of transitives (6.65) and the secondary objects of ditransitives (6.66). Incorporation of derived objects is discussed in §6.3.3.

(6.65) Nga-**kakkin**-kalng.
1SG.NF-flesh-get.PST
'I got meat.' [IK1-160429_0001/01:14:36]

(6.66) Nganj-**kakkin**-rnirlakka burru=rnungu.
1SG.FUT-flesh-send.NP arm=he.GEN
'I'll send him/her meat, the arm/flipper part.'
[IK1-180601_1SY1/01:35:35–38]

When the Theme is a body part in a possessive construction, and thus allows for possessor raising (see §4.6.2), it may also be incorporated, with the possessor indexed in the object slot (6.67). Similar structure is found in Wubuy, where the possessum can be incorporated both in a possessor raising construction and without possessor raising (Baker et al. 2010).

(6.67) Ka-**bun-birr**-djarrang.
       3SG.NF-3SG.OBJ-hand-eat.PST
       'It burnt her on the hand.' [IK1-160712_0001/14:41]

The absolutive pattern for noun incorporation is typologically very common (e.g. Massam 2009: 1089 and references therein). Incorporation of adjuncts, however, is seldom attested. Adjuncts can incorporate in Chukchi, for instance (Spencer 1995). Within the Gunwinyguan family, incorporation of instrumentals and locatives is found in Wubuy (B. Baker 2014a). In Kunbarlang locatives can be incorporated into a variety of verbs if they describe essive location (6.68) or source (6.69).

(6.68) Ngadda-**yalbi**-djanganj   Malabunuwa.
        1PL.EXCL.NF-country-stand.PST M
        'We were staying at Malabunuwa country.' [IK1-160510_0001/01:54–56]

(6.69) a. Kadda-**ngambi**-djukkumung.
            3PL.NF-water-pull_out.PST
            'They pulled it out of the water.' [Coleman 2010: 18]

        b. Ka-burrun-**nguluk**-kalng.
            3SG.NF-3DU.OBJ-ash-get.PST
            '[The devil] took them two out of the ashes.' [IK1-180601_1SY1/06:31]

Example (6.69b) shows that the Theme is indexed in the object slot, while the Source is incorporated. Example (6.70) shows that when Source is encoded paraphrastically, it appears with the locative demonstrative:

(6.70) Ka-burrun-kalng   **karra**   nguluk ka-burrun-kinjeng.
        3SG.NF-3DU.OBJ-get.PST DEM.MED.LOC   ash   3SG.NF-3SG.OBJ-cook.PST
        '[The devil] took them two out of the ashes, he'd cooked them.'
                                                    [IK1-180601_1SY1/06:52–56]

Example (6.71) further shows that the Source (just like all other Kunbarlang incorporation, for instance, see examples (6.61b), (6.63a), (6.63b), (6.68)) may be doubly expressed, and then the external locative obligatorily has *korro* or *karra*. It seems to be a particular property of placenames that they can be used without *korro*/*karra* (6.68).

(6.71) Ka-**yambi**-yuwa   nayi djabirrk *(**karra**)   **baladji**.
        3SG.NF-swag-lie.NP   NM.I dress   DEM.MED.LOC   bag
        'The dress is in the bag.' [IK1-180529_1SY1/55:28–34]

As I have mentioned above, another Gunwinyguan language that allows the incorporation of locatives is Wubuy (6.72).

(6.72) Wubuy (B. Baker 2014a: 237)
   wirri-**wala**-jabijgaa   ana-ngagara   (a-wa̱lak-guy)
   3PL/NEUT-log-go.in.CAUS.PC   NEUT.TOP-bones   NEUT.OBL-hollow.log-ALL
   'They put the bones in the hollow log (NEUT).'

For comparison, Bininj Kunwok only allows incorporation of absolutive arguments, with several extensions: the essive locatives can incorporate into verbs of stance and waiting, and the verb *dowen* 'die' can incorporate the goal (with the meaning 'be dying for/of'); there are also cases suggestive of the A-argument incorporation, but they all admit of alternative analyses (Evans 2003a: 468–71).

6.3.2 External modification

In terms of the possibilities of external modification, however, Kunbarlang is considerably more moderate than Bininj Kunwok, which allows modification of the incorporated noun by adjectives, demonstratives, numerals, possessives, proper names, relative clauses, and in addition to that construal of the incorporated noun as conjoined with a freestanding nominal (Evans 2003a: 452–3). By contrast, Kunbarlang only allows modification by adjectives (6.73a) and possessives (6.73b), as well as doubling by an external noun, often more specific (6.66, repeated below).

(6.73) a. Kanjyuwa ngudda-**yambi**-kanj **na-rleng**.
      PROH   2PL.NF-swag-take.NP   I-much
      'Don't bring too many things!'   [20060614IB/00:50]

   b. Nga-**djakbu**-karlangwanj **kun-ngadju**.
      1SG.NF-step-follow.NP   IV-she.GEN
      'I'm following in her footsteps.'   [IK1-180601_1SY1/01:23:55]

(6.66) Nganj-**kakkin**-rnirlakka **burru=rnungu**.
   1SG.FUT-flesh-send.NP   arm=he.GEN
   'I'll send him/her meat, the arm/flipper part.'
   [IK1-180601_1SY1/01:35:35–38]

Modification by demonstratives and numerals seems ill-formed, as is coordination with external material. Example (6.74) shows that a second independent predicate is obligatory if coordination is to be done.

(6.74) Ka-bun-djanga-djarrang la karra kunbid
3SG.NF-3SG.OBJ-foot-eat.PST CONJ DEM.MED.LOC hand

 *(ka-bun-birr-djarrang).
 3SG.NF-3SG.OBJ-hand-eat.PST

'S/he got burned on the foot and on the hand.' [IK1-180522_3SY1/18:33–43]

This may reflect the syntactic restriction on extraction from a coordinate island, on a syntactic movement theory such as M. C. Baker's (1996). It would require much further work to establish every detail of syntactic functioning of Kunbarlang incorporation.

6.3.3 Interaction with argument derivation

Similarly to Bininj Kunwok, in Kunbarlang comitative objects can incorporate (6.75) and (6.9), repeated below.

(6.75) Nganj-**lerrk**-**walkki**-**wonj** bi-rnungu balanda.
   1SG.FUT-word-COM-return.NP DAT-he.GEN whitefella

  'I'll translate for the whitefella.' [IK1-180601_1SY1/01:16:32–37]

(6.9) Ka-bun-**bardi**-**walkki**-**rnay** kunbareng.
  3SG.NF-3SG.OBJ-liquid-COM-see.PST alcohol

  '[The policeman] saw him/her with grog.' [IK1-180601_1SY1/01:22:08–11]

Benefactive objects, however, cannot incorporate. While the benefactive prefix *marnanj-* can co-occur in a verbal word with an incorporated noun, they necessarily deal with distinct arguments (6.76a):

(6.76) a. Nganj-ka nganj-**marnanj**-**bardi**-kali njunjuk.
    1SG.FUT-go.NP 1SG.FUT-BEN-liquid-get.NP water

   'I'll go fetch some water for him/her/it.' [IK1-180605_1SY1/30:02–05]

  b. *Nganj-bardi-marnanj-ka.
    1SG.1SG-liquid-BEN-go.NP

   intended: 'I'll go for water.' [ibid./29:24–28]

Forms like (6.76b) are ungrammatical. Notice also that the ordering of the benefactive and the incorporated noun as in (6.76a) mirror the semantic composition of the verb: [[get-water] for-someone].

6.3.4 Productivity

The variety of forms with incorporated nominals in Kunbarlang is vast. However, incorporation seems not entirely productive. Rather, sometimes one finds gaps that are currently hard to explain by factors other than some degree of lexicalisation of which verb stems can incorporate which nouns. Consider example (6.77b): while we can see independently that *-kali* 'to get' can incorporate nouns (6.76a), (6.77a) and that *dulk-* is the incorporated form of 'tree; stick' (6.62), (6.63d), their combination is ungrammatical.

(6.77) a. Ngorro   njunjuk   ka-**bardi**-kalng.
        DEM.MED.IV water   3SG.NF-liquid-get.PST
        'This is the water that he brought.'   [IK1-170522_1SM1/07:16–19]

   b. *Kinj-dulk-kali!
      2SG.FUT-tree-get.NP
      intended: 'Get some branches!'   [IK1-180601_1SY1/01:38:28–38]

In the next section I turn to another class of bound morphemes with lexical meaning— the incorporated adverbials.

6.4 Adverb incorporation

The "middlefield" of the verb, as I shall call the slots between the benefactive and the comitative prefixes, contains incorporated nominals, described in §6.3, and incorporated adverbials, such as *warribo-* in (6.78).

(6.78) Nga-**warribo**-djarrang: yimarnek   man-ngaybu   la   mukka   man-rnungu.
        1SG.NF-INADV-eat.PST   like   III-I.GEN   CONJ   it.III III-he.GEN
        'I ate the wrong food: I thought it was mine, but it was his.'
                                                          [IK1-180601_1SY1/38:48–55]

The verbal template from Chapter 5 is repeated here as figure 6.1 for convenience, with the adverbial slots in boldface.

Incorporating adverbs are a semantically heterogeneous class of elements that modify the description of the event or its participants, including the quantificational nuances. They are bound morphemes that appear only within verbal words, so the characterisation of them as *incorporating* refers purely to their positioning inside of the verbal word, as opposed to other free adverbs (and not to a productive relation between the same adverbial element being bound or freestanding, as is the case with incorporated nominals, §6.3). Only three of these morphemes are known to appear

-10	-9	-8	-7	-6	-5	-4	-3	-2	-1	0	+1	+2
Subject	Object	Benefactive	Delimitative	Directionals	Incorp. Qfr.	Inadvertitive	Incorp. noun	Incompletive	Comitative	Stem	RR	TAM

Fig. 6.1: Verbal template in Kunbarlang

inside or outside of the verb, viz. *kaburrk* 'two', *mulmul* 'many', and *warribo-* in the reduplicated form *warriwarribo* 'sloppily'. Table 6.2 lists the incorporating adverbs with their meanings and the glosses used for them.

Tab. 6.2: Kunbarlang incorporating adverbs

Adverb	Meaning	Gloss
baba	each/separately	each
(ka)burrk	together; two	COLL
mulmul	many	many
mun	thither	THITH
nganj	hither	HITH
rnak	only	LIM
warribo	wrongly	INADV
woh	partially	INCP

Kunbarlang incorporating adverbs can co-occur within a single verb, as in (6.79), although I have never recorded a verb that had more than two. The ordering between them largely follows the template, with little permutation possible; I talk about the ordering for individual adverbials below.

(6.79) Kanjbarra-**nganj-rnak**-ka.
3DU.FUT-HITH-LIM-go.NP

'They two will just come together.' [IK1-170530_1SY2/53:35]

Incorporating adverbs differ in their scope possibilities, i.e. what bits of information they can modify. Thus, some modify the properties of the event, scoping over the verb's stem. Others modify descriptions of certain participants, having scope over corresponding arguments of the verb. In what follows, I discuss each of the incorporating adverbs in turn, illustrating their usage and scopal properties.

6.4.1 *baba-* 'separately, each'

The incorporating adverb *baba-* is a distributive universal quantifier (6.80; see also §4.7.3.2) in slot -5 in the verbal template (figure 6.1):

(6.80) a. Kabarra-**baba**-kalng   neyang.
            2DU.NF-DISTR-get.PST   food
            'They two each got some food, separately.'   [IK1-160429_0001/ 36:23]

        b. Kadda-nganj-**baba**-kidanj.
            3PL.NF-HITH-DISTR-go.PST
            'They all came separately.'   [ibid./08:58]

Its semantics is to pair an object or an event type in its scope (the so-called SHARE) to each of the distributive KEYS (Gil 1995), such as the agent of the event. Thus, in (6.80b) the use of *baba-* specifies the event of arriving (the share) as distributed over the plural subject (the key). Similarly, (6.80a) describes the event of getting food as distributed over the dual subject. Example (6.81) shows the object (expressed here by the numeral *nakudji* 'one') as the share.

(6.81) Na-buk   ka-rnak-mulmul-kalng,   bedbe **na-kudji** kadda-**baba**-kalng.
        I-person 3SG.NF-LIM-many-get.PST   they   I-one   3PL.NF-DISTR-get.PST
        'He just caught plenty [of fish], and they've got one each.'
                                                                  [IK1-160722_0001/23:22–52]

In the above examples (6.80–6.81) the key is always the subject, but with the ditransitives the goal (i.e. the primary object) can be the key as well (6.82):

(6.82) Ngudda   ki-ngaddu-**baba**-wuy   djarrang.
        you.SG   2SG.NF-1PL.EXCL.OBJ-DISTR-give.PST   horse
        'You (SG) gave **us each** a horse.'   [IK1-160503_0001/02:52–03:08]

The theme, i.e. the primary object of a transitive verb in (6.83), can also be construed as the key (esp. once the subject is singular and does not override the object for being the key):

(6.83) Nga-**baba**-kalng.
        1SG.NF-DISTR-get.PST
        'I got some of each.'   [IK1-160429_0001/59:06–12]

This example describes a situation constructed with the help of construction blocks: the agent had three piles of blocks in front of them, and took one block from each pile. Here, the taking events (the share) are distributed over the object items (the key).

Among the incorporated adverbials, *baba-* has been found in variable ordering with the hither directional *nganj-*.

6.4.2 *kaburrk-* 'collectively'

The adverb *kaburrk-* in slot -5 is the only incorporating adverb that is freely found outside of the verb, in which case it is the numeral 'two' (§4.7.2.1.1). As the prefix, it sometimes appears in the audibly short form *burrk-* (6.84) due to lenition of its first syllable in the intervocalic position. Its semantics is that of a collective marker, meaning that the agents carry out the action together.

(6.84)   Kanjbarra-nganj-rnak-ka   kanjbarra-**burrk**-djin.
         3DU.FUT-HITH-LIM-go.NP   3DU.FUT-COLL-eat.NP
         'They two will just come and eat together.'   [IK1-170530_1SY2/53:34–39]

Being a collective marker, it is semantically incompatible with distributivity.

(6.85)   *Na-kudji~kudji   kadda-**kaburrk**-warre.
         I-DISTR~one   3PL.NF-COLL-move.NP
         Intended: 'Everyone is walking by themselves.'   [IK1-170610_1SY1/24:50–53]

It can, however, co-occur with the distributive *baba-* (§6.4.1) if an appropriate construal is available (6.86):

(6.86)   Kadda-**kaburrk**-**baba**-warre.
         3PL.NF-COLL-DISTR-move.NP
         'Different groups (*kaburrk*) are walking separate from each other (*baba*).'
         [IK1-170610_1SY1/20:52–54]

When co-occurring, *kaburrk-* precedes *baba-*. The groups in (6.86) can be larger than two members, which shows that *kaburrk-* is collective, rather than dual. Besides the subject, it can also modify the primary object (6.87):

(6.87)   Ka-nganun-**kaburrk**-wuy.
         3SG.NF-1DU.EXCL.OBJ-COLL-give.PST
         'S/he gave us two something to share.'   [IK1-180524_SY2/43:23]

6.4.3 *mulmul-* 'many'

The prefix *mulmul-* 'many' is a quantifier (6.88) with lexically restricted combinatorics. It only combines with the verbs *-ka* 'to go' (6.88a) and *-kali* 'to get' (6.88b) and scopes over the intransitive subject of the former or the object of the latter (see also §4.7.2.2).

(6.88) a. Kadda-nganj-**mulmul**-kidanj.
3PL.NF-HITH-many-go.PST
'a lot of people came.' [IK1-160802_0001/14:21]

b. Kadda-**mulmul**-kalng apple kadda-wu-djinj.
3PL.NF-many-get.PST ENG 3PL.NF-give-REFL.PST
'They've got many apples and are sharing them (amongst themselves).'
[IK1-160429_0001/01:28:33–37]

Section §4.7.2 describes this prefix within the system of other bound and free quantifiers.

6.4.4 *nganj-* 'HITHer'

There are two directional prefixes placed in slot -6 in Kunbarlang: *nganj-* 'HITH' and *mun-* 'THITH'. The prefix *nganj-* 'HITH' is rather frequent and is primarily used with motion and other dynamic verbs. With these, it adds the semantic component of motion directed towards a deictic center, which may or may not coincide with the speaker. Thus, the pair in (6.89) shows a contrast between an example without *nganj-* that refers to a non-specific direction of returning (6.89a) and an example with *nganj-* that refers to an event of returning to the place which is the current stage of the action unfolding at that point in the narrative (6.89b):

(6.89) a. **Ka-wom** ngorro ka-bardi-kalng njunjuk.
3SG.NF-return.PST DEM.MED.IV 3SG.NF-liquid-get.PST water
'S/he went back to get water.' [IK1-170516_1SY1/12:08–12]

b. **Ka-nganj-wom** ngorro ka-burrun-yalbi-yawam.
3SG.NF-HITH-return.PST DEM.MED.IV 3SG.NF-3DU.OBJ-country-seek.PST
'When he came back he looked for those two (but they were not there).'
[20150212AS01/05:01–04]

Similar to the Bininj Kunwok 'hither'-directional *m-* (Evans 2003a: 489–90), the Kunbarlang *nganj-* allows occasional extension of the meaning into non-dynamic, non-directional event descriptions. Example (6.90) shows an instance of such extension with the verb *-yuwa* 'to lie', where the use of *nganj-* probably highlights the mutual proximity of the two participants:

(6.90) Pat la   Stacey **ka-nganj-yuwa**   la   na-wuk-ma.
       P   CONJ S   3SG.NF-HITH-lie.NP CONJ I-person-CONTR
       'Pat and Stacey are neighbours (i.e., live near each other).'
       [IK1-160513_0011/00:44–50]

This prefix typically precedes the other incorporated adverbs, but also has been found in variable ordering with the delimitative *rnak-* (see §6.4.6 for examples).

6.4.5 *mun-* 'THITHer'

Unlike the 'hither' prefix *nganj-* (§6.4.4), the 'thither' prefix *mun-* (6.91) is very infrequent.

(6.91) a. ...la   ngadda-**mun**-bing-bi   ngadda-maddjing.
            CONJ 1PL.EXCL.NF-THITH-exit.PST-THITH   1PL.EXCL.NF-pierce.PST
           '...and we got close [to that crocodile] and we speared it.'
           [20060620IB04/09:12–15]
      b. Nga-**mun**-rnirlakwang   kikakkin.
         1SG.NF-THITH-send.PST   meat
         'I sent (someone) meat.'   [IK1-160503_0001/24:32–34]

There are few examples of this prefix (only four tokens in narratives currently), which makes it difficult to determine the semantics of *mun-* precisely. Two out of the four tokens feature the allative clitic *bi-* (§7.6) on the verb (6.91a), and the other two—on a locative pronoun (6.92), suggesting that there is a strong semantic connection between them.

(6.92) Kabbala kenda-**bi**   ka-**mun**-kidanj=kulkkulk.
       boat   DEM.PROX.LOC-THITH   3SG.NF-THITH-go.PST=run
       'A boat was going from this way.'   [20060620IB03/06:30–33]

The interpretation of (6.92), with the boat approaching the place where the speaker was, suggests that the deictic center assumes the perspective of the grammatical subject (rather than the speaker).

6.4.6 *rnak-* 'just'

The deLIMitative prefix *rnak-* in slot -7 has a wide range of discourse uses, which are fairly close to the English adverb *just*.[19] Effectively, through association with its scope, it has the following meaning: consider things of the same kind as the phrase in scope describes; substituting them in place of scope makes false statements. Thus, in (6.93) the prefix associates with the Recipient phrase *ngalbuk bi-ngadju* 'for herself', and has the effect of exclusion of other, potential, Recipients, such as "for me", set up in the left context:

(6.93) Nga-ngunda=barr   ngayi   ngana-djanganj   ka-marnbum   bi-ngaybu
        1SG.NF-do.PST=open   I   1DU-sibling   3SG.NF-make.PST DAT-I.GEN

    neyang,   la   ka-**rnak**-marnbum   ngal-buk bi-ngadju.
    food   CONJ   3SG.NF-LIM-make.PST   II-person DAT-she.GEN

'I thought sister made food for me, but she only made it for herself.'
[IK1-160513_0021/22:25–35]

The prefix is not grammatically restricted in its association: it may associate with a range of verb's arguments, as well as with the verb stem, i.e. the event description, itself. Example (6.94) illustrates this by showing a ditransitive verb with *rnak-* (a) and a selection of felicitous continuations (b–e) which all highlight different possible construals of (a), viz. the focus on subject, primary and secondary objects, or the entire event description.[20]

(6.94)   IK1-160503_0001/46:50–01:00:20

    a. Ngayi   nga-buddu-**rnak**-wuy   djarrang...
        I   1SG.NF-3PL.OBJ-LIM-give.PST horse

    'ONLY[I gave them a horse].' (i.e. 'I was the only one who gave them a horse', or 'They were the only ones I gave a horse to', or 'It was only horse that I gave them', or 'All I did was give them a horse')

    b. SUBJECT:

        ngunda **ki**-buddu-wuni   djarrang.
        not   3SG.IRR.PST-3PL.OBJ-give.IRR.PST horse

    'S/he didn't give them a horse.'

---

19 The Bininj Kunwok prefix *djal-* 'just' is very similar to *rnak-* (Evans 2003a: 515ff.).

20 These continuations were all constructed by me and offered to my consultant to judge if they made sense when said together with the sentence containing *rnak-* (6.94a). I have also verified that the speaker rejected contradictory Kunbarlang statements (like, *I gave them a horse, but I didn't give them a horse*) as non-sensical.

c. PRIMARY OBJECT/RECIPIENT:

ngunda   ngay-**ngun**-wuni.
not   1SG.IRR.PST-2SG.OBJ-give.IRR.PST
'I didn't give one to you.'

d. SECONDARY OBJECT/THEME:

ngunda   ngay-buddu-wuni   **durduk**.
not   1SG.IRR.PST-2SG.OBJ-give.IRR.PST   dog
'I didn't give them a dog.'

e. ENTIRE EVENT:

ngunda   **ngay-wuni**   neyang.
not   1SG.IRR.PST-give.IRR.PST   food
'I didn't feed it.'

The ordering of *rnak-* with respect to the other middlefield prefixes is often flexible (6.95).

(6.95) a. Kadda-**rnak-nganj**-kidanj.
          3PL.NF-LIM-HITH-go.PST
          'They just came suddenly.' [IK1-160513_0001/54:19–22]

    b. Kanjbarra-**nganj-rnak**-ka kanjbarra-kaburrk-djinj.
       3DU.FUT-HITH-LIM-go.NP   3DU.FUT-COLL-eat.NP
       'They (two) will just come and eat together.' [IK1-170530_1SY2/53:34–39]

However, the delimitative appears to be rigidly ordered preceding the incompletive *woh-* (§6.4.8).

6.4.7 *warribo-* 'INADvertently'

The inadvertitive prefix *warribo-* is related to the free-standing adverb *warriwarribo* 'sloppily' and conveys that something about the event is wrong or sloppy. It does not contribute any more specific or complex information, and the appropriate interpretation must be arrived at via the relevant context. In effect, the scope of this adverb is always over the event as a whole, rather than its individual participants; cf. Bicevskis's (2012: 80–86) analysis of the corresponding modifier *warrgah-* found in Bininj Kunwok (Kundjeihmi and Kune) and Dalabon, where she argues that it scopes over the entire stative (sub)event.

(6.96) a. Kabarra-marnanj-bing old man kakkak Bungorro.
3DU.NF-BEN-exit.PST ENG ENG MMB B
'They two came to the old man Bungorro.' [IK1-160624_0021/03:35–38]

b. Ka-buddu-marnanj-**warribo**-bing.
3SG.NF-3PL.OBJ-BEN-INADV-exit.PST
'S/he came to the wrong people.' [IK1-160628_0001/52:46–48]

A speaker in the discussion of (6.97) comments that it could describe any kind of mistake at all—e.g. the wrong kind of meat, the wrong piece, unintentionally getting meat instead of rice, etc.

(6.97) Nga-**warribo**-kalng nayi kikakkin.
1SG.NF-INADV-get.PST NM.I meat
'I wrongly got the meat.' [IK1-160429_0001/01:16:15–17]

6.4.8 *woh-* 'incompletely'

The contribution of the incompletive prefix *woh-* can be described as 'incompletely', 'unthoroughly' or 'halfway'. Effectively, in the majority of uses it can be translated as 'not all'. That is, adding it to the verb describes the event as incomplete, an action only partially carried out or its result merely temporary and transient. Example (6.98) illustrates its use to describe a partially affected theme:

(6.98) Man-kudji kurrambalk ka-bun-**woh**-djarrang
III-one house 3SG.NF-3SG.OBJ-INCP-eat.PST

la kadda-ngulukdombum.
CONJ 3PL.NF-extinguish.PST
'A certain house only burnt down partially, they've put out the fire.'
[IK1-170530_1SY2/13:48–54]

With plural arguments the effect of *woh-* is similarly that of partial quantification (6.99):

(6.99) a. Kadda-rninganj kadda-**woh**-djanganj.
3PL.NF-sit.PST 3PL.NF-INCP-stand.PST
'They were sitting and then part of them stood up.'
[IK1-180601_1SY1/29:23]

b. Kinj-**woh**-bunj=ngurr   la   na-yika   ngayi
   2SG.FUT-INCP-hit.NP=rippled   CONJ   I-some   I

   nganj-bunj=ngurr.
   1SG.FUT-hit.NP=rippled

   'You wash some [of the dishes] and I shall do the rest.'
   [IK1-170530_1SY2/20:23–27]

In some cases this prefix may communicate an air of negligence, such as 'lying around' in (6.100a), or a temporary result state, which probably relates semantically to the idea of negligence, not putting in enough effort for a proper permanent result (6.100b).

(6.100) a. Marrek barda ngemek ki-**woh**-yung   korro
           not   what   yet   3SG.IRR.NP-INCP-lie.IRR.NP   DEM.MED.LOC

           welenj.
           road

           'There is nothing else lying around on the road.'
           [IK1-170610_2SM1/11:07–11]

       b. Nga-**woh**-marnbum.
           1SG.NF-INCP-make.PST

           'I made it only temporary [will make a permanent one later].'
           [IK1-150725_0011/12:56]

The prefix *woh-* normally follows all other prefixes in the middlefield.

6.5 Coverb constructions

Kunbarlang is the only Gunwinyguan language that has coverb constructions (6.101), in the narrow sense that will be defined below.

(6.101) Nga-**warrenj**=**yerri**   kurrula.
        1SG.NF-move.PST=dream   saltwater

        'I dreamt of the sea.'   [IK1-150802_1PN2/19:54]

These coverb constructions are formed by combining an inflecting "light" verb with an uninflecting coverb. In (6.101), the verb *-warre* 'to move' is combined with the coverb *yerri*, with the resulting predicate meaning 'to dream'. Thus, coverb constructions are a type of complex predication. By *complex predicate* I mean here structures where "the information normally associated with the [lexical—IK] head of a verbal predicate is spread over several parts of the predicate" (Bowern 2014: 264).

The light verb in the Kunbarlang construction is drawn from a set of 14 verbs (see table 6.3), all of which have simple stems (see the introduction to chapter 5 for simple and complex stems) and can otherwise be used as predicates on their own.[21] The coverb is drawn from a closed class of items in the order of one hundred, whose distribution is restricted to this function. Many of them are listed in tables 6.4–6.8 later in this section. As is discussed in §3.2.5.1, coverbs are analysed here as lexical clitics: they have rich lexical content, but very rigid placement immediately following the verb (with the caveat that monosyllabic ideophonic ones are occasionally attested in the immediate preverbal position). Their clitic behaviour is also manifest in the manner assimilation that can happen between the consonants at the point of nexus (§2.7.4). Nothing can intervene between the two parts of this construction; see (6.102) and §3.2.5.1 for more examples.

(6.102) *Nga-**warrenj** kurrula **yerri**.
1SG.NF-move.PST saltwater dream
intended: 'I dreamt of the sea.' [IK1-150802_1PN2/20:52]

This section focuses on the complex predicate formation, relation of the coverb construction to other predicates (§6.5.1), and its place within the context of the Gunwinyguan family and other neighbouring languages, esp. Mawng (§6.5.2).

Kunbarlang coverbs cannot appear by themselves. When asked about some coverb, speakers would usually recognize it and produce a full coverb construction, rather than give translations, explanations or examples for the coverb alone. The light verb and the coverb form a tight morphosyntactic unit. Not only can they not be interrupted by other material, but also the light verb cannot be gapped under coordination, such as contrastive focus (6.103):

(6.103) a. Nga-**kali**=**karlirrk** dolobbo.
1SG.NF-get.NP=drag stringybark
'I'm dragging bark.' [IK1-150802_1PN2/13:32]

b. Nga-**kali**=**kerd** dolobbo.
1SG.NF-get.NP=carry stringybark
'I'm carrying bark.' [list_cvc.xls]

---

21 The lexical content of the light verbs is remarkably uniform across Australian languages: they are the frequent verbs with generic meanings, such as 'say / do', 'sit / be', 'stand', 'become', 'fall', 'go', 'carry', 'take', 'hit', 'catch / get', 'put', 'give', 'throw' and 'spear' (McGregor 2002: 104); Kunbarlang set conforms to this observation. Across languages of the world, verbs with these meanings often serve as light verbs, auxiliaries or verb proforms, or grammaticalise as markers of voice, tense and aspect (Heine & Kuteva 2002).

Tab. 6.3: Light verbs of the coverb constructions

verb	meaning
-bunj	'to hit'
-dja	'to stand'
-ka	'to go'
-kali	'to get'
-karrme	'to hold'
-kelkwunj	'to tease'
-maddje	'to pierce'
-ngale	'to spread, move along'
-ngundje	'to say; to do'
-rdam	'to put'
-rna	'to sit'
-rnanj	'to see'
-warre	'to occur; to move'
-yuwa	'to lie (down)'

   c. *Nga-kali=karlirrk, ngunda ~~ngarra-kalbing~~ =kerd.
    1SG.NF-get.NP=drag not (1SG.IRR.NP-get.IRR.NP) carry
    intended: 'I'm dragging it, not carrying it.' [IK1-150805_0001/15:22–28]

(6.104) Nga-**kali**=**karlirrk**, ngayi ngunda ngarra-**kalbing**=**kerd**.
    1SG.NF-get.NP=drag I not 1SG.IRR.NP-get.IRR.NP=carry
    'I'm dragging it, not carrying it.' [IK1-150805_0001/16:01]

In the first two examples in (6.103) the two coverb constructions use the same light verb *kali* 'get', but different coverbs. Example (6.103c) shows that the light verb cannot be elided under identity (shown schematically in ~~strikethrough~~), leaving the coverb behind. On the other hand, ellipsis of the verb is allowed in other constructions with a direct object (6.105):

(6.105) Nukka ka-bunj=beleybeley, la marrek ~~ki-bu~~ kunbid.
    he 3SG.NF-hit.NP=clap CONJ not 3SG.IRR.NP-hit.IRR.NP hand
    'He's clapping something, but not hands.' [IK1-150805_0001/11:06–16]

Most of the light verbs, as well as most of the coverbs, participate in several combinations. However, coverbs are used at most with three or four verbs, and cross-classing usually is insufficient to determine their semantic contribution with certainty. Moreover, coverbs are not used outside the coverb construction, which complicates the task of isolating their meaning. Some are only recorded in one construction (6.106), and their meaning has to be stipulated, to an extent.

(6.106) Ka-**maddjing**=**rdorr**   barndang.
3SG.NF-pierce.PST=goad trouble
'S/he started trouble.'   [list_cvc.xls]

The coverbs are very diverse formally, many of them mono- or disyllabic, but a few are quite large (6.107).

(6.107) Ka-ngan-marnanj-**kalng**=**kubirribirrkuk**.
3SG.NF-1SG.OBJ-BEN-get.PST=steal
'S/he / it stole it from me.'   [IK1-160715_0001/09:36–39]

They are also very diverse with respect to the effect they have on resulting predicate semantics and event structure. There is not a single uniform pattern. Some of the coverbs have a very transparent contribution, akin to adverbial modification; consider the coverb *mulmul*, which 'adds' the meaning 'underwater' to the base light verb (6.108):

(6.108) a. Ka-**karrme**=**mulmul**.
3SG.NF-hold.NP=underwater
'He's holding it underwater.'   [IK1-150803_1PN1/16:48]

b. Ka-**warre**=**mulmul**.
3SG.NF-occur.NP=underwater
'He's diving.'   [list_cvc.xls]

By contrast, complex predicates built with some other coverbs, such as *karndjurrk* 'single_file' or *kolk* 'cut', are harder to relate to the light verb (6.109). Interestingly, these are frequently the ones where the coverb does not cross-combine with other verbs.

(6.109) a. Kadda-**maddje**=**karndjurrk**   kadda-ka.
3PL.NF-pierce.NP=single_file 3PL.NF-go.NP
'They are walking in a single file.'   [IK1-170610_1SY1/29:09]

b. Kadda-**djanganj**=**kolk**.
3PL.NF-stand.PST=cut
'They cut it down [the tree].'   [IK1-150804_0001/44:40–42]

Comparing (6.108) and (6.109), one can see that in the former, *mulmul* narrows down the situation described by the light verb (e.g. holding underwater is a type of holding); however, being in single file (*karndjurrk*) is not a type of piercing, nor is cutting down a tree a type of standing.

It is fairly tricky to reason about the change in transitivity and aspectual class change in coverb constructions. Many of the ones that appear to change in transitivity compared to the base light verb do not easily take human objects (e.g. as in (6.109)): *-maddje* 'to pierce' → *-maddje=karndjurrk* 'to form a single file'; *-dja* 'to stand' → *-dja=kolk* 'to cut/chop down'); thus, object agreement prefixes, which would provide the most reliable evidence for their transitivity, are not readily available. In terms of the aspectual class (Aktionsart), there are no good tests for that in Kunbarlang at the moment. One can only rely on the semantics apparent in translations. Based on that, it does seem that the structure of the event can change considerably. One example is *-dja=kolk* in (6.109b): it appears that a stative event of standing, which only has one participant, changes to an accomplishment with an agent and a patient. Similarly, example (6.110) shows a posture base verb *-rna* 'to sit', which has only one participant and is presumably stative, turning into an achievement with two participants *-rna=bard* 'to acquire':

(6.110) Neyang **ka-rninganj=bard** kandidjawa.
         food   3SG.NF-sit.PST=acquire bread
         'He bought food, flour.'   [20060620IB04/11:59–12:03]

Further work is required to explore event structure in Kunbarlang and syntax and semantics of individual coverb constructions.

6.5.1 Structural parallels

Kunbarlang coverb constructions have an interesting place in the broader picture of predicate formation in Gunwinyguan languages. When I emphasised the uniqueness of the Kunbarlang coverb construction in the beginning of §6.5, I did so because of its highly regularised structure. At the same time, closely related constructions are attested in many Gunwinyguan languages. In the ensuing discussion, two phenomena are central: (i) Gunwinyguan complex stems, and (ii) excorporation.

Recall the discussion at the beginning of Chapter 5 concerning the structure of the complex stems, consisting of a prepound and a thematic. *Thematics* are monomorphemic verbal roots that determine the conjugation class. *Prepounds* are elements to the immediate left of the thematic that come from various historical sources and form lexicalised complex stem combinations together with thematics. Other Gunwinyguan languages have similar structures. I find that a number of Kunbarlang coverbs are clear cognates to morphemes found as prepounds in other languages. For instance, Bininj Kunwok has a verb *djelh.me* 'to drip', whose prepound corresponds to the Kunbarlang coverb *djerl* 'drip' (6.111a); Dalabon has a verb *karrhkarrh.mû* 'to shake', corresponding to the Kunbarlang coverb *karrkarr* 'shake'; and Ngandi has a verb *wurlup-dhu* 'to bathe, be immersed', corresponding to the Kunbarlang coverb *rlubburlub* 'splash' (6.111b). I talk about cognacy with other Gunwinyguan morphemes, as well as other sources of coverbs in more detail below.

(6.111) a. Tea ka-**dja**=**djerl**.
ENG 3SG.NF-stand.NP=drip
'Tea is dripping.' [IK1-150802_1PN2/37:34]

b. Nawalak ka-**rna**=**rlubburlub**.
child 3SG.NF-sit=splash
'The baby sits splashing/playing in water.' [Coleman 2010: 110]

Furthermore, a few of the Kunbarlang coverbs can appear in either position: as a coverb or as a prepound within a complex stem. One such coverb is *larl* 'open' (6.112a), which has a cognate in Dalabon (6.112c), and as a prepound in Kunbarlang combines with the thematic *-ma* meaning 'to divide, separate' (6.112b).[22]

(6.112) a. Ka-djarda-**karrmeng**=**larl**.
3SG.NF-mouth-hold.PST=open
'S/he opened the door.' [list_cvc.xlc]

b. Ngarrki-**larlma**.
1.INCL.FUT-divide.NP
'We'll divide it.' [IK1-170620_1SY2/13:13]

c. Dalabon (Evans, Merlan & Tukumba 2004: 199)
Yila-h-**larlh.miyan**.
1PL-R-open.FUT
'We'll prise it open.' [glosses mine—IK]

Next, there is the phenomenon of EXCORPORATION, found at least in Rembarrnga (McKay 2008), Ngalakgan (Baker & Harvey 2003), Dalabon (Evans, Fletcher & Ross 2008), and some varieties of Bininj Kunwok (Kuninjku, Kunwinjku, and Manyallaluk Mayali; Evans 2017, also 2003a: 587). In this construction, "otherwise bound verb roots… can optionally appear externally to the rest of the verb word" (B. Baker 2014b: 147); an example from Ngalakgan is in (6.113):

(6.113) Ngalakgan (Baker & Harvey 2003: 14)

a. Burru-worrowk-mi+ny
3PL-gallop-AUX+PP
'They galloped.'

b. Worrowk burru-mi+ny.
gallop 3PL-AUX+PP
'They galloped.'

---

22 The thematics in (6.112b) and (6.112c) are also cognate, in fact.

Unlike the Kunbarlang coverbs (but similar to Kunbarlang preverbs, see §3.2.5.2), excorporated prepounds in other Gunwinyguan languages appear to the left of the inflecting verb left behind (6.113b). In this particular example, -*mi* does not have lexical content on its own, so the string *burruminy* is not a word by itself. There is not enough information about these constructions in the aforementioned languages, but it appears that they differ from the rigid Kunbarlang coverb construction. Thus, in Ngalakgan the two constituents cannot be permuted or interrupted by other material, but the prepound part can sometimes appear alone (Baker & Harvey 2003: 14–15). In Rembarrnga, the prepound may be separated from the inflected verb by other material (McKay 2008: 9). In both Rembarrnga (ibid.) and Dalabon (Evans 2017: 330), the prepound may recur both outside and inside the inflected verb. My understanding of the literature is that in all of the cited languages, excorporation serves a stylistic purpose, perhaps making narration more vivid and dramatic. This is in striking contrast with Kunbarlang where for many lexicalised meanings, this is the only available expression, and not a stylistic variant. It is almost certain that the predicate-forming structures discussed above—complex stems, (Kunbarlang) coverb constructions, and excorporation—are very closely related historically, presenting slightly different ways of combining a lexical component (i.e. the prepound/coverb) with a structural component (the thematic) to produce a complex predicate. It will require a separate investigation to establish the diachronic pathways between these structures.

Further corroboration of the idea that coverbs and prepounds are functionally very similar comes from the fact that in Kunbarlang all light verbs in the coverb construction have simple stems. Attempts to build coverb constructions with complex stems are rejected by my informants, e.g. (6.114).

(6.114) a. Kikka kadda-**kel.kidanj** ngob.
 they 3PL.NF-fear.go.PST all
 'They fled (in fear).' [IK1-170607_1SM1/49:09]

 b. Ka-**ka**=**kulkkulk** munguy.
 3SG.NF-go.NP=run a_lot
 'S/he goes running always/every day.' [IK1-160719_0011/06:09]

 c. *Kadda-kel.kidanj=kulkkulk.
 3PL.NF-fear.go.PST=run
 'They fled, running in fear.' [IK1-160728_0001/01:15–20]

The verb -*kelkidanj* 'flee.PST' in (6.114a) has a complex stem, with the prepound *kel* 'fear' and the thematic -*ka* 'to go'. That thematic, when used as a simple stem, can form a coverb construction meaning 'to run' (6.114b). However, their combination is impossible.

6.5.2 Etymology

I have discussed above a family of complex predicate constructions, in Gunwinyguan languages, which appear very closely connected as a collection of morphosyntactic solutions to the singular task of forming a predicate from two lexical heads. I do not attempt here to reconstruct the diachrony of the Kunbarlang construction arising. However, I shall review the coverb construction in Mawng, which is structurally very similar to the Kunbarlang one. Next, I shall demonstrate some lexical correspondence between Kunbarlang, Mawng, and some other Gunwinyguan languages, and make a suggestion that Kunbarlang might have developed the coverb construction from the original Gunwinyguan option for variable prepound placement in the contact situation with Mawng, perhaps from the need to accommodate for lexical exchange with the latter.

Before discussing Mawng, I would like to point out that in 1960s, i.e. in the earliest extensive records, the coverb construction was already attested in Kunbarlang (6.115).

(6.115) Ngayi nga-bum=ngurr   kun-mak.
        I   1SG.NF-hit.PST=rippled IV-good

'I did the washing very well.'   [Kinslow Harris 1969b: 33; gloss mine—IK]

Its extent, however, is not known. The two constructions that appear in Kinslow Harris's examples are -*bunj=ngurr* 'to wash' and -*ka=kulkkulk* 'to run'.

6.5.2.1 Mawng coverb constructions

Mawng coverb constructions essentially show very similar structural properties to the Kunbarlang ones (Singer 2016: §3.1.2):
- they form a tight morphosyntactic unit
  - they are strictly adjacent: all postverbal clitics must attach after the coverb, without breaking the complex (6.116a)[23] (Singer 2016: 118 fn. 10)
  - the verb-coverb boundary is subject to morphophonemic integration
- they are often non-transparent semantically, with high degree of idiomatisation
- they often feature lexicalised agreement (one quarter of coverb constructions; Singer 2005: 6) (6.116b)

---

[23] The non-obvious glosses for the Mawng examples are: EMPH1 backgrounding suffix for verbs, PHAB past habitual, P.SEQ sequential particle.

(6.116) Mawng (Singer 2006)

a. Pa **ani-wu-k** **pirl**=ga=pa ja nganaparru
P.SEQ 3.MA>3.LL-hit-PP cross_water=H=EMPH1 MA buffalo
y-a-ngkung-ka.
3.MA-go$_1$-PHAB-HITH
'So the buffalo crossed over (a body of water) and was headed this way.'
[p. 71; "=" for the clitic separator and boldface mine—IK]

b. **Anny-arlukpa-n** **rtap** ja Yumparrparr.
3.MA>3.LL-move_foot-PP slip MA giant
'Yumparrparr slipped.' [p. 292; boldface mine—IK]

In example (6.116a) the postverbal clitics, directional *ga* 'hither' and backgrounding *pa*, attach to the verb-coverb complex, i.e. after the coverbs, rather than to the light verb. Example (6.116b) shows the so-called *lexicalised agreement*: the light verb agrees as if with a land gender object, while no such object is overtly present in the sentence, nor does the same verb have such agreement when used by itself.

Interestingly, "[i]t is acceptable for some Mawng coverbs to precede rather than follow the verb" (albeit this is rare in spontaneous speech), which is a bit more freedom of placement than there is for coverbs in Kunbarlang (Singer 2006: 77). In the following section I discuss the lexical similarities between Mawng and Kunbarlang.

6.5.2.2 Lexical correspondence

Out of approximately a hundred coverbs known in Kunbarlang at least 18 are common with Mawng (Singer et al. 2015). The correspondences between Kunbarlang and Mawng are shown in table 6.4. This list is not necessarily exhaustive, these are just the correspondences I have identified to date.

Singer (2005) provides independent evidence that nouns were the source of some coverbs in Mawng. I take this as a piece of evidence to support the hypothesis that the direction of borrowing is from Mawng into Kunbarlang. Further suggestion along these lines comes from the fact that fewer of the Kunbarlang coverbs have cognates in the closer related Gunwinyguan languages: eleven in Bininj Kunwok (Evans 1991), seven in Dalabon (Evans, Merlan & Tukumba 2004), three in Ngandi (Heath 1978). Every pair of these other languages (except Dalabon~Ngandi) shares at least one of these morphemes; for instance, Mawng and Bininj Kunwok share as many as five. The same caveat holds for Gunwinyguan correspondences as for Mawng, mentioned above: these lists are indicative rather than exhaustive. In the following tables I show Kunbarlang coverbs that have correspondence with words in Bininj Kunwok (table 6.5), Dalabon (table 6.6), and Ngandi (table 6.7).

---

24 Initial glides of many coverbs in Mawng undergo hardening after a consonant final verb (e.g. *wu~pu*).

Tab. 6.4: Kunbarlang coverbs with correspondence in Mawng

Kunbarlang	meaning	Mawng	meaning
buk	blow, spit	wu_2[24]	blow
barrbarr	flat	parrparr	be extended, stretch
berlbberl	ooze	pirlpirl	flow
bokob	float	pagap	float
djerr	hold tightly	jir(r)	hold tightly
djab	move	yap_2	move from one spot to another
djerl	drip	djirl	drip
djorrord	limp	jarrart	limp
dob	pop, burst	rtap	explode
dowdow	shake	tawktawk	shake
kabbirrk	trip up	kapirrk	trip over
karlk	walk in line	kalk	be in line
larl	open	larl	lie open
mabularr	calm	mapularr	calm
madmad	fly	matmat	fly
marrmarr	happy	marrmarr	happy
mulmul	underwater	murlmurl	dive in
rlubburlub	splash	wurlupurlup	bathe, swim

Tab. 6.5: Kunbarlang coverbs with correspondence in Bininj Kunwok

Kunbarlang	meaning	Bininj Kunwok	meaning	category
barr	display	barrme	be open	intr. verb[25]
barr	display	barrhbun	dawn, (day) break	intr. verb
borrkborrk	play	borrk-	play, dance	N/V
buk	blow, spit	buhme	blow	trans. verb
djerl	drip	djelhme	drip	intr. verb
kidjihkidji	tickle	gidjigidjikme	tickle	intr. verb
kolk	cut	golkme	cut	trans. verb
kulkkulk	run	gurlhgurlme	run fast (of water)	intr. verb
larl	open	larlma	separate	trans. verb
marrmarr	happy	marrmarrme	be happy	intr. verb
wayud	wave	waidan	wave	trans. verb
yerri	dream	bengyirri[26]	daydream	intr. verb

Tab. 6.6: Kunbarlang coverbs with correspondence in Dalabon

Kunbarlang	meaning	Dalabon	meaning	category
barr	display	barr(mû)	open	intr. verb
borrng	snore	borrmû	snore	intr. verb
djorrord	limp	djorrordmû	be lame	intr. verb
karrkarr	shake	karrhkarrhmû	shake off (dirt)	trans. verb
kulkkulk	run	kurlhkurlhno	fast pace, run	noun
kulkkulk	run	kurlhkurlhmû	run along	intr. verb
larl	open	larlarl(mû)	be open/ready to split	intr. verb
larl	open	larlhmang	(prise) open	trans. verb
wirrkwirrk	scrape	wirrkmû	scrape clean	trans. verb

Tab. 6.7: Kunbarlang coverbs with correspondence in Ngandi

Kunbarlang	meaning	Ngandi	meaning	category
buk	blow, spit	buh-dhu	blow	intr. verb
kolk	cut	gulk-dhu	cut	trans. verb
rlubburlub	splash	wurlup-dhu	bathe, be immersed	intr. verb

It has been previously observed in languages of northern Australia that coverbs are freely borrowed (Bowern 2014: 288). Furthermore, McConvell (2010) discusses the scenario where a language has developed coverb constructions as the means to accommodate loans (in Gurindji, for borrowings from non-Pama-Nyungan languages). It would take much more diachronic work to thoroughly describe the evolution of the Kunbarlang coverb construction; however, I would like to make the following suggestion in light of the facts reviewed in this section, viz. (i) the morphosyntactic variety of complex predicate structures within the Gunwinyguan family (§6.5.1), and (ii) the particular structural and lexical affinity between Kunbarlang and Mawng. It appears plausible that Kunbarlang has developed the coverb construction as a regularised way of borrowing lexicon from Mawng. Simultaneously, a subset of inherited Gunwinyguan morphemes (which are prepounds in other Gunwinyguan languages), have also got fixed as coverbs in Kunbarlang. Perhaps there were loans from contact languages other than Mawng—further etymological research is required to shed light on that. Thus, we have today's picture of a rigid construction in Kunbarlang where the coverbs come from a variety of sources.

Finally, table 6.8 provides those 36 Kunbarlang coverbs for which no correspondences in other languages have been established at the moment of writing.

---

25 The dictionary says "transitive verb", which is likely a typo.
26 The part *beng* presumably is the nominal root meaning 'hearing; intelligence', and thus the Bininj Kunwok verb might evoke the image of the sleep of reason.

Tab. 6.8: Kunbarlang coverbs without established correspondence

Coverb	Meaning
bard	acquire
berrulk	cough
bordobordo	shake head
budj	thud
bulilibbulilib	slide
dakkardak	block
durdulk	rub, stroke
didik	stretch
dilirr	drift
djakdjak	sift
djirrdjirr	slide and fall
karlirrk	drag
karndjurrk	single file
karrik	paddle
kerd	carry
kubirribirrkuk	steal
lorr	lean (against something)
makoberl	envy
marr	tease[a]
mawiwird	whistle
melmel	(lightning) strike
molek	(make) noise
mung	suck
munumunu	roll up
ngerrk	growl
ngid	proud of obj.
ngurr	wash
njawnjaw	chew
nunu	squeeze
rdak	obstruct
rdorr	goad
rdurdu	thunder
wadbuk	splash
wadbukwadbuk	fan, blow
worrworr	shake (trans.)
yulyulk	put under

[a] It seems probable that *marr* and *marrmarr* 'happy' are related, but since they occur in different constructions and the synchronic relation is unclear, I included *marr* here for the sake of completeness. The constructions are: *-kelkwunj=marr* 'to tease' vs. *-ngundje=marrmarr* 'to be happy'.

7 Clause structure

This chapter is focused on the structure of simple clauses. There are two main types of simple clauses: the bulk of the chapter deals with clauses built around verbal predicates, and section 7.7 is about the stative clauses, the majority of which have nominal predicates. The analytical comparative constructions cross-cut the distinction, but they are presented all together in §7.7.4 for the sake of presentation coherency. This chapter is structured as follows. In section 7.1 I discuss clausal word order, which is relatively free in Kunbarlang, and its relation to information structure. Section 7.2 presents the analytical viewpoint constructions that express imperfectivity and duration. Negation strategies, which require a change in the mood of the clause to irrealis, are discussed in §7.3. In §7.4 I turn to the formation of questions, which may, but do not have to include a question particle (in the case of polar questions) or a question word at the front (in constituent questions). Then I show how imperatives are formed in Kunbarlang (§7.5): there is no dedicated imperative mood, so positive imperatives use the future tense of the verb, and negative imperatives employ a construction with a prohibitive particle and a present tense verb. Section 7.6 is about the directional clitics in Kunbarlang. The following section (§7.7) brings together discussion of the ascriptive (§7.7.1), possessive (§7.7.2), locative and existential clauses (§7.7.3), and the expression of comparative and superlative degrees (§7.7.4). Finally, the last section of this chapter (§7.8) gives a brief overview of the reference tracking patterns and strategies to mark coreference that are found in Kunbarlang. In the next chapter, I turn to a discussion of multiclausal constructions found in Kunbarlang (chapter 8).

This discussion of clausal structure, especially for the verbal predicate clauses, relies heavily on the discussion of verbal morphology in chapter 5. The topics most important for navigating the clausal constructions are verbal agreement and tense (§§5.2–5.5), and the exposition of grammatical relations (§5.1).

7.1 Word order and information structure

In section 3.4 I argued that Kunbarlang might be a language of the pronominal argument type. This means that the arguments of the verbal predicate are the bound pronouns on the verb, and all free NPs are but adjuncts. This view has immediate consequences for any discussions of word order. If the bound pronouns on a verb are its true arguments, then given the structure of the verbal template in Kunbarlang (see Table 5.1 on page 162) it has rigid SOV order at its core. However, even if free NPs are syntactic adjuncts coindexed with personal prefixes or licensed by applicatives, it does not mean that their order with respect to each other and the verb is not relevant or interesting. The narrow syntactic 'computation' may be confined to the inflected verb form in Kunbarlang, but the 'encyclopedic information' that occurs in adjunct positions is without a doubt immediately relevant for communicative purposes, and especially so in the view of absence of any verb-internal means of manipulating and accentuating information structure and discourse structure. In this section I discuss the two primary means to that end: word order and intonation patterns. In the ensuing discussion of word order, I talk about subject and object noun phrases, which should be understood as 'the noun phrase coindexed with the subject (or, respectively, object) bound pronoun'.

As has been emphasised throughout this grammar, a defining feature of Kunbarlang is polysynthesis. It has been observed in a variety of other polysynthetic languages that their constituent order is often based on pragmatic factors rather than grammatical relations (Fortescue, Mithun & Evans 2017: 4–5), and this has been tied to the richness of their morphology (ibid.: 2). The freedom of word order in the Australian context has been primarily discussed for the dependent-marking languages (Nordlinger 2014: §3) under the agenda of nonconfigurationality (initiated in Hale's work, such as the seminal 1983 paper). However, head-marking languages have also been described in these terms, including such Gunwinyguan languages as Bininj Kunwok (Evans 2003a: 549ff.) and Wubuy (Heath 1986).

Kunbarlang is similar in this respect, in that it has 'free' word order.[1] This means that the word order in Kunbarlang does not serve to encode grammatical function as it does, for instance, in English or French. Kinslow Harris (1969b: 31–2, 1969a: 78–9) describes Kunbarlang transitive clauses as SVO by default (7.1), with ample room for reordering.

(7.1) Ngadbe wularrud ngada-djarrang kikakinj.
we.EXCL.PL already 1PL.EXCL.NF-eat.PST meat
'Long ago we ate meat.' [Kinslow Harris 1969b: 32; gloss mine—IK]

Kinslow Harris's data are very valuable, since she was collecting data from non-English speakers, as I discuss in §1.4. She does not report any specific proportions within her data, so that is ultimately up to her analysis, but it is very important that her data are free from potential English influence.

Coleman (1982: 51), describes Kunbarlang verbal clauses as having a prevailing tendency for SVO (7.2a), with SOV signalling focus on the object (7.2b).

(7.2) Coleman 1982: 53, 72 (glossing mine—IK)
    a. [Ngayi]$_S$ ku-rleng nga-mabulunj [dred na-kerrkung]$_O$.
       I IV-much 1SG.NF-like.NP dress I-new
      'I very much want a new dress.'

---

[1] Very often in natural discourse in Kunbarlang the clauses consist of a single verb. The discussion in this section is concerned with the subset of the clauses that have overt NP arguments.

b. [Ngayi]ₛ [barbung]ₒ nga-kalng.
   I   fish   1SG.NF-get.PST
   '(It was) fish (that) I got.'

The considerable freedom of ordering of clausal constituents, whereby a tendency for SVO is nevertheless discernible, is essentially what I have found in my field work. Thus, in a simple transitive clause with an overt subject and an overt object there is no fixed predetermined order of the verb, subject and object. The pair of examples (7.3) show two of the possible orders, viz. SVO and OVS. Both examples were elicited with picture prompts (rather than an English prompt or a linguist-constructed Kunbarlang prompt).[2]

(7.3) a. [Ninda   ngarrken]ₛ ka-buddu-karlangwanj   [kaburrk
         DEM.PROX.I   creature   3SG.NF-3PL.OBJ-chase.NP   two
         djarrangalanj]ₒ.
         boy
         'This bird is chasing two boys.'   [IK1-170609_2SM1/01:01:38–45]

    b. [Nukka nayi kirdimarrk]ₒ kanj-bun-beye   [nayi nakarlyung]ₛ.
       he   NM.I man   3SG.FUT-3SG.OBJ-bite.NP NM.I crocodile
       'The crocodile is going to bite the man.'   [ibid./52:46–53]

An example of a verb-initial order VSO from a narrative is given in (7.4):

(7.4) Ka-bun-wardam   [balanda]ₛ   [kirdimarrk]ₒ.
      3SG.NF-3SG.OBJ-ask.PST   whitefella   man
      'Whitefellas [the police] asked him [the aboriginal man].'
                                               [20060831IB10/01:14–15]

In direct elicitation of the word order permutations in a three-word sentence, all six options are judged well-formed (7.5), if the speaker is alerted to the fact that the linguist is attempting different ways to express the same idea (but see §7.1.1 below).

(7.5) Field notes 2015-07-20, PN:

    a. Djarrangalanj ka-maddjing   mankuli.
       boy   3SG.NF-pierce.PST   green.turtle
       'A boy speared a turtle.'   (SVO)

---

[2] The pictures were generously shared with me by Evan Kidd and Rachel Nordlinger, who created them for an experimental study of the word order in Murrinhpatha. See more in §7.1.1.

b. Djarrangalanj mankuli kamaddjing. (SOV)

c. Mankuli djarrangalanj kamaddjing. (OSV)

d. Kamaddjing mankuli djarrangalanj. (VOS)

e. etc...

This does not amount, however, to saying that the word order is completely unconstrained. Rather, Kunbarlang word order is largely driven by the information flow in the discourse, or the information structure (Baker & Mushin 2008). Looking at the basic function of predicating a property of something, one finds a topic–comment structure in Kunbarlang, the topics preceding the comment (7.6).

(7.6) a. [Manyalk]$_{topic}$ [mukka Yirriddja]$_{comment}$. [Narrambareng]$_{topic}$ [nukka
honey_type it.III   Y   honey_type   he

Duwa]$_{comment}$.
D

'The honey in the branches is Yirriddja moiety. The honey in the ground is Duwa moiety.' [20060620IB03/02:56–03:07]

b. Ngayi [kodbarre korro   kaddum]$_{topic}$, barninda, [ka-ngundje
   I   house   DEM.MED.LOC   top   IGNOR   3SG.NF-do.NP

yimarne mulubin]$_{comment}$.
like   blood

'In my picture, the roof of the house is, whatsit, red.' [lit. 'I, house on top, whatsit, does like blood.']   [IK1-170610_2SM1/01:45–02:00]

The topic–comment structure can, and often is, overridden by discourse-pragmatic needs, e.g. prominent information can be placed clause-initially even if it is not topical; see section §7.1.2 below. Example (7.6b) shows additionally that aboutness topics may be preceded by frame-setting topics, in this case the pronoun *ngayi* 'I' serves to set the frame 'in my picture'. Notice also that the phrase that constitutes the comment is a verbal phrase, spelling out what is lexicalised in English as the adjective 'red'.

Besides some regularities that stem from the information structure principles, there are also certain lexical classes with specific ordering preferences. Connectors are normally placed between the constituents that they connect (7.7), question words (§4.5.4) are preferentially placed clause-initially (7.8), the universal quantifier *ngob* (§4.7.3.1) is most often found in immediate post-verbal position (even though it can float around; 7.9).

(7.7) Nga-mankang **la** bedbe-rrema   kadda-nganj-bing   bonj.
     1SG.NF-fall.PST CONJ they-CONTR   3PL.NF-HITH-exit.PST   exactly

'I landed and they arrived too.'   [20060620IB03/11:57–12:03]

(7.8) **Na-kaybi** ki-rnay karra welenj?
I-who 2SG.NF-see.PST DEM.MED.LOC road
'Who did you see in the street?' [IK1-160811_0001/38:02–05]

(7.9) a. Ka-burrun-marnanj-worrmeng **ngob**.
3NSG.NF-3NSG.OBJ-BEN-kindle.PST all
'They made fire for all of that other mob.' [IK1-160510_0001/04:49–51]

b. Korro hall **ngob** djidda-rna.
DEM.MED.LOC ENG all 2PL.FUT-sit.NP
'Go to the hall you all!' [20060614IB/00:25–27; translation mine—IK]

Having established that word order does not serve to encode grammatical functions in Kunbarlang, I show in the next section that there still is a default order, namely, SVO. But before proceeding to the specific topics in Kunbarlang word order, an important caveat must be clarified. Word order is not the only correlate of information structure rendering, the other one of high importance being the intonation. A thorough study of word order and information structure, including instrumental measures and large corpus statistics, as well as controlled experiments, would be a subject for a separate full-scale study. As this is only one topic in the present grammar, I rely primarily on my direct perception of the intonational patterns, such as pitch movement and intonation contours.

7.1.1 Subject–Verb–Object as the default word order

Singer (n.d.) points out that "strong tendencies in word ordering have been found in all recently published analyses of word order in Australian languages... In most cases, these ordering tendencies are not only correlated to discourse-pragmatic factors but to grammatical function as well". Even though, as we have seen, the constituents encoding core grammatical functions may occur in various orders in the Kunbarlang clause, I argue here that SVO is the most neutral order. Recent experimental work on Murrinhpatha has used a picture paradigm to investigate word order in isolation of the context (Nordlinger & Kidd 2018). In Nordlinger & Kidd's (2018) design, a set of pictures controlled for a number of factors (animacy, number, left-to-right linear order of figures in the picture) was presented to Murrinhpatha native speakers to elicit sentence production.[3] The pictures are unrelated and do not form a narrative, thus the sentences produced by the speakers can be assumed to be out-of-the-blue and

---

[3] The authors' original paradigm involves eye-tracking of the speakers gaze alongside with the production, which I do not discuss here.

without contextual information structure biases. Some of the findings in this study are that there is no "basic word order" as such in Murrinhpatha production, but there are certain tendencies. In particular, subjects tend to precede objects, but animate objects tend to precede inanimate subjects. I show below that there are similar tendencies in Kunbarlang. In fact, I argue that there is a stronger tendency for SVO, not just subject before object.

The order SVO in Kunbarlang is (impressionistically) very prevalent in production during elicitation, but this is always open to the interpretation that the English prompts could be responsible for at least a proportion of such sentences. To tap into this issue and gain some preliminary insight into the word orders in out-of-the-blue production unbiased by the prompts, I used the same stimuli, which the authors generously made available to me. I instructed the speakers I worked with to name the participants in the situation described, so most of the responses have at least two overt noun phrases.[4] I report on one of the subsets of pictures that was used in elicitation with four different speakers, yielding 50 responses. Out of those, 14 had to be left out because they contained less than two NPs or other errors. Considering the remaining 36 responses with both subject and object present, SVO sentences comprise approximately 69% (n=25), OVS approximately 28% (n=10), and the only produced SOV sentence amounts to ~3%. All examples with the OVS order include either a lower animate acting on a human (7.3b) or an inanimate agent (7.10).

(7.10)   [Manda   kundulk]$_O$ ka-bum   [nawordewordekken]$_S$.
         DEM.PROX.III   tree   3SG.NF-hit.PST   lightning
         'Lightning strikes this tree.'   [IK1-170609_2SM1/01:01:12–18]

I conclude that there is a preference for SVO in the absence of information structural and other contextual pressures. However, there is also a strong tendency for post-verbal inanimate agents (particularly striking with human objects), which normally overrides the default order. Obviously, this elicitation does not directly address the question of whether during the decades of contact there has been a perceptible influence of the English word order on the Kunbarlang word order tendencies. Two considerations, however, speak against SVO being an artifact of the contact with English. One is that the English patterns cannot explain the strict systematicity of all four speakers' OVS responses to the stimuli with low animacy agents, which therefore indicates genuinely autonomous Kunbarlang ordering in those cases, thus supporting the viability of autonomous ordering principles elsewhere. The other consideration has to do with Kinslow Harris's (1969b) analysis of SVO as the basic pattern, which is based on her recordings of non-English speakers, as I have discussed above.

---

4 A few sentences contain more, because they include, for instance, a description of an instrument. I did not analyse the nominals beyond the S and O ones.

Let us now consider the opposite aspect, viz. the interpretation of sentences. I find that even though an object-first order is possible (such as OVS in (7.3b) or (7.10)), it is usually rejected out-of-the-blue. I conclude that from the comprehension point of view, the preferred interpretation of sentences with the sequence NP–V–NP is SVO (cf. a similar remark about the flexibility of the Russian word order by Comrie (1989: 88)). Thus, a fronted object order is marked and requires certain licensing (such as contextual prominence or inherent prominence due to the patient being higher on the animacy hierarchy than the agent, as in (7.3b)). Consider example (7.11), modified from previously elicited examples to the OVS order and presented to a speaker. Even despite the possibility of such word order in principle, the speaker judged the example as semantically odd, interpreting it as SVO by default.

(7.11) #Mayi   murrkidj ka-bun-rladbum   ngalwundji.
       NM.III   potato   3SG.NF-3SG.OBJ-overcook.PST   girl
       '#The potato overcooked the girl.'   [IK1-160712_0001/15:48–16:04]

In this section I have described SVO as the default, or neutral, word order in Kunbarlang. In natural connected discourse, however, pragmatic and contextual factors often yield mutations of that order. In Kunbarlang, similar to a number of Australian languages, there are dedicated constructions that express various discourse functions. In section §7.1.2 I discuss the most prominent one: the clause-initial position.

7.1.2 The initial position

The clause-initial position has been noted in Australianist literature as pragmatically distinguished. Simpson & Mushin (2008), surveying a number of word order studies in individual Australian languages, conclude that

> there is consensus that whatever core constituent occurs *clause-initially* has some pragmatic importance or prominence. This importance is usually to signal that the information in question is brought to the forefront of the hearer's attention, perhaps by emphasis or contrast, because it's either non-recoverable (i.e., new) or it runs counter to expectations (i.e., it changes the interlocutor's knowledge state) and is thus prominent. (Simpson & Mushin 2008: 27)

I find that in Kunbarlang the clause-initial position is also prominent. There is no unique discourse-pragmatic function associated with it; however, two functions are particularly noticeable, viz. new information focus and contrast. The first one is exemplified by the set of question-answer pairs (7.12–7.15). Notice that the focused constituent in the answer always occurs clause-initially. The prominent constituent, placed in that position, bears higher pitch accent with a falling contour.

(7.12) Q: Na-kaybi nayi kirdimarrk ki-rlemang?
            I-who   NM.I man   2SG.NF-punch.PST
            'Which man did you punch?'   [IK1-160829_0001/53:03–06]

   A1: **Nawamud**, or   **Nabangardi** nga-rlemang.
         N   ENG N   1SG.NF-punch.PST
         'I punched Nawamud or Nabangardi.'   [ibid./53:08–12]

   A2: **Ninda**   kirdimarrk nga-rlemang.
         DEM.PROX.I   man   1SG.NF-punch.PST
         'I punched this man [pointing].'   [ibid./54:14–17]

   A3: **Ninda**   nga-rlemang.
         DEM.PROX.I   1SG.NF-punch.PST
         'I punched him [pointing].'   [ibid./54:25–27]

(7.13) Q: Ki-bum   kundulk or   barda ki-rlemang?
            2SG.NF-hit.PST stick   ENG what   2SG.NF-punch.PST
            'Did you hit him/her/it with a stick or with what?'
                                                          [IK1-160829_0001/51:44–46]

   A: **Kunbid** nga-rlemang.
         hand   1SG.NF-punch.PST
         'I punched him/her/it with my hand.'   [ibid./51:47–48]

(7.14) Q: Karrakenda nayi kirdimarrk ki-rlemang?
            where   NM.I man   2SG.NF-punch.PST
            'Where did (it happen that) you punch the man?'
                                                          [IK1-160829_0001/50:37–40]

   A: **Karra**   **kodbarre** nga-rlemang.
         DEM.MED.LOC   house   1SG.NF-punch.PST
         'I punched him at home.'   [ibid./50:53–56]

(7.15) Q: Na-kaybi ka-ngan-marnanj-kalng   nayi nga-djanga-rda-yi?
            I-who   3SG.NF-1SG.OBJ-BEN-get.PST   NM.I 1SG.NF-foot-enter-REFL.NP
            'Who took my shoes?'   [IK1-160811_0001/46:21–36]

   A: **Nukka** ka-kalng   bi-nungku   **nayi ka-nganj-kankinj**
         he   3SG.NF-get.PST   DAT-you.SG.GEN   NM.I   3SG.NF-HITH-take.PST
         neyang.
         food
         'He who brought us food took them on you (to your detriment).'
                                                          [ibid./46:56–47:20]

These examples illustrate constituent questions to various grammatical functions: the primary object (7.12), the instrument (7.13), the locative adjunct (7.14) and the subject (7.15). Regardless of the grammatical function, however, the focus of the answer preferentially occurs in the clause-initial position in Kunbarlang. This placement is only preferential, but not obligatory. Thus, as an alternative to the OV order answers in (7.12) the order VO (7.16) is also possible in response to (7.12Q):

(7.16) Nga-rlemang   **Nabangardi.**
        1SG.NF-punch.PST N
        'I punched Nabangardi.'   [IK1-160829_0001/53:53–55]

The subject question-answer pair in (7.15) shows a further interesting variation of the construction. The subject there is a relative clause headed by the pronoun *nukka* 'he'. This head appears in the clause-initial prominent position, whereas the modifier clause is shifted to the end of the clause, presumably due to its heaviness.[5]

Example (7.17) shows that an embedded object can front and appear in the clause-initial position, if there is appropriate context. The resulting order is O–V_{matr}–V_{emb} with the matrix verb separating the embedded verb from its fronted object. In the absence of supporting context, however, the sentence-initial word is construed as the subject of the matrix verb, which in this case yields an infelicitous reading 'the barramundi told me that *p*' (7.17a). I consider this subject construal out-of-context, even in the face of pragmatic implausibility, to be further evidence for SVO preference in Kunbarlang.

(7.17) IK1-160512_0001/47:00–49:46:

   a. %**Bilmu**   ka-ngan-marnanj-ngunda   ka-kalng.
      barramundi 3SG.NF-1SG.OBJ-BEN-do.PST   3SG.NF-get.PST
      'S/he told me that s/he caught barramundi.'
      Infelicitous unless in the right context, such as the question in (b).
      Speaker's comment: "It's just like saying, bilmu told you."

   b. Barda nayi barbung ka-kalng?
      what NM.I fish   3SG.NF-get.PST
      'What sort of fish did s/he catch?'

---

[5] Relative clauses in subject position are usually embedded (i). See §8.4 on relativisation in Kunbarlang.

(i) Na-kaybi-nuk   [$_{RC}$nayi ka-mangarninjdjanganj]   ka-ngan-rluklung,   la
    I-who-INDF   NM.I   3SG.NF-sing.PST   3SG.NF-1SG.OBJ-wake.PST   CONJ
    nga-wakwanj.
    1SG.NF-ignorant.NP
    'Someone who was singing woke me up, but I don't know [who that was].'
                                                          [IK1-160822_0001/11:30–39]

All of the above examples show the attraction of the new information focus to the clause-initial position, diagnosed by the question-answer pairs. The other significant function that appears in the clause-initial position is contrast. On the one hand, I find that the contrastive/emphatic pronouns with the suffix -*ma* (§4.5.1.2) overwhelmingly occur in the clause-initial position (7.18).

(7.18) Kadda-kidanj, **nganj-ma** ngondo   bonj   nga-rnak-rninganj.
       3PL.NF-go.PST I-CONTR   DEM.PROX.IV exactly 1SG.NF-LIM-sit.PST
       'They went, and I just stayed in this country.'   [20060620IB03/33:53–58]

Out of 35 examples with -*ma*-marked pronouns drawn at random,[6] 26 have them in the initial position (approximately 75%). Three examples in the sample involve the reciprocal construction "V la *pro*-ma" 'V each other' (§6.1.3), which really is a different function of these forms. With the exclusion of these three, the proportion of the clause-initial ones is even higher, namely 82% (26/32). For comparison, out of 35 examples of various personal pronouns not marked for any communicative function, only 19 occur clause-initially (54%).

Further examples of constituents bearing contrast being placed in the initial position come from non-pronominal contrastive constituents that receive the contrast prominence through syntagmatic oppositions. Consider (7.19), which contraposes women with men in regards to the treatment they receive from the mythical giant *mankurdel*. In the first clause, the noun *barramimbanj* 'woman' is topical, placed in the clause-initial position; it is paired with the contrastive focus *kirdimarrk* 'man', placed in the initial position of the second clause.[7]

(7.19) [**Barramimbanj**]$_{CT}$ || karlu   ngunda
       woman   NEG.PRED not

    ki-buddu-bakbelbu   ngayi barramimbanj ||
    3SG.IRR.NP-3PL.OBJ-throw_down.IRR.NP NM.PL woman

    only [**kirdimarrk**]$_{CF}$ ka-buddu-bakbelbunj.
    ENG   man   3SG.NF-3PL.OBJ-throw_down.NP

'As for women, he doesn't throw the women down, it's only the men that he throws down.'   [20060901IB08/00:29–00:35]

---

[6] This is roughly half of all instances of such pronouns in the corpus. I have analysed the first half of the output of ELAN search function, which yielded a mixture of speakers and recording occasions. I have omitted examples from elicitation, and thus only spontaneous narrative/dialogue is included.

[7] My analysis of *kirdimarrk* 'man' as focal is based on its association with the exhaustive particle 'only'. Furthermore, I assume here that CONTRAST is an information-structural feature in its own right, which allows for pairing contrastive elements without necessarily matching their TOPICality or FOCality.

Contrastive focus constituents are also placed in the clause-initial position. In (7.20A) the object that is under contrastive focus is placed in the beginning of the clause, just after the conjunction *la*.[8]

(7.20) IK1-160628_0001/16:19–48

    Q: Yidok ka-burrun-beyang nayi durduk?
        Q   3SG.NF-3DU.OBJ-bite.PST NM.I dog
        'Did that dog bite both the man and the woman?'

    A: Karlu, la [barramimbanj]$_{CF}$ ka-bun-rnak-beyang.
        NEG.PRED CONJ woman   3SG.NF-3SG.OBJ-LIM-bite.PST
        'No, it only bit the woman.'

These two discourse-pragmatic functions, contrast (which can be topic or focus) and new information focus, cover the vast majority of noun phrases (other than the subject) in the clause-initial position. They certainly do not account for every single example that one can encounter, but as was mentioned earlier, such a level of detail is unfeasible within the scope of the present grammar. I observe that the functions discussed here are consistent with the broader picture reported in Simpson & Mushin 2008 and elsewhere (e.g. Singer n.d.), both in terms of the heterogeneity of this position and in terms of the particular types of prominent information. I assume for now that (i) the other functions that may be connected to the Kunbarlang initial position are also expressing prominence and (ii) that the subjects and aboutness topics do not have to be prominent to occur in that position (in virtue of SVO and the topic–comment structure being the defaults; see §7.1.1). Effectively, prominence of a constituent allows it to occur in the initial position, potentially overriding the default placement. The opposite, far right end of the clause, which hosts the so-called "afterthoughts", is discussed in the next section.

7.1.3 Afterthoughts

Afterthought, or the right-dislocated, position is another pragmatically significant position recognised in a variety of Australian languages. Baker & Mushin define it as the "position, where a (typically phrasal) constituent is informationally connected to a preceding utterance (e.g., it refers to a discourse entity which was also referred to

---

[8] With respect to connectors I take a different approach to Simpson & Mushin (2008). They count the connectors as one of classes of items that fill the clause-initial position, but I regard them as external to clause.

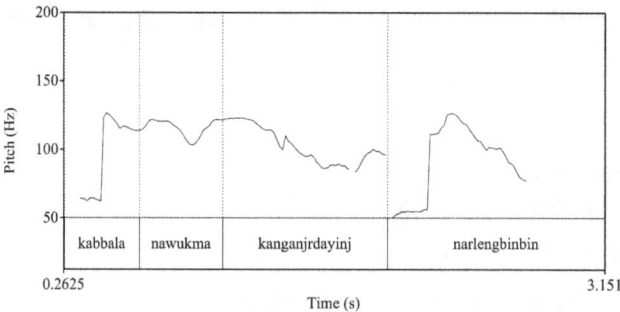

Fig. 7.1: Pitch contour of an afterthought

in the previous utterance), but is offset prosodically from that preceding utterance" (2008: 10). Kunbarlang uses the right-dislocated position in this function, too (7.21).[9]

(7.21) Ngadda-nganj-mayinj, kabbala na-wuk-ma
1PL.EXCL.NF-HITH-cross.PST boat[I] I-person-CONTR

ka-nganj-rda-yinj, **na-rlengbinbin**.
3SG.NF-HITH-put-REFL.PST I-big

'We came across and there was a boat coming in, a big one.'

[IK1-160510_0001/02:27–33]

The pitch contour for (7.21) is shown in figure 7.1 (without the first verb). Even though there is no prolonged pause before the afterthought, the pitch reset is clearly visible.

Being a clarificatory device or hosting appositional modifiers, the afterthoughts in Kunbarlang are a prime source of discontinuous but coreferential nominal material. While looking—from the point of view of word order—like classic discontinuous NPs, such right-dislocated nominals are considered by some researchers to constitute a separate phenomenon from discontinuity proper (e.g. Schultze-Berndt & Simard 2012). I analyse such appositional modifiers in the right periphery as separate, but coreferential, noun phrases. Singer (2006: 99–100) pursues the same analysis for Mawng discontinuous nominals (7.22). The word order in the Kunbarlang NP is taken up further in §7.1.4, and NP constituency is discussed in §4.4.

---

9 Notice an interesting instance of the pronoun *nawukma* 'he.CONTR' determining the noun *kabbala* 'boat' (class I).

(7.22) Mawng (Singer 2006: 99)
Yungku   marrik manga-niki-ng   **mata ma-lakpi.**
firewood[VEG] NEG   3.NMA>3VEG-carry-IRR VEG VEG-heavy
'She shouldn't carry heavy firewood.'

The afterthoughts in Kunbarlang may, but do not necessarily have to, co-refer with some nominal material from the main/preceding part of the utterance. They just broadly refer to some discourse entity, and thus can also elaborate on other kinds of referents, such as those represented in the pronominal prefixes on verbs; cf. (7.23), where the only nominal material referring to the subject of the throwing is right-dislocated to the afterthought position.

(7.23) Like yimarne ka-yuwa=rdurdu   yimarne balmad bonj   kuyi
       ENG like   3SG.NF-lie.NP=thunder like   rain   exactly NM.IV
       ka-buddu-bakbelbunj   ngayi kirdimarrk ‖ **nayi mankurdel.**
       3SG.NF-3PL.OBJ-throw_down.NP NM.PL man   NM.I giant
'It's like when the thunder roars, when it's wet season, that's how [it sounds like when] he throws the people down; the giant.' [20060901IB08/00:18–25]

7.1.4 Word order in the noun phrase

Flexible word order and the possibility of linear discontinuity of noun phrases have been suggested as two of the hallmarks of nonconfigurationality and a number of Australian languages have been argued, due to these features, to lack NPs altogether (e.g. Kalkatungu (Blake 1983: 145), Wubuy (Heath 1986: 377–81) or Bininj Kunwok (Evans 2003a: 229–31); see also an overview and references in Nordlinger 2014: §6). Some more recent work on other Australian languages has argued for the existence of noun phrases and discussed their organisational principles. The results of both individual languages studies and typological investigations (see, respectively, Schultze-Berndt & Simard 2012 for Jaminjung and Louagie & Verstraete 2016 for a sample of a 100 Australian languages) point towards the conclusion that the characterisation of Australian languages as generally lacking NP structures may be premature and unwarranted. A closer inquiry into the conditions on NP discontinuity suggests that what at a first glance may look like one disrupted NP, could often more fruitfully be analysed rather as two co-referential constituents. In particular, the by now familiar discourse-pragmatic factors (such as focusing or topicalising a certain fragment of information) can favour encoding of referring expressions via such independent but co-referential constituents over a single longer unit (see e.g. Schultze-Berndt & Simard 2012).

I find that the order of the elements in the Kunbarlang noun phrase is relatively restricted. This has been expressed in §4.4.1 in terms of a descriptive noun phrase template, which is repeated in (7.27) below. The bulk of the modifiers precede the head noun. Similar to the order of the verb's arguments, discussed above, in elicitation a variety of orders of an adjective, a noun marker and the head noun are available (7.24, repeated from (3.47)). One categorical restriction is that the noun markers are not allowed in the NP-final position (7.24e–f).

(7.24) a. Belebbele **nayi** nadjorleng   NOUN-NM-ADJ
crab_apple NM.I I-ripe

ka-mankang   korro   lorre.
3SG.NF-fall.PST DEM.MED.LOC ground

'A ripe crab apple fell to the ground.'   [IK1-150728_001/06:00–02]

b. na-djorleng **nayi** belebbele   ADJ-NM-NOUN
I-ripe   NM.I crab_apple

'the ripe crab apple'   [IK1-150728_001]

c. **kuyi** hospital ku-buke   NM-NOUN-ADJ
NM.IV hospital IV-old

'the old hospital'   [20060620IB03/25:02–04]

d. **nayi** na-rlengbinbin nguya   bi-ngadju   NM-ADJ-NOUN
NM.I I-big   patriclan DAT-she.GEN

'her big patriclan'   [20150413IOv01/07:50]

e. *na-djorleng belebbele   **nayi**   ADJ-NOUN-NM
I-ripe   crab_apple NM.I

intended: 'a ripe crab apple'   [IK1-150728_001]

f. *belebbele   na-djorleng **nayi**   NOUN-ADJ-NM
crab_apple I-ripe   NM.I

intended: 'a ripe crab apple'   [IK1-150728_001]

However, outside of elicitation of the permutations, i.e. in cohesive context, there are several noticeable regularities concerning the word order in the Kunbarlang noun phrase. They include the following ones:
1. noun markers are prohibited NP-finally (see (7.24) above)
2. relative clauses are normally postnominal (example (7.25) and §8.4 on RCs)
3. in the possessive constructions, the *bi*-marked possessors follow and the agreeing ones precede the head noun (7.26)
4. interpretive effects of the noun marker position, described in detail in §4.3

(7.25) barrayidjidj [$_{RC}$ngayi kanjbadda-nganj-ka malayi]
kids　　　　 NM.PL　 3PL.FUT-HITH-go.NP　 tomorrow
'the kids that will come tomorrow'　　　　 [IK1-160505_0011/33:53–34:00]

The head noun *barrayidjidj* 'kids' in (7.25) is the head of the relative clause, which follows it immediately. In the two examples in (7.26) the same speaker uses two different possessive contructions to talk about his language, and accordingly uses the different word order: the *bi*-marked possessor occurs after the head noun *lerrk* 'word' (7.26a) and the agreeing possessor precedes the head noun (7.26b).

(7.26) a. **lerrk**　　**bi-ngaybu** kuyi　 ngayi, Kunbarlang
　　　　 word[IV]　 DAT-I.GEN　 NM.IV　 I　　　 K
　　　　 'my language, Kunbarlang'　　　　　　　　　 [RS1-140/00:47–50]

　　　 b. Kunkurduwala kuyi　 **kun-ngaybu lerrk**
　　　　 K　　　　　　　　 NM.IV　 IV-I.GEN　　 word[IV]
　　　　 'Kun-kurduwala, my language.'　　　　　 [20070108IB01/02:32–35]

Again, the ordering in the possessive constructions is not categorical, but the *bi*-possessors follow the head noun in 84% of examples and the agreeing ones precede the head in 87% of examples, revealing a very strong tendency.

Kunbarlang noun phrases are very short in natural discourse, rarely having one or two modifiers. However, in §4.4 I argued that when attributive modifiers are present, their order is not at all random, but rather is governed by an information structure-sensitive syntactic system. I only repeat the most general points here, referring the reader to that section for more details. At the surface level of description, modifiers follow the maximal NP template in (7.27), with a few reasonably systematic exceptions.

(7.27) pronoun — demonstrative — quantifier — NM — GEN-possessor — HEAD NOUN
　　　 — adjective — DAT-possessor — RC

The exceptions, however, are systematic enough to motivate a different analysis than the surface template above. One of them has to do with adjective placement in front of the noun, which is associated with an emphatic interpretation, which I identify as focus on the preposed adjective. The other is the observation that increasing the number of modifiers leads to the situation whereby they have to be introduced by additional linker noun markers. These considerations are reflected in a configurational hierarchical account of the NP, presented in section 4.4.3. Rather than repeat that here, I shall restate the surface ordering facts in a way both more general and more satisfactory than (7.27).

The leftmost part of the NP is for determining pronouns and demonstratives. Then there can be quantifiers or focused adjectives. A noun marker indicating definiteness

(§4.3.1) comes close to the head noun; a genitive possessor may intervene. The noun is obligatory, although it may be phonologically null. It is followed by one or more of the dative possessor, adjective phrases, and relative clauses. This description is schematised in (7.28), somewhat reminiscent of McGregor's (1990: 253) functional NP template for Gooniyandi in that it sometimes makes reference to the element's function, rather than formal category.

(7.28) (Det) — (Quant) — (FocAdjP) — (NM) — (Gen-PR) — N — (Dat-PR) · (AdjP) · (RC)

As argued in §4.4.3, however, a hierarchical account of the NP structure is superior, since it captures the combinatorial behaviour of the noun markers and opens a possibility for a principled account of the placement of adjectives with respect to the noun. See also Kapitonov (submitted) for a more detailed discussion of these aspects of syntax and semantics of adjectives and noun markers.

7.2 Aspectual constructions

As discussed above (e.g. §5.3), the verbal morphology only specifies the tense and mood of the clause, but not the aspect. There are, however, other expressive means that convey (some) viewpoint aspect information: the imperfective auxiliary construction (IAC; §7.2.1) and the stylistic lengthening §7.2.2.

7.2.1 The imperfective auxiliary construction

Viewpoint aspect is not a morphological category in Kunbarlang, but there is a construction which expresses imperfective aspect. This construction involves the verbs *-dja* 'to stand', *-rna* 'to sit', *-yuwa* 'to lie', and *-warre* 'to move' in auxiliary-like functions. They are fully inflected and combined with the semantically main verb (or nominal predicate—see (7.31c)), which also is fully inflected.[10] The two verbs have identical subjects (and thus, subject prefixes) and identical tense/mood specification. The auxiliary verb comes before the main verb.

---

[10] Similar constructions, albeit with a diverse range of functions, have been described in a number of Australian languages, including Garrwa, Kalkatungu, Ngan'gityemerri, Waanyi, Wambaya, and Yukulta, and treated as a type of serial verb construction (see Laughren 2016 and references therein.)

(7.29) Ngadda-djanganj   ngadda-rnay   la   ka-warrenj
        1PL.EXCL.NF-stand.PST 1PL.EXCL.NF-see.PST CONJ 3SG.NF-move.PST

   ka-yidjung.
   3SG.NF-sink.PST

   'We were standing there watching the boat sink.'   [20060620IB03/10:30–33]

Mismatch of the tense features of the auxiliary and the main verb is prohibited, e.g. (7.30) shows that present tense auxiliary is ruled out with a past tense main verb (even though present tense is fine in this construction, as (7.33b) shows).

(7.30) Na-kaybi ngondo   {**ka-rninganj** | *ka-rna}   ka-nganj-**kanginj**
        I-who   DEM.PROX.IV 3SG.NF-sit.PST   3SG.NF-sit.NP 3SG.NF-HITH-take.PST

   kuyi   kuwalak?
   NM.IV   rock

   'Who was bringing all these rocks here?'
                                        [IK1-170602_1SY2/36:34–40, 37:50–53]

The meaning of this construction is, essentially, the IMPERFECTIVE. It is used to specify the viewpoint aspect as unbounded, i.e. that the reference time is included as a subset into the event time. More specifically, it can realise a number of aspectual meanings, such as PROGRESSIVE (7.31a), HABITUAL (7.31b),[11] or STATIVE (7.31c). Similar constructions, with varying syntax and auxiliary sets, are found in other languages of the region, for instance: Nakkara (Eather 2011: 403–10), Gurr-goni (Green 1995: §5.3), Ndjébbana (McKay 2000: 286–7), Bininj Kunwok (esp. Kuninjku and Kune; Evans 2003a: 371, 659–61, Mawng (Singer 2006: 130–2)).

(7.31) a. Ngadda-maddjing   ngadda-karlangwa::ng   **ka-rninganj**
            1PL.EXCL.NF-pierce.PST 1PL.EXCL.NF-follow.PST 3SG.NF-sit.PST

       ka-burrdji-yinj   la   ngadda-mun-bing-bi
       3SG.NF-wrap-REFL.PST   CONJ 1PL.EXCL.NF-THITH-exit.PST-THITH

       ngadda-maddjing || ngadda-burrdjing.
       1PL.EXCL.NF-pierce.PST   1PL.EXCL.NF-wrap.PST

       'We speared it, then we chased it. It **was getting wrapped around** [with a rope], and we got close to that crocodile and we speared it. We wrapped [the rope] around the crocodile.'   [20060620IB04/09:08–17]

---

11 It is not clear what the masculine pronoun *nukka* in this example refers to.

b. Nukka **ngadda-warrenj** **ngadda-kalng** kiyurlu la
he 1PL.EXCL.NF-move.PST 1PL.EXCL.NF-get.PST egg CONJ
na-walak~walak.
I-RDP~small

'That's where we used to get those seagull eggs and the baby ones too.'
[20060620IB04/07:37–43; translation mine—IK]

c. And balkkime ngorro **ngarrk-dja** **ngarrak-djarrak**, and
and now DEM.MED.IV 1.INCL.NF-stand.NP 1.INCL-healthy and
balkkime kenda ngarrk-dja.
now DEM.PROX.LOC 1.INCL.NF-stand.NP

'And today those of us still alive, and today we are here.'
[IK1-160424_0001/01:55–02:00]

The respective postures (or motion) conveyed by the auxiliary appear to be implied and cancellable. That is, while the subject of the action may be construed as being in a particular posture (7.32), or wandering (7.31b) during the event, often that original meaning is incompatible with the type of the event. That is a sign that the original posture/motion meaning may sometimes be bleached and the aspectual contribution of the auxiliary is central in this construction. In particular, the incompatibility is evident in cases where a posture verb accompanies a motion predicate, as in the examples in (7.33).

(7.32) **Kadda-djanganj kadda-kelkkuyinj** la Georgina **ka-djanganj**
3PL.NF-stand.PST 3PL.NF-work.PST CONJ G 3SG.NF-stand.PST
ka-burrun-**rnay**.
3SG.NF-3DU.OBJ-see.PST

'They were digging and Georgina was watching them.'
[20060814IB01/00:39–42; translation mine—IK]

(7.33) a. **Kadda-rninganj kadda**-nganj-**kidanj**.
3PL.NF-sit.PST 3PL.NF-HITH-go.PST

'Everyone was coming [separately, rather than arrived together].'
[IK1-160429_0001/07:33–35]

b. Kukkangundje **kadda-rna kadda-wonj** karra yalbi.
maybe 3PL.NF-sit.NP 3PL.NF-return.NP DEM.MED.LOC country

'Maybe they're going back home.' [IK1-170615_1SY2/06:52–55]

The interaction of this construction with the Aktionsart has not been studied systematically, for the want of a good understanding of Kunbarlang Aktionsart. However, all examples in the corpus are compatible with the hypothesis that the imperfective auxiliary construction requires the eventuality of the verb phrase to be DURATIVE (which corroborates the analysis advanced here of this construction as imperfective). Thus, one finds examples where it is plausible to think that the underlying eventuality is a state (7.31c), an activity (7.32) or an accomplishment (7.31a), but there are no compelling examples of achievements. Although there are no "starred" examples, there is one suggestive case from an elicitation (7.34). When asked about the possibility of using *nga-warrenj nga-rnay* [1SG.NF-move.PST 1SG.NF-see.PST] in the context which forced the achievement reading of the main verb ('find' rather than 'see, watch'), the speaker repeated that with an extra conjunction *la* in between, which indicates that these belong to separate clauses.

(7.34) Nga-warrenj nga-yawang la babi la **nga-warrenj** la
1SG.NF-move.PST 1SG.NF-seek.PST CONJ later CONJ 1SG.NF-move.PST CONJ
nga-rnay.
1SG.NF-see.PST
'I was looking for it and then (**I was browsing and**) **I found it**.'
[IK1-170610_1SY2/54:02–10]

This is consistent with the above interpretation of this construction as specifying unbounded aspect. This view further predicts that if an achievement verb was to be used in an imperfective auxiliary construction, the resulting reading would have to be iterative or habitual (see de Swart 1998 on aspectual coercion). This prediction seems to be borne out: example (7.31b) is understood as a habitual, and (7.35) as iterative.

(7.35) **Ka-warrenj** **ka-rlakwang** mayi mamukunbid, ngunda barbung
3SG.NF-move.PST 3SG.NF-throw.PST III fishing_rod not fish
ki-kala, karlu.
3SG.IRR.PST-get.IRR.PST NEG.PRED
'S/he was casting the fishing rod, but did not catch any fish.'
[IK1-160722_0001/06:09–44]

In terms of intonation, the two verbs are included within a single contour and pronounced without pauses. The pitch contour for (7.36) is shown in figure 7.2.[12]

(7.36) And nga-nganj-kanginj kenda-wu **nga-djanganj**
and 1SG.NF-HITH-take.PST DEM.PROX.LOC-ELA 1SG.NF-stand.PST
nga-bum=ngurr karra yalbi.
1SG.NF-hit.PST=rippled DEM.MED.LOC country
'I took them here and washed them at home.'
[20060814IB03/01:00–02; translation mine—IK]

---

[12] The main verb in (7.36), *nga-bum=ngurr* 'I washed', is itself a complex one, more specifically, a coverb construction (§6.5).

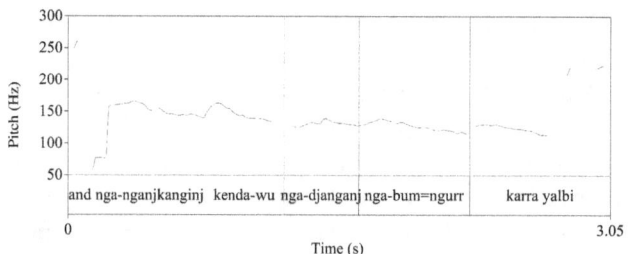

Fig. 7.2: Pitch contour of the IAC [20060814IB03/01:00]

Ross (2011: 257–79) shows that in Dalabon (and Kayardild) there are multi-verb intonational phrases which include under a single contour verbs describing tightly connected events. In the next subsection I turn to a prosodic means of expressing prolonged duration of an event.

7.2.2 Stylistic lengthening

Kunbarlang speakers employ another prosodic device to indicate extended duration of an event, namely stylistic lengthening. In this case, the vowel of the final syllable of the verb is pronounced with an emphatically long duration (7.31a), (7.37).

(7.37) Ngadda-burl-**karrme::** ngob ngorro ngadda-marnbunj yimarne
1PL.EXCL.NF-fist-hold.NP all DEM.MED.IV 1PL.EXCL.NF-make.NP like
ka-ngundje kurrana.
3SG.NF-do moon
'We knead it all for a while, then we make it into a round shape.'
[IK1-160726_0021/00:34–41]

The extent of the lengthening is illustrated in the following pair of waveform diagrams, taken from a recording of one male speaker. The words pictured are a near-minimal pair: they involve the verb *-djin* 'to eat/consume' (7.38), referring to a human's consumption of a liquid in one instance and to a fire burning in the other.

(7.38) a. Ka-bardi-**djarrang**.
3SG.NF-liquid-eat.PST
'He drank it.' [20060606IB02/09:49]

b. Ka-bun-**djarra::ng**.
3SG.NF-3SG.OBJ-eat.PST
'It was cooking.' [ibid./01:06]

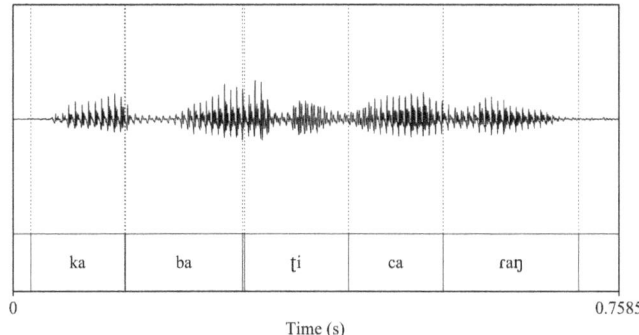

Fig. 7.3: Waveform of *ka-bardi-djarrang* [20060606IB02/09:49]

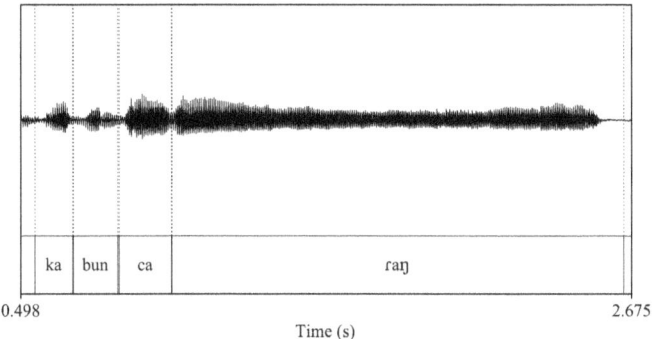

Fig. 7.4: Waveform of *ka-bun-djarrang* with stylistic lengthening [20060606IB02/01:06]

Figure 7.3 shows a token of *ka-bardi-djarrang* 's/he drank', spoken in a regular way. The final syllable [raŋ] here is 0.17s in length (duration of the whole word is 0.69s). In contrast, figure 7.4 shows a token of *ka-bun-djarra::ng* 'it was burning/cooking' with the lengthening. Duration of the whole word is 2.1 seconds, including the final syllable [ra::ŋ] of 1.6s.

This kind of vowel lengthening is one of the characteristic intonational patterns in Australian languages (see, e.g. Fletcher & Butcher (2014: 124) and references therein; phonological structure of such lengthening in Bininj Kunwok is analysed by Bishop (2002: §2.3.6)).

In Kunbarlang this formal means of signalling temporal extent of an event can, and often is, combined with the imperfective auxiliary construction, described above. Examples of this can be found in (7.31a) and (7.39).

(7.39) Ka-warrenj   ka-yunga::nj.
       3SG.NF-move.PST   3SG.NF-lie.PST
       'It [the crocodile] was lying down.'   [20060620IB04/08:55–09:00]

7.3 Negation

Negation is formed using one of the two negative particles, *ngunda* (7.40a–b) or *merrek* (7.40c), which immediately precede the verb (7.40) or the nominal predicate (see examples below).

(7.40) a. And malayi   **ngunda** kirri-nganj-wo   kenda?
           ENG tomorrow   not   2SG.IRR.NP-HITH-return.IRR.NP   DEM.PROX.LOC
           'And tomorrow you are not coming back here?'
                                                          [IK1-160828_0011/00:26–29]

       b. Ngayi **ngunda** ngay-kala   munun,   la   nga-kalng
           I   not   1SG.IRR.PST-get.IRR.PST   dugong   CONJ 1SG.NF-get.PST
           barbung.
           fish
           'I didn't catch dugong, but I caught some fish.'
                                                          [IK1-160626_0001/42:21–43:11]

       c. Kaburrk kirdimarrk **marrek** ki-bun-rnani   la
           two   man   not   3SG.IRR.PST-3SG.OBJ-see.IRR.PST   CONJ
           na-wuk-ma.
           I-person-CONTR
           'The two men did not see each other.'   [IK1-160523_0011/12:41–54]

The verb form is sensitive to the polarity of the clause: it is obligatorily irrealis under negation, marked in the subject prefix and in the verbal stem form. This can be clearly seen in (7.40b), where the first of the two conjoined clauses is negative polarity and the verb is marked for irrealis past (*ngay-kala*), but the second clause is positive and the verb is marked for realis past (*nga-kalng*). For more on the verb tense/mood morphology see §5.4 and for the semantics of these forms, §5.5. The unusual reciprocal construction in (7.40c) is described in detail in §6.1.3.2.

Of the two particles, *marrek* is shared with Bininj Kunwok and Mawng; I am not aware of any counterparts of *ngunda* in other languages. The latter is also more frequently used, and perhaps there is an air of it being 'more properly' Kunbarlang. There is however no semantic difference between the two, and speakers will often alternate between them and/or allow substitution (7.41).

(7.41) Ngal-buk **ngunda** ki-djarri   barbung.
        II-person not   3SG.IRR.NP-eat.IRR.NP fish

   Marrek ki-mabulu.
   not   3SG.IRR.NP-like.IRR.NP

   'She doesn't eat fish. She doesn't like it.'   [IK1-160722_0011/02:05–23]

In terms of the verb's paradigm, the tense categories are reduced under negation (although this is the property of the irrealis mood and not peculiar to negation alone; §5.4). While there are three tense forms in the realis (past, present and future), only past and non-past are distinguished in the irrealis.[13]

These negative particles always scope over the interrogatives, yielding the 'negative indefinite pronoun' effect, i.e. the narrow scope existential reading ((7.42); see §4.5.4 for more).

(7.42) a. **Ngunda na-kaybi** ki-buddu-rnani.
          not   I-who   3SG.IRR.PST-3PL.OBJ-see.IRR.PST

   'S/he didn't see anyone.'   [IK1-160628_0001/09:29–31]

   b. **Marrek barda** ngemek ki-woh-yung   korro
      not   what   yet   3SG.IRR.NP-INCP-lie.IRR.NP DEM.MED.LOC

      welenj.
      road

      'There is nothing else lying around on the road.'
                                                   [IK1-170610_2SM1/11:07–11]

In such constructions the negative particle and the interrogative together have to precede the verb (7.43):

(7.43) a. Merrek karrakenda ngarra-kidang.
          not   where   1SG.IRR.NP-go.IRR.NP

   'I can't go anywhere.'   [IK1-180525_1DDj1/29:20]

   b. *Ngarra-kidang   merrek karrakenda.
       1SG.IRR.NP-go.IRR.PST   not   where

      intended: 'I can't go anywhere.'   [ibid./29:40–46]

Nominal predicates are similar to the verbal ones in that either *merrek* or *ngunda* may be used (7.44):

---

[13] This is consistent with the observation that the future tense contrast is susceptible to neutralisation in negative contexts, as opposed to the past (Ultan 1978: 95).

(7.44) a. Ninda **merrek marrkidjbu**.
DEM.PROX.I not witch_doctor
'He's not a witch doctor.' [IK1-160829_0001/01:14:37]

b. Nukka **ngunda durduk**, nukka kornobolo.
he.I not dog he.I wallaby
'It's not a dog, it's a wallaby.' [IK1-160630_0001/01:00–02]

In addition to that, however, the predicative negation marker *karlu* can be used with nominals, both in constituent negation (7.45) and with nominal predicates (7.46). See §4.4 for more details.

(7.45) a. **Karlu nayi wombat** kenda Mardbalk.
no NM.I wombat DEM.PROX.LOC S.Goulburn
'There are no wombats here on South Goulburn Is.'
[IK1-160802_0001/27:48–55]

b. Manda mayi kundulk ka-karrme ma-rleng mayi burru,
DEM.PROX.III NM.III tree 3SG.NF-hold.NP III-much NM.III arm
la **karlu mayi maworord**.
CONJ NEG.PRED NM.III leaf
'This tree has many branches, but it has no leaves.'
[IK1-170522_1SM1/44:50–53, 45:35–46]

(7.46) Nukka **karlu djerli**, nukka nayi manberrk korro
he.I NEG.PRED mangrove_monitor he.I NM.I bush DEM.MED.LOC
ka-yuwa.
3SG.NF-lie.NP
'This is not the mangrove monitor, this one lives in the woodland.'
[IK1-160624_0021/07:35–41]

In subordinate clauses, if the matrix predicate is negated, the sentential complement is obligatorily inflected for the same tense/mood value as the matrix verb (7.47):

(7.47) a. Ka-mulmul-kalng banikkin, la ngunda **ki-mabulu**
3SG.NF-many-get.PST dish CONJ not 3SG.IRR.NP-like.IRR.NP
ki-bu=ngurr.
3SG.IRR.NP-hit.IRR.NP=rippled
'S/he has got a lot of dishes but doesn't want to wash them.'
[IK1-170608_1SY1/17:51–56]

b. *Ngunda ki-mabulu **kanj-bunj**=ngurr.
   not   3SG.IRR.NP-like.IRR.NP 3SG.FUT-hit.NP=rippled
   intended: 'S/he does not want to wash it.' [ibid./18:50–59]

The literal structure of (7.47a) is hard to render in English, but it could be along the lines of saying "she doesn't want [that] she **would wash** them". The ungrammatical variant in (7.47b) shows that it is not possible to use a realis form as complement to an irrealis one. This phenomenon of tense/mood agreement is considered in greater detail in section §8.3.

As will be shown in §7.5, the prohibitive particle in the negative imperatives does not create negative polarity and the verb forms are morphosyntactically realis.

7.4 Questions

Questions can be categorised by the type of the answer that they require, which correlates with the formal means of constructing them. Polar (also known as *yes/no*) questions and constituent (also known as *wh*-questions) questions can be formed in Kunbarlang, and are described in the two following sections. I have not been able to identify a reliable way to ask an alternative question, such as *Does she like cats or dogs?* That is probably related to the lack of a dedicated disjunction strategy.

7.4.1 Polar questions

Polar questions are the ones that require *yes* or *no* for the answer (hence their other name, *yes/no* questions).

(7.48) Q: Sandra ka-kinje neyang?
        S   3SG.NF-cook.NP food
        'Is Sandra cooking food?' [IK1-170613_1SM1/29:49–53]

      A: Yoh, ngal-buk=bonj ka-kinje neyang.
         yes II-person=exactly 3SG.NF-cook.NP food
         'Yes, it is she who is cooking food.' [ibid./29:53–57]

There is no evidence of high rising tunes in questions in other Australian languages (see, e.g. Fletcher & Butcher 2014: §5.2). For Kuninjku it has even been reported that in a small corpus of recordings all polar questions displayed a phrase-final fall (Bishop 2002: 96–7). At the same time, however, a study of Dyirbal reports suspended F0 declination in 88% of interrogative intonation phrases in a corpus. This contrasts to Dyirbal declarative phrases, where a comparable proportion of phrases shows steady declination (King 1994: 145). The author suggests that the cue to differentiation between declaratives and interrogatives in Dyirbal may lie in the presence or absence of F0 declination.

My impression is that Kunbarlang questions have a distinct tune from declaratives, and that this tune is the main formal way to mark an utterance as interrogative. However, at the present stage the individual pitch contours that I have examined are not informative. Thus, this impression remains to be verified in a controlled instrumental study of Kunbarlang intonation.

The yes/no questions can also contain the question particle *yidok* (7.49). This particle does not seem to be obligatory under any circumstances.[14]

(7.49) a. **Yidok** ka-burrun-beyang, nayi durduk?
　　　　Q　　3SG.NF-3DU.OBJ-bite.PST　NM.I dog
　　　　'Did that dog bite them two?'　　　　[IK1-160628_0001/06:19–29]

    b. Karlu, la barramimbanj ka-bun-rnak-beyang.
　　　　NEG.PRED CONJ woman 3SG.NF-3SG.OBJ-LIM-bite.PST
　　　　'No, it only bit the woman.'　　　　[ibid./06:42–48]

The marker *yidok* is restricted to matrix clauses, i.e. it cannot be used to embed a question like the English *whether* (7.50a). No complementizer is used at all when a question needs to be embedded under a verb like *-wakwanj* '(to be) ignorant' (7.50b).

(7.50) a. *Nga-wakwanj **yidok** mayi birradja Mary ka-kinjang
　　　　1SG.NF-ignorant.NP Q NM.III rice M 3SG.NF-cook.PST
　　　　balkkime.
　　　　today
　　　　intended: 'I don't know whether Mary cooked rice today.'
　　　　　　　　　　　　　　　　　　[IK1-160812_0001/04:32–48]

    b. Nga-wakwanj manda birradja mayi Mary ka-kinjang.
　　　　1SG.NF-ignorant.NP DEM.PROX.III rice NM.III M 3SG.NF-cook.PST
　　　　'I don't know whether Mary cooked RICE.'　　[ibid./04:50–55]

7.4.2 Constituent questions

Constituent questions are used to request specific information, rather than a *yes* or *no*. They are formed with the help of interrogatives, which are listed and described in §4.5.4.

---

14 Mawng has a particle *kurlingka* with similar function.

(7.51) Q: **Na-kaybi** ki-marnanj-lerrk-rdayinj?
　　　　I-who　　2SG.NF-BEN-word-enter.PST
　　　　'Who did you call (on the phone)?'　　　　[IK1-160628_0001/03:41–43]

　　A: Ngayi Ngalngarridj nga-marnanj-lerrk-rdayinj.
　　　　NM.II　N　　　　　1SG.NF-BEN-word-enter.PST
　　　　'I called Ngalngarridj.'　　　　[ibid./04:01–04]

The new information that constitutes the focus of the answer—*Ngalngarridj*, in the case of (7.51A),—is characteristically found in the preverbal position (see §7.1 for more on word order). The answer can be elliptical and include only that new information (7.52A):

(7.52) Q: Ngudda **birlinj ka-ngundje** nayi ka-bakki-dja　　　　kaddum?
　　　　you　　how　　3SG.NF-do.NP NM.I 3SG.NF-vertical-stand.NP above
　　　　'In your picture, what are the chimneys like?' [lit. 'What is it doing, that which stands up at the top?']　　　　[IK1-170610_2SM1/00:12–16]

　　A: Kaburrk, na-walk~walak.
　　　　two　　　I-PL~small
　　　　'Two, small ones.'　　　　[ibid./00:18–23]

The construction *birlinj ka-ngundje*, as in (7.52Q), is the major periphrastic way to inquire about any property of a referent, in particular, qualities and quantity. In terms of the word order, the interrogative expressions tend to occur clause initially, possibly preceded by sentence external topics (7.52Q). The fronting, however, is not obligatory, and the interrogative may as well occur elsewhere (7.53):

(7.53)　Ka-kidanj　　**na-kaybi** ka-yawanj　　wam?
　　　　3SG.NF-go.PST I-who　　3SG.NF-seek.NP honey
　　　　'Who went to look for honey?'　　　　[IK1-180524_1SY1/06:40–42]

The particle *yidok* cannot be used in a constituent question (7.54):

(7.54) *****Yidok** Jamie **barda** ka-kinjang?
　　　　Q　　J　　what　3SG.NF-cook.PST
　　　　intended: 'What did Jamie cook?' or 'Did Jamie cook something?'
　　　　　　　　[IK1-170614_1PG1/14:33–35]

7.5 Imperatives

Imperatives are defined here functionally, after König & Siemund (2007: 303), as "the constructions dedicated to the expression of the directive speech acts, i.e. orders and requests, but also invitations... etc." In Kunbarlang there are positive imperatives, which express a directive to perform a certain action, and negative imperatives, which express a directive not to perform a certain action. Except for the specialised imperative negator, there are no dedicated imperative forms, and regular agreement morphology is used.

The positive imperative uses the future realis form of the verb (7.55), i.e. the second person prefix is drawn from the future series (tables 5.2/5.7) and the verbal stem is in the non-past realis form.

(7.55) Ngabba, karrard, **ngundji-n**-rnanj!
father mother 2DU.FUT-1SG.OBJ-see.NP
'Mommy, Daddy, look at me!' [IK1-160613_0001/06:08–11]

The second person singular subject of the imperative has a phonologically reduced form with the first person object (7.56), as always in the future forms (see table 5.7).[15]

(7.56) Barda ninda ki-karrme? **Nj-ngan**-rdukbanjdje!
what DEM.II 2SG.NF-hold.NP 2SG.FUT-1SG.OBJ-show.NP
'What have you got? Show it to me!' [IK1-160613_0001/01:19–02:12]

Negative imperatives use a dedicated prohibitive negator not used elsewhere, *kanj-yuwa* 'PROH',[16] and the usual negators found in declarative sentences (*marrek* and *ngunda*) are prohibited. The verbal stem is in the non-past realis form, as in the positive imperatives, but the personal prefixes are drawn from the non-future realis set (7.57).[17]

---

15 There is one unusual occurrence of a non-reduced form, which may well be hypercorrect, as one of the nasal clusters does not sound simplified, also unusually:

(i) Kinj-ngan-ngeme! [kiɲan'ŋeme]
2SG.FUT-1SG.OBJ-paint
'Paint me!' [IK1-160712_0001/11:07]

16 Curiously, this prohibitive (negative imperative) marker is homonymous with the future tense form of the verb *-yuwa* 'to lie' with a third person singular subject: *kanj-yuwa* (3SG.NF-lie.NP) 'S/he / it will lie down'. One might speculate that, by analogy with the use of the future tense forms for imperatives, this is an OPTATIVE, which is now undergoing grammaticalisation into a complex prohibitive construction. Incidentally, Mawng negative imperatives have the same structure as the Kunbarlang ones (Singer 2006: 72).

17 The form *-madde* is the Kunkurduwala variant of *-maddje*.

(7.57) a. **Kanjyuwa ki**-buddu-wunj bakki.
PROH 2SG.NF-3PL.OBJ-give.NP tobacco
'Don't give tobacco to that mob!' [IK1-160613_0001/15:42–44]

b. Ngadda-marnanj-ngunda "**kanjyuwa ki**-mulmul-kali la
1PL.EXCL.NF-BEN-do.PST PROH 2SG.NF-many-get.NP CONJ
kaburrk **kinj**-madde".
two 2SG.FUT-pierce.NP
'We told him, *Don't get a lot [of stingray]—just get two.*'
[20150413IOv01/03:31–33]

Despite its formal resemblance of the third person future tense form of *-yuwa* 'to lie down', the prohibitive particle is not a morphosyntactically active verb. For one, it is not sensitive to the person and number features of the event participants. The mismatch is obvious with the second person subject of the imperative, and the prohibitive particle does not change with different persons of the object either. Thus, with a first person object informants reject *nganjyuwa* [1SG.FUT.lie.NP] (7.58):

(7.58) Kanjyuwa ki-ngan-rnanj!
PROH 2SG.NF-1SG.OBJ-see.NP
'Don't look at me!' [IK1-180521_1SY1/25:15]

There is also an uninflecting imperative interjection *djadji* 'come here!' (7.59):

(7.59) **Djadji** ngarrki-karluwa!
come_here 1.INCL.FUT-dig.NP
'Come here, let's dig [for water]!' [20060606IB02/12:58]

Since there are no dedicated morphological forms for imperatives (nor hortatives, nor optatives), there are no grounds to postulate first or third person imperatives.

7.6 Directionals

There are several morphemes in Kunbarlang that serve to express the directional, or more broadly, locative, meanings. Two of them—the verbal prefixes *mun-* 'THITH' and *nganj-* 'HITH'—are discussed in §6.4. The other two are the clitics *=bi* 'THITH' (7.60) and *=way* 'HITH' (7.61). These clitics attach to verbs (7.60a), (7.61b) and to demonstratives (7.60b):

(7.60) a. Ki-ngan-marnanj-ngunda   nganj-**mun**-ka=**bi**   malayi
           2SG.NF-1SG.OBJ-BEN-do.PST   1SG.FUT-THITH-go=THITH   tomorrow
           Budawin.
           Port_Darwin
           'You told me, *I'm going to Darwin tomorrow.*'   [IK1-180516_1PN2/17:20–25]

   b. Korro=**bi**   ka-ka   kun-barrkidbe yalbi.
       DEM.MED.LOC=THITH   3SG.NF-go.NP   IV-other   country
       'S/he's going to another country.'   [ibid./37:38–43]

(7.61) IK1-180529_1SY1/01:32:42–50

   a. Ka-ngan-rnirlakwang.
       3SG.NF-1SG.OBJ-send.PST
       'S/he sent me.' [no direction or location specified]

   b. Ka-ngan-rnirlakwang=**way**.
       3SG.NF-1SG.OBJ-send.PST=HITH
       'S/he sent me over here.'

Example (7.61) offers a minimal pair, where the addition of the clitic =*way* adds a locational specification 'towards the deictic centre'. These clitics seem to be going out of use. They are not used in spontaneous speech very frequently, and although in elicitations they are recognised and judgements are offered with confidence, those judgements are not always consistent. For these reasons, the rules described below are a good approximation of the present-day system, but they can also be found violated in some elicitation recordings—possibly due to some discourse conditions on their use that are hard to control for in elicitation. It is not inconceivable that the decline of the system has to do—in one way or another—with the complexity of the deixis encoded, as discussed below.

The directional clitics have a strong tendency to cliticise onto the verbs with a directional prefix (7.62a–b). Moreover, by default the prefix and the clitic match in the direction they encode (7.62c–d; although see more below):

(7.62) IK1-180518_1SY1/01:43–02:49

   a. ?? Ka-ka=bi.
        3SG.NF-go.NP=THITH
        intended: 'S/he's going away.'

   b. ?? Ka-ka=way.
        3SG.NF-go.NP=HITH
        'S/he's coming here.'

c. *Ka-mun-ka=way.
   3SG.NF-THITH-go.NP=HITH

d. *Ka-nganj-ka=bi.
   3SG.NF-HITH-go.NP=THITH

In fact, the requirement that a prefix be present in the verb for the clitic to attach is somewhat variable. Thus, one speaker shows no sensitivity to that requirement whatsoever, while another consistently observes it.[18] For instance, the sentence in (7.63) is volunteered (and later confirmed) by the former of the two, but ruled out by the latter:

(7.63) %Kinj-rdam=bi   korro   yirrk!
       2SG.FUT-put.NP=HITH DEM.MED.LOC inside
       'Take/put it inside!'   [IK1-180516_1PN2/30:08; IK1-180518_1SY-01/06:22]

Further complications arise with respect to the deictic centre. As is pointed out in §6.4, the direction of motion is determined relative to a deictic centre, which may or may not coincide with the speaker of the utterance. Interestingly, some examples suggest that more than one deictic centre can be encoded if both a prefix and a clitic are present. Consider (7.64), which may be uttered by a speaker standing outside of a building to an addressee who is inside of the building:

(7.64) Kinj-**mun**-rdam=**way**   kenda   rlobberl nganj-kali.
       2SG.FUT-THITH-put.NP=HITH DEM.PROX.LOC outside   1SG.FUT-get.NP
       'Pass it on here outside, I'll get it.'   [IK1-180518_1SY1/35:02–06]

In (7.64) there is a mismatch between the directional prefix and clitic. It can be interpreted to serve a creative purpose, however, indicating that for the verb's subject (i.e. the addressee of the imperative utterance) the action is elative, but from the speaker of the utterance's point of view the action is allative.

As is discussed in §6.4.5, there is a certain asymmetry between the directional prefixes, such that the hither *nganj-* occurs more frequently than the thither *mun-*, and the default interpretation of directed actions in the absence of either prefix is the elative. This does not seem to be the case with the clitics, which are equally infrequent. Another manifestation of the asymmetry in prefixes is the fact that *nganj-*, but not *mun-*, can combine with stative (posture) verbs (7.65). It is not clear to me whether there is any semantic import of *nganj-* in such cases.

---

18 Data from other speakers are more sporadic at the moment, but are in agreement with the requirement.

(7.65) Korro-bi   ka-**nganj-yuwa**.
        DEM.MED.LOC=THITH 3SG.NF-HITH-lie.NP
        'S/he stays/sleeps over there.'   [IK1-180518_1SY1/31:33]

More generally, the verbs that can be prefixed with the directionals are those that admit of some kind of directionality as part of their meaning. Accordingly, -*kanj* 'to take' can have a directional prefix, but -*bularrbunj* 'to finish' or -*warre* 'to move' cannot. Likewise, -*rduka* 'to look' can receive the directional prefix, but -*rnanj* 'to see' cannot (7.66):

(7.66) a. Ka-**nganj-rduka**(=way)   ka-ngarrku-rnanj.
          3SG.NF-HITH-look.NP(=HITH)   3SG.NF-1DU.OBJ-see.NP
          'S/he's looking this way and seeing us two.'
                                                   [IK1-180520_DDj1/16:52–17:47]

      b. *Ka-nganj-**rnanj**(=way).
         3SG.NF-HITH-see.NP(=HITH)
         'S/he's looking/facing this way.' [perhaps similar to the badness of the English *s/he sees this way*]   [ibid./18:37–53]

Among the nominals the situation is not completely clear cut either. The clitics are normally only found on demonstratives (7.67) and are banned from proper and common nouns and from personal pronouns (7.68).

(7.67) Ngarrki-kinje   neyang ngorro   ngarrki-wu-dji
       1.INCL.FUT-cook.PST   food   DEM.MED.IV   1.INCL.FUT-give-REFL.NP
       korro=way   **kenda**=way.
       DEM.MED.LOC=HITH   DEM.PROX.LOC=HITH
       'We'll make food and then share it/exchange it with each other [lit. 'give it to ourselves that way and this way'].'   [IK1-180522_2SM1/16:52–17:02]

(7.68) a. Malayi   nganj-mun-ka=bi   **Mardbalk**=(*bi).
          tomorrow   1SG.FUT-THITH-go.NP=THITH S.Goulburn= THITH
          'Tomorrow I'm going to South Goulburn island.'
                                                   [IK1-180516_1PN2/38:06–15]

      b. *Nga-ka   **kodbarre**=way.
         1SG.NF-go.NP   house=HITH
         intended 'I'm going towards the house.'   [IK1-180518_1SY1/12:23–25]

      c. *nukka=bi; *ngudda=way.
         he=THITH   you=HITH
         intended: 'to him; from you.'   [IK1-180520_1DDj1/11:26, 11:57]

However, there is one example in a spontaneous exchange between two speakers where =*bi* is used metaphorically, cliticised on the noun *balanda* 'whitefella; English' meaning '[translate it] into English' (7.69).

(7.69) Korro   la   **balanda=bi**   kinj-yolyolme
        DEM.MED.LOC   CONJ   whitefella=THITH   2SG.FUT-talk.about.NP

        kanjbarra-burrbunj.
        3DU.FUT-know.NP

'Say it in English so they can understand.'   [20060606IB02/11:32–35]

Apparently, the form *balandabi* in (7.69) means 'away, from the agent's point of view, into the foreign language'.

7.7 Stative clause types

This section focuses on stative clauses: ascriptive (§7.7.1), possessive (§7.7.2), locative and existential (§7.7.3), and comparative (§7.7.4). Ascriptive clauses have a nominal predicate with a posture verb copula (omitted in the present tense). Possessive clauses come in two varieties, depending on the semantic definiteness of the possessum; one type is formally identical to ascriptive clauses, the other uses the verb -*karrme* 'to hold'. Locative and existential clauses are built around a posture verb copula with a locational complement. Comparative clauses use verbal predicates.

7.7.1 Ascriptive clauses

Ascriptive clauses assert some property of an object. The property is expressed by a nominal, i.e. a noun (7.70) or an adjective (7.71). There is no copula in the present tense. The order of the constituents seems to be always topic–comment.

(7.70) a. Ninda   nayi   yiwarrudj=rnungu.
            DEM.PROX.I   NM.I   church=he.GEN

           'This [man] is a priest.'   [Field notes, 2015-08-02, SM]

      b. Nginda   barramimbanj   korl   didja.
          DEM.PROX.II   woman   school teacher

           'This woman is a teacher.'   [IK1-160616_0001/48:42]

(7.71) a. Mary kin-kodjkodjburrinj.
M II-smart
'Mary is smart.' [IK1-170616_1SY1/10:53–55]

b. Mukka kandiddjawa **man-rayek djininj**.
it.III damper III-hard properly
'This damper is **really hard**.' [IK1-180524_1SY2/20:36–41]

c. Yimarne kadda-ngunda=barr **na-bareng**, but nukka ngorro
like 3PL.NF-do.PST=open I-dangerous ENG he DEM.MED.IV
karlu, nukka ngorro **na-mak, Christian man**.
NEG.PRED he DEM.MED.IV I-good ENG ENG
'They thought he was **dangerous**, but he wasn't, he was **good, a Christian man**.' [IK1-160624_0001/03:05–12]

Notice also the null anaphora in the first clause of (7.71c), where *nabareng* 'dangerous' is predicated of a discourse topic (this is from a passage about the arrival of Reverend James Watson, the founder of Warruwi Mission), but there is no overt subject noun or pronoun until the next clause (*nukka* 'he').

Kunbarlang is a language that uses zero copulas for predicate nominals in the present tense (Stassen 2013b). In the non-present tenses overt copulas are used in Kunbarlang. There are five known verbs used in the copular function: the three posture verbs *-dja* 'to stand', *-rna* 'to sit', and *-yuwa* 'to lie', the generic existential/motion verb *-warre* (which I gloss as 'move'), and another verb with a very general meaning 'to say; do; perform' *-ngundje*. Different subtypes of non-verbal predicates make use of different subsets of these copular verbs. Ascriptive clauses have been recorded with the posture verb *-rna* 'to sit' (7.72a) and the verb *-ngundje* 'to do' (7.72b). See §7.7.3 for examples of locative and existential sentences, where other posture verbs are also used.

(7.72) a. Kikka ngorro **ka-rninganj ki-wanjak**, ngadda-karrmeng.
she DEM.MED.IV 3SG.NF-sit.PST II-little 1PL.EXCL.NF-get.PST
'She was little [when] we got her.' [20060620IB03/29:17–22]

b. **Nga-ngunda ngarra-wanjak**.
1SG.NF-do.PST 1SG-little
'I was little.' [RS1-140/19:32]

No copula is required in the present tense with negation, where either the negative particle *ngunda* or the predicative negator *karlu* is used:

(7.73) a. Nukka **ngunda na-bareng**.
he not I-dangerous
'He [the dog] is not dangerous.' [IK1-180524_1SY2/12:57]

b. Nukka **karlu** **na-bareng**.
   he   NEG.PRED I-dangerous
   'He [the dog] is not dangerous.' [ibid./13:11]

7.7.2 Possessive clauses

This section describes ways of encoding predicative possession, i.e. cases when ownership of some entity (the *possessum*) is predicated of a *possessor* (Stassen 2013a). Adnominal/attributive possession is discussed in §4.6. In the typological literature a distinction is sometimes made between indefinite and definite predicative possession, which refers to the definiteness of the possessum (Stassen 2013a). The distinction is illustrated with English, which uses different constructions for the two types, the indefinite possessum in (7.74a) and the definite one in (7.74b):

(7.74) a. Erwin has a cat.
       b. This cat is Erwin's.

Kunbarlang uses different constructions for the two types as well. I discuss them in turn below.

7.7.2.1 Indefinite possessum

Kunbarlang uses two constructions to express possession of a semantically indefinite item. The first one involves the transitive verb *-karrme* 'hold' (7.75). This is a 'have'-type possessive (Freeze 1992, Stassen 2013a), which uses a transitive verb.

(7.75) Kukkangundje **ka-karrme**   budjibudji.
       maybe   3SG.NF-hold.NP cat
       'Maybe he has a cat.' [IK1-160513_0011/08:40–42]

This construction is used for metaphorical extension of possession as well, for instance, part-whole descriptions of inanimate entities. Example (7.76) illustrates that, and also shows that absence of possession can be expressed using constituent negation (see also §7.3).

(7.76) Manda   mayi   kundulk **ka-karrme**   ma-rleng mayi   burru, la
       DEM.PROX.III NM.III tree   3SG.NF-hold.NP III-much NM.III arm   CONJ
       karlu   mayi   maworord.
       NEG.PRED   NM.III leaf
       'This tree has many branches, but it doesn't have any leaves.'
       [IK1-170522_1SM1/44:50–53, 45:35–46]

Another negation strategy for this possessive construction is negating the verbal predicate -*karrme* (7.77):

(7.77) **Ngunda ngarrak-karrme** mayi neyang.
not 1.INCL.IRR.NP-hold.IRR.NP NM.III food
'We don't have food.' [IK1-160802_0011/06:23–40]

Besides the 'have'-type possessive, (indefinite) predicative possession can be expressed in Kunbarlang with the adnominal possessive construction (7.78). This seems to be a rather infrequent strategy in Kunbarlang, as well as probably a typological rarum. Stassen (2009: §4) lists a number of languages that employ their respective adnominal possessive constructions for predicative possession; however, all of those languages except Gumbaynggirr use an overt copula 'be'/'exist'.

(7.78) Ngana-kalbi-yinj ngorro balkkime
1DU.EXCL.NF-get-REFL.PST DEM.MED.IV now

nawalak bi-nganungka.
child DAT-we.DU.EXCL.GEN

'We got married, now **we've got kids**.' [lit. 'my and his/her children']
[20150413IOv01/07:56–59]

It is clear that semantically the highlighted fragment in (7.78) is a proposition, not a referential phrase. In the discussion of adnominal/attributive possession in §4.6 (see esp. §4.6.2.1) I also show that these constructions sometimes appear more semantically complex than mere attribution of possession.

7.7.2.2 Definite possessum

Expression of definite predicative possession largely draws on the resources available for attributive possession (§4.6). Thus, a typical example of a possessive clause just uses the possessive noun phrase as its predicate (7.79). In fact, grammatically this is a subtype of ascriptive clauses, singled out here only on semantic grounds.

(7.79) a. Kirnda ngorro Karrabbu **ngayi kun-ngaybu yalbi**.
DEM.AFOR.LOC DEM.MED.IV K I IV-I.GEN country
'That Karrabbu is my country.' [20060620IB03/33:27–33]

b. Manda mayi neyang **man-ngaybu**.
DEM.PROX.III NM.III food III-I.GEN
'This food is mine.' [IK1-170522_1SM1/24:52]

Negation of definite possession is made by the negative particle scoping over the possessive (7.80; more on negation in section 7.3):

(7.80) Ninda   djurra **ngunda bi-ngaybu**.
       DEM.PROX.I paper not   DAT-I.GEN
       'The book is not mine.'   [IK1-160618_0001/01:47]

In tenses other than present, the verb -*karrme* 'to hold' is added (7.81), which is otherwise used in the indefinite possessum constructions described in §7.7.2.1 above.

(7.81) Ninda   durduk **ngayi bi-ngaybu nga-karrmeng** la   balkkime
       DEM.PROX.I dog   I   DAT-I.GEN 1SG.NF-hold.PST CONJ now
       ngorro   ki-nungku.
       DEM.MED.IV I/II-you.GEN
       'This dog was mine and now it is yours.'   [IK1-170522_2SM1/31:51–38:12]

7.7.3 Locative and existential clauses

In some languages location and existence are expressed with different constructions, due to the fact that they have slightly different pragmatics, arising form a different presuppositional viewpoint (Partee & Borschev (2002) call it the *Perspectival Centre*). In locative constructions the existence of the THING is presupposed, and its location is at issue. In existential constructions, on the other hand, the existence of the LOCATION is presupposed, and the object that is present or non-present there is central to the assertion. In Kunbarlang these constructions seem to have the same expression.

7.7.3.1 The form of locative and existential clauses

The general pattern for this semantic type of clause is FIGURE–(COPULA)–GROUND. In contrast to the ascriptive clauses, the copula in the locative and existential clauses is normally present in all tenses, i.e. not omitted in the present (7.82). The locative expression is most often introduced by the medial locative demonstrative *korro/karra* (see §4.5.3 for more details), or else can be unmarked if it is an inherently locational expression, as in (7.86) below.

(7.82) Nayi manburrba **ka-yuwa**   korro   baladji.
       NM.I clothes   3SG.NF-lie.NP DEM.MED.LOC bag
       'The dress is in the bag.'   [Field notes 2015-08-02, SM]

Example (7.83) shows examples of negative existentials, where the predicative negator *karlu* serves as the only copula, whether in the present (7.83a) or in the past tense (7.83b), and example (7.84) shows co-occurrence of copula and *karlu*.

(7.83) a. **Karlu nakarlyung** korro njunjuk.
NEG.PRED crocodile DEM.MED.LOC water
'There's no crocodiles in the water [so you can swim].'
[IK1-160429_0011/11:23–27]

b. Nga-mabuluy ngay-kangkayi karnda=way la
1SG.NF-like.PST 1SG.IRR.PST-go.IRR.PST DEM.DIST.LOC=HITH CONJ
karlu kabbala.
NEG.PRED boat
'[Yesterday] I wanted to go to the mainland, but there was no boat.'
[IK1-170613_1SM1/45:20–40]

(7.84) Kordokmeng **karlu nakarlyung ka-rninganj** ngadda-ngambiwang.
first NEG.PRED crocodile 3SG.NF-sit.PST 1PL.EXCL.NF-swim.PST
'There used to be no crocodiles and we used to swim across.'
[20060620IB03/04:56–05:01]

Similar to other stative clauses, the copula encodes the tense of the clause, cf. example (7.85) in the past tense:

(7.85) Bread **ka-yunganj** karra burrubburrkang, la karlu.
bread 3SG.NF-lie.PST DEM.MED.LOC bag CONJ NEG.PRED
'The bread was in the bag, but now it's not [there].'
[IK1-150803_1PN1/01:05:05–19]

The copulas used in locatives and existentials are more varied than those used in ascriptive clauses (§7.7.1), specifically, they can be different posture verbs and the verb *-warre* 'to move'. In the examples above it was *-yuwa* 'to lie'. The other ones are *-rna* 'to sit' (7.86a) and *-dja* 'to stand' (7.86b). The choice of the copula is further discussed in §7.7.3.2 below.

(7.86) a. Kinbadda-rleng marnilikarn kaddum **kadda-rna**.
PL-many star above 3PL.NF-sit.NP
'There are many stars in the sky.' [IK1-160616_0001/44:58]

b. Barrayidjyidj **kadda-dja** rlobberl.
kids 3PL.NF-stand.NP outside
'The kids are outside.' [IK1-160618_0001/09:41]

7.7.3.2 Choice of the copula

Establishing the precise conditions that influence the choice of the copula would need further detailed lexico-semantic research, but some preliminary generalisations can be made from the examples available in my data. It appears that the primary factor which determines the choice of the copula is the ontological type of the figure, sometimes in conjunction with its physical position (in cases when the figure can assume various positions). Below I describe which figures/positions are typical of each copular verb.

The verb *-yuwa* 'to lie' is used for the figures that have a 'lying' posture, i.e. a salient horizontal axis (such as crocodiles (7.87a); but cf. (7.84) above with the most versatile copula *-rna* 'to sit'), or do not have any inherent posture at all (such as clothing (7.82) or water (7.87b)).

(7.87) a. Yidok   nakarlyung **ka-yuwa**   korro   njunjuk?
        Q   crocodile   3SG.NF-lie.NP DEM.MED.LOC water
        'Are there crocodiles in the water?'   [IK1-160429_0011/13:14–18]

     b. Djadji   ngudji-nganj-ka,   ngondo   kyui   njunjuk
        come_here   2DU.NF-HITH-go.NP DEM.PROX.IV NM.IV water
        ka-yuwa   bi-ngarrku.
        3SG.NF-lie.NP DAT-we.INCL.GEN
        'Come here you two, there's water for us.'   [IK!-160610_0001/27:07–20]

The verb *-yuwa* 'to lie' also extends to mean 'to sleep', and via that meaning further to 'to live/stay [somewhere]' (7.88):

(7.88) Nginda   ngayingana ngayi kin-ngadju nawalak **kadda-baba-yuwa**.
       DEM.PROX.II mother   NM.PL I/II-she.GEN child   3PL.NF-DISTR-lie.NP
       'Her kids live separately.'   [IK1-160819_0001/42:48–43:10]

The verb *-dja* 'to stand' is used for temporary location of people (7.86b) and for the figures that are standing upright, such as large animals (7.89):

(7.89) Na-rleng nganabbarru **ka-dja**   korro   manberrk.
       I-much   buffalo   3SG.NF-stand.NP DEM.MED.LOC bush
       'There are many buffalos on the mainland.' [IK1-160715_0001/01:37:22–40]

Inanimate figures can also be localised with this verb, if their position is upright:

(7.90) Window **ka-dja**   la   karnda=way   nayi curtain.
       window 3SG.NF-stand.NP CONJ DEM.DIST.IV=HITH NM.I curtain
       'There's a window and behind it a curtain.'   [IK1-170526_1SY2/13:16–26]

The verb *-rna* 'to sit' seems to have the most abstract semantics of the three posture verbs. It can be used in existentials with the figures that typically have some other postures and positions, e.g. the crocodiles (who normally "lie" rather than "sit") in example (7.84). It can be used for abstract objects that do not have a distinct position, such as the stars in the sky (7.86a). It also extends to meaning of 'to live [somewhere]' (7.91):

(7.91)   Budawin **ka-rna**,   but ka-yuwa   hospital, ka-warrmi.
         Darwin   3SG.NF-sit.NP but 3SG.NF-lie.NP hospital 3SG-sick
         'She lives in Darwin, but is now at the hospital sick.'
         [IK1-170610_2SM1/19:41–47]

Sometimes still another verb is used as an existential copula, viz. *-warre* 'to move'. Its core meaning is non-directed motion, although the motion component may be absent in certain combinations. An example of its existential use is in (7.92):

(7.92)   Nukka-dju djarrangalanj kenda   ngunda **ki-warre**.
         he-COLL   boy   DEM.PROX.LOC   not   3SG.IRR.NP-move.IRR.NP
         'There's no boys like that here.'   [IK1-170607_1SM1/43:24–30]

These posture/motion verbs are also used in the analytic aspectual construction (§7.2.1). Similar polyfunctionality of a set of posture and motion verbs has been described for many Australian languages, including Maningridan languages (Gurr-goni, Green 1995: §5; Nakkara, Eather 2011: 371–2, 403–10; Ndjébbana, McKay 2000: 286, 291), and also for Ngan'gityemerri and other Daly languages (Reid 2002).

7.7.4 Comparative and superlative clauses

In Kunbarlang there are no morphological means to mark comparative and superlative degrees. Instead, the relevant meanings are inferred from the usage of the positive form of gradable predicates (primarily, gradable adjectives). Thus, in example (7.93) the comparative meaning arises from the coordination of two ascriptive clauses with antonymic predicates, *-djuhmi* 'short' and *-kukkarlyung* 'long'. Likewise, the superlative semantics is inferred from the contextual use of the general purpose intensifier *djininj* 'properly' (7.94; see §7.7.4.2 below).

(7.93)   Kundulk bi-nungku   man-**djuhmi**, la   mayi   bi-ngaybu
         tree   DAT-you.GEN III-short   CONJ NM.III DAT-I.GEN
         man-**kuk-karlyung**.
         III-length-big
         'My stick is longer than yours.' [lit. 'Your stick is short and mine is long.']
         [IK1-160818_0001/19:54–20:02]

(7.94) John, nukka na-**karlirayek djininj**.
         J   he   I-strong   properly
        'John is the strongest one.' [IK1-160802_0021/19:53–58]

The data from Kunbarlang gradable predicates are very interesting, as they contribute to the growing literature on *degree-less* languages, i.e. languages that do not have any degree constructions but only the implicit comparison (see Beck et al. 2009, Bochnak 2015, Bowler 2016). This work, and its extension in Kapitonov 2019b, adds to the description of comparison in Australian languages, a topic that too often receives little attention in grammatical descriptions. Below I provide an overview of how comparative and superlative meanings are expressed in Kunbarlang (§7.7.4.1 and §7.7.4.2, resp.).

7.7.4.1 Comparative clauses

Typologically speaking, Kunbarlang belongs to the languages that express comparison with IMPLICIT, or CONJOINED, constructions.[19] This means that there are no dedicated comparison words or morphemes, but instead the comparative semantics is inferred from the way clauses are combined. The subtypes of the implicit comparison that are encountered in the data are these: antonyms (7.93, 7.95, 7.97a), negation of a quality (7.96, 7.97b), *ngemek* 'still, yet' (7.98), and *budarr*, a Mawng loan (7.99). I shall exemplify and discuss them in turn.

A major strategy is the conjunction of two antonymic descriptions, as in (7.95); see also examples (7.93) above and (7.97a) below.

(7.95) Ngudda ki-kelkkuyinj   **kun-kuk-karlyung**, la   ngayi nga-kelkkuyinj
        you.SG 2SG.NF-work.PST   IV-length-big   CONJ   I   1SG.NF-work.PST
        kun-djuhmi.
        IV-short
        'You have worked here longer than I have.' [lit. 'You worked long and I worked short.']   [IK1-160802_0011/55:46–56:10]

An alternative to conjoined antonyms is the conjunction of a positive and a negative statement (7.96):

(7.96) Ngalbangardi kin-**kuk-karlyung**, la   Ngalngarridj **karlu**.
        N   II-length-big   CONJ N   NEG.PRED
        'Ngalbangardi is taller than Ngalngarridj.' [lit. 'Ngalbangardi is tall and Ngalngarridj is not.']   [IK1-160816_0001/01:28:34–40]

---

[19] For a typological overview see Stassen 1985, Bobaljik 2012 and references therein.

There are no comparative forms of proportional quantifiers ('many' ~ 'more'). The respective meaning is expressed just as comparison of qualities, with antonyms ('many' ~ 'few'; 7.97a) or negation (7.97b).

(7.97)　IK1-160818_0001/22:49–23:31

    a.　Ngalbangardi　ka-karrme　　　　na-**rleng**　durduk,　Ngalngarridj
　　　　　N　　　　　　 3SG.NF-hold.NP　I-many　　dog　　　 N

       na-**worrkbam**　ka-karrme.
　　　　I-few　　　　3SG.NF-hold.NP

    'Ngalbangardi has more dogs than Ngalngarridj.' [lit. 'Ngalbangardi's got many dogs, and Ngalngarridj few.']

    b.　Ngalbangardi　ka-karrme　　　nayi　na-**rleng**　durduk,　Ngalngarridj
　　　　　N　　　　　　 3SG.NF-hold.NP　I　　I-many　　dog　　　 N

       djal　**karlu**.
　　　　merely　NEG.PRED

    'Ngalbangardi has more dogs than Ngalngarridj.' [lit. 'Ngalbangardi's got many dogs, and Ngalngarridj not.']

A different way to form an implicit comparative in Kunbarlang is to reiterate the same description or quantifier with the word *ngemek* 'ngemek' (7.98). It affords a concessive flavour akin to how *yet* may be used in English:

(7.98)　Bedbe　kadda-kalng　　　na-**rleng**,　la　　ngayi　**ngemek**　nga-kalng
　　　　 they　 3PL.NF-get.PST　I-many　　 CONJ　I　　 yet　　　 1SG.NF-get.PST

    na-**rleng**　bonjbonj.
　　　I-many　　RDP~exactly

    'I caught more [fish] than they did.' [lit. 'They got plenty, yet I got plenty, too.']
                                                              [IK1-160802_0011/41:26–31]

Finally, some speakers may occasionally loan a word from Mawng, such as *wutarr* (Mawng orthography, rendered as *budarr* in Kunbarlang examples) meaning 'a little bit more':[20]

---

[20] This word in Mawng is used in kin term formation, e.g. to derive 'second eldest child' from 'the eldest child' (Ruth Singer, p.c.). This is one of the ways in which the elaborate kinship systems in Australian languages can get recruited for the less elaborate areas of comparison and quantification. Another notable example is that the noun for 'mother', which often becomes a "lexicalized superlative", used with concrete objects but not abstract ideas (Umpila and Cape York Creole, Peter Sutton p.c.; Burarra, Margaret Carew p.c.; Arrernte and Western Desert language, Jenny Green p.c.; also Woiwurrung: *bababi djinang* 'big toe' (lit. 'mother foot'), as the biggest toe, and perhaps *babadi marnung* 'thumb' (lit. 'mother hand') (Blake 1991). But also in English, e.g. *the mother of all bombs* (thanks to Pattie Epps for pointing this out).

(7.99) Ninda   kinbadda-djuhmi la   narnda=bi   na-kuk-karlyung
        DEM.PROX.I   3PL-short   CONJ   DEM.DIST.I=THITH   I-length-big

  budarr,   la   narnda=bi   na-kuk-karlyung djininj.
  next_in_line   CONJ   DEM.DIST.I=THITH   I-length-big   properly

  'They$_j$ are short, and this guy$_k$ is **next tall**, and this guy$_l$ is very tall.'
  [IK1-160802_0011/01:00:26–52]

The last word in (7.99), *djininj* 'properly', is the intensifier that is used in construction of the Kunbarlang superlatives, to which I turn next.

7.7.4.2 Superlative clauses

The superlative construction is formed with the intensifier *djininj* 'really; very; properly' (7.99). Just as in the comparative clauses, the semantics here is inferred, rather than encoded with any dedicated, conventional means. The superlative can be shown to be ABSOLUTE rather than RELATIVE, i.e. expressing a high degree of a quality but not necessarily the unique maximum. Thus, the following dialogue (7.100) shows that the uniqueness presupposition is absent from Kunbarlang superlative clauses. The sentence that functionally serves as a superlative question 'Which X is the P-est one?' literally just asks 'Which X is really/very P?' (7.100). If the speaker is presented with a set of alternatives, he or she would identify the relevant (here, biggest) referent and pointing to it, saying something that literally means 'This one is very P' (7.100b). The possibility of the continuation (7.100c), which says about another referent that it is 'also very P', confirms the lack of uniqueness component in the meaning of an utterance like (7.100b).

(7.100) IK1-160816_0001/01:23:53–01:27:45

  a. QUESTION:

  Karra kenda nayi   barbung ki-**ngana djininj**?
  where   NM.I   fish   II-big   properly

  'Which fish is very big?' (literal)
  OR 'Which is the biggest fish?' (pragmatic)

  b. ANSWER:

  Ninda$_j$ ki-**ngana djininj**...
  DEM.PROX.I II-big   properly

  'This one is very big...'
  OR 'This one is the biggest...'

c. ANSWER [CTD.]:
   …La   ninda$_k$ ki-ngana djininj   bonjbonj.
   CONJ DEM.PROX.I II-big   RDP~exactly   properly

   '…And this [other] one is very big, too.'
   #'…And this [other] one is the biggest, too.'

Relative superlatives (such as the superlative in English) have the uniqueness entailment, which renders the superlative+additive continuation in the translation of (7.100c) anomalous (indicated by the hash-mark). However, the continuation in Kunbarlang is fine, since the Kunbarlang superlative is an absolute one and does not entail uniqueness.

7.8 Anaphora and reference maintenance

This section gives a brief summary of the ways to track reference in Kunbarlang discourse. The reader interested in an extensive analysis of person reference and other communicative practices in an Australian language is referred to Garde (2013), who studied the topic in Bininj Kunwok in enviable depth. For cross-references to the parts of this grammar that describe anaphoric and coreference constructions in Kunbarlang, see the end of this section.

In Kunbarlang, noun phrases are used very sparingly in discourse. Personal prefixes in the verb prevail as the reference tracking device, i.e. one finds what can be considered very extensive zero anaphora. Full noun phrases are given as the first mention, and afterwards the referent does not have to have any nominals referring to it, with a few exceptions. The main kinds of these exceptions are:
- contrastive focus, which can only be achieved with the use of overt nominals, and
- oblique case positions, where a pronoun (and possibly other nominals) occurs to mark a grammatically obligatory case.

Essentially, these exceptions—illustrated below—are precisely those cases where verbal morphology is insufficient to convey some information, and so a nominal is obligatory. Example (7.101) shows focus on the first person subject, which is contrasted with another referent mentioned earlier in the text.

(7.101) La   **ngarrka-ma**   ngarrki-kali   mulurr   ngarrki-ka.
         CONJ we.INCL-CONTR   1.INCL.FUT-get.NP driftwood   1.INCL.FUT-go.NP

         'And US MOB, we'll get driftwood and we'll go.'   [20150212AS01/04:02–06]

The pair of examples in (7.102) (repeated from (4.64)) illustrate the point about case positions. These are several consecutive clauses from a narrative, where the speaker expresses a phrase with the same sense ('they say to me') in two slightly different ways.

In (7.102a), there is a verb *-ngundje* 'to say/do', which requires dative case marking on the addressee; here a free pronoun is obligatory, at least as an exponent of case. By contrast, in (7.102b), the speaker adds an applicative to the verb, making it *-marnanj-ngundje* 'to say to (someone)', which indexes the addressee participant in the object slot; here the pronoun is not required (in fact, here it is prohibited; see §4.2 for details.)

(7.102) a. Kadda-ngundje **bi-ngaybu** "kikka Ngal-Bangardi ka-wokdja
　　　　　3PL.NF-say.NP DAT-I.GEN she.II N 3SG.NF-speak.NP

　　　　　Kunbarlang kun-mak ngadda-ngayinj".
　　　　　Kunbarlang IV-good 1PL.EXCL.NF-hear.PST

　　　　　'They tell me: "We heard that Ngal-Bangardi speaks Kunbarlang well."'
　　　　　[20070108IB01/25:21–26; translation mine—IK]

　　　b. Yoh, nga-ngunda, ngayi ngorro teach im.
　　　　　yes 1SG.NF-say.PST I DEM.MED.IV [Kriol]

　　　　　Ka-**ngan-marnanj**-ngunda "Ah aku!"
　　　　　3SG.NF-1SG.OBJ-BEN-say.PST ah ok

　　　　　'"Yes", I told them, "I teach her." They said to me "Ah okay!"'
　　　　　[ibid./25:26–29; translation mine—IK]

The above discussion was concerned with the cases of obligatory use of referring expressions. When not obligatory, they are very seldom used. This can be appreciated in any of the three text samples included in Appendix A. After the first mentions established referents rarely ever get mentioned by referring expressions again, and usually if they do, they do for a reason. For instance, *kandiddjawa* 'damper', the topic of Text A.2, is mentioned with a free NP in the first clause (A.31) and then only 13 clauses later, as *manda ngorro kandiddjawa* [DEM.PROX.III DEM.MED.IV bread] 'this damper' in (A.44). The possible reason is that in the first part of the text, the damper is construed generically, but later on the narrator switched to the actual situation and refered to the specific damper that she was making at that moment.

Another example is found in the game-based dialogue in Text A.3. One of the first established referents, *nayi kabakkidja kaddum* [NM.I 3SG.NF-stand_vertically.NP above] 'chimneys (lit. that which stands up at the top)' in (A.49), only get described by modifiers without any nouns or pronouns, until some 12 clauses later (A.57) players spot the difference. Then one of the speakers uses a pronoun (*nukka* 'he.I') to refer to the chimneys and convey a sense of contrast.

This style of reference maintenance, whereby tracking mainly is not done with (pro)nouns, but rather with agreement, zero anaphora, and/or inference, seems typical of Australian languages. It is reported in such distant languages as Bininj Kunwok, Guugu Yimithirr, Ngarinyin (see Garde 2013: §5.2 for discussion and references), and Bardi (Bowern 2012: 286).

That does not mean, however, that in Kunbarlang nouns and pronouns are omitted whenever possible—just most of the time. Example (7.103) below (repeated from (4.55)) shows that a speaker may choose to insert a pronoun without any obvious compelling reason to: the first person referent is referred to only through the verb for a while (7.103a), and then a free pronoun is added (7.103b).

(7.103) a. Ngadda-rda-yinj, ngadda-djarrang,
1PL.EXCL.NF-put-REFL.PST 1PL.EXCL.NF-eat.PST

ngadda-makarninjdjanganj.
1PL.EXCL.NF-sing.PST

'We went in, we ate and we sang.' [IK1-160624_0001/01:18–22]

b. Ngemek **ngadbe** ngadda-makarninjdjanganj.
yet we.EXCL.PL 1PL.EXCL.NF-sing.PST

'We sang more.' [ibid./01:23–25]

Kunbarlang has several strategies for expressing coreference. All of them are discussed elsewhere, so here I merely list them and give cross-references to other parts of the grammar. One is the 'aforementioned' series of demonstratives (§4.5.3), which seemingly are passing out of use. A more actively used demonstrative with anaphoric functions is the class IV medial demonstrative *ngorro*. In its anaphoric use it always combines with other demonstratives or personal pronouns; in §4.5.3 I suggest that *ngorro* imparts the feature of givenness to the resulting pronominal complex.

Anaphoric binding constructions, i.e. reflexives and reciprocals, are detailed in §6.1.3. The main one is a verbal suffix that has both interpretations (the reciprocal arguably being a special case of the reflexive). There are, moreover, two non-verbal constructions: an anaphoric intensifier *bidju*, used for reflexives (§6.1.3.1), and a typologically rare analytic reciprocal construction that appears to have developed from a biclausal one (§6.1.3.2).

8 Complex syntax

The inner clausal structure and syntactic processes that happen within a single clause are covered in chapter 7. The present chapter concludes the description of Kunbarlang by discussing structures that involve more than one clause. There are two main classes of such structures: clausal coordination and subordination. Coordination is the subject of §8.1. It is done in Kunbarlang via juxtaposition of clauses or with the help of the conjunction *la*. This construction with *la*, however, has a wider range of functions than mere logical conjunction. One of its frequent uses is to encode causal relations (see §8.1 and §8.5.1). The subsequent section (§8.2) provides some typological and Australianist background to contextualise the ensuing discussion of subordinate structures in Kunbarlang. Subordination in Kunbarlang is represented by a range of finite subordinate clauses that can be verbal complements (§8.3), relative clauses modifying nouns (§8.4), or adverbial clauses (§8.5). There is rather little morphological marking (or lexical complementizers) for any of the subordinate clause types in Kunbarlang. It is interesting, therefore, to investigate the formal means signalling subordination (§§8.3.2–8.3.3) and diagnostics for particular structures (§8.4.2). Similar to many other languages (e.g. German or Swahili), there is some form-function overlap between the types of subordinate clauses, whereby some of the adverbial clause functions are served by free relatives (§§8.5.2–8.5.3).

8.1 Clausal coordination

In contrast to the various types of subordinate clauses described in sections 8.3–8.5 below, where the two combined clauses are not equal in their status (asymmetry), clausal coordination involves a set of clauses in a symmetrical relation. There are two main ways to coordinate clauses in Kunbarlang: juxtaposition (8.1) and coordinating with the conjunction *la* 'CONJ' (8.2).[1]

(8.1) Ka-burrun-kalng   kenda   ngorro   kadda-yunganj.
       3NSG.NF-3NSG.OBJ-get.PST DEM.PROX.LOC DEM.MED.IV 3PL.NF-lie.PST
       'They [Aboriginal people] got them [whitefellas], and they [the whitefellas] slept there.'   [IK1-160510_0001/05:22–25]

---

1 The same particle is used in Mawng (Singer et al. 2015) and in Eastern dialects of Bininj Kunwok, while in the other dialects the prevailing coordinator is *dja* (Alex Marley, p.c.).

(8.2) a. Nayi na-buk bidju bi-rnungu nayi mutikang ka-marnbum
NM.I I-person EMPH DAT-he.GEN NM.I car 3SG.NF-make.PST
la ka-rdakdjung bonj~bonj.
CONJ 3SG.NF-break.PST RDP~exactly

'The guy fixed his car, and/but it broke again.'

[IK1-180606_1SM1/29:05–19]

b. Ngunda kidda-ngulukdombuni **la** ka-bun-djarrang
not 3PL.IRR.PST-extinguish.IRR.PST CONJ 3SG.NF-3SG.OBJ-eat.PST
ngob.
all

'They did not put the fire out and it [the house] burnt down completely.'

[IK1-170530_1SY2/15:16–20]

Because of the extent of pro-drop in Kunbarlang, taken together with the fact that every verb must indicate its subject's person and number, it is not meaningful to contrast clausal coordination and VP-coordination when the subject is the same for two or more verbs. Thus, (8.3), containing only two fully inflected and juxtaposed verbs, can be analysed either way.

(8.3) Kadda-ngambiwam kadda-bukayinj.
3PL.NF-swim.PST 3PL.NF-rise.PST

'They swam and got out onto the shore.' [IK1-160510_0001/03:51]

The only Kunbarlang coordinator, the particle *la*, is not hard-wired with any discourse relations (like for instance contrast, or adversativity, as in the case of the English *but*). Besides the most typical use as a logical conjunction (as in the majority of the above examples) it can connect things that are in contrast (8.4) or even in a relation more typical for adverbial clauses, that of reason (e.g. 8.5), where it connects a consequence and its reason; see more examples in §8.5.1.

(8.4) Na-buk yimarnek ki-buddu-karlkkandji **la** kadda-rnay la
I-person like 3SG.NEG-3PL.OBJ-stalk.IRR.PST CONJ 3PL.NF-see.PST CONJ
kadda-bum.
3PL.NF-hit.PST

'He was going to sneak up on them, but they saw him and beat him.'

[IK1-160712_0001/00:40–01:40]

(8.5) Ngandji-ka **la** kadda-dja kabarr-ngan-midjbunj.
1PL.EXCL.FUT-go.NP CONJ 3PL.NF-stand.NP 3NSG.NF-1NSG.EXCL.OBJ-wait.NP

'We (exclusive) shall go, because [lit. 'and'] they are waiting for us.'

[IK1-180529_1SY1/01:56:31–34]

The particle *la* can be used in a (weak) disjunction (8.6), too:

(8.6) **Ngunda birlinj** kidda-ngundje la kidda-woh-kidang.
not how 3PL.IRR.PST-do.IRR.NP CONJ 3PL.IRR.PST-INCP-go.IRR.NP
'They can neither do anything nor walk properly.' [20060614IB/01:21–24]

Examples of coordination of constituents below the clause level can be found in §3.2.10.

8.2 Subordination: preliminaries

As an introduction to the ensuing discussion of the subordinate clauses in Kunbarlang I first give a brief overview of the types of subordination and of the formal means employed in subordinate constructions, both from the point of view of broader typology and from the Australianist perspective. Then I outline the distinctions between the main types of subordinate clauses in Kunbarlang and describe each type in turn.

Considering the full array of subordinate structures, Thompson, Longacre & Hwang (2007: 238) note that "[t]here are three devices which are typically found among languages of the world for marking subordinate clauses": (i) subordinating morphemes, (ii) special verb forms, and (iii) word order. In the typological literature three types of subordinate clauses are usually recognised (see e.g. Lehmann 1988 or Diessel 2001, among many others):

(i)   complement clauses   (section 8.3; Noonan 2007)
(ii) adverbial clauses   (section 8.5; Thompson, Longacre & Hwang 2007)
(iii) relative clauses   (section 8.4; Andrews 2007)

Diessel (2001: 435–6) offers the following distinguishing criteria for the three types. On the level of syntax, complement clauses are complements, while both adverbial and relative clauses are adjuncts. Semantically speaking, complement clauses are arguments of some matrix predicate, and the other two (being syntactic adjuncts) are modifiers: adverbial clauses modify the main clause or its verb phrase, and relatives modify a nominal constituent in the main clause. Finally, from the point of view of characteristic morphosyntactic marking, relative clauses contain a gap or a relative pronoun; adverbial clauses usually have an adverbial subordinator, which indicates the semantic relation between the main and the subordinate clause; and complement clauses are marked by a complementizer (including zero, as a special case). I shall use some of these criteria in the analysis of Kunbarlang below.

It has been noted in the typological literature that the distribution of subordination across languages of various structural profiles is not even. Specifically, there were claims that polysynthetic languages do not have (or only show weak development of) subordinate structures, and in particular non-finite constructions (Mithun 1984a, M. C. Baker 1996). Recent work on the Gunwinyguan languages has shown these generalisations to be overly strong: Nordlinger & Saulwick (2002) demonstrate that Rembarrnga has infinitives (even two types thereof), and Evans (2006) documents a wide variety of subordination strategies in Dalabon. On this spectrum, Kunbarlang falls into an intermediate position. There are no infinitives: all well-formed verbs must be finite. There are not many dedicated strategies to *mark* subordination either, save for a few subordinating conjunctions. However, syntactically Kunbarlang has all three structural types of subordinate clauses, all of them built with finite verbs. I give examples of these types and criteria for their recognition presently, after a brief exposition of the topic of subordination in the broad Australian context.

One of the topics in subordination that has received much attention in the Australianist literature is relative clause formation. In a very influential paper, Hale (1976) described a type of subordinate clause that is linearly unembedded within, or adjacent to, the matrix clause. He called this type the *adjoined relative clause* (henceforth AdjRC).[2] The focus of his paper was on Warlpiri and Kaytetye, although he mentions a number of other languages where similar structures have been found. In Warlpiri, futhermore, the AdjRC can serve functionally as a relative clause or as a temporal adverbial clause, specific examples often being ambiguous between the two readings (termed *NP-relative* and *T-relative*, respectively). The significance and impact of that work, as well as a recent revision of the adjoined relative clause hypothesis (Nordlinger 2006), is further explored in the section on Kunbarlang relative clauses (§8.4; see also Nordlinger 2014: 248–252 and references therein). Kunbarlang does not have the prototypical AdjRC-type clause, yet headless relatives fulfil the function of some adverbial subordinate clauses (see §8.5 for further detail).

Looking beyond the adjoined relative clause and similar constructions, one finds a wide variety of formal devices signalling subordination. In Thompson, Longacre & Hwang's (2007) terms, they fall primarily into two classes: special verb forms and subordinating morphemes. The first class is exemplified by Gooniyandi, where the verb of the subordinate clause must be in a non-indicative mood (McGregor 1988). The second class is represented both by dedicated complementizing morphemes (such as the subordinating prefixes in Dalabon (Evans 2006)) and by functional extensions of other types of morphology, perhaps most notably of case markers (known as the 'c-complementizing case', see Dench & Evans 1988). For an overview of major research topics in subordination in Australian indigenous languages, and for further references, see Nordlinger 2014: §7. Austin 1988 is a collection of original papers on various topics concerning complex sentences in a number of typologically and genetically diverse Australian languages.

---

[2] An important diagnostic is the possibility of the construction where the nominal head is linearly disjoint from the clause modifying it. Whereas in Warlpiri the AdjRC has to occur peripherally, Kaytetye shows both the possibility for the disjoint construction and that for linear integration of the RC within the matrix clause.

Even in closely related languages there can be a significant degree of variation. For instance, Dalabon and Bininj Kunwok, which belong to the same branch of the Gunwinyguan family as Kunbarlang, noticeably differ in the array of available formal means of marking subordination: whereas Bininj Kunwok reveals "a paucity of formally distinct subordinating structures" (Evans 2003a: 628, 646), Dalabon "possesses an elaborated set of structural options for signalling subordination overtly on the verb" (Evans 2006: 55). It should be pointed out, on the other hand, that the availability of those diverse subordinating structures is independent of their use by the speakers: in a two hundred clause Dalabon corpus surveyed by Evans (2006) only 3.9% of clauses are subordinate.

Kunbarlang is more similar to Bininj Kunwok than to Dalabon, in that it does not have an elaborate array of dedicated subordinating structures. However, the three major types of subordinate clauses can be recognized, according to the following criteria. COMPLEMENT CLAUSES (8.7) are complements of a matrix predicate, i.e. they are subcategorised for by a small set of matrix verbs that take clausal complements (see §8.3 for full description of this class).

(8.7) Nga-**mabulunj** [kanj-ka barbung].
1SG.NF-like.NP 3SG.FUT-go.NP fish
'I **want** him/her [to go fishing].' [IK1-170615_1SY2/25:52–54]

RELATIVE CLAUSES contain a gap in the relativisation site, which cannot be filled (as (8.8) shows; see §8.4 for more detail). They are adjuncts modifying nominals (headed RCs) or—in case there is no nominal head—themselves appear in the positions of noun phrases, i.e. as arguments or adjuncts of any predicate, without being restricted to the set of complement-taking verbs.

(8.8) Ka-maddjinj ka-mankang korro [kuyi ngadbe
3SG.NF-pierce.PST 3SG.NF-fall.PST DEM.MED.LOC NM.IV we.EXCL.PL

ngadda-rninganj (*korro)].
1PL.NF-sit.PST DEM.MED.LOC

'They shot it and it fell down to [where we were staying (*there)].'
[IK1-160701_0001/08:26–35]

Posture verbs like -*rna* 'to sit; live' normally can take a locative phrase, but (8.8) suggests that there is an obligatory gap in the position that is relativised over. See §8.4.2 for more details.

ADVERBIAL CLAUSES come in two main varieties: some are introduced by dedicated subordinating conjunctions (8.9); others are a residue class, formally identical to headless relatives, and distinguished as adverbial clauses on a functional basis, rather than formally. The subordinate clause in (8.8) above is an example of a free relative that functionally is a locative adverbial clause.

(8.9) Kirdimarrk   ka-rdulkkarrawarribin   [warri   na-buk=bonj
       man   3SG-tired   because   I-person=exactly
       ka-djung   wirdidj].
       3SG.NF-stab.PST   fire
       'The man is tired [because he was chopping firewood].'
                                                          [IK1-170607_1SM1/56:52–57]

These three types are discussed in detail in the sections that follow (§§8.3–8.5).

8.3 Complement clauses

Finite clauses in Kunbarlang can be complements to thought and speech verbs, as discussed in the bulk of this section, and to the verb *-marnbunj* 'to make', thus forming causatives. These analytic causatives are presented in §8.3.1, distinguished on functional grounds. In section 8.3.2 I provide a list of the functional elements that can appear between the matrix and the subordinate clause similar to complementizers. Section 8.3.3 discusses the tense/mood forms of complement clauses expressing desires.

A small set of thought and speech verbs in Kunbarlang are able to take subordinate clauses as complements. The most notable ones among them are: *-burrbunj* 'to know', *-burrdjuwa* 'to divulge; to tell', *-mabulunj* 'to want; to like', *-ngundje* 'to say / do', *-wardam* 'to ask (inquire)', and *-wakwanj* 'to not know'. The adjectives *-mak* 'good' and *-warri* 'bad' can also function as propositional attitude matrix predicates, in which case they inflect for class IV (8.10).

(8.10) Kun-**mak**   [kuyi   ngundji-nganj-kaburrk-ka].
       IV-good   NM.IV   2DU.FUT-HITH-COLL-go.NP
       'It's **good** [that you two will come together].'   [IK1-160505_0011/28:39–42]

Speech verbs embed reported speech clauses. In Kunbarlang there is a strong preference for DIRECT reported speech: this is the case when some utterance is reproduced verbatim. In particular, all indexicals (such as pronouns, for instance) must be interpreted relative to the reported situation and not the utterance situation. Consider (8.11):

(8.11) Ngabbard   ka-ngan-marnanj-**ngunda**   [kenda   kinj-rna
       father   3SG.NF-1SG.OBJ-BEN-do.PST   DEM.PROX.LOC   2SG.FUT-sit.NP
       karra   karlu   barndang].
       DEM.MED.LOC   NEG.PRED   trouble
       'My father **told** me [to stay here and not get into trouble].' [lit. 'told me: *Stay here, out of trouble!*']
                                                                    [IK1-180524_1SY2/34:47–52]

In (8.11) one can tell that the subordinate clause is direct speech, because the second person subject pronoun *kinj-* '2SG' refers to the same individual as the matrix clause benefactive object (i.e. the speaker of (8.11)), rather than to the utterance addressee. In other words, the matrix predicate here 'shifts' the setting in which that subject pronoun (and other indexicals) is to be understood. The intonational contours are varied: sometimes the direct speech of the subordinate clause is set off from the main by the pause, as in (8.12), but in some examples it is a single intonational contour.

(8.12) Babi   la   ka-bun-**wardam** || [bardarnungu ki-kalng   nayi
        later CONJ 3SG.NF-3SG.OBJ-ask.PST   why   2SG.NF-get.PST   NM.I

        carrot?]
        ENG

        'And then he **asked** her, [*Why did you buy the carrot?*]'
                                                                     [IK1-170615_1SY1/05:07–11]

Occasionally, however, the speech in the subordinate clause is INDIRECT, as in example (8.13). The fact that the embedded verb *ka-karrme* 'he has' has a third person pronominal prefix shows that this is indirect speech, otherwise the prefix would have been *nga-*, for the first person.

(8.13) La   ngunda ki-burrbuni   nayi   norno, babi   la
        CONJ   not   3SG.IRR.PST-know.IRR.PST   NM.I   snake   later CONJ

        ka-bun-marnanj-**ngunda**   [norno **ka**-karrme].
        3SG.NF-3SG.OBJ-BEN-do.PST   snake   3SG.NF-hold.NP

        'She did not know (that he had) that snake, but later he$_j$ **told** her [that he$_j$ had a snake].'   [IK1-170615_1SY1/04:21–30]

The remaining matrix verbs are exemplified below: *-burrbunj* 'to know; to think' (8.14),[3] *-mabulunj* 'to like; to want' (8.16), and *-wakwanj* 'to not know; to be ignorant' (8.17).

(8.14) Pat ka-**burrbunj**,   [na-kaybi   kanj-bun-rna~rna~rnanj   nayi
        P   3SG.NF-think.PST   I-who   3SG.FUT-3SG.OBJ-RDP~RDP~see.NP   NM.I

        ki-rnungu   ka-karrme   norno].
        I/II-he.GEN 3SG.NF-hold.NP   snake

        'Pat **thought**, [who would look after the snake that he has got]?'
                                                                     [IK1-170615_1SY1/01:39–51]

---

3 This example may perhaps be classified as *free indirect discourse* (FID) for its combination of the author's and the protagonist's speech: the indexicals are interpreted as in the indirect speech (for instance, not first but third person form of the verb *ka-karrme*), but the presence of the interrogative is rather characteristic of the direct reported speech (see Reboul, Delfitto & Fiorin 2016 for an overview of FID and further references). I refrain here from postulating this as a separate class of reported speech constructions in Kunbarlang. More data would be needed for an appropriate analysis.

(8.15) Nganj-**burrdjuwa** [kuyi ngadda-karrmeng Yiwarrudj
1SG.FUT-divulge.NP NM.IV 1PL.EXCL.NF-hold.PST church

kenda=bonj Warruwi].
DEM.PROX.LOC=exactly W

'I'll **tell** [how we had the Mission Centennial here at Warruwi].'

[IK1-160719_0001/00:13–19]

(8.16) La nga-**mabulunj** [na-kaybi-nuk kanj-bun-wunj neyang Fluffy
CONJ 1SG.NF-like.NP I-who-INDF 3SG.FUT-3SG.OBJ-give.NP food F

kuyi nganj-ka].
NM.IV 1SG.FUT-go.NP

'And I **would like** [someone to feed Fluffy when I'm gone].'

[IK1-160513_0011/01:58–02:21]

(8.17) ...la nga-**wakwanj** [barda ki-karrme]...
CONJ 1SG.NF-ignorant.NP what 2SG.NF-hold.NP

'...but I **do not know** [what you have]' [IK1-170615_1SY1/04:14]

8.3.1 Causatives

Causatives in Kunbarlang are formed analytically, using the verb *-marnbunj* 'to make' as the matrix causative verb. The caused event is expressed with a full clause directly following that matrix verb, as in (8.18). The clause that encodes the caused event is in brackets.

(8.18) Ngayi nga-**marnbum** [nayi nawalak ka-malakkidjanganj].
I 1SG.NF-make.PST NM.I child 3SG.NF-laugh.PST

'I made the child laugh.' [IK1-160505_0011/01:20:29–38]

The causation does not have to be volitional. Consider example (8.19b), where *kanak* 'sun' denotes the causer in a direct, non-volitional causative situation:[4]

(8.19) a. Picture ka-walarrbum ngob.
ENG 3SG.NF-white.PST all

'The picture is bleached.' [IK1-160523_0011/35:47–8]

---

4 The concept of 'white' is lexicalised as a verb in Kunbarlang, rather than an adjective.

b. Kanak ka-**marnbum**   [ka-walarrbum   nayi badjubadju].
       sun   3SG.NF-make.PST   3SG.NF-white.PST   NM.I shirt
       'The sun bleached out the shirt.'   [ibid./39:46–54]

   c. *Kanak ka-walarrbum   badjubadju.
        sun   3SG.NF-white.PST   shirt
        intended: 'The sun bleached out the shirt.'   [ibid./39:36]

The causee, i.e. the subject of the caused event verb, is indexed as the object in the verb *-marnbunj*. This is shown in (8.20), where the causee is first person. This example provides good evidence that these causatives are complex clauses (and not pairs of two distinct finite clauses), because the argument structure of the matrix clause does not make sense without the complement clause.

(8.20) Kurrana ka-**ngan-marnbunj**   [nga-walarrbunj].
        moon   3SG.NF-1SG.OBJ-make.NP   1SG.NF-white.NP
        'The moon makes me shine and appear white.'   [IK1-160523_0011/42:55]

Either of the higher or the lower verb can be negated with the expected difference in the reading. Consider the following paradigm in (8.21), with negation scoping over the causation event (b) or the caused event (c).[5]

(8.21) Field notes 2015-07-24, SY

   a. Nga-marnbu-djinj   nganj-djin.
       1SG.NF-make-REFL.PST   1SG.FUT-eat.NP
       'I made myself eat it.'

   b. **Ngunda ngarra-marnbu-dji**   nganj-djin.
       not   1SG.IRR.NP-make-REFL.IRR.NP   1SG.FUT-eat.NP
       'I didn't make myself eat it.'

   c. Nga-marnbu-djinj   **ngunda ngarra-djang**.
       1SG.NF-make-REFL.PST   not   1SG.IRR.NP-eat.IRR.NP
       'I made myself not want to eat.'

In the typological literature a conceptual distinction is made between *direct* and *indirect* causation (e.g. Shibatani & Pardeshi 2002; see also Horrack 2018: 68–71). The former prototypically involves a single event with immediate physical involvement of

---

5 Note the contrast of this pattern to the irrealis spreading found in the desire constructions (§8.3.3). In the Kunbarlang causatives, it is possible that only the matrix verb is in the irrealis, while in desire constructions the embedded verb has to be in the irrealis whenever the matrix one is.

the causer and (a fully patientive) causee (e.g. *The moon makes me shine*). The latter prototypically consists of two sub-events, each with its own agent (e.g. *Mother made me eat porridge*). In Kunbarlang there is no morphosyntactic difference between direct and indirect causation. However, indirect causation, probably partially due to its more pragmatic, open-to-interpretation nature, can be expressed with the verb *-ngundje* 'say; do', as in (8.22):

(8.22) Ngunda   ki-mabuluni   ki-buni=ngurr,   babi
       not   3SG.IRR.PST-like.IRR.PST   3SG.IRR.PST-hit.IRR.PST=rippled   later
       la   **nga-marnanj-ngunda ka-bum=ngurr**.
       CONJ   1SG.NF-BEN-do.PST   3SG.NF-hit.PST=rippled

'He did not want to wash [the dishes], but later **I told him to** and he washed them.'   [IK1-170608_1SY1/24:53–25:22]

Since there is no lability in Kunbarlang (see, for instance, §6.2), no predicate can just take an extra causer and become a causative predicate, hence the ungrammaticality of (8.19c). Kunbarlang does not have any productive morphological means of marking causativity, unlike some other Gunwinyguan languages. For instance, causative suffixes are found in Anindilyakwa (van Egmond 2012: 172ff.) and Wubuy (Horrack 2014), but in other languages complex predicate formation serves this function: in Bininj Kunwok, verbal incorporation into the verbs *-we* 'to throw', *-wo* 'give' and the transitive thematic *-ke* forms causatives (Evans 2003a: 539ff), and in Rembarrnga incorporation into *-ga* 'to take' and *-wa* 'to follow' has the same function (Saulwick 2003: ch. 8). Kunbarlang shows reflexes of these structures in some lexicalised causatives, where the thematic is *-wunj* 'to give'. Known verbs that contain this as the causative thematic are *-djuhmiwunj* 'to shorten', *-kelkwunj* 'to soften', *-makwunj* 'to decorate', *-monekwunj* 'to warm someone up', *-morewunj* 'to fold; to muster', *-rayekwunj* 'to tighten; to fix in a position', *-worlngunj* 'to (re)heat', and probably also *-djawunj* 'to feed' and *-djurrkwunj* 'to annoy'. Some of the prepounds are easily identifiable as adjectives (*-djuhmi* 'short', *-mak* 'good', *-more* 'close together', *-rayek* 'hard') or adverbs (*monek* 'warm'). Even though not productively, a few of these stems participate in a lexicalised causative-inchoative alternation, achieved by varying the thematic. Compare the causative formation from the adjectival prepound *rayek* 'hard' in (8.23a) and the corresponding inchoative formation (8.23b):

(8.23) a. Nga-**rayek.wunj**   ninda   door la   ka-bilibilayi.
          1SG.NF-tighten.NP DEM.PROX.I ENG   CONJ   3SG.NF-sway.NP
         'I'm jamming the door, because it is swinging open.'
                                               [IK1-180521_2SY1/14:54–59]

       b. Ngunda ngarra-mabulu   mayi   ka-**rayek.minj**.
          not   1SG.IRR.NP-like.IRR.NP   NM.III 3SG.NF-harden.PST
         'I don't like [bread] which has dried/hardened.'
                                              [IK1-160827_0001/22:55–58]

Tab. 8.1: Combinations of the major matrix predicates and subordinate clause markers

	marnbunj 'make'	mabulunj 'like; want'	ngundje 'say; do'	wakwanj 'not know'	burrbunj 'know'	wardam 'ask'
kuyi	-	✓	✓	✓	✓	✓
EmQu	-	?	-	✓	✓	✓
yidok	-	?	-	-	-	✓
yimarne(k)	-	✓	✓	%	?	-

In all of these verbs (except 'to feed', 'to annoy' and 'to reheat') prepounds are able to combine with the inchoative thematic -*mi*, yielding respective readings.

8.3.2 Elements functioning as complementizers

There are no dedicated complementizers for sentential complements in Kunbarlang. However, there are three functional elements that can occur in embedded clauses, effectively as complementizers. They are:
- *kuyi*—the class IV noun marker (§4.3; examples (8.10) and (8.15) above)
- *yidok*—the interrogative particle also used in root polar questions (§7.4.1; example (8.24) below)
- *yimarne(k)*—the similative and quotative particle (examples (8.4) or (8.29))

(8.24) Ka-ngan-**wardam** [yidok shop ka-bum=dol].
3SG.NF-1SG.OBJ-ask.PST Q ENG 3SG.NF-hit.PST=obstruct
'S/he **asked** me [whether the shop was closed].' [IK1-180604_1SM1/24:47–51]

The subordinate clause can be an indirect question, with a *wh*-pronoun at its left edge (as in examples (8.14) and (8.25)).

(8.25) Nga-**wakwanj** [na-kaybi ka-kinjang mayi birradja].
1SG.NF-ignorant.NP I-who 3SG.NF-cook.PST NM.III rice
'I **don't know** [who cooked the rice].' [IK1-160805_0001/22:47–23:09]

Every predicate can only select a subset of these complementizing markers/constructions to combine with. The causative matrix verb *-marnbunj* 'to make' (§8.3.1) can only take bare complement clauses. Table 8.1 summarises the combinations (*EmQu* stands for 'embedded question' and the % sign means that speakers are divided on the combinability of *-wakwanj* with *yimarne(k)*).

There are three combinations in table 8.1 that I am not certain about, although I think they are impossible; these are indicated by the question marks. However, it is important to note that these complementizer-like elements are completely optional.

Any of these predicates can take a subordinate clause complement without additional marking.

8.3.3 Tense and mood forms in the expressions of desires

There are no infinitives in Kunbarlang, i.e. all verb forms are finite (see §8.2; also chapters 3 and 5). Thus, there are no equivalents to control or raising constructions. In the majority of cases the use of the tenses and moods is absolute, i.e. not dependent on the neighbouring verbs (including the matrix verb; see §5.5 on tense and mood semantics). There is, however, one interesting exception to this generalisation, viz. constructions with the matrix verb -*mabulunj* 'to want; to like'.

I distinguish the following 3 cases of its use with a clausal complement:
- actual wishes, which are expressions of desire in the present, or a fulfilled desire in the past
- counterfactual wishes, which are akin to counterfactual conditionals (§8.5.4.2) in the sense that they express desires impossible to fulfil at the relevant point in time
- negative wishes, which involve negation of the matrix verb and the spreading of the irrealis marking into the subordinate clause (*mood spreading*, as I call it)

In expression of the actual wishes, the subordinate verb is in the realis mood, and its tense depends on that of the matrix verb in a straightforward way: if -*mabulunj* is non-past, the subordinate verb is in the future (8.26a); if -*mabulunj* is in the past, the subordinate verb is in the past (8.26b).

(8.26) a. Djidda-nganj-ka=way **nga-mabulunj** [**ngarrki-rna**
 2PL.FUT-HITH-go.NP=HITH 1SG.NF-like.NP 1.INCL.FUT-sit.NP
 ngarrki-wokdja].
 1.INCL.FUT-talk.NP
 'Come over, I'd **like** [**to sit and talk** with you].' [200150413IOv01/10:47]

b. Ngayi **nga-mabuluy** [**nga-djarrang** ngorro].
 I 1SG.NF-like.PST 1SG.NF-eat.PST DEM.MED.IV
 'I **wanted** [**to eat**, so I ate].' [IK1-170613_1SM1/35:26]

Example (8.26b) highlights an important feature of the desire constructions in Kunbarlang: the speaker must convey whether the wish is consummated or not (unlike in English, where a verb such as *want* does not require—or indeed make it possible—to express the outcome of the wishing). Contrast (8.26b), where the realis past form of the subordinate verb entails that the wish was fulfilled, with a past tense counterfactual wish in (8.27), which unambiguously indicates that the wishing was in vain:

(8.27) **Nga-mabuluy** [**ngay-djarri**]   la   karlu,
        1SG.NF-like.PST 1SG.IRR.PST-eat.IRR.PST CONJ NEG.PRED

   kadda-djarda-bum=dol   kuyi   shop.
   3PL.NF-mouth-hit.PST=obstruct NM.IV   ENG

   'I **wanted** [**to eat**], but no, the shop was closed.'   [IK1-170613_1SM1/36:13–20]

Example (8.27) shows the irrealis past form, which the subordinate verb takes in past tense counterfactual wishes. Present tense counterfactual wishes, in turn, employ the irrealis non-past form. The irrealis mood is obligatory, as illustrated in (8.28):

(8.28) IK1-170614_1PG1/48:20–50:11

   a. Benbe   **nga-mabuluy**   [**ngay-kangkayi**   korro
       yesterday   1SG.NF-like.PST   1SG.IRR.PST-go.IRR.PST   DEM.MED.LOC

       mandandi] la   karlu   kabbala.
       mainland   CONJ NEG.PRED boat

       'Yesterday I **wanted** [**to go** to the mainland], but didn't have a boat.'

   b. *Benbe   **nga-mabuluy**   [**nganj-ka** /   **nga-kidanj**   korro
       yesterday   1SG.NF-like.PST   1SG.FUT-go.NP   1SG.NF-go.PST   DEM.MED.LOC

       mandandi] la   karlu   kabbala.
       mainland   CONJ NEG.PRED boat

       intended: 'Yesterday I wanted to go to the mainland, but didn't have a boat.'

The subject of the subordinate clause does not have to co-refer with the matrix subject:

(8.29) Nga-**mabuluy**   [yimarne   ki-kangkayini   barbung]   la
        1SG.NF-like.PST   like   3SG.IRR.PST-go.IRR.PST   fish   CONJ

   ka-ngunda   karlu   ngunda   ngarra-mabulu.
   3SG.NF-do.PST   NEG.PRED   not   1SG.IRR.NP-like.IRR.NP

   'I **wanted** [**him to go fishing**], but he said *No I don't want to*.'
                                                          [IK1-170615_1SY2/33:26–56]

The embedded clause subject is not constrained by the higher clause configuration, but rather freely indicated by the personal prefix. In this respect, Kunbarlang can be said to not have any *control verbs*.[6]

We see from the above discussion that the use of the realis or irrealis mood of the subordinate verb can differentiate the actual and counterfactual wishes, while the

---

[6] This might be a corollary of not having infinitive forms in Kunbarlang.

matrix verbs remains in the realis. In the negative wishes, however, we find a tense and mood agreement between the matrix and the subordinate verbs. Similar to English, where the negation normally appears in the higher clause regardless of its actual scope, in Kunbarlang the negation is also found in the higher clause. Since verbs in scope of negation must be in the irrealis form (see §7.3), the matrix verb is irrealis. What is interesting is that the subordinate verb must also be in the irrealis (8.30). This seems to be motivated morphosyntactically, rather than semantically.

(8.30) a. Ka-mulmul-kalng banikkin, la ngunda **ki-mabulu**
 3SG.NF-many-get.PST dish CONJ not 3SG.IRR.NP-like.IRR.NP
 [**ki-bu**=ngurr].
 3SG.IRR.NP-hit.IRR.NP=rippled
 'S/he has got a lot of dishes but doesn't **want** [to **wash** them].'
 [IK1-170608_1SY1/17:51–56]

b. *Ngunda ki-mabulu **kanj-bunj**=ngurr.
 not 3SG.IRR.NP like.IRR.NP 3SG.FUT-hit.NP=rippled
 intended: 'S/he does not want to wash it.' [ibid./18:50–59]

This pattern contrasts with that in the causatives, where the negation-triggered irrealis is confined to that verb which is in the scope of negation (see §8.3.1). Furthermore, in desire constructions, if there are several subordinate verbs, the negation spreads over all of them (8.31):

(8.31) Ngunda ngarra-**mabulu** [malayi **ngarra-kidang**
 not 1SG.IRR.NP-like.IRR.NP tomorrow 1SG.IRR.NP-go.IRR.NP
 ngarra-rda-yi school].
 1SG.IRR.NP-put-REFL.IRR.NP ENG
 'I don't want to go to school tomorrow.'
 [IK1-160704_0001/01:26:59 and notes]

A more literal rendition of (8.31) could be something along the lines of 'I don't want it that tomorrow I would go and I would enter school.' As this example shows, in case there are juxtaposed subordinate verbs, they all take on the irrealis form. The tense of the subordinate verb also needs to correspond to that of the matrix one. Thus, while the above examples show the non-past irrealis forms (for future temporal point), example (8.32) below is in irrealis past (as a report of a negative wish at a past temporal point):

(8.32) Benbe   ninda   ngunda **ki-mabuluni**
       yesterday DEM.PROX.I   not   3SG.IRR.PST-like.IRR.PST
  [**ki-buni**=ngurr].
  3SG.IRR.PST-hit.IRR.PST=rippled
  'This guy did not want to wash [the dishes] yesterday [implies: and did not do them].'   [IK1-170608_1SY1/22:51–58]

The inference that the dishes were never done is not an entailment, and can be cancelled, as shown by (8.33), an elaboration on (8.32):

(8.33) a. Ngunda ki-mabuluni   ki-buni=ngurr,   **babi**
          not   3SG.IRR.PST-like.IRR.PST 3SG.IRR.PST-hit.IRR.PST=rippled later
    la   nga-marnanj-ngunda **ka-bum=ngurr**.
    CONJ   1SG.NF-BEN-do.PST   3SG.NF-hit.PST=rippled
    'He did not want to wash [the dishes], but later I told him to and he washed them.'   [IK1-170608_1SY1/24:53–25:22]
  b. *Benbe   ngunda ki-mabuluni   ka-bum=ngurr.
     yesterday not   3SG.IRR.PST-like.IRR.PST 3SG.NF-hit.PST=rippled
     intended: 'He did not want to, but washed [the dishes].'   [ibid./24:15–20]

8.4 Relativisation

Relative clauses are a type of subordinate clause which modify a main clause noun phrase (or some other aspect of the matrix clause, such as its temporal point). Thus, semantically they are used to characterise a participant of one event (the matrix clause event) through their participation in another event, described by the relative clause, which is subordinate (for various definitions and discussion see Keenan & Comrie 1977, Andrews 2007, Lander 2012: §0.1.1, among many others). Thus, prototypical relative clauses are clausal modifiers for nominals, although other kinds exist as well. Consider a Kunbarlang example (8.34):

(8.34) Mukka **mabudj**   [mayi ka-rna   ka-ngarrkun-wunj]
       it.III cheeky_yam   NM.III 3SG.NF-sit.NP 3SG.NF-1.INCL.OBJ-give.NP
       man-warri.
       III-bad
  'The cheeky yam that he's always giving us is rubbish.'
                        [IK1-180606_2SY1/01:16:59–17:05]

In (8.34), the main proposition is *That cheeky yam is rubbish*, expressed in Kunbarlang: *Mayi mabudj manwarri*. Its subject, *mayi mabudj* 'the cheeky yam' is modified by the relative clause *mayi ka-rna ka-ngarrkun-wunj* 'which he's always giving us'. The relative clause makes the reference more specific by describing the yam as the object in the situation of giving. This section goes into the details of how such clauses are built in Kunbarlang and what different types there are.

Languages vary in the strategies used for relative clause formation, but remarkably, all natural languages seem to have some kind of relativisation (Polinsky 2016: 20).[7] Typological classifications include the following dimensions (cf. Bianchi 2002: 197; de Vries (2002: 17–18) offers a comprehensive list of 11 parameters):
– presence or absence of a head noun (i.e. headed vs. free relatives);
– the nature of the relativisation site (the position/grammatical function in the subordinate clause that corresponds to the characterised participant): a gap or a resumptive pronoun;
– the nature of the relative pronoun: phonologically overt or a null one;
– the syntactic relation between the head and the relative clause

It is important to keep in mind that relativisation in Australian languages has been the subject of some controversy: some have interpreted Hale's (1976) seminal paper on the 'adjoined relative clause' (AdjRC) to mean that there are no relative clauses in Warlpiri and other languages of the continent, and probably even no syntactic subordination (cf. the discussion by Nordlinger (2006), who calls this type of subordination 'general modifying subordinate clause'). The structure that Hale described is a polyfunctional subordinate clause type that can have both adverbial and relative interpretations, and that—in the relative clause function—may be linearly disjoint from its head (8.35),[8] indeed with a preference to appear on the edge of the matrix clause.

(8.35) Warlpiri (Hale 1976: 78)

ŋatjulu-ḷu ø-na **yankiri** pantu-ṇu, [kutja-lpa ŋapa ŋa-ṇu].
I-ERG AUX emu spear-PST COMP-AUX water drink-PST
'I speared the **emu** which was/while it was drinking water.'

Example (8.35) illustrates two important characteristics of the AdjRC. One is the lack of linear adjacency between the head and the RC. The other is the interpretation, ambiguous between a relative ('NP-relative') and a co-temporal adverbial ('T-relative'). Over time it has become the prevailing view that there is one major and uniform type

---

[7] Notice that this holds also of Pirahã, a Mura language of Brazil that has been the subject of much debate regarding embedding, which, however, has relativisation of the CORRELATIVE type (Everett 1986: 275–7).
[8] The transcription and glosses are original, boldface and bracketing mine—IK.

of clause combination in Australian languages, one involving some kind of adjunction (instead of syntactic subordination). Recently, Nordlinger (2006) revisited the issue and forcefully argued (in particular, based on Wambaya data) for the following theses:
- Hale's (1976) term *embedded*, a linear order notion, should not be confused with *subordinate*, a structural notion, so the fact that Hale describes clauses as not being embedded in the main clause, does not necessarily mean they are not subordinate structures
- despite the fact that many constructions share certain features of the AdjRC, the actual structures across different languages are much more diverse
- for a given structure, having properties of the AdjRC does not preclude syntactic subordination, and a subordinate analysis is appropriate at least for some Australian languages

With this in mind, I turn to Kunbarlang relativisation. I will arrive at conclusions similar to Nordlinger's (2006): I find certain features of the AdjRC archetype in Kunbarlang, too, but argue that the Kunbarlang relative structures are truly subordinate. In what follows, I first present the taxonomy of Kunbarlang relative clauses (§8.4.1) and then argue for their true subordinate status (§8.4.2). The accessibility of various grammatical functions for relativisation is discussed in §8.4.3.

8.4.1 Types of Kunbarlang relative clauses

There are no dedicated morphosyntactic markers of relativisation in Kunbarlang: neither relative pronouns (words like the English *which*) nor complementizers (words like the English *that* in *the cat that meows*). The verb in the relative clause does not have any marking. Best diagnostics are syntactic, and are discussed in detail in §8.4.2. However, typically a noun marker (§4.3) is found with a relative clause, signalling that a fragment that looks like a clause is in fact nominal material syntactically.

I divide the relative constructions in Kunbarlang into two major types: the headed RCs (§8.4.1.1) and the free RCs (§8.4.1.2), based on the presence of a head noun in the matrix clause. The following sections discuss them in turn.

8.4.1.1 Headed relative clauses
A typical headed relative clause in Kunbarlang is exemplified in (8.36) and (8.38). Throughout this section I will enclose relative clauses in examples in square brackets with the subscript "RC": [$_{RC}$...]. Besides that, heads are highlighted with **boldface** when they are present.

(8.36) Ngayi   mimdom-mimdom   kadda-mabuluy   nayi   **djurra**   [_RC_ngayi
       NM.PL   RDP~old.person   3PL.NF-like.PST   NM.I   paper   I
       nga-buddu-wuy].
       1SG.NF-3PL.OBJ-give.PST

'The elders liked the **book** [that I gave them].'   [IK1-160505_0011/7:03–7:25]

The substring of (8.36) that we are interested in here is *nayi djurra ngayi nga-buddu-wuy* 'the book that I gave them'. It showcases all the ingredients of a Kunbarlang noun phrase that contains a headed relative clause: a NOUN MARKER *nayi*, a head noun (*djurra* 'paper, book') and a fragment that would be a well-formed finite clause on its own: *ngayi ngabudduwuy* 'I gave [it] to them'. The relative clause predicate is finite, the full NP is absent from the relativisation site, but it is not at all unusual for a nominal phrase that encodes an argument to not be present. The noun marker agrees in the noun class with the head noun.

Consider another example of a headed relative clause from spontaneous discourse (8.37):

(8.37) ...kadda-kalng || na-buk-ma   dead body   la   **kirdimarrk**   [_RC_nayi
        3PL.NF-get.PST   I-person-CONTR   ENG ENG   CONJ   man   NM.I
        ka-nganda.rlakwang].
        3SG.NF-hurl.PST

'...they took the dead body and the man who threw the spear.'
[20060620IB03/18:37–18:46]

Again, in (8.37) one finds all the characteristic features of a Kunbarlang RC. The difference from (8.36) is that the head noun *kirdimarrk* 'man' is directly followed (rather than preceded) by the noun marker (*nayi*); then a clause (in this case consisting of a single verb *ka-ngandarlakwang* 's/he hurled it') follows the noun marker. The full NP is again absent from the relativisation site, namely the subject of the subordinate clause, but the subject agreement for that argument is in place and in its usual form. As far as the position of the noun markers is concerned, they enjoy the same freedom of placement as in other types of NPs. In example (8.41a) below the noun marker *mayi* occurs twice: immediately preceding the head noun and between the head and the rest of the relative clause. The general schema for the prototypical headed RC in Kunbarlang is thus as follows:
- NM—Head—RC (8.36)
- Head—NM—RC (8.37)
- NM—Head—NM—RC (8.40b)

In locative relative relatives, the medial locative demonstrative *korro/karra* is found instead of the noun marker (8.38).

(8.38) Kadda-kidanj kun-barrkidbe **yalbi** [korro njunjuk ka-yuwa].
3PL.NF-go.PST IV-other country DEM.MED.LOC water 3SG.NF-lie.NP
'They went to another country where there is water.'
[IK1-160726_0001/07:29–40]

Examples of headed relative clauses that do not use a single noun marker seem extremely rare (8.39) and are corrected to include one or two noun markers in elicitation (e.g. (8.40)).

(8.39) Ngadda-bardidjarrang **cuppa tea** [RCkabba-ngarrun-wuy].
1PL.EXCL.NF-drink.PST ENG ENG 3NSG.NF-1NSG.OBJ-give.PST
'We drank a cup of tea that they gave us.' [20060901IB02/01:09–11]

(8.40) IK1-170620_1SY1/05:22–36

a. *Kadda-kalng **kirdimarrk** [RCka-ngandarlakwang].
3SG.NF-get.PST man 3SG.NF-hurl.PST
intended: 'They took the man who threw the spear.'

b. Kadda-nganj-kidanj kadda-kalng nayi **kirdimarrk** [RCnayi
3PL.NF-HITH-go.PST 3SG.NF-get.PST NM.I man NM.I
ka-ngandarlakwang].
3SG.NF-hurl.PST
'They came and took the man who threw the spear.'

As (8.40) shows, when offered relative clauses constructed without noun markers at all, a speaker would correct it, so that in this particular case there are two noun markers, one on either side of the head noun.

The following examples show noun marker agreement with the head for classes III (8.41a) and IV (8.41b):

(8.41) a. Ngal-buk marrek ki-djang mayi **kandiddjawa**
II-person not 3SG.IRR.NP-eat.IRR.NP NM.III bread
[RCmayi ngarrka ngarrk-karrme] la ngundjida-wunj mayi
NM.III we.INCL 1.INCL.NF-hold.NP CONJ 2PL.FUT-give.NP NM.III
kandiddjawa [RCngal-buk ka-nganj-kankinj].
bread II-person 3SG.NF-HITH-take.PST
'She won't eat the **bread** [that we have], give her the **bread** [that she brought].' [IK1-160505_0011/55:23–36]

b. Ngondo **njunjuk** [kuyi nayi kirdimarrk ka-bardi-rdam].
DEM.PROX.IV water NM.IV NM.I man 3SG.NF-liquid-put.PST
'This is the **puddle** [that the man poured].' [ibid./01:04:24–29]

The fact that the noun markers agree with the head noun puts them closer to relative pronouns than relative complementizers (according to a classic diagnostic due to Kayne (1975)), but given their wider distribution, i.e. the ability to occur in all NPs, they cannot be classified as proper relative pronouns, in the sense of that being their defining function. Furthermore, their freedom of placement on both sides of the head noun is untypical of relative pronouns.

In terms of respective arrangement of the head and the RC, from a typological viewpoint, one can say that Kunbarlang headed relative clauses are POSTNOMINAL, or HEAD-INITIAL. In elicitations, however, other syntactic types were recorded as well: CIRCUMNOMINAL (HEAD-INTERNAL; 8.42) and, sometimes, PRENOMINAL (HEAD-FINAL; 8.43).[9]

(8.42) a. Ngayi mimdom-mimdom   kadda-mabuluy [$_{RC}$ngudda **djurra**
          NM.PL RDP~old.person   3PL-like.PST   you   paper
          ki-buddu-wuy].
          2SG.NF-3PL.OBJ-give.PST
          'The elders liked the **books** that you gave them.'
          [IK1-160505_0011/9:12–18]

    b. Ngayi nganj-bunj   [$_{RC}$nayi benbe   **durduk**
       I   1SG.FUT-hit.NP   NM.I   yesterday dog

       ka-ngan-beyang]   malayi.
       3SG.NF-1SG.OBJ-bite.PST tomorrow
       'I'll hit tomorrow the **dog** that bit me yesterday.'
       [IK1-160822_0001/12:48]

In both examples in (8.42) the head noun (shown in boldface print) is located linearly within the relative clause, unlike being on its left edge, as in all examples shown previously, or its right edge, as in (8.43).

(8.43) Nginda   kanj-kinje   [$_{RC}$nayi ninda
       DEM.PROX.II 3SG.FUT-cook.NP NM.I   DEM.PROX.I

       ka-djarramarramaddjiyinj] nayi   **barbung**.
       3SG.NF-buy.PST   NM.I   fish
       'She will cook the **fish** that he bought.'   [IK1-160701_0001/17:48–53]

---

9 Sometimes speakers accept examples and translate them, but would not repeat (e.g. 8.42), but other times they repeat as well (e.g. 8.43). Crucially, these examples always had to be first constructed by the linguist.

It must be pointed out that both head-final and especially head-internal RCs mainly occur in elicitation. That is, Kunbarlang appears to allow construction of circumnominal and prenominal RCs, but perhaps these types are not as natural as the postnominal RCs. At the same time, such a preference might have been shaped by the contact with English, which only has postnominal RCs. There are, however, occasional spontaneous examples like (8.44), which I also analyse as relative clauses.

(8.44) Karrakenda [_{NP}mukka [_{RC}kabarra-bum] **marderr**]? — Manda.
        where   it.III   3DU.NF-hit.PST   creek   DEM.PROX.III
        'Where is the **creek** that they two made? — There.'
        [20150212AS01/02:06–09]

The verb of the relative clause precedes the head noun *marderr* 'creek', and thus it is an example of a head-final RC.[10] Finally, note that similarly to relative clauses, attributive adjectives in Kunbarlang are postnominal by default, according to my analysis of the noun phrase in §4.4.3.

I have established that Kunbarlang RCs are primarily head-initial, but can also be head-internal and head-final. These are all subtypes of EMBEDDED RCs, in the terminology of de Vries (2002).[11] The embedded RCs are those which form a constituent with the head, or at least are linearly adjacent to the head. While a full-blown paradigm of constituency tests is not available at the moment, some observations on linear order suggest that unity of the head and the relative clause is found at least sometimes. The examples to this point are (8.42b) for head-internal and (8.45) for head-initial RCs. Notice that in both of them the matrix clause material surrounds the relative clause: the RC separates the matrix adverb *malayi* 'tomorrow' from the rest of the matrix clause.

(8.45) Ngayi nganj-bunj   nayi   **durduk**   [_{RC}nayi benbe
        I   1SG.FUT-hit.NP   NM.I   dog   NM.I   yesterday

        ka-ngan-beyang]   malayi.
        3SG.NF-1SG.OBJ-bite.PST   tomorrow
        'I will hit the **dog** [that bit me yesterday] tomorrow.'
        [IK1-160811_0001/01:27:30]

De Vries (2002) further contrasts embedded RCs with CO-RELATIVES. These latter ones include EXTRAPOSED (or *right-dislocated*) relative clauses and Hale's (1976) adjoined relative clause. Unlike the linearly contiguous embedded RCs, the head of a co-relative

---

10 Notice, however, that from a structural point of view (8.44) admits of a head-internal construal as well. In order to tell such cases apart, one needs evidence from adverb placement; cf. (8.42b).
11 In his thesis on the syntax of relative clauses de Vries (2002) offers a systematisation of the proliferated terminology in this field; cf. his Figure 1 on page 21.

is linearly disjoint with the RC (and thus does not form a constituent together with the RC). It is possible to form co-relatives in Kunbarlang as well. In the following examples (subject relative (8.46a) and object relative (8.46b)) the head is separated from the relative clause by the matrix verb.[12]

(8.46) a. Ngayi nayi **kornobolo** nga-djung [_RC_ nayi
I NM.I wallaby 1SG.NF-stab.PST NM.I

ka-bardi-djarrang].
3SG.NF-liquid-eat.PST

'I speared a **wallaby** [that was drinking].' [IK1-160827_0001/48:06–14]

b. Ngayi nayi **kornobolo** nga-kinjang [_RC_ nayi ngudda
I NM.I wallaby 1SG.NF-cook.PST NM.I you

ki-djung].
2SG.NF-stab.PST

'I cooked the **wallaby** [that you speared].' [ibid./47:36–47]

In terms of semantic interpretation, all examples so far have shown RESTRICTIVE RCs. Restrictive RCs narrow down or specify the reference of the head noun, rather than just add some extra information about it. Consider the sentence (8.47):

(8.47) Nganj-buddu-wunj nayi kadda-buyu-bunjdje (ngayi) **barrayidjidj**
1SG.FUT-3PL.OBJ-give.NP NM.I 3PL.NF-PLURAC~lick.NP NM.PL kids

[_RC_ ngayi kanjbadda-nganj-ka malayi].
NM.PL 3PL.FUT-HITH-go.NP tomorrow

'I'm going to give a lolly to the **kids** that come tomorrow [i.e., whoever comes tomorrow, and only those ones].' [IK1-160505_0011/33:49–35:01]

As the comment in the translation explains, the relative clause specifies the reference of the head noun *barrayidjidj* 'kids'. Thus, it can be seen as providing an answer to the question 'Which kids am I going to give a lolly?', along the lines of 'Exactly those kids that will come tomorrow, and no other ones'. An alternative meaning, if the RC could be interpreted as a NON-RESTRICTIVE one, would have been 'I'm going to give a lolly to the kids, who will come tomorrow', i.e. there is a set of kids defined by the context, and I will give all of them lollies, and there is additional knowledge that those kids will come tomorrow. However, that is not a possible interpretation in Kunbarlang, according to the speakers' judgements.

---

[12] It is worth mentioning that the only examples of co-relatives in Kunbarlang I am aware of come from elicitation, just like the head-internal and head-final RCs.

Further evidence against non-restrictive RCs in Kunbarlang is scarce. Example (8.48a) is suggestive, as it shows impossibility to attach a relative clause to the first person pronoun *ngayi* 'I'. This is likely prohibited for the reason that uniquely referring NPs only allow non-restrictive modification. Example (8.48b) shows that attachment to pronouns should not be a problem per se.

(8.48) a. Ngayi (*nayi) nga-rna Mardbalk, nga-kalng kaburrk
I NM.I 1SG.NF-sit.NP M 1SG.NF-get.PST two
mudikang.
car
'I stay at Warruwi, I've got two cars.'
NOT: '*I, who live in Warruwi, have two cars.'
[IK1-160818_0021/49:12–45]

b. **Nukka** [RCnayi Warruwi ka-rna] ka-kalng kaburrk
he NM.I W. 3SG.NF-sit.NP 3SG.NF-get.PST two
mutikang.
car
'This man who lives in Warruwi has got two cars.' [Informant's translation: "He staying at Warruwi, he got two vehicle."] [ibid./47:11–15]

Having presented the headed RCs in Kunbarlang, I turn to the free relatives.

8.4.1.2 Free relative clauses

A free relative clause is one where there is no nominal head but the clause itself appears in a position where a noun can appear—as an argument or an adjunct to a verb. An example from spontaneous Kunbarlang discourse is in (8.49):

(8.49) Kadda-maddjing ka-mankang korro [RCngadbe
3PL.NF-pierce.PST 3SG.NF-fall.PST DEM.MED.LOC we.EXCL.PL
ngadda-rninganj].
1PL.EXCL.NF-sit.PST
'They shot [that plane] and it fell down (to) where we were staying.'
[20060620IB03/6:12–6:19]

In (8.49) the string *ngadbe ngadda-rninganj* 'we were staying' should be considered a free relative clause with locative meaning (i.e. functionally, an adverbial clause). It combines with the locative demonstrative *korro* (in the present case interpreted as 'to'), i.e. here the clause is found in the environment typical of nominals. On the other hand, the specification of the location of the stay is missing, although the predicate *-rna* 'sit; live', when used in the sense 'stay, live', normally subcategorises for a locative adjunct; cf. (8.50):

(8.50) Kadda-rninganj **korro** **rlobbel-rlobbel** kadda-rdukidanj
 3PL.NF-sit.PST DEM.MED.LOC RDP~outside 3PL.NF-look.PST
 bi-rnungu.
 DAT-he.GEN

 'They were sitting outside looking for him/waiting for him.'
 [20060620IB06/2:14–2:19]

But in (8.49), the locative adjunct of 'stayed' is relativised over, which makes the clause available to combine with *korro*. There are no formal indicators of its status as a relative clause other than its syntactic position following the demonstrative *korro* (which effectively functions as a locative preposition): in particular, there is no (overt) complementizer or relative pronoun.

Unlike the relativisation of the Locative thematic role, however, relativisation of other roles involves the use of a noun marker (8.51a). The variant in (8.51b) shows that the noun marker is obligatory. It may be the case that the demonstrative *korro* creates the required nominal context in an example like (8.49), but in its absence a noun marker is required for the same purpose.

(8.51) a. Dukulu ka-rlakwang bi-ngaybu [_RC_ nayi nga-kodjkodj-rda-yi].
 wind 3SG.NF-throw.PST DAT-I.GEN NM.I 1SG.NF-head-put-REFL.NP

 'Wind blew my hat off.' [lit. 'Wind threw off my (thing) that I insert my head into.'] [IK1-160805_0001/1:18:48–1:19:09]

 b. *Dukulu ka-rlakwang bi-ngaybu [nga-kodjkodj-rda-yi].
 wind 3SG.NF-throw.PST DAT-I.GEN 1SG.NF-head-put-REFL.NP

 intended: 'Wind blew my hat off me.' [IK1-160811_0001/01:05:20–30]

Example (8.51a) shows another use of free relatives—the formation of descriptions for novel concepts. Consider the noun phrase meaning 'my hat'. Morphosyntactically, *nayi nga-kodjkodjrdayi* is a combination of a noun marker with a verb/clause, which literally means "that [which] I insert head [into]". The phrase clearly refers to an entity, and the whole sentence cannot be interpreted as an asyndetic clausal conjunction 'Wind blew [it] off me; I put my head in [it]'. Both this structure and this use resemble the clauses with noun class markers in Ngan'gityemerri, which are also like relative clauses (Reid 1997).

Such relative clauses as in (8.51a) can have possessors, which further demonstrates their ontological status as referring expressions. The possessor in (8.51a) is *bingaybu*, the dative form of the first person pronoun. Example (8.52) manipulates the person of the possessor to rule out the possibility of the dative pronoun being construed as the affected argument (maleficiary):

(8.52) Dukulu   ka-rlakwang   **bi-rnungu**   [_RC_ nayi   ka-nga-nuy
         wind   3SG.NF-throw.PST   DAT-he.GEN   NM.I   3SG.NF-1SG.OBJ-give.PST

         nga-kodjkodj-rda-yinj].
         1SG.NF-head-put-REFL.PST

'Wind blew his hat off me.' [lit. 'Wind blew off **his** whatever he gave me that I put on.'] [IK1-160811_0001/01:19:11]

The possessor phrase in (8.52) is *birnungu* 'his', which confirms that a free relative clause in Kunbarlang can be a referring expression. Besides the meaning of the sentence, the possessor interpretation of that pronoun (rather than affected maleficiary) is evidenced by the person mismatch of this possessor pronoun and the personal prefixes on the embedded verb (which refers to the actual wearer).

Another example of this concept formation via free relative clauses is in (8.53), repeated from (8.47) above:

(8.53) Nganj-buddu-wunj   [_RC_ nayi   kadda-buyu-bunjdje]   (ngayi)
        1SG.FUT-3PL.OBJ-give.NP   NM.Cli   3PL.NF-PLURAC~lick.NP   NM.PL

        barrayidjidj   ngayi   kanjbadda-nganj-ka   malayi.
        kids   NM.PL   3PL.FUT-HITH-go.NP   tomorrow

'I'm going to give lolly to those kids that come tomorrow [whoever comes tomorrow, and only those ones].' [IK1-160505_0011/33:49–35:01]

In (8.53), the NP with the meaning '(a) lolly' is a free relative clause. In the discussion about how to express the concept of candy/lolly the speaker literally said the following: "when we say 'lolly', that's *nayi kaddabuyubunjdje*, like 'the one they chew' " (IK1-160505_0011/25:15), a commentary that suggests transparency of that structure to the speakers of Kunbarlang. It is worth noticing, too, that the expression was given with the noun marker—additional (even though somewhat indirect) evidence that the noun marker belongs to the relative clause, rather than being a fragment of some other preceding constituent.

Finally, turning KINSHIP VERBS (§3.2.4.1) into referential expressions is still another use of Kunbarlang free RCs (8.54).

(8.54) Ngayi,   Ngalbangardi,   Nakangila   la   [_RC_ ngayi   kabarra-rna],
        I   N   N   CONJ   NM.II   3DU.NF-sit.NP

        ngadda-rna.
        1PL.EXCL.NF-sit.NP

'I, Ngalbangardi, Nakangila and **his partner**, we are sitting here.'
[IK1-160726_0021/01:29–37]

The verb *-rna* 'to sit' in (8.54) is relativised, which enables it to be conjoined with other nouns within an argumental position.

8.4.2 Arguments for relativisation in Kunbarlang

There are a number of arguments in favour of postulating truly subordinate relative structures in Kunbarlang, as opposed to parataxis. These arguments may be grouped as follows:
- syntactic
  - RCs are clauses that appear in nominal environments
    * after/together with the noun markers (especially the headed RCs)
    * after the locative demonstrative *korro* (see §8.4.1.2)
  - it is impossible to overtly fill the relativisation site (see (8.55) below)
  - unavailability of the relativised argument for other operations (see (8.56) below)
  - the possibility to linearly embed the subordinate clause within the matrix clause (suggestive, but not compelling; (8.45))
- semantic: relative clause interpretation (less compelling than the syntactic arguments)
  - restrictive modification (cf. the discussion of (8.47) above)
  - anti-iconic temporal sequencing (8.57)
  - temporal restrictions with destruction verbs (8.58)

In the naturally occurring Kunbarlang relativisation there is no full NP in the position that is relativised over. Furthermore, in elicitation attempts to fill in that gap are prohibited. Consider the pair of examples in (8.55): the first one (8.55a) shows that the adverbial phrase *korro* 'there' can appropriately express location with the verb *-rna* 'sit'; the second one, a free relative clause in (8.55b), shows that when the location is relativised, *korro* becomes inappropriate.

(8.55) a. Ngadbe   ngadda-rninganj   **korro.**
       we.EXCL.PL   1PL.EXCL.NF-sit.PST   DEM.MED.LOC
       'We stayed over there.'   [IK1-160701_0001/09:54]

   b. Ka-maddjinj   ka-mankang   korro   [_{RC} kuyi   ngadbe
      3SG.NF-pierce.PST   3SG.NF-fall.PST   DEM.MED.LOC   NM.IV   we.EXCL.PL

      ngadda-rninganj (*__korro__)].
      1PL.NF-sit.PST   DEM.MED.LOC
      'They shot it and it fell down to where we were staying (*there).'
                                                                      [ibid./08:26–35]

I conclude that the relativisation site is a special position: the absence of the full NP in that position is principled and related to its subordinate syntactic status, but not reducible to a pro-drop and parataxis interpretation.

There is further evidence to that conclusion. In formal theories of the semantics of relativisation, it is standardly analysed in terms of an operator that binds into the relativisation site: λx[Jack built x],—thus turning a clause into a predicate.[13] I use this idea to construct the test as follows. If there is no relativisation but just parataxis with pro-drop of the relevant argument, then that argument must be freely available for binding by other operators. One such operator is the reflexive, which binds the verb's object (see §6.1.3). The parataxis view predicts that a putative relative clause can contain a reflexive; the relativisation view predicts incompatibility of the two. The data strongly support the relativisation view; consider (8.56):

(8.56) IK1-170620_1SY1/12:43–13:45

    a. Nga-yawanj nayi **doctor** [RCnayi ngayi nga-rdukkumung].
        1SG.NF-seek.NP NM.I ENG NM.I I 1SG.NF-cut.PST
        'I am looking for the doctor who I cut.'

    b. *Nga-yawanj nayi **doctor** [RCnayi ngayi nga-rdukkumi-**yinj**].
        1SG.NF-seek.NP NM.I ENG NM.I I 1SG.NF-cut-REFL.PST
        intended: 'I am looking for a doctor; I cut myself.'
        CF. *I am looking for a/the doctor who I cut myself.

    c. Ngayi nga-yawanj doctor **la** nga-rdukkumi-**yinj**.
        I 1SG.NF-seek.NP ENG CONJ 1SG.NF-cut-REFL.PST
        'I am looking for a doctor because I cut myself.'

The example at issue is (8.56a): we are testing if it has to have a relative clause construal (*the doctor who I cut*) or can be construed paratactically, with the object of the second clause routinely pro-dropped (*I'm looking for a/the doctor; I cut [him/her/it]*). If parataxis was possible in this structure, nothing would prevent reflexivisation of the second clause verb. However, (8.56b) shows that it is out (as its translation shows, this is exactly parallel to what happens in relative clauses in English, as well).[14] The only way to express the idea of *two events that do not share a participant* is to coordinate clauses (8.56c).[15]

Finally, I adduce two suggestive facts about the temporal interaction of the matrix and the relative clauses. One is the possible anti-iconic temporal sequencing of the clauses, which is thought to be a characteristic of subordinate structures (see footnote 21 on page 348). In example (8.57) the preceding (matrix) clause is in the future tense and the second (relative) clause is in the past, thus reverting the natural temporal progression.

---

13 See e.g. Heim & Kratzer (1998: ch.5).
14 As suggested above, a formal analysis would suggest that two operators compete for one object and thus fail. This is known as the NO VACUOUS QUANTIFICATION/ABSTRACTION constraint (Potts 2002, citing Bittner 1999).
15 See also §8.5.1 on purpose/reason clauses.

(8.57) Ngayi **nganj-kinje** nayi **kornobolo** [_RC_ nayi ngudda **ki-djung**].
I 1SG.FUT-cook.NP NM.I wallaroo NM.I you.SG 2SG.NF-stab.PST
'I will cook the wallaroo that you speared.' [IK1-160505_0011/38:25–29]

Building on this idea, one also finds that the extralinguistic knowledge of the natural progression of events constrains the temporal relation between clauses. Example (8.58) illustrates this for the natural progression of catching and cooking game:

(8.58) Ngayi nga-kinjang nayi **kornobolo** [_RC_ nayi ki-djung /
I 1SG.NF-cook.PST NM.I wallaby NM.I 2SG.NF-stab.PST
#kinj-djuwa].
2SG.FUT-stab.NP
'I cooked the wallaby that you {speared / #will spear}.'
[IK1-160505_0011/42:00–07]

On a paratactic reading, one could expect (8.58) with the future form *kinj-djuwa* 'you will spear it' to mean *I cooked a wallaby; you are going to spear a wallaby/something/it*. However, speakers do not accept such interpretation, and the infelicity suggests that there is a shared participant, i.e. the second clause is a relative that modifies the matrix clause object.

8.4.3 Accessibility hierarchy

In terms of Keenan & Comrie's (1977) ACCESSIBILITY HIERARCHY (8.59),[16] Kunbarlang relativisation with a gap can target positions up to the Possessor (as there are no constructionalised comparatives, see §7.7.4).

(8.59) SUBJECT > DIRECT OBJ > INDIRECT OBJ > OBLIQUE > POSSESSOR > STD. OF COMPAR.

In the terminology adopted in the present grammar (see §5.1), Keenan & Comrie's direct object corresponds to the primary object of monotransitives and the secondary object of ditransitives, and Keenan & Comrie's indirect object corresponds to the primary object of ditransitives, and their oblique corresponds to the benefactive and locative adjuncts.

The standard of comparison is not a grammatical function that is available in Kunbarlang (see §7.7.4). All other functions can be relativised. I give examples below in two groups, showing that both headed and free RCs can be formed from all those functions.

---

16 OBJ stands for 'object', STD. OF COMPAR. stands for 'standard of comparison'.

8.4.3.1 Headed relative clauses

Headed relative clauses in Kunbarlang can be formed from the subject (8.60b), the secondary object (Theme) of a ditransitive (8.61) (monotransitive objects are amply exemplified elsewhere in this section, e.g. (8.58)), the primary object (Recipient) of a ditransitive (8.62), the locative adjunct (8.63) and the benefactive object (8.64) (both Keenan & Comrie's (1977) oblique), and the possessor (8.65)–(8.66).

(8.60) a. Na-kaybi ka-ngan-marnanj-kalng nayi nga-djanga-rda-yi?
I-who 3SG.NF-1SG.OBJ-BEN-get.PST NM.I 1SG.NF-foot-put-REFL.NP
'Who took my shoes?' [lit. 'Who took it on me, that which I insert my feet into?']

b. **Nukka** ka-kalng bi-nungku [_{RC}nayi ka-nganj-kankinj neyang].
he 3SG.NF-get.PST DAT-you.GEN NM.I 3SG.NF-HITH-take.PST food
'The guy who brought us food got your shoes.' [lit. '**He** got them on you [who brought food].'] [IK1-160811_0001/46:21–47:20]

(8.61) Ngayi mimdom-mimdom kadda-mabuluy nayi **djurra** [_{RC}ngayi nga-buddu-wuy].
NM.PL RDP~old.person 3PL.NF-like.PST NM.I paper I 1SG.NF-3PL.OBJ-give.PST
'The elders liked the book that I gave them.' [IK1-160505_0011/7:03–7:25]

(8.62) Nga-karlmurdubbebeminj nayi **kirdimarrk** [_{RC}nayi nga-wuy djurra].
1SG.NF-forget.PST NM.I man NM.I 1SG.NF-give.PST paper
'I forgot the man who I gave the book to.' [IK1-170621_1SY1/14:02–06]

(8.63) Ka-rna karra **yalbi** [_{RC}karra ngadda-ka].
3SG.NF-sit.NP DEM.MED.LOC country DEM.MED.LOC 1PL.EXCL.NF-go.NP
'S/he lives in the country where we are going.' [IK1-170620_1SY1]

(8.64) Nj-ngan-rdukbanjdje **kirdimarrk** [_{RC}nayi ngudda ki-marnanj-kali barbung].
2SG.FUT-1SG.OBJ-show.NP man NM.I you.SG 2SG.NF-BEN-get.NP fish
'Show me the man that you are getting fish for.' [IK1-170621_1SY1/21:10]

(8.65) Nayi   djamun   ka-bun-wardam   **kirdimarrk**   [_RC_ nayi
        NM.I   policeman   3SG.NF-3SG.OBJ-ask.PST   man   NM.I
        kadda-kalng=kubirribirrkuk kabbala].
        3PL.NF-get=steal   boat
        'The policeman asked the man whose boat was stolen.'   [IK1-170621_1SY1]

Possessor relativisation in (8.65) is interesting in that it is almost identical in form to a subject RC. The masculine singular form of the noun marker (*nayi*) prevents the head noun *kirdimarrk* from being construed as a possible subject of the verb *kaddakalng*. If the noun marker had been plural (*ngayi*), however, the NP would have been ambiguous between 'the men whose boat was stolen' and 'the men who stole the boat'. In the case of possessor relativisation, a resumptive pronoun is permitted in the RC (bolded in (8.66)), which is typical of the grammatical roles low on the scale, according to Keenan & Comrie (1977).

(8.66) Nayi   djamun   ka-bun-wardam   **kirdimarrk**   [_RC_ nayi
        NM.I   policeman   3SG.NF-3SG.OBJ-ask.PST   man   NM.I
        kadda-kalng=kubirribirrkuk kabbala **kin-rnungu**].
        3SG.NF-get=steal   boat   I/II-he.GEN
        'The policeman asked the man whose boat was stolen.'   [IK1-170621_1SY1]

8.4.3.2 Free relative clauses

Free relative clauses in Kunbarlang can be formed from the subject (8.67), the primary object of a monotransitive (8.68) and the secondary object (Theme) of a ditransitive (8.69), the primary object (Recipient) of a ditransitive (8.70), the locative adjunct (8.71) and the possessor (8.72)–(8.73). I treat the relative clauses that begin with a demonstrative like the proximal class I *ninda* (e.g. (8.70), (8.72)) as free relatives, since they do not have a noun head.

(8.67) [_RC_ Ka-ngan-karrmeng]   ka-karlmu-karrmeng ka-kidanj.
              3SG.NF-1SG.OBJ-hold.PST   3SG.NF-ear-hold.PST 3SG.NF-go.PST
        'My father drove away.'   [Field notes 2016-04-27, SY]

(8.68) Ngayi nganj-kinje   [_RC_ nayi kinj-djuwa].
        I   1SG.FUT-cook.NP   NM.I 2SG.FUT-stab.NP
        'I'll cook whatever you spear.'   [IK1-160505_0011/40:56]

(8.69) Nga-rlakwang [RCnayi ngudda ki-ngan-wuy].
1SG.NF-throw.PST NM.I you.SG 2SG.NF-1SG.OBJ-give.PST
'I threw out what you gave me.' [IK1-170621_1SY1/17:30]

(8.70) Ninda nga-karlmurdubbebeminj [RCninda nayi nga-wuy
DEM.PROX.I 1SG.NF-forget.PST DEM.PROX.I NM.I 1SG.NF-give.PST
djurra].
paper
'I forgot who I gave the book to.' [IK1-170621_1SY1/14:54–15:00]

(8.71) Na-kaybi ka-ngan-marnanj-kalng [RCnayi nga-djanga-rda-yi]?
I-who 3SG.NF-1SG.OBJ-BEN-get.PST NM.I 1SG.NF-foot-put-REFL.NP
'Who took my shoes?' [lit. 'Who took it on me, that which I insert my feet into?']
[IK1-160811_0001/46:21–35]

(8.72) Nayi djamun ka-bun-wardam [RCninda
NM.I policeman 3SG.NF-3SG.OBJ-ask.PST DEM.PROX.I

kadda-kalng=kubirribirrkuk kabbala].
3SG.NF-get=steal boat
'The policeman asked the one whose boat was stolen.' [IK1-170621_1SY1]

Similarly to the headed example of the possessor RC above (8.65)–(8.66), in the possessor free relative a resumptive pronoun is permitted (8.73):

(8.73) Nayi djamun ka-bun-wardam [RCninda
NM.I policeman 3SG.NF-3SG.OBJ-ask.PST DEM.PROX.I

kadda-kalng=kubirribirrkuk kabbala **kin-rnungu**].
3SG.NF-get=steal boat I/II-he.GEN
'The policeman asked the one whose boat was stolen.' [IK1-170621_1SY1]

8.5 Adverbial clauses

Adverbial clauses are the clauses used as modifiers of predicates or propositions, such as the purpose clause in brackets in (8.74).

(8.74) Nga-yawanj   story mankurddel [**anu**   nganj-yolyolme
 1SG.NF-seek.NP ENG   giant   so_that   1SG.FUT-talk_about.NP
 bi-nungudbe].
 DAT-you.PL.GEN

'I am looking for the story about *mankurddel* [e.g. in a book], so that I can tell you [that story about him].' [IK1-170602_1SY1/08:29–41]

Here I generally follow Diessel's (2001) operational definition of adverbial clauses: he points out that they need to be distinguished (i) from other types of subordination (i.e. relative and complement clauses) and (ii) from clausal coordination. Contrasting adverbial clauses with other subordinate clauses, I assume that complement clauses are complements, while relative and adverbial clauses are adjuncts. Relatives, however, modify nouns, while adverbial clauses modify predicates/propositions. In addition to that, an externally headed relative clause contains a gap that cannot be filled, while an adverbial one does not have to have a gap.[17] See more on relativisation in §8.4.

With coordination, however, the picture is less clear, as Diessel (2001: 437) himself admits (see his paper for further references):[18] "Following recent crosslinguistic work on clause combining, I assume that (adverbial) subordination and (clausal) coordination form a continuum rather than two distinct types of interclausal connections." I classify juxtaposition and clauses connected with *la* 'CONJ' as coordinate structures, and it will be clear below that such structures can have the function of adverbial clauses.

As with the sentential complements (§8.3), the only formal marking of subordination of an adverbial clause found in Kunbarlang are free subordinating morphemes. Moreover, generally the functions that are typically carried out by subordinate adverbial clauses in the world's languages, are often expressed in Kunbarlang with coordination or juxtaposition, rather than subordination.[19] The following functional types of adverbial clauses have a conventionalised, if not always unique, form of expression in Kunbarlang:

(i)   purpose and cause
(ii) locative
(iii) time
(iv) conditional

---

[17] In fact, time and locative adverbial clauses in Kunbarlang are formally built as headless relatives. I single them out as functionally distinct headless relative clauses.

[18] Diessel cites a range of (morpho-)syntactic tests that help place a given construction towards one or the other end of the continuum (2001: 437–8), but application of these to Kunbarlang is also a task for future work.

[19] Thompson, Longacre & Hwang (2007: 241) cite Otomanguean languages as an example of "languages in which juxtaposition of clauses with certain aspect markers is more commonly exploited as a signal of clause relationships than are subordinating constructions."

8.5.1 Purpose and cause clauses

There are two subordinators for expression of intention or prior cause, *anu* 'so that' and *warri* 'because'. They are both infrequent, and other ways of indicating causal relations are often used (see below).

(8.75) Ka-ngan-yawanj [anu nganj-balkkikarrme].
3SG.NF-1SG.OBJ-seek.NP so_that 1SG.FUT-help.NP
'S/he is looking for me **so that I would help her/him**.'
[IK1-170602_1SY1/44:32–46]

The subordinator *anu* expresses a genuine purpose relation and is not compatible with a simple sequence of two events (8.76a), where the simple temporal connective is appropriate (8.76b):

(8.76) a. *Ka-warrenj ka-yawang sunglass anu ka-rnay.
3SG.NF-move.PST 3SG.NF-seek.PST ENG so_that 3SG.NF-see.PST
intended: 'S/he was looking for the glasses, then s/he found them.'
[IK1-170602_1SY1/43:02–13]

b. Ka-warrenj ka-yawang sunglass babi la ka-rnay.
3SG.NF-move.PST 3SG.NF-seek.PST ENG later CONJ 3SG.NF-see.PST
'S/he was looking for the glasses, then s/he found them.'
[ibid./41:59–42:05]

The subordinator *warri*, which expresses the reason/cause, can introduce finite clauses, as in (8.77a), or nominals, as in (8.77b).[20]

(8.77) a. Kun-barlang ngay-rnak-wokdji [warri ngayi
IV-Warlang 1SG.IRR.PST-LIM-speak.IRR.PST because I

ngarra-barlang].
1SG-Warlang
'I would just speak Kunbarlang **because I'm a Warlang man**.'
[RS1-140/20:48–53]

b. Nga-rnay kunwaral ka-djanganj nga-nganj-wom
1SG.NF-see.PST spirit 3SG.NF-stand.PST 1SG.NF-HITH-return.PST
warri munun.
because darkness
'I saw a spirit standing and returned **because of the darkness**.'
[IK1-160610_0001/45:48–46:03]

---

20 Given that the whole event of the example (8.77b) takes place in the past, *munun* is unlikely to be a predicative nominal '(it) was dark', as a copula would be expected in that case (see §7.7.1).

In addition to using the subordinating connectives *anu* and *warri*, the meaning of intention or causality can be encoded via, and inferred from, clause coordination with *la*. It is remarkable that the clause that expresses the cause usually linearly follows the one that expresses the effect, which is the reverse order compared to the real-world events.[21] Consider examples in (8.78):

(8.78) a. Nga-mabulunj nganj-yuwa [la ngunda ngay-yu
1SG.NF-like.NP 1SG.FUT-lie.NP CONJ not 1SG.IRR.PST-lie.IRR.PST

djininj].
properly

'I want to sleep, [because; lit. 'and'] I didn't sleep enough.'
[IK1-160704_0001/38:23]

b. Burdubburdub ngay-kangkayini barbung la balkkime
often 1SG.IRR.PST-go.IRR.PST fish CONJ now

nga-rnak-rna karra yalbi [la
1SG.NF-LIM-sit.NP DEM.MED.LOC country CONJ

nga-buddu-wuy nayi kabbala].
1SG.NF-3PL.OBJ-give.PST NM.I boat

'I used to go fishing a lot, but now I don't go anymore, [because; lit. 'and'] I sold the boat.' [IK1-160819_0001/38:14–39:05]

c. Narno ka-yuwa korro ku-djorlok
snake 3SG.NF-lie.NP DEM.MED.LOC IV-deep

la ka-wungmi.
CONJ 3SG.NF-breath_smokes.NP

'The snake is in his hole because it's winter-time (frosty breath).'
[Kinslow Harris 1969b: 42; gloss mine—IK]

Additionally, connectives are sometimes borrowed from English to express the reason/cause relations, as in (8.79). Borrowing of semantically specific subordinators is not typologically unusual (Thompson, Longacre & Hwang 2007: 267–9).

(8.79) Karlu ngayi ngunda ngarra-mabulu ngarra-rna
NEG.PRED I not 1SG.IRR.NP-like.IRR.NP 1SG.IRR.NP-see.IRR.NP

because nga-kelbungu nayi norno, nga-kelhme.
ENG 1SG.NF-afraid.NP NM.I snake 1SG.NF-fear.NP

'No, I said, *I don't want to see it because I'm scared of snakes, I'm afraid.*'
[20060814IB01/02:11–17]

---

[21] The anti-iconic order of the clauses is more characteristic of subordinate structures than of coordination, according to Diessel (2001).

Finally, clause juxtaposition without any formal indication of the purposive semantics can also be used, in which case the relation is only inferred.[22] The verb *-ka* 'to go' is one that is frequently used in such a way (8.80):

(8.80) Nakodjok ka-kidanj   barbung kanj-kali.
       N   3SG.NF-go.PST   fish   3SG.FUT-get.NP
       'Nakodjok has gone (to) get (some) fish.'   [Coleman 1982: 152; gloss mine]

8.5.2 Locative clauses

The locative adverbial clauses in Kunbarlang are formally similar to relative clauses (§8.4) introduced by *korro* 'DEM.MED.LOC' (8.81). I mention them here as a distinct conventional way to realise the function of a locative adverbial.

(8.81) a. Wadjbud   ka-bukayinj   [korro   ngurrum   ka-dja].
          beach   3SG.NF-rise.PST DEM.MED.LOC casuarina 3SG.NF-stand.NP
          'He landed at the beach **where there are casuarinas**.'
                                              [IK1-160624_0001/02:09–12]

   b. Kadda-kidanj   kun-barrkidbe yalbi   [korro   njunjuk
      3PL.NF-go.PST IV-other   country DEM.MED.LOC   water
      ka-yuwa].
      3SG.NF-lie.NP
      'They went to another country, **where there is water**.'
                                              [IK1-160726_0001/07:30–40]

In these constructions there are no lexicalised/grammaticalised semantic distinctions, such as distance or direction.

8.5.3 Time clauses

Time adverbial clauses in Kunbarlang are classified as class IV, since they describe the abstract notion of time (see §4.1). Thus, the time adverbial clause is introduced by the class IV noun marker *kuyi* and are formally similar to class IV headless relative clauses (8.82):[23]

---

[22] Probably such inferences are essentially conversational implicatures, but I have not done proper diagnostics, such as cancellation of the alleged implicature.
[23] This parallels exactly the time clause formation in Swahili, where there is a relative clause marker on the verb for class 16 (time/place), but no overt head noun which that marker would be agreeing with (i):

(8.82) a. Kukka ngorro [**kuyi** ka-warr-mi nayi mankurddel].
it.IV DEM.MED.IV NM.IV 3SG.NF-bad-INCH.NP NM.I giant
'That's what happens when the mankurddel dies.'
[20060901IB08/02:19–22]

b. Ngadda-djarri [**kuyi** ngorro manberrk].
1PL.EXCL.IRR.PST-eat.IRR.PST NM.IV DEM.MED.IV bush
'We used to eat [all of that] when [we were] on the mainland.'
[20060620IB03/17:02–05]

c. Kinj-rnanj mayi birradja, [**kuyi** kanj-burleng-mi ngob]
2SG.FUT-see.NP NM.III rice NM.IV 3SG.FUT-dry-INCH.NP all
kinj-ngulukdombunj mayi wirdidj.
2SG.FUT-extinguish.NP NM.III fire
'Watch the rice, when it's absorbed all water turn off the heat.'
[IK1-170525_1JW1/14:31–16:54]

However, very often similar meanings are expressed via juxtaposition/coordination of clauses, rather than subordination (8.83–8.86). There may be a logical connector such as *la* (8.83), *babi la* (8.84) or *ngorro* (8.85; see §4.5.3.1 for more on this demonstrative), or may be none (8.86). The clausal conjunct that corresponds to the temporal adverbial clause in the English translation is in bold.

(8.83) |¹ Ngayi nga-marnbum marlorlorr |² **la ki-nganjkidanj**.
Ngayi nga-marnbum marlorlorr la ki-nganj-kidanj.
I 1SG.NF-make.PST fighting_spear CONJ 2SG.NF-HITH-go.PST
'I was making a spear and you came.'
PROMPT: 'I was trimming a fighting spear **when you came up**.'
[IK1-160827_0001/49:35–38]

(8.84) |¹ Kangan-midjbum |² **nga-bing** |³ babi la ka-yunganj.
Ka-ngan-midjbum nga-bing babi la ka-yunganj.
3SG.NF-1SG.OBJ-wait.PST 1SG.NF-exit.PST later CONJ 3SG.NF-lie.PST
'She was waiting for me, I got there, and she went to bed.'
PROMPT: 'She was waiting for me, and **when I got home**, she went to sleep.'
[IK1-170615_1SY2/42:25–32]

(i) u-li-**po**-fik-a...
2SG-PST-REL.16-arrive-FV
'When you arrived...' [Marten 2013: 55]

(8.85) |¹ Ngadda-rninganj |² **ngorro war ka-bing**.

Ngadda-rninganj   ngorro   war   ka-bing.
1PL.EXCL.NF-sit.PST DEM.MED.IV ENG 3SG.NF-exit.PST
'We were staying [there] **when war arrived**.' [20060620IB03/05:30–37]

(8.86) |¹ **Kardokkardok nga-nganjwom** |² nga-rnay ka-yunganj |³ babi la nga-rluklung |⁴ ka-rdolkkidanj.

Kardokkardok nga-nganj-wom   nga-rnay   ka-yunganj   babi
afternoon   1SG.NF-HITH-return.PST   1SG.NF-see.PST 3SG.NF-lie.PST later

la   nga-rluklung   ka-rdolkkidanj.
CONJ 1SG.NF-wake.PST   3SG.NF-get_up.PST

'I got back in the afternoon, I saw she was still in bed, later I woke her up and she got up.'

PROMPT: '**When I returned** she was sleeping, so I woke her up.'
[IK1-170615_1SY2/36:40–38:56]

The connectives, when present, reflect a plausible logical relation between the clauses. For instance, in (8.83) it is a simple conjunction of the events, whereas in (8.84) it is temporal succession.

8.5.4 Conditional adverbial clauses

Following common practice in linguistics (see von Fintel 2011 for an overview), I distinguish between REAL (also known as INDICATIVE) and COUNTERFACTUAL (also known as SUBJUNCTIVE) conditionals. Their expression in Kunbarlang is similar, but not identical, and I shall review them in turn.

8.5.4.1 Real conditionals

Real conditionals are those which express an open possibility, i.e. where the protasis (the *if*-clause) describes some possible state of affairs. There is no specialised subordinator in Kunbarlang for use in the protasis or in the apodosis (*then*-clause) of a real conditional. However, the protasis is always marked by the class IV noun marker *kuyi* (the same as in the temporal adverbials), or by the irrealis form of the verb, or both (as in (8.87)). Sometimes the verb in the apodosis is also in the irrealis, and sometimes the apodosis includes the class IV demonstrative *ngorro* (8.88a below).

(8.87) Durduk djidda-rdam korro yirrk.
dog 2PL.FUT-put.NP DEM.MED.LOC inside

[**Kuyi ki-ngan-beye**]$_{prot}$ [nganj-bunj]$_{apod}$.
NM.IV 3SG.IRR.NP-1SG.OBJ-bite.IRR.NP 2SG.FUT-hit.NP

'Keep that dog inside! **If it bites me**, I will kill it.'

[IK1-160828_0001/03:15–41]

The apparent obligatoriness of the protasis marking via at least one feature (i.e. *kuyi* or irrealis) accords with Comrie's (1986: 87) typological observation that "[o]vert marking of the protasis seems to be the commonest situation cross-linguistically". Both strategies (that is, morphological and lexical marking) are well-attested. Example (8.88) shows that just one of the markers suffices: while (8.88a) has *kuyi* and the verb is in realis, (8.88b) only features irrealis marking but no *kuyi*.

(8.88) a. Kuyi ngudda kinj-rnekbe nayi djang, ngarrki-warrmi
NM.IV you.SG 2SG.FUT-step.NP NM.I dreaming.site 1.INCL.FUT-die.NP

ngob, ngarrka **ngorro** ngarrki-warrmi.
all we.INCL DEM.MED.IV 1.INCL.FUT-die.NP

'If you step on that dreaming site, we all will die.'

[IK1-160802_0001/40:58–41:12]

b. **Kirri-mabulu** kirri-karrme (la ngunda
2SG.IRR.NP-like.IRR.NP 2SG.IRR.NP-hold.IRR.NP CONJ not

ki-ngun-beye).
3SG.IRR.NP-2SG.OBJ-bite.IRR.NP

'If you want to, you can hold it (it won't bite you).'

[IK1-170615_1SY1/19:40]

Although the apodosis does not require any marking (cf. (8.87)), it may be marked via the irrealis form of the verb, as in (8.88b), or contain the class IV demonstrative *ngorro* in its discourse cohesion function, as in (8.88a).

8.5.4.2 Counterfactual conditionals

Counterfactual conditionals stand in contrast to the real ones in that the state of affairs described by them is known to be contrary to the fact. Like with the real conditionals, there is no dedicated subordinator for the counterfactuals in Kunbarlang. Both the protasis and the apodosis are in the irrealis past form (8.89), and the protasis may contain *kuyi* (8.89a) or the similative particle *yimarne* 'like' (8.89b).

(8.89) a. **Kuyi ngarrki-kangkayini** hammer **ngay-karrmili** or
NM.IV 1.INCL.IRR.PST-go.IRR.PST hammer 1SG.IRR.PST-hold.IRR.PST or

rrabbi... la karlu.
file CONJ NEG.PRED

'If we had have been going to go, I would've taken a hammer or a file... but nothing.' [20060814IB02/01:12–18]

b. Ngudda benbe **yimarne** ki-nganj-**kangkayini**
you.SG yesterday like 2SG.IRR.PST-HITH-go.IRR.PST

ngay-ngun-**wuni** bilmu
1SG.IRR.PST-2SG.OBJ-give.IRR.PST barramundi

ki-djarri.
2SG.IRR.PST-eat.IRR.PST

'Had you come yesterday, I would've given you barramundi to eat.'
[IK1-170609_1SY2/10:43–54]

Both examples in (8.89) describe situations that are only hypothetical, but are known to be contrary to the fact. Marking counterfactual conditionals is one of the major functions of the irrealis past (§5.5.2.1), along with counterfactual wishes, negation and past habituals.

In concluding the discussion of the Kunbarlang adverbial clauses, I would like to point out that a whole range of (functionally) adverbial clauses are formally headless relatives (discussed back in §8.4.1.2): this is true at least of the temporal, locative and some conditional clauses. This is not at all unusual in the languages of the world, cf. the following quote from a typologically-oriented work on conditionals: "Some lexical protasis markers are relative pro-forms, the protasis being a free relative clause. An example are German *wenn*-clauses, which abstract out of the protasis clause the sum of conditions that are sufficient for the truth of the antecedent. Plugging them into another clause makes the proposition of the latter depend on precisely these conditions" Zaefferer (1991: 217). Just like in Kunbarlang, in German the same form of a free (i.e. headless) relative clause can describe the temporal location of the matrix clause it modifies *or* the conditions under which the situation described by the matrix clause holds. Notice that the German *wenn* 'when; if' displays the same polyfunctionality, as a temporal and a conditional subordinator, as the Kunbarlang *kuyi*, reflecting a general close affinity between conditional and temporal/modal meanings.[24]

---

[24] See Zaefferer (1991) for discussion and references to formal analyses that aim to capture this aspect of conditional semantics.

9 Conclusion

In this chapter I provide a summary of the book and outline some further research directions. In a way, I attempt to portray Kunbarlang in a few strokes, highlighting its most crucial properties and placing them in the areal and theoretical-typological context. At the same time, this chapter serves to highlight the main analytical changes that the grammar underwent compared to my PhD thesis (Kapitonov 2019a), on which this book is based.

This book offers a description of the grammar of Kunbarlang, a Gunwinyguan language of northern Australia, whose number of speakers has decreased dramatically in the last several decades. As is explained in the Introduction, the description and analysis are based on three principal sources: the groundwork laid by previous research (most importantly, Coleman 1982), my original field work in the Northern Territory, and recordings made by other scholars. In terms of organisation, the description progresses from smaller units to increasingly larger units of analysis: beginning with phonetics and phonology, it then moves to morphology and morphosyntax of the Kunbarlang lexical categories, and afterwards to intra-clausal and inter-clausal syntax of this language. Semantics of the grammatical categories and constructions is treated in parallel with discussion of their morphosyntax.

The analysis reveals a constellation of features both similar to many genetically and areally related languages and distinct from them, ultimately combining to create the unique and fascinating personality of Kunbarlang, just like it happens with every human language. Basic alignment in Kunbarlang is nominative-accusative, and for the objects it is secundative, equating the goal, rather than the theme, of ditransitives with the sole object of a monotransitive (§3.1). In the most general terms, Kunbarlang is a typical language of its family (Gunwinyguan) and area (central-western Arnhem Land). That is, Kunbarlang is a polysynthetic agglutinating language with a noticeable asymmetry between the morphologically rich verb structure (which is holophrastic and self-sufficient, and central to the organisation of the clause) and the near absense of morphology in the nominal domain. Indeed, nominal morphology of Kunbarlang stands out among the Gunwinyguan languages in how minimalistic it is. The only categories that are obligatorily expressed in the noun phrase is noun class (also known as grammatical gender; §4.1) and case. Noun class systems are frequently found in non-Pama-Nyungan languages, including in the majority of Gunwinyguan languages. On the other hand, and quite unusually, Kunbarlang lacks case marking on nominals other than pronouns (where by nominals I mean the constituents of the noun phrase), and the three-case system itself is more compact than in most Australian languages (§4.2). This contrast to the other Gunwinyguan languages is complemented by the highly organised syntax of the noun phrase. While its family-mates have figured prominently in the literature for their lack of NP construal, I provide a novel account of Kunbarlang here, on which not only is the NP construal supported (as recognised already in Kapitonov 2019a), but also a hierarchical analysis of its word order and communicative organisation is advanced. Moreover, I argue that noun markers serve a dual function as definite articles and linker articles (§4.3).

Accordingly, the Kunbarlang analytic case marking construction—the way noun phrases are licensed in certain oblique and adjunct positions—is quite unique (§4.4.2). This aspect of the very economical role of case in grammatical role marking distinguishes it from most Australian languages. Yet in this domain there are clear similarities to other Australian languages, too, such as the licensing of some adjunct noun phrases via verbal applicative morphemes, or the relationship between the noun phrases and the personal prefixes in the verb. A major change in the present description compared to Kapitonov 2019a happened in the conceptualisation of argumenthood: as it is argued extensively in §3.4, in a sense *all* free nominal phrases are syntactic adjuncts, while it is the bound pronouns on the verb that are its true arguments. This *pronominal argument* view of argument structure realisation is argued to afford considerable advantages for understanding of the surface 'nonconfigurational' patterns, as well as facts of 'agreement'.

Adding to the list of interesting features related to how argument structure is reflected in the verb, I should point out some facts about the paradigmatic morphology of the personal prefixes. In all Gunwinyguan languages mono- and ditransitive verbs can index two arguments via personal prefixes, and it is a family trait that there is a high proportion of indivisible subject/object portmanteaux in this part of the paradigm. I have argued in this grammar that Kunbarlang (along with Warray) stands out in the family in that its complex transitive paradigms can be analysed as fully separable into subject and object exponents (§5.2.1). This analysis comes at the price of postulating exuberant allomorphy, but I show that even that allomorphy reveals systematic patterns. In the course of investigating semantics and distribution of the individual exponents, I have found that the third person singular marking in Kunbarlang is general in its meaning, and not specifically singular (§5.2.2). This is but one part of an intricate system of neutralisations in the person-number paradigm of the bound pronouns.

The highlights of the Kunbarlang verbal inflection other than agreement concern its composite TAM system. *Composite* here means that the TAM value encoding of a given verbal form is distributed between the subject personal prefix and the tense/mood suffix. All verb forms in Kunbarlang are finite. This inflection, when the values are combined, encodes mood (reality status) and tense, but neither viewpoint aspect nor illocutionary force (§5.3 and §5.4). Some aspectual distinctions can be expressed via an auxiliary verb construction (that uses mainly posture verbs, there are no dedicated auxiliaries; §7.2.1) or prosodically, by vowel lengthening (§7.2.2). Temporal and aspectual semantics is an area where more work is always welcome. Some directions for such research in Kunbarlang are the workings of Aktionsart and interaction of lexical aspect of predicates with the TAM categories; a better understanding of temporal and modal semantics of what I called here realis future; and, combining temporal structure and argument structure analyses, a wholistic picture of event structure of both simple and complex predicates (see below).

In the realm of derivation Kunbarlang also has interesting features: argument structure derivations (§6.1), noun incorporation (§6.3), adverbial affixes (§6.4; but no affixal verbs or adjectives), and rather unique complex predicate constructions (§3.2.5 and §6.5). The inventory of argument structure operations is typical of the Gunwinyguan family: benefactive, comitative and reflexive/reciprocal; unlike some Gunwinyguan languages, Kunbarlang does not have morphological causatives. The description of argument structure derivations has been made more precise since the thesis version of the grammar, especially in what concerns the reflexive/reciprocal.

Speaking about deriving predicates, there are two classes of elements that collocate with verb stems to form complex predicates in two related, yet distinct constructions. One class (free preverbs; §3.2.5.2) is sourced as loans from English, and is the only way to borrow predicates, as verbs cannot be borrowed into Kunbarlang directly. The other class (enclitic coverbs; §3.2.5.1 and §6.5) contains a number of cognates to coverbs in some other Gunwinyguan languages, as well as the Iwaidjan language Mawng, with which Kunbarlang has been in close contact for a long time. The patterns of preverb and coverb constructions in Kunbarlang are quite unique typologically on a world-wide scale, but also show interesting differences to cognate patterns of nearby languages. Further research on microvariation in the syntax of these and related complex predicate constructions in these genetically and areally connected languages is currently underway. Another remaining issue is further detail of the interaction between the valency-changing operations and the effects of this interaction on argument realisation.

At the level of syntactic phrases and clause organisation, Kunbarlang shows its own particular set of manifestations of surface nonconfigurationality. These include extensive zero anaphora (§7.8), quite free, information structure-sensitive word order (§7.1) and apparently discontinuous noun phrases (§4.4.4). However, it is argued here for strong NP integrity, rather than purely semantically construed coherence among nominal elements (§4.4), and there are other configurational-type features, such as true subordination, including relative clauses with gaps (§8.4). This is an important finding in light of the previous research on nonconfigurationality and on the adjoined relative clause in Australian languages. Subordinate constructions are not heavily used in Kunbarlang discourse, in line with what has been observed in other polysynthetic languages, yet there is an inventory of diverse subordinate structures (§§8.3–8.5). The distinction between adverbial subordinate clauses and clausal coordination can be explored in more detail. Despite the said freedom of word order in the clause, I show that Kunbarlang has a tendency for subject–verb–object order (§7.1.1).

It is not only in morphology and syntax that Kunbarlang has features of interest, but in phonology as well. The phonological inventory of Kunbarlang (§2.1) is standard both for an Australian language in general and for Arnhem Land more specifically (e.g. it has a five-vowel system, whereas outside of the north three-vowel systems are more common). As mentioned above, Kunbarlang has minimal morphophonemics, resembling in this respect the closely related Bininj Kunwok. Two aspects of its morphophonology are quite striking, however. One has to do with clusters of nasals that may occur on morpheme boundaries (§2.7.3). Such clusters are not tolerated when an inflectional morpheme is involved, and are simplified. These simplification rules are remarkable in that they contradict the Australian-wide generalisations about harmonic cluster resolution. Additionally, it seems that the nasal clusters that occur between derivational morphemes and stems do not simplify, even when they are very marked on that Australian-wide harmonic scale. The other surprising behaviour is found with retroflex consonants. While in most Australian languages retroflexion is lost following heterorganic consonants, in Kunbarlang it is largely retained (§2.5.2.1). Further work, especially involving high quality recordings and instrumental investigation, would be very important for a better understanding of Kunbarlang morphophonology and phonetic realisations more generally. Another area where further research is much needed is stress: both its acoustic correlates and the metrical structure.

I tried to make this description of Kunbarlang theory-neutral, so that it would be useful for a broad linguistic audience, and thus deliberately avoided getting deep into theoretical issues. It is clear, however, that across all areas of Kunbarlang grammar there are data of keen theoretical interest. Thus, a general direction for future work is a more in-depth theoretical analysis of the many interesting issues left. Is the morphological template all that there is to the verb's organisation, or does it have a hierarchical, syntax-like structure? In particular, what is the nature of noun incorporation—is it syntactic? What are further details of the hierarchical organisation of noun phrases, beyond the initial proposals made here? Likewise, in referential semantics, what is the referential and discourse import of the determining pronouns and of noun markers more precisely? How did the coverb constructions develop historically, what were the directions of borrowing of coverbs between the Gunwinyguan and the Iwaidjan languages?

It is my hope that the work presented here will be of use and interest to a wide community; that it may help Kunbarlang people keep their language strong and pass it on to next generations; that it will enrich linguists' understanding of the typological diversity and the regularities underlying human language, and inform our theoretical inquiry; that it can spark interest in other scholars to continue investigation of this fascinating language, and can serve as a useful basis for such research. It is also my hope that the Kunbarlang language thrives in the years to come.

A Texts

A.1 Trip to the mainland

This is a fragment of a spontaneous narrative told by two Kunbarlang speakers in a traditional fashion of narration with turn-taking. The storytellers are Ngalwamud Rita Djitmu and Ngalwamud Linda Najinga, recounting memories of their trip from Warruwi to Nakalarramba, Mayirri and Kurridja in Kunbarlang country on the mainland, which took place in December 1974, overlapping with cyclone Tracy. The recording is archived as IK1-160624_0021.

(A.1) Start yimarne karri-wam Nakalarramba.
ENG like 1PL.INCL-go.PST N
'Start from how we went to Nakalarramba.'
[LN; *karri-wam* is a Kunwinjku verb, the gloss is mine—IK]

(A.2) Ngadda-kidanj Nakalarramba.
1PL.EXCL.NF-go.PST N
'We went to Nakalarramba.' [RDj]

(A.3) And walk ngarrk-ngunda.
ENG ENG 1.INCL.NF-do.PST
'And we walked.' [LN]

(A.4) Heading to ngarrk-ngunda Mayirri.
ENG ENG 1.INCL.NF-do.PST M
'We were heading to Mayirri.' [LN]

(A.5) Mayirri, then start ka-ngunda kubbunj kabarra-bum old man,
M ENG ENG 3SG.NF-do.PST canoe 3DU.NF-hit.PST ENG ENG
mammam, two, two mammam, Kodjok and Kunarr mammam.
MF ENG ENG MF K ENG K MF
'[We were/arrived at] Mayirri, then they two started to make a canoe, the two old men, two grandpa's, Kodjok and Kunarr.' [LN]

(A.6)   Yoh.
        yes
        'Yes.'   [RDj]

(A.7)   And   kakkak   Mayawadjba   and   Kaun   babi,   karri-wam,   eh
        ENG   MM   M   ENG   K   later   1PL.INCL-go.PST   ah
        "karri-wam"   —   ngarrk-kidanj.
        1PL.INCL-go.PST   1.INCL.NF-go.PST
        'And then also with granny Mayawadjba and Kaun, we went.'
                          [LN; *karri-wam* is a Kunwinjku verb, notice the self-repair]

(A.8)   Ngarrk-kidanj.
        1.INCL.NF-go.PST
        'We went.'   [RDj]

(A.9)   Kabarra-marnbum   kubbunj,   kabarra-baybum   then   walk   ngarrk-ngunda
        3DU.NF-make.PST   canoe   3DU.NF-leave.PST   ENG   ENG   1.INCL.NF-do.PST
        ngarrk-kidanj.
        1.INCL.NF-go.PST
        'They two made the canoe, then they left it and we went on foot.'   [LN]

(A.10) Heading   ngarrk-ngunda   Kurridja.
        ENG   1.INCL.NF-do.PST   K
        'We were heading to Kurridja.'   [LN]

(A.11) From   karrakenda,   Mayirri?
        ENG   where   M
        'From where, from Mayirri?'   [RDj]

(A.12) Yoh,   from   Mayirri   mukka   ngorro   kubbunj   ngarrk-baybum   then
        yes   ENG   M   it.III   DEM.MED.IV   canoe   1.INCL.NF-leave.PST   ENG
        walk.
        ENG
        'Yes, from Mayirri, we left that canoe there, then walked.'   [LN]

(A.13) Kabarra-ngunda two mammam ngarrk-ka   ngorro   Kurridja,
       3DU.NF-do.PST ENG MF   1.INCL.NF-go.NP DEM.MED.IV K
       then walk ngarrk-ngunda.
       ENG ENG 1.INCL.NF-do.PST
       'The two grandpa's said, *We're going to Kurridja*, then we walked.'   [LN]

(A.14) Walk ngadda-ngunda.
       ENG 1PL.EXCL.NF-do.PST
       'We walked.'   [RDj]

(A.15) Walk ngadda-ngunda   then ngadda-kidanj.
       ENG 1PL.EXCL.NF-do.PST ENG 1PL.EXCL.NF-go.PST
       'We walked and then we came.'   [LN]

(A.16) Ngadda-kidanj   ngadda-rninganj   then.
       1PL.EXCL.NF-go.PST 1PL.EXCL.NF-sit.PST ENG
       'We came and then we stayed.'   [LN]

(A.17) Ngadda-kidanj   kabarra-ngunda two old people.
       1PL.EXCL.NF-go.PST 3DU.NF-do.PST ENG ENG ENG
       'We came and the two old men said:'   [LN]

(A.18) Kenda   ngorro   ngarrki-rna   nunu.
       DEM.PROX.LOC DEM.MED.IV   1.INCL.FUT-sit.NP   all
       "We are all going to stay here."   [LN]

(A.19) Ngadda-rninganj   korro   kabbal   Kurridja,
       1PL.EXCL.NF-sit.PST   DEM.MED.LOC   floodplain K
          ngadda-marnbum   dolobbo.
          1PL.EXCL.NF-make.PST stringybark
       'We stayed at the floodplain Kurridja, we made [shelter from] bark.'   [LN]

(A.20) Ngadda-rninganj   djanbe,   kurrambalk   la   balabbala.
         1PL.EXCL.NF-sit.PST platform shelter   CONJ   bed
         'We stayed on wooden platforms, with a shade and a bed.'   [LN]

(A.21) Nukka   ngorro   cyclone ngorro   ka-nganj-kidanj   ready
         he.I   DEM.MED.IV   ENG   DEM.MED.IV   3SG.NF-HITH-go.PST   ready

         ngorro   John   Hunter   ka-nganj-kidanj   ka-ngunda
         DEM.MED.IV   J   H   3SG.NF-HITH-go.PST   3SG.NF-do.PST

         kin-burnunga   two   old   people   ka-nganj-ka   dukulu.
         I/II-they.DU.GEN   ENG   ENG   ENG   3SG.NF-HITH-go.NP   wind
         'That cyclone was ready and approaching, and then John Hunter came and
         told the two old men that wind was coming.'   [LN]

(A.22) And   then   [...]   kabarra-marnanj-ngunda   that   two   mammam: bonj
         ENG   ENG   3DU.NF-BEN-do.PST   ENG   ENG   MF   exactly

         ngandjidda-rna   kun-mak.
         1PL.EXCL.FUT-sit.NP   IV-good
         'And then the two grandpa's told him: "Ok, we'll be fine."'   [LN]

(A.23) Kabarra-djabbalawum,   ngorro   ngadda-rninganj   kun-mak.
         3DU.NF-tell.PST   DEM.MED.IV   1PL.EXCL.NF-sit.PST   IV-good
         'They two told him that we were fine there.'   [RDj]

(A.24) And   kabarra-wom   ngorro   walk   kabarra-ngunda   Mayirri
         ENG   3DU.NF-return.PST   DEM.MED.IV   ENG   3DU.NF-do.PST   M

         kubbunj   kabarra-marnbum   mukka   ngorro   kabarra-rninganj.
         canoe   3DU.NF-make.PST   it.III   DEM.MED.IV   3DU.NF-sit.PST
         'And they two went back to Mayirri for that canoe they were making.' [LN]

(A.25) Ngarrka-wu[?]   ngorro   ngarrk-rninganj   nunu   korro
         we.INCL-LIM?   DEM.MED.IV   1.INCL.NF-sit.PST   all   DEM.MED.LOC

         kabbal.
         floodplain
         'We were staying on the floodplain.' (Probably: 'The rest of us remained on the
         floodplain.')   [LN]

(A.26) Yoh, ngorro   kabbal   ngadda-rninganj.
        yes   DEM.MED.IV floodplain 1PL.EXCL.NF-sit.PST
        'Yes, we stayed on a floodplain then.'   [RDj]

(A.27) Kabarra-marnbum   mukka   ngorro   kubbunj, ngorro
        3DU.NF-make.PST   it.III DEM.MED.IV   canoe   DEM.MED.IV
          kabarra-ngorrodjanganj.
          3DU.NF-turn_around.PST
        'They fixed/finished that canoe and then they came around.'   [LN]

(A.28) Yoh, kabarra-ngorrodjanganj   korro   creek.
        yes   3DU.NF-turn_around.PST   DEM.MED.LOC   ENG
        'Yes, they came around up the creek.'   [RDj]

(A.29) Kurridja   creek   kabarra-ngorrodjanganj   Mayirri   kabarra-nganj-kidanj
        K   ENG   3DU.NF-turn_around.PST   M   3DU.NF-HITH-go.PST
          kabarra-bing   Kurridja.
          3DU.NF-exit.PST   K
        'They came from Mayirri and up the Kurridja creek and arrived and landed at
        Kurridja.'   [LN]

(A.30) Kunkarrnim, yoh, kabarra-walkki-bukayinj   mukka   ngorro   kubbunj.
        K   yes   3DU.NF-COM-rise.PST   it.III   DEM.MED.IV   canoe
        'They landed with that canoe at Kunkarrnim.'   [LN]

A.2 Making damper

This is a procedural text on making damper, the classic yeast-free bread of the outback cuisine, which is baked in hot ashes. The recording is made with Ngalngarridj Sandra Makurlngu at Bottle Rock, Warruwi, on June 26th, 2016. The recording is archived as IK1-160726_0021.

(A.31) Nganj-yolyolhme   bonj~bonj   kuyi   ngadda-burlkarrme   mayi
       1SG.FUT-tell_about.NP RDP~exactly   NM.IV   1PL.EXCL.NF-knead.NP   NM.III

   kandiddjawa.
   bread

'I am going to tell again how we make damper'.

(A.32) Ngadda-rdam   mayi   kadda-ngundje balanda   mayi   plain   one
       1PL.EXCL.NF-put.NP   NM.III 3PL.NF-do   whitefella   NM.III   ENG   ENG

   la   mayi   ka-ngukbudjuwa   korro   self-raising.
   CONJ   NM.III 3SG.NF-heave.NP   DEM.MED.LOC   ENG

'We put what in English is called plain [flour] and the "heaving" one, the self-raising.'

(A.33) Ka-bunj   ngob, ngorro   kongon   ngadda-rdam.
       3SG.NF-hit.NP   all   DEM.MED.IV   milk   1PL.EXCL.NF-put.NP

'You mix them, then we add milk'.

(A.34) Ka-marnbunj   ngob.
       3SG.NF-make.NP   all

'You mix them.'

(A.35) Ngorro   ngadda-burlkarrme.
       DEM.MED.IV   1PL.EXCL.NF-knead.NP

'Then we knead it.'

(A.36) Ngadda-burlkarrme::   ngob   ngorro   ngadda-marnbunj   yimarne
       1PL.EXCL.NF-knead   all   DEM.MED.IV   1PL.EXCL.NF-make.NP   like

   ka-ngundje   kurrana.
   3SG.NF-do.NP   moon

'We knead it all for a while, then we make it into a round shape [lit. 'like the moon'].'

(A.37) Bonj   ngorro   la   ngadda-rdam   korro   nguluk.
       exactly   DEM.MED.IV   CONJ   1PL.EXCL.NF-put.NP   DEM.MED.LOC   ash

'Well, then we put it into the hot ashes.'

(A.38) Ka-bun-djinj werrk kaddum babi la kuyi
3SG.NF-3SG.OBJ-eat.NP immediately above later CONJ NM.IV
karnda=way=wali ngadda-ngorrordam ka-bun-djinj
DEM.DIST.LOC=HITH=turn 1PL.EXCL.NF-turn.NP 3SG.NF-3SG.OBJ-eat.NP
ngob.
all

'It bakes first on the top and then on the other side in turn, we turn it around and it bakes completely.'

(A.39) Bonj ngorro ka-bun-djinj, man-djorleng, la
exactly DEM.MED.IV 3SG.NF-3SG.OBJ-eat.NP III-ripe CONJ
ngadda-nguluk-kali.
1PL.EXCL.NF-ash-get.NP

'Then it bakes, and when it's ready, we take it out from the ashes.'

(A.40) Ka-yuwa, ngadda-rdukku~rdukkume, ngorro ngadda-djinj,
3SG.NF-lie.NP 1PL.EXCL.NF-RDP~cut.NP DEM.MED.IV 1PL.EXCL.NF-eat.NP
share ngadda-ngundje.
share 1PL.EXCL.NF-do.NP

'It sits [cooling down], we cut it in pieces, then we eat it, we share it.'

(A.41) Kenda ngadda-nganj-kidanj Ngaminali.
DEM.PROX.LOC 1PL.EXCL.NF-HITH-go.PST Ng

'We came here to Ngaminali [Bottle Rock]'.

(A.42) Ngadda-rna ngadda-kinje.
1PL.EXCL.NF-sit.NP 1PL.EXCL.NF-cook.NP

'We are cooking.'

(A.43) Ngayi, Ngalbangardi, Nakangila la ngayi kabarra-rna,
I N N CONJ NM.II 3DU.NF-sit.NP
ngadda-rna.
1PL.EXCL.NF-sit.NP

'I, Ngalbangardi, Nakangila and his partner, we are sitting here.'

(A.44)   Ngadda-midjbunj   manda   ngorro   kandiddjawa,
         1PL.EXCL.NF-wait.NP   DEM.PROX.III   DEM.MED.IV   bread
         ka-bun-djinj.
         3SG.NF-3SG.OBJ-eat.NP
         'We are waiting for this damper, it's baking.'

(A.45)   Kanj-bun-djinj   ngob babi la   nganj-nguluk-kali   ngorro.
         3SG.FUT-3SG.OBJ-eat.NP   all   later CONJ 1SG.FUT-ash-get.NP   DEM.MED.IV
         'It is going to bake through. Afterwards I'll pull it out.'

(A.46)   Ngandjidda-rdukku~rdukkume,   ngandjidda-djinj,   babi   ngorro
         1PL.EXCL.FUT-RDP~cut.NP   1PL.EXCL.FUT-eat.NP   later   DEM.MED.IV
         la   ngandjidda-rdokme   korro   yalbi.
         CONJ   1PL.EXCL.FUT-leave.NP   DEM.MED.LOC   country
         'We shall cut it into pieces and eat it, and after that we shall go back home.'

(A.47)   Yoh,   kun-mak.
         yes   IV-good
         'Yes, good.'

A.3 Spot-the-Difference game dialogue

This is a fragment of a dialogue elicited with the help of Spot-the-Difference picture sets (originally designed by Masha Kyuseva for elicitation of physical properties descriptions; see Kyuseva 2020). Two Kunbarlang speakers, Ngalngarridj Sandra Makurlngu and Nakodjok George Manmurulk, each had a picture from a pair of similar-looking pictures with some manipulated differences, such as the size or number of items shown. Their task was to find as many differences as they could without looking at each other's pictures, but through discussing them. The recording is archived as IK1-170610_2SM1.

(A.48)   Mayi   kodbarre. Manda   mayi   kodbarre ka-dja.
         NM.III   house   DEM.PROX.III   NM.III   house   3SG.NF-stand.NP
         'The house. There's that house.'   [GM]

(A.49) Ngudda birlinj ka-ngundje   nayi ka-bakkidja   kaddum?
       you.SG how   3SG.NF-do.NP NM.I 3SG.NF-stand_vertically.NP above
       'In your picture, what are the chimneys like?' [lit. 'What is it doing, that which
       stands up at the top?']'   [GM]

(A.50) Kaburrk, na-walk~walak.
       two   I-RDP~small
       'Two, small ones.'   [SM]

(A.51) Mandjad?
       straight
       'Straight?'   [GM]

(A.52) Na-kudji... ay, kaburrk, na-walk~walak.
       I-one   ah two   I-I-RDP-small
       'One... ah, two, little ones.'   [SM]

(A.53) La   ngudda birlinj?
       CONJ you.SG how
       'What about you?'   [SM]

(A.54) Na-kudji, nayi... na-rlengbinbin.
       I-one   NM.I   I-big
       'One, it is a... big one.'   [GM]

(A.55) Yoh. La   na-barrkidbe birlinj ka-ngundje? Na-wanjak?
       yes CONJ I-other   how   3SG.NF-do.NP I-little
       'And what is the other like? Little one?'   [SM]

(A.56) Yoh, na-wanjak.
       yes I-little
       'Yes, a little one.'   [GM]

(A.57) Aku, la ngayi nukka ka-birrinja.
ah CONJ I he.I 3SG.NF-same.NP
'Ah! But mine are similar.' [SM]

(A.58) Nayi na-rlengbinbin, na-barrkidbe na-wanjak.
NM.I I-big I-other I-little
'A big one, and the other a little one.' [GM]

(A.59) Ngayi nukka ka-birrinja.
I he.I 3SG.NF-same.NP
'I have similar ones.' [SM]

(A.60) Birlinj, kodbarre bonj~bonj?
how house RDP~exactly
'What else, the house itself?' [GM]

(A.61) Ngudda nj-ngan-wardam.
you.SG 2SG.FUT-1SG.OBJ-ask.NP
'You ask me!' [GM]

(A.62) Ngayi kodbarre korro kaddum, barninda, ka-ngundje yimarne
I house DEM.MED.LOC above IGNOR 3SG.NF-do.NP like
  mulubin.
  blood
'In my picture, the roof of the house is red.' [SM]

(A.63) La nayi ngarrki-rdabirrdjuwa, na-kudji.
CONJ NM.I 1.INCL.NF-open.NP I-one
'And one door.' [SM]

(A.64) Nukka=bonj ka-birrinja.
he.I=exactly 3SG.NF-same.NP
'This one is the same.' [GM]

(A.65) Nayi norno kenda ka-dja kaburrk bala na-kudji.
NM.I snake DEM.PROX.LOC 3SG.NF-stand.NP two LNK I-one
'Of the snakes, there are three.' [GM]

(A.66) Kuyi ngudda?
NM.IV you.SG
'In your picture?' [GM]

(A.67) Yoh.
yes
'Yes.' [SM]

(A.68) Ngayi kaburrk nayi norno.
I two NM.I snake
'In mine, two snakes.' [GM]

(A.69) La ngemek nayi kadda-karebihbimbunj, or ngarrk-karebihbimbunj,
CONJ yet NM.I 3PL.NF-write.NP ENG 1.INCL.NF-write.NP
yiwanj ka-bakkidja korro kundulk ku-wanjak.
DISC.PTCL 3SG.NF-stand_vertically.NP DEM.MED.LOC tree IV-little
'And also the pencils that sit on top of the little log.' [SM]

(A.70) Kaburrk bala na-kudji.
two LNK I-one
'Three.' [SM]

(A.71) Ngayi nukka ngayi ngarrk-karebihbimbunj kundulk kaburrk.
I he.I NM.PL 1.INCL.NF-write.NP tree two
'I have two pencils on the log.' [GM]

(A.72) Kaburrk; ngayi kaburrk bala na-kudji.
two I two LNK I-one
'Two; I've got three.' [SM]

(A.73) Yiwanj...
DISC.PTCL
'Then...' [SM]

(A.74) La   mayi   kundulk ka-dja   mayi   kaburrk.
CONJ NM.III tree   3SG.NF-stand.NP NM.III two
'And there are two trees.' [GM]

(A.75) Kaburrk bonj~bonj.
two   RDP~exactly
'Also two.' [GM]

(A.76) Ka-birrinja?
3SG.NF-same.NP
'The same?' [GM]

(A.77) Yoh, ka-birrinja   kaburrk.
yes 3SG.NF-same.NP two
'Yes, also two.' [SM]

(A.78) Aku.
DISC.PTCL
'I see!' [GM]

(A.79) Burru=ngadju.
arm=she.GEN
'The branches [lit. 'her arms'].' [SM]

(A.80) Man-kudji burru=ngadju ka-karrme   kaburrk la   kaburrk, ay
III-one   arm=she.GEN   3SG.NF-hold.NP   two   CONJ two   ah
       ka-rnak-birrinja,   kaburrk la   kaburrk.
       3SG.NF-LIM-same.NP   two   CONJ two
'One of them has four branches, ah, just the same, four.' [SM]

(A.81) Yoh, ka-rnak-birrinja ngobbu.
yes 3SG.NF-LIM-same.NP both
'Yes, both are just the same.' [GM]

Bibliography

Alpher, Barry, Nicholas Evans & Mark Harvey. 2003. Proto Gunwinyguan verb suffixes. In Nicholas Evans (ed.), *The non-Pama-Nyungan languages of northern Australia: Comparative studies of the continent's most linguistically complex region*, 305–352. Canberra: Pacific Linguistics.

Andrews, Avery. 2007. Relative clauses. In Timothy Shopen (ed.), *Language typology and syntactic description*. Vol. II: *Complex constructions*, second edition, chap. 4, 206–236. Cambridge/New York: Cambridge University Press.

Austin, Peter K. (ed.). 1988. *Complex sentence constructions in Australian languages* (Typological Studies in Language 15). Amsterdam/Philadelphia: John Benjamins Publishing Company.

Austin, Peter K. 1995. Double case marking in Kanyara and Mantharta languages, Western Australia. In Frans Plank (ed.), *Double case: Agreement by Suffixaufnahme*, chap. 13, 363–379. New York/Oxford: Oxford University Press.

Austin, Peter K. & Joan Bresnan. 1996. Non-configurationality in Australian Aboriginal languages. *Natural Language and Linguistic Theory* 14(2). 215–68.

Baker, Brett. 1999. *Word structure in Ngalakgan*. University of Sydney dissertation. http://hdl.handle.net/2123/408 (October 2018).

Baker, Brett. 2004. Stem forms and paradigm reshaping in Gunwinyguan. In Claire Bowern & Harold Koch (eds.), *Australian languages: Classification and the comparative method*, 313–340. John Benjamins.

Baker, Brett. 2008a. The interpretation of complex nominal expressions in Southeast Arnhem Land languages. In Ilana Mushin & Brett Baker (eds.), *Discourse and grammar in Australian languages* (Studies in Language Companion 104), 135–166. Amsterdam/Philadelphia: John Benjamins.

Baker, Brett. 2008b. *Word structure in Ngalakgan*. Stanford, CA: CSLI Publications.

Baker, Brett. 2014a. Incorporation in Wubuy. In Lauren Gawne & Jill Vaughan (eds.), *Selected papers from the 44th conference of the Australian Linguistic Society*, 231–260.

Baker, Brett. 2014b. Word structure in Australian languages. In Harold Koch & Rachel Nordlinger (eds.), *The languages and linguistics of Australia*, chap. 4, 139–213. Berlin/Boston: Walter de Gruyter GmbH.

Baker, Brett & Mark Harvey. 2003. Word structure in Australian languages. *Australian Journal of Linguistics* 23(1). 3–33.

Baker, Brett & Mark Harvey. 2010. Complex predicate formation. In Mengistu Amberber, Brett Baker & Mark Harvey (eds.), *Complex predicates: cross-linguistic perspectives on event structure*, chap. 1, 13–47. Cambridge.

Baker, Brett, Kate Horrack, Rachel Nordlinger & Louisa Sadler. 2010. Putting it all together: Agreement, incorporation, coordination and external possession in Wubuy (Australia). In Miriam Butt & Tracy Holloway King (eds.), *Proceedings of the LFG10 conference*. Stanford, CA: CSLI Publications.

Baker, Brett & Ilana Mushin. 2008. Discourse and grammar in Australian languages. In Ilana Mushin & Brett Baker (eds.), *Discourse and grammar in Australian languages* (Studies in Language Companion 104), 1–23. Amsterdam/Philadelphia: John Benjamins.

Baker, Brett & Rachel Nordlinger. 2008. Noun-adjective compounds in Gunwinyguan languages. In Miriam Butt & Tracy Holloway King (eds.), *Proceedings of LFG08 conference*, 109–128. Stanford: CSLI Publications.

Baker, Mark C. 1988. *Incorporation: a theory of grammatical function changing*. Chicago: Chicago University Press.

Baker, Mark C. 1996. *The polysynthesis parameter*. Oxford: Oxford University Press.

Barwise, Jon & Robin Cooper. 1981. Generalized quantifiers and natural language. *Linguistics and Philosophy* 4(2). 159–219.

Beck, Sigrid, Sveta Krasikova, Daniel Fleischer, Remus Gergel, Stefan Hofstetter, Christiane Savelsberg, John Vanderelst & Elisabeth Villalta. 2009. Crosslinguistic variation in comparison constructions. *Linguistic Variation Yearbook* 9. 1–66.

Bianchi, Valentina. 2002. Headed relative clauses in generative syntax—Part I. *Glot International* 6(7). 197–204.

Bicevskis, Katie. 2012. *Incorporated modifier scope in Gunwinyguan languages*. University of Melbourne Postgrad Dip Thesis.

Bickel, Balthasar. 2010. Grammatical relations typology. In Jae Jung Song (ed.), *The Oxford handbook of language typology*, 399–444. Oxford.

Bishop, Judith. 2002. *Aspects of intonation and prosody in Bininj Gun-wok: an autosegmental-metrical analysis*. University of Melbourne PhD thesis.

Bittner, Maria. 1999. Concealed causatives. *Natural Language Semantics* 7(1). 1–78.

Blake, Barry J. 1983. Structure and word order in Kalkatungu: The anatomy of a flat language. *Australian Journal of Linguistics* 3(2). 143–75.

Blake, Barry J. 1991. Woiwurrung. In Robert M. W. Dixon & Barry J. Blake (eds.), *The handbook of Australian languages*. Vol. 4: *The Aboriginal language of Melbourne and other sketches*, 31–124. Melbourne: Oxford University Press.

Blake, Barry J. 1994. *Case*. Cambridge University Press.

Blake, Barry J. 2001. The noun phrase in Australian languages. In Jane Simpson, David Nash, Peter Austin & Barry Aplher (eds.), *Forty years on: Ken Hale and Australian languages*, 415–425. Canberra: Pacific Linguistics.

Bobaljik, Jonathan David. 2012. *Universals in comparative morphology*. Cambridge, MA: MIT Press.

Bochnak, M. Ryan. 2015. The Degree Semantics Parameter and cross-linguistic variation. *Semantics and Pragmatics* 8(6). 1–48. https://doi.org/10.3765/sp.8.6.

Boersma, Paul & David Weenink. 2016. *Praat: doing phonetics by computer [Computer program]*. Version 6.0.19. http://www.praat.org (July 2016).

Boneh, Nora & Edit Doron. 2010. Modal and temporal aspects of habituality. In Edit Doron, Malka Rappaport-Hovav & Ivy Sichel (eds.), *Syntax, lexical semantics, and event structure*, 338–363. Oxford: Oxford University Press.

Bowern, Claire. 2012. *A grammar of Bardi*. Berlin/Boston: De Gruyter Mouton.

Bowern, Claire. 2014. Complex predicates in Australian languages. In Harold Koch & Rachel Nordlinger (eds.), *The languages and linguistics of Australia*, chap. 6, 263–295. Berlin/Boston: Walter de Gruyter GmbH.

Bowler, Margit. 2016. The status of degrees in Warlpiri. In Mira Grubic & Anne Mucha (eds.), *Proceedings of the semantics of African, Asian and Austronesian languages 2*. Universität Potsdam.

Bowler, Margit & Ivan Kapitonov. Forthcoming. Quantification in Australian languages. In Claire Bowern (ed.), *Handbook of Australian languages*. Oxford University Press.

Bruening, Benjamin. 2008. *The Scope Fieldwork Project*. http://udel.edu/~bruening/scopeproject/scopeproject.html (1 July, 2015).

Bruening, Benjamin. 2009. Selectional asymmetries between CP and DP suggest that the DP Hypothesis is wrong. In *University of pennsylvania working papers in linguistics*. http://repository.upenn.edu/pwpl/vol15/iss1/5.

Butcher, Andrew. 1995. The phonetics of neutralisation. The case of Australian coronals. In J. Windsor Lewis (ed.), *Studies in general and English phonetics: Essays in honour of Professor J.D. O'Connor*, 10–38. London: Routledge.

Caha, Pavel. 2009. *The nanosyntax of case*. Universitetet i Tromsø PhD thesis. https://munin.uit.no/bitstream/handle/10037/2203/thesis.pdf?sequence=1 (30 October, 2017).

Capell, Arthur. 1940. The classification of languages in North and North-west Australia. *Oceania* 10(3). 241–272.

Capell, Arthur & Heather E. Hinch. 1970. *Maung grammar, text and vocabulary*. The Hague/Paris: Mouton.
Chafe, Wallace L. 1976. Givenness, contrastiveness, definiteness, subjects, topics and point of view. In Charles N. Li (ed.), *Subject and topic*, 27–55. New York: Academic Press.
Chomsky, Noam & Morris Halle. 1968. *The sound patterns of English*. New York, NY: Harper & Row.
Cinque, Guglielmo. 2005. Deriving Greenberg's Universal 20 and its exceptions. *Linguistic Inquiry* 36(3). 315–332.
Coleman, Carolyn. 1982. *A grammar of Gunbarlang: with special reference to grammatical relations*. Australian National University Sub-thesis.
Coleman, Carolyn. 2010. Kun-barlang—English dictionary. Unpublished Draft.
Coleman, Carolyn. N.d. Key ideas: Kun-barlang word grammar. Ms.
Comrie, Bernard. 1985. *Tense*. Cambridge University Press.
Comrie, Bernard. 1986. Conditionals: A typology. In Elizabeth Closs Traugott, Alice ter Meulen, Judy Snitzer Reilly & Charles A. Ferguson (eds.), *On conditionals*, 77–99. Cambridge: Cambridge University Press.
Comrie, Bernard. 1989. *Language universals and linguistic typology: Syntax and morphology*. 2nd edn. Oxford: Basil Blackwell.
Crain, Stephen & Rosalind Thornton. 1998. *Investigations in Universal Grammar: A guide to experiments on the acquisition of syntax and semantics*. MIT Press.
Crowell, Thomas Harris. 1979. *A grammar of Bororo*.
Dahl, Östen. 1985. *Tense and aspect systems*. Basil Blackwell.
Davis, Henry & Lisa Matthewson. 2003. Quasi objects in St'át'imcets: On the (semi-)independence of Agreement and Case. In Andrew Carnie, Heidi Harley & MaryAnn Willie (eds.), *Formal approaches to function in grammar: In honor of eloise jelinek*, 79–106. Amsterdam/Philadelphia: John Benjamins Publishing Company.
Davis, Henry & Lisa Matthewson. 2009. Issues in Salish syntax and semantics. *Language and Linguistics Compass* (3). 1097–1166. https://doi.org/10.1111/j.1749-818x.2009.00145.x.
Dench, Alan & Nicholas Evans. 1988. Multiple case-marking in Australian languages. *Australian Journal of Linguistics* 8. 1–47.
Diessel, Holger. 1999. *Demonstratives: Form, function, and grammaticalization* (Typological Studies in Language 42). Amsterdam/Philadelphia: John Benjamins Publishing Company.
Diessel, Holger. 2001. The ordering distribution of main and adverbial clauses: a typological study. *Language* 77(3). 433–455. http://www.jstor.org/stable/3086939.
Dixon, Robert M. W. 1972. *The Dyirbal language of Northern Queensland*. Cambridge: Cambridge University Press.
Dixon, Robert M. W. 1980. *The languages of Australia*. Cambridge: Cambridge University Press.
Dixon, Robert M. W. 2002. *Australian languages: their nature and development*. Cambridge University Press.
Donaldson, Tamsin. 1980. *Ngiyambaa: The language of the Wangaaybuwan*. Cambridge University Press.
Dryer, Matthew S. 1986. Primary objects, secondary objects, and antidative. *Language* 62(4). 808–845.
Dryer, Matthew S. 2007. Noun phrase structure. In Timothy Shopen (ed.), *Language typology and syntactic description*. Vol. II: *Complex constructions*, second edition, 151–205. Cambridge/New York: Cambridge University Press.
Eather, Bronwyn. 1990. *A grammar of Nakkara (Central Arnhem Land Coast)*. Australian National University PhD thesis.
Eather, Bronwyn. 2011. *A grammar of Nakkara (Central Arnhem Land coast)* (Outstanding grammars from Australia 7). Lincom Europa.

van Egmond, Marie-Elaine. 2012. *Enindhilyakwa phonology, morphosyntax and genetic position*. University of Sydney dissertation.
ELAN. 2020. *ELAN [Computer software]*. Version 6.0. Nijmegen: Max Planck Institute for Psycholinguistics, The Language Archive. https://archive.mpi.nl/tla/elan (June 2021).
Erteschik-Shir, Nomi. 2007. *Information structure*. Oxford: Oxford University Press.
Evans, Nicholas. 1991. *Mayali Dictionary*. Part III of the consultancy report 'Study and production of an orthography for the Gun-djeihmi Language, Alligator Rivers Region, Phase II', prepared for ANPWS.
Evans, Nicholas. 1992. Macassan loanwords in Top End languages. *Australian Journal of Linguistics* 12. 45–91.
Evans, Nicholas. 1995a. A-quantifiers and scope in Mayali. In Emmon Bach, Eloise Jelinek, Angelika Kratzer & Barbara Hall Partee (eds.), *Quantification in natural languages* (Studies in Linguistics and Philosophy 54), 207–270. Dordrecht: Springer.
Evans, Nicholas. 1995b. *Kayardild*. Mouton.
Evans, Nicholas. 2000. Kinship verbs. In Petra M. Vogel & Bernard Comrie (eds.), *Approaches to the typology of word classes* (Empirical Approaches to Language Typology 23), 103–172. Berlin/New York: Mouton de Gruyter.
Evans, Nicholas. 2001. The last speaker is dead – long live the last speaker! In Paul Newman & Martha Ratliff (eds.), *Linguistic fieldwork*, 250–281. Cambridge: Cambridge University Press.
Evans, Nicholas. 2002. The true status of grammatical object affixes: Evidence from Bininj Gun-wok. In Nicholas Evans & Hans-Jürgen Sasse (eds.), *Problems of polysynthesis* (Studia Typologica 4), 15–50. Berlin: Akademie Verlag.
Evans, Nicholas. 2003a. *Bininj gun-wok: a pandialectal grammar of Mayali, Kunwinjku and Kune*. Canberra: Pacific Linguistics.
Evans, Nicholas. 2003b. Introduction: Comparative non-Pama-Nyungan and Australian historical linguistics. In Nicholas Evans (ed.), *The non-Pama-Nyungan languages of northern Australia: Comparative studies of the continent's most linguistically complex region*, 3–25. Canberra: Pacific Linguistics.
Evans, Nicholas. 2006. Who said polysynthetic languages avoid subordination? Multiple subordination strategies in Dalabon. *Australian Journal of Linguistics* 26(1). 31–58.
Evans, Nicholas. 2008. Reciprocal constructions: towards a structural typology. In Ekkehard König & Volker Gast (eds.), *Reciprocals and reflexives: cross-linguistic and theoretical explorations*, 169–92. Berlin: Mouton de Gruyter.
Evans, Nicholas. 2017. Polysynthesis in Northern Australia. In Michael Fortescue, Marianne Mithun & Nicholas Evans (eds.), *The Oxford handbook of polysynthesis*, chap. 19, 313–335. Oxford University Press.
Evans, Nicholas, Dunstan Brown & Greville G. Corbett. 2001. Dalabon pronominal prefixes and the typology of syncretism: a Network Morphology analysis. In Geert Booij & Jaap van Marle (eds.), *Yearbook of Morphology 2000*, 187–232. Kluwer.
Evans, Nicholas, Dunstan Brown & Greville G. Corbett. 2002. The semantics of gender in Mayali: partially parallel systems and formal implementation. *Language* 78(1). 111–155. http://www.jstor.org/stable/3086647.
Evans, Nicholas, Janet Fletcher & Belinda Britt Ross. 2008. Big words, small phrases: Mismatches between pause units and the polysynthetic word in Dalabon. *Linguistics* (46). 89–129. https://doi.org/10.1515/LING.2008.004.
Evans, Nicholas, Alice Gaby & Rachel Nordlinger. 2007. Valency mismatches and the coding of reciprocity in Australian languages. *Linguistic Typology* 11. 541–597.

Evans, Nicholas, Stephen C. Levinson, Nick J. Enfield, Alice Gaby & Asifa Majid. 2004. Reciprocal constructions and situation type. In Asifa Majid (ed.), *Field manual*, vol. 9, 25–30. Nijmegen: Max Planck Institute for Psycholinguistics. https://doi.org/10.17617/2.506955.

Evans, Nicholas & Alexandra Helen Marley. Forthcoming. The Gunwinyguan languages. In Claire Bowern (ed.), *Handbook of Australian languages*. Oxford University Press.

Evans, Nicholas & Francesca Merlan. 2003. Dalabon verb conjugations. In Nicholas Evans (ed.), *The non-Pama-Nyungan languages of northern Australia: Comparative studies of the continent's most linguistically complex region*, 269–283. Canberra: Pacific Linguistics.

Evans, Nicholas, Francesca Merlan & Maggie Tukumba. 2004. *A first dictionary of Dalabon (Ngalkbon)*. Maningrida: Maningrida Arts & Culture.

Everett, Daniel. 1986. Pirahã. In Desmond C. Derbyshire & Geoffrey K. Pullum (eds.), *Handbook of Amazonian languages*, vol. 1, 200–325. Berlin: Mouton de Gruyter.

von Fintel, Kai. 2011. Conditionals. In Klaus von Heusinger, Claudia Maienborn & Paul Portner (eds.), *Semantics: an international handbook of meaning*, vol. 2 (Handbücher zur Sprach- und Kommunikationswissenschaft 33.2), chap. 59, 1515–1538. Berlin/Boston: de Gruyter Mouton.

Fletcher, Janet & Andrew Butcher. 2014. Sound patterns of Australian languages. In Harold Koch & Rachel Nordlinger (eds.), *The languages and linguistics of Australia*, chap. 3, 91–138. Berlin/Boston: Walter de Gruyter GmbH.

Fletcher, Janet & Nicholas Evans. 2002. An acoustic phonetic analysis of intonational prominence in two Australian languages. *Journal of the International Phonetic Association* 32(2). 123–140. https://doi.org/10.1017/S0025100302001019.

Forrester, Katerina. 2015. *The internal structure of the Mawng noun phrase*. University of Melbourne Honours thesis.

Fortescue, Michael, Marianne Mithun & Nicholas Evans. 2017. Introduction. In Michael Fortescue, Marianne Mithun & Nicholas Evans (eds.), *The Oxford handbook of polysynthesis*, chap. 1, 1–16. Oxford University Press.

Freeze, Ray. 1992. Existentials and other locatives. *Language* 68(3). 553–595.

Gaby, Alice & Ruth Singer. 2014. Semantics of Australian languages. In Harold Koch & Rachel Nordlinger (eds.), *The languages and linguistics of Australia*, chap. 7, 295–327. Berlin/Boston: Walter de Gruyter GmbH.

Garde, Murray. 2013. *Culture, interaction and person reference in an Australian language: An ethography of Bininj Gunwok communication* (Culture and Language Use 11). Amsterdam/Philadelphia: John Benjamins Publishing Company.

Gil, David. 1995. Universal quantifiers and distributivity. In Emmon Bach, Eloise Jelinek, Angelika Kratzer & Barbara Hall Partee (eds.), *Quantification in natural languages*, chap. 10, 321–362. Kluwer.

Green, Rebecca. 1995. *A grammar of Gurr-goni (North Central Arnhem Land)*. Australian National University PhD thesis.

Hale, Kenneth. 1973. Person marking in Warlpiri. In Stephen Anderson & Paul Kiparsky (eds.), *A Festschrift for Morris Halle*, 308–344. New York: Holt, Rinehart & Winston.

Hale, Kenneth. 1976. The adjoined relative clause in Australia. In Robert M. W. Dixon (ed.), *Grammatical categories in Australian languages*, 78–105. Canberra: AIAS.

Hale, Kenneth. 1983. Warlpiri and the grammar of non-configurational languages. *Natural Language and Linguistic Theory* 1(1). 5–47.

Hale, Kenneth. 2003. On the significance of Eloise Jelinek's Pronominal Argument Hypothesis. In Andrew Carnie, Heidi Harley & MaryAnn Willie (eds.), *Formal approaches to function in grammar: In honor of Eloise Jelinek*, 11–43. John Benjamins.

Hamel, Patricia J. 1994. *A grammar and lexicon of Loniu, Papua New Guinea* (Pacific Linguistics, Series C 103). Canberra: ANU.

Hamilton, Philip James. 1993. Intrinsic markedness relations in segment structure. *Toronto Working Papers in Linguistics*. 79–95.
Hamilton, Philip James. 1996. *Phonetic constraints and markedness in the phonotactics of Australian Aboriginal languages*. University of Toronto dissertation.
Harvey, Mark. 1997. Nominal classification and gender in Aboriginal Australia. In Mark Harvey & Nicholas Reid (eds.), *Nominal classification in Aboriginal Australia*, 17–62. Philadelphia, PA: John Benjamins.
Harvey, Mark. 2003. An initial reconstruction of Proto Gunwinyguan phonology. In Nicholas Evans (ed.), *The non-Pama-Nyungan languages of northern Australia: Comparative studies of the continent's most linguistically complex region*, chap. 8, 205–268. Canberra: Pacific Linguistics.
Harvey, Mark. N.d. Warray grammar. Unpublished ms.
Harvey, Mark & Robert Mailhammer. 2017. Reconstructing remote relationships. *Diachronica* 34(4). 470–515. https://doi.org/10.1075/dia.15032.har.
Harvey, Mark & Nicholas Reid. 1997a. Introduction. In Mark Harvey & Nicholas Reid (eds.), *Nominal classification in Aboriginal Australia*, 1–15. Philadelphia, PA: John Benjamins.
Harvey, Mark & Nicholas Reid (eds.). 1997b. *Nominal classification in Aboriginal Australia*. Philadelphia, PA: John Benjamins.
Haspelmath, Martin. 1997. *Indefinite pronouns*. Oxford: Clarendon Press.
Haspelmath, Martin. 2005. Argument marking in ditransitive alignment types. *Linguistic Discovery* 3. https://doi.org/10.1349/PS1.1537-0852.A.280.
Heath, Jeffrey. 1978. *Ngandi grammar, texts, and dictionary*. Canberra: Australian Institute of Aboriginal Studies.
Heath, Jeffrey. 1984. *Functional grammar of Nunggubuyu*. Canberra: Australian Institute of Aboriginal Studies.
Heath, Jeffrey. 1986. Syntactic and lexical aspects of nonconfigurationality in Nunggubuyu (Australia). *Natural Language and Linguistic Theory* 4. 375–408.
Heim, Irene & Angelika Kratzer. 1998. *Semantics in generative grammar*. Blackwell.
Heine, Bernd & Tania Kuteva. 2002. *World lexicon of grammaticalization*. Cambridge University Press.
Himmelmann, Nikolaus P. 1996. Demonstratives in narrative discourse: A taxonomy of universal uses. In Barbara Fox (ed.), *Studies in anaphora* (Typological Studies in Language 33), 205–254. Amsterdam/Philadelphia: John Benjamins Publishing Company.
Himmelmann, Nikolaus P. 1997. *Deiktikon, Artikel, Nominalphrase: zur Emergenz syntaktischer Struktur*. Max Niemeyer Verlag.
Himmelmann, Nikolaus P. 2001. Articles. In Martin Haspelmath, Ekkehard König, Wulf Oesterreicher & Wolfgang Raible (eds.), *Language typology and language universals*, 831–841. Berlin: de Gruyter.
Horrack, Kate. 2014. He jumped off the bridge CAUS she told him to: Indirect speech as a means of expressing indirect causation in Wubuy. In Lauren Gawne & Jill Vaughan (eds.), *Selected papers from the 44th conference of the Australian Linguistic Society, 2013*, 211–230.
Horrack, Kate. 2018. *Argument realisation in Wubuy*. University of Melbourne dissertation.
Iatridou, Sabine. 2000. The grammatical ingredients of counterfactuality. *Linguistic Inquiry* 31(2). 231–270.
Ihsane, Tabea & Geneveva Puskás. 2001. Specific is not Definite. *Generative Grammar in Geneva* 2. 39–54. http://archive-ouverte.unige.ch/unige:93392.
Jelinek, Eloise. 1984. Empty categories, case and configurationality. *Natural Language and Linguistic Theory* 2(1). 39–76.
Kapitonov, Ivan. 2016a. *Kunbarlang, central Arnhem Land*. Collection IK1 at catalog.paradisec.org.au [Open Access]. https://catalog.paradisec.org.au/collections/IK1.

Kapitonov, Ivan. 2016b. *Number in Person's Disguise: Kunbarlang Impoverishment*. Talk at New Fields for Morphology. University of Melbourne. https://www.academia.edu/30430933/Number_in_Persons_Disguise_Kunbarlang_Impoverishment.

Kapitonov, Ivan. 2019a. *A grammar of Kunbarlang*. University of Melbourne PhD thesis.

Kapitonov, Ivan. 2019b. Degrees and scales of Kunbarlang. In M. Ryan Bochnak, Miriam Butt, Erlinde Meertens & Mark-Matthias Zymla (eds.), *Proceedings of TripleA 5: Fieldwork perspectives on the semantics of African, Asian and Austronesian languages*, 91–105. Tübingen. https://doi.org/10.15496/publikation-36875.

Kapitonov, Ivan. Submitted. Definiteness, information structure, and determiner spreading in the Kunbarlang noun phrase.

Kayne, Richard S. 1975. *French syntax: The transformational cycle*. Cambridge, MA: MIT Press.

Keenan, Edward L. 2012. The quantifier questionnaire. In Edward L. Keenan & Denis Paperno (eds.), *Handbook of quantifiers in natural language* (Studies in Linguistics and Philosophy 90), chap. 1, 1–20. Springer.

Keenan, Edward L. & Bernard Comrie. 1977. Noun phrase accessibility and Universal Grammar. *Linguistic Inquiry* 8(1). 63–99.

Keenan, Edward L. & Denis Paperno. 2012. Introduction. In Edward L. Keenan & Denis Paperno (eds.), *Handbook of quantifiers in natural language* (Studies in Linguistics and Philosophy 90), v–viii. Springer.

King, Heather B. 1994. The interrogative intonation of Dyirbal. In *SST 1994 Proceedings*, vol. 1, 144–149. http://www.assta.org/sst/SST-94-Vol-l/cache/SST-94-VOL1-Chapter6-p14.pdf (26 February, 2019).

Kinslow Harris, Joy. 1969a. *Descriptive and comparative study of the Gunwingguan languages, Northern Territory*. Australian National University dissertation.

Kinslow Harris, Joy. 1969b. Preliminary grammar of Gunbalang. In Joy Kinslow Harris, Stephen A. Wurm & Donald C. Laycock (eds.), *Papers in Australian linguistics no. 4* (Pacific Linguistics, Series A 17), 1–49. Canberra: Linguistic Circle of Canberra. https://doi.org/10.15144/PL-A17.

König, Ekkehard & Peter Siemund. 2007. Speech act distinctions in grammar. In Timothy Shopen (ed.), *Language Typology and Syntactic Description*. Vol. I: *Clause structure*, second edition, chap. 5, 276–324. Cambridge/New York: Cambridge University Press.

König, Ekkehard, Peter Siemund & Stephan Töpper. 2013. Intensifiers and reflexive pronouns. In Matthew S. Dryer & Martin Haspelmath (eds.), *The world atlas of language structures online*. Leipzig: Max Planck Institute for Evolutionary Anthropology. http://wals.info/chapter/47.

Krifka, Manfred. 2008. Basic notions of information structure. *Acta Linguistica Hungarica* 55. 243–276. https://doi.org/10.1556/ALing.55.2008.3-4.2.

Kyuseva, Maria. 2020. *Size and shape specifiers in Russian Sign Language: A morphological analysis*. University of Melbourne & University of Birmingham dissertation. http://hdl.handle.net/11343/241476.

Ladefoged, Peter. 2003. *Phonetic data analysis: An introduction to fieldwork and instrumental techniques*. Blackwell Publishing.

Lakoff, George. 1986. Classifiers as a reflection of the mind. In Collete G. Craig (ed.), *Noun classes and categorization*, 13–51. Amsterdam: John Benjamins.

Lander, Yury A. 2012. *Релятивизация в полисинтетическом языке: адыгейские относительные конструкции в типологической перспективе [Relativization in a polysynthetic language: Adyghe relative constructions in a typological perspective]*. Russian State University for the Humanities dissertation.

Laughren, Mary. 2016. Serial verbs in Waanyi and its neighbours. In Peter K. Austin, Harold Koch & Jane Simpson (eds.), *Language, land & song: Studies in honour of Luise Hercus*, chap. 13, 172–193. London: EL Publishing. http://www.elpublishing.org/PID/2013.

Lazard, Gilbert. 2006. More on counterfactuality, and on categories in general. *Linguistic Typology* 10. 61–66.
Lehmann, Christian. 1988. Towards a typology of clause linkage. In John Haiman & Sandra A. Thompson (eds.), *Clause combining in grammar and discourse* (Typological Studies in Language 18), 181–225. Amsterdam/Philadelphia: John Benjamins Publishing Company.
Lewis, David K. 1986. *On the plurality of worlds*. Oxford: Blackwell.
Louagie, Dana. 2020. *Noun phrases in Australian languages: A typological study* (Pacific Linguistics 662). De Gruyter.
Louagie, Dana & Jean-Christophe Verstraete. 2016. Noun phrase constituency in Australian languages: A typological study. *Linguistic Typology* 20(1). 25–80. https://doi.org/10.1515/lingty-2016-0002.
Lyons, Christopher. 1999. *Definiteness*. Cambridge University Press.
Mallinson, Graham & Barry J. Blake. 1981. *Language typology: Cross-linguistic studies in syntax*. North-Holland Publishing Company.
Mansfield, John B. 2016. Borrowed verbs and the expansion of light verb phrases in Murrinhpatha. In Felicity Meakins & Carmel O'Shannessy (eds.), *Loss and renewal: Australian languages since contact*. Berlin: De Gruyter.
Marley, Alexandra Helen. 2020. *Kundangkudjikaberrk: Variation and change in Bininj Kunwok, a Gunwinyguan language of Northern Australia*. Australian National University PhD thesis. https://doi.org/10.25911/5fbf76787f833.
Marten, Lutz. 2013. Structure and interpretation in Swahili existential constructions. *Rivista di Linguistica* 25(1). 45–73.
Massam, Diane. 2009. Noun incorporation: essentials and extensions. *Language and Linguistics Compass* 3(4). 1076–1096. https://doi.org/10.1111/j.1749-818X.2009.00140.x.
Matthewson, Lisa. 2004. On the methodology of semantic fieldwork. *International Journal of American Linguistics* 70(4). 369–415.
McConvell, Patrick. 1985. The origin of subsections in Northern Australia. *Oceania* 56(1). 1–33.
McConvell, Patrick. 2006. Grammaticalization of demonstratives as subordinate complementizers in Ngumpin-Yapa. *Australian Journal of Linguistics* 26(1). 107–137.
McConvell, Patrick. 2010. Contact and Indigenous languages in Australia. In Raymond Hickey (ed.), *The handbook of language contact*, 770–794. Oxford University Press.
McConvell, Patrick. 2018. Introduction: Revisiting Aboriginal social organisation. In *Skin, kin and clan: The dynamics of social categories in Indigenous Australia*, chap. 1, 1–20. Canberra: Australian National University Press.
McGregor, William B. 1988. Mood and subordination in Kuniyanti. In Peter K. Austin (ed.), *Complex sentence constructions in Australian languages* (Typological Studies in Language 15), 37–67. Amsterdam/Philadelphia: John Benjamins Publishing Company.
McGregor, William B. 1990. *A functional grammar of Gooniyandi*. Amsterdam/Philadelphia: John Benjamins.
McGregor, William B. 1996. The grammar of nominal prefixing in Nyulnyul. In Hilary Chappell & William McGregor (eds.), *The grammar of inalienability: A typological perspective on body part terms and the part-whole relation*, 251–292. Berlin/New York: Mouton de Gruyter.
McGregor, William B. 2002. *Verb classification in Australian languages* (Empirical Approaches to Language Typology 25). Berlin / New York: Mouton de Gruyter.
McKay, Graham Richard. 2000. Ndjébbana. In Robert M. W. Dixon & Barry J. Blake (eds.), *The handbook of Australian languages*. Vol. 5: *Grammatical sketches of Bunuba, Ndjébbana and Kugu Nganhcara*, 155–354. Melbourne: Oxford University Press.
McKay, Graham Richard. 2008. Cohesive features in Rembarrnga narratives. In Timothy Jowan Curnow (ed.), *Selected papers from the 2007 conference of the Australian Linguistic Society*.

Meakins, Felicity & Rob Pensalfini. 2016. Gender bender: Superclassing in Jingulu gender marking. In Felicity Meakins & Carmel O'Shannessy (eds.), *Loss and renewal: Australian languages since contact*, chap. 13, 425–452. Berlin: De Gruyter.

Merlan, Francesca. 2003. The genetic position of Mangarrayi: Evidence from nominal prefixation. In Nicholas Evans (ed.), *The non-Pama-Nyungan languages of northern Australia: Comparative studies of the continent's most linguistically complex region*, chap. 12, 353–367. Canberra: Pacific Linguistics.

Mithun, Marianne. 1984a. How to avoid subordination. In *Bls*, 73–85.

Mithun, Marianne. 1984b. The evolution of noun incorporation. *Language*. 847–894.

Murasugi, Kumiko. 2014. Noun incorporation, nonconfigurationality and polysynthesis. In Andrew Carnie, Yosuke Sato & Dan Siddiqi (eds.), *The Routledge handbook of syntax*, chap. 14, 283–303. Routledge.

Mushin, Ilana. 1995. Epistememes in Australian languages. *Australian Journal of Linguistics* 15(1). 1–31.

Mushin, Ilana & Jane Simpson. 2008. Free to bound to free? Interactions between pragmatics and syntax in the development of Australian pronominal systems. *Language* 84(3). 566–596. https://doi.org/0.1353/lan.0.0048.

Nichols, Johanna & Balthasar Bickel. 2013a. Locus of marking in possessive noun phrases. In Matthew S. Dryer & Martin Haspelmath (eds.), *The world atlas of language structures online*. Leipzig: Max Planck Institute for Evolutionary Anthropology. http://wals.info/chapter/24.

Nichols, Johanna & Balthasar Bickel. 2013b. Locus of marking in the clause. In Matthew S. Dryer & Martin Haspelmath (eds.), *The world atlas of language structures online*. Leipzig: Max Planck Institute for Evolutionary Anthropology. http://wals.info/chapter/23.

Nichols, Johanna & Balthasar Bickel. 2013c. Possessive classification. In Matthew S. Dryer & Martin Haspelmath (eds.), *The world atlas of language structures online*. Leipzig: Max Planck Institute for Evolutionary Anthropology. http://wals.info/chapter/59.

Nikolaeva, Irina. 2016. Analyses of the semantics of mood. In Jan Nuyts & Johan van der Auwera (eds.), *The Oxford handbook of modality and mood*, chap. 5, 68–85. Oxford: Oxford University Press.

Noonan, Michael. 2007. Complementation. In Timothy Shopen (ed.), *Language typology and syntactic description*. Vol. II: *Complex constructions*, second edition, chap. 2, 52–150. Cambridge/New York: Cambridge University Press.

Nordlinger, Rachel. 1998. *Constructive case: Evidence from Australian languages* (Dissertations in Linguistics). Stanford: CSLI Publications.

Nordlinger, Rachel. 2006. Spearing the Emu drinking: Subordination and the adjoined relative clause in Wambaya. *Australian Journal of Linguistics* 26(1). 5–29.

Nordlinger, Rachel. 2011. Transitivity in Murrinh-Patha. *Studies in Language* 35(3). 702–734.

Nordlinger, Rachel. 2014. Constituency and grammatical relations in Australian languages. In Harold Koch & Rachel Nordlinger (eds.), *The languages and linguistics of Australia*, chap. 5, 215–261. Berlin/Boston: Walter de Gruyter GmbH.

Nordlinger, Rachel & Evan Kidd. 2018. *An experimental study of word order in Murrinhpatha*. Talk at ALW 2018.

Nordlinger, Rachel & Adam Saulwick. 2002. Infinitives in polysynthesis: the case of Rembarrnga. In Nicholas Evans & Hans-Jürgen Sasse (eds.), *Problems of polysynthesis* (Studia Typologica 4), 185–201. Berlin: Akademie Verlag.

Nouwen, Rick. 2020. E-Type pronouns: Congressmen, sheep, and paychecks. In Daniel Gutzmann, Lisa Matthewson, Cécile Meier, Hotze Rullmann & Thomas E. Zimmerman (eds.), *The Wiley Blackwell companion to semantics*. https://doi.org/10.1002/9781118788516.sem091.

O'Keeffe, Isabel. 2016. *Multilingual manyardi/kun-borrk: Manifestations of multilingualism in the classical song traditions of western Arnhem Land*. University of Melbourne dissertation.

O'Keeffe, Isabel, Carolyn Coleman & Ruth Singer. toappear. The expression of emotions in Kunbarlang and its neighbours in the multilingual context of western and central Arnhem Land. *Pragmatics and Cognition*.

O'Keeffe, Isabel, Carolyn Coleman, Ruth Singer, Linda Barwick, Janet Mardbinda & Talena Wilton. 2017. *Documentation of Kunbarlang*. Endangered Languages Archive. http://hdl.handle.net/2196/1edca13c-736f-4f46-8bce-82429702aaf3 (8 April, 2021).

Osborne, C. R. 1974. *The Tiwi language*. Grammar, myths and dictionary of the Tiwi language spoken on Melville and Bathurst Islands, northern Australia (Australian Aboriginal Studies No. 55 / Linguistic Series No. 21). Canberra: Australian Institute of Aboriginal Studies.

Parncutt, Amy. 2015. *Towards a phonological typology of reduplication in Australian languages*. University of Queensland Honours.

Partee, Barbara H. & Vladimir Borschev. 2002. Genitive of negation and scope of negation in Russian existential sentences. In Jindřich Toman (ed.), *Annual workshop on formal approaches to Slavic linguistics: the second Ann Arbor meeting 2001*, 181–200. Ann Arbor: Michigan Slavic Publications.

Partee, Barbara Hall. 1995. Quantificational structures and compositionality. In Emmon Bach, Eloise Jelinek, Angelika Kratzer & Barbara Hall Partee (eds.) (Studies in Linguistics and Philosophy 54), 541–601. Dordrecht: Springer.

Payne, Doris L. & Immanuel Barshi. 1999. External possession: What, where, how, and why. In Doris L. Payne & Immanuel Barshi (eds.), *External possession*, 3–29. Amsterdam/Philadelphia: John Benjamins Publishing Company.

Pensalfini, Rob. 2004. Towards a typology of configurationality. *Natural Language and Linguistic Theory* 22(2). 359–408.

Poignant, Roslyn. 1996. *Encounter at Nagalarramba*. Canberra: National Library of Australia.

Polinsky, Maria. 2016. *Deconstructing ergativity: Two types of ergative languages and their features*. New York, NY: Oxford University Press.

Potts, Christopher. 2002. No vacuous quantification constraints in syntax. In Masako Hirotani (ed.), *Proceedings of the Northeast Linguistic Society (NELS) 32*, vol. 2, 451–470. Amherst, MA: GLSA Publications.

Reboul, Anne, Denis Delfitto & Gaetano Fiorin. 2016. The semantic properties of free indirect discourse. *Annual Review of Linguistics* 2. 255–71. https://doi.org/10.1146/annurev-linguistics-011415-040722.

Reid, Nicholas. 1997. Class and classifier in Ngan'gityemerri. In Mark Harvey & Nicholas Reid (eds.), *Nominal classification in Aboriginal Australia*, 165–228. Philadelphia, PA: John Benjamins.

Reid, Nicholas. 2002. Sit right down the back: Serialized posture verbs in Ngan'gityemerri and other Northern Australian languages. In John Newman (ed.), *The linguistics of sitting, standing and lying*, 239–267. Amsterdam/Philadelphia: John Benjamins Publishing Company.

Riedel, Kristina. 2009. *The syntax of object marking in Sambaa: A comparative Bantu perspective*. Universiteit Leiden PhD thesis. https://www.lotpublications.nl/Documents/213_fulltext.pdf.

Ross, Belinda Britt. 2011. *Prosody and grammar in Dalabon and Kayardild*. University of Melbourne dissertation.

Saulwick, Adam. 2003. *Aspects of the verb in Rembarrnga, a polysynthetic language of northern Australia: Grammatical description, texts and dictionary*. University of Melbourne dissertation.

Schultze-Berndt, Eva & Candide Simard. 2012. Constraints on noun phrase discontinuity in an Australian language: the role of prosody and information structure. *Linguistics* 50(5). 1015–1058.

Schweiger, Fritz. 1995. Suffixaufnahme and related case marking patterns in Australian languages. In Frans Plank (ed.), *Double case: Agreement by Suffixaufnahme*, chap. 12, 339–362. New York/Oxford: Oxford University Press.

Shibatani, Masayoshi & Prashant Pardeshi. 2002. The causative continuum. In Masayoshi Shibatani (ed.), *The grammar of causation and interpersonal manipulation* (Typological Studies in Language 48), 85–126. Amsterdam/Philadelphia: John Benjamins Publishing Company.
Simpson, Jane. 1991. *Warlpiri morpho-syntax: A lexicalist approach* (Studies in Natural Language and Linguistic Theory 23). Springer.
Simpson, Jane & Ilana Mushin. 2008. Clause-initial position in four Australian languages. In Ilana Mushin & Brett Baker (eds.), *Discourse and grammar in Australian languages* (Studies in Language Companion 104), 25–57. Amsterdam/Philadelphia: John Benjamins.
Singer, Ruth. 2001. *The inclusory construction in Australian languages*. University of Melbourne Honours thesis. http://hdl.handle.net/11343/39215.
Singer, Ruth. 2005. Argument to coverb: tracing the development of Mawng coverb constructions. Ms.
Singer, Ruth. 2006. *Agreement in Mawng: Productive and lexicalised uses of agreement in an Australian language*. University of Melbourne dissertation.
Singer, Ruth. 2011. Strategies for encoding reciprocity in Mawng. In Nicholas Evans, Alice Gaby, Stephen C. Levinson & Asifa Majid (eds.), *Reciprocals and semantic typology*, chap. 14, 233–249. John Benjamins Publishing Company.
Singer, Ruth. 2016. *The dynamics of nominal classification: Productive and lexicalised uses of gender agreement in Mawng* (Pacific Linguistics 642). Boston/Berlin: De Gruyter Mouton.
Singer, Ruth. N.d. Initial position as a heterogeneous category: use of word order and intonation to express object focus in Mawng. Ms.
Singer, Ruth, Nita Garidjalalug, Heather Hewett, Peggy Mirwuma & Phillip Ambidjambidj. 2015. *Mawng dictionary*. Version 1.0. http://www.mawngngaralk.org.au/main/dictionary.php.
Spencer, Andrew. 1995. Incorporation in Chukchi. *Language* 71(3). 439–489. http://www.jstor.org/stable/416217.
Stassen, Leon. 1985. *Comparison and Universal Grammar*. Oxford: Basil Blackwell.
Stassen, Leon. 2009. *Predicative possession*. Oxford/New York: Oxford University Press.
Stassen, Leon. 2013a. Predicative possession. In Matthew S. Dryer & Martin Haspelmath (eds.), *The world atlas of language structures online*. Leipzig: Max Planck Institute for Evolutionary Anthropology. http://wals.info/chapter/117.
Stassen, Leon. 2013b. Zero copula for predicate nominals. In Matthew S. Dryer & Martin Haspelmath (eds.), *The world atlas of language structures online*. Leipzig: Max Planck Institute for Evolutionary Anthropology. http://wals.info/chapter/120.
Stoakes, Hywel M. 2013. *An acoustic and aerodynamic analysis of consonant articulation in Bininj Gun-wok*. University of Melbourne dissertation.
Stokes, Judith. 1982. A description of the mathematical concepts of Groote Eylandt Aborigines. In S. Hargrave (ed.), *Language and culture* (Work Papers of the SIL, Australian Aborigines Branch B 8), 33–152. Darwin: SIL.
de Swart, Henriëtte. 1998. Aspect shift and coercion. *Natural Language & Linguistic Theory* 16(2). 347–385. http://www.jstor.org/stable/4047954.
TFS Working Group. 2012. *Feeding Fluffy*. http://totemfieldstoryboards.org/stories/feeding_fluffy/ (25 February, 2016).
Thompson, Sandra A., Robert E. Longacre & Shin Ja J. Hwang. 2007. Adverbial clauses. In Timothy Shopen (ed.), *Language typology and syntactic description*. Vol. II: *Complex constructions*, second edition, chap. 5, 237–300. Cambridge/New York: Cambridge University Press.
Ultan, Russell. 1978. The nature of future tenses. In Joseph H. Greenberg, Charles A. Ferguson & Edith A. Moravcsik (eds.), *Universals of human language*. Vol. 3: *Word structure*, 83–123. Stanford CA: Stanford University Press.
Verstraete, Jean-Christophe. 2005. The semantics and pragmatics of composite mood marking: The non-Pama-Nyungan languages of northern Australia. *Linguistic Typology* 9. 223–268.

de Vries, Mark. 2002. *The syntax of relativization*. Universiteit van Amsterdam dissertation. http://www.let.rug.nl/dvries/pdf/proefschrift-mdevries.pdf.
Watters, John R. 2003. Grassfields Bantu. In Derek Nurse & Gérard Philippson (eds.), *The Bantu languages* (Routledge Language Family Descriptions 4), chap. 14, 225–256. London/New York: Routledge.
Wickham, Hadley. 2016. *Ggplot2: elegant graphics for data analysis*. Springer-Verlag New York. https://ggplot2.tidyverse.org.
Zaefferer, Dietmar. 1991. Conditionals and unconditionals: Cross-linguistic and logical aspects. In Dietmar Zaefferer (ed.), *Semantic universals and universal semantics* (Groningen-Amsterdam Studies in Semantics 12), 210–236. Berlin / New York: Foris Publications.

Index

bidju 64, 118, 193, 227–230, 316
bonj 40, 63, 64, 70, 71, 75–77, 93, 96, 108, 109, 116, 118, 119, 122, 123, 129, 155, 168, 188, 192, 193, 208, 209, 213, 216, 219, 227–230, 272, 278, 281, 293, 310, 312, 316, 320, 322, 361, 363, 364, 367, 369
yimarne 24, 52, 57, 60, 131, 155, 192, 248, 272, 281, 288, 302, 316, 327, 352, 358, 363, 367
yiwanj 146, 192, 210, 228, 239, 368, 369

adnominal pronouns 107–109, 114, 117, 280
animacy 115, 117, 119, 136, 143, 144, 190–192, 194, 218, 242, 274, 275, 303, 307
Anindilyakwa 8, 9, 153, 199, 200, 215, 220, 226, 324
applicative 78, 79, 166, 167, 169, 215–220, 223, 237, 239, 240
Arrernte 310
article 68, 95–102, 112, 155
aspect
– Aktionsart 261, 286, 287
– viewpoint 13, 198, 284–290
assimilation 29, 30, 41, 44–47, 196
asyndetic pronominal coordination 125–127
Athabaskan 175
auxiliary *see* aspect > viewpoint

Bantu 133, 175
Bardi 313
Bininj Kunwok 3, 4, 6, 8, 9, 12, 15, 19, 20, 25, 36, 39, 40, 56, 60, 61, 64, 66, 81, 90–92, 100, 123, 125, 150, 162, 164, 166, 170, 185, 187, 189, 193–195, 198–201, 212, 215, 216, 219, 226, 235, 241, 242, 246, 247, 252, 254, 255, 261, 262, 265–267, 270, 281, 285, 289, 290, 312, 313, 315, 319, 324, 357
Bororo 149
borrowing 45, 50, 51, 63, 66, 68, 102, 234, 265, 267, 348, *see also* loan
Burarra 310

Cape York Creole 310
causative 225, 322–325
causative-inchoative alternation 234, 324
Chukchi 245
clusivity 115, 116, 119, 175, 176, 179, 186
conditional 204, 211–213, 351–353

consonant clusters 16, 19, 21, 27, 30, 41–44
counterfactual
– conditional 205, 212, 351–353
– wish 326, 327

Dalabon 7–9, 12, 16, 17, 37, 60, 64, 84, 173, 187, 198–201, 216, 222, 255, 261–263, 265, 267, 288, 318, 319
demonstratives 71, 108, 112, 128–134, 300, 314, 332, 337, 351
determiner *see* adnominal pronouns, article, demonstratives
determining pronouns *see* adnominal pronouns
dialect 5, 6, 241, 296
Djinang 155

ellipsis 54, 106, 231, 258, 259, 295
English 3, 4, 13, 51, 63, 66–68, 72, 81, 100, 101, 114, 137, 153, 172, 208, 211, 227, 235, 254, 270, 272, 274, 294, 301, 303, 310, 312, 316, 326, 331, 335, 341, 348

focus 105, 110, 111, 135, 155, 158, 227, 254, 258, 275, 277–279, 283, 295, 312
free indirect discourse *see* reported speech
future tense 201–203, 209–211, 213, 326, 328

Garrwa 284
gender (grammatical) *see* noun class
Generalized Quantifier theory 150, 151
German 227, 353
Gooniyandi 153, 284, 318
Gumbaynggirr 304
Gurr-goni 285, 308
Guugu Yimithirr 313

habitual 47, 203, 205, 208, 212, 213, 285, 287
Hausa 99
hortative 210
Hungarian 117

ideophone 64
idioms 65, 146, 147, 219, 220, 239
imperative 198, 204, 210, 213, 296–297
(im)perfective *see* aspect > viewpoint
inchoative 50, 53, 55, 153, *see also* causative-inchoative alternation
inclusory construction 62, 78, 80, 126–128

instrument 170–172, 277
Iwaidja 233, 234

Jaminjung 113, 281
Jawoyn 8, 12, 200
Jiwarli 94

Kalkatungu 107, 114, 284
Kanyara languages 94
Kayardild 166, 288
Kaytetye 318
kinship 4, 6, 86, 142, 143, 310
– verbs 60–62, 339
Kundedjnjenghmi 12
Kundjeyhmi 12, 241
Kune 3, 5, 8, 241
Kungarakany 7, 8, 241
Kuninjku 3, 8, 17, 37, 241, 262, 293
Kunwinjku 1, 8, 12, 241, 262, 358, 359

Latin 117
loan 50, 51, 66–68, 72, 85, 165, 267, 309, 310,
    see also borrowing
location and direction 67, 73, 74, 92, 130, 132,
    133, 137–139, 170, 171, 230, 245, 252, 253,
    277, 297–301, 305–308, 332, 337, 338, 340,
    349
Loniu 148

Mangarayi 7–9, 199, 200, 241
Marra 45, 97
Mawng 1–5, 9, 12, 45, 96, 97, 125, 130, 133, 147,
    155, 158, 212, 215, 233, 234, 258, 264–267,
    280, 281, 285, 290, 294, 296, 309, 310, 315,
    356
Mayali 8, 241, 262
Mengerrdji 12
modality 9, 202, 204, 207, 211, 213, 214
– deontic 213
– epistemic 58, 204, 213, 214
mood 9, 162, 173–178, 198, 201–214, 291–293,
    326–329
– composite 162, 175, 201
– spreading 326, 328, 329
Murrinhpatha 166, 271, 273, 274

Nakkara 36, 147, 285, 308
Ndjébbana 3, 4, 12, 80, 147, 154, 189, 285, 308

neutralisation
– of apical contrast 31, 34, see also retroflex > in
    heterorganic clusters
– of number see number > neutralisation
Ngalakgan 8, 9, 36, 37, 56, 97, 199, 200, 241,
    262, 263
Ngan'gityemerri 284, 308, 338
Ngandi 8, 9, 15, 199–201, 215, 226, 241, 261,
    265, 267
Ngarinyin 313
Ngiyambaa 46
nonconfigurationality 78, 82, 102, 103, 113, 270,
    281, 355
Northern Straits Salish 81
noun class 52, 54, 84–92, 117, 132, 133, 142, 332
– morphology 54, 87–91, 241
noun marker 68–70, 95–102, 105, 108–112, 282,
    325, 331–333, 338, 339, 349, 351
number
– -lessness 179, 186, 188–189, 193
– neutralisation 119, 174, 179, 185, 188, 189, 195
numerals 72, 100, 155
Nunggubuyu see Wubuy

operator scope see scope

past tense 201, 203–205, 207, 212, 305, 306,
    326–328
Persian 205
pluractionality 46, 47, 209, 336, 339
polarity see negation
Polish 117
prepound 64, 164, 234, 261–264, 267, 324, 325
present tense 201, 208, 209, 213, 302, 305, 327
prohibitive 209, 293, 296–297
Pronominal Argument Hypothesis 78–83, 269
proprietive use of possessives 146–147
proto-Gunwinyguan 7, 8, 63, 88, 91, 131, 196,
    198–201

quantifier scope see scope

reality status see mood
Rembarrnga 8, 16, 84, 199, 200, 262, 263, 318,
    324
reported speech 210, 320, 321
resultative 89, 153
retroflex 18, 21, 29–31
– in heterorganic clusters 29–31

Russian 227, 275

sandhi 42, 44, 45, 66
scope 71, 82, 97, 134, 135, 140, 155, 159, 212, 213, 249, 250, 252, 254, 255, 291, 328
secondary predicate 164, 241
St'át'imcets 79, 170
status *see* mood
superclassing 86, 87, 90, 91, 142
suppletion 88, 93, 241, 243
Swahili 349
syllable
– lengthening 288, 289
– structure 19, 24–28, 32, 35
– syllabification 19, 27, 34
syncretism 87, 91, 116, 120, 178, 186

thematic 164, 195–197, 199, 200, 234, 261–263, 324, 325
Tiwi 7, 148, 149
topic (information structure) 272, 278, 279, 295, 301, 302

truth value judgement 11, 151, 152

Umpila 310
unregistered arguments 79, 169–172

variation 5, 17–21, 30, 31, 39, 64, 66, 67, 126, 131, 142, 154, 172, 196, 204, 221, 223, 240, 251, 253, 262, 278, 283, 290, 291, 299, 302, 319, 325

Waanyi 284
Wambaya 284
Warlpiri 78, 79, 81, 170, 225, 318, 330
Warray 8, 9, 173, 200, 220, 355
Woiwurrung 310
Wubuy 8–10, 15, 56, 97, 127, 167, 195, 199, 200, 215, 216, 220, 226, 244–246, 270, 281, 324

Yir Yoront 155
Yukulta 284

www.ingramcontent.com/pod-product-compliance
Lightning Source LLC
Chambersburg PA
CBHW080834230426
43665CB00021B/2836